Readings in
International Political
Economy

Readings in International Political Economy

David N. Balaam
Department of Politics and Government

Michael Veseth
*Department of Economics
and Director of the Political Economy Program*

University of Puget Sound

Prentice Hall, Upper Saddle River, New Jersey 07458

Library of Congress Cataloging-in-Publication Data

Readings in international political economy / edited by David N.
  Balaam and Michael Veseth.
      p.   cm.
  Includes bibliographical references.
  ISBN 0–13–149600–X
  1. International economic relations.   I. Balaam, David N.,   II. Veseth, Michael.
  HF1359.R4   1996
  337—dc20   95–34434
                                                                                  CIP

Acquisitions editor: Jennie Katsaros
Editorial/production supervision
  and interior design: Darrin Kiessling
Copy editor: Elise Paxson
Cover director: Jayne Conte
Buyer: Bob Anderson

©1996 by Prentice-Hall, Inc.
Simon & Schuster/A Viacom Company
Upper Saddle River, New Jersey 07458

Printed in the United States of America
10 9 8 7 6 5 4 3 2 1

ISBN 0-13-149600-X

Prentice-Hall International (UK) Limited, *London*
Prentice-Hall of Australia Pty. Limited, *Sydney*
Prentice-Hall Canada Inc., *Toronto*
Prentice-Hall Hispanoamericana, S.A., *Mexico*
Prentice-Hall of India Private Limited, *New Delhi*
Prentice-Hall of Japan, Inc., *Tokyo*
Simon & Schuster Asia Pte. Ltd., *Singapore*
Editora Prentice-Hall do Brasil, Ltda., *Rio de Janeiro*

Contents

PART II   IPE Structures: Production, Money, Power, and Knowledge   85

PART III   State-Market Tensions Today   199

PART IV   IPE North and South

PART V   Global Problems Today

Preface

This reader was put together with several objectives in mind. First, in conjunction with our text *An Introduction to International Political Economy* (Prentice-Hall, 1996) we have attempted to fill a gap in the international political economy (IPE) literature available to undergraduates. The number of IPE texts and edited readers has grown significantly in the past ten years. However, based on our experience teaching introductory IPE courses mainly to freshmen and sophomores, material written for lower division–introductory courses is almost nonexistent. Thus, we have edited this reader with an introductory-level audience in mind. We wish to provide instructors who choose to use our text with a reader that offers them a more detailed examination of the theoretical approaches to IPE, IPE structures, state-market relations, and contemporary North-South problems and issues. We have also tried to accommodate instructors from different disciplines who either want to teach the subject or know more about it.

Yet another reason for putting together these articles was to produce a reader that would stand on its own. For the most part, IPE constitutes an eclectic effort on the part of theorists and practitioners from different disciplines to understand a field of study in which politics, economics, sociology, history, and other disciplines overlap with one another. We felt strongly that students taking an IPE course, whether in Political Science, Economics, History, Sociology, or in any other field, would benefit from a reader that exposed them to some of the classic IPE pieces and to works that covered many of the more common and controversial subjects within the field.

A number of criteria influenced our choice of readings. First, we felt it necessary and beneficial to students to select some classic works in the field. In Part I, students are exposed first-hand to the writings of Friedrich List, Adam Smith, and Karl Marx, probably the three most influential theorists in the field. Their works instill in students not only an appreciation of the views of these "masters," but also a sense of history. Those already familiar with the IPE literature will recognize throughout the reader the contemporary works of more recent influential writers and theorists from different disciplines, such as Andre Gunder Frank, Joseph S. Nye, Jr., Garrett Hardin, and David P. Calleo. In conjunction with the instructor's presentation or discussions, students will have the opportunity to explore a number of topics and to judge for themselves what the author meant.

Second, we attempted to select works that were written in a straightforward manner and that challenged introductory students but did not leave them or their instructors bored or put off either by the subject, the writing, or the length of the piece. In a few cases we edited the reading down to a more manageable length for both the introductory student and instructors who may not be acquainted with the approaches or issues.

Third, we chose readings that applied one or more of the theoretical approaches to IPE in such a way that students would be able to recognize these approaches and apply them to specific problems and issues. These works provide students with an opportunity to raise a number of questions about approaches, particular issues, and/or how well these approaches help explain particular issues.

Fourth, many of the works we chose deal with more than one IPE approach and multiple concepts. Focusing on any IPE issue usually raises questions that require the use of several different approaches or concepts to describe and explain that issue. In Part II, we offer selections that discuss the international production (trade), finance, technology, and national security structures that serve as a backdrop for many IPE problems and issues. Part III emphasizes the extent to which problems associated with production, finance, security, and technology are confronted by different nations, their decision-makers, and also other international and subnational groups and individuals. Multiple approaches and concepts also play a large role in the selections of Part IV, which deal with a variety of interrelated problems such as hunger, development, population, and environmental issues.

Fifth, in selecting these works we made a conscious effort to represent economic liberal, mercantilist, and structuralist (Marxist) ideas. There is no effort here to support one outlook over another. It is our desire that instructors and students will spend some time discussing the different assumptions and values associated with each ideological perspective.

Sixth, and finally, we also consciously made an effort to choose material that would be accessible to different academic disciplines, especially Political Science, Economics, Sociology, and History, to name some of the disciplines most often interested in IPE. It has been our experience in teaching IPE courses that some students prefer the works of the discipline with which they identify while shying away from the works of unfamiliar disciplines. We have chosen works that for the most part do not assume specialized training or detailed background in the issue under study or the discipline most often associated with that issue. For instance, Paul Volcker and Toyoo Gyohten discuss monetary issues in language that most lower-division undergraduate students should be able to understand. It is our hope that as students encounter the ideas and concepts of other disciplines they will be excited—at least inquisitive—about them, instead of threatened by them. Some works such as the writings of Adam Smith will be more difficult to understand than other works. In the cases of the original writings we have complemented these works with those of a more recent vintage so as to demonstrate how these ideas are played out in the international political economy today.

Acknowledgments

Putting together this reader was a cooperative effort between the editors, who were assisted by some of their colleagues at the University of Puget Sound. Many of those we teach with in the International Political Economy program at the university were consulted as to which articles or writings worked best when they taught their IPE classes. These colleagues are Nancy Bristow, Karl Fields, Leon Grunberg, Sunil Kukreja, Elizabeth Norville, Lisa Nunn, Ross Singleton, David Smith, and David Sousa. We wish to thank all of them for their support in this project, especially for their willingness to "drop things and go dig up that piece." All of us have benefited from a Hewlett Foundation grant that funded a faculty IPE seminar in the Spring of 1992. These funds also made it possible for David P. Calleo and Susan Strange, among others, to visit the campus in support of our new IPE program. We would also like to thank the people at Prentice-Hall for their support through all phases of this project, especially Jennie Katsaros and Michael Bickerstaff.

Finally, we wish to thank all our students who, for the past three years, have helped "test" some of this material with frank and honest comments. Stacey Lorenz, Cory Graff, and Sarah Drummond assisted the editors with manuscript preparation. This reader is dedicated to all of our students, those who now and in the future we hope will enjoy learning about and trying to make sense of the international political economy.

David N. Balaam and Michael Veseth

Readings in
International Political
Economy

Part I

Perspectives on International Political Economy

The world is a complicated place, characterized at all levels by elements of interdependence. We depend on one another in many ways at many levels. The world of human existence is therefore filled with elements of tension, fault lines where differing and sometimes conflicting interests, points of view, or value systems come into contact with one another. It is the purpose of the humanities and the social sciences to improve our understanding of the human condition by analyzing the causes of these tensions and their consequences—how they are resolved. International Political Economy contributes to this work by focusing in a particular piece of the fault line that has traditionally been of interest to social scientists.

Because it is useful, especially at the start, to use a simple vocabulary to discuss new ideas, let us agree to think about international political economy (IPE) as the *field of study that analyzes the problems and questions that arise from the parallel existence and dynamic interaction of "state" and "market" in the modern world.*[1] The first set of readings introduces the main perspectives that have shaped IPE for the past 200 years and provides a peek at the historical context within which these ideas developed.

By way of introduction to the topic of IPE, Miles Kahler explores many of the "sea-changes" that have occurred in the international political economy throughout the postwar (World War II) years. Writing in 1990, Kahler addresses

1

one of the major events that to this day influences developments in the IPE—the collapse of the Soviet Union and the presumed end of the Cold War. Although the significance of this event remains yet to be determined, it continues to underscore many of the political and economic conditions discussed in the rest of this reader. Since the end of the Cold War, international political economic issues have moved higher onto the agendas of nation-states and other actors in the international system. States such as Japan that have become economically stronger play bigger roles in the international political economy. Meanwhile, most nations find it necessary to compete economically with one another in an environment that reflects "the intensified internationalization of financial markets and the globalization of production."

The other selections in this part of the reader offer students the chance to sample the works of Friedrich List, Adam Smith, and Karl Marx, three classic political economists whose works are associated with each of the three basic approaches to IPE: mercantilism, economic liberalism, and structuralism. To demonstrate how each of these approaches is applied to contemporary problems and issues, we have chosen another selection by a more contemporary writer.

The ideas of mercantilism are most often associated with Friedrich List (1789–1846).[2] List, born in Germany, served as an office clerk and became a government official and university professor. After the Napoleonic wars (1815) he was elected president of an association whose goal it was to abolish internal customs duties between the German states. List supported political union of all German states. After being committed to jail and hard labor for supporting Commercial Union, he escaped to Paris but returned to his native Württemberg where the King exiled him. List traveled to the United States and made friends with such noted people as President Jackson, Henry Clay, and James Madison, among others. In the United States he began a German newspaper and published a series of letters dealing with tariff issues between the United States and Great Britain. He attacked Adam Smith's "cosmopolitan system of free trade" and strongly urged trade protection in support of domestic industries. List then worked on several publications while developing his argument about the necessity of protection and the benefits of an industrial society. President Jackson appointed him Consul for the United States at Hapsburg, but the Senate at Hapsburg refused to ratify his appointment. He later returned as U.S. Consul at Leipzig and supported the development of a national German railway system. List wrote numerous tracts on commercial relations between Germany and other European countries and the United States. He favored the development of a national manufacturing power base supported by imports of raw materials and protection of native industries. According to List, protection would be necessary until a nation reached the stage of development in which it was strong enough to conduct free trade on a politically and economically equal basis with other nations.

List returned to Leipzig and in 1841 began publishing parts of his most famous work *The National System of Political Economy,* a chapter of which we have chosen for this reader. A popular read, List's work was bitterly criticized by the English and attacked for its emphasis on strengthening Germany at the exclusion of other countries. List continued writing for several magazines and visiting other countries where he became known for his support of national economic interests. On his last visit to England he worried that repeal of the Corn Laws (shifting government support away from agriculture to industry) would weaken German manufacturing industries and lead to Britain's manufacturing supremacy of the continent. Poor health and depression led to his death in 1846.

James Fallows is the editor of *The Atlantic Monthly* magazine. In this selection, Fallows argues that Japan and other countries, particularly many of the Newly Industrialized Countries (NICs), have been influenced profoundly by the views of List. Fallows nicely outlines the major differences in the thought of Anglo-American economic liberals, who have admired Adam Smith, and the mercantilist views of nations such as Japan and the NICs, who have studied and applied some of the ideas of List in their struggle to compete with the more mature industries of the U.S. and European industrial powers. In effect, Fallows argues that Great Britain and the United States have mythologized Smith. Contrary to their claim that their industries matured in economic liberal policies, to develop they actually adopted mercantilist practices more in keeping with List than the economic liberal Smith.

Adam Smith (1723–1790) was a Scottish political economist and moral philosopher. His most important works were *Inquiry into the Nature and Causes of the Wealth of Nations* (1776), a seminal work of classical political economy, and *Theory of Moral Sentiments* (1759), a classic work of moral philosophy. *The Wealth of Nations* focuses on issues related to wealth and efficiency, developing systematically the laissez-faire (i.e., the state should leave the market alone) ideas with which Smith is most closely associated. *Theory of Moral Sentiments,* however, presents an equally powerful vision of the ethical and moral issues that underlie political and economic life. Although Smith is best known for *The Wealth of Nations,* it is important to bear in mind that his views about markets and wealth were conditioned by his deep ethical convictions about the limits of selfish individual action.

Smith was strongly influenced by the leading economic liberals of his day, especially his friend David Hume, one of the major thinkers of the Scottish Enlightenment, and his teacher, Francis Hutcheson. As tutor to Henry Scott, 3rd duke of Buccleuch, Smith toured France and Switzerland, meeting many of the leading thinkers of the physiocratic school, which based its approach to political economy on the concepts of natural law, wealth, and order. Smith was particularly influenced by François Quesnay and Anne Robert Jacques Turgot. Smith's views had enormous influence in his lifetime, and still influence politics, economics, and philosophy today. His ideas are so popular in many nations that they are often referred to as the "dominant" or "popular" school. Several members of the administration of U.S. President Ronald Reagan, for example, proudly wore neckties bearing Adam Smith's image, as a symbol of their dedication to the idea of limiting the role of the state and letting market forces play a greater role in shaping public policies.

In the 1930s in the United States, the ideas of John Maynard Keynes (1883–1946) shaped economic liberal thought a great deal. Keynes was the son of Cambridge political economist John Neville Keynes and husband of the Russian ballerina Lydia Lopokova. Keynes was a political economist, government official, patron of the arts, and originator of what we now call the Keynesian school of economic analysis. It can be argued that Keynes was the most influential political economist of the 20th century and perhaps, along with Sigmund Freud, Albert Einstein, Pablo Picasso, and a few others, one of the most influential persons of this century. Keynes's great influence stems in part from his participation in three of the defining events of the century: negotiation of the Treaty of Versailles at the end of World War I, the Great Depression of the 1930s, and the Bretton Woods conference (1944), which established the monetary and trade structure of the international system after World War II.

Robert Skidelsky of the University of Warwick is the leading biographer of John Maynard Keynes. "Keynes's Middle Way" is taken from the second volume of his biography of Keynes, *John Maynard Keynes: The Economist as Savior 1920–1937*. The heart of this essay is the discussion of Keynes's famous speech "The End of Laissez Faire," in which he details the faults of the market of his day. Lord Skidelsky frames this discussion, however, in the context of Keynes's views of other systems of political economy—communism, socialism, fascism—and their faults. In the end, Skidelsky finds Keynes to be a complicated person, trying to find a middle way between the extremes of individual and society and trying to guide capitalism through a dangerous set of barriers. Keynes's attempts to save the market by introducing state actions to stabilize it demonstrates how much the concept of liberalism had changed from the way Smith conceived of it.

Today Keynes is associated with the rise of big government in Britain and the United States. It is true that he advocated government intervention to correct the fatal flaws he saw in capitalism, especially those stemming from fear, uncertainty, and doubt—three characteristics of life during the 1930s. However, as Robert Skidelsky points out, in his own writing Keynes made clear that he sought to strengthen the market through state actions, not replace it with the state. Many of the institutions and practices that we take for granted today are the legacy of Keynes's ideas, including unemployment benefits, social security insurance, bank deposit insurance, and the system of international finance institutions that were established at the 1944 Bretton Woods conference.

Karl Marx (1818–1883) was the son of a lawyer. Educated at the universities of Bonn and Berlin, he received a doctorate in philosophy. He became an editor of a liberal-democratic journal and left Germany for Paris when Prussian authorities suppressed his journal. In Paris, Marx met Friedrich Engels, the son of a wealthy textile manufacturer. One of Marx's most famous works is *The*

Communist Manifesto (1848), which he wrote with Engels for the Communist League in London. In 1849, Marx was expelled from Prussia after being acquitted for high treason. He settled in London and wrote numerous works, including *Das Capital*, his most famous. In the *Manifesto* he outlines how the economy conditions political and social relations. The economy serves as the structure upon which the wealthy bourgeoisie or owners of the means of production exploit the working class proletariat, eventually resulting in revolution and a transformation of capitalist society to a socialist society. Marx argued that because the state (government) was composed of the bourgeoisie, it supported their effort to suppress the proletariat. The bourgeoisie would do anything to stamp out the revolutionary spirit of the proletariat. Marx hints at the role imperialism and colonialism play in helping sustain the bourgeoisie, thereby postponing the day when they would "dig their own grave."

Marx's ideas have influenced and shaped the views of many socialists, communists, neo-Marxists, and structuralists the world over. There exist a great many variations of Marxist thought depending on the local (national) conditions to which his ideas are applied; thus the reference to Marxist-Leninist, Marxist-Maoist, etc. Marx's ideas have also shaped the views of many structural international political economists who, although they might not be Marxists per se, use his critique of the relationship of the oppressor to the oppressed in the international system at large to explain such problems as the underdevelopment of less developed countries (LDCs). Andre Gunder Frank's work, for instance, is often cited to explain why some of the Latin American nations have not developed, and more importantly, why they have *become* underdeveloped. Frank's argument is that these LDCs were once developed countries in their own right, to the extent that they were self-sufficient and at one time had great civilizations. But exposure to capitalist economies through trade and foreign investment has caused them to revert into an underdeveloped status.

In this part of the reader we explore still another approach to IPE: rational-choice theory. Rational-choice theory provides a tool for political economists to better understand some aspects of individual and social behavior. In "The Politics of Market Socialism," Andrei Shleifer and Robert W. Vishny apply the tools of rational-choice analysis to the issue of the transition some countries are making from communism to market socialism or to some other form of national political economy. Communism, or the classical socialist system, is a system of political economy with power and authority concentrated in the state, and especially in the communist party. Market socialism, in contrast, is characterized by less severe centralization. Whereas many resources are collectively owned, resulting in a socialist system, decision-making is decentralized in the market, leading to greater efficiency. Many people assume that market socialism will be more efficient than communism because of the lack of a communist bureaucracy. The authors suggest that this conclusion may be wrong because the interests and incentives of decision-makers under democracy, although different from those of a dictator, are not necessarily more efficient than a dictator. No democratic government is likely to place enough emphasis on economic efficiency, they argue, and the government of a nation employing market socialism is likely to have even greater opportunity to sacrifice economic efficiency for political ends. Thus, the authors argue, market socialism may be a system of political economy that is more subject to abuse of state power than either of its main alternatives.

NOTES

1. This is the definition used by Robert Gilpin in his influential book, *The Political Economy of International Relations,* (Princeton: Princeton University Press, 1987) p. 8.
2. A good deal of this history is taken from the Introduction of *The National System of Political Economy* by Reprints of Economic Classics (New York: Augustus M. Kelleyk, 1966).

1. The International Political Economy

Miles Kahler

For much of the 1980s, absent upheavals to match the oil price shocks of the 1970s, the international political economy was overshadowed by the volatility of East-West relations. This surface calm disguised sea-changes in international economic relations, changes profound in their effects on world politics and irreversible in the medium term. Some of these changes have been glacial in pace and difficult to discern. Other events that appeared cataclysmic, such as the stock market crash of October 1987, are as difficult to assess as heat lightning in a summer sky: an illusory warning or a genuine harbinger of storms to come? International economic trends that now seem irreversible may also disappear when nations—at least larger nations—alter their economic course. Margaret Thatcher and Deng Xiaoping, for example, have drastically changed domestic economic policies and international economic orientation after decades in which both were regarded as immovable. The plight of the Organization of Petroleum Exporting Countries during the 1980s demonstrates, however, that the economic destinies of apparently powerful actors can be strongly affected by both the strategies of other nations and the behavior of international markets.

Four sea-changes in the international political economy will be discussed in the first section of this essay. The relative absence of change in the political organization of international economic relations—the dog that has not barked—will be briefly noted in the second section. Third, changes in the relationship between states and markets will be examined, particularly the intensified internationalization of financial markets and the globalization of production. Finally, an assessment will be attempted of the importance of all these changes for both the character of world politics and the future U.S. policy.

STRUCTURAL CHANGE: SHIFTS IN POWER AND PLACE

The term "structural" is used here to signify changes in relative economic weight among the key players in the international economy and in their positions within the overlapping fields of economic relations (the trading or financial systems, for example). Two sea-changes became unmistakably clear in the 1980s—the rise of Japan and the divided economic prospects of the developing countries. The implications of two others—the leap toward further integration of the European Community and a more thoroughgoing incorporation of some centrally planned economies into the international economic order—will be fully apparent only in the next decade.

The rise of Japan has been an almost continuous process since the proclamation of the "Japanese miracle" in the early 1960s, but in its earlier manifestations, Japanese economic might expressed itself principally in a powerful export drive in manufactures. During the 1970s, that drive produced an array of trade disputes with the United States and Europe. In the decade that began with the publication of *Japan as Number One*,[1] however, Japan's economic reach expanded into high-technology industrial sectors and international finance, an expansion that fundamentally changed its bilateral relationship with the United States. As the Reagan administration's strategy of fiscal expansion produced massive American borrowing abroad, it became clear that Japan was home to the largest pool of exportable capital in the world economy. A share of that capital served to finance a yawning American payments deficit; other shares financed both a boom in foreign direct investment (in North America and Southeast Asia) and a more active stance in the debt crisis and development lending.[2]

To some—let us call them the optimists—the new financial clout of Japan, added to an existing manufacturing prowess that increasingly encroaches on U.S. high-tech preserves, is not a serious concern. This group has advanced two broad arguments. A number of commentators claim that Japan's ascendancy is transitory. Bill Emmott of *The Economist* has argued this most forcefully: Japan's savings rate and its external surpluses will erode with the aging of Japan's population and the emergence of new competitors in Asia; Japan's window of opportunity is a narrow one and may not outlast the century. According to this view, Japan will gradually come to look like other industrialized countries. A stronger yen has already increased the volume of manufactured imports; external pressures (and pressures from its own consumers) may force higher public spending, a greater attention to consumer welfare, and a weakening of powerful lobbies (such as the agricultural lobby) that would erode Japan's peculiar pattern of policy and its position in the international economy.

A second group of optimists argues that the international implications of Japan's rise have been overstated, since its "power portfolio"—heavily dependent on a cluster of export industries and its capital exports—is not diversified in the fashion of the United States. Hence, Japan will continue to need American military protection and American markets as much as the United States needs Japanese capital and technology. The result: an intensification of interdependence rather than American dependence on Japan.[3]

For many of these observers, the United States must "manage" the bilateral relationship as well as Japan's new role in the world economy until Japan's economic trajectory converges with that of other industrialized economies. Increasingly, however, a second set of arguments has been heard both in the United States and in Europe. Framed in military metaphors, such as "containment," and hedged by homilies on the importance of U.S.–Japanese ties, these new "revisionist" critics paint a more ambiguous portrait of Japanese aims and capabilities: the ambitious hegemonic power-to-be rather than the acquiescent partner. Japan not only is seen as the first plausible aspirant to that role in the economic sphere since 1945; it also is viewed as a new-model political economy, one that does *not* work like Western economies, and one that will remain closed unless more forceful pressure is exerted by its trading partners or an entirely new structure of managed trade is created.[4]

A second sea-change was less apparent to Americans in the 1980s: the widening gap in economic performance within the developing world. The 1970s seemed to herald an irreversible push toward economic and political influence on the part of the Third World as a collectivity, as well as on the part of "new influentials," such as Saudi Arabia and Brazil. The 1980s saw the deflation of those hopes with the collapse and only partial recovery of commodity (including oil) prices, the shocks of high real interest rates, and an abrupt decline in bank lending in the early 1980s. The lingering debt crisis destroyed the image of a homogeneous Third World, an image that may never have corresponded with reality. In the 1980s heavily indebted countries in Latin America and Sub-Saharan Africa experienced the worst decade in terms of economic performance since the Great Depression; the countries of Asia maintained higher growth rates and export performance. The divide is no longer between middle-income and poor developing countries (the Third and Fourth Worlds of the 1970s): India's performance in the 1980s was stronger than Peru on most measures; China's better than Brazil's.

Is this new divide the result of indebtedness, taken on in the preceding period of high commodity prices and easy credit, coupled with drastically altered world economic conditions in the early 1980s (high real interest rates, deep recession, plummeting commodity prices) that were beyond the control of developing economies? Or is indebtedness itself a principal symptom of a syndrome of national economic policies that were not successfully altered in the 1980s, an alteration made even more difficult by the burden of debt? Whatever explanation is advanced, the North-South cleavage changed in the 1980s. Conflicts continue between successful exporters, such as South Korea or Taiwan, and the industrialized countries, responding to their threatened industries. The larger debtors have repeatedly gone to the brink with their creditors, private and public. These patterns of conflict, however, rarely overlap: developing countries no longer aspire to a unified bargaining stance across issue-areas. While some newly industrializing countries (NICs) confront a transition to rich country status, other developing countries scramble to escape decades of economic stagnation and an increasingly marginal status in the world economy.

Looking to the immediate future, two sea-changes in the world economy appear likely to occur in the 1990s. The communist states were long excluded (and excluded themselves) from full participation in the institutions of international economic management. The Cold War and the organization of their economies by central planning rather than market principles made integration with the capitalist world economy difficult. Although some socialist states (notably Yugoslavia and Romania) found their way into the International Monetary Fund (IMF), the World Bank, and the General Agreement on Tariffs and Trade (GATT) after demonstrating their independence from the Soviet Union, it was not until the entry of Hungary and China into the Bretton Woods institutions in the 1980s that greater participation was clearly linked to a wider program of internal economic reforms. Now Poland has been tipped as a major recipient of IMF and World Bank lending, and the Soviet Union has made clear its own closer integration with the capitalist West.

This new wave of institutional participation and economic integration does not resemble the ties established during the last superpower thaw, the years of détente in the early 1970s. Then the communist regimes carefully controlled imports of technology and, less carefully, imports of capital to bolster an existing state-dominated mode of development. The pattern that is likely to emerge in the 1990s will couple closer integration with both domestic economic reforms, particularly decentralization, and institutional commitments that will make controlling the terms of integration more difficult and, possibly, more difficult to reverse. The current quandaries of Chinese policymakers suggest that the process may well be characterized by stops and starts, particularly when the political effects of economic liberalization become clearer. The fact that political upheaval did not bring a sharp turning away from the policies of economic openness in China suggests, however, the powerful internal allies that such a strategy can create in a relatively short period of time.

The significance of renewed momentum toward closer economic integration on the part of the European Community is less clear, and it will depend in part on the future course of events in Eastern Europe and the Soviet Union. The Single European Act will clearly have a substantial impact in the area of "negative integration": removal of remaining barriers to the free movement of goods, capital, and labor within the European Community. Its results in other spheres appear more conditional. Movement toward an economic and monetary union, surpassing the relative success of the European Monetary System, could founder on British opposition and German lack of enthusiasm. More important, dramatic changes in Eastern Europe could absorb the energies of Community members, particularly Germany, at a time when the inclusion of new members might slow the motor of integration in any case. In addition, the tug to the East could shift European attention from the international economic sphere, where Community institutions have reinforced common policies, to the political and strategic sphere, where joint positions have been harder to construct.

THE ORGANIZATION OF INTERNATIONAL ECONOMIC RELATIONS: THE WEIGHT OF THE PAST

In contrast to these structural shifts in the centers of international economic power and the continuing evolution of market integration that is considered below, it is worth noting that international institution-building and institutional change have not kept pace. The international organizations that crowned the postwar international economic order remain in place; their persistence symbolizes that the international rules of the game have not collapsed during two decades of economic shock. Nevertheless, their role has been repeatedly questioned and even ignored during the past decade. Even such an apparent exception as the role played by the IMF and the World Bank in managing the debt crisis appears less exceptional in the most recent phase of the crisis, as banks and debtors have moved independently toward debt reduction. Throughout the crisis, the United States, attuned to the interests of its commercial banks, has announced the close of one phase of the international debt strategy and the opening of the next.

The GATT has served as a useful locus for agreements on trade liberalization; negotiations under its aegis have also served as a means of staving off protectionist demands in the United States and other industrialized countries. Its greatest triumph—dramatic lowering of tariffs among Europe, Japan, and the United States—had been accomplished by the end of the 1970s, however, and during the 1980s, crucial trade bargains were often struck outside the GATT. (Voluntary restraints on Japanese automobile exports to the United States were only one example.) Although the most recent trade negotiations, the Uruguay Round, have widened the trade liberalization agenda to include agriculture and services as well as strengthening the GATT, the success of the negotiations remains in doubt.

Official American attitudes toward international economic institutions are certainly warmer now than they were at the beginning of the 1980s: President Bush's proposal to use the World Bank and the IMF to assist Poland is only the latest indication of this trend. Nevertheless, the overall stance of the United States and the other major capitalist countries has been measured for two reasons: their self-proclaimed fiscal bind, which (they claim) makes it increasingly difficult to extract resources from legislatures and electorates to support international institutions, and their ideological resistance to public intervention in international markets. Thus, despite the debt trap described above, public resources have provided only a small fraction of the lending that commercial banks had formerly offered to the indebted developing economies. The creditor nations have carefully avoided establishing new international mechanisms to reverse net capital outflows from the debtor countries. The industrialized states have invested new energy in another sphere of international economic policy, economic policy coordination, since the Plaza Agreement of 1985. Those steps have not, however, been incorporated in a new institutional framework, and the involvement of existing organizations, such as the IMF, has been peripheral. This reluctance to construct new institutions or to revise existing ones is apparent across international economic relations.

The most important threat to the institutional fabric, however, is neither a scarcity of resources nor ideological skepticism. The threat arises, paradoxically, from one indicator of institutional success: the growing—and increasingly heterogeneous—membership of these organizations. Developing countries, including such long-standing holdouts as Mexico, are acceding to the GATT in increasing numbers; socialist states have gained entry to the key organizations or, like the Soviet Union, are seeking membership. Apart from the challenges to cooperative solutions that sheer numbers pose for these organizations, heterogeneity of political and economic systems calls into question postwar principles of organization, such as nondiscrimination and liberalization, in a world that is no longer dominated by mixed economies of the "Atlantic" variety. Doubts about the incorporation of Japan and the East Asian NICs were noted above; the possibilities for short-term transformation in the Council for Mutual Economic Assistance (COMECON) economies can also be viewed with skepticism. Can an international order be created with this degree of national diversity? It is a question that was originally avoided by the self-exclusion of many developing countries and the division of the world between American and Soviet blocs. In the 1990s, the question will require an answer.

THE POWER OF STATES AND THE FORCE OF MARKETS

Underlying these concerns over the repositioning of states in the international economy and the efficacy of international institutions are the ongoing integration of international markets and the changing strategies of international corporations. Integration has grown most rapidly in the financial markets, where the growth of international financial transactions has consistently outstripped the growth of world trade.[5] The level of international financial integration was clearly demonstrated in the synchronized crashes that followed Wall Street's plunge in October 1987. The interconnectedness of such markets has existed since the birth of capitalism, but the current speed of transmission, closely tied to advances in computer and telecommunications technology, and the scale of financial flows across national boundaries are clearly unprecedented and deserve the label of sea-change.

The implications of financial integration for the global economy and the international financial system are not clear: the Federal Reserve successfully reestablished financial confidence in October 1987; central bank consultation has addressed the question of an international lender of last resort. Whether such mechanisms could withstand a more severe or sustained shock is less certain. For national governments, however, the effects are not obscure: their autonomy in setting economic policies is increasingly constrained, as capital controls become less effective and financial markets read their political and economic missteps with shorter and shorter time lags. Proponents of market perfection view this as a positive development, one that will keep wayward governments on the path of policy rectitude. A less optimistic view would note the blindness of the financial markets in the years preceding the debt crisis, and their tendency to overshoot in both the optimistic and the pessimistic directions on the basis of often incomplete information.

International markets for goods were marked during the 1980s by both liberalization and greater management of trade on the part of governments responding to protectionist pressures. The early years of the decade—years of deep recession, sharp upward movements of the dollar, and an unprecedented American current account deficit—witnessed a move toward greater American and European efforts to allocate international market shares in key sectors, such as steel and autos. The often predicted collapse of the trading system did not occur, however: a threat of uncontrollable protectionist pressures in the early 1980s spurred governments to open the Uruguay Round of trade negotiations. Despite rising trade barriers in certain sectors, the growth of world trade resumed after the 1981–1982 recession, and the principal targets of protectionist measures, particularly Japan and the NICs, continued their export success. Industrialized governments also moved to lower trade barriers with some of their principal trading partners: the United States and Canada, Australia and New Zealand, the 1992 project of the European Community.

Technology had not undermined closure so clearly as in the financial markets, but governments did confront greater sophistication on the part of traders if their attempts to restrain trade distorted the market too greatly: in developing countries, whole sectors moved to the black market economy in part to evade import and export controls; in such sophisticated sectors as semiconductors, "gray markets" quickly developed to satisfy demand in the United States after the 1986 U.S.–Japan Semiconductor Agreement.

Although the postwar international economic order had always included an ideological commitment by the dominant powers to liberalization in the movement of goods and capital, the free movement of labor has remained a jealously guarded sphere of national authority. In the last decade, however, it has become increasingly clear that better international communication and burgeoning mass tourism have undermined barriers to immigration at a time when the disparities between rich and poor countries remain enormous. Even a society as hostile to immigration as Japan has found it impossible to stop illegal immigration when its own businesses collude to gain cheap labor. Outside the richest countries, brain drains and labor outflows become serious restraints on national governments, particularly in the developing world; economic downturns and political repression no longer produce only the temporarily unemployed or refugees who later return to their homes. Another option, permanent emigration, is now available, as Central America, Peru, China, and East Germany have all learned of late.

The differing pace of integration in markets for capital, goods, and labor has influenced the increasingly complex strategies of transnational corporations. The global organization of production in certain sectors, such as oil, extends back many decades; but the 1980s was the decade in which the global factory came into its own. Seeking ways to put their capital and rapidly eroding technological advantages together with low-cost labor, firms in the industrialized countries developed suppliers and production sites throughout the world. They attempted to improve their competitive position through cooperative arrangements (such as licensing agreements and joint ventures) with firms that may appear to be their rivals in other settings. The pursuit of such strategies, by global giants as well as middling firms, has further blurred the distinction between "home" country and "host" country. These crosscutting corporate interests have also complicated any definition of national economic interest. Should the United States encourage Japanese investment in smaller, American, high-technology firms, for example? Are American corporations in Japan part of the U.S. economy situated abroad, or are they essentially Japanese firms? Such a web of private connections at first appears to create important pressures for liberalization in government policies: the complexity of relations among firms makes efforts at international restriction less likely to be effective or beneficial. On the other hand, nationalist political responses to these new relationships—particularly foreign investment—could provoke a backlash that will create renewed pressure for controls.

SEA-CHANGES AND THE TRANSFORMATION OF WORLD POLITICS

That this intensified if uneven integration of markets in capital, goods, and labor could be reserved by some future shock—major financial crisis, global economic depression, or war—is a possibility that has haunted liberal memories since the end of World War II. A more pertinent question is whether such dis-integration could arise from the actions of governments, perhaps through unwitting exercises in economic brinksmanship that end up unraveling, in a perverse game of tit for tat, the fabric of economic openness. Few governments are willing to argue any longer for the benefits of economic closure, whatever their skepticism about the stability of markets or the effects of external liberalization on more vulnerable groups or sectors. Governments will certainly continue to shape the rules of the game to protect the interests of politically powerful and less mobile sectors of the economy. Calculated measures in favor of dis-integration, however, seem unlikely.

If the configurations described persist, some might be tempted to argue that they will constitute a sea-change in the very character of world politics, profound enough to contribute to an "end of history." Such predictions would have seemed outlandish at the beginning of the 1980s, when the newest chapter of the Cold War intensified concerns over military dangers. Today, however, one may well ask whether relations among states are not characterized by a permanent shift toward goals of economic welfare and a concomitant rise in the importance of economic resources and economic instruments in interstate competition. Such a change is linked not only to those international economic developments already mentioned, but also to reduction in superpower rivalry and widespread, if not yet universal, internal political liberalization. Foreign policy elites may not yet be ready to accept arguments made by Paul Kennedy (among others) regarding the inherent liabilities of imperial policies, but they can hardly see any gains accruing from traditional military competition in an era when governments, in order to remain in power, must respond to their populations' outspoken desires for economic well-being.

Arguments in favor of such a benign transformation in the character of world politics can be challenged on at least three grounds. First, even if "welfarist" concerns come to dominate the domestic politics of most societies, they might produce more, rather than less, international conflict. If elites depend more on economic performance for their internal hold on power, redistributional questions may loom larger than ever in the international arena. This domestic political dynamic, coupled with the internationalization of national economies, may cause some states to define their security requirements more broadly rather than less: Japanese semiconductors may be added to Persian Gulf oil as critical constituents of national economic well-being and security. Second, elites are rarely sensitive politically to a general notion of economic welfare. Rather, they will make efforts to satisfy the economic demands of certain constituencies within their societies instead of others, thereby maintaining distributional conflicts between classes and groups. Those internal conflicts may then drive states in the direction of more conflictual foreign policies. Finally, and most important, people are not interested only in issues affecting their material well-being: nationalism and religion have resurfaced as explosive issues and major concerns in the wake of the political liberalization that we are seeing—most dramatically in Eastern Europe—and may be reflected in the international behavior of states as well.

Thus, without lapsing into a Spenglerian pessimism that risks becoming as fashionable as the most recent hype over the new era of good feelings, we should see changes in the international economy not as producing an inevitable resolution to age-old problems of interstate conflict, but as intimately tied to that conflict, as they have been since the birth of capitalism. The ever changing economic fortunes of nation-states affect their strategic position as well as their perception of national security. Internationalized though they may be, markets will continue to confront fragmented political authority. Whatever the sea-changes in the international economy, they will take place within these deeply embedded features of international relations, for they have not yet transformed them.

INTERNATIONAL ECONOMIC CHANGE AND AMERICAN POLICY

The balance between persistence and change in the international economy confronts the United States with particular challenges. Both the goals that the United States has pursued since 1945 and the instruments that it has employed to reach those goals may be called into question. One preeminent national aim has been a liberal world economy, in which any government controls and interventions that affect the free movement of goods and capital are reduced. This goal has always been qualified: the United States not only has imposed such controls itself (whether as instruments of national strategy or as responses to domestic demands), it also has recognized that completely liberalized markets might be politically insupportable.

The goal of a liberal world economy is now questioned for two reasons. First, those who view Japan and the NICs through revisionist eyes argue that the United States has become a liberal dupe in a world that does not operate according to neoclassical economic principles. As economic exchanges with the socialist economies grow, such complaints are likely to surge. Such criticisms could lead policy in several directions: protectionism, industrial policy, or reciprocal liberalization with "like-minded" countries (for example, the free trade agreement with Canada).

The second reason for viewing liberalization more skeptically derives from the reconsideration of market deregulation that is now under way. The infallible wisdom of markets, even markets untouched by political manipulation or monopolistic behavior, is less likely to be taken for granted in the future. An economic shock (a second, more severe financial crash, for example) would only add support to such criticisms.

A global rather than a regionalized world economy has been a second overarching goal of the United States; this goal has been closely related to the multilateral structure of international economic institutions and such norms as nondiscrimination in trade. Since the economic shocks of the 1970s, some observers have predicted a world economy divided into regional blocs; some of the sea-changes described above—the consolidation of Europe and the rise of Japan—may point in that direction. The United States has endorsed certain regional groupings, particularly the European Economic Community, for their value in offsetting Soviet power. If the Soviet military threat fades and regionalization takes a form that appears damaging to American economic interests, that support may disappear. The United States may need to specify its economic interests in either a global or a regionalized economic order on purely economic grounds.

In advancing its goals in the international economic arena, the United States also faces choices concerning the instruments that it employs. The role of collaboration among governments (within or outside established international institutions) must be assessed as an alternative to either unilateral measures by the United States to impose its policy preferences (for example, threats of trade sanctions to open markets) or the avoidance of political intervention in international markets. It seems unlikely that either the immiseration of parts of the world or the integration of the socialist economies can be dealt with in the absence of sustained cooperation on the part of the major industrialized countries. Throughout the 1980s, the United States was skeptical of international institutions that were often portrayed as either bloated bureaucracies or unwanted restraints on American action. A reassessment has already begun: unilateral American action is likely to be less effective, and the workings of an untrammeled market may be less desirable than innovation (or renovation) of mechanisms for international collaboration.

In any collaborative initiatives that are undertaken, the United States faces a final choice—the claims of leadership that it will make and the price that it is willing to pay for those claims. Japan has now become the largest donor of foreign aid. The Bush administration has signaled its willingness to have the European Community lead in organizing economic assistance for Eastern Europe. Our fiscal deadlock has made it difficult for the United States to lead on issues of international economic importance. In a regionalized world economy, demands would not be so great: each major actor—Japan, Europe, the United States—would tend its own backyard. If such a fragmented world is not the future that we desire, then the United States will need economic instruments for a world in which military instruments may become increasingly unsuited. If the threat of Soviet military power recedes, then a central question will be what price the United States and its taxpayers are willing to pay in order to possess those instruments and, with them, a central role in sustaining an altered international economic order.

NOTES

1. Ezra Vogel, *Japan as Number One* (Cambridge, Mass.: Harvard University Press, 1979).
2. Economist Lawrence Krause has summarized some of the latest indicators of Japan's economic power: "When measured in a common currency, Japanese per capita income is already larger than in the United States, and the rising yen is increasing the gap. . . . Japan is the largest creditor nation in the world. Seven of the eight largest commercial banks in the world are Japanese. Three of the five largest insurance companies are Japanese, including the largest (Nippon Life). The largest brokerage firm is Japanese (Nomura). . . . In 1987, the total value of equities in the Tokyo market exceeded that in New York, even before the crash, and the drop was larger in New York than in Tokyo." See his "Changing America and the Economy of the Pacific Basin," in Robert A. Scalapino et al., eds., *Pacific-Asian Economic Policies and Regional Interdependence* (Berkeley, Calif.: Institute of East Asian studies, 1988), pp. 48–49.
3. For example, see Joseph S. Nye, Jr., "Understating U.S. Strength, " *Foreign Policy*, no. 72 (Fall 1988), pp. 118–125; and Samuel P. Huntington, "The U.S.—Decline or Renewal?" *Foreign Affairs*, vol. 67, no. 2 (Winter 1988/89), pp. 90–92.
4. Although the diagnoses and prescriptions of these observers differ considerably, the Japanese have singled out a "Gang of Four" who espouse this more pessimistic view: James Fallows, Chalmers Johnson, Clyde Prestowitz, and Karel van Wolferen. For an excellent summary, see Chalmers Johnson, "Rethinking Japanese Politics: A Godfather Reports," *Freedom at Issue* (November–December 1989), pp. 5–11.
5. Ralph Bryant, *International Financial Intermediation* (Washington, D.C.: Brookings Institution, 1987).

2. The Theory of the Powers of Production and the Theory of Values

Friedrich List

Adam Smith's celebrated work is entitled, "The Nature and Causes of the Wealth of Nations." The founder of the prevailing economical school has therein indicated the double point of view from which the economy of nations, like that of private separate individuals, should be regarded.

The causes of wealth are something totally different from *wealth itself.* A person may possess wealth, i.e. exchangeable value; if, however, he does not possess the power of producing objects of more value than he consumes, he will become poorer. A person

From *The National System of Political Economy,* Second Book, chapter 12, pp. 133–148.

may be poor; if he, however, possesses the power of producing a larger amount of valuable articles than he consumes, he becomes rich.

The power of producing wealth is therefore infinitely more important than *wealth itself;* it insures not only the possession and the increase of what has been gained, but also the replacement of what has been lost. This is still more the case with entire nations (who cannot live out of mere rentals) than with private individuals. Germany has been devastated in every century by pestilence, by famine, or by civil or foreign wars; she has, nevertheless, always retained a great portion of her powers of production, and has thus quickly reattained some degree of prosperity; while rich and mighty but despot- and priest-ridden Spain, notwithstanding her comparative enjoyment of internal peace,[1] has sunk deeper into poverty and misery. The same sun still shines on the Spaniards, they still possess the same area of territory, their mines are still as rich, they are still the same people as before the discovery of America, and before the introduction of the Inquisition; but that nation has gradually lost her powers of production, and has therefore become poor and miserable. The War of Independence of the United States of America cost that nation hundreds of millions, but her powers of production were immeasurably strengthened by gaining independence, and it was for this reason that in the course of a few years after the peace she obtained immeasurably greater riches than she had ever possessed before. If we compare the state of France in the year 1809 with that of the year 1839, what a difference in favour of the latter! Nevertheless, France has in the interim lost her sovereignty over a large portion of the European continent; she has suffered two devastating invasions, and had to pay milliards of money in war contributions and indemnities.

It was impossible that so clear an intellect as Adam Smith possessed could altogether ignore the difference between wealth and its causes and the overwhelming influence of these causes on the condition of nations. In the introduction to his work, he says in clear words in effect: "Labour forms the fund from which every nation derives its wealth, and the increase of wealth depends first on the *productive power* of labour, namely on the degree of skill, dexterity, and judgment with which the labour of the nation is generally applied, and secondly on the proportion between the number of those employed productively and the number of those who are not so employed." From this we see how clearly Smith in general perceived that the condition of nations is principally dependent on the sum of their *productive powers.*

It does not, however, appear to be the plan of nature that complete sciences should spring already perfected from the brain of individual thinkers. It is evident that Smith was too exclusively possessed by the cosmopolitical idea of the physiocrats, "universal freedom of trade," and by his own great discovery, "the division of labour," to follow up the idea of the importance to a nation of its *powers of production.* However much science may be indebted to him in respect of the remaining parts of his work, the idea "division of labour" seemed to him his most brilliant thought. It was calculated to secure for his book a name, and for himself posthumous fame.

---

1. This is true respecting Spain up to the period of her invasion by Napoleon, but not subsequently. Our author's conclusions are, however, scarcely invalidated by that exception.—TR.

He had too much worldly wisdom not to perceive that whoever wishes to sell a precious jewel does not bring the treasure to market most profitably by burying it in a sack of wheat, however useful the grains of wheat may be, but better by exposing it at the forefront. He had too much experience not to know that a *débutant* (and he was this as regards political economy at the time of the publication of his work) who in the first act creates a *furore* is easily excused if in the following ones he only occasionally raises himself above mediocrity; he had every motive for making the introduction to his book, the doctrine of division of labour. Smith has not been mistaken in his calculations; his first chapter has made the fortune of his book, and founded his authority as an economist.

However, we on our part believe ourselves able to prove that just this zeal to put the important discovery "*division of labour*" in an advantageous light, has hindered Adam Smith from following up the idea "*productive power*" (which has been expressed by him in the introduction, and also frequently afterwards, although merely incidentally) and from exhibiting his doctrines in a much more perfect form. By the great value which he attached to his idea "*division of labour*" he has evidently been misled into representing labour itself as the "fund" of all the wealth of nations, although he himself clearly perceives and also states that the productiveness of labour principally depends on the degree of skill and judgment with which the labour is performed. We ask, can it be deemed scientific reasoning if we assign as the cause of a phenomenon that which in itself is the result of a number of deeper lying causes? It cannot be doubted that all wealth is obtained by means of mental and bodily exertions (labour), but yet from that circumstance no reason is indicated from which useful conclusions may be drawn; for history teaches that whole nations have, in spite of the exertions and of the thrift of their citizens, fallen into poverty and misery. Whoever desires to know and investigate how one nation from a state of poverty and barbarism has attained to one of wealth and prosperity, and how another has fallen from a condition of wealth and well-being into one of poverty and misery, has always, after receiving the information that labour is the cause of wealth and idleness the cause of poverty (a remark which King Solomon made long before Adam Smith), to put the further question, what are the causes of labour, and what the causes of idleness?

It would be more correct to describe the limbs of men (the head, hands, and feet) as the causes of wealth (we should thus at least approach far nearer to the truth), and the question then presents itself, what is it that induces these heads, arms, and hands to produce, and calls into activity these exertions? What else can it be than the spirit which animates the individuals, the social order which renders their energy fruitful, and the powers of nature which they are in a position to make use of? The more a man perceives that he must provide for the future, the more his intelligence and feelings incite him to secure the future of his nearest connections, and to promote their well-being; the more he has been from his youth accustomed to forethought and activity, the more his nobler feelings have been developed, and body and mind cultivated, the finer examples that he has witnessed from his youth, the more opportunities he has had for utilising his mental and bodily powers for the improvement of his condition, also the less he has been restrained in his legitimate activity, the more successful his past endeavours have been, and the more their fruits have been secured to him, the more he has been able to obtain public recognition and esteem by orderly conduct and activity, and the less his mind suffers from prejudices, superstition, false notions, and ignorance, so much the more will he exert his mind and limbs for the object of production, so much the more will he be able to accomplish, and so much the better will he make use of the fruits of his labour. However, most depends in all these respects on the conditions of the society in which the individual has been brought up, and turns upon this, whether science and arts flourish, and public institutions and laws tend to promote religious character, morality and intelligence, security for person and for property, freedom and justice; whether in the nation all the factors of material prosperity, agriculture, manufactures, and trade, have been equally and harmoniously cultivated; whether the power of the nation is strong enough to secure to its individual citizens progress in wealth and education from generation to generation, and to enable them not merely to utilise the natural powers of their own country to their fullest extent, but also, by foreign trade and the possession of colonies, to render the natural powers of foreign countries serviceable to their own.

Adam Smith has on the whole recognised the nature of these powers so little, that he does not even assign a productive character to the mental labours of those who maintain laws and order, and cultivate and promote instruction, religion, science, and art. His investigations are limited to that human activity which creates material values. With regard to this, he certainly recognises that its productiveness depends on the "skill and judgment" with which it is exercised; but in his investigations as to the causes of this skill and judgment, he does not go farther than the division of labour, and that he illustrates solely by exchange, augmentation of material capital, and extension of markets. His doctrine at once sinks deeper and deeper into materialism, particularism, and individualism. If he had followed up the idea *"productive power,"* without allowing his mind to be dominated by the idea of "value," "exchangeable value," he would have been led to perceive that an independent *theory of the "productive power"* must be considered by the side of a *"theory of values"* in order to explain the economical phenomena. But he thus fell into the mistake of explaining mental forces from material circumstances and conditions, and thereby laid the foundation for all the absurdities and contradictions from which his school (as we propose to prove) suffers up to the present day, and to which alone it must be attributed that the doctrines of political economy are those which are the least accessible to the most intelligent minds. That Smith's school teaches nothing else than the theory of values, is not only seen from the fact that it bases its doctrine everywhere on the conception of "value of exchange," but also from the definition which it gives of its doctrine. It is (says J.B. Say) that science which teaches how riches, or exchangeable values, are produced, distributed, and consumed. This is undoubtedly not the science which teaches how the *productive powers* are awakened and developed, and how they become repressed and destroyed. M'Culloch calls it explicitly *"the science of values,"* and recent English writers *"the science of exchange."*

Examples from private economy will best illustrate the difference between the theory of productive powers and the theory of values.

Let us suppose the case of two fathers of families, both being landed proprietors, each of whom saves yearly 1,000 thalers and has five sons. The one puts out his savings at interest, and keeps his sons at common hard work, while the other employs his savings in educating two of his sons as skilful and intelligent landowners, and in enabling the other three to learn a trade after their respective tastes; the former acts according to the theory of values, the latter according to the theory of productive powers. The first at his death may prove much richer than the second in mere exchangeable value, but it is quite otherwise as respects productive powers. The estate of the latter is divided into two parts, and every part will by the aid of improved management yield as much total produce as the whole did before; while the remaining three sons have by their talents obtained abundant means of maintenance. The landed property of the former will be divided into five parts, and every part will be worked in as bad a manner as the whole was heretofore. In the latter family a mass of different mental forces and talents is awakened and cultivated, which will increase from generation to generation, every succeeding generation possessing more power of obtaining material wealth than the preceding one, while in the former family stupidity and poverty must increase with the diminution of the shares in the landed property. So the slaveholder increases by slavebreeding the sum of his values of exchange, but he ruins the productive forces of future generations. All expenditure in the instruction of youth, the promotion of justice, defence of nations, etc. is a consumption of present values for the behoof of the productive powers. The greatest portion of the consumption of a nation is used for the education of the future generation, for promotion and nourishment of the future national productive powers.

The Christian religion, monogamy, abolition of slavery and of vassalage, hereditability of the throne, invention of printing, of the press, of the postal system, of money, weights and measures, of the calendar, of watches, of police, the introduction of the principle of freehold property, of means of transport, are rich sources of productive power. To be convinced of this, we need only compare the condition of the European states with that of the Asiatic ones. In order duly to estimate the influence which liberty of thought and conscience has on the productive forces of nations, we need only read the history of England and then that of Spain. The publicity of the administration of justice, trial by jury, parliamentary legislation, public control of State administration, self-administration of the commonalities and municipalities, liberty of the press, liberty of association for useful purposes, impart to the citizens of constitutional states, as also to their public functionaries, a degree of energy and power which can hardly be produced by other means. We can scarcely conceive of any law or any public legal decision which would not exercise a greater or smaller influence on the increase or decrease of the productive power of the nation.[1]

If we consider merely bodily labour as the cause of wealth, how can we then explain why modern nations are incomparably richer, more populous, more power-

---

1. Say states in his *Economie Politique Pratique*, vol. iii. p. 242, "Les lois ne peuvent pas créer des richesses." Certainly they cannot do this, but they create productive power, which is more important than riches, i.e. than possession of values of exchange.

ful, and prosperous than the nations of ancient times? The ancient nations employed (in proportion to the whole population) infinitely more hands, the work was much harder, each individual possessed much more land, and yet the masses were much worse fed and clothed than is the case in modern nations. In order to explain these phenomena, we must refer to the progress which has been made in the course of the last thousand years in sciences and arts, domestic and public regulations, cultivation of the mind and capabilities of production. The present state of the nations is the result of the accumulation of all discoveries, inventions, improvements, perfections, and exertions of all generations which have lived before us; they form the *mental capital of the present human race*, and every separate nation is productive only in the proportion in which it has known how to appropriate these attainments of former generations and to increase them by its own acquirements, in which the natural capabilities of its territory, its extent and geographical position, its population and political power, have been able to develop as completely and symmetrically as possible all sources of wealth within its boundaries, and to extend its moral, intellectual, commercial, and political influence over less advanced nations and especially over the affairs of the world.

The popular school of economists would have us believe that politics and political power cannot be taken into consideration in political economy. So far as it makes only values and exchange the subjects of its investigations, this may be correct; we can define the ideas of value and capital, profit, wages, and rent; we can resolve them into their elements, and speculate on what may influence their rising or falling etc. without thereby taking into account the political circumstances of the nation. Clearly, however, these matters appertain as much to private economy as to the economy of whole nations. We have merely to consider the history of Venice, of the Hanseatic League, of Portugal, Holland, and England, in order to perceive what reciprocal influence material wealth and political power exercise on each other.

The school also always falls into the strangest inconsistencies whenever this reciprocal influence forces itself on their consideration. Let us here only call to mind the remarkable dictum of Adam Smith on the English Navigation Laws.[2]

The popular school, inasmuch as it does not duly consider the nature of the powers of production, and does not take into account the conditions of nations in their aggregate, disregards especially the importance of developing in an equal ratio agriculture, manufactures and commerce, political power and internal wealth, and disregards especially the value of a manufacturing power belonging specially to the nation and fully developed in all its branches. It commits the error of placing manufacturing power in the same category with agricultural power, and of speaking of labour, natural power, capital etc. in general terms without considering the differences which exist between them. It does not perceive that between a State devoted merely to agriculture and a State possessing both agriculture and manufactures, a much greater difference exists than between a pastoral State and an agricultural one. In a condition of merely agricultural industry, caprice and slavery, superstition and igno-

2. *Wealth of Nations*, Book IV. chap. ii.

rance, want of means of culture, of trade, and of transport, poverty and political weakness exist. In the merely agricultural State only the least portion of the mental and bodily powers existing in the nation is awakened and developed, and only the least part of the powers and resources placed by nature at its disposal can be made use of, while little or no capital can be accumulated.

Let us compare Poland with England: both nations at one time were in the same stage of culture; and now what a difference. Manufactories and manufactures are the mothers and children of municipal liberty, of intelligence, of the arts and sciences, of internal and external commerce, of navigation and improvements in transport, of civilisation and political power. They are the chief means of liberating agriculture from its chains, and of elevating it to a commercial character and to a degree of art and science, by which the rents, farming profits, and wages are increased, and greater value is given to landed property. The popular school has attributed this civilising power to foreign trade, but in that it has confounded the mere exchanger with the originator. Foreign manufactures furnish the goods for the foreign trade, which the latter conveys to us, and which occasion consumption of products and raw materials which we give in exchange for the goods in lieu of money payments.

If, however, trade in the manufactures of far distant lands exercises admittedly so beneficial an influence on our agricultural industry, how much more beneficial must the influence be of those manufactures which are bound up with us locally, commercially, and politically, which not only take from us a small portion, but the largest portion of their requirements of food and of raw materials, which are not made dearer to us by great costs of transport, our trade in which cannot be interrupted by the chance of foreign manufacturing nations learning to supply their own wants themselves, or by wars and prohibitory import duties?

We now see into what extraordinary mistakes and contradictions the popular school has fallen in making material wealth or value of exchange the sole object of its investigations, and by regarding mere bodily labour as the sole productive power.

The man who breeds pigs is, according to this school, a productive member of the community, but he who educates men is a mere non-productive. The maker of bagpipes or jews-harps for sale is a productive, while the great composers and virtuosos are non-productive simply because that which they play cannot be brought into the market. The physician who saves the lives of his patients does not belong to the productive class, but on the contrary the chemist's boy does so, although the values of exchange (viz. the pills) which he produces may exist only for a few minutes before they pass into a valueless condition. A Newton, a Watt, or a Kepler is not so productive as a donkey, a horse, or a draught-ox (a class of labourers who have been recently introduced by M'Culloch into the series of the productive members of human society).

We must not believe that J.B. Say has remedied this defect in the doctrine of Adam Smith by his fiction of "*immaterial goods*" or products; he has thus merely somewhat varnished over the folly of its results, but not raised it out of its intrinsic absurdity. The mental (immaterial) producers are merely productive, according to his views, because they are remunerated with values of exchange, and because their attainments have been obtained by sacrificing values of exchange, and *not because they produce productive powers.*[3] They merely seem to him an accumulated capital. M'Culloch goes still further; he says that man is as much a product of labour as the machine which he produces, and it appears to him that in all economical investigations he must be regarded from this point of view. He thinks that Smith comprehended the correctness of this principle, only he did not deduce the correct conclusion from it. Among other things he draws the conclusion that eating and drinking are productive occupations. Thomas Cooper values a clever American lawyer at 3,000 dollars, which is about three times as much as the value of a strong slave.

The errors and contradictions of the prevailing school to which we have drawn attention, can be easily corrected from the standpoint of *the theory of the productive powers.* Certainly those who fatten pigs or prepare pills are productive, but the instructors of youths and of adults, virtuosos, musicians, physicians, judges, and administrators, are productive in a much higher degree. The former *produce values of exchange,* and the latter *productive powers,* some by enabling the future generation to become producers, others by furthering the morality and religious character of the present generation, a third by ennobling and raising the powers of the human mind, a fourth by preserving the productive power of his patients, a fifth by rendering human rights and justice secure, a sixth by constituting and protecting public security, a seventh by his art and by the enjoyment which it occasions fitting men the better to produce values of exchange. In the doctrine of mere values, these *producers of the productive powers* can of course only be taken into consideration so far as their services are rewarded by values of exchange; and this manner of regarding their services may in some instances have its practical use, as e.g. in the doctrine of public taxes, inasmuch as these have to be satisfied by values of exchange. But whenever our consideration is given to the nation (as a whole and in its international relations) it is utterly insufficient, and leads to a series of narrow-minded and false views.

The prosperity of a nation is not, as Say believes, greater in the proportion in which it has amassed more wealth (i.e. values of exchange), but in the proportion in which it has more *developed its powers of production.* Although laws and public institutions do not produce immediate values, they nevertheless produce productive powers, and Say is mistaken if he maintains that nations have been enabled to become wealthy under all forms of government, and that by means of laws no wealth can be created. The foreign trade of a nation must not be estimated in the way in which individual merchants judge it, solely and only according to the theory of values (i.e. by regarding merely the gain at any particular moment of some material advantage); the nation is bound to keep steadily in view all these conditions on which its present and future existence, prosperity, and power depend.

The nation must sacrifice and give up a measure of material property in order

---

3. From the great number of passages wherein J.B. Say explains this view, we merely quote the newest—from the sixth volume of *Economie Politique Pratique,* p. 307: "Le talent d'un avocat, d'un médecin, qui a été acquis au prix de quelque sacrifice et qui produit un revenu, est une valeur capitale, non transmissible à la vérité, mais qui réside néanmoins dans un corps visible, celui de la personne qui le possède."

to gain culture, skill, and powers of united production; it must sacrifice some present advantages in order to insure to itself future ones. If, therefore, a manufacturing power developed in all its branches forms a fundamental condition of all higher advances in civilisation, material prosperity, and political power in every nation (a fact which, we think, we have proved from history); if it be true (as we believe we can prove) that in the present conditions of the world a new unprotected manufacturing power cannot possibly be raised up under free competition with a power which has long since grown in strength and is protected on its own territory; how can anyone possibly undertake to prove by arguments only based on the mere theory of values, that a nation ought to buy its goods like individual merchants, at places where they are to be had the cheapest—that we act foolishly if we manufacture anything at all which can be got cheaper from abroad—that we ought to place the industry of the nation at the mercy of the self-interest of individuals—that protective duties constitute monopolies, which are granted to the individual home manufacturers at the expense of the nation? It is true that protective duties at first increase the price of manufactured goods; but it is just as true, and moreover acknowledged by the prevailing economical school, that in the course of time, by the nation being enabled to build up a completely developed manufacturing power of its own, those goods are produced more cheaply at home than the price at which they can be imported from foreign parts. If, therefore, a sacrifice of *value* is caused by protective duties, it is made good by the gain of a *power of production*, which not only secures to the nation an infinitely greater amount of material goods, but also industrial independence in case of war. Through industrial independence and the internal prosperity derived from it the nation obtains the means for successfully carrying on foreign trade and for extending its mercantile marine; it increases its civilisation, perfects its institutions internally, and strengthens its external power. A nation capable of developing a manufacturing power, if it makes use of the system of protection, thus acts quite in the same spirit as that landed proprietor did who by the sacrifice of some material wealth allowed some of his children to learn a productive trade.

Into what mistakes the prevailing economical school has fallen by judging conditions according to the mere theory of values which ought properly to be judged according to the theory of powers of production, may be seen very clearly by the judgment which J.B. Say passes upon the bounties which foreign countries sometimes offer in order to facilitate exportation; he maintains that "*these are presents made to our nation.*" Now if we suppose that France considers a protective duty of twenty-five per cent sufficient for her not yet perfectly developed manufactures, while England were to grant a bounty on exportation of thirty per cent, what would be the consequence of the "present" which in this manner the English would make to the French? The French consumers would obtain for a few years the manufactured articles which they needed much cheaper than hitherto, but the French manufactories would be ruined, and millions of men be reduced to beggary or obliged to emigrate, or to devote themselves to agriculture for employment. Under the most favourable circumstances, the present consumers and customers of the French agriculturists would be converted into competitors with the latter, agricultural production would be increased, and the consumption lowered. The necessary consequence would be diminution in value of the products, decline in the value of property, national poverty and national weakness in France. The English "present" in mere value would be dearly paid for in loss of power; it would seem like the present which the Sultan is wont to make to his pashas by sending them valuable *silken cords*.

Since the time when the Trojans were "presented" by the Greeks with a wooden horse, the acceptance of "presents" from other nations has become for the nation which receives them a very questionable transaction. The English have given the Continent presents of immense value in the form of subsidies, but the Continental nations have paid for them dearly by the loss of power. These subsidies acted like a bounty on exportation in favour of the English, and were detrimental to the German manufactories. If England bound herself to-day to supply the Germans gratuitously for years with all they required in manufactured articles, we could not recommend them to accept such an offer. If the English are enabled through new inventions to produce linen forty per cent cheaper than the Germans can by using the old process, and if in the use of their new process they merely obtain a start of a few years over the Germans, in such a case, were it not for protective duties, one of the most important and oldest branches of Germany's industry will be ruined. It will be as if a limb of the body of the German nation had been lost. And who would be consoled for the loss of an arm by knowing that he had nevertheless bought his shirts forty per cent cheaper?

If the English very often find occasion to offer presents to foreign nations, very different are the forms in which this is done; it is not unfrequently done against their will; always does it behove foreign nations well to consider whether or not the present should be accepted. Through their position as the manufacturing and commercial monopolists of the world, their manufactories from time to time fall into the state which they call "glut," and which arises from what they call "overtrading." At such periods everybody throws his stock of goods into the steamers. After the lapse of eight days the goods are offered for sale in Hamburg, Berlin, or Frankfort, and after three weeks in New York, at fifty per cent under their real value. The English manufacturers suffer for the moment, but they are saved, and they compensate themselves later on by better prices. The German and American manufacturers receive the blows which were deserved by the English—they are ruined. The English nation merely sees the fire and hears the report of the explosion; the fragments fall down in other countries, and if their inhabitants complain of bloody heads, the intermediate merchants and dealers say, "The crisis has done it all!" If we consider how often by such crises the whole manufacturing power, the system of credit, nay the agriculture, and generally the whole economical system of the nations who are placed in free competition with England, are shaken to their foundations, and that these nations have afterwards notwithstanding richly to recompense the English manufacturers by higher prices, ought we not then to become very sceptical as to the propriety of the commercial conditions of nations being regulated according to the mere theory of values and according to cosmopolitical principles? The prevailing economical school has never deemed it expedient to elucidate the causes and effects of such commercial crises.

The great statesmen of all modern nations, almost without exception, have comprehended the great influence of manufactures and manufactories on the wealth, civilisation, and power of nations, and the necessity of protecting them. Edward III comprehended this like Elizabeth; Frederick the Great like Joseph II; Washington like Napoleon. Without entering into the depths of the theory, their foreseeing minds comprehended the nature of industry in its entirety, and appreciated it correctly. It was reserved for the school of physiocrats to regard this nature from another point of view in consequence of a sophistical line of reasoning. Their castle in the air has disappeared; the more modern economical school itself has destroyed it; but even the latter has also not disentangled itself from the original errors, but has merely advanced somewhat farther from them. Since it did not recognise the difference between productive power and mere values of exchange, and did not investigate the former independently of the latter, but subordinated it to the theory of values of exchange, it was impossible for that school to arrive at the perception how greatly the nature of the agricultural productive power differs from the nature of the manufacturing productive power. It does not discern that through the development of a manufacturing industry in an agricultural nation a mass of mental and bodily powers, of natural powers and natural resources, and of instrumental powers too (which latter the prevailing school terms "capital"), is brought to bear, and brought into use, which had not previously been active, and would never have come into activity but for the formation and development of an internal manufacturing power; it imagines that by the establishment of manufacturing industry these forces must be taken away from agriculture, and transferred to manufacture, whereas the latter to a great extent is a perfectly new and additional power, which, very far indeed from increasing at the expense of the agricultural interest, is often the means of helping that interest to attain a higher degree of prosperity and development.

3. How the World Works

James Fallows

In Japan in the springtime of 1992 a trip to Hitotsubashi University, famous for its economics and business faculties, brought me unexpected good luck. Like several other Japanese universities, Hitotsubashi is almost heartbreaking in its cuteness. The road from the station to the main campus is lined with cherry trees, and my feet stirred up little puffs of white petals. Students glided along on their bicycles, looking as if they were enjoying the one stress-free moment of their lives. They probably were. In sur-

From "How the World Works," by James Fallows. *The Atlantic Monthly,* December 1993, pp. 61–87. Reprinted by permission.

veys huge majorities of students say that they study "never" or "hardly at all" during their university careers. They had enough of that in high school.

I had gone to Hitotsubashi to interview a professor who was making waves. Since the end of the Second World War, Japanese diplomats and businessmen have acted as if the American economy should be the model for Japan's own industrial growth. Not only should Japanese industries try to catch up with America's lead in technology and production but also the nation should evolve toward a standard of economic maturity set by the United States. Where Japan's economy differed from the American model—for instance, in close alliances between corporations which U.S. antitrust laws would forbid—the difference should be considered temporary, until Japan caught up.

Through the 1980s a number of foreign observers challenged this assumption, saying that Japan's economy might not necessarily become more like America's with the passing years. Starting in 1990 a number of Japanese businessmen and scholars began publicly saying the same thing, suggesting that Japan's business system might be based on premises different from those that prevailed in the West. Professor Iwao Nakatani, the man I went to Hitotsubashi to meet, was one of the most respected members of this group, and I spent the afternoon listening to his argument while, through the window, I watched petals drifting down.

On the way back to the station I saw a bookstore sign advertising Western-language books for sale. I walked to the back of the narrow store and for the thousandth time felt both intrigued and embarrassed by the consequences of the worldwide spread of the English language. In row upon row sat a jumble of books that had nothing in common except that they were published in English. Self-help manuals by Zig Ziglar. Bodice-rippers from the Harlequin series. A Betty Crocker cookbook. The complete works of Sigmund Freud. One book by, and another about, Friedrich List.

Friedrich List! For at least five years I'd been scanning used-book stores in Japan and America looking for just these books, having had no luck in English-language libraries. I'd scoured stores in Taiwan that specialized in pirated reprints of English-language books for about a tenth their original cost. I'd called the legendary Strand bookstore, in Manhattan, from my home in Kuala Lumpur, begging them to send me a note about the success of their search (it failed) rather than make me wait on hold. In all that time these were the first books by or about List I'd actually laid eyes on.

One was a biography, by a professor in the north of England. The other was a translation, by the same professor, of a short book List had written in German. Both were slim volumes, which, judging by the dust on their covers, had been on the shelf for years. I gasped when I opened the first book's cover and saw how high the price was—9,500 yen, about $75. For the set? I asked hopefully. No, apiece, the young woman running the store told me. Books are always expensive in Japan, but even so this seemed steep. No doubt the books had been priced in the era when one dollar was worth twice as many yen as it was by the time I walked into the store. I opened my wallet, pulled out a 10,000-yen note, took my change and the biography, and left the store. A few feet down the sidewalk I turned around, walked back to the store, and used the rest of my money to buy the other book. I would always have regretted passing it up.

Why Friedrich List? The most I had heard about List in the preceding five years, from economists in Seoul and Osaka and Tokyo, the more I had wondered why I had virtually never heard of him while studying economics in England and the United States. By the time I saw his books in the shop beneath the cherry trees, I had come to think of him as the dog that didn't bark. He illustrated the strange self-selectivity of Anglo-American thinking about economics.

I emphasize "Anglo-American" because in this area the United Kingdom and the United States are like each other and different from most of the rest of the world. The two countries have dominated world politics for more than a century, and the dominance of the English language lets them ignore what is being said and thought overseas—and just how isolated they have become. The difference shows up this way: The Anglo-American system of politics and economics, like any system, rests on certain principles and beliefs. But rather than acting as if these are the best principles, or the ones their societies prefer, Britons and Americans often act as if these were the *only possible* principles and no one, except in error, could choose any others. Political economics becomes an essentially religious question, subject to the standard drawback of any religion—the failure to understand why people outside the faith might act as they do.

To make this more specific: Today's Anglo-American world view rests on the shoulders of three men. One is Isaac Newton, the father of modern science. One is Jean-Jacques Rousseau, the father of liberal political theory. (If we want to keep this purely Anglo-American, John Locke can serve in his place.) And one is Adam Smith, the father of laissez-faire economics. From these founding titans come the principles by which advanced society, in the Anglo-American view, is supposed to work. A society is supposed to understand the laws of nature as Newton outlined them. It is supposed to recognize the paramount dignity of the individual, thanks to Rousseau, Locke, and their followers. And it is supposed to recognize that the most prosperous future for the greatest number of people comes from the free workings of the market. So Adam Smith taught, with axioms that were enriched by David Ricardo, Alfred Marshall, and the other giants of neoclassical economics.

The most important thing about this summary is the moral equivalence of the various principles. Isaac Newton worked in the realm of fundamental science. Without saying so explicitly, today's British and American economists act as if the economic principles they follow had a similar hard, provable, undebatable basis. If you don't believe in the laws of physics—actions create reactions, the universe tends toward greater entropy—you are by definition irrational. And so with economics. If you don't accept the views derived from Adam Smith—that free competition is ultimately best for all participants, that protection and interference are inherently wrong—then you are a flat-earther.

Outside the Unite States and Britain the matter looks quite different. About science there is no dispute. "Western" physics is the physics of the world. About politics there is more debate: with the rise of Asian economies some Asian political leaders, notably Lee Kuan Yew, of Singapore, and several cautious figures in Japan, have in effect been saying that Rousseau's political philosophy is not necessarily the world's philosophy. Societies may work best, Lee and others have said, if they pay less attention to the individual and more to the welfare of the group.

But the difference is largest when it comes to economics. In the non-Anglophone world Adam Smith is merely one of several theorists who had important ideas about organizing economies. In most of East Asia and continental Europe the study of economics is less theoretical than in England and America (which is why English-speakers monopolize Nobel Prizes) and more geared toward solving business problems. In Japan economics has in effect been considered a branch of geopolitics—that is, as the key to the nation's strength or vulnerability in dealing with other powers. From this practical-minded perspective English-language theorists seem less useful than their challengers, such as Friedrich List.

TWO CLASHING WORLD VIEWS

Britons and Americans tend to see the past two centuries of economics as one long progression toward rationality and good sense. In 1776 Adam Smith's *The Wealth of Nations* made the case against old-style mercantilism, just as the Declaration of Independence made the case against old-style feudal and royal domination. Since then more and more of the world has come to the correct view—or so it seems in the Anglo-American countries. Along the way the world has met such impediments as neo-mercantilism, radical unionism, sweeping protectionism, socialism, and, of course, communism. One by one the worst threats have given way. Except for a few lamentable areas of backsliding, the world has seen the wisdom of Adam Smith's ways.

Yet during this whole time there has been an alternative school of thought. The Enlightenment philosophers were not the only ones to think about how the world should be organized. During the eighteenth and nineteenth centuries the Germans were also active—to say nothing of the theorists at work in Tokugawa Japan, late imperial China, czarist Russia, and elsewhere.

The Germans deserve emphasis—more than the Japanese, the Chinese, the Russians, and so on—because many of their philosophies endure. These did not take root in England or America, but they were carefully studied, adapted, and applied in parts of Europe and Asia, notably Japan. In place of Rousseau and Locke the Germans offered Hegel. In place of Adam Smith they had Friedrich List.

The German economic vision differs from the Anglo-American in many ways, but the crucial differences are these:

"Automatic" Growth versus Deliberate Development.   The Anglo-American approach emphasizes the unpredictability and unplannability of economics. Technologies change. Tastes change. Political and human circumstances change. And because life is so fluid, attempts at central planning are virtually doomed to fail. The best way to "plan," therefore, is to leave the adaptation to the people who have their own money at stake. These are the millions of entrepreneurs who make up any country's economy. No planning agency could have better information than they about the direction things are moving, and no one could have a stronger incentive than those who hope to make a profit and avoid a loss. By the logic of the Anglo-American system, if each individual does what is best for him or her, the result will be what is best for the nation as a whole.

Although List and others did not use exactly this term, the German school was more concerned with "market failures." In the language of modern economics these are the cases in which normal market forces produce a clearly undesirable result. The standard illustration involves pollution. If the law allows factories to dump pollutants into the air or water, then every factory will do so. Otherwise, their competitors will have lower costs and will squeeze them out. This "rational" behavior will leave everyone worse off. The answer to such a market failure is for the society—that is, the government—to set standards that all factories must obey.

Friedrich List and his best-known American counterpart, Alexander Hamilton, argued that industrial development entailed a more sweeping sort of market failure. Societies did not automatically move from farming to small crafts to major industries just because millions of small merchants were making decisions for themselves. If every person put his money where the return was greatest, the money might not automatically go where it would do the nation the most good. For it to do so required a plan, a push, an exercise of central power. List drew heavily on the history of his times—in which the British government deliberately encouraged British manufacturing and the fledgling American government deliberately discouraged foreign competitors.

This is the gist of List's argument, from *The Natural System of Political Economy*, which he wrote in five weeks in 1837:

> The cosmopolitan theorists [List's term for Smith and his ilk] do not question the importance of industrial expansion. They assume, however, that this can be achieved by adopting the policy of free trade and by leaving individuals to pursue their own private interests. They believe that in such circumstances a country will automatically secure the development of those branches of manufacture which are best suited to its own particular situation. They consider that government action to stimulate the establishment of industries does more harm than good. . . .
>
> The lessons of history justify our opposition to the assertion that states reach economic maturity most rapidly if left to their own devices. A study of the origin of various branches of manufacture reveals that industrial growth may often have been due to chance. It may be chance that leads certain individuals to a particular place to foster the expansion of an industry that was once small and insignificant—just as seeds blown by chance by the wind may sometimes grow into big trees. But the growth of industries is a process that may take hundreds of years to complete and one should not ascribe to sheer chance what a nation has achieved through its laws and institutions. In England Edward III created the manufacture of woolen cloth and Elizabeth founded the mercantile marine and foreign trade. In France Colbert was responsible for all that a great power needs to develop its economy. Following these examples every responsible government should strive to remove those obstacles that hinder the progress of civilisation and should stimulate the growth of those economic forces that a nation carries in its bosom.

Consumers versus Producers.   The Anglo-American approach assumes that the ultimate measure of a society is its level of consumption. Competition is good, because it kills off producers whose prices are too high. Killing them off is good, because more-efficient suppliers will give the consumer a better deal. Foreign trade is very good, because it means that the most efficient suppliers in the whole world will be able to compete. It doesn't even matter why competitors are willing to sell for less. They may really be more efficient; they may be determined to dump their goods for reasons of their own. In either case the consumer is better off. He has the ton of steel, the cask of wine, or—in today's terms—the car or computer that he might have bought from a domestic manufacturer, plus the money he saved by buying foreign goods.

In the Friedrich List view, this logic leads to false conclusions. In the long run, List argued, a society's well-being and its overall wealth are determined not by what the society can *buy* but by what it can *make*. This is the corollary of the familiar argument about foreign aid: Give a man a fish and you feed him for a day. Teach him how to fish and you feed him for his life.

List was not concerned here with the morality of consumption. Instead he was interested in both strategic and material well-being. In strategic terms nations ended up being dependent or independent according to their ability to make things for themselves. Why were Latin Americans, Africans, and Asians subservient to England and France in the nineteenth century? Because they could not make the machines and weapons Europeans could.

In material terms a society's wealth over the long run is greater if that society also controls advanced activities. That is, if you buy the ton of steel or cask of wine at bargain rates this year, you are better off, as a consumer, right away. But over ten years, or fifty, you and your children may be stronger as both consumers and producers if you learn how to make the steel and wine yourself. If you can make steel rather than just being able to buy it, you'll be better able to make machine tools. If you're able to make machine tools, you'll be better able to make engines, robots, airplanes. If you're able to make engines and robots and airplanes, your children and grandchildren will be more likely to make advanced products and earn high incomes in the decades ahead.

The German school argued that emphasizing consumption would eventually be self-defeating. It would bias the system away from wealth creation—and ultimately make it impossible to consume as much. To use a homely analogy: One effect of getting regular exercise is being able to eat more food, just as an effect of steadily rising production is being able to consume more. But if people believe that the reason to get exercise is to permit themselves to eat more, rather than for longer-term benefits, they will behave in a different way. List's argument was that developing productive power was in itself a reward. "The forces of production are the tree on which wealth grows," List wrote in another book, called *The National System of Political Economy*.

> The tree which bears the fruit is of greater value than the fruit itself. . . . The prosperity of a nation is not . . . greater in the proportion in which it has amassed more wealth (ie, values of exchange), but in the proportion in which it has more *developed its powers of production*.

Process versus Result.   In economics and politics alike the Anglo-American theory emphasizes how the game is played, not who wins or loses. If the rules are fair, then the best candidate will win. If you want better politics or a stronger economy, you should concentrate on reforming the rules by which political and economic struggles are waged. Make sure everyone can vote; make sure everyone can bring new products to market. Whatever people choose under those fair rules will by definition be the best result. Abraham Lincoln or Warren Harding, Shakespeare or *Penthouse*—in a fair system whatever people choose will be right.

The government's role, according to this outlook, is not to tell people how they should pursue happiness or grow rich. Rather, its role is that of referee—making sure no one cheats or bends the rules of "fair play," whether by voter fraud in the political realm or monopoly in the economic.

In the late twentieth century the clearest practical illustration of this policy has been the U.S. financial market. The government is actively involved—but only to guard the process, not to steer the results. It runs elaborate sting operations to try to prevent corporate officials from trading on inside information. It requires corporations to publish detailed financial reports every quarter, so that all investors will have the same information to work from. It takes companies to court—IBM, AT&T,— whenever they seem to be growing too strong and stunting future competitors. It exposes pension-fund managers to punishment if they do not invest their assets where the dividends are greatest.

These are all ways of ensuring that the market will "get prices right," as economists say, so that investments will flow to the best possible uses. Beyond that it is up to the market to decide where the money goes. Short-term loans to cover the budget deficits in Mexico or the United States? Fine. Long-term investments in cold-fusion experimentation? Fine. The market will automatically assign each prospect the right price. If fusion engines really would revolutionize the world, then investors will voluntarily risk their money there.

The German view is more paternalistic. People might not automatically choose the best society or the best use of their money. The state, therefore, must be concerned with both the process and the result. Expressing an Asian variant of the German view, the sociologist Ronald Dore has written that the Japanese—"like all good Confucianists"—believe that "you cannot get a decent, moral society, not even an efficient society, simply out of the mechanisms of the market powered by the motivational fuel of self-interest." So, in different words, said Friedrich List.

Individuals versus the Nation.   The Anglo-American view focuses on how individuals fare as consumers and on how the whole world fares as a trading system. But it does not really care about the intermediate levels between one specific human being and all five billion—that is, about communities and nations.

This criticism may seem strange, considering that Adam Smith called his mighty work *The Wealth of Nations*. It is true that Smith was more of a national-defense enthusiast than most people who now invoke his name. For example, he said that the art of war was the "noblest" of the arts, and he approved various tariffs that would keep defense-related industries strong—which in those days meant sailcloth making. He also said that since defense "is of much more importance than opulence, the act of navigation is, perhaps, the wisest of all the commercial regulations of England." This "act of navigation" was, of course, the blatantly protectionist legislation designed to restrict the shipment of goods going to and from England mostly to English ships.

Still, the assumption behind the Anglo-American model is that if you take care of the individuals, the communities and nations will take care of themselves. Some communities will suffer, as dying industries and inefficient producers go down, but other communities will rise. And as for nations as a whole, outside the narrow field of national defense they are not presumed to have economic interests. There is no general "American" or "British" economic interest beyond the welfare of the individual consumers who happen to live in America or Britain.

The German view is more concerned with the welfare, indeed sovereignty, of people in groups—in communities, in nations. This is its most obvious link with the Asian economic strategies of today. Friedrich List fulminated against the "cosmopolitan theorists," like Adam Smith, who ignored the fact that people lived in nations and that their welfare depended to some degree on how their neighbors fared. In the real world happiness depends on more than how much money you take home. If the people around you are also comfortable (though, ideally, not as comfortable as you), you are happier and safer than if they are desperate. This, in brief, is the case that today's Japanese make against the American economy: American managers and professionals live more opulently than their counterparts in Japan, but they have to guard themselves, physically and morally, against the down-and-out people with whom they share the country.

In the German view, the answer to this predicament is to pay explicit attention to the welfare of the nation. If a consumer has to pay 10 percent more for a product made by his neighbors than for one from overseas, it will be worse for him in the short run. But in the long run, and in the broadest definitions of well-being, he might be better off. As List wrote in *The National System of Political Economy,*

> Between each individual and entire humanity, however, stands the NATION, with its special language and literature, with its peculiar origin and history, with its special manners and customs, laws and institutions, with the claims of all these for existence, independence, perfection, and continuance for the future, and with its separate territory; a society which, united by a thousand ties of mind and of interests, combines itself into one independent whole.

Economic policies, in the German view, will be good or bad depending on whether they take into account this national economic interest. Which leads to

Business as Peace versus Business as War.   By far the most uplifting part of the Anglo-American view is the idea that everyone can prosper at once. Before Adam Smith, the Spanish and Portuguese mercantilists viewed world trade as a kind of battle. What I won, you lost. Adam Smith and David Ricardo demonstrated that you and I could win at the same time. If I bought your wine and you bought my wool, we would both have more of what we wanted, for the same amount of work. The result would be the economist's classic "positive sum" interaction. Your well-being and my well-being added together would be greater than they were before our trade.

The Germans had a more tragic, or "zero sum"–like, conception of how nations dealt with each other. Some won; others lost. Economic power often led to political power, which in turn let one nation tell others what to do. Since the Second World War, American politicians have often said that their trading goal is a "level playing field" for competition around the world. This very image implies a horizontal relationship among nations, in which they all good-naturedly joust as more or less equal rivals. "These horizontal metaphors are fundamentally misleading," the American writer John Judis has written in the magazine *In These Times.*

> Instead of being grouped horizontally on a flat field, nations have always been organized vertically in a hierarchical division of labor. The structure of the world economy more accurately resembles a pyramid or a cone rather than a plane. In the 17th century, the Dutch briefly stood atop the pyramid. Then, after a hundred year transition during which the British and French vied for supremacy, the British emerged in 1815 as the world's leading industrial and financial power, maintaining their place through the end of the century. Then, after about a forty-year transition, the U.S. came out of World War II on top of the pyramid. Now we are in a similar period of transition from which it is likely, after another two decades, that Japan will emerge as the leading industrial power.

The same spirit and logic run through List's arguments. Trade is not just a game. Over the long sweep of history some nations lose independence and control of their destiny if they fall behind in trade. Therefore nations must think about it strategically, not just as a matter of where they can buy the cheapest shirt this week.

In *The Natural System of Political Economy,* List included a chapter on this theme, "The Dominant Nation." Like many other things written about Britain in the nineteenth century, it makes bittersweet reading for twentieth-century Americans. "England's manufactures are based upon highly efficient political and social institutions, upon powerful machines, upon great capital resources, upon an output larger than that of all other countries, and upon a complete network of internal transport facilities," List said of the England of the 1830s, as many have said of the United States of the 1950s and 1960s.

> A nation which makes goods more cheaply than anyone else and possesses immeasurably more capital than anyone else is able to grant its customers more substantial and longer credits than anyone else. . . . By accepting or by excluding the import of their raw materials and other products, England—all powerful as a manufacturing and commercial country—can confer great benefits or inflict great injuries upon nations with relatively backward economies.

This is what England lost when it lost "dominance," and what Japan is gaining now.

Morality versus Power.   By now the Anglo-American view has taken on a moral tone that was embryonic when Adam Smith wrote his book. If a country disagrees with the Anglo-American axioms, it doesn't just disagree: it is a "cheater." Japan "cheats" the world trading system by protecting its rice farmers. America "cheats" with its price supports for sugar-beet growers and its various other restrictions on trade. Malaysia "cheated" by requiring foreign investors to take on local partners. And on and on. If the rules of the trading system aren't protected from such cheating, the whole system might collapse and bring back the Great Depression.

In the German view, economics is not a matter of right or wrong, or cheating or playing fair. It is merely a matter of strong or weak. The gods of trade will help those who help themselves. No code of honor will defend the weak, as today's Latin Americans and Africans can attest. If a nation decides to help itself—by protecting its own industries, by discriminating against foreign products—then that is a decision, not a sin.

WISHING AWAY REALITY

Why bring the Germans into it? Because they had a lasting effect—outside the Anglo-American bloc. With the arrival of Commodore Matthew Perry and his American warships in 1853, the Japanese realized that the Western world had far outstripped them in both commercial and military technology. Throughout the rest of Asia were examples of what happened to countries that were weaker than the Europeans or the Americans: they turned into colonies. Through the rest of the nineteenth century Japan's leaders devoted themselves to modernizing the country, so that it would no longer be vulnerable. During the decades of sustained creativity known as the Meiji era, from 1868 to 1912, Japanese scholars, industrialists, and administrators carefully studied Western theories about how economies grew. In the writings of List and other continental theorists they found a set of prescriptions more persuasive than the laissez-faire teachings of Adam Smith.

The most important part of the German-Asian argument is its near invisibility in the English-speaking world, especially the United States. The problem is not that Americans don't accept the German analysis: in many ways it is flawed. The problem is that they don't know that it exists. For instance, a popular dictionary of economics, edited by American and British economists and published in 1991, has a long explanation of the Laffer curve but no mention of List.

Some "real" economists are not quite so closed-minded. Since at least the early 1980s economists at several American universities have, in essence, rediscovered Friedrich List. (But not at all universities. In 1992 Robert Wade, the author of the influential book *Governing the Market*, went looking in the MIT library for List's work. Wade previously had been teaching in Korea, and there he had found plenty of copies of List's works in every campus bookstore. But in the catalogue of MIT's vast library system Wade found an entry for just a single volume by List, *The National System of Political Economy*, in an edition published in 1885. When Wade finally obtained the book, he found that it had last been checked out in 1966.) They have examined more and more failures in the Anglo-American model. They have found more and more evidence that "cheating," in the form of protectionism, can increase a nation's wealth.

But very little of this news has trickled down to the realms where economics is usually discussed—newspaper editorials, TV talk shows, and the other forms of punditry that define reasonable and unreasonable ideas. When Americans talk about wealth, poverty, and their nation's place in the world, they often act as if Adam Smith's theories were the only theories still in play.

After the World Bank's meeting in Bangkok in 1991 an editorial writer for *The Wall Street Journal* proclaimed that "with a few sickly exceptions, such as the decaying Communist holdouts of China and Vietnam, it seems that the ideas of Adam Smith, of Alfred Marshall, of Milton Friedman, have triumphed. We are all capitalists now."

This is true only if we accept the most vulgar and imprecise statement of what being a capitalist means. The economies that have grown most impressively over the past generation—from Germany to Thailand to Korea to Japan—all certainly believe in competition. Toyota and Nissan grow strong fighting each other. Daewoo and Hyundai compete on products from cars to computers to washing machines. But it would be very hard to find a businessman or an official in these countries who would say, with a straight face, that these industries grew "automatically" or in a "natural" way.

Two years ago another *Wall Street Journal* item, this one a review of a book on trade, said,

> [The author] puts it well: "The benefits of unilaterally adopting free trade now are greater than the benefits of multilateral adoption of free trade ten or fifteen years from now." Ask Hong Kong, which has totally shunned retaliation and not coincidentally has had the highest growth rate in the world over the past three decades.

Yes, indeed—ask Hong Kong. Since the end of the Second World War its policy has generally been laissez-faire. Compared with the rest of Asia, Hong Kong interferes less, plans less, and leaves market forces more on their own. What has been the result? During the 1980s the real earnings of Hong Kong's people rose more slowly than those of the people of Korea, Singapore, Thailand, and Taiwan. It is a busy, bustling entrepôt of merchants, especially those handling commerce in and out of China. But as an industrial center it is falling behind its neighbors.

In the mid-1980s David Aikman, a journalist for *Time,* wrote a book about the "miracle" economies of Asia. The successes of Taiwan and Hong Kong, he wrote, "demonstrate just how faithful, consciously or not, the rulers of these two countries have been to American conceptions of free enterprise."

Despite Hong Kong's lack of regulations, though, and despite the small businesses that abound in Taiwan, to say that either of these places behaves in an "American" way is to drain the term of all meaning. For example, as late as 1987 most imports of steel into Taiwan had to be approved by the nation's big steel maker, China Steel. The United States, too, protects its steel industry, but this is presumably not what the author meant in saying that Taiwan had been "faithful" to American concepts of free enterprise.

"There is a great deal of misinformation abroad about the trade regimes of

[Taiwan and Korea], misinformation which is cultivated by the governments to conceal how much real protection there has been," the economist Robert Wade wrote in an exhaustive study that concentrated on Taiwan and rebutted virtually everything in Aikman's book.

> East Asian trade regimes are inconsistent in important ways with even a modified version of the standard economist's account of what a good trade regime looks like. . . . It is amazing and even scandalous that the distinguished academic theorists of trade policy . . . . *have not tried* to reconcile these facts about East Asian trade regimes with their core prescriptions [emphasis added]. . . .

Anyone who reads American or British newspapers or listens to political speeches in English could provide other examples. But they're not necessary. The Anglo-American theories have obviously won the battle of ideas—when that battle is carried out in English. The concepts of consumer welfare, comparative advantage, and freest possible trade now seem not like concepts but like natural laws. But these concepts are detached from historical experience.

WHEN WE ACTED THE WAY THEY DO

In 1991 the economic historian William Lazonick published an intriguing book, *Business Organization and the Myth of the Market Economy*. It examined the way industrial economies had behaved during the years when they became strongest—England in the eighteenth and nineteenth centuries, the United States in the nineteenth and twentieth centuries, and Japan from the late nineteenth century on.

These countries varied in countless ways, of course. The United Kingdom had a huge empire; the United States had a huge frontier; Japan had the advantage of applying technology the others had invented. Yet these success stories had one common theme, Lazonick showed. None of the countries conformed to today's model of "getting prices right" and putting the consumer's welfare first. All had to "cheat" somehow to succeed.

Friedrich List had railed on about exactly this point in the 1840s, when England was the only industrial success story to observe. The British were just beginning to preach free-trade theory in earnest. They abolished the famous Corn Laws in 1846, exposing their inefficient domestic farmers to competition from overseas. Yet over the previous 150 years England had strong-armed its way to prosperity by violating every rule of free trade. It would be as if Japan, in the 1990s, finally opened its rice market to competition, in the name of free trade—and then persuaded itself that it had been taking a hands-off approach to industry for the previous 150 years. When England was building its technological lead over the rest of the world, Lazonick said, its leaders did not care just about the process of competition. They were determined to control the result, so that they would have the strongest manufacturers on earth.

British economists began talking about getting prices right only after they succeeded in promoting their own industries by getting prices wrong. Prices were wrong in that cheap competition from the colonies was forbidden. They were wrong in that the Crown subsidized and encouraged investment in factories and a fleet. They were right in that they made British industry strong.

By the time Adam Smith came on the scene, Lazonick said, the British could start lecturing other countries about the folly of tariffs and protection. Why should France (America, Prussia, China . . .) punish its consumers by denying them access to cheap, well-made English cloth? Yet the British theorists did not ask themselves why their products were so advanced, why "the world market . . . in the late eighteenth century was *so uniquely under British control.*" The answer would involve nothing like laissez-faire.

The full answer would instead include the might of the British navy, which by driving out the French and Spanish had made it easier for British ships to dominate trade routes. It would involve political measures that prevented the Portuguese and Irish from developing textile industries that could compete with England's. It would include the Navigation Acts, which ensured a British monopoly in a number of the industries the country wanted most to develop. The answer involved land enclosure and a host of other measures that allowed British manufacturers to concentrate more capital than they could otherwise have obtained.

Lazonick summed up this process in a passage that exactly describes the predicament of the United States at the end of the twentieth century.

> The nineteenth-century British advocated laissez-faire because, given the advanced economic development that their industries had already achieved, they thought that their firms could withstand open competition from foreigners. [They wanted] to convince other nations that they would be better off if they opened up their markets to British goods. . . . [They] accepted as *a natural fact of life* Britain's dominant position as the "workshop of the world" [emphasis added]. They did not bother to ask how Britain had attained that position. . . .
>
> But the ultimate critique of nineteenth-century laissez-faire ideology is *not* that it ignored the role of national power in Britain's past and present. Rather, the ultimate critique is that laissez-faire failed to comprehend Britain's economic future—a future in which, confronted by far more powerful systems of national capitalism, the British economy would enter into a long-run relative decline from which it has yet to recover.

America's economic history follows the same pattern. While American industry was developing, the country had no time for laissez-faire. After it had grown strong, the United States began preaching laissez-faire to the rest of the world—and began to kid itself about its own history, believing its slogans about laissez-faire as the secret of its success.

The "traditional" American support for worldwide free trade is quite a recent phenomenon. It started only at the end of the Second World War. This period dominates the memory of most Americans now alive but does not cover the years of America's most rapid industrial expansion. As the business historian Thomas McCraw, of the Harvard Business School, has pointed out, the United States, which was born in the same year as *The Wealth of Nations*, never practiced an out-and-out mercantilist policy, as did Spain in the colonial days. But "it did exhibit for 150 years after the Revolution a pronounced tendency toward protectionism, mostly through the device of the tariff."

American schoolchildren now learn that their country had its own version of the Smith-List debate, when Thomas Jefferson and Alexander Hamilton squared off on what kind of economy the new nation should have. During George Washington's first term Hamilton produced his famous "Report on Manufactures," arguing that the country should deliberately encourage industries with tariffs and subsidies in order to compete with the mighty British. Jefferson and others set out a more pastoral, individualistic, yeoman-farmer vision of the country's future. As everyone learns in class, Hamilton lost. He was killed in a duel with Aaron Burr; he is not honored on Mount Rushmore or in the capital, as Jefferson is; he survives mainly through his portrait on the $10 bill. Yet it was a strange sort of defeat, in that for more than a century after Hamilton submitted his report, the United States essentially followed his advice.

In 1810 Albert Gallatin, a successor of Hamilton's as Secretary of the Treasury, said that British manufacturers enjoyed advantages that could keep Americans from ever catching up. A "powerful obstacle" to American industry, he said, was "the vastly superior capital of Great Britain which enables her merchants to give very long term credits, to sell on small profits, and to make occasional sacrifices."

This, of course, is exactly what American manufacturers now say about Japan. Very little has changed in debates about free trade and protectionism in the past 200 years. If the antique language and references to out-of-date industries were removed from Hamilton's report of 1791, it could have been republished in 1991 and would have fit right into the industrial-policy debate. "There is no purpose to which public money can be more beneficially applied, than to the acquisition of a new and useful branch of industry" was the heart of Hamilton's argument—and, similarly, of many modern-day Democratic Party economic plans.

In the years before the American Revolution most leaders in the Colonies supported the concept of British protectionist measures. They were irritated by new taxes and levies in the 1760s and 1770s—but they had seen how effective Britain's approach was in developing industries. Through the nineteenth century the proper level of a national tariff was on a par with slavery as a chronically divisive issue. Northerners generally wanted a higher tariff, to protect their industries; farmers and southerners wanted a lower tariff, so that they could buy cheaper imported supplies. Many politicians were unashamed protectionists. "I don't known much about the tariff," Abraham Lincoln said, in what must have been an aw-shucks way. "But I know this much. When we buy manufactured goods abroad we get the goods and the foreigner gets the money. When we buy the manufactured goods at home, we get both the goods and the money." The United States had, just before Lincoln's term, forced the Japanese to accept treaties to "open" the Japanese market. These provided that Japan could impose a tariff of no more than five percent on most imported goods. America's average tariff on all imports was almost 30 percent at the time.

In the 1880s the University of Pennsylvania required that economics lecturers not subscribe to the theory of free trade. A decade later William McKinley was saying that the tariff had been the crux of the nation's wealth: "We lead all nations in agriculture; we lead all nations in mining; we lead all nations in manufacturing. These are the trophies which we bring after twenty-nine years of a protective tariff." The national tariff level on dutiable goods had varied, but it stayed above 30 percent through most of the nineteenth century. When the United States began to preach or practice free trade, after the Second World War, the average duty paid on imports fell from about nine percent in 1945 to about four percent in the late 1970s.

In addition to the tariff, nineteenth-century America went in heavily for industrial planning—occasionally under that name but more often in the name of national defense. The military was the excuse for what we would now call rebuilding infrastructure, picking winners, promoting research, and coordinating industrial growth. As Geoffrey Perret has pointed out in *A Country Made by War,* many evolutions about which people now say "That was good for the country" occurred only because someone could say at the time "This will be good for the military"—giving the government an excuse to step in.

In the mid-nineteenth century settlers moving west followed maps drawn by Army cartographers, along roads built by Army engineers and guarded by Army forts. At the end of the century the U.S. Navy searched for ways to build bigger, stronger warships and along the way helped foster the world's most advanced steel industry.

Just before Thomas Jefferson took office as President, the U.S. government began an ambitious project to pick winners. England surpassed America in virtually every category of manufacturing, and so, to a lesser degree, did France. Wheels turned and gears spun throughout Europe, but they barely did so in the new United States. In 1798 Congress authorized an extraordinary purchase of muskets from the inventor Eli Whitney, who was at the time struggling and in debt. Congress offered him an unprecedented contract to provide 10,000 muskets within twenty-eight months. This was at a time when the average production rate was one musket per worker per week. Getting the muskets was only part of what Congress accomplished: this was a way to induce, and to finance, a mass-production industry for the United States. Whitney worked round the clock, developed America's first mass-production equipment, and put on a show for the congressmen. He brought a set of disassembled musket locks to Washington and invited congressmen to fit the pieces together themselves—showing that the age of standardized parts had arrived.

"The nascent American arms industry led where the rest of manufacturing followed," Perret concluded. "Far from being left behind by the Industrial Revolution the United States, in a single decade and thanks largely to one man, had suddenly burst into the front rank." America took this step not by waiting for it to occur but by deliberately promoting the desired result.

For most of the next century and a half the U.S. government was less interested in improving the process of competition than in achieving a specific result. It cared less about getting prices right and more about getting ahead. This theme runs through the Agriculture Extension Service, which got information to farmers more rapidly than free-market forces might have; the shipbuilding programs of the late nineteenth century, which stimulated the machine-tool and metal-working industries; aircraft-building contracts; and medical research.

What America actually did while industrializing is not what we tell ourselves about industrialization today. Consumer welfare took second place; promoting production came first. A preference for domestic industries did cost consumers money. A heavy tariff on imported British rails made the expansion of the American railroads in the 1880s costlier than it would otherwise have been. But this protectionist policy coincided with, and arguably contributed to, the emergence of a productive, efficient American steel industry. The United States trying to catch up with Britain behaved more or less like the leaders of Meiji (and postwar) Japan trying to catch up with the United States. Alexander Hamilton, dead and unmourned, won.

Thomas McCraw says that the American pattern was not some strange exception but in fact the norm. The great industrial successes of the past two centuries— America after its Revolution, Germany under Bismarck, Japan after the Second World War—all violated the rules of laissez-faire. Despite the obvious differences among these countries, he says, the underlying economic strategy was very much the same.

4. Of the Different Progress of Opulence in Different Nations

Adam Smith

OF THE NATURAL PROGRESS OF OPULENCE

The great commerce of every civilised society is that carried on between the inhabitants of the town and those of the country. It consists in the exchange of rude for manufactured produce, either immediately, or by the intervention of money, or of some sort of paper which represents money. The country supplies the town with the means of subsistence and the materials of manufacture. The town repays this supply by sending back a part of the manufactured produce to the inhabitants of the country. The town, in which there neither is nor can be any reproduction of substances, may very properly be said to gain its whole wealth and subsistence from the country. We must not, however, upon this account, imagine that the gain of the town is the loss of the country. The gains of both are mutual and reciprocal, and the division of labour is in this, as in all other cases, advantageous to all the different persons employed in the various occupations into which it is subdivided. The inhabitants of the country purchase of the town a greater quantity of manufactured goods, with the produce of a

From "Of the Different Progress of Opulence in Different Nations," in *The Wealth of Nations*, by Adam Smith. (London: J. M. Dent & Sons: 1964) pp. 217–412.

much smaller quantity of their own labour, than they must have employed had they attempted to prepare them themselves. The town affords a market for the surplus produce of the country, or what is over and above the maintenance of the cultivators, and it is there that the inhabitants of the country exchange it for something else which is in demand among them. . . .

That order of things which necessity imposes in general, though not in every particular country, is, in every particular country, promoted by the natural inclinations of man. If human institutions had never thwarted those natural inclinations, the towns could nowhere have increased beyond what the improvement and cultivation of the territory in which they were situated could support; till such time, at least, as the whole of that territory was completely cultivated and improved. Upon equal, or nearly equal profits, most men will choose to employ their capitals rather in the improvement and cultivation of land than either in manufactures or in foreign trade. The man who employs his capital in land has it more under his view and command, and his fortune is much less liable to accidents than that of the trader, who is obliged frequently to commit it, not only to the winds and the waves, but to the more uncertain elements of human folly and injustice, by giving great credits in distant countries to men with whose character and situation he can seldom be thoroughly acquainted. The capital of the landlord, on the contrary, which is fixed in the improvement of his land, seems to be as well secured as the nature of human affairs can admit of. The beauty of the country besides, the pleasures of a country life, the tranquillity of mind which it promises, and wherever the injustice of human laws does not disturb it, the independency which it really affords, have charms that more or less attract everybody; and as to cultivate the ground was the original destination of man, so in every stage of his existence he seems to retain a predilection for this primitive employment. . . .

According to the natural course of things, therefore, the greater part of the capital of every growing society is, first, directed to agriculture, afterwards to manufactures, and last of all to foreign commerce. This order of things is so very natural that in every society that had any territory it has always, I believe, been in some degree observed. Some of their lands must have been cultivated before any considerable towns could be established, and some sort of coarse industry of the manufacturing kind must have been carried on in those towns, before they could well think of employing themselves in foreign commerce.

But though this natural order of things must have taken place in some degree in every such society, it has, in all the modern states of Europe, been, in many respects, entirely inverted. The foreign commerce of some of their cities has introduced all their finer manufactures, or such as were fit for distant sale; and manufactures and foreign commerce together have given birth to the principal improvements of agriculture. The manners and customs which the nature of their original government introduced, and which remained after that government was greatly altered, necessarily forced them into this unnatural and retrograde order. . . .

The general industry of the society never can exceed what the capital of the society can employ. As the number of workmen that can be kept in employment by any particular person must bear a certain proportion to his capital, so the number of those that can be continually employed by all the members of a great society must bear a certain proportion to the whole capital of that society, and never can exceed that proportion. No regulation of commerce can increase the quantity of industry in any society beyond what its capital can maintain. It can only divert a part of it into a direction into which it might not otherwise have gone; and it is by no means certain that this artificial direction is likely to be more advantageous to the society than that into which it would have gone of its own accord.

Every individual is continually exerting himself to find out the most advantageous employment for whatever capital he can command. It is his own advantage, indeed, and not that of the society, which he has in view. But the study of his own advantage naturally, or rather necessarily, leads him to prefer that employment which is most advantageous to the society. . . .

The produce of industry is what it adds to the subject or materials upon which it is employed. In proportion as the value of this produce is great or small, so will likewise be the profits of the employer. But it is only for the sake of profit that any man employs a capital in the support of industry; and he will always, therefore, endeavour to employ it in the support of that industry of which the produce is likely to be of the greatest value, or to exchange for the greatest quantity either of money or of other goods.

But the annual revenue of every society is always precisely equal to the exchangeable value of the whole annual produce of its industry, or rather is precisely the same thing with that exchangeable value. As every individual, therefore, endeavours as much as he can both to employ his capital in the support of domestic industry, and so to direct that industry that its produce may be of the greatest value; every individual necessarily labours to render the annual revenue of the society as great as he can. He generally, indeed, neither intends to promote the public interest, nor knows how much he is promoting it. By preferring the support of domestic to that of foreign industry, he intends only his own security; and by directing that industry in such a manner as its produce may be of the greatest value, he intends only his own gain, and he is in this, as in many other cases, led by an invisible hand to promote an end which was no part of his intention. Nor is it always the worse for the society that it was no part of it. By pursuing his own interest he frequently promotes that of the society more effectually than when he really intends to promote it. I have never known much good done by those who affected to trade for the public good. It is an affectation, indeed, not very common among merchants, and very few words need be employed in dissuading them from it. . . .

What is prudence in the conduct of every private family can scarce be folly in that of a great kingdom. If a foreign country can supply us with a commodity cheaper than we ourselves can make it, better buy it of them with some part of the produce of our own industry employed in a way in which we have some advantage. The general industry of the country, being always in proportion to the capital which employs it, will not thereby be diminished, no more than that of the above-mentioned artificers; but only left to find out the way in which it can be employed with the greatest advantage. It is certainly not employed to the greatest advantage when it is thus directed towards an object which it can buy cheaper than it can make. The value of its annual produce is certainly more or less diminished when it is thus turned away from producing commodities evidently of more value than the commodity which it is directed to produce. According to the supposition, that commodity could be purchased from foreign countries cheaper than it can be made at home. It could, therefore, have been purchased with a part only of the commodities, or, what is the same thing, with a part only of the price of the commodities, which the industry employed by an equal capital would have produced at home, had it been left to follow its natural course. The industry of the country, therefore, is thus turned away from a more to a less advantageous employment, and the exchangeable value of its annual produce, instead of being increased, according to the intention of the lawgiver, must necessarily be diminished by every such regulation.

By means of such regulations, indeed, a particular manufacture may sometimes be acquired sooner than it could have been otherwise, and after a certain time may be made at home as cheap or cheaper than in the foreign country. But though the industry of the society may be thus carried with advantage into a particular channel sooner than it could have been otherwise, it will by no means follow that the sum total, either of its industry, or of its revenue, can ever be augmented by any such regulation. The industry of the society can augment only in proportion as its capital augments, and its capital can augment only in proportion to what can be gradually saved out of its revenue. But the immediate effect of every such regulation is to diminish its revenue, and what diminishes its revenue is certainly not very likely to augment its capital faster than it would have augmented of its own accord had both capital and industry been left to find out their natural employments. . . .

5. Keynes's Middle Way

Robert Skidelsky

Victorian governments believed that an economy prospers best when left to the free play of market forces. From this followed the golden rule of "non-interference" or *laissez-faire*. Economic policy, in the sense of a commitment to certain outcomes for the economy as a whole, did not exist. The idea that the economy should be "managed" to secure "objectives" like full employment, stable prices, a healthy balance of payments, a satisfactory growth rate and so on would have struck the Victorians as incomprehensible or merely fanciful. Goods and capital were left free to flow where they would. The government raised taxes to pay for its own upkeep, including defence and law and order, but not to influence the volume of activity. There was no monetary policy, the supply of domestic currency being regulated by the "automatic" mechanism of the gold standard. Governments made no attempt to prevent, and little to mitigate, unemployment. There was a business cycle, but the unemployed sooner or later seemed to disappear of their own accord—either back into jobs or on to ships taking them to North America or Australia. There were no attempts to "restructure" British industry or agriculture to make them more competitive: the market system was supposed to take care of this. The *laissez-faire* consensus had started to break down by the end of the nineteenth century. The Right advocated protection of British industry against foreign competition; the Left called for higher income and inheritance taxes to pay for social services. Economists were hostile to the first, but accepted an economic case for the second. In general, there was little disposition to tamper with a system which had brought the British economy growing prosperity in the nineteenth century. *Laissez-faire* was validated by success, just as later it was ruined by failure.

Keynes rejected *laissez-faire* as a policy before he developed a convincing economic theory explaining why *laissez-faire* would not work. Economists have taken this as a sign of his "intuitions" running ahead of his theory, but this characterisation is too one-sided. From 1924 to 1929 Keynes developed a powerful critique of *laissez-faire*, but it was not specifically economic-theoretical, though it carried a strong theoretical charge. It was directed to showing that the presuppositions of *laissez-faire*—the psychological and organisational conditions which had made it work as a policy in the nineteenth century—had passed away. The idea that the nineteenth century was a special case in economic history thus makes its appearance in Keynes's thinking before the idea that classical economics—the *theory* of the "special case"—was itself a "special case" of a more general theory of economic behaviour applicable to the more usual condition of mankind. Psychological and institutional *observation* was the foundation of Keynesian economics.

In chapter 2 of *The Economic Consequences of the Peace* Keynes explained the precariousness of the nineteenth-century achievement under four headings: "population," "organisation," "the psychology of society," and "the relation of the old world to the new." The basic argument was that the increasing prosperity of Europe's growing population had depended on a worldwide system of free imports and capital exports made possible by peace and security, and on a social and moral equipoise which produced contented workers so long as the rich saved, and rendered the duty of saving "nine-tenths of virtue." This whole "complicated and artificial" system depended on precarious balances which were already endangered before the war, and which the war had shattered: the class balance between capital and labour, the psychological or moral balance between saving and consumption, and the balance of trade and capital transfers between Europe and America. The epoch, that is, for which *laissez-faire* had been tolerable as a policy, and for which "classical economics" had provided a tolerably accurate stylisation, was already doomed before the First World War delivered the knock-out blow. The question for thought and action was how Europe, including Britain, was to maintain its existing and still growing population when the mechanisms of fine and semi-automatic adjustment between global supplies of, and demands for, money, goods and labour had broken down. The older school of states-manship and economics said: restore these mechanisms as quickly as possible. Keynes replied that they could not be restored, or could only be partially restored, and any-way the best chance of restoring them had been destroyed by the peacemakers at Ver-sailles.

As the 1920s unfolded, Keynes shifted his emphases within this general ap-proach. The problem of population remained a preoccupation till at least the late 1920s, demanding a "population policy." In the early 1920s he concentrated on the need for a monetary policy. Instability in the value of money was undermining the so-cial contract on which capitalism was based. Workers' acquiescence in a modest re-ward depended on capitalists—entrepreneurs and investors—doing their duty of pro-ducing wealth. Inflation and deflation cut the moral link between effort and reward, leading to the unjustified enrichment of some and the unjustified impoverishment of others; hence the supreme importance of price stability for the virtue of the system. "Any important change in the cost of living and general price level, whether up or down, will endanger industrial peace," Keynes wrote just before Britain went back to gold. In 1924 he started questioning whether a mature economy like Britain could any longer provide enough investment opportunities to absorb the historically given rate of domestic saving. Should savings be allowed to drift abroad or should the govern-ment take active measures to provide for their employment at home? He also pointed to the increasing unwillingness of modern societies—Britain being the society he knew best—to adjust their internal structures to the ebb and flow of money and trade. Stability of internal economic conditions was the essential requirement of social sta-bility; this precluded a *laissez-faire* attitude to the three chief determinants of the stan-dard of life: population, money, and saving and investing.

Unlike Marx, Keynes did not regard the "organisation" of society as deter-mining its psychology: that is, its beliefs and expectations. They influence each other. Nor did he accept, or even understand, the core Marxist proposition that firms which covered their costs were exploiting the worker. But under capitalism there is a double problem of legitimacy. The first arises, as we have seen, from instability of money, which cuts off effort from reward. The second is more fundamental. In Keynes's view capitalism's driving force is a vice which he called "love of money." Material outcomes are the measure of its success—or failure. As long as it fulfilled its historic task of pro-ducing wealth for all it was reasonably secure. But, if wealth-creation faltered, capi-talism was vulnerable to creed-based systems, which appealed to more worthy mo-tives. As a piece of social machinery for getting mankind from poverty to affluence capitalism was the best on offer. But its success was no more assured than its failure. To succeed it had to be able to take on new forms in new habitats. The economist's task was to discern the form or style suitable to the age—a matter of aesthetics and logic.

Keynes always stressed the crucial importance of "vigilant observation" for suc-cessful theory-construction—theory being nothing more, in his view, than a stylised representation of the dominant tendencies of the time, derived from reflection on the salient facts. It is fascinating to observe how Keynes's imagination and logical power acting on the data of experience gradually yield a distinctive understanding of the *modus operandi* of modern economic life to which the adjective "Keynesian" is correctly applied.

Implicit in all this is a crucial shift in view concerning the relationship between the economy and the polity. Nineteenth-century economists had looked to a liberal political system—one dominated by the business class—to underwrite economic prosperity. Keynes was the first economist to argue that economic prosperity was the only secure guarantee of a liberal political system.

Keynes's understanding of the diseases of modern capitalism, and the remedies for them, was not developed in isolation. Michael Freeden has rightly drawn attention to "the context of the production and dissemination of Liberal ideas that was taking place at the time he [Keyes] was developing his own theories." Keynes and Henderson both understood that new theories about controlling the business cycle might provide Liberalism with an alternative to the protectionism of the right and the redistributionism of the left, especially if dramatised as an unemployment policy. Lloyd George seemed to grasp this, Asquith did not. That is why the man of ideas was drawn, despite the past, to the man of action.

The period 1924–9 marks Keynes's maximum involvement in the politics of the Liberal Party. He quite explicitly set out to supply the Party with a new philosophy of government. But, with the historical Liberal party in decline, Keynes also came to see his reconstructed liberalism as the common ground of a two-party system, with the Liberal Party "supplying Conservative governments with Cabinets, and Labour governments with ideas." In the 1930s this Liberal context disappeared, and Keynes did not add importantly to the political philosophy he had developed in the 1920s.

What Freeden calls the "production and dissemination" of Liberal ideas took place through three overlapping institutional networks in each of which Keynes played a leading part: the Liberal Summer Schools meeting alternately in Oxford and Cambridge from 1922 onwards, the weekly journal the *Nation*, and the Lloyd George-financed Liberal Industrial Inquiry, whose report *Britain's Industrial Future* was published in 1928.

Keynes's involvement in the politics of Liberalism raises the question of the relationship between Keynes's Liberalism and that body of ideas known as the New or social Liberalism which flourished before 1914 and is distinguished from the classical or individualistic Liberalism which preceded it. "From 1906 to 1914," wrote Hubert Henderson, "a common economic policy united the parties of the Left—the development of the social services involving public expenditure, and the raising of the money by stiffer taxes on wealth." To this tradition, Ramsay Muir and the "Manchester Liberals" added industrial democracy, as a way out of the class struggle, and also to limit the growth of private and public power. Peter Clarke sees Keynes's Middle Way as being continuous with this tradition, particularly with its political goal of a Labour–Liberal partnership. Michael Freeden, on the other hand, sees Keynes as the intellectual progenitor of a new "centrist Liberalism," grafting technocratic solutions to specific problems on to an individualist stem. By confining state intervention to spaces left vacant by private enterprise, by "jettisoning redistribution as a major field of socioeconomic policy" and by "de-democratising" policymaking in favour of expert control, Keynes repudiated the distinctive features of the pre-war "new" Liberalism. This is also the interpretation of Maurice Cranston.

Freeden and Cranston are more nearly right than Clarke. However, the matter is not quite straightforward. There were similarities as well as differences between Keynes's Liberalism and the tradition of social Liberalism. The issues can be summarised under four heads.

First, and most obviously, Keynes added macroeconomic stabilisation to the pre-war Liberal agenda and, in fact, gave it priority. Post-war Liberalism, he said, must address itself to new, not old, problems. The short-run instability of capitalism was a greater threat to the social order than any long-run inequity in the distribution of wealth and income. The greatest economic evils, Keynes proclaimed, were the fruits of "risk, uncertainty, and ignorance." The state's main economic duty was to offset the effects of these by monetary policy and capital spending. Keynes also understood that to emphasise social reform while business confidence was low would prevent the recovery of private investment needed to lift the economy out of the slump. Questions of social justice had to be shelved as long as businessmen lacked the confidence to invest. This is a clear line, though one to which the left has often been blind.

However, it was not just that Keynes downgraded social reform as a priority; it was never a passion with him. Elizabeth Johnson may exaggerate when she writes that, for Keynes, "social injustice existed only in there not being enough jobs to go round," but his rather complacent reflections on the pre-war social order—"escape was possible, for any man of capacity or character at all exceeding the average, into the middle and upper classes . . ."—hardly suggest a burning dissatisfaction with it. The truth is that Keynes's notion of inequity was largely limited to the existence of windfall or unjustified gains and losses. Justice to Keynes involved the maintenance of existing group norms and the fulfilment of settled expectations. His notion of it was contractual, or commutative, rather than substantive. He regarded as unjust the arbitrary shifts in wealth and incomes caused by avoidable business fluctuations—shifts unrelated to effort and beyond the control of ordinary prudence. That is why he sympathised so strongly with the miners at the time of the General Strike in 1926—victims of the return to the gold standard in 1925. The insight that what groups of workers really feared was the loss of *relative* position would inform his discussion of wage behaviour in the *General Theory*. What Keynes did, in essence, was to transfer the problem of social justice from the microeconomy to the macroeconomy. Injustice becomes a matter of uncertainty, justice a matter of contractual predictability. Redistribution plays a minor part in his social philosophy, and then only as an adjunct to the machinery of macroeconomic stabilisation, not as a means to an ideal end.

Secondly, Keynes's emphasis on stabilisation policy is connected to what may be called his short-termism. Its philosophic basis was the principle of "moral risk," which he got from Burke and Moore, and which tells us it is more rational to aim for a smaller good with a high probability of attainment than for a larger one with a low probability of attainment. This was the guiding principle of his statesmanship. It inoculated him equally against communism and the sacrificial thinking implicit in much of orthodox economics. It explains why Keynes tended to take the economic structure as given, and try to find a way round the rocks rather than try to pulverise them. Expediency is raised to a high principle of statecraft. "It is fatal," he wrote, "for a capitalist government to have principles. It must be opportunistic in the best sense of the word, living by accommodation and good sense. If any monarchical, plutocratic or other analogous form of government has principles, it will fall." Keynes's scepticism about the benefits of large-scale social change was matched by an extraordinary optimism about the possibility of intelligent management of short-run problems.

Thirdly, it was Keynes's statism and elitism which distanced him above all from the pre-war New Liberals. The New Liberals valued democracy as an end in itself and wanted to extend it to control private and public concentrations of power. Keynes's purposes required a managerial state. Moreover, since it was a state driven, in its economic functions, by updated economic theory, it was a technical or expert state. Thus Keynes welcomed the coming to power of a new class of Platonic Guardians. He wrote in 1925, "I believe that the right solution [to the economic question] will involve intellectual and scientific elements which must be above the heads of the vast mass of more or less illiterate voters." Beatrice Webb could not have put it better.

A final point to note is the difference in intellectual style between Oxford and Cambridge. "What a home of diseased thought Oxford is," Keynes had written to his father in 1906 after reading a book on logic by the philosopher Horace Joseph. Oxford was the centre of the New Liberalism of the pre-war era. Not only was Oxford (by Cambridge standards) ignorant of economics, but the Oxford-based attack on *laissez-faire* was couched in a mixture of Hegelian and biological language which Keynes and his generation at Cambridge found repellent. The epistemological assault on Bradley's doctrine of "internal relations," led by Moore and Russell, carried over to the social ethics associated with T. H. Green, L. T. Hobhouse and J. A. Hobson. Against the view that the good of the individual and the good of the whole are organically connected, Keynes emphasised that good states of mind could be enjoyed by individuals in isolation from social states of affairs. Yet one must be aware of the connections as well as the differences. There was a large trace of Hegelianism in Moore's doctrine of "organic unities;" and by the 1920s Keynes was willing to acknowledge that many processes of production and consumption were "organic" rather than atomistic.

Keynes's 1924 Sidney Ball lecture, "The End of *Laissez-Faire*," delivered at Oxford on 6 November 1924 and published in 1926, provides the framework within which his arguments developed over the next five years. Like all his best work, it is full of sparkling prose and arresting ideas. He seems to have read, or at least delved, quite widely in the history of economic and political thought: the essay version is sprinkled with references to Locke, Hume, Rousseau, Paley, Bentham, Godwin, Burke and Coleridge, as well as to the nineteenth-century political economists. An important source was Leslie Stephen's *English Thought in the Eighteenth Century*. But no less characteristically its superb style hides a deal of hasty argument. As Schumpeter remarks, Keynes never gave himself the extra fortnight needed to perfect his occasional pieces.

Keynes traced the origins of *laissez-faire* thinking to the eighteenth-century view that social well-being resulted from individual calculations of self-interest. "Suppose that by the working of natural laws individuals pursuing their own interests with enlightenment in conditions of freedom always tend to promote the general interest at the same time! Our philosophical difficulties are resolved. . . . The political philosopher could retire in favour of the businessman—for the latter could attain the philosopher's *summum bonum* by just pursuing his own private profit." The synthesis between the two received further powerful reinforcement in Darwin's theory of natural selection. "The principle of the survival of the fittest could be regarded as a vast generalisation of the Ricardian economics. Socialist interferences became, in the light of this grander synthesis, not merely inexpedient but impious, as calculated to retard the onward movement of the mighty process by which we ourselves had risen like Aphrodite from the primeval slime."

The trouble is that Keynes fails to develop any sustained critique of this set of doctrines. This is the hole at the heart of the essay. He lumps together, in briefest summary, objections to *laissez-faire* which may be philosophical or merely practical ("the prevalence of ignorance over knowledge"), moral objections (the "cost . . . of the competitive struggle" and the "tendency for wealth to be distributed where it is not appreciated most"), and objections which stem from changed techniques of production (economies of scale) leading to monopoly. As a result we are left in the dark about whether the *laissez-faire* project cannot, as a matter of fact, be realised in given circumstances, whether it cannot be realised under any conceivable or probable set of circumstances, or whether it would be wrong to try to realise it, even if it could be.

Rather than pursuing these questions, Keynes explains the continued resilience of *laissez-faire* ideas by the "poor quality of its opponent proposals—protectionism on the one hand, and Marxian socialism on the other." Protectionism is treated a little more gently than the year before; but "Marxist socialism must always remain a portent to the historians of opinion—how a doctrine so illogical and so dull can have exercised so powerful and enduring influence over the minds of men and, through them, the events of history." Keynes, as Donald Winch has remarked, was always "notoriously tone deaf as far as Marx was concerned." Nor did the war experience greatly increase the appeal of "centralised social action on a great scale," since "the dissipation of effort was . . . prodigious, and the atmosphere of waste and not counting the cost . . . disgusting to any thrifty or provident spirit."

The conclusion Keynes draws from all this is that the question of the proper sphere of individual and state action cannot be settled on abstract grounds. Each age, he implies, needs to distinguish for itself between what the state ought to do and what can be left to the individual; or, in Bentham's terms, between the Agenda and Non-Agenda of government. "Perhaps the chief task of economists at this hour is to distinguish afresh the *Agenda* of government from the *Non-Agenda;* and the companion task of politics is to devise forms of government within a democracy which shall be capable of accomplishing the *Agenda*." This is a misleading way of stating the task. The Agenda of government cannot be laid down apart from considering what "governments in a democracy" can successfully accomplish; political theorists, not just economists, have to work it out.

Keynes then develops what looks like a public-goods argument for state intervention. "We must aim," he wrote, "at separating those services which are technically social from those which are technically individual." The most important items on the Agenda relate "not to those activities which private individuals are already fulfilling, but to those functions which fall outside the sphere of the individual, to those decisions which are made by no one if the State does not make them." Remedy for the evils arising from "risk, uncertainty and ignorance" required "deliberate control of the currency and of credit by a central institution, and . . . the collection and dissemination of . . . business facts." He proposed in addition a "coordinated act of intelligent judgement" concerning the aggregate volume of savings and their distribution between home and foreign investment, and a population policy "which pays attention to innate quality as well as to . . . numbers." Keynes does not explain why the last two goods are *technically* social—that is, why private individuals cannot provide savings and children in the amounts they desire. We have here a good example of the difficulty of trying to build collectivist conclusions on individualistic premises.*

Keynes's public goods are to be provided by the state. But when he talks about the state the private–public distinction on which the argument hinges breaks down because of the existence of intermediate institutions. Keynes points to the growth of "semi-autonomous bodies within the State" like the "universities, the Bank of England, the Port of London Authority, even perhaps the railway companies," as well as to mixed forms of industrial organisation, such as joint-stock institutions, "which when they have reached a certain age and size [tend] to approximate to the status of public corporations rather than that of individualistic private enterprise." Echoing the ideas of the Managerial Revolution, soon to receive their classic exposition by James Burnham, Keynes pointed out that corporations of a certain age and size were owned by anonymous shareholders, but were actually run by managers increasingly sensitive to the public implications of their activities. The Bank of England, the rights of whose shareholders "have already sunk to the neighbourhood of zero," was merely an extreme instance of institutions which were "socialising themselves." The growth of these "semi-autonomous bodies," Keynes suggested, harked back to "medieval conceptions of separate autonomies."

Most people, of course, do not think of the state as including private bodies. Keynes was suggesting that the rise of planning and administration within the private sphere pointed to the fracturing of sovereignty, *de facto* if not yet *de jure*, in reversal of

---

*The technical argument that markets cannot provide certain goods in the quantity they are desired rests heavily on the "free rider" problem: the lack of incentive for individuals to pay voluntarily for goods in which there are no private property rights. Defence is a classic example. In the pure logic of the case, if a country's defence system had to be provided by voluntary contribution, expenditure on defence would be zero, since everyone would share in it whether they contributed or not. So it must be provided by compulsory contribution (taxes) in amounts decided by collective choice. But this argument cannot be applied to saving or population, since individuals do not have to share their savings or children with anyone else. Keynes is saying something different: that there is an optimal quantity of population or saving different from the desired quantity as reflected in individual decisions. But do these optima exist? Later he was to say that the community as a whole cannot achieve its desired level of saving if its income is subject to large fluctuation. This *is* a technical economic argument, which was lacking from the 1924 statement.

the whole tendency since the Middle Ages for property to become fully privatised, with its public functions being taken over by the Crown. The classical liberal idea of a sovereign but limited state, and an untrammelled market was yielding to new corporatism, in which the state (in the narrow sense) was simply one—a *primus inter pares*—in the order of corporations or associations.

What is striking is not Keynes's recognition that the growth of private power posed new questions for the relationship between the state and the economy—this recognition was widespread in the political thought of the time—but his way of resolving the issue. Old-fashioned liberals still aimed to pulverise private power by trust-busting; social liberals wanted to subject it to "democracy"—whether by decision-sharing, profit-sharing or wider share ownership. Socialists saw it as furnishing a justification for nationalisation. These were all efforts to secure accountability, whether to consumers, workers or electors. Keynes had no real interest in them. He was no pluralist. He welcomed the "aggregation of production" as tending to stabilise the economy; he accepted uncritically the view that captains of industry were constrained, by the size of their undertakings, to serve the public interest; and he assumed, without further argument, that an interconnected elite of business managers, bankers, civil servants, economists and scientists, all trained at Oxford and Cambridge and imbued with a public service ethic, would come to run these organs of state, whether private or public, and make them hum to the same tune. He wanted to decentralise and devolve only down to the level of Top People.

Keynes's anti-market, anti-democratic bias was driven by a belief in scientific expertise and personal disinterestedness which now seems alarmingly naive. This runs like a leitmotiv through his work and is *the* important assumption of his political philosophy. Economic progress, he emphasised, depends "on our willingness to entrust to science those things which are properly the concern of science;" the principles of central banking, he was to say a little later, should be "utterly removed from popular controversy and . . . be regarded as a kind of beneficent technique of scientific control such as electricity or other branches of science are." He contrasted the "scientific spirit" with the "sterility of the purely party attitude." He recognised the problem of combining "representative institutions and the voice of public opinion with the utilisation by governments of the best technical advice," yet in economic policy he looked forward to the "euthanasia of politics." Although his language was sometimes extreme, this, as Noel Annan has pointed out, was the authentic voice of "Our Age." It approximated to what actually happened in the "consensus years" of the 1950s and 1960s. The consensus broke down only when the experts started to disagree, and it became apparent, as it always should have been, that policy is a handmaiden of politics.

With technical questions removed from party warfare, political debate would, Keynes suggested, largely revolve round the nature of the ideal society of the future. The basic divide, he felt, would be over the scope to be allowed "to the money-making and money-loving instincts as the main motive force of the economic machine." Capitalism could be made an efficient technique of production; but the motives it relied upon might still be felt to be morally objectionable. "Our problem is to work out a social organisation which shall be as efficient as possible without offending our no-tions of a satisfactory way of life." If this was a problem for society, it was a personal problem for Keynes, the speculator who was also a disciple of G.E. Moore.

"The End of *Laissez-Faire*" is a flawed production; but it remains the most im-pressive short attempt on record to define a social and economic philosophy fit for the time of troubles framed by the two world wars. Nearly seventy years after it was writ-ten its spaciousness, humanity and sheer linguistic vivacity still shine brightly. Its faults are shortness and hastiness. Every proposition cries out for development, criticism, re-finement. Had he lived longer, Keynes would surely have been tempted to embed his economic theory (which came later) in a culminating work of political and social phi-losophy to rival and confront Hayek's *Constitution of Liberty*. For the argument is not over. Capitalism may have vanquished socialism, but the debate between *laissez-faire* and Keynes's philosophy of the Middle Way is still fiercely joined.

6. Manifesto of the Communist Party†

Karl Marx
Friedrich Engels

A spectre is haunting Europe—the spectre of Communism. All the Powers of old Eu-rope have entered into a holy alliance to exorcise this spectre: Pope and Czar, Met-ternich and Guizot, French Radicals and German police-spies.

Where is the party in opposition that has not been decried as Communistic by its opponents in power? Where the Opposition that has not hurled back the branding reproach of Communism, against the more advanced opposition parties, as well as against its reactionary adversaries?

Two things result from this fact.

I. Communism is already acknowledged by all European Powers to be itself a Power.

II. It is high time that Communists should openly, in the face of the whole world, publish their views, their aims, their tendencies, and meet this nursery tale of the Spec-tre of Communism with a Manifesto of the party itself.

From *Manifesto of the Communist Party*, by Karl Mark and Friedrich Engels. 1888.

†The English text of the *Communist Manifesto* that follows was authorized by Engels in 1888. Engels himself chose the translator, Samuel Moore, who had translated volume 1 of *Capital*. . . .

To this end, Communists of various nationalities have assembled in London, and sketched the following Manifesto, to be published in the English, French, German, Italian, Flemish and Danish languages.

I. BOURGEOIS AND PROLETARIANS

The history of all hitherto existing society is the history of class struggles.

Freeman and slave, patrician and plebeian, lord and serf, guild-master and journeyman, in a word, oppressor and oppressed, stood in constant opposition to one another, carried on an uninterrupted, now hidden, now open fight, a fight that each time ended, either in a revolutionary re-constitution of society at large, or in the common ruin of the contending classes.

In the earlier epochs of history, we find almost everywhere a complicated arrangement of society into various orders, a manifold gradation of social rank. In ancient Rome we have patricians, knights, plebeians, slaves; in the Middle Ages, feudal lords, vassals, guild-masters, journeymen, apprentices, serfs; in almost all of these classes, again, subordinate gradations.

The modern bourgeois society that has sprouted from the ruins of feudal society has not done away with class antagonisms. It has but established new classes, new conditions of oppression, new forms of struggle in place of the old ones.

Our epoch, the epoch of the bourgeoisie, possesses, however, this distinctive feature: it has simplified the class antagonisms. Society as a whole is more and more splitting up into two great hostile camps, into two great classes directly facing each other: Bourgeoisie and Proletariat.

From the serfs of the Middle Ages sprang the chartered burghers of the earliest towns. From these burgesses the first elements of the bourgeoisie were developed.

The discovery of America, the rounding of the Cape, opened up fresh ground for the rising bourgeoisie. The East-Indian and Chinese markets, the colonisation of America, trade with the colonies, the increase in the means of exchange and in commodities generally, gave to commerce, to navigation, to industry, an impulse never before known, and thereby, to the revolutionary element in the tottering feudal society, a rapid development.

The feudal system of industry, under which industrial production was monopolised by closed guilds, now no longer sufficed for the growing wants of the new markets. The manufacturing system took its place. The guild-masters were pushed on one side by the manufacturing middle class; division of labour between the different corporate guilds vanished in the face of division of labour in each single workshop.

Meantime the markets kept ever growing, the demand ever rising. Even manufacture no longer sufficed. Thereupon, steam and machinery revolutionised industrial production. The place of manufacture was taken by the giant, Modern Industry, the place of the industrial middle class, by industrial millionaires, the leaders of whole industrial armies, the modern bourgeois.

Modern industry has established the world-market, for which the discovery of

America paved the way. This market has given an immense development to commerce, to navigation, to communication by land. This development has, in its turn, reacted on the extension of industry; and in proportion as industry, commerce, navigation, railways extended, in the same proportion the bourgeoisie developed, increased its capital, and pushed into the background every class handed down from the Middle Ages.

We see, therefore, how the modern bourgeoisie is itself the product of a long course of development, of a series of revolutions in the modes of production and of exchange.

Each step in the development of the bourgeoisie was accompanied by a corresponding political advance of that class. An oppressed class under the sway of the feudal nobility, an armed and self-governing association in the mediaeval commune; here independent urban republic (as in Italy and Germany), there taxable "third estate" of the monarchy (as in France), afterwards, in the period of manufacture proper, serving either the semi-feudal or the absolute monarchy as a counterpoise against the nobility, and, in fact, corner-stone of the great monarchies in general, the bourgeoisie has at last, since the establishment of Modern Industry and of the world-market, conquered for itself, in the modern representative State, exclusive political sway. The executive of the modern State is but a committee for managing the common affairs of the whole bourgeoisie.

The bourgeoisie, historically, has played a most revolutionary part.

The bourgeoisie, wherever it has got the upper hand, has put an end to all feudal, patriarchal, idyllic relations. It has pitilessly torn asunder the motley feudal ties that bound man to his "natural superiors," and has left remaining no other nexus between man and man than naked self-interest, than callous "cash payment." It has drowned the most heavenly ecstasies of religious fervour, of chivalrous enthusiasm, of philistine sentimentalism, in the icy water of egotistical calculation. It has resolved personal worth into exchange value, and in place of the numberless indefeasible chartered freedoms, has set up that single, unconscionable freedom—Free Trade. In one word, for exploitation, veiled by religious and political illusions, it has substituted naked, shameless, direct, brutal exploitation.

The bourgeoisie has stripped of its halo every occupation hitherto honoured and looked up to with reverent awe. It has converted the physician, the lawyer, the priest, the poet, the man of science, into its paid wage-labourers. . . .

The bourgeoisie cannot exist without constantly revolutionising the instruments of production, and thereby the relations of production, and with them the whole relations of society. Conservation of the old modes of production in unaltered form, was, on the contrary, the first condition of existence for all earlier industrial classes. Constant revolutionising of production, uninterrupted disturbance of all social conditions, everlasting uncertainty and agitation distinguish the bourgeois epoch from all earlier ones. All fixed, fast-frozen relations, with their train of ancient and venerable prejudices and opinions, are swept away, all new-formed ones become antiquated before they can ossify. All that is solid melts into air, all that is holy is profaned, and man is at last compelled to face with sober senses, his real conditions of life, and his relations with his kind.

The need of a constantly expanding market for its products chases the bourgeoisie over the whole surface of the globe. It must nestle everywhere, settle everywhere, establish connexions everywhere.

The bourgeoisie has through its exploitation of the world-market given a cosmopolitan character to production and consumption in every country. To the great chagrin of Reactionists, it has drawn from under the feet of industry the national ground on which it stood. All old-established national industries have been destroyed or are daily being destroyed. They are dislodged by new industries, whose introduction becomes a life and death question for all civilised nations, by industries that no longer work up indigenous raw material, but raw material drawn from the remotest zones; industries whose products are consumed, not only at home, but in every quarter of the globe. In place of the old wants, satisfied by the productions of the country, we find new wants, requiring for their satisfaction the products of distant lands and climes. In place of the old local and national seclusion and self-sufficiency, we have intercourse in every direction, universal inter-dependence of nations. And as in material, so also in intellectual production. The intellectual creations of individual nations become common property. National one-sidedness and narrow-mindedness become more and more impossible, and from the numerous national and local literatures, there arises a world literature.

The bourgeoisie, by the rapid improvement of all instruments of production, by the immensely facilitated means of communication, draws all, even the most barbarian, nations into civilisation. The cheap prices of its commodities are the heavy artillery with which it batters down all Chinese walls, with which it forces the barbarians' intensely obstinate hatred of foreigners to capitulate. It compels all nations, on pain of extinction, to adopt the bourgeois mode of production; it compels them to introduce what it calls civilisation into their midst, *i.e.*, to become bourgeois themselves. In one word, it creates a world after its own image.

The bourgeoisie has subjected the country to the rule of the towns. It has created enormous cities, has greatly increased the urban population as compared with the rural, and has thus rescued a considerable part of the population from the idiocy of rural life. Just as it has made the country dependent on the towns, so it has made barbarian and semibarbarian countries dependent on the civilised ones, nations of peasants on nations of bourgeois, the East on the West.

The bourgeoisie keeps more and more doing away with the scattered state of the population, of the means of production, and of property. It has agglomerated population, centralised means of production, and has concentrated property in a few hands. The necessary consequence of this was political centralisation. Independent, or but loosely connected provinces, with separate interests, laws, governments and systems of taxation, became lumped together into one nation, with one government, one code of laws, one national class-interest, one frontier and one customs-tariff. . . .

We see then: the means of production and of exchange, on whose foundation the bourgeoisie built itself up, were generated in feudal society. At a certain stage in the development of these means of production and of exchange, the conditions under which feudal society produced and exchanged, the feudal organisation of agri-

culture and manufacturing industry, in one word, the feudal relations of property became no longer compatible with the already developed productive forces; they became
so many fetters. They had to be burst asunder; they were burst asunder.

Into their place stepped free competition, accompanied by a social and political constitution adapted to it, and by the economical and political sway of the bourgeois class.

A similar movement is going on before our own eyes. Modern bourgeois society with its relations of production, of exchange and of property, a society that has
conjured up such gigantic means of production and of exchange, is like the sorcerer,
who is no longer able to control the powers of the nether world whom he has called
up by his spells. For many a decade past the history of industry and commerce is but
the history of the revolt of modern productive forces against modern conditions of
production, against the property relations that are the conditions for the existence of
the bourgeoisie and of its rule. It is enough to mention the commercial crises that by
their periodical return put on its trial, each time more threateningly, the existence of
the entire bourgeois society. In these crises a great part not only of the existing products, but also of the previously created productive forces, are periodically destroyed.
In these crises there breaks out an epidemic that, in all earlier epochs, would have
seemed an absurdity—the epidemic of over-production. Society suddenly finds itself
put back into a state of momentary barbarism; it appears as if a famine, a universal
war of devastation had cut off the supply of every means of subsistence; industry and
commerce seem to be destroyed; and why? Because there is too much civilisation, too
much means of subsistence, too much industry, too much commerce. The productive
forces at the disposal of society no longer tend to further the development of the conditions of bourgeois property; on the contrary, they have become too powerful for
these conditions, by which they are fettered, and so soon as they overcome these fetters, they bring disorder into the whole of bourgeois society, endanger the existence
of bourgeois property. The conditions of bourgeois society are too narrow to comprise the wealth created by them. And how does the bourgeoisie get over these crises?
On the one hand by enforced destruction of a mass of productive forces; on the other,
by the conquest of new markets, and by the more thorough exploitation of the old
ones. That is to say, by paving the way for more extensive and more destructive crises,
and by diminishing the means whereby crises are prevented. . . .

In proportion as the bourgeoisie, *i.e.*, capital, is developed, in the same proportion is the proletariat, the modern working class, developed—a class of labourers, who
live only so long as they find work, and who find work only so long as their labour increases capital. These labourers, who must sell themselves piecemeal, are a commodity, like every other article of commerce, and are consequently exposed to all the
vicissitudes of competition, to all the fluctuations of the market.

Owing to the extensive use of machinery and to division of labour, the work of
the proletarians has lost all individual character, and, consequently, all charm for the
workman. He becomes an appendage of the machine, and it is only the most simple,
most monotonous, and most easily acquired knack, that is required of him. Hence,
the cost of production of a workman is restricted, almost entirely, to the means of subsistence that he requires for his maintenance, and for the propagation of his race. But

the price of a commodity, and therefore also of labour, is equal to its cost of production. In proportion, therefore, as the repulsiveness of the work increases, the wage decreases. Nay more, in proportion as the use of machinery and division of labour increases, in the same proportion the burden of toil also increases, whether by prolongation of the working hours, by increase of the work exacted in a given time or by increased speed of the machinery, etc.

Modern industry has converted the little workshop of the patriarchal master into the great factory of the industrial capitalist. Masses of labourers, crowded into the factory, are organised like soldiers. As privates of the industrial army they are placed under the command of a perfect hierarchy of officers and sergeants. Not only are they slaves of the bourgeois class, and of the bourgeois State; they are daily and hourly enslaved by the machine, by the overlooker, and, above all, by the individual bourgeois manufacturer himself. The more openly this despotism proclaims gain to be its end and aim, the more petty, the more hateful and the more embittering it is.

The less the skill and exertion of strength implied in manual labour, in other words, the more modern industry becomes developed, the more is the labour of men superseded by that of women. Differences of age and sex have no longer any distinctive social validity for the working class. All are instruments of labour, more or less expensive to use, according to their age and sex.

No sooner is the exploitation of the labourer by the manufacturer, so far, at an end, and he receives his wages in cash, than he is set upon by the other portions of the bourgeoisie, the landlord, the shopkeeper, the pawnbroker, etc.

The lower strata of the middle class—the small tradespeople, shopkeepers, and retired tradesmen generally, the handicraftsmen and peasants—all these sink gradually into the proletariat, partly because their diminutive capital does not suffice for the scale on which Modern Industry is carried on, and is swamped in the competition with the large capitalists, partly because their specialised skill is rendered worthless by new methods of production. Thus the proletariat is recruited from all classes of the population.

The proletariat goes through various stages of development. With its birth begins its struggle with the bourgeoisie. At first the contest is carried on by individual labourers, then by the workpeople of a factory, then by the operatives of one trade, in one locality, against the individual bourgeois who directly exploits them. They direct their attacks not against the bourgeois conditions of production, but against the instruments of production themselves; they destroy imported wares that compete with their labour, they smash to pieces machinery, they set factories ablaze, they seek to restore by force the vanished status of the workman of the Middle Ages. . . .

But with the development of industry the proletariat not only increases in number; it becomes concentrated in greater masses, its strength grows, and it feels that strength more. The various interests and conditions of life within the ranks of the proletariat are more and more equalised, in proportion as machinery obliterates all distinctions of labour, and nearly everywhere reduces wages to the same low level. The growing competition among the bourgeois, and the resulting commercial crises, make the wages of the workers ever more fluctuating. The unceasing improvement of machinery, ever more rapidly developing, makes their livelihood more and more precarious; the collisions between individual workmen and individual bourgeois take more and more the character of collisions between two classes. Thereupon the workers begin to form combinations (Trades' Unions) against the bourgeois; they club together in order to keep up the rate of wages; they found permanent associations in order to make provision beforehand for these occasional revolts. Here and there the contest breaks out into riots.

Now and then the workers are victorious, but only for a time. The real fruit of their battles lies, not in the immediate result, but in the ever-expanding union of the workers. This union is helped on by the improved means of communication that are created by modern industry and that place the workers of different localities in contact with one another. It was just this contact that was needed to centralise the numerous local struggles, all of the same character, into one national struggle between classes. But every class struggle is a political struggle. And that union, to attain which the burghers of the Middle Ages, with their miserable highways, required centuries, the modern proletarians, thanks to railways, achieve in a few years.

This organisation of the proletarians into a class, and consequently into a political party, is continually being upset again by the competition between the workers themselves. But it ever rises up again, stronger, firmer, mightier. It compels legislative recognition of particular interests of the workers, by taking advantage of the divisions among the bourgeoisie itself. Thus the ten-hours' bill in England was carried.

Altogether collisions between the classes of the old society further, in many ways, the course of development of the proletariat. The bourgeoisie finds itself involved in a constant battle. At first with the aristocracy; later on, with those portions of the bourgeoisie itself, whose interests have become antagonistic to the progress of industry; at all times, with the bourgeoisie of foreign countries. In all these battles it sees itself compelled to appeal to the proletariat, to ask for its help, and thus, to drag it into the political arena. The bourgeoisie itself, therefore, supplies the proletariat with its own elements of political and general education, in other words, it furnishes the proletariat with weapons for fighting the bourgeoisie. . . .

Finally, in times when the class struggle nears the decisive hour, the process of dissolution going on within the ruling class, in fact within the whole range of old society, assumes such a violent, glaring character, that a small section of the ruling class cuts itself adrift, and joins the revolutionary class, the class that holds the future in its hands. Just as, therefore, at an earlier period, a section of the nobility went over to the bourgeoisie, so now a portion of the bourgeoisie goes over to the proletariat, and in particular, a portion of the bourgeois ideologists, who have raised themselves to the level of comprehending theoretically the historical movement as a whole.

Of all the classes that stand face to face with the bourgeoisie today, the proletariat alone is a really revolutionary class. The other classes decay and finally disappear in the face of Modern Industry; the proletariat is its special and essential product.

The lower middle class, the small manufacturer, the shopkeeper, the artisan, the peasant, all these fight against the bourgeoisie, to save from extinction their existence as fractions of the middle class. They are therefore not revolutionary, but conservative. Nay more, they are reactionary, for they try to roll back the wheel of history. If by chance they are revolutionary, they are so only in view of their impending transfer into the proletariat, they thus defend not their present, but their future interests, they desert their own standpoint to place themselves at that of the proletariat.

The "dangerous class," the social scum, that passively rotting mass thrown off by the lowest layers of old society, may, here and there, be swept into the movement by a proletarian revolution, its conditions of life, however, prepare it far more for the part of a bribed tool of reactionary intrigue.

In the conditions of the proletariat, those of old society at large are already virtually swamped. The proletarian is without property; his relation to his wife and children has no longer anything in common with the bourgeois family-relations; modern industrial labour, modern subjection to capital, the same in England as in France, in America as in Germany, has stripped him of every trace of national character. Law, morality, religion, are to him so many bourgeois prejudices, behind which lurk in ambush just as many bourgeois interests.

All the preceding classes that got the upper hand, sought to fortify their already acquired status by subjecting society at large to their conditions of appropriation. The proletarians cannot become masters of the productive forces of society, except by abolishing their own previous mode of appropriation, and thereby also every other previous mode of appropriation. They have nothing of their own to secure and to fortify, their mission is to destroy all previous securities for, and insurances of, individual property. . . .

Though not in substance, yet in form, the struggle of the proletariat with the bourgeoisie is at first a national struggle. The proletariat of each country must, of course, first of all settle matters with its own bourgeoisie.

In depicting the most general phases of the development of the proletariat, we traced the more or less veiled civil war, raging within existing society, up to the point where that war breaks out into open revolution, and where the violent overthrow of the bourgeoisie lays the foundation for the sway of the proletariat. . . .

The essential condition for the existence, and for the sway of the bourgeois class, is the formation and augmentation of capital; the condition for capital is wage-labour. Wage-labour rests exclusively on competition between the labourers. The advance of industry, whose involuntary promoter is the bourgeoisie, replaces the isolation of the labourers, due to competition, by their revolutionary combination, due to association. The development of Modern Industry, therefore, cuts from under its feet the very foundation on which the bourgeoisie produces and appropriates products. What the bourgeoisie, therefore, produces, above all, is its own grave-diggers. Its fall and the victory of the proletariat are equally inevitable.

II. PROLETARIANS AND COMMUNISTS

In what relation do the Communists stand to the proletarians as a whole?

The Communists do not form a separate party opposed to other working-class parties.

They have no interests separate and apart from those of the proletariat as a whole.

They do not set up any sectarian principles of their own, by which to shape and mould the proletarian movement.

The Communists are distinguished from the other working-class parties by this only: 1. In the national struggles of the proletarians of the different countries, they point out and bring to the front the common interests of the entire proletariat, independently of all nationality. 2. In the various stages of development which the struggle of the working class against the bourgeoisie has to pass through, they always and everywhere represent the interests of the movement as a whole.

The Communists, therefore, are on the one hand, practically, the most advanced and resolute section of the working-class parties of every country, that section which pushes forward all others; on the other hand, theoretically, they have over the great mass of the proletariat the advantage of clearly understanding the line of march, the conditions, and the ultimate general results of the proletarian movement.

The immediate aim of the Communists is the same as that of all the other proletarian parties: formation of the proletariat into a class, overthrow of the bourgeois supremacy, conquest of political power by the proletariat. . . .

The distinguishing feature of Communism is not the abolition of property generally, but the abolition of bourgeois property. But modern bourgeois private property is the final and most complete expression of the system of producing and appropriating products, that is based on class antagonisms, on the exploitation of the many by the few.

In this sense, the theory of the Communists may be summed up in the single sentence: Abolition of private property.

We Communists have been reproached with the desire of abolishing the right of personally acquiring property as the fruit of a man's own labour, which property is alleged to be the groundwork of all personal freedom, activity and independence.

Hard-won, self-acquired, self-earned property! Do you mean the property of the petty artisan and of the small peasant, a form of property that preceded the bourgeois form? There is no need to abolish that; the development of industry has to a great extent already destroyed it, and is still destroying it daily.

Or do you mean modern bourgeois private property?

But does wage-labour create any property for the labourer? Not a bit. It creates capital, *i.e.*, that kind of property which exploits wage-labour, and which cannot increase except upon condition of begetting a new supply of wage-labour for fresh exploitation. Property, in its present form, is based on the antagonism of capital and wage-labour. Let us examine both sides of this antagonism.

To be a capitalist, is to have not only a purely personal, but a social *status* in production. Capital is a collective product, and only by the united action of many members, nay, in the last resort, only by the united action of all members of society, can it be set in motion.

Capital is, therefore, not a personal, it is a social power.

When, therefore, capital is converted into common property, into the property of all members of society, personal property is not thereby transformed into social property. It is only the social character of the property that is changed. It loses its class-character. . . .

The average price of wage-labour is the minimum wage, *i.e.,* that quantum of the means of subsistence, which is absolutely requisite to keep the labourer in bare existence as a labourer. What, therefore, the wage-labourer appropriates by means of his labour, merely suffices to prolong and reproduce a bare existence. We by no means intend to abolish this personal appropriation of the products of labour, an appropriation that is made for the maintenance and reproduction of human life, and that leaves no surplus wherewith to command the labour of others. All that we want to do away with, is the miserable character of this appropriation, under which the labourer lives merely to increase capital, and is allowed to live only in so far as the interest of the ruling class requires it. . . .

You are horrified at our intending to do away with private property. But in your existing society, private property is already done away with for nine-tenths of the population; its existence for the few is solely due to its non-existence in the hands of those nine-tenths. You reproach us, therefore, with intending to do away with a form of property, the necessary condition for whose existence is the non-existence of any property for the immense majority of society.

In one word, you reproach us with intending to do away with your property. Precisely so; that is just what we intend. . . .

Communism deprives no man of the power to appropriate the products of society; all that it does is to deprive him of the power to subjugate the labour of others by means of such appropriation. . . .

The communists are further reproached with desiring to abolish countries and nationality.

The working men have no country. We cannot take from them what they have not got. Since the proletariat must first of all acquire political supremacy, must rise to be the leading class of the nation, must constitute itself *the* nation, it is, so far, itself national, though not in the bourgeois sense of the word.

National differences and antagonisms between peoples are daily more and more vanishing, owing to the development of the bourgeoisie, to freedom of commerce, to the world-market, to uniformity in the mode of production and in the conditions of life corresponding thereto.

The supremacy of the proletariat will cause them to vanish still faster. United action, of the leading civilised countries at least, is one of the first conditions for the emancipation of the proletariat.

In proportion as the exploitation of one individual by another is put an end to, the exploitation of one nation by another will also be put an end to. In proportion as the antagonism between classes within the nation vanishes, the hostility of one nation to another will come to an end. . . .

When people speak of ideas that revolutionise society, they do but express the fact, that within the old society, the elements of a new one have been created, and that the dissolution of the old ideas keeps even pace with the dissolution of the old conditions of existence. . . .

But whatever form they may have taken, one fact is common to all past ages, *viz.*, the exploitation of one part of society by the other. No wonder, then, that the social consciousness of past ages, despite all the multiplicity and variety it displays, moves within certain common forms, or general ideas, which cannot completely vanish except with the total disappearance of class antagonisms.

The Communist revolution is the most radical rupture with traditional property relations; no wonder that its development involves the most radical rupture with traditional ideas.

But let us have done with the bourgeois objections to Communism.

We have seen above, that the first step in the revolution by the working class, is to raise the proletariat to the position of ruling class, to win the battle of democracy.

The proletariat will use its political supremacy to wrest, by degrees, all capital from the bourgeoisie, to centralise all instruments of production in the hands of the State, *i.e.*, of the proletariat organised as the ruling class; and to increase the total of productive forces as rapidly as possible. . . .

7. The Development
of Underdevelopment

Andre Gunder Frank

We cannot hope to formulate adequate development theory and policy for the majority of the world's population who suffer from underdevelopment without first learning how their past economic and social history gave rise to their present underdevelopment. Yet most historians study only the developed metropolitan countries and pay scant attention to the colonial and underdeveloped lands. For this reason most of our theoretical categories and guides to development policy have been distilled exclusively from the historical experience of the European and North American advanced capitalist nations.

Since the historical experience of the colonial and underdeveloped countries has demonstrably been quite different, available theory therefore fails to reflect the past of the underdeveloped part of the world entirely, and reflects the past of the world as a whole only in part. More important, our ignorance of the underdeveloped countries' history leads us to assume that their past and indeed their present resembles ear-

From "The Development of Underdevelopment," by Andre Gunder Frank. *Monthly Review,* September 1966, pp. 111–123. Reprinted by permission.

lier stages of the history of the now developed countries. This ignorance and this assumption lead us into serious misconceptions about contemporary underdevelopment and development. Further, most studies of development and underdevelopment fail to take account of the economic and other relations between the metropolis and its economic colonies throughout the history of the worldwide expansion and development of the mercantilist and capitalist system. Consequently, most of our theory fails to explain the structure and development of the capitalist system as a whole and to account for its simultaneous generation of underdevelopment in some of its parts and of economic development in others.

It is generally held that economic development occurs in a succession of capitalist stages and that today's underdeveloped countries are still in a stage, sometimes depicted as an original stage, of history through which the now developed countries passed long ago. Yet even a modest acquaintance with history shows that underdevelopment is not original or traditional and that neither the past nor the present of the underdeveloped countries resembles in any important respect the past of the now developed countries. The now developed countries were never *under*developed, though they may have been *un*developed. It is also widely believed that the contemporary underdevelopment of a country can be understood as the product or reflection solely of its own economic, political, social, and cultural characteristics or structure. Yet historical research demonstrates that contemporary underdevelopment is in large part the historical product of past and continuing economic and other relations between the satellite underdeveloped and the now developed metropolitan countries. Furthermore, these relations are an essential part of the structure and development of the capitalist system on a world scale as a whole. A related and also largely erroneous view is that the development of these underdeveloped countries, and within them of their most underdeveloped domestic areas, must and will be generated or stimulated by diffusing capital, institutions, values, etc., to them from the international and national capitalist metropoles. Historical perspective based on the underdeveloped countries' past experience suggests that on the contrary, economic development in the underdeveloped countries can now occur only independently of most of these relations of diffusion.

Evident inequalities of income and differences in culture have led many observers to see "dual" societies and economies in the underdeveloped countries. Each of the two parts is supposed to have a history of its own, a structure, and a contemporary dynamic largely independent of the other. Supposedly only one part of the economy and society has been importantly affected by intimate economic relations with the "outside" capitalist world; and that part, it is held, became modern, capitalist, and relatively developed precisely because of this contact. The other part is widely regarded as variously isolated, subsistence-based, feudal, or pre-capitalist, and therefore more underdeveloped.

I believe on the contrary that the entire "dual" society thesis is false and that the policy recommendations to which it leads will, if acted upon, serve only to intensify and perpetuate the very conditions of underdevelopment they are supposedly designed to remedy.

A mounting body of evidence suggests, and I am confident that future historical research will confirm, that the expansion of the capitalist system over the past centuries effectively and entirely penetrated even the apparently most isolated sectors of
the underdeveloped world. Therefore the economic, political, social, and cultural institutions and relations we now observe there are the products of the historical development of the capitalist system no less than are the seemingly more modern or capitalist features of the national metropoles of these underdeveloped countries.
Analogous to the relations between development and underdevelopment on the international level, the contemporary and underdeveloped institutions of the so-called
backward or feudal domestic areas of an underdeveloped country are no less the product of the single historical process of capitalist development than are the so-called
capitalist institutions of the supposedly more progressive areas. I should like to sketch
the kinds of evidence which support this thesis and at the same time indicate lines
along which further study and research could fruitfully proceed.

The Secretary General of the Latin American Center for Research in the Social Sciences writes in that Center's journal: "The privileged position of the city has
its origin in the colonial period. It was founded by the Conqueror to serve the same
ends that it still serves today; to incorporate the indigenous population into the economy brought and developed by that Conqueror and his descendants. The regional
city was an instrument of conquest and is still today an instrument of domination."[1]
The Instituto Nacional Indigenista (National Indian Institute) of Mexico confirms this
observation when it notes that "the mestizo population, in fact, always lives in a city,
a center of an intercultural region, which acts as the metropolis of a zone of indigenous population and which maintains with the underdeveloped communities an intimate relation which links the center with the satellite communities."[2] The Institute
goes on to point out that "between the mestizos who live in the nuclear city of the region and the Indians who live in the peasant hinterland there is in reality a closer economic and social interdependence than might at first glance appear" and that the
provincial metropoles "by being centers of intercourse are also centers of exploitation."[3]

Thus these metropolis-satellite relations are not limited to the imperial or international level but penetrate and structure the very economic, political, and social
life of the Latin American colonies and countries. Just as the colonial and national
capital and its export sector become the satellite of the Iberian (and later of other)
metropoles of the world economic system, this satellite immediately becomes a colonial and then a national metropolis with respect to the productive sectors and population of the interior. Furthermore, the provincial capitals, which thus are themselves
satellites of the national metropolis—and through the latter of the world metropolis—are in turn provincial centers around which their own local satellites orbit. Thus,
a whole chain of constellations of metropoles and satellites relates all parts of the
whole system from its metropolitan center in Europe or the United States to the far-
thest outpost in the Latin American countryside.

When we examine this metropolis-satellite structure, we find that each of the satellites, including now underdeveloped Spain and Portugal, serves as an instrument to suck capital or economic surplus out of its own satellites and to channel part of this surplus to the world metropolis of which all are satellites. Moreover, each national and local metropolis serves to impose and maintain the monopolistic structure and exploitative relationship of this system (as the Instituto Nacional Indigenista of Mexico calls it) as long as it serves the interests of the metropoles which take advantage of this global, national, and local structure to promote their own development and the enrichment of their ruling classes.

These are the principal and still surviving structural characteristics which were implanted in Latin America by the Conquest. Beyond examining the establishment of this colonial structure in its historical context, the proposed approach calls for study of the development—and underdevelopment—of these metropoles and satellites of Latin America throughout the following and still continuing historical process. In this way we can understand why there were and still are tendencies in the Latin American and world capitalist structure which seem to lead to the development of the metropolis and the underdevelopment of the satellite and why, particularly, the satellized national, regional, and local metropoles in Latin America find that their economic development is at best a limited or underdeveloped development.

That present underdevelopment of Latin America is the result of its centuries-long participation in the process of world capitalist development, I believe I have shown in my case studies of the economic and social histories of Chile and Brazil.[4] My study of Chilean history suggests that the Conquest not only incorporated this country fully into the expansion and development of the world mercantile and later industrial capitalist system but that it also introduced the monopolistic metropolis-satellite structure and development of capitalism into the Chilean domestic economy and society itself. This structure then penetrated and permeated all of Chile very quickly. Since that time and in the course of world and Chilean history during the epochs of colonialism, free trade, imperialism, and the present, Chile has become increasingly marked by the economic, social, and political structure of satellite underdevelopment. This development of underdevelopment continues today, both in Chile's still increasing satellization by the world metropolis and through the ever more acute polarization of Chile's domestic economy.

The history of Brazil is perhaps the clearest case of both national and regional development of underdevelopment. The expansion of the world economy since the beginning of the sixteenth century successively converted the Northeast, the Minas Gerais interior, the North, and the Center-South (Rio de Janeiro, São Paulo, and Paraná) into export economies and incorporated them into the structure and development of the world capitalist system. Each of these regions experienced what may have appeared as economic development during the period of its golden age. But it was a satellite development which was neither self-generating nor self-perpetuating. As the market or the productivity of the first three regions declined, foreign and domestic economic interest in them waned and they were left to develop the underdevelopment they live today. In the fourth region, the coffee economy experienced a similar though not yet quite as serious fate (though the development of a synthetic coffee substitute promises to deal it a mortal blow in the not too distant future). All of this historical evidence contradicts the generally accepted theses that Latin America suffers from a dual society or from the survival of feudal institutions and that these are important obstacles to its economic development.

During the First World War, however, and even more during the Great Depression and the Second World War, São Paulo began to build up an industrial establishment which is the largest in Latin America today. The question arises whether this industrial development did or can break Brazil out of the cycle of satellite development and underdevelopment which has characterized its other regions and national history within the capitalist system so far. I believe that the answer is no. Domestically the evidence so far is fairly clear. The development of industry in São Paulo has not brought greater riches to the other regions of Brazil. Instead, it has converted them into internal colonial satellites, de-capitalized them further, and consolidated or even deepened their underdevelopment. There is little evidence to suggest that this process is likely to be reversed in the foreseeable future except insofar as the provincial poor migrate and become the poor of the metropolitan cities. Externally, the evidence is that although the initial development of São Paulo's industry was relatively autonomous it is being increasingly satellized by the world capitalist metropolis and its future development possibilities are increasingly restricted.[5] This development, my studies lead me to believe, also appears destined to limited or underdeveloped development as long as it takes place in the present economic, political, and social framework.

We must conclude, in short, that underdevelopment is not due to the survival of archaic institutions and the existence of capital shortage in regions that have remained isolated from the stream of world history. On the contrary, underdevelopment was and still is generated by the very same historical process which also generated economic development: the development of capitalism itself. This view, I am glad to say, is gaining adherents among students of Latin America and is proving its worth in shedding new light on the problems of the area and in affording a better perspective for the formulation of theory and policy.[6]

The same historical and structural approach can also lead to better development theory and policy by generating a series of hypotheses about development and underdevelopment such as those I am testing in my current research. The hypotheses are derived from the empirical observation and theoretical assumption that within this world-embracing metropolis-satellite structure the metropoles tend to develop and the satellites to underdevelop. The first hypothesis has already been mentioned above: that in contrast to the development of the world metropolis which is no one's satellite, the development of the national and other subordinate metropoles is limited by their satellite status. It is perhaps more difficult to test this hypothesis than the following ones because part of its confirmation depends on the test of the other hypotheses. Nonetheless, this hypothesis appears to be generally confirmed by the non-autonomous and unsatisfactory economic and especially industrial development of Latin America's national metropoles, as documented in the studies already cited. The most important and at the same time most confirmatory examples are the metropolitan regions of Buenos Aires, and São Paulo, whose growth only began in the nineteenth century, was therefore largely untrammeled by any colonial heritage, but was and remains a satellite development largely dependent on the outside metropolis, first of Britain and then of the United States.

A second hypothesis is that the satellites experience their greatest economic development and especially their most classically capitalist industrial development if and when their ties to their metropolis are weakest. This hypothesis is almost diametrically opposed to the generally accepted thesis that development in the underdeveloped countries follows from the greatest degree of contact with and diffusion from the metropolitan developed countries. This hypothesis seems to be confirmed by two kinds of relative isolation that Latin America has experienced in the course of its history. One is the temporary isolation caused by the crises of war or depression in the world metropolis. Apart from minor ones, five periods of such major crises stand out and are seen to confirm the hypothesis. These are the European (and especially Spanish) depression of the seventeenth century, the Napoleonic Wars, the First World War, the Depression of the 1930s, and the Second World War. It is clearly established and generally recognized that the most important recent industrial development—especially of Argentina, Brazil, and Mexico, but also of other countries such as Chile—has taken place precisely during the periods of the two world wars and the intervening Depression. Thanks to the consequent loosening of trade and investment ties during these periods, the satellites initiated marked autonomous industrialization and growth. Historical research demonstrates that the same thing happened in Latin America during Europe's seventeenth-century depression. Manufacturing grew in the Latin American countries, and several, such as Chile, became exporters of manufactured goods. The Napoleonic Wars gave rise to independence movements in Latin America, and these should perhaps also be interpreted as in part confirming the development hypothesis.

The other kind of isolation which tends to confirm the second hypothesis is the geographic and economic isolation of regions which at one time were relatively weakly tied to and poorly integrated into the mercantilist and capitalist system. My preliminary research suggests that in Latin America it was these regions which initiated and experienced the most promising self-generating economic development of the classical industrial capitalist type. The most important regional cases probably are Tucamán and Asunción, as well as other cities, such as Mendoza and Rosario, in the interior of Argentina and Paraguay during the end of the eighteenth and the beginning of the nineteenth centuries. Seventeenth- and eighteenth-century São Paulo, long before coffee was grown there, is another example. Perhaps Antioquia in Colombia and Puebla and Querétaro in Mexico are other examples. In its own way, Chile was also an example, since before the sea route around the Horn was opened this country was relatively isolated at the end of a long voyage from Europe via Panama. All of these regions became manufacturing centers and even exporters, usually of textiles, during the periods preceding their effective incorporation as satellites into the colonial, national, and world capitalist system.

Internationally, of course, the classic case of industrialization through non-participation as a satellite in the capitalist world system is obviously that of Japan after the Meiji Restoration. Why, one may ask, was resource-poor but unsatellized Japan able to industrialize so quickly at the end of the century while resource-rich Latin American countries and Russia were not able to do so and the latter was easily beaten by Japan in the War of 1904 after the same forty years of development efforts? The second hypothesis suggests that the fundamental reason is that Japan was not satellized either during the Tokugawa or the Meiji period and therefore did not have its development structurally limited as did the countries which were so satellized.

A corollary of the second hypothesis is that when the metropolis recovers from its crisis and re-establishes the trade and investment ties which fully re-incorporate the satellites into the system, or when the metropolis expands to incorporate previously isolated regions into the worldwide system, the previous development and industrialization of these regions is choked off or channeled into directions which are not self-perpetuating and promising. This happened after each of the five crises cited above. The renewed expansion of trade and the spread of economic liberalism in the eighteenth and nineteenth centuries choked off and reversed the manufacturing development which Latin America had experienced during the seventeenth century, and in some places at the beginning of the nineteenth. After the First World War, the new national industry of Brazil suffered serious consequences from American economic invasion. The increase in the growth rate of Gross National Product and particularly of industrialization throughout Latin America was again reversed and industry became increasingly satellized after the Second World War and especially after the post-Korean War recovery and expansion of the metropolis. Far from having become more developed since then, industrial sectors of Brazil and most conspicuously of Argentina have become structurally more and more underdeveloped and less and less able to generate continued industrialization and/or sustain development of the economy. This process, from which India also suffers, is reflected in a whole gamut of balance-of-payments, inflationary, and other economic and political difficulties, and promises to yield to no solution short of far-reaching structural change.

Our hypothesis suggests that fundamentally the same process occurred even more dramatically with the incorporation into the system of previously unsatellized regions. The expansion of Buenos Aires as a satellite of Great Britain and the introduction of free trade in the interest of the ruling groups of both metropoles destroyed the manufacturing and much of the remainder of the economic base of the previously relatively prosperous interior almost entirely. Manufacturing was destroyed by foreign competition, lands were taken and concentrated into latifundia by the rapaciously growing export economy, intra-regional distribution of income became much more unequal, and the previously developing regions became simple satellites of Buenos Aires and through it of London. The provincial centers did not yield to satellization without a struggle. This metropolis-satellite conflict was much of the cause of the long political and armed struggle between the Unitarists in Buenos Aires and the

Federalists in the provinces, and it may be said to have been the sole important cause of the War of the Triple Alliance in which Buenos Aires, Montevideo, and Rio de Janeiro, encouraged and helped by London, destroyed not only the autonomously developing economy of Paraguay but killed off nearly all of its population unwilling to give in. Though this is no doubt the most spectacular example which tends to confirm the hypothesis, I believe that historical research on the satellization of previously relatively independent yeoman-farming and incipient manufacturing regions such as the Caribbean islands will confirm it further.[7] These regions did not have a chance against the forces of expanding and developing capitalism, and their own development had to be sacrificed to that of others. The economy and industry of Argentina, Brazil, and other countries which have experienced the effects of metropolitan recovery since the Second World War are today suffering much the same fate, if fortunately still in lesser degree.

A third major hypothesis derived from the metropolis-satellite structure is that the regions which are the most underdeveloped and feudal-seeming today are the ones which had the closest ties to the metropolis in the past. They are the regions which were the greatest exporters of primary products to and the biggest sources of capital for the world metropolis and were abandoned by the metropolis when for one reason or another business fell off. This hypothesis also contradicts the generally held thesis that the source of a region's underdevelopment is its isolation and its pre-capitalist institutions.

This hypothesis seems to be amply confirmed by the former super-satellite development and present ultra-underdevelopment of the once sugar-exporting West Indies, Northeastern Brazil, the ex-mining districts of Minas Gerais in Brazil, highland Peru, and Bolivia, and the central Mexican states of Guanajuato, Zacatecas, and others whose names were made world famous centuries ago by their silver. There surely are no major regions in Latin America which are today more cursed by underdevelopment and poverty; yet all of these regions, like Bengal in India, once provided the life blood of mercantile and industrial capitalist development—in the metropolis. These regions' participation in the development of the world capitalist system gave them, already in their golden age, the typical structure of underdevelopment of a capitalist export economy. When the market for their sugar or the wealth of their mines disappeared and the metropolis abandoned them to their own devices, the already existing economic, political, and social structure of these regions prohibited autonomous generation of economic development and left them no alternative but to turn in upon themselves and to degenerate into the ultra-underdevelopment we find there today.

These considerations suggest two further and related hypotheses. One is that the latifundium, irrespective of whether it appears today as a plantation or a hacienda, was typically born as a commercial enterprise which created for itself the institutions which permitted it to respond to increased demand in the world or national market by expanding the amount of its land, capital, and labor and to increase the supply of its products. The fifth hypothesis is that the latifundia which appear isolated, subsistence-based, and semi-feudal today saw the demand for their products or their productive capacity decline and that they are to be found principally in the above-named former agricultural and mining export regions whose economic activity declined in general. These two hypotheses run counter to the notions of most people, and even to the opinions of some historians and other students of the subject, according to whom the historical roots and socioeconomic causes of Latin American latifundia and agrarian institutions are to be found in the transfer of feudal institutions from Europe and/or in economic depression.

The evidence to test these hypothesis is not open to easy general inspection and requires detailed analyses of many cases. Nonetheless, some important confirming evidence is available. The growth of the latifundium in nineteenth-century Argentina and Cuba is a clear case in support of the fourth hypothesis and can in no way be attributed to the transfer of feudal institutions during colonial times. The same is evidently the case of the post-revolutionary and contemporary resurgence of latifundia, particularly in the north of Mexico, which produce for the American market, and of similar ones on the coast of Peru and the new coffee regions of Brazil. The conversion of previously yeoman-farming Caribbean islands, such as Barbados, into sugar-exporting economies at various times between the seventeenth and twentieth centuries and the resulting rise of the latifundia in these islands would seem to confirm the fourth hypothesis as well. In Chile, the rise of the latifundium and the creation of the institutions of servitude which later came to be called feudal occurred in the eighteenth century and have been conclusively shown to be the result of and response to the opening of a market for Chilean wheat in Lima.[8] Even the growth and consolidation of the latifundium in seventeenth-century Mexico— which most expert students have attributed to a depression of the economy caused by the decline of mining and a shortage of Indian labor and to a consequent turning in upon itself and ruralization of the economy—occurred at a time when urban population and demand were growing, food shortages were acute, food prices skyrocketing, and the profitability of other economic activities such as mining and foreign trade declining.[9] All of these and other factors rendered hacienda agriculture more profitable. Thus, even this case would seem to confirm the hypothesis that the growth of the latifundium and its feudal-seeming conditions of servitude in Latin America has always been and is still the commercial response to increased demand and that it does not represent the transfer or survival of alien institutions that have remained beyond the reach of capitalist development. The emergence of latifundia, which today really are more or less (though not entirely) isolated, might then be attributed to the causes advanced in the fifth hypothesis—i.e., the decline of previously profitable agricultural enterprises whose capital was, and whose currently produced economic surplus still is, transferred elsewhere by owners and merchants who frequently are the same persons or families. Testing this hypothesis requires still more detailed analysis, some of which I have undertaken in a study on Brazilian agriculture.[10]

All of these hypotheses and studies suggest that the global extension and unity of the capitalist system, its monopoly structure and uneven development throughout its history, and the resulting persistence of commercial rather than industrial capitalism in the underdeveloped world (including its most industrially advanced countries) deserve much more attention in the study of economic development and cultural change than they have hitherto received. Though science and truth know no national boundaries, it is probably new generations of scientists from the underdeveloped countries themselves who most need to, and best can, devote the necessary attention to these problems and clarify the process of underdevelopment and development. It is their people who in the last analysis face the task of changing this no longer acceptable process and eliminating this miserable reality.

They will not be able to accomplish these goals by importing sterile stereotypes from the metropolis which do not correspond to their satellite economic reality and do not respond to their liberating political needs. To change their reality they must understand it. For this reason, I hope that better confirmation of these hypotheses and further pursuit of the proposed historical, holistic, and structural approach may help the peoples of the underdeveloped countries to understand the causes and eliminate the reality of their development of underdevelopment and their underdevelopment of development.

NOTES

1. *América Latina*, Año 6, No. 4 (October–December 1963), p. 8.
2. Instituto Nacional Indigenista, *Los centros coordinadores indigenistas* (Mexico, 1962), p. 34.
3. Ibid., pp. 33–34, 88.
4. "Capitalist Development of Underdevelopment in Chile" and "Capitalist Development of Underdevelopment in Brazil," in *Capitalism and Underdevelopment in Latin America* (New York & London: Monthly Review Press, 1967 and 1969).
5. Also see "The Growth and Decline of Import Substitution," *Economic Bulletin for Latin America*, 9, No. 1 (March 1964), and Celso Furtado, *Dialectica do Desenvolvimiento* (Rio de Janeiro: Fundo de Cultura, 1964).
6. Others who use a similar approach, though their ideologies do not permit them to derive the logically following conclusions, are Aníbal Pinto, *Chile: Un caso de desarrollo frustrado* (Santiago: Editorial Universitaria, 1957); Celso Furtado, *The Economic Growth of Brazil* (Berkeley: University of California Press, 1963); and Caio Prado Júnior, *Historia Económica do Brasil*, 7th ed. (São Paulo: Editora Brasiliense, 1962).
7. See for instance Ramiro Guerra y Sánchez, *Sugar and Society in the Caribbean* (New Haven: Yale University Press, 1964).
8. Mario Góngora, *Origen de los "inquilinos" de Chile central* (Santiago: Editorial Universitaria, 1960); Jean Borde and Mario Góngora, *Evolución de la propiedad rural en el Valle del Puango* (Santiago: Instituto de Sociología de la Universidad de Chile); and Sergio Sepúlveda, *El trigo chileno en el mercado mundial* (Santiago: Editorial Universitaria, 1959).
9. Woodrow Borah makes depression the centerpiece of his explanation in "New Spain's Century of Depression," *Ibero-Americana*, No. 35 (Berkeley, 1951). François Chevalier speaks of turning in upon itself in the most authoritative study of the subject, "La formación de los grandes latifundios en México," *Problemas Agrícolas e Industriales de México*, 8, No. 1, 1956.
10. "Capitalism and the Myth of Feudalism in Brazilian Agriculture," in *Capitalism and Underdevelopment in Latin America*.

8. The Politics of Market Socialism

Andrei Shleifer
Robert W. Vishny

One of the most enduring proposals in modern economics is market socialism: an economy in which firms are owned and controlled by the government but then sell their products to consumers in competitive markets. A reasonable person might expect that recent events in eastern Europe would put this proposal to permanent and well-deserved rest. Instead, these events seem to have given hope to the market socialists. After all, eastern European countries are starting out with virtually all firms controlled by the state. In contrast to capitalist economies, where in order to get to market socialism the state must first nationalize the economy, in eastern Europe and Russia this step was completed decades ago. If only privatization can be stopped, eastern Europe presents mouthwatering possibilities for experimentation with market socialism. Peculiar as it may seem, the escape from socialism has only encouraged many socialists.[1]

This paper takes another stab at the problem of market socialism. We focus on an issue that is often mentioned, but rarely seriously discussed in the debates over market socialism. Under all forms of market socialism, from Lange (1936) to the present, the state ultimately controls the firms, and hence politicians' objectives must determine resource allocation. Market socialists have traditionally assumed that politicians will pursue an efficient resource allocation, and only paid lip service to the idea that the state becomes "bureaucratized." They dismiss the tragic socialist experience as irrelevant because totalitarian systems are not what they have in mind. Rather, market socialists count on a democratic socialist government that pursues efficiency. The question of what such a government will maximize is therefore absolutely central to the discussion of market socialism.

We begin by reviewing the debate over market socialism, pointing out the essential role played by assumptions about the objectives of the government. We then discuss a series of economies: totalitarian socialism, democratic socialism, and de-

Andrei Shleifer is Professor of Economics, Harvard University, Cambridge, Massachusetts. Robert W. Vishny is Professor of Finance, University of Chicago, Chicago, Illinois.

We are grateful to Alberto Alesina, Alan Krueger, Carl Shapiro, and Timothy Taylor for helpful suggestions.

From "The Politics of Market Socialism," by Andrei Shleifer and Robert W. Vishny. *Journal of Economic Perspectives*, Vol. 8, No. 2, Spring 1994, pp. 165–176. Reprinted by permission.

1. Examples include Yunker (1992), Bardhan and Roemer (1992), and papers collected in Bardhan and Roemer (1993).

mocratic capitalism. Our argument against democratic market socialism is basically twofold. First, we argue that *no* democratic government is likely to place sufficient weight on economic efficiency, regardless of whether the economy is capitalist or socialist. Second, we claim that the damage from the government pursuing its "political" objectives will be much greater under socialism than under capitalism because, under socialism, the government has a greater ability to determine outcomes at the firm level.

THE MARKET SOCIALISM DEBATE

Analytical debate over market socialism started with Barone (1908 [1935]), who pointed out that the Central Planner, like the Walrasian Auctioneer, can solve *n* equations with *n* unknowns and so determine prices that simultaneously clear all markets. The state can then control firms and make lump sum redistributions to promote equality, and still get efficient outcomes for any distribution of income.

Barone's argument invited objections from von Mises (1920 [1935]) and Hayek (1935), who argued that the state does not have the necessary information to determine equilibrium prices. These objections, however, were effectively rebutted by Lange (1936), whose paper remains the most coherent and articulate case for market socialism. Lange argued that, while it is true that the state has only limited information, so does the Walrasian Auctioneer. The process of price adjustment in a market economy, according to Lange, takes the form of price increases on goods that are in excess demand, and price declines on goods that are in excess supply. The Central Planner can follow exactly the same procedure: raising prices in response to shortages and cutting prices in response to surpluses. Lange thus established quite convincingly that a benevolent Central Planner can, in principle, clear markets.

Not satisfied with establishing the equivalence between market and socialist resource allocation, Lange went on to present several reasons why socialism is superior. First, the state can distribute income more equitably. Second, since the state controls all firms, it can solve the problem of externalities. Third, since the state sets prices and determines entry, it can avoid monopolies. Aside from excessive prices, monopolies in Lange's model have two disadvantages. They are responsible for rigid prices and therefore contribute to business cycles; and they are only interested in preserving economic rents and hence are incapable of innovation. By crushing monopolies, the socialist state can both solve the business cycle problem and increase the rate of innovation.

Lange's arguments rely heavily on the government's pursuit of efficiency. His basic argument that the government raises prices of goods in short supply presumes that it actually wants to do so—rather than to maintain shortages. The pursuit of income redistribution, of internalizing externalities, and of competition rather than monopoly all presume efficiency-maximizing politicians. Indeed, Lange makes this assumption quite explicitly. For example, he writes: "The decision of the managers of production are no longer guided by the aim of maximizing profit. Instead, certain rules are imposed on them by the Central Planning Board which aim at satisfying consumers' preferences in the best way possible" (Lange, 1936–1938, p. 75).

The actual experience of socialist countries has, of course, been rather different. Instead of raising prices to clear markets, socialist governments typically maintain shortages of many goods for years. Some socialist dictators have pursued economic equality, though murder and repression by others have produced more equality of incomes than of welfare. The notion that the government solves the externality problem is belied by the experience with pollution, which seems to be worse in socialist than in comparably rich market economies (Grossman and Krueger, 1991). Also, monopolies, at least as measured by concentration, are much more common in socialist than in market economies (International Monetary Fund, 1991). Finally, practically no one believes that technological progress has been faster under socialism.

Market socialists familiar with this experience blame it on totalitarian government, and then get on with the business of praising market socialism in a democratic state. Lange (1936, pp. 109–110) briefly mentions the dangers of the state becoming bureaucratized, but does not spend much time on this problem: "It seems to us, indeed, that the *real danger of socialism is bureaucratization of economic life* [italics Lange's], and not the impossibility of coping with the problem of allocation of resources. Unfortunately, we do not see how the same, or even greater, danger can be averted under monopolistic capitalism. Officials subject to democratic control seem preferable to private corporation executives who practically are responsible to nobody."

One obvious problem with this statement is Lange's denial of the importance of incentive and control mechanisms in market economies, including boards of directors, management ownership, large blockholders, takeovers, banks, and bankruptcy (Stiglitz, 1991). Subsequent market socialists have indeed focused on this issue, and have added to Lange's model of market socialism incentives for enterprise managers comparable to those in market economies; for example, a group of socially-owned large banks might have a controlling interest in large companies (Bardhan and Roemer, 1992). In practice, such market-oriented incentive schemes for managers of state enterprises are very uncommon, and are often removed by politicians when managers begin to actually maximize profits (Nellis, 1988). But even more important than the question of incentives for the agent—that is, the manager—is the question of the objectives of the principal—that is, the government. Lange's most controversial assertion is that democratic control of corporate managers will lead to good outcomes, which is effectively a claim that politicians pursue economic efficiency.

In the following 50 years, the discussion of market socialism (except in the public choice literature[2]) has largely swallowed the assumption that the government would maximize efficiency, and proceeded to discuss the more technical issues, such as the ability of the state to complete the markets, or the relative efficiency of various price adjustment schemes. Hayek's warning (1944) that even democratic socialists turn into

---

2. The classic work is Buchanan and Tullock (1962). Mueller (1989) surveys the theory and evidence on what governments actually do.

Hitlers and Mussolinis made a relatively bigger impression on the public opinion than on the economics profession. An analytical discussion of the objectives of a socialist government is still missing. The rest of the paper tries to fill this gap, by discussing first the likely objectives of a socialist dictator, and then turning to the unlikely ideal of democratic socialism.

TOTALITARIAN SOCIALISM

We begin by considering an ideal dictator, who is completely secure from political or military challenges. This dictator does not need to worry about keeping down unemployment, building up defense, paying off or killing off political competitors, feeding the population or any other problems. A strictly rational dictator in such a position would maximize personal wealth, which the dictator can either put in a Swiss bank account or use to build monuments, such as armies, cathedrals, or industrial plants. The question is: does the pursuit of this objective lead to efficient outcomes?

At first glance, one might think that the unthreatened dictator is just a shareholder in the whole economy, and therefore should be interested in maximizing the value of his shares—that is, the profits of all the firms. Moreover, the dictator would internalize the externalities resulting from the operations of these firms and hence produce an even more efficient outcome than the market. But this is only true if the dictator takes prices as given. In fact, of course, such a dictator would control prices as well as production decisions. In this case, profit maximization would call for creation of monopolies in all industries (assuming that the dictator cannot perfectly price discriminate). Far from designing a competitive market equilibrium, the unthreatened dictator would strive for a highly monopolistic and inefficient economy—in stark contrast to Lange's insistence that socialism *prevents* monopolistic tendencies. This result, incidentally, finds empirical support in the tendency of European monarchs to create monopolies precisely to maximize personal revenues (Ekelund and Tollison, 1981).

This model seems to better describe the conduct of capitalist dictators, such as Ferdinand Marcos in the Philippines and monarchs in the age of mercantilism, than that of socialist dictators. In socialist countries, rather than observing market-clearing monopoly prices, we see a shortage of most goods. Shleifer and Vishny (1992) address this issue in a model in which a socialist dictator maximizes his income, but is prevented by the constraint of secrecy from openly putting monopoly profits in his pocket. In that paper, we show that the dictator would behave very similarly to a monopolist, but with one important exception. Instead of charging monopoly prices, the dictator would choose to charge low prices, to create a shortage, and then collect bribes from the rationed consumers. In such a model, a socialist dictator constrained by secrecy would allocate resources very similarly to a capitalist dictator, except for the way in which income is collected.

This simple model has several empirical implications consistent with the experience of socialist countries. First, it explains why shortages in socialist economies are so pervasive, since bribe collection afforded by a shortage is the main mechanism for the dictator and his ruling elite to receive income. Second, the model explains why despite shortages, prices in socialist economies are often not raised for years, even on consumer luxuries for which income distribution arguments cannot justify artificially low prices. For example, Russian communists kept the prices of cars and apartments fixed for decades despite years-long waiting lists. Raising prices would eliminate bribe income, contrary to the interest of the ruling elite. Third, the model explains the tendency of socialist economies to produce many goods monopolistically, since monopoly prevents competition in bribes that would bring prices down to competitive levels. In sum, the socialist dictator model goes some way toward explaining why the inefficiency of socialist economies is so much larger than Lange predicted.

While modeling a socialist dictator as maximizing his wealth oversimplifies reality, more realistic models would probably imply an even smaller interest in efficiency on his part. Most dictators, for example, are politically insecure, and hence pursue the personal security of themselves and their supporters. To this end, they spend enormous resources on armies and police, refocus production on military rather than consumer goods, organize firms to make them easy to control and managed by supporters rather than experts, alter prices to transfer resources to their followers and often kill millions of opponents. These are more serious costs to economic efficiency than those caused by secure, wealth-maximizing dictators.

DEMOCRACY AND ECONOMIC EFFICIENCY

Market socialists will deem the above discussion historically relevant, at best, but surely immaterial to their visions of democratic socialism, in which the government is extremely responsive to the will of the people. So let us consider the case of a democratically elected socialist government in control of a nation's firms. Most market socialists presume that such a government will strive for efficient resource allocation. How likely is this objective to occur?

Before proceeding with this question, we must mention three issues that we will *not* address. First, Hayek (1944) has followed the inspiration of Smith (1776 [1976]) and argued that democracy is impossible in a country where a single leader has all the power that comes with controlling capital. We are sympathetic to Hayek's argument. But in this paper, we will grant market socialists the possibility of democratic socialism, and only examine its consequences. Second, Stigler (1965) has complained that even economists skeptical about the state, such as Adam Smith, usually focus on the state's intentions rather than its ability to implement the announced goals. While Stigler is right that even a benevolent state might have serious implementation problems, that is not our focus here.

Third, and most important, market socialists often obfuscate the importance of politicians' intentions by imagining complex corporate governance structures. Thus Bardhan and Roemer (1992) imagine a system in which the government controls banks, which also have other shareholders, and that in turn control enterprises. Our view on this issue is simple, but realistic: no matter what smoke and mirrors are used, as long as the government remains in ultimate control of enterprises, which it does by definition in all market socialists' schemes, its objectives are going to be the ones that are maximized. Any manager who dares to stand up to the government, or to the bank controlled by the government, will be acting against personal interest. Similarly, no manager of a bank controlled by the government will refuse to lend money to a large state enterprise when the government that hired him "advises" in favor of the loan. The right focus is therefore on the objectives of the government, regardless of the governance structure through which these objectives are implemented.

The futility of trying to insulate public firms from political pressures is best illustrated by the experience of public enterprises in western Europe, where democratic institutions are strong and hence the conditions for such insulation are ideal (see Bardhan and Roemer, 1994). Despite extensive mechanisms for independent governance, most public firms in western Europe are subject to heavy-handed government interference. Just recall the experience of British Coal, where the Parliament refused to accept layoffs from enormously inefficient coal mines. Or consider the failure of Air France to cut labor, as the government opted for strikers' support and fired the manager. In countries with weaker democratic institutions, such as Italy, as well as many countries in Africa, Asia, and eastern Europe, public enterprises are simply used by politicians to gain political support, and the concept of government non-interference is totally foreign. The experience with public enterprises suggests grave skepticism about the possibility of insulating public firms from the objectives of the government.

So what objective will the government inherit from the democratic process? Two leading models of democratic decision-making are majority voting and pressure groups. Neither model predicts that the democratic government will maximize economic efficiency, although they differ in the nature of deviations from efficiency that they predict.

The majority voting model predicts that the majority will redistribute resources from the minority to itself even at the cost of reduced efficiency. The reason for inefficiency is that majority voting schemes do not weigh the intensity of preferences. As a result, if a majority can obtain a gain as a result of a redistribution from a minority, it will do so even if the costs to the minority exceed the benefits to the majority. In other words, majority voting does not lead to efficient outcomes (Tullock, 1959).

This prediction of majority voting seems to hold true in a variety of cases. Most democratic countries (whether capitalist or socialist) practice progressive taxation, often sharply progressive. Industrial workers sometimes gang up on farmers and expropriate their crops and land even when this strategy leads to devastating losses to farmers and meager benefits to workers. A majority of tenants in a city routinely impose inefficient rent control on the minority of landlords. Ethnic majorities throughout the world force minority businesses to charge prices below cost, hire members of the majority, and pay exorbitant taxes (Sowell, 1990). In light of the multiple examples of the tyranny of the majority, the claim that a majority will elect a government committed to economic efficiency is simply false.

An alternative model for democratic politics is the interest group model (Olson,

1965; Becker, 1983). In this model, interest groups form and pressure the government to pursue policies that benefit these groups at the expense of the rest of the population. Interest group politics leads to efficient resource allocation only under very restrictive conditions. First, forming an interest group and collecting contributions must be completely costless, so that the free rider and other problems are circumvented. In this case, all groups that have a common interest will form. Second, there should be no resource cost of lobbying the government; that is, interest groups should simply bid in cash, which they raise in a non-distortionary fashion, for the policies they want. If both of these conditions hold, then the interest groups model predicts efficient outcomes simply because the interest groups that put a higher value on a policy will bid more for it. Thus, if an industry wants protection that reduces efficiency, the consumer lobby will value free trade more than the industry, pay more for it, and thus ensure free trade. The public interest model with costless group formation and lobbying reduces to an efficient auction of policy choices.

Of course, organizing interest groups is actually quite expensive, because the free rider program discourages joining (Olson, 1965). Many interest groups in which benefits are small and diffuse, such as "consumers for free trade," simply do not form. The interest groups that do form and lobby the government are generally small groups with concentrated benefits, such as "automobile industry for protection." As a result, the organized minorities tend to gang up on the disorganized majority, creating an inefficient resource allocation. Moreover, the assumption of costless lobbying is also false, as rent-seeking can absorb substantial resources.

Examples of inefficiencies resulting from interest group politics are numerous; they form the substance of a vast public choice literature. The well-organized managers of the military-industrial complex can form a lobby that makes sure that the state allocates to them, and not to other firms, the majority of state credits. Farmers, doctors and other groups form effective lobbies that raise prices and redistribute public resources to themselves. Many industries demand and receive protection. We are unaware of any evidence that interest group politics leads to anything like the efficient outcome.

In a provocative but ultimately unpersuasive article, Wittman (1989) argues that the two biases—from majority voting and from interest group pressures—should cancel each other out. Specifically, the majority will vote against candidates who are too favorable to the interests of well-organized minority groups. An example might be that consumers would always vote against protectionist presidential candidates.

However, it is hard to see why these two deviations from efficiency in democratic politics should cancel out in any exact sense. In fact, sometimes the majority is better organized. For example, the majority of the population may be employed in import-competing industries, and hence the majority would favor protection. The disorganized minority that is not employed in such industries will then bear the double cost of neither getting higher wages nor having access to cheap imports. Or consider the case of "democracy" in post-communist Russia, where something close to the majority of the population benefits from state subsidies to inefficient industrial enterprises, and is also vastly better organized through industrial lobbies than the remainder of the population. This majority can then extract tremendous resources from the rest of the population at a huge cost to efficiency.

In sum, there is no presumption that democratic politics will lead to anything like an efficiency-pursuing government (see also Kornai, 1993). Vast amounts of evidence from the United States and western European democracies confirm this point. Even Sweden, long the darling of all socialists, has been suffering from a "crisis" brought about by heavy government intervention in the economy, and has been trying to restore "a highly competitive market system" (Lindbeck et al., 1993). Indeed, the very few governments in the world that might appear to pursue something resembling efficiency, such as those of Korea and Taiwan, are very far from democratic. And even market socialists no longer wish to bet on an enlightened dictator.

DEMOCRATIC SOCIALISM VS. DEMOCRATIC CAPITALISM

A market socialist would intercede at this point (if not earlier) and note, quite correctly, that the inefficiencies of democratic politics plague capitalist as well as socialist economies. After all, protection, subsidies, and state loans to declining firms are common in capitalist economies as well. Why, then, is democratic politics a special problem for democratic socialism?

The public choice literature establishes that democratic politics do not lead to governmental interest in efficiency, regardless of the economic system. To establish our main point—that democratic socialism must be a less efficient economic system than democratic capitalism—we must show that a democratic government does more damage under socialism than under capitalism.

Our argument boils down to a single assertion: when the government controls firms, it has considerably more ability to convince them to pursue its political objectives than when the government must persuade private shareholders. Becker (1983) is characteristically perceptive: "Even though Schumpeter and others have identified selfish pressure groups with democratic capitalism, I believe that pressure groups of workers, managers, intellectuals, etc, have an incentive to be more rather than less active under democratic and other forms of socialism because a larger fraction of resources is controlled by the State under socialism than under capitalism."

Let's examine this argument for the superiority of democratic capitalism in greater detail. Suppose the government wants a firm owned by private shareholders to do something that they might not want to do if they maximized profits, such as employ extra people, pay extra wages, undertake a "socially desirable" investment project, produce output for the war effort, and so on. If the government does not control this firm through regulation, it must pay the shareholders the opportunity cost of meeting the government's wishes, since these shareholders, rather than the government, have the control rights over the decisions of the firm. For example, governments often pay firms to maintain employment through tax breaks, procurement contracts and so on. And however the government raises money to make those payments—whether through taxes, borrowing, or the printing press—it is likely to encounter some opposition from the broader public. As a result, such political interference in privately-owned firms is rather limited.

Of course, governments often find a cheaper way to get firms to pursue political objectives—through regulation. Regulation gives the governments some control rights over firms whose profits are privately owned, so that it can compel them to follow the political will without compensating shareholders. By effectively expropriating the wealth of a few shareholders rather than taxing a broader segment of the population, the government faces a lower political price of enforcing inefficient allocations through regulation. Nonetheless, as with any form of taxation, regulation is not free to politicians.

Under true market socialism, the government both owns the cash flows from firms and controls their decisions. In this case, when the government makes a firm produce inefficiently, the Treasury pays the opportunity cost of such production. From this viewpoint, market capitalism and market socialism appear quite similar: under capitalism, the government must pay shareholders to pursue politically motivated policies and must raise taxes to do it; under socialism, the Treasury gives up profits because of the same politically motivated policies, and hence must pay for the foregone profits by raising taxes. Since a democratically elected government bears the political cost of having to raise taxes in either case, its willingness to enforce economic inefficiency might be similar under socialism and capitalism.

But there is a critical difference between capitalism and socialism. Under socialism, the government is much richer relative to the wealth of the economy than under capitalism: it owns the cash flow of most or all of the firms in the economy. As a result, the government can afford many more politically motivated inefficient projects that lose money than it could in a capitalist economy. For example, the Soviet government could use the wealth from the country's natural resources to build an extremely inefficient, militaristic economy. Many African countries wasted their mineral and agricultural wealth on failed industrialization. When, in contrast, resources are privately owned, the government cannot as easily spend them to pursue its objectives. Surely it can tax and regulate to extract some wealth, but that gives it much less wealth than owning all the assets to begin with.

Moreover, the private owners of the assets often use both economic mechanisms and the political process to keep their wealth away from the government. No matter how eager the United States Congress and the President are to spend more money, their political ability to raise tax revenues is limited. As a result, the U.S. government is much poorer, relative to the U.S. economy, than the Russian government is relative to the Russian economy, and therefore has many fewer resources to expend on inefficient projects than the Russian government does, relative to the economy. The reason that democratic socialist economies must be much less efficient than market economies is not that the democratic process leads to worse government *objectives* under socialism than under capitalism, but that the government can afford to pay for much more politically motivated inefficiency under socialism than under capitalism.

CONCLUSION

Under both capitalism and socialism, the democratic process does not generate governmental objectives consistent with the pursuit of efficiency. But under socialism, the government turns these inefficient objectives into much more damage to the economy than does a capitalist government. The theoretical case for economic efficiency under democratic socialism simply does not work.

For the purposes of our argument here, we have granted market socialists the assumptions that democratic socialism will not degenerate into totalitarianism and that it has the power to implement its plans. Removing either of these assumptions, or adding the actual economic record of socialism in the Soviet Union and eastern Europe, would only strengthen the case for democratic capitalism.

In this context, it is instructive to keep in mind who the supporters of "market socialism" in eastern Europe are. The supporters, who inevitably talk about Sweden, tend to be former communist officials and managers of doomed state enterprises—the people who stand to personally benefit the most from continued government ownership. It is unfortunate that, like the Soviet communists in the 1930s, these advocates of market socialism are getting support from idealists in the West.

REFERENCES

Bardhan, Pranab, and John E. Roemer, "Market Socialism: A Case for Rejuvenation," *Journal of Economic Perspectives*, Summer 1992, 6:3, 101–16.

Bardhan, Pranab K., and John E. Roemer, *Market Socialism: The Current Debate*. New York: Oxford University Press, 1993.

Barone, Enrico, "The Ministry of Production in the Collectivist State," (1908). Reprinted in Hayek, Friedrich A., *Collectivist Economic Planning: Critical Studies on the Possibilities of Socialism*. London: G. Routledge, 245–90. [1935].

Becker, Gary S., "A Theory of Competition Among Pressure Groups for Political Influence," *Quarterly Journal of Economics*, August 1983, 98:3, 371–400.

Buchanan, James M., and Gordon Tullock, *The Calculus of Consent*. Ann Arbor: University of Michigan Press, 1962.

Ekelund, Robert B., and Robert D. Tollison, *Mercantilism as a Rent-Seeking Society*. College Station: Texas A & M University Press, 1981.

Grossman, Gene, and Alan B. Krueger, "Environmental Impact of a North-American Free Trade Agreement," NBER Working Paper #3914, Cambridge, 1991.

Hayek, Friedrich A., *Collectivist Economic Planning*. London: Routledge and Kegan Paul, 1935.

Hayek, Friedrich A., *The Road to Serfdom*. Chicago: University of Chicago Press, 1944.

International Monetary Fund (IMF), *A Study of the Soviet Economy*, Volume 3, Washington, D.C., 1991.

Kornai, János, "Market Socialism Revisited." In Bardhan, Pranab K., and John E. Roemer, eds., *Market Socialism: The Current Debate*. New York: Oxford University Press, 1993, 42–68.

Lange, Oskar, "On the Economic Theory of Socialism: Part One/Part Two," *Review of Economic Studies*, 1936–37, 4:1, 53–71, and 4:2, 123–42. Reprinted in Lange, Oskar, and Fred M. Taylor, *On the Economic Theory of Socialism* (1938). New York: McGraw Hill, [1964].

Lindbeck, Assar, et al., "Options for Economic and Political Reform in Sweden," *Economic Policy*, October 1993, *17*, 219–64.

Mises, Ludwig v., "Economic Calculation in the Socialist Commonwealth," (1920). In Hayek, Friedrich A., *Collectivist Economic Planning: Critical Studies on the Possibilities of Socialism.* London: G. Reutledge, [1935], 87–130.

Mueller, Dennis C., *Public Choice II.* Cambridge, UK: Cambridge University Press, 1989.

Nellis, John, "Contract Plans and Public Enterprise Performance," Staff Working Paper 119, Washington, D.C., The World Bank, 1988.

Olson, Mancur, *The Logic of Collective Action.* Cambridge: Harvard University Press, 1965.

Shleifer, Andrei, and Robert W. Vishny, "Pervasive Shortages Under Socialism," *Rand Journal of Economics*, Summer 1992, *23*:2, 237–46.

Smith, Adam, *The Wealth of Nations*, (1776). Chicago: University of Chicago Press, [1976].

Sowell, Thomas, *Preferential Policies: An International Perspective.* New York: Morrow, 1990.

Stigler, George J., "The Economist and the State," *American Economic Review*, March 1965, *55*, 1–18.

Stiglitz, Joseph E., "W[h]ither Socialism?: Perspectives from the Economics of Information," mimeo, Stanford University, 1991, forthcoming as Wicksell Lectures.

Tullock, Gordon, "Some Problems of Majority Voting," *Journal of Political Economy*, December 1959, *67*, 571–79.

Wittman, Donald, "Why Democracies Produce Efficient Results," *Journal of Political Economy*, December 1989, *97*:6, 1395–1424.

Yunker, James A., *Socialism Revised and Modernized: The Case for Pragmatic Market Socialism.* New York: Praeger, 1992.

Part II

IPE Structures: Production, Money, Power, and Knowledge

Part II presents a number of works that focus on the four primary IPE structures or sets of relationships that tie together nation-states with other national and international actors and national and global markets. These structures are the international production (trade), finance, security, and technology structures. The reader should not confuse these structures with a "structuralist" approach or analysis as discussed in Part I. What we mean by *structure* in this case is a set of international relationships or the foundation on which actors try to influence and shape state and market activities. Along with the mercantilist and liberal approaches, the structuralist approach focuses on dependency relationships built into a capitalist IPE that organizes the production, finance, security, and knowledge structures in certain ways. These structures are also important underlying foundations of some of the IPE problems and issues, discussed later in this reader, that face the Northern industralized nations, the Southern developing nations, and that help characterize many of the problems that challenge all of these nations and other actors in the international political economy.

The production structure focuses on what is produced, where, under what conditions, how it is sold, to whom, and for how much. Often viewed as an "international division of labor," the production structure involves international trade—some of the oldest and controversial issues of IPE. Peter F. Drucker's work on trade incorporates some of the positive aspects of trade that are usually found in economic liberal arguments, namely that it contributes to economic growth and helps integrate the national economies of the world into a global economy. However, what concerns Drucker is that the face of trade has changed so much and so quickly. Large amounts of investment monies are available today. Trade no longer takes the form of an exchange of goods but also services. And more and different types of firms such as manufacturers, designers, and university research labs are forming alliances, all of which make it more difficult for states to insulate their national economies from international developments and to manage trade in a way that allows them to derive benefits from trade. Instead of trying to protect itself even more, Drucker suggests that the more exposed an economy is to the global market, the more likely it will be to gain from trade.

Karl J. Fields examines a mercantilist trend that many argue is occurring not only in Asia but the world over—the formation of regional trading blocs. Although there are many liberal reasons to create a bloc, namely that trade barriers between partners are lowered and production efficiencies emphasized, trade "blocs tend to beget blocs." For a variety of political and economic reasons, states feel compelled to manage trade and form regional blocs. Recently there has been a good deal of press attention on the competition between the United States and its effort to create an "American" trade bloc via the North American Free Trade Agreement (NAFTA), the European Union, and Japan. Fields argues that the Japanese economy is likely to shape developments in Asia and that this could take the form of an "informal yen bloc" in that region. Even so, there are many political problems within the region that Japan must overcome, including its own reluctance to lead such a bloc, if it is to organize others to compete with the United States and Western Europe.

A second structure is the international monetary structure. Paul A. Volcker and Toyoo Gyohten were actively involved in most of the important international monetary policies and events of the postwar era, Volcker as chairman of the Board of Governors of the U.S. Federal Reserve System (1979–1987) and Gyohten as an important official in Japan's Ministry of Finance. In this chapter from their book, *Changing Fortunes: The World's Money and the Threat to American Leadership,* Volcker and Gyohten reflect on the Bretton Woods system, the market-based system of flexible exchange rates that replaced it, and the prospects for the future. Volcker especially considers the implications of global financial markets for the United States, concluding that the dollar's diminished status in international finance does not necessarily indicate a diminished role for the United States in world affairs. Gyohten takes a somewhat different approach, focusing on the problems of cooperation and coordination among the United States, Japan, and German governments. In Gyohten's dream future, the three currencies circulate as legal tender in all three countries, uniting formally the three major economies, which are united in their interdependence anyway. This reading provides interesting reflections from the U.S. and Japanese viewpoints on monetary problems of the present, the legacy of the past, and the prospects for the future of the international monetary system.

The world has changed dramatically in the past 20 years. The Bretton Woods institutions that figure importantly in international trade and finance have changed too, but have they changed enough? This is the question asked by Harvard political economist Jeffrey Sachs in his *The Economist* essay "Beyond Bretton Woods: A New Blueprint." *The Economist* is the influential British newsweekly that has stood foursquare for economic liberalism for more than a century. Sachs has been active as an advisor to Poland and other formerly communist countries regarding economic reforms and market liberalizations. The needs of these transition economies is therefore on his list of matters requiring attention, but he finds a great many areas in which renewed global efforts are necessary. Can the International Monetary Fund (IMF), World Trade Organization (WTO), and World Bank address these problems successfully? Should they be reformed? Is a new Bretton Woods necessary to create new institutions for the 21st century?

The Bretton Woods meetings in 1944 were "the most ambitious economic negotiations the world has ever seen" according to *The Economist*. In the brief essay "Bretton Woods Revisited: A Gift from the Cold War," *The Economist* ponders the real basis for the Bretton Woods international economic order. What made the international system work during the postwar years? Was it Bretton Woods and its global institutions, including the World Bank, IMF, and the General Agreement on Tariffs and Trade (GATT)? Or was it the United States acting as a Cold War hegemon? What will become of the international economic order now that the Cold War is over and the United States is free to turn its attention away from global security issues and toward its pressing domestic needs? (Note: for another view of these issues, see reading number 34 by David P. Calleo).

Sir William Arthur Lewis was born in St. Lucia in the Caribbean in 1915 and has written extensively about the problems of economic development. The essay included here is from his 1977 book, *The Evolution of the International Economic Order*. Lewis received the Nobel Prize in Economics in 1979 for his work in this field. This essay stresses several themes that Lewis finds important. The dilemmas of LDCs are closely related to their population growth rates and to the difficulties they incur as their economies shift from a rural to urban-industrial basis. These forces, Lewis argues, assist in creating a dependence on foreign funds, which has important consequences for both less- and more-developed nations. Fluctuations in international financial markets add risk and uncertainty to the problems of all nations. The international economic order must be structured in a way that minimizes these fluctuations, so that nations can be free from the problems of global finance and can more adequately address any number of issues, especially population, that hold the keys to their future.

The international security structure is the foundation for war and peace in the international political economy. It defines the sets of relationships, agreements, understandings, and rules of behavior that affect the safety and security of states, groups, and individuals within the IPE. It is composed of such formal security alliances as the North Atlantic Treaty Organization (NATO), but also less visible arrangements such as the decade-long détente (peaceful coexistence or relaxation of tension) between the United States and the Soviet Union in the 1970s. Underwriting any security structure has always been the ability of each nation or actor to transform resources into weapons that could be used to repel an aggressor or deter an opponent from initiating an attack. Mercantilists (and political realists) usually focus on the necessity of states to secure themselves in a "self help" international political economy in which nation-states are sovereign actors and the security of no state is guaranteed. The more money and military weapons a state has, the more power it has, and thus the more likely it is to be able to secure itself.

Joseph S. Nye, Jr., argues that the elements that make states powerful in the international political economy are changing in response to a shift that is occurring in the elements of power: from primarily hard-military types of power to softer "co-optive" measures states use to secure themselves. Nye suggests that this development has consequences for how we think about managing the international security structure. He rejects the classic "balance-of-power" system of a mercantilist-realist outlook. He also rejects the "hegemony" or domination by one state argument often made by mercantilists, liberals, and structuralists. Nye argues that neither of these types of arrangements adequately captures the true nature of the international security structure today, which he labels "transnational interdependence." This article ends abruptly, but Nye elaborates more on this theme in Part V of this reader (see reading number 33 "What New World Order?").

Martin and Susan J. Tolchin would agree with Nye that what makes nations powerful today is more than military power. Yet the "new globalism" of international economic interdependence limits the sovereignty of states and can threaten the security of any state that is too dependent on other states for sophisticated technologies used to make component parts of today's modern weapons system. Tolchin and Tolchin focus on how the international security structure shapes and is shaped by developments in the international technology and knowledge structure. Their outlook on the international security structure is decidedly mercantilist in nature. Foreigners are investing heavily in U.S. corporations that produce technologies used in U.S. military weapons. A certain amount of knowledge and control over these technologies is lost to other nations, some of whom cannot be trusted. The Tolchins recommend that the United States government adopt a "realeconomik" (the United States first) policy in order to make its industrial base less dependent on semiconductors and new technologies from other nations.

"Who Are the Copy Cats Now?" is a brief but provocative piece from *The Economist*. Science and technology are more important than ever, the article argues, but a close examination of recent trends indicates that innovation patterns have changed. Once known for its facile ability to adapt and adopt foreign technologies, Japan is now becoming the source of new innovations, which are not always made available to foreign firms. How should governments respond to the changing IPE of science and technology? The state has always had an important influence on patterns of development of science and technology. Should U.S. policies be more like those of Japan? The reader of this article is encouraged to weigh the consequences of different state roles in this critical market area, and to arrive at an independent judgment.

9. Trade Lessons
from the World Economy

Peter F. Drucker

ALL ECONOMICS IS INTERNATIONAL

In recent years the economies of all developed nations have been stagnant, yet the world economy has still expanded at a good clip. And it has been growing faster for the past 40 years than at any time since modern economies and the discipline of economics emerged in the eighteenth century. From this seeming paradox there are lessons to be learned, and they are quite different from what practically everyone asserts, whether they be free traders, managed traders or protectionists. Too many economists, politicians and segments of the public treat the external economy as something separate and safely ignored when they make policy for the domestic economy. Contrary lessons emerge from a proper understanding of the profound changes in four areas—the structure of the world economy, the changed meaning of trade and investment, the relationship between world and domestic economies, and the difference between workable and unworkable trade policies.

The segments that comprise the world economy—the flows of money and information on the one hand, and trade and investment on the other—are rapidly merging into one transaction. They increasingly represent different dimensions of cross-border alliances, the strongest integrating force of the world economy. Both of these segments are growing fast. The center of world money flows, the London Interbank Market, handles more money in one day than would be needed in many months—perhaps an entire year—to finance the real economy of international trade and investment. Similarly, the trades during one day on the main currency markets of London, New York, Zurich and Tokyo exceed by several orders of magnitude what would be needed to finance the international transactions of the real economy.

Today's money flows are vastly larger than traditional portfolio investments made for the sake of short-term income from dividends and interest. Portfolio money flows were once the stabilizers of the international economy, flowing from countries of low short-term returns to countries of higher short-term returns, thus maintaining an equilibrium. They reacted to a country's financial policy or economic condition. Driven by the expectation of speculative profits, today's world money flows have become the great destabilizers, forcing countries into precipitous interest rate hikes that

Peter F. Drucker is Clarke Professor of Social Science and Management at the Claremont Graduate School in Claremont, California.

throttle business activity, or into overnight devaluations that drag a currency below its trade parity or purchasing-power parity, thus generating inflationary pressures. These money flows are a pathological phenomenon. They underline the fact that neither fixed nor flexible foreign exchange rates (the only two known systems) really work. Contemporary money flows do not respond to attempted government restrictions such as taxes on money-flow profits; the trading just moves elsewhere. All that can be done as part of an effective trade policy is to build resistance into the economy against the impact of the flows.

Information flows in the world economy are probably growing faster than any category of transactions in history. Consisting of meetings, software, magazines, books, movies, videos, telecommunications and a host of new technologies, information flows may already exceed money flows in the fees, royalties and profits they generate. Unlike money flows, information flows have benign economic impacts. In fact, few things so stimulate economic growth as the rapid development of information, whether telecommunications, computer data, computer networks or entertainment media. In the United States, information flows—and the goods needed to carry them—have become the largest single source of foreign currency income. But just as we do not view medieval cathedrals economically—although they were once Europe's biggest generators of economic activity next to farming, and its biggest nonmilitary employer—information flows have mostly social and cultural impacts. Economic factors like high costs restrain rather than motivate information flows.

The first lesson is that these two significant economic phenomena—money flows and information flows—do not fit into any theory or policy. They are not even transnational; they are nonnational.

WHAT TRADE DEFICIT?

For practically everyone international trade means merchandise trade, the import and export of manufactured goods, farm products and raw materials. But international trade is increasingly services trade—little reported and largely unnoticed. The United States has the largest share of the trade in services among developed countries, followed by the United Kingdom. Japan is at the bottom of the list. The services trade of all developed countries are growing fast, and it may equal or overtake their merchandise trade within ten years. Knowledge is the basis of most service exports and imports. As a result, most service trade is based on long term commitments, which makes it—excluding tourism—impervious to foreign exchange fluctuations and changes in labor costs.

Even merchandise trade is no longer confined to the sale and purchase of individual goods. Increasingly it is a relationship in which a transaction is only a shipment and an accounting entry. More and more merchandise trade is becoming "structural" and thereby impervious to short-term (and even long-term) changes in the traditional economic factors. Automobile production is a good example. Plant location decisions by manufacturers and suppliers are made at the time of product design. Until the model is redesigned, say in ten years, the plants and the countries specified in the original design are locked in. There will be change only in the event of a catastrophe such as a war or fire that destroys a plant. Or take the case of a Swiss pharmaceutical company's Irish plant. Rather than sell a product, it ships chemical intermediates to the company's finished-product plants in 19 countries on both sides of the Atlantic. For this the company charges a "transfer" price, which is a pure accounting convention having as much to do with taxes as with production costs. The traditional factors of production are also largely irrelevant to what might be called "institutional" trade, in which businesses, whether manufacturers or large retailers, buy machinery, equipment and supplies for new plants or stores, wherever located, from the suppliers of their existing plants, that is, those in their home countries.

Markets and knowledge are important in these types of structural and institutional trade decisions; labor costs, capital costs and foreign exchange rates are restraints rather than determinants. More important, neither type of trade is foreign trade, except in a legal sense, even when it is trade across national boundaries. For the individual business—the automobile manufacturer, the Swiss pharmaceutical company, the retailer—these are transactions within its own system.

Accounting for these developments, U.S. trading activity is more or less in balance. The trade deficit bewailed in the media and by public and private officials is in merchandise trade, caused primarily by an appalling waste of petroleum and a steady decline in the volume and prices of farm exports. The services trade account has a large surplus. According to little-read official figures, published every three months, the services trade surplus amounts to two-thirds of the merchandise trade deficit. Moreover, government statisticians acknowledge gross underreporting of service exports, perhaps by as much as 50 percent.

THE COMING OF ALLIANCES

Traditional direct investment abroad to start or acquire businesses continues to grow. Since the 1980s direct investment in the United States by Europeans, Japanese, Canadians and Mexicans has grown explosively. But the action is rapidly shifting to alliances such as joint ventures, partnerships, knowledge agreements and outsourcing arrangements. In alliances, investment is secondary, if there is any at all. A recent example is the dividing up of design and production of an advanced microchip between Intel, a U.S.-based microchip *designer*, and Sharp, the Japanese electronics *manufacturer*. Both will share the final product. There are alliances between scores of university research labs and businesses—pharmaceutical, electronic, engineering, food processing and computer firms. There are alliances in which organizations outsource support activities; a number of American hospitals, and some in the United Kingdom and Japan, let independent suppliers do their maintenance, housekeeping, billing and data processing, and increasingly let them run the labs and the physical therapy and diagnostic centers. Computer makers now outsource the data processing for their own businesses to contractors like Electronic Data Systems, the company Ross Perot built and sold to General Motors. They are also entering alliances with small, independent software designers. Commercial banks are entering alliances with producers and managers of mutual funds. Small and medium-sized colleges are entering alliances with one another to do paperwork jointly.

Some of these alliances involve substantial capital investment, as in the joint ventures of the 1960s and 1970s between Japanese and U.S. companies to produce American-designed goods in Japan for the Japanese market. But even then the basis of the alliance was not capital but complementary knowledge—technical and manufacturing knowledge supplied by the Americans, marketing knowledge and management supplied by the Japanese. More and more, investment of whatever size is symbolic—a minority share in each other's business is regarded as "bonding" between partners. In many alliances there is no financial relationship between the partners. (There is apparently none between Intel and Sharp.)

Alliances, formal and informal, are becoming the dominant form of economic integration in the world economy. Some major companies, such as Toshiba, the Japanese electronics giant, and Corning Glass, the world's leading maker of high-engineered glass, may each have more than 100 alliances all over the world. Integration in the Common Market is proceeding far more through alliances than through mergers and acquisitions, especially among the middle-sized companies that dominate most European economies. As with structural and institutional trade, businesses make little distinction between domestic and foreign partners in their alliances. An alliance creates a relationship in which it does not matter whether one partner speaks Japanese, another English and a third German or Finnish. And while alliances increasingly generate both trade and investment, they are based on neither. They pool knowledge.

THE VITAL LINK

For developed economies, the distinction between the domestic and international economy has ceased to be a reality, however much political, cultural or psychological strength remains in the idea. An unambiguous lesson of the last 40 years is that increased participation in the world economy has become the key to domestic economic growth and prosperity. Since 1950 there has been a close correlation between a country's domestic economic performance and its participation in the world economy. The two major countries whose economies have grown the fastest in the world economy, Japan and South Korea, are also the two countries whose domestic economies have grown the fastest. The same correlation applies to the two European countries that have done best in the world economy in the last 40 years, West Germany and Sweden. The countries that have retreated from the world economy (most notably the United Kingdom) have consistently done worse domestically. In the two major countries that have maintained their participation rate in the world economy within a fairly narrow range—the United States and France—the domestic economy has put in an average performance, neither doing exceptionally well nor suffering persistent malaise and crisis like the United Kingdom.

The same correlation holds true for major segments within a developed economy. In the United States, for instance, services have tremendously increased their world economy participation in the last 15 years; finance, higher education and information are examples. American agriculture, which has consistently shrunk in terms of world economy participation, has been in continual depression and crisis, masked only by ever-growing subsidies.

Conversely, there is little correlation between economic performance and policies to stimulate the domestic economy. The record shows that a government can harm its domestic economy by driving up inflation. But there is not the slightest evidence that any government policy to stimulate the economy has an impact, whether it be Keynesian, monetarist, supply-side or neoclassical. Contrary to what some economists confidently promised 40 years ago, business cycles have not been abolished. They still operate pretty much the way they have for the past 150 years. No country has been able to escape them. When a government policy to stimulate the economy actually coincided with cyclical recovery (which has been rare), it was by pure coincidence. No one policy shows more such coincidences than any other. And no policy that "worked" in a given country in recession A showed any results when tried again in the same country in recession B or recession C. The evidence not only suggests that government policies to stimulate the economy in the short term are ineffectual but also something far more surprising: they are largely irrelevant. Government, the evidence shows clearly, cannot control the economic weather.

The evidence of the past four decades does show convincingly that participation in the world economy has become the controlling factor in the domestic economic performance of developed countries. For example, a sharp increase in manufacturing and service exports kept the U.S. economy from slipping into deep recession in 1992, and unemployment rates for adult men and women never reached the highs of earlier post-World War II recessions. Similarly, Japan's sharply increased exports have kept its current recession from producing unemployment figures at European levels of eight to ten percent.

WHAT WORKS, WHAT DOES NOT

The evidence is crystal clear that both advocates of managed trade and conventional free traders are wrong in their prescriptions for economic growth. Japan's industrial policy of attempting to select and support "winning" business sectors is by now a well-known failure. Practically all the industries the Japanese Ministry of International Trade and Industry (MITI) picked—such as supercomputers and pharmaceuticals—have been at best also-rans. The Japanese businesses that succeeded, like Sony and the automobile companies, were opposed or ignored by MITI. Trying to pick winners requires a fortune-teller, and the world economy has become far too complex to be outguessed. Japan's economy benefited from a competency—an extraordinary ability to miniaturize products—that was virtually unknown to MITI. Pivotal economic events often take place long before we notice their occurrence. The available data simply do not report important developments such as the growth of the service trade, of structural and institutional trade, of alliances.

Still, the outstanding overall performance of Japan and other Asian countries cannot be explained away as merely a triumph of conventional free trade. Two common economic policies emerge from a recent World Bank study of eight East Asian "superstars"—Japan, South Korea, Hong Kong, Taiwan, Singapore, Malaysia, Thailand and Indonesia. First, they do not try to manage short-term fluctuations in their domestic economies; they do not try to control the economic weather. Moreover, not one of the East Asian economies took off until it had given up attempts to manage domestic short-term fluctuations. All eight countries focus instead on creating the right economic climate. They keep inflation low. They invest heavily in education and training. They reward savings and investment and penalize consumption. The eight started modernizing their economics at very different times, but once they got going, all have shown similar growth in both their domestic and international economies. Together they now account for 21 percent of the world's manufactured goods exports, versus nine percent 30 years ago. Five percent of their populations live below the poverty line, compared with about 40 percent in 1960, and four of them—Japan, Hong Kong, Taiwan and Singapore—rank among the world's richest countries. Yet the eight are totally different in their culture, history, political systems and tax policies. They range from laissez-faire Hong Kong to interventionist Singapore to statist Indonesia.

The second major finding of the World Bank study is that these eight countries pursue policies to enhance the competitiveness of their industries in the world economy with only secondary attention to domestic effect. These countries then foster and promote their proven successes in the world economy. Though MITI neither anticipated nor much encouraged Japan's world market successes, the whole Japanese system is geared to running with them. Japan offers its exporters substantial tax benefits and credits, which remain scarce and expensive for domestic businesses, and it deliberately keeps prices and profits high in a protected domestic market in order to generate cash for overseas investment and market penetration.

The same lessons were being taught until recently by the two countries in the West that showed similar growth: West Germany and Sweden. These countries, too, have very different domestic policies. But both created and maintained an economic growth climate, and through the same measures: control of inflation, high investment in education and training, a high savings rate obtained by high taxes on consumption and fairly low taxes on savings and investment. Both also gave priority to the world economy in governmental and business decisions. The moment they forgot this—when the trade unions a few years back began to subordinate Germany's competitive standing to their wage demands, and the Swedes subordinated their industries' competitive standing to ever-larger welfare spending—their domestic economies went into stagnation.

An additional lesson of the world economy is that investment abroad creates jobs at home. In both the 1960s and the 1980s, expanded U.S. business investments overseas spurred rapid domestic job creation. The same correlation held for Japan and Sweden, both of which invested heavily in overseas plants to produce goods for their home markets. In manufacturing—and in many services, such as retailing—investment per worker in the machinery, tools and equipment of a new facility is three to five times annual production. Most of this productive equipment comes from institutional trade (that is, from the home country of the investor), and most of it is produced by high-wage labor. The initial employment generated to get the new facility into production is substantially larger than the annual output and employment during its first few years of operation.

The last 40 years also teach that protection does not protect. In fact, the evidence shows quite clearly that protection hastens decline. Less-protected U.S. farm products—soybeans, fruit, beef and poultry—have fared a good deal better on world markets than have the more subsidized traditional crops, such as corn, wheat and cotton. Equally persuasive evidence suggests that the American automobile industry's share of its domestic market went into a precipitous decline as soon as the U.S. government forced the Japanese into "voluntary" export restraints. That protection breeds complacency, inefficiency and cartels has been known since before Adam Smith. The counterargument has always been that it protects jobs, but the evidence of the last 40 years strongly suggests that it does not even do that.

FREE TRADE IS NOT ENOUGH

The world economy has become too important for a country not to have a world-economy policy. Managed trade is a delusion of grandeur. Outright protectionism can only do harm, but simply trying to thwart protectionism is not enough. What is needed is a deliberate and active—indeed, aggressive—policy that gives the demands, opportunities and dynamics of the external economy priority over domestic policy demands and problems. For the United States and a number of other countries, it means abandoning ways of thinking that have dominated American economics perhaps since 1933, and certainly since 1945. We still see the demands and opportunities of the world economy as externalities. We usually do not ask whether domestic decisions will hurt American competitiveness, participation and standing in the world economy. The reverse must become the rule: will a proposed domestic move advance American competitiveness and participation in the world economy? The answer to this question determines what are the right domestic economic policy and business decisions. The lessons of the last 40 years teach us that integration is the only basis for an international trade policy that can work, the only way to rapidly revive a domestic economy in turbulence and chronic recession.

10. Circling the Wagons: The Trend Toward Economic Regionalism and Its Consequences for Asia*

Karl J. Fields

The Asian economic zone will outdo the North American economic zone and European zone at the beginning of the twenty-first century and assume a very crucial role.
—Kiichi Miyazawa (June 1991)[1]

Over a hundred years ago, settlers trekked across the great expanse of the American heartland in covered wagons and handcarts. In a situation of virtual anarchy, and in the absence of other forms of security, it became common practice on these Westward journeys to "circle up" the wagons at night as a means of protection against outside threats.

Although the end of the Cold War has perhaps eased the threat of global war, the decline of American hegemony and the uncertainty of a new world order remind us that anarchy is as much a part of the international system as it was of the American West. Vulnerable nation-states in the great expanse of this global anarchy are also inclined to protect their interests by circling up.

Economic regionalism and trading blocs—its institutional manifestation—are born of fear and uncertainty. West Europeans formed the European Community (EC)—the oldest, largest, and most successful trading bloc—in the wake of the Second World War because they feared the consequences of a third. Since the 1980s, the driving force behind their renewed efforts to further economic integration was European fear of Soviet military might and Japanese economic prowess. More recently, Germany's reunification has proved a further "catalyst" for European integration as "the only way to provide neighbors with leverage over the new German colossus."[2]

Like the American West of a century ago, the anarchical global arena also prompts those outside the circle to seek others with shared interests with whom to counter-consolidate. The result is the creation of additional groups designed to compete with or withstand the initial grouping.

In short, blocs tend to beget blocs; ample evidence of this tendency can be found

*Revised version of a paper delivered at the Sino-American-European Conference on Contemporary China, Taipei, August 17–19, 1992. The author wishes to acknowledge the helpful comments of Michael Veseth on an earlier draft of this article.

From "Circling the Wagons: The Trend Toward Economic Regionalism and Its Consequences for Asia," by Karl J. Fields. *Issues and Studies*, Vol 28, No 12, December 1992. Reprinted by permission.

in the growing economic regional integration and the formation of regional trading blocs in the world today.[3] One recent study found thirty-two trading blocs in the current international system.[4] Another places the number of preferential trading arrangements at twenty-three, involving 119 countries and more than 80 percent of the world's international trade in goods.[5] Capturing more headlines (though less empirical confirmation), observers now point to the emergence of three "super" regions of economic integration, Europe, North America, and Asia. While there is general consensus on this trend, defining these regions and determining the consequences of their integration are subject to very wide interpretation.

In spite of (or perhaps even because of) the Danish "no" vote in June and the feeble French "oui" in September to the Maastricht accords on economic and political union,[6] the economic integration of (at least) Western Europe would seem inevitable. If the original twelve members of the EC are able to merge with members of the European Free Trade Area (EFTA), they would combine to create a market of 380 million people, accounting for nearly 50 percent of world trade.[7] If central (what used to be eastern) European countries join this common market, there will be over 850 million relatively well-educated and relatively prosperous producers and consumers capable of virtual self-sufficiency.[8]

Faced with this prospect, the two countries with the largest bilateral trading relationship in the world—the United States and Canada—implemented a free trade agreement in 1989. One year later, formal negotiations began which—if ratified—would link these two countries with Mexico in a North American Free Trade Area (NAFTA) of 360 million people from the Yukon to the Yucatan, with a combined gross national product (GNP) of over US$6 trillion and nearly one-fourth of total world trade.[9] President George Bush has offered to extend NAFTA to include Latin American countries in what could conceivably become a free trade area embracing the entire Western Hemisphere (WHFTA).[10]

What does this mean for East Asia?[11] More than any other region in the world, the countries of East Asia have blossomed under the aegis of the U.S.-sponsored General Agreement on Tariffs and Trade (GATT) with its mandate of expanding unfettered world commerce. In the face of this "head-to-head" competition with two other institutionalized and potentially self-sufficient trading blocks,[12] will the Asia-Pacific region be compelled to circle up as well? If so, what would or should such a bloc look like? If not, what other options are available to this dynamic region of export-led capitalist development?

Trends toward economic regionalism in Europe and America will continue, and perhaps even accelerate, pressuring an increasing number of East Asian countries to integrate in a similar way. However, for a variety of reasons, the degree, and in fact the type of integration likely to occur in East Asia in this last decade of the twentieth century will be very different from its American and European counterparts. In short, historical legacies (distrust of Japanese hegemony outside Japan and reluctance within Japan to bear hegemonic public goods), situational imperatives (disparities among the various countries), and heterogeneous economic ties (dependencies on markets external to the region) will lead to a hybrid regional integration in East Asia characterized by overlapping sub-regional (and supra-regional) bilateral and multilateral arrangements.

THE GATHERING STORM

Trading Blocs and Their Consequences

A trading bloc is a broadly-based preferential economic relationship among a group of countries. While economic integration can, and does, often flow naturally from open market transactions, the presence of a bloc implies the concentration is the consequence of government policy or other intentional noneconomic factors such as common language or culture.[13]

Brand distinguishes five degrees of trade integration that—in ascending order of integration—include: *preferential trade arrangements* (extending members freer access to markets); *free trade areas* (eliminating tariffs among members, but maintaining origi nal tariffs against nonmembers); *customs unions* (freeing trade among members and erecting a common tariff wall against all nonmembers); *common markets* (removing restrictions on the internal movement of the means of production); and *economic unions* (unifying fiscal, monetary, and social policies within the common market).[14] The NAFTA arrangement among the United States, Canada, and Mexico, if approved, would be a free trade area, as the U.S. Canada pact already is. The twelve-member EC, as now constituted, approaches a common market and aspires to become a genuine economic union.

The phrase "trading bloc," particularly in liberal trade circles, carries with it the negative connotation of zero-sum protectionism. Much of this infamy stems from the association of the term with the protectionist blocs formed in the wake of the financial crashes and global Great Depression in the late 1920s and early 1930s. Adopting trade policies of economic nationalism, the dominant powers of the day circled their wagons (Japanese Greater East Asian Co-Prosperity Sphere, the British Empire, the French Union, Germany and central Europe, and the United States with a revived Monroe Doctrine) in an effort to minimize imports and preserve jobs. The blocs were so effective in achieving the former goal they brought exports to a virtual standstill, exacerbating the economic consequences of the depression. Ultimately, these economic blocs gave way to the formation of military alliances and the outbreak of World War II.[15]

It was in this context that technocrats and visionaries met at Bretton Woods after the war to create a system that would prevent a recurrence of these events. Armed with a religious sense of mission and the liberal canons of comparative advantage and non-discrimination, the unchallenged American hegemon imposed a system of "unilateral global Keynesianism" and institutionalized it under GATT.[16] Based on the principles of most favored nation (MFN) and mutual reciprocity, GATT's objective of expanding global trade through reducing tariffs and other trade barriers was remarkably successful. Tariffs on manufactured good were cut from a global average of 40 percent in 1947 to less than 5 percent in 1990.[17]

During the 1980s, events conspired to spell the doom of GATT and its liberal trading order. The relative and absolute decline of the United States as the global economic hegemon has meant that while it may still be capable of "imperial overreach" in a military sense,[18] GATT's hegemonic sponsor can no longer fulfill its roles of promoting free traders by carrying free riders or pulling the world out of recession on the strength of its import market. In addition, it became increasingly obvious that multilateral GATT proceedings were ill-prepared to resolve the issue of non-tariff barriers. With no one country able or willing to impose a universal system, narrow self-interest dictated bilateral trade negotiations and regional economic integration. This regionalism further stymied the functioning of GATT as internal commitments deemed necessary to bloc cohesion became more imperative than the promotion of global trade efficiency. The recent foundering of "yet another round" of the Uruguay round of GATT negotiations prompted one observer to rename this hallowed postwar institution the "General Agreement to Talk and Talk."[19]

From the outset, GATT provisions have tolerated the formation of free trade areas and customs unions when the ultimate objective of these blocs is a complete political union.[20] Thurow argues, however, that a common market as large as the EC violates the spirit of GATT and the planned inclusion of associate members to the EC violates the letter of GATT law. North Americans, he points out, have not even bothered with this "legal fig leaf" as they negotiate NAFTA and as the United States pushes its bilateral Structural Impediment talks with the Japanese.[21]

This economic regionalism will likely endure and gain in strength. What does this circling of wagons mean for global economic efficiency and political stability? The classic danger of trading blocs is that trade will be diverted from efficient nonmembers to less efficient bloc members leading to a net decline in global trade efficiency.[22] Further, as blocs form they tend to adopt the policies of the most protectionist members as the path of least resistance. Also, regional integration, particularly of the tripolar variety anticipated, would operate most perniciously against the world's poorest and most dependent nations, those in most desperate need of trade.[23] Finally, and most dangerously, history has demonstrated economic blocs can provide justification for countervailing blocs, destroying liberal trade institutions and feeding the escalating fires of protectionism and trade wars, with potentially disastrous economic, social, and ultimately international political consequences.

If properly managed, however, it is argued that the potential costs of trading blocs can be minimized while the potential benefits in an imperfect post-GATT world can be substantial. Most observers believe that while a certain amount of trade diversion is probably unavoidable, regional free trade areas cannot afford to cease trading with other regions. Thurow contends three regional trade arrangements will form in the 1990s, around Europe, North America, and Japan, but refers to them as "quasi-trading blocs" in order to "distinguish them from the trading blocs of the 1930s." These quasi-blocs of the 1990s, he argues, "will attempt to manage trade, but they will not attempt to reduce or eliminate it as the trading blocs of the 1930s did."[24] Johnson argues competition among and within these three regions may in fact be as great a stimulus to growth as the liberal trade regime that preceded it.[25]

Moreover, there is no question that preferential trade arrangements generate huge increases in trade among participants. A 1988 study commissioned by the European Community estimated that EC92 would create 2 million jobs, boost corporate profits by nearly 2 percent and gross domestic product by 5 percent, and cut consumer prices by 6 percent and industrial production costs by 7 percent. Similarly, it is estimated that by 1999 the Canada-U.S. free trade pact will have raised U.S. GNP by 1 percent and the Canadian GNP by 5 percent and have created a total of nearly one and a half million jobs in both countries.[26]

Trading blocs are particularly useful in eliminating import quotas and other non-tariff barriers among member countries, and as such may in fact offer "a supplemental, practical route to the universal free trade that GATT favored as the ultimate goal."[27] Free trade within regions and managed trade between them may prove to be a necessary and workable intermediate step between national economies and a single world economy, cementing pro-liberal sentiment at national and regional levels.[28]

A final justification that may prove more compelling than all others is political. Whatever the economic costs or gains, European unity makes good political sense and, despite the trepidations of Margaret Thatcher and now many other Europeans, is "one of the most encouraging developments in Western history."[29] The greater amity among the United States and its Latin American neighbors that could result from voluntary economic integration in the Western Hemisphere is also long overdue.

Further economic integration into some form of regional blocs over the course of the next decade is inevitable, but not inimicable to the expansion of global welfare if managed properly.

European and North American Blocs

The EC is the oldest, largest, and most effective of all trading blocs. Its origins lie in the European Coal and Steel Community established in 1951, and the European Economic Community and European Atomic Energy Community created under the 1957 Treaties of Rome. The fundamental objectives of these regimes—binding German industry to the rest of Europe and restarting economic growth in the region—were largely accomplished without achieving the degree of economic and political integration that some hoped would naturally flow from interdependence.[30]

Since the mid-1980s, however, the regional integration of Europe has taken on new life and new urgency. Under the standard of "European Community 1992," the EC initiated a series of measures designed to remove all barriers to the movement of capital, goods, and people and the creation of a genuine common market. In December 1991, EC representatives (if not their national constituencies) agreed in treaties on a European monetary union (EMU) and political union (EPU) to form a new federation anchored by a single currency (ECU) and central bank by the end of this century.[31] The decline of the United States, the rise of Japan, the disintegration of the Soviet Empire, and the reunification of Germany spurred the Community to redouble its efforts to circle the wagons in a way that was deemed neither possible nor necessary under the bipolar "old world order."

These efforts, since 1985, it is argued, are,

> a disjunction, a dramatic new start, rather than the fulfillment of the original effort to construct Europe. . . . Nineteen ninety-two is a vision as much as a program—a vision of Europe's place in the world. The vision is already producing a new awareness of European strengths and a seemingly sudden assertion of the will to exploit those strengths in competition with the United States and Japan.[32]

And a formidable competitor it is. With a GNP exceeding US$4 trillion and total world trade valued at nearly US$2.8 trillion, this is the largest "common" market in the world.[33] With European Free Trade Area members now candidates for merger and central European and North African countries also knocking at the door, this region's economic clout can only expand.

While initial fears of "Fortress Europe" have diminished somewhat, concern in the United States, Asia, and elsewhere about protectionism within the bloc is well-founded. "Economic gains not shared with outsiders," Thurow argues, are "the glue necessary to politically weld together" these disparate European nations.[34] If integration brings no special privileges, why participate? While EC demands of reciprocity will certainly discriminate against outsiders unwilling to conform to European standards, the strongest glue binding the EC together has been the subsidy programs under the Common Agriculture Policy (CAP). Arguing that Italy and France would not have joined the Community without them, Brand notes that these subsidies for production and export eat up 60 percent of the EC budget and persist as the EC's single most difficult international problem.[35]

Responding to both the rise of Japan and a resurgent Europe as economic competitors, the Reagan and Bush administrations have sought to play midwife to a trading bloc larger than the EC in size, population, and wealth. Reagan first proposed the idea of a North American common market during his 1980 election campaign, envisioning it to include the United States, Canada, Mexico, and the Caribbean nations.[36] President Reagan launched the Caribbean Basin Initiative (CBI) in 1983, extending trade preferences and access to U.S. markets to the 50 million people in the Caribbean and Central America. Discussions for a Canadian-U.S. Free Trade Area (FTA) began in 1986, and the FTA went into effect on January 1, 1989. The agreement calls for the gradual reduction of tariffs in three stages over the course of the decade until all commodities and ultimately capital and labor would be free flowing.[37]

In June 1990, Presidents Carlos Salinas and Bush committed to negotiate a bilateral free trade agreement between Mexico and the United States. Canada joined the discussions three months later, and the three nations have been working toward the creation of a North American Free Trade Area (NAFTA). Formal talks began in June 1991, and trilateral negotiations were completed in August. If in fact the accord can meet the approval of legislative bodies in all three countries, implementation could come as early as 1993.[38] In May 1992, the Bush administration announced that it would begin to negotiate a free trade pact with Chile as soon as NAFTA is enacted as "a first step toward setting up a free trade bloc with all of South America."[39]

The United States and Canada comprise the world's largest and eighth largest economies and are ranked first and second in the world in terms of purchasing power. They have a combined population of 270 million and combined world trade valued at nearly US$1.2 trillion. The Canadian province of Ontario alone received more U.S. exports than all of Japan during the 1980s.[40] A combined NAFTA would have 360 million people creating more than US$6 trillion in economic activity, more than one-and-a-half times that of the EC.[41] Merging the remainder of the Caribbean and Latin America could create an Americas bloc of 600 million people and would give the region, like a European bloc, near self-sufficiency in both markets and means of production.

While NAFTA negotiators have claimed that any free trade arrangement will not be protectionist, outsiders—particularly East Asian nations dependent on the North American market—are concerned that higher local content requirements or preferential trade and investment policies will restrict their access to the North American market. U.S. trade officials have offered little evidence to allay these concerns, and America's willingness to pursue aggressive unilateralism in trade negotiations with Japan and other East Asian countries gives Asian nations both reason for apprehension and motivation to respond.

THE EAST ASIAN RESPONSE

East Asia has been alarmed by the regional integration of the economies of Europe and the Americas. While calls to circle up the wagons in Asia have increased, the particular nature of the Asian political economy is producing different consequences.

East Asia lacks the geopolitical circumstances and shared economic and cultural interests integrating the regions of Europe and North America. Despite the absence of these factors or any formal trading bloc, intra-regional trade, investment, and financial ties are nonetheless increasing rapidly in the region, regardless of how the area is defined geographically.[42] Pacific Basin trade surpassed transatlantic trade for the first time in 1983, and trade among East Asian countries will surpass trans-Pacific trade during this decade. Since 1989, Japan's trade with Asia has been greater than its trade with North America, though the United States is still Japan's single largest market.[43]

This pattern of integration also holds true for the East Asian Newly Industrializing Economies (EANIEs) and the Association of Southeast Asian Nations (ASEAN). From 1970 through 1987, Japan's trade with ASEAN grew eight fold, trade between Japan and North America grew ten fold, between the EANIEs and ASEAN fifteen fold, between Japan and the EANIEs eighteen fold, and between the EANIEs and North America forty-eight fold.[44] This increase in intra-Asian trade has cut the EANIEs' dependence on the U.S. market from one-half to one-third of total exports. But like Japan, the United States remains the largest market for the EANIEs.

While the pace of East Asian intra-regional trade and investment has accelerated more rapidly than trans-Pacific trade since 1985, the North American market
still looms largest. Frankel finds that while East Asian intra-regional trade grew from
33 percent of these countries' total trade in 1980 to 37 percent in 1989, the "bias" of
this trade (measured in terms of ratio of the proportion of intra-regional trade to the
region's share of world trade) actually declined over the course of the decade and the
intensification of trade bias during this period was actually much greater in the EC
and NAFTA regions.[45] Frankel concludes that in terms of trade, the United States
and Canada should be considered full partners in any Pacific bloc and that this
broader Pacific bloc has the strongest trade bias of any region.[46] When North America is included, the percentage of intra-regional trade practically doubles, to over two-
thirds of total trade.[47] The same holds true of investment, with Okita finding that
fully 80 percent of foreign investment within this Pacific region comes from other
countries within the region.[48]

Despite the continued importance of North America and particularly the
United States to East Asian trade and investment patterns, there is no question that
"Japan, rather than the U.S., is now the dominant economic player in Asia. Japan is
the region's technology leader, its primary supplier of capital goods, its dominant exporter, its largest annual foreign direct investor and foreign aid supplier, and increasingly a vital market for imports."[49] Without deliberate governmental efforts to link the
region through institutional means, these trade, aid, and investment ties are serving
to naturally integrate the economies of East Asia vertically and horizontally with
Japan at the core.

This process of Japanese-led regional integration has its origins in the nineteenth century and reached its first crest under Imperial Japan's Greater East Asian
Co-Prosperity Sphere in the 1930s.[50] The most recent integration boom, however,
may be dated not from some Japanese imperial plot, but rather the 1985 Plaza Accord that revalued the Japanese yen against the U.S. dollar by some 60 percent. This
revaluation of the Japanese currency combined with rising domestic labor and land
prices and increased foreign pressure to expand imports and liberalize capital markets pushed Japanese transnationals to penetrate regional markets and seek cheaper
offshore production sites in the region for re-import as well as export to third countries.

Japanese government and businesses have worked in tandem, integrating
Japan's neighbors into an informal grouping by proffering aid, loans, technology
transfers, direct investment, and preferential access to the Japanese market.[51] From
1984 to 1989, Japanese investment in the EANIEs grew by roughly 50 percent per
year and by roughly 100 percent per year in the ASEAN economies.[52] In 1991, a new
Japanese factory opened every three days in Thailand.[53]

Many now speak of the region as a multi-tiered division of labor or "flying
geese" pattern (to use the Japanese term) with Japan on top trailed by the EANIEs,
the lower income ASEAN countries, and the Leninist laggards.[54] Though this division of labor has been predominantly vertical in the past, increasingly Taiwan and
South Korea—facing the same external and internal pressures as the lead goose—are

also moving production offshore through direct investment in Southeast Asia and the mainland Chinese seaboard. In 1988, Taiwan led all other investors in Thailand in terms of number of investments, and was the largest investor in the Philippines and second largest investor in Indonesia in terms of total value.[55] In 1991, Indonesia received over US$1 billion in foreign investment each month with other Asian countries as its top three investors.[56] The EANIEs and ASEAN economies, while remaining dependent on the Japanese for capital goods, have also been able to increase their exports of finished manufactured products to the Japanese market.

While Japan's economic clout and "long experience in creating institutions and formulating policies" may make it seem "the ideal motive force for directing an Asian regional division of labor,"[57] not all (or even many) of Japan's Asian neighbors concur. Aware of these concerns, Japan traditionally deferred to the wishes and concerns of other regional actors and assumed the role of low-key advocate for some form of "soft" regionalism. Stirred by the fears of the EC and NAFTA as potentially discriminatory trading blocs, Japan since the late 1980s has begun to assume a station concomitant with its economic status in the region. Japan's Ministry of International Trade and Industry (MITI), Ministry of Finance, and Economic Planning Agency all created committees and commissioned reports during the period 1987–88 aimed at enhancing Asian economic integration.[58]

The consequence of these growing regional ties is the emergence of an informal yen bloc of comparable proportions (if not equal institutionalization) to the European and North American trade blocs. It has a GNP of over US$4 trillion compared to US$4.6 trillion for the EC and roughly US$6 trillion for NAFTA.[59] Led by the sophisticated prongs of Japanese trading companies and the subtle undertows of overseas Chinese investors, this dynamic East Asian region will continue to integrate, and as Kiichi Miyazawa predicted in June 1991, will likely "outdo the North American economic zone and European zone at the beginning of the twenty-first century and assume a very crucial role."[60]

Asian government officials, business leaders, and futurists have struggled to keep pace with events in attempting to chart and manage the course of this regional integration. True certainly of efforts in the other regions as well, formal efforts to institutionalize the Asian regional economy have faced particularly daunting obstacles in the form of historical legacies, economic and ideological differences, and ambiguous geographical boundaries. Before turning to these obstacles, it is worthwhile examining the formal efforts of institutionalizing the integration process in East Asia both for what these efforts tell about the difficulty of overcoming these impediments and the ultimate and divergent course of East Asian integration.

Concrete proposals for some form of "Pacific OECD" have been tossed around the Pacific region for nearly three decades with the Australians, Japanese, and (sometimes) Americans as major promoters. . . .[61]

Ambivalence toward an exclusive East Asian club reflects a debate over two very different alternatives of regional integration in Asia. The first, with the Asian Pacific Economic Cooperation Forum (APEC) as its institutional manifestation, calls for a broad, almost open-ended regionalism including the United States and Canada, and conceivably the entire Pacific Basin. Some have speculated there may be only two trading blocs in the twenty-first century: one European, the other Pacific.[62] Such a Pacific bloc would have a GNP of well over US$10 trillion and would account for nearly half of the global volume of trade.[63]

The second option, with the proposed East Asian Economic Caucus (EAEC) as its formal expression, would be smaller and more exclusive, but with Japan and the EANIEs at its center and ASEAN, Indochina, and the Chinese seaboard at the perimeter, it would be a very formidable contender. The uncertainty of the new world order combined with the inevitability of increased integration of some form in Asia, render either of these alternatives distinct possibilities. But a third, hybrid outcome is much more likely in the short run, and is much healthier for both East Asia and the global economy.

THE TIES THAT BIND

The continued economic integration of the Asian region is inevitable. But for at least three reasons, the nature of this integrative process will likely be very different from the deliberate, self-contained, and more nearly homogeneous integration taking place in Europe and North America.

The first obstacle to the formation of a regional trading bloc is the great diversity among the nations involved, particularly when the region is defined broadly. While the cultural and ideological differences are certainly greater than either a European or any version of an Americas bloc,[64] it is the economic disparity within the region that will prove the most difficult to overcome. Income levels in the region vary sharply, with GNP per capita in 1991 ranging from over US$25,000 in Japan to barely US$400 in mainland China,[65] and with wages roughly 27 times higher in Japan.[66] As one observer noted, "If one of the tests of regional integration is the free movement of labor, and approximate equality of working conditions in different countries, then the Asia-Pacific region must be decades, if not centuries, away from achieving such integration."[67]

In a recent conference on Asian regionalism, Valery Giscard d'Estaing argued that this disparity made an EC type of regionalism in Asia highly unlikely. He noted in the EC, dominant Germany is responsible for less than 30 percent of the EC's total GNP, whereas Japan is responsible for fully 80 percent of the EC's total GNP, whereas Japan is responsible for fully 80 percent of Asia's GNP.[68] The vertical nature of the "flying geese" complementarity between resource rich and resource poor nations in the region also makes it politically very difficult to create a trading bloc. Unlike the EC where economic gains are made in intra-industry trade specialization, integration in Asia threatens a division of labor much less profitable to those on the bottom.[69]

The solution some have offered to this problem of diversity is to shrink the perimeters of the region to embrace only Asia or even capitalist East Asia. But the leader of such a bloc would certainly be Japan, and this is a prospect that stirs fear (or at least reluctance) in the hearts of many Asians, both inside and outside Japan, for several reasons.

Most Asians have bitter memories of Japan's military domination of Asia in the 1930s and 1940s. While regional groupings work best with a leader (Germany in the EC, the United States in NAFTA), there is no enthusiasm anywhere in Asia for a militarily strong Japan and little more interest in Japanese political leadership.[70] In a *Nihon Keizai* poll conducted in February and March 1992, some 449 scholars and businessmen in eleven Asian countries and Australia were asked a number of questions concerning Japan's role in Asia. Nearly 80 percent of those questioned were in favor of a regional economic bloc with Japan participating and over 90 percent of those surveyed in Indonesia, Thailand, and the Philippines indicated they would welcome Japanese leadership of such a bloc. However, 78 percent of mainland Chinese and 54 percent of South Koreans rejected Japanese leadership. Some 90 percent of all respondents said they would like their country to strengthen economic ties with Japan, but only 10 percent wanted stronger political ties and none wanted military ties.[71]

This reluctance for Japanese leadership seems just as strong within Japan, as one observer notes:

> The absence of a supranational guiding hand [in Asia] has not come about by accident. The difficulty in setting up any form of Asian economic grouping is that Japan would have to play the leading role and nobody wants that, least of all, it seems, the Japanese. The economic leviathan is a political pygmy. And this inversion affects every aspect of integration—political, economic, financial, and military.[72]

Despite its economic dominance of the region, Japan is not even prepared economically to pilot an Asian bloc with the relatively free flow of labor and trade such a bloc would entail. To do so, Japan would have to be prepared (economically and culturally) to digest foreign labor on an unprecedented scale as well as replace the United States as the primary market for East Asian exports and investments. While only Japan among the Asian countries has the necessary wealth to support a persistent trade deficit, this would require it to shift from a strategy of producer-oriented capitalism to one of consumer-oriented capitalism, a change that will be some time in coming.[73]

Japan's share of world imports actually declined during the 1980s, and its per capita imports in 1988 were only US$752 compared to US$3,076 for West Germany, US$2,651 for the United Kingdom, US$2,572 for France, and US$1,484 for the United States.[74] Although EANIE and ASEAN manufactured exports have been making inroads into the Japanese market, most of these transactions involve Japanese companies at both ends.[75] Moreover, EANIE and ASEAN dependence on Japanese industrial goods is actually widening their bilateral trade gaps. A MITI white paper recently concluded that the EANIEs will continue to post larger trade deficits with Japan through the 1990s, and that the ASEAN economies will soon be in deficit as well.[76]

This is closely related to a final reason why Asia is not likely to experience self-contained economic regionalism in the near future. Even if the fear and loathing of Japanese regional hegemony could be overcome, the very nature of East Asian dynamism precludes this kind of inward-looking strategy. The East Asian developmental miracles have been predicated on export-oriented growth, and the consumer markets of North America and Europe have ingested the overwhelming majority of these exports. During the 1980s, U.S. imports from the EANIEs, ASEAN, and mainland China were 50 percent more than those of neighboring Japan, and Asian dependence on the U.S. market actually grew over the course of the decade.[77] While the American twin deficits guarantee this trend cannot continue for long, the North American and European markets remain vital to Asia. Even Malaysia, the country most actively pushing for an exclusive East Asian bloc, still has its major markets in the West, with 30 percent of its total trade in 1991 conducted with the United States and the EC.[78]

For these (and other) reasons, both the intentional efforts and natural tendencies toward the integration of the Asian economies have begun, and will continue, to create a hybrid regional integration characterized by overlapping sub-regional (and supra-regional) bilateral and multilateral arrangements. These mini-regions, or what the *Nihon Keizai* refers to as "spontaneous economic spheres" and Singapore ambassador-at-large Tommy Koh describes as "expanding and intersecting circles," may best be labeled (at the risk of yet another acronym) sub-regional free trade areas (SRFTA). . . .

Such SRFTAs promise much good and little ill for East Asia, and the possibilities for this kind of regionalism are practically endless. The formation of these SRFTAs will have positive consequences both inside and outside the region. Internally, these diverse ties and sub-regional free trade zones will reap economic, and often times more important political benefits. Externally, the dynamism and wealth of a region advocating multilateralism will temper any trend toward global protectionism of the severity of the 1930s, with its disastrous economic and political consequences.[79]

The result of regional economic integration in East Asia and worldwide will be an international trade regime characterized by relatively free trade within the regions and "managed" but at least manageable trade without. The wagons will inevitably circle, but like their predecessors in the American Far West, these protective rings may only be temporary gatherings as a prelude to greener and more open climes.

NOTES

1. As quoted in Kenneth Pyle, "How Japan Sees Itself," *The American Enterprise*, November/December 1991, 33.
2. Elizabeth Pond, "Germany in the New Europe," *Foreign Affairs* 71, no. 2 (Spring 1992): 114.
3. The analysis of this trend has blossomed into a growth industry in the social sciences. See, for example, Jagdish Bhagwati, "Departures from Multilateralism: Regionalism and Aggressive Unilateralism," *The Economic Journal* 100 (December 1990): 1304–17; Norman S. Fieleke, "One Trading World, or Many: The Issue of Regional Trading Blocs," *New England Economic Review*, May/June 1992, 3–20; Chalmers A. Johnson, "Where Does

Mainland China Fit in a World Organized into Pacific, North American, and European Regions?" *Issues & Studies* 27, no. 8 (August 1991): 1–17; Kazuo Nukazawa, "Interdependence and Regionalism," *Journal of International Affairs* 42 (Fall 1988): 43–51; Lester C. Thurow, *Head to Head: The Coming Economic Battle among Japan, Europe and America* (New York: William Morrow and Company, 1992).

4. Joseph L. Brand, "The New World Order," *Vital Speeches of the Day* 58 (December 15, 1992): 155–60.

5. Fieleke, "One Trading World, or Many," 3–20.

6. European Community (EC) "spin doctors" argued the defeat of EC92 in the Danish referendum would in fact galvanize support among the other eleven members of the community for further integration. See *Christian Science Monitor* June 10, 1992. In the wake of the narrow margin of French support and further grumbling within the community, these spin doctors are less sanguine.

7. Fieleke, "One Trading World, or Many," 14; George T. Treverton, "The New Europe," *Foreign Affairs* 71, no. 1 (Fall 1991/92): 94.

8. A *Beijing Review* article notes that of the three regions, the European Community is already the most self-reliant, with member countries absorbing 58 percent of EC exports in 1987. The comparable figures for North America were 39 percent and for East Asia 44 percent in the same year. Wang Juyi, "An Analysis of the Three Economic Rims," *Beijing Review* 32, no. 11 (March 20–26, 1989): 17.

9. Earl H. Fry, "A Continent of Free Trade: Negotiations Toward a North American Free Trade Agreement," *Journal of State Government* 64 (October/December 1991): 128; Fieleke, "One Trading World, or Many," 15.

10. Bhagwati, "Departures from Multilateralism," 1311.

11. For the purposes of this paper, East Asia refers to Japan; the four East Asian Newly Industrializing Economies (EANIEs) of South Korea, Taiwan, Hong Kong, and Singapore; and the four Association of Southeast Asian Nations (ASEAN) states of Thailand, Indonesia, Malaysia, and the Philippines. In certain specified contexts it will include Russia and the Leninist command economies of North Korea, mainland China, and Indochina. Australasia includes, in addition to all the countries noted above, Australia and New Zealand. The Pacific Basin adds to these the countries of North America (Canada, the United States, and Mexico) and in certain specified contexts the countries of Central and South America bordering the Pacific.

12. The term "head-to-head" is taken from Thurow, *The Coming Economic Battle*.

13. Jeffrey A. Frankel, "Is Japan Creating a Yen Bloc in East Asia and the Pacific?" *NBER Working Paper Series* (National Bureau of Economic Research, Cambridge, Mass.), no. 4050 (April 1992): 1.

14. Brand, "The New World Order," 156.

15. Robert Gilpin, *The Political Economy of International Relations* (Princeton, N.J.: Princeton University Press, 1987): 190; Thurow, *The Coming Economic Battle*, 55–56.

16. Thurow, *The Coming Economic Battle*, 56.

17. Susan Lee, "Are We Building New Berlin Walls?" *Forbes*, January 7, 1991, 88.

18. Paul Kennedy, *The Rise and Fall of the Great Powers: Economic Change and Military Conflict from 1550–2000* (New York: Random House, 1987).

19. Brand, "The New World Order," 157.

20. See Thurow, *The Coming Economic Battle*, 59. Bhagwati notes this escape clause was included to allow and facilitate European integration because the United States felt it could tolerate an imperfect economic union "in the cause of what it saw as a politically beneficial union." Bhagwati, "Departures from Multilateralism," 1304.

21. Thurow, *The Coming Economic Battle*, 59, 76.

22. Lee, "Are We Building New Berlin Walls?" 87.

23. Brand, "The New World Order," 159.

24. Thurow, *The Coming Economic Battle*, 66.

25. Johnson, "Where Does Mainland China Fit?" 16.

26. As cited by Wang, "An Analysis of the Three Economic Rims," 17.

27. Bhagwati, "Departures from Multilateralism," 1308.

28. See note 15 above; Thurow, *The Coming Economic Battle*, 82.

29. See note 27 above.

30. Wayne Sandholtz et al., *The Highest Stakes: The Economic Foundations of the New Security System* (New York: Oxford University Press, 1992), 75.

31. Treverton, "The New Europe," 94.

32. Sandholtz et al., *The Highest Stakes*, 73.

33. Brand, "The New World Order," 156; Fieleke, "One Trading World, or Many," 12.

34. Thurow, *The Coming Economic Battle*, 68.

35. Brand, "The New World Order," 156.

36. Wang, "An Analysis of the Three Economic Rims," 15.

37. Brand, "The New World Order," 158; Wang, "An Analysis of the Three Economic Rims," 15.

38. Fry, "A Continent of Free Trade," 128.

39. *New York Times*, May 14, 1992.

40. Fieleke, "One Trading World, or Many," 15; Fry, "A Continent of Free Trade," 128.

41. Blayne Cutler, "North American Demographics," *American Demographics*, March 1992, 38.

42. See note 13 above.

43. Chalmers A. Johnson, "Japan in Search of a 'Normal' Role" (Unpublished manuscript, May 1992), 30.

44. Saburo Okita, "Japan's Role in Asia-Pacific Cooperation," *Annals of the American Academy of Political and Social Science* 513 (January 1991): 26.

45. It is worth noting, however, that the intra-regional trade bias in East Asia was higher in 1980 than it was in the other two regions and, despite a decline in this bias over the decade, remained higher than that of the EC even by 1989 (1.85 for East Asia compared to 1.77 for the EC). Frankel attributes this higher figure to the networks of overseas Chinese and the role of Japanese capital in the region. Frankel, "Is Japan Creating a Yen Bloc?" 10; *Far Eastern Economic Review*, December 19, 1991, 69.

46. Frankel, "Is Japan Creating a Yen Bloc?" 4, 11.

47. Kym Anderson, "Is an Asian-Pacific Trade Bloc Next?" *Journal of World Trade* 25 (August 1991): 31.

48. As cited by Anderson in ibid.

49. Sandholtz et al., *The Highest Stakes*, 27.

50. Cumings notes "in this decade what we might call the 'natural economy' of the [Northeast Asian] region was created; although it was not natural, its rational division of labor and set of possibilities have skewed East Asian development ever since." Bruce Cumings, "The Origins and Development of the Northeast Asian Political Economy: Industrial Sectors, Product Cycles and Political Consequences," in *The Political Economy of the New Asian Industrialism*, ed. Frederic Deyo (Ithaca, NY: Cornell University Press, 1987), 55.

51. Pyle, "How Japan Sees Itself," 33.

52. Sandholtz et al., *The Highest Stakes*, 27.

53. See note 1 above.

54. See, for example, Okita, "Japan's Role in Asia-Pacific Cooperation"; Johnson, "Where Does Mainland China Fit?"; and Christopher Howe, "China, Japan and Economic Interdependence in the Asia Pacific Region," *The China Quarterly*, no. 124 (December 1990): 662–93.

55. Karl Fields, "DFI Diplomacy: The Politics of Taiwan's Outward Investment" (Unpublished manuscript, November 1991), 8.

56. Brand, "The New World Order," 159.
57. See note 1 above.
58. John Greenwood, "Potential for an Asian Free Trade Area," *Business Economics,* January 1990, 33.
59. *Free China Journal,* May 15, 1992, 8; Fry, "A Continent of Free Trade," 128.
60. See note 1 above.
61. *Far Eastern Economic Review,* June 8, 1989, 51, 56.
62. Johnson, "Where Does Mainland China Fit?" 14.
63. *Far Eastern Economic Review,* November 14, 1991, 27.
64. Nukazawa, "Interdependence and Regionalism," 48.
65. I am indebted to Harmon Zeigler and his "PC Globe" database for these numbers.
66. *Far Eastern Economic Review,* April 25, 1991, 54.
67. *Far Eastern Economic Review,* June 8, 1989, 76.
68. *Free China Journal,* May 22, 1992, 7.
69. Anderson, "Is an Asian-Pacific Trade Bloc Next?" 39.
70. Howard H. Baker, Jr. and Ellen L. Frost, "Rescuing the U.S.-Japan Alliance," *Foreign Affairs* 71, no. 2 (Spring 1992): 104.
71. As cited by Johnson, "Japan in Search of a 'Normal' Role," 32.
72. *Far Eastern Economic Review,* June 8, 1989, 88.
73. Thurow, *The Coming Economic Battle,* 250–51.
74. Okita, "Japan's Role in Asia-Pacific Cooperation," 30; *Far Eastern Economic Review,* June 15, 1989, 59.
75. A 1990 study concluded that 70 percent of Japan's worldwide trade involves a Japanese company at each end of the transaction, typically an overseas Japanese subsidiary exporting finished goods back to its domestic parent. In the EC, the corresponding figure is less than 50 percent and in the United States only 20 percent. (*Far Eastern Economic Review,* October 11, 1990, 72).
76. *Far Eastern Economic Review,* May 21, 1992, 38.
77. *Far Eastern Economic Review,* October 11, 1990, 73.
78. *Far Eastern Economic Review,* April 16, 1992, 50.
79. In fact, there is evidence that this notion of sub-regional cooperation is also appealing to Europeans wary of the confines of a United States of Europe. *The Economist* proposes an ECA (Europe of Consenting Adults) in which European states would be free to "pick and choose" when and where they want to cooperate, through intertwined spheres of alliances and agreements (*The Economist,* June 24, 1992, 60). *Die Zeit* also endorses sub regionalism with a metaphor of a spacious cathedral housing many chapels (as cited in *World Press Review,* November 1991).

OTHER REFERENCES

Jacquemin, Alexis, and Andre Sapir. "Europe Post-1992: Internal and External Liberalization." *AEA Papers and Proceedings* 81 (May 1991): 166–70.

Kellas, James G . "European Integration and the Regions." *Parliamentary Affairs* 44 (April 1991): 226–39.

McCracken, Paul W. "Will the Third Great Wave Continue?" *The American Enterprise,* March/April 1991, 52–57.

Scalapino, Robert A. "Regionalism in the Pacific: Prospects and Problems for the Pacific Basin." *The Atlantic Community Quarterly* 26 (Summer 1988): 174–88.

Taira, Koji. "Japan, an Imminent Hegemon?" *Annals of the American Academy of Political and Social Science* 513 (January 1991): 151–63.

11. A New World Order or a New Nationalism

Paul A. Volcker
Toyoo Gyohten

PAUL VOLCKER

Almost a year has passed since Toyoo Gyohten and I ended our Princeton seminar. Much has happened in that time, all of it reinforcing the sense of changing fortunes that has characterized our lives, and we now review our thoughts and look toward the future.

In these pages, we have recorded some of the false starts, the misunderstandings, the genuine political and economic strains that have recurred in international monetary affairs, and in our economic life more broadly, since World War II. The mechanics of the Bretton Woods system broke down. Oil crises unsettled our sense of economic security. The United States faced the most serious inflationary threat in its history. Huge burdens of debt have come to be a drag on growth in many countries, including the United States. There have been enormous fluctuations in exchange rates. Protectionist pressures, after receding for decades, now seem to be growing stronger.

But for all of that, what stands out so boldly today is how much has been accomplished. The vision of those men and women who built the postwar world has been largely realized. The sudden end of the Cold War is a stunning fact of life. That is surely a tribute to the steadfastness of the United States and its allies in maintaining their military defenses, a matter beyond the scope of this book. But it is equally true that that effort could not have been sustained, and that victory won, without the success of the postwar economic order. Never have so many nations and so many people—in North America, in Europe, and in East Asia—enjoyed such an increase in prosperity and personal freedom as during the past forty-five years.

The triad of fundamental ideas supporting that achievement—political democracy, respect for human rights, and reliance on a market system with private property—is ascendent almost everywhere. Now, in Latin America, in Eastern Europe, and most significantly, within the borders of the old USSR itself, there are enormous new opportunities for replicating the success of the highly developed trilateral world. Even in China and Africa, stirrings of constructive change and progress are apparent.

As an American, I take it almost as an article of faith (a faith that in this case can be backed by facts) that the United States, as the dominant world power after

World War II and for decades afterwards, was the driving force toward a liberal trading order and the freedom of international investment. At critical points it provided the margin of official assistance that underlay much of our collective success. All that seemed relatively simple and straightforward to those of us coming of age after years of depression and war. The United States, after all, produced most of the steel in the world and most of the cars. We had invented television and the computer. We probably also invented business schools; certainly they prospered mightily in the United States, and carried the image of being at the leading edge of management science.

When I was starting out on my career, productivity teams from other countries were ubiquitous in the United States. I recall first meeting Japanese in the 1950s when they seemed to descend on us in waves, barely speaking English, but determined to learn about the American banking and financial system. And it was American professors, we now know, who first taught the Japanese how to develop and maintain quality in the products of their industries.

Now, the picture looks quite different. In purely statistical terms, the Germans, the Japanese, and several other countries have higher average incomes than the Americans at current exchange rates. Those statistics are no doubt misleading; taking account of the relatively low cost of food and housing here, the average American still enjoys the highest standard of living of any large national group. Moreover, the recovery and growth of other, poorer countries was after all a conscious object of American policy after the devastation of World War II. This is therefore a measure of policy success rather than defeat.

Nonetheless, it seems plain that the United States is not doing all it can and should to maintain the strength of its own economy. Perhaps it is inevitable and desirable that others who have started so far below us have had faster productivity growth than the United States. But we cannot be satisfied that for twenty years our own productivity, overall, has been growing at little more than 1 percent a year, less than half that of the earlier postwar period. Our business schools still seem to be thriving, as they concentrate on teaching more and more rarefied techniques of financial manipulation, but our manufacturing industries are not. We used to think there was an insatiable demand for American goods, limited only by everyone else's power to buy them. Now, we wonder whether we can compete in world markets. In one respect the tables have turned more or less completely: Now it is we who look to Japan, curious about its management techniques, about quality circles, and about the merits of a long view in business and government decision making. We are more humble—or should be—about setting out our financial system as a model of stability and efficiency.

The size and persistence of our trade deficit and our chronically low savings rate certainly suggest something is not right. In some recent years, to finance our investment and government deficits, we have had to borrow abroad or sell some of our assets in amounts close to the total of all the personal savings generated in the United States. Even with that borrowing, the United States has been investing in plant and equipment only about as much as Japan, a country with a population half that of the United States. Persuasive arguments can be made that the United States still has technological leadership; we are certainly ahead in basic research. But it is also a fact that the United States has fallen well behind both Germany and Japan (by about a third) in research and development spending relative to our total output. On recent trends of productivity and growth, the Japanese economy will actually be larger than that of the United States in twenty or thirty years.

I don't want to exaggerate the point. Trends like that do not go on forever. There is room for doubt about whether we are measuring productivity in our large service industries correctly, and there are bright signs of improved competitive performance in some manufacturing industries. I, for one, do not believe in the inexorable economic decline of the United States, relative or otherwise.

There also is little question that, just at the point of enormous new opportunities for the world, the mood in the United States has turned querulous and inward. Some of that may be a passing phase. The absence of a typically strong recovery from extended recession and the evident and costly financial strains after years of excessive debt creation have us psychologically on edge. But it is also true that the sense of frustration and temptations to turn protectionist have been building for some time and seem related to our economic performance over a longer term.

One set of statistics, for all the doubts about the precise accuracy of the data, is particularly telling. Read literally, they say that the real hourly and weekly earnings of the average production worker in the United States are lower today than twenty-five years ago. Sophisticated economists can tell us that the statisticians may not have measured correctly all the improvements in medical care or the efficiency of computers or other factors that make life better—but neither do they measure the costs of increasing crime and greater urban congestion and the evidence of eroding educational standards. Taken altogether, it's hard to refute the sense that progress for the average American for almost a generation has been extremely limited at best.

That, I suspect, goes a long way toward explaining the paradox of why, as a country, we feel so much more burdened by our international responsibilities just as they are lightening. Defense costs in recent years have been a substantially smaller piece of a bigger GNP than during most postwar years; yet the pressures to cut military spending were intense even before the breakup of the Soviet Union. For some time, we have, relative to our size, scored near the bottom of the international league in providing development assistance. We gripe more about the two tenths of a percent of GNP we provide in aid today (heavily concentrated in Israel and Egypt) than we did about the 2 percent of GNP we provided during the peak years of the Marshall Plan.

Even now, with prospects that defense spending can be prudently cut way below earlier levels, we seem to be looking to others to carry the bulk of the load of assisting the new democracies to get on their feet.

To our credit, objective observers still agree that the United States has the most open markets of any leading countries. But the direction of change is not so reassuring: Compared to ten or twenty years ago it is our barriers that have been increasing. Now various estimates suggest up to 30 percent of our imports are subject to some kind of quantitative restriction. Most other nations, including Japan, have been moving toward more open markets. No doubt it is still enormously difficult for American as well as Asian and European firms to break into Japanese markets for manufactured goods even though tariffs and quotas are almost gone. But if Japanese society and culture remain substantially export driven and import resistant, I am aware of no evidence that unfair trading practices have been increasing. As a matter of fact Japanese imports of manufactured goods have been substantially increasing.

Although more marked here, the pattern of slower growth and protectionist pressures is not confined to the United States. For nearly two decades, expansion in the industrialized world has been less robust. Both unemployment and inflation are larger problems than they were in the 1950s and 1960s. The fact that, after five years of effort, the current, highly ambitious Uruguay Round of negotiations on further lowering trade barriers remains in doubt is perhaps symptomatic of a certain broader malaise of spirit.

The question can legitimately be asked whether all this is related to, and aggravated by, the breakdown of the disciplines implied by the Bretton Woods monetary system and the subsequent volatility of exchange rates that began in the early 1970s. In approaching that question, I have long believed that the United States, in shaping its "domestic" policy, would have been well served by paying more attention to the desirability of exchange rate stability. Certainly in the early stages of the Vietnam War, when serious inflationary pressures began during the mid-1960s, more attention to defending the dollar by more restrained fiscal and monetary policies would have helped stabilize the economy. In retrospect, it is also clear that, had we done more to defend the dollar abroad before and after the two dollar devaluations in the early 1970s, we might well have prevented inflation from becoming so entrenched. Later in that decade, crises in the exchange markets finally did help precipitate a full-scale attack on inflation.

But that was late in the day, and it took long and difficult years to restore a sense that inflation had again been brought under at least some measure of control. Greater confidence in the stability of prices has fortunately permitted the American monetary authorities a needed degree of flexibility in dealing with the present sluggishness of business activity. The larger lesson is that confidence is a valuable thing, and once lost, is hard to regain.

The strongly appreciating dollar was giving a very different sort of signal through the first half of the 1980s, and the appropriate response was less clear-cut. . . . An effort to moderate the extreme strength of the dollar by greater easing of American monetary policy seemed potentially self-defeating in terms of other objectives, and in particular the need to keep inflation at bay. What should have been brought to bear, in my judgment, was fiscal policy. In the short run we were indeed uncertain whether fiscal tightening would, by producing lower interest rates, lower the value of the dollar or, by increasing confidence in the management of American economic policy, strengthen it further. But, over time, I believe lower interest rates would have brought the dollar down to a more realistic value. Smaller budget deficits would have reduced our dependence on foreign capital, improved the climate for domestic investment, and reduced the risks in easing monetary policy. Unfortunately, to this day, that fiscal discipline has not been achieved.

What American experience strongly suggests—and what the experiences of a number of other countries confirm—is that whatever its economic merits, the flexible use of fiscal policy is politically difficult. This difficulty is what limits so sharply the potential for the international coordination of economic policies, although there will be occasions when the central banks can and should act in complementary ways.

In the absence of closer coordination of monetary and fiscal policies, flexibility in exchange rates has seemed a logical necessity. But in practice floating exchange rates have not produced anything like the stability and orderly conditions in exchange markets that its more ardent proponents envisaged. Until the most recent years, the actual trend was toward more volatility, not less. Daily changes of a percent or more between the dollar and other key currencies are not at all unusual. Over a few weeks or months, the changes sometimes have cumulated to 10 percent or more. Cyclical changes in the value of the dollar have ranged to 50 percent or more against the yen and the mark. Such volatility has been especially disappointing while economic trends in the world's major countries have actually been converging, and they have shared success in bringing down inflation.

What is less clear is how the ups and downs of exchange rates have affected the sum of things we really care about: growth in trade and economic activity, the level of prices and productivity. By and large, all the statistics and equations of the most sophisticated econometricians have not been able to arrive at conclusive results. That does not surprise me too much; in a world in which so many things are happening at once, it is hard to pin down the effects of any one factor. But the logic of the situation suggests to me that, over a long period of time, the costs in economic efficiency must be substantial.

The economic case for an open economic order rests, after all, largely on the idea that the world will be better off if international trade and investment follow patterns of comparative advantage; that countries and regions concentrate on producing what they can do relatively efficiently, taking account of their different resources, the supply and skills of their labor, and the availability of capital. But it is hard to see how business can effectively calculate where lasting comparative advantage lies when relative costs and prices among countries are subject to exchange rate swings of 25 to 50 percent or more. There is no sure or costless way of hedging against all uncertainties; the only sure beneficiaries are those manning the trading desks and inventing the myriad of new devices to reduce the risks—or to facilitate speculation.

But these risks and costs seem to be driving more of the industrial investment of operating businesses in developed countries toward producing for local or regional markets. In other words, the decisions in the real world are often defensive and are designed to escape exchange rate uncertainties and protectionist pressures rather than to maximize efficiency. That inevitably leads to diluting some of the important benefits of open markets, which is maintaining tough competition among the world's dominant producers.

There cannot be much doubt either that economic management is greatly complicated by large changes in exchange rates that take place independently of differences in economic performance, or greatly exaggerate them. Small countries may be most vulnerable, but large ones are by no means protected from huge swings. One case in point is the dislocations suffered by American industry because of the extreme strength of the dollar during the mid-1980s. Moreover, the sense of irrationality and helplessness associated in the minds of businessmen with widely fluctuating exchange rates easily translates into political pressures for protection against foreign competition.

In sum, the fact that the world has had a mostly unmanaged system of floating exchange rates over the past twenty years while it also experienced slower growth, greater inflation, and stronger pressures for protectionism does not strike me as entirely accidental. No doubt other factors have also played an important role, notably the oil crises of the 1970s and worldwide tendencies toward lower savings and less fiscal discipline. But on the evidence, it is hard to believe that we have found anything like an optimal set of international monetary arrangements.

American experience over the postwar period illustrates a related point that now seems generally accepted. While devaluation (or appreciation) of a currency may be appropriate and even necessary to help deal with the consequences of past inflation or serious international imbalances, it cannot be a substitute for more fundamental policies to restore competitiveness, to enhance productivity and savings, and to maintain stability. Repeated time and again, devaluations represent in effect a kind of abdication from necessary policy decisions, and in the end only complicate the job of maintaining growth and stability.

One of the ironies of the story of this book is that, after repeated depreciation of the dollar since 1971 to the point where it is 60 percent lower against the yen and 53 percent lower against the deutsche mark, the American trade and current account deficits are nevertheless much higher than anything imagined in the 1960s. Conversely, among the major industrialized countries, those with the most strongly appreciating currencies enjoy higher savings rates, stronger productivity, more competitive industries, and finally, the strongest trade balances.

Taking all this into account and looking ahead, one logical option might seem to be to restore a system of fixed exchange rates, with specified par values and rules of the game under the firm control of an international organization—a modernized Bretton Woods. Essentially, that is what the Committee of Twenty spent a couple of years discussing in the early 1970s. I confess to a certain nostalgia for the intellectual coherence and logic involved in such a highly organized system. But even with that bias, I cannot come close to convincing myself that such arrangements are a practical possibility in today's much more complicated world.

Bretton Woods, after all, did not last very long, even with the potential advantage of a strong, self-confident, stable, and outward-looking nation providing the reserve currency and dedicated for many years to making the system work. No doubt the United States could have—and, to my mind, to its own advantage should have—done more in the late 1960s and early 1970s to protect and sustain the stability of the dollar at the center of the system. But in the longer frame of history, and given much more even distribution of economic power among the United States, Japan, and Europe, it would be unrealistic to rely so heavily on the policies of a single nation and its currency for the stability of a highly structured system.

A theoretical alternative to a stable national currency maintained by a benign and dominant national power would be the creation of a powerful world central bank, able to issue its own currency and to enforce agreed rules. In an embryonic way, the International Monetary Fund already can exercise some of those functions. But it does so in a much more constrained framework than a true central bank, very much subject to the ability of its principal members to reach a consensus through cumbersome procedures. After so much negotiating effort to bring the Special Drawing Rights into being, their relative disuse illustrates the difficulties. The idea of sovereign governments delegating so much authority to a supranational world central bank—or of the markets accepting its liabilities as true and easily usable international money—simply does not provide today, nor will it for years to come, a realistic base for planning, however intellectually attractive the idea may seem.

A different answer may be quite possible within a group of countries closely tied both politically and economically. The European Community, against the bulk of skeptical expert opinion, has succeeded in operating within that area a fixed exchange rate system for more than a decade. It has done so while almost entirely eliminating controls on capital movements and in the face of violent fluctuations in interest and exchange rates in the wider world. For a period of more than three years there have been no changes at all in official currency values among members of the European exchange rate mechanism.

That success has been possible because within the area there has, in fact, been a dominant economic power and a predominant currency—West Germany and the deutsche mark. With only limited exceptions, the nations of the Community have, in fact, been willing to nail their currencies to the strong mast of the DM. They have done so in the conviction that fixed intra-European currency values are a critical complement to an economically unified common market, dependent for its operation on large flows of trade among the members. As long as the German economy has remained strong and its currency a bastion of stability, the constraints implied for domestic monetary policy for the other members of the European exchange rate mechanism have seemed worth the protection against inflation and instability.

A basic difficulty with that arrangement, as with the Bretton Woods system in practice, is that it is heavily dependent on the policies, circumstances, and judgments of one country and one national central bank—the Deutsche Bundesbank. As I write, the internal pressures on German prices and wages, on the German budget, and on German interest rates growing out of the reconstruction of the old East Germany underscore the point. That is, of course, a historically unique circumstance, and for a time at least, the other members of the European Community seem fully prepared to bear the consequences for their own monetary policies of extraordinarily high German interest rates. But the situation illustrates why many members of the Community, in a longer-term framework, feel it necessary and appropriate to move toward collective responsibility for decisions that affect interest rates, monetary policy, and by extension the economic direction and indeed the health of the Community as a whole.

The logic of the situation—the desire for fixed exchange rates and the consequent need for coordinated monetary policy and appropriate political authority—has driven the Community to accept the concept of a regional central bank and a common currency before the end of the century. Tough conditions have been set down. Individual countries cannot adopt the common currency without meeting strict criteria for the convergence of their inflation levels, budget deficits, and interest rates. The basic mandate to be given the European Central Bank has already been carefully spelled out: It will promote price stability. Furthermore, while the new bank will draw upon each of the central banks of the Community's member nations to make up its own governing body and implement its policy decisions, the whole European central banking system is designed to be remarkably independent of national or partisan political influence. Indeed, assuming the European Central Bank goes forward as planned, it is likely to precede any equally strong focus of political authority and decision making on a European scale. That, in itself, raises interesting questions of coordinating largely national fiscal policies with a single regional monetary policy, and ultimately, of the appropriate form of public and political accountability.

Full resolution of those questions remains for the future. What is not in doubt is that the world, economically speaking, is drifting into regional areas. The European Community is by far the most developed. It has already passed far beyond the simple idea of a common external tariff into a broader community dealing with problems of competition, financial regulation, the environment, and much more. Now that the aim of a common currency has been clearly set out, some members plainly want a stronger political federation as well.

The United States itself has negotiated a free trade area with Canada, and is in the process of such negotiations with Mexico. There are hints, at least, that the region might be extended through Latin America, where some much more limited regional arrangements are already being put in place. And all of that activity has begun to provoke thinking among some Asian countries that they too, for defensive reasons, should consider an East Asian trading area despite their historic suspicions of Japan.

These emerging economic and trading areas would have been anathema to American postwar planners. They had before them the example of the "imperial preferences" developed by Britain in the interwar years, and the network of bilateral trading arrangements developed by Germany and others. All of that was, quite rightly, considered discriminatory and protectionist, carrying the seeds of political antagonism as well as economic inefficiency. To be sure, it was not so long after Bretton Woods and the GATT were negotiated that the United States supported the creation of the European Common Market. But that was considered a tolerable deviation from the multilateral norm, justified by the overriding political purpose of European reconciliation and the creation of a strong Western Europe.

Today, a more general economic rationale for regional trading areas is being advanced, with increasing intellectual support from both the academic community and practical politicians. In a world otherwise under protectionist pressure (and now with the Uruguay Round in jeopardy), the argument runs that regional free trade areas are the only available path to freer trade. Because they will likely encompass particularly close trading partners, they might also provide a natural focus for efforts to stabilize exchange rates within the area, shielding a substantial amount of world trade from the vicissitudes of freely floating exchange rates. Neither Canada nor Mexico, nor for that matter the United States, is at all likely to envisage a common currency in North America. But the fact is that both of those neighboring countries, with a very large portion of their trade with the United States, are already motivated to stabilize their currencies against the U.S. dollar. If the North American free trade area itself proves durable, I would not be surprised to see both countries eventually refix their currencies against the dollar, as the Mexican peso was fixed during most of the post-war period.

But for all the advantages presented by regional areas, the drift in that direction leaves me uneasy. By their nature, free trade areas and common markets are Janus-like. The benign liberal countenance faces inward, to members of the group. Within the area, barriers are eliminated. If the practical effect is to head off unilateral protectionist measures, that would be a clear gain. But the dark side is discrimination against those outside. That threat need not be serious if—and it is the "if" that is really in question—the trade, financial, and monetary barriers against others remain low. But there are those in Europe and America who view these areas as the means and justification for maintaining barriers against outsiders and even increasing them. For example, one argument goes that if we in the United States open our market to cheap Mexican labor, we ought to restrict the access of the Asians or at least opt out of further multilateral liberalization. As the reaction of some Asian countries suggests, this implicit threat seems real. The natural response to one trading area is, as a matter of self-protection, to build another.

As a practical matter, it is Japan and some smaller countries left out of regional arrangements that have in the past seemed potentially most threatened. Today, the greatest risk may be elsewhere. It would be unfortunate, to state it mildly, if preoccupation with regional areas and the inevitable internal tensions that arise within them reduce the opportunities for the emerging Eastern European democracies and the new Commonwealth republics of the former Soviet Union to find markets in the established industrialized world. For all the talk of financial and technical assistance, their reconstruction and eventual prosperity must rest on access to markets in Europe, North America, and Japan, which will in turn encourage the new investment and new technology they need.

Quite obviously, the success or failure of the current GATT negotiations will be vitally important to the prospects for maintaining and enhancing an open, prosperous world economy. That point is made in every international seminar, at every summit and G-7 meeting, in every editorial in the establishment press, here and abroad. Yet the oratory and the ink have not yet resolved the remaining points at issue, which carry large political freight, however small they may seem relative to what is at stake for those not directly involved. The risks of failure are particularly great precisely because that failure would come in the context of sluggish economic growth, spreading free trade agreements, and a greater willingness to skirt the existing rules of international trade. In that environment a failure would not imply just the maintenance of the status quo, but the clear probability that protectionist forces would gain the upper hand.

The developments and dilemmas we have reviewed in this book require other constructive responses, and they can be shaped at the very least into a modest agenda.

- *The GATT.* The existing Article XXIV of the General Agreement on Tariffs and Trade provides some protections against the aggressive use of common markets and free trade areas to discriminate against others, including a prohibition against raising the average level of tariffs to outsiders. But restraints on nontariff barriers have been less effective in this context than in others. Consistent with both the spirit of the GATT and the stated intentions of European and North American leaders, the rules against nontariff barriers should be clarified, tightened, and enforced. Ideally, any existing regional quotas and other nontariff barriers should be converted to tariffs and reduced over time.

- *A Pacific Community.* More promising than potential rivalries between American and East Asian trading areas would be the larger concept embracing both shores of the Pacific. The basin encompasses Japan; Southeast Asia; the four "tigers" of Hong Kong, Korea, Singapore, and Taiwan; and Australia and New Zealand, as well as the Americas. That large area already accounts for more than 40 percent of all world trade, and it has been the most rapidly growing segment, expanding by about 8.5 percent a year in real terms in the decade of the 1980s. It includes some of the most open markets in all the world—and also some of the most protected. It is also beset by recurrent, and now almost continuous, bilateral conflicts about trade, mutual suspicions, and outright misunderstandings. The bickering and name-calling between Japanese and Americans is the most obvious case in point, but it is not the only one.

The region may be too large and diverse to think in terms of a full-scale free trade agreement. But the bare bones of a political framework already exist for enhancing regional cooperation. Our mutual dependence on trade with each other and the growing amounts of direct investment are plain to all. Surely, those regional concerns provide opportunities for jointly resolving disputes, resisting protectionist pressures, and reaching common understandings on the treatment of foreign investment. Concentration on opportunities to improve the environment and economic development, which, by their nature, transcend national policies, can help place our often emotional trade disputes in a broader perspective. And, in time, China could become a partner.

- *Exchange Rates and International Monetary Relations.* Within regions we should aim for progress toward stabilization as the Europeans have done, although not necessarily in the same way. The regions have different problems and traditions, but Europe, the Americas, and East Asia each have important characteristics, including a dominant currency and strong intra-regional trade patterns, that should facilitate exchange-rate stability. Regional arrangements—perhaps informal outside of Europe—would fall far short of a fully articulated international system. It would, however, provide a base for more effectively reducing exchange rate volatility among regions. In time, the new Commonwealth of Independent States might also provide a focus for a currency area.

The kind of coordination I foresee would not require an elaborate institutional structure. Indeed, the strength of the G-5 or G-7, to my mind, rests on its informality and flexibility. I am not . . . convinced that elaborate schemes of statistical indicators are practical or that a special secretariat would be particularly useful. Nor would I wish to impair the independence and authority of central banks, undermining the usefulness of the most flexible tool of general economic policy. Indeed, without some method of insulating central banks from partisan political pressures and focussing attention on the need for price stability, efforts to stabilize exchange rates are likely to fail.

What seems to me possible within that framework is the development of some reasoned and broad judgments about what range of exchange rate fluctuation among the regions is reasonable and tolerable, and what is not. I am thinking of ranges significantly broader than the plus or minus 5 percent that was meant to trigger consultation in the Louvre agreement. At the same time, unlike the Louvre, governments should stand ready to support a broad and agreed range by more than just intervention in currency markets. They would have to be prepared to support their agreements in the short term with changes in monetary policy, and in the medium and longer term by a willingness to alter the basic orientation of their fiscal policies as well. Judgments about which country should move, and by how much and when, would be taken in the light of the existing economic situation, drawing in part on the wisdom of international institutions.

For the whole idea to have any meaning, governments would have to accept that strong pressures on exchange rates would be a prime indicator of the need for policy action. The agreed ranges would also have to be publicly known. The official statement of a target zone would influence market expectations, helping to stabilize trading activity. That has certainly been the experience within Europe, where exchange rates are fixed within a narrow range. But that result will be achieved only if the target zone for any country or region is in fact taken seriously in the conduct of monetary policy and in developing general economic policies.

• Finally, for the sake of completeness, I should note the importance of other matters on the international economic agenda that have not been the central focus of this book. In the financial area, there is need to broaden and reinforce the work already done to achieve more consistent capital and reporting standards for financial institutions and to provide transitional technical and financial support to the new democracies.

All that has no pretensions to adding up to a new Bretton Woods, neither in detail nor in the building of institutions. But at the same time, it is rather straightforward and manageable. together with the successful completion of the GATT negotiations, I, for one, would feel a lot more confident that we would be equipped to seize the enormous opportunities before us.

The danger is that somehow, with Soviet communism collapsed, with the threat of nuclear disaster reduced if not eliminated, and seemingly secure in our military might, we will fail to seize those opportunities. We in the United States are becoming absorbed in our own affairs and preoccupied with internal pressures and strains— with crime and drugs, with the cost of health care and our eroding infrastructure, with educational shortcomings and lingering recession. Our partners in Europe and Japan have preoccupations of their own.

My point is not that those problems can be neglected. They obviously need attention and they should get it. But it seems to me entirely wrong to think that those domestic concerns somehow compete against our international responsibilities, and that they justify pulling back from a cooperative world order. On the contrary, international cooperation will more than pay its own way. The simple fact is that, with the end of the Cold War, the cost of providing national security is dropping sharply, by amounts that will be many times larger than the potential costs of assisting in a constructive, peaceful transition for the emerging democracies of Eastern Europe and the new Commonwealth of Independent States. It is a safe bet that, in a cooperative framework, other countries will provide a larger share of the needed assistance than they did in past decades, and that Japan in particular would feel its responsibilities and act upon them.

But the stakes are not simply financial or budgetary. Far more important, a world of open trade, of greater financial and exchange rate stability, of more international investment in new and old economies, is important to us as a nation. It is important to our own economic welfare and standard of living and important to the kind of world in which we want to live. Of course, we need to respond to our domestic priorities for their own sake. But we need to do so as well to provide a foundation of public support for policies that can look outward, policies that recognize that, in the end, our own success will be bound up with that of others.

Certainly, we live in a world of more dispersed power, a world in which Japan and Europe will both have more to say and the resources to back up what they say. The time may be gone when the United States can pull very far out in front in insisting upon its own ideas. But the force of leadership and example will still be decisive. And I don't think it is sheer nostalgia that suggests a special responsibility still lies with the United States—the responsibility, more often than not, to set the agenda, to call the meetings, to provide a spur for action, and, if really necessary, at times even to provide a large share of the needed resources. That, in a quite different sphere, seems to me the lesson of what happened so dramatically when Saddam Hussein threatened the Middle East, and what happened afterward when everyone looked to the United States as the catalyst of a broader peace in that region.

The days of a simple Pax Americana, to the extent it ever existed, are past. But neither is there any justification for thinking that somehow we are drained and exhausted by international responsibilities, by unfair foreign trading practices, or by domestic problems. On the contrary, we are still the richest and strongest country in the world. What we need to do is to restore a sense of confidence in that strength and stability. Then, my sense is that other nations—old allies and new democracies alike, the now-rich and the still-struggling—will still welcome a constructive lead from the United States. To fail in that responsibility would be to jeopardize all the bright prospects before us. But the simple fact is that, at this time of really unprecedented opportunity, the challenge lies well within our capacity to meet it.

TOYOO GYOHTEN

The issue of the international monetary system has been very popular since the day the Bretton Woods system collapsed, but we have to distinguish between two interrelated elements of any system. One is the role played by currency and particularly by reserve currencies. The other is the exchange rate arrangements among different currencies.

Under the classical gold standard, gold was the only reserve currency, and it had a fixed exchange rate with all currencies. Under the Bretton Woods system, both gold and the dollar were reserve currencies, and the rate between them was fixed at $35 an ounce. The U.S. government guaranteed the conversion between gold and the dollar. In other words, the U.S. government made the dollar as good as gold. The exchange rate between the dollar and the other currencies was a sort of adjustable peg, and countries could change their currencies' exchange rates against the dollar only when their payments position was in fundamental disequilibrium and the IMF approved. In the floating system we have multiple reserve currencies—the dollar, the yen, and the deutsche mark (with the mark to be replaced by a single European currency when and if one is created). The reason we think of a different system is that we complain about the present one and recall the successes of the gold standard and Bretton Woods in their heyday. Paul Volcker has argued that it is too much to ask one country to bear all the responsibilities of maintaining and operating the system, but that is exactly what did happen when Britain ran the gold standard late in the nineteenth century and the United States the Bretton Woods system between the years of 1945 and 1965. In those times, both nations had the dominant economic, military, and political power to act as hegemon, and they had a strong external current account position to finance the system through the normal ups and downs of business and trade cycles. It was not necessary for the finance to be based only on a surplus of goods; often they ran a trade deficit that was more than offset by their overseas earnings and other international profits. Both also maintained appropriate domestic policies that did not swing too heavily toward inflation or deflation. When these conditions vanished, the system collapsed.

Our experiences make it absolutely clear that the current system—or non-system, to be precise—was not the result of anyone's choice. It was inevitable when the Bretton Woods system became unsustainable. What is wrong with the current non-system is its lack of stability and predictability in exchange rates, which seems to hurt the stable growth of trade and investment. It would be intriguing to analyze technically whether this really is a theoretically valid correlation, but past performance in the real world seems to confirm it in practice. Simply consider the Bretton Woods period from 1960 to 1973, and the period of our non-system from 1973 to 1987. During the Bretton Woods period, the average GNP growth of the OECD countries was

4.8 percent a year; in the second period it declined to 2.6 percent. Annual inflation accelerated from 4.3 percent to 6.8 percent. The export volume of those countries grew by 8.8 percent annually under Bretton Woods, but only by 4.2 percent in the second period, while the annual growth of import volume declined from 9.3 percent to 3.7 percent. Under the present non-system, world economic performance has certainly been poorer, the volatility of everyone's external accounts has been aggravated, and the threat of protectionism certainly has increased.

Does the poor performance of our present non-system argue in favor of a new one? The system itself is not the ultimate goal. Its sustainability really depends on whether the countries can take advantage of it to maximize their national welfare and improve growth, price stability, employment, and so on. Countries need to be convinced, after considering their economic and political costs and benefits, that the balance of advantages gives them an incentive to stay.

In fact, we already are in a system of multicurrency reserves. The dollar, the mark, and the yen represent the countries with the three largest economies in today's world. The United States, Germany, and Japan also are different because they alone maintain autonomous fiscal and monetary policies and are strong enough economically to let the exchange rates of their currencies fluctuate. Other, less powerful countries surrender some control over domestic policy in order to maintain stable exchange rates; this is certainly the case for all the non-German countries in the European Monetary System.

One problem in constructing a system based on the United States, Germany, and Japan is that none of them has the kind of broad, hegemonic power that Britain and the United States had in the old days. Another problem is that the relative international roles of the three main currencies do not reflect their economic fundamentals. For example, the dollar's role is probably excessive because of noneconomic factors such as the security role of the United States, the economic role of its large and open market, and the historic use of the dollar in the international banking system. The discrepancy is even more pronounced when the share of each currency's international reserves is contrasted with figures for the economy each currency represents. As of 1989, the dollar accounted for 60 percent of world reserves, the mark 19 percent, and the yen 9 percent. But the U.S. gross national product in 1988 was $4.9 trillion and exports $322 billion, compared to a GNP for Japan of $2.9 trillion and exports of $265 billion, and Germany's $1.2 trillion and $323 billion. This discrepancy between the currencies' reserve role and the countries' economic fundamentals is one drawback to achieving a stable relationship among these currencies upon which to base a new monetary system.

Having said that, I have to admit that there seems no alternative but to accept the present multicurrency system. To replace the present system with gold, a new issue of Special Drawing Rights, or any other newly created asset seems totally unrealistic and could be devastating in generating a new wave of inflation that could swamp the world's economies. The price of gold would have to be raised by a very large amount to ensure enough reserves to replace dollars, marks, and yen. Alternatively, we would have to create an enormous amount of SDRs, and that would be as politically unacceptable as it would be economically impractical.

That means the three major currency countries need first of all to increase their efforts to achieve as much balance as possible in their external accounts, whether they are in deficit like the United States or in surplus like Japan. It would of course be unrealistic to expect them all to hit a zero balance, but their continuing effort to reduce those imbalances would stabilize the system. They also must continue to make efforts to keep their capital and financial markets open, efficient, and credible, which will mean greater efforts by Japan and Germany than the United States. With all these efforts, a better balance would be created between the international role of these currencies and the economic fundamentals of the countries issuing them. Let me make it clear that I am not suggesting three currency regions or blocs. On the contrary, I think the institutionalization of separate currency blocs has no global merit, even though there is a trend toward regionalization in Europe and North America. I would not object to a closer regional cooperation as long as those regions remain open to the rest of the world without discriminating against outsiders. But if those two regions try to become more solidified as currency or economic blocs, it is inevitable that the Asia-Pacific region will feel a greater pressure and even a threat, which will probably tend to strengthen its regional ties. I do not want to see that happen, because the most important source of dynamism in the Asia-Pacific region is both its diversity and its openness to the rest of the world.

Working out arrangements to maintain a steady exchange rate relationship among the three main currencies would be even more difficult and probably impossible in today's political climate. Although target zones, reference ranges, and numerous technical ideas are forever being discussed, all of them are essentially the same, because when the actual exchange rate reaches its limit, some mechanism presupposes a defense at that limit. So there really are only two exchange rate arrangements: fixed rates and floating rates. To create a fixed arrangement among three currencies, many questions would have to be settled, none of them easy.

Is it possible to discover, let alone agree on, an equilibrium exchange rate among these three currencies? That rate must not only satisfy their three separate national interests but also be internationally compatible so that it can be sustained.

Can the exchange rates also be made flexible enough to adjust to external shocks and change in economic fundamentals that might affect only one of the three, such as the effect on the mark of the absorption of East Germany? When such things happen, exchange rates often must be adjusted. One lesson of Bretton Woods is that a new system would have to include the mechanism for doing so smoothly and quickly.

Could the three countries yield autonomy over their own monetary policies and commit themselves to an unlimited amount of intervention if they had to do so, in order to defend the parities they had agreed on? For example, when the United States runs an external deficit and the dollar falls in the market, Japan and Germany would be obligated to buy dollars to defend the parities of the three currencies.

Is it possible to agree on a method for settling accounts by trading assets so that obligatory intervention becomes possible? Unless the United States agrees to settle its deficits by paying them in foreign currencies, SDRs, or some other non-dollar asset,

Japan and Germany certainly will not commit themselves to unlimited intervention simply by accumulating depreciating dollars.

Huge capital flows influence exchange rates, especially in today's deregulated and globalized market; is it possible to control them? This raises one more allied but special problem. Although the exchange rate is certainly a far more important economic indicator than, for example, the price of coffee beans or wool, in today's world market currency nevertheless is traded just as if it were a commodity. As a result, there is an almost constant danger of overshooting. In the market itself, traders strongly prefer volatility, because they make more money out of it than from stability. Businessmen, by contrast, prefer stability because it allows them to plan ahead.

These problems, which are of fundamental importance but often excruciatingly technical, would have to be resolved before we could seriously think of a fixed exchange rate arrangement among three currencies. So my conclusion is that under the current three-currency system, we have to stick with floating rates. But they still must be managed in some way, because the essential problem we face is that while rates may float, they refuse to stabilize. I therefore think it would be useful to create a kind of triumvirate of the United States, Japan, and Europe, perhaps with Germany as the representative of Europe if that is what the Europeans want. The central banks would of course have to be represented on this triumvirate because we are dealing with currencies, but the finance ministries must also be there because they represent elected governments. They are able to speak about political dynamics but not much else; central bankers are good at talking about markets but not much else. We would also need a third representative on each triumvir who would see the situation from a more objective and even a theoretical point of view, and he might well be an academic. Of course, if international institutions, particularly the IMF, can act as truly neutral umpires, their participation would also be quite useful. The group should meet regularly, and also whenever emergencies arise.

This triumvirate should try to reach agreement on desirable and sustainable exchange rates for their currencies under the prevailing situation. From my personal experience of G-7 meetings, whenever we discussed our exchange rates, I had the feeling that if the representatives could have discarded the political constraints imposed upon them by restrictive national interests, they could have held fairly agreeable discussions using common sense about the appropriate value of currencies at any given time. (For example, the rates prevailing as this is written—about 125 yen and 1.50 deutsche marks to the dollar—would attract broad agreement among such a group.) When they agreed that prevailing rates were not consistent with economic fundamentals, they could agree on measures to rectify the situation. In addition to overseeing the exchange rate, the triumvirate would engage in regular, mutual peer pressure about macroeconomic and microeconomic policy with a view to achieving better international balance and sustainable noninflationary growth.

In conducting the meetings, I have a bold proposal that would mark a considerable departure from current practice. I believe it would give greater legitimacy and force to the triumvirate's decisions if a full account of their discussions is given to the public. While I agree with Paul Volcker that informality and confidentiality secure frankness in discussion, the most frustrating element of all those G-5 and G-7 meetings was that although we discussed, and discussed, and discussed, when it came down to implementation, there was no broad support at home for the basic agreements we reached in our small, closed forum. One way to stimulate and then mobilize public support is to let the public know what its representatives have discussed about decisions affecting its own economy. Although they would not be meeting under the glare of television lights in a fully open forum, they would know they were speaking on the record. After the inevitable false starts and misunderstandings of the learning process, I hope and believe that as the public and the politicians came to know what their representatives said in these forums, and what other representatives said about the policies of each country, a broader basis of support would develop for what was decided.

In this kind of an open forum, the representatives would certainly be under a different kind of pressure. Granted, they might be more nationalistic and play to their home audiences in a demonstration of loyalty to their own countries. But there would be a crucial difference as they came to realize that their audience was not only their own countrymen but the world as a whole. They would know that the force and validity of their arguments would be judged by a global jury. They also would know that purely selfish and parochial arguments would not only invite international sneers but also reprisals that would surely counter their national interests.

Their focus might change from one meeting to another. On one occasion, the major concern might be global inflation and on another it might be aggravating international imbalances or global lack of capital. At all meetings, each representative would also focus on what his country might do to improve matters, either by shifting the exchange rate or changing domestic policy. One very crucial condition for all arguments: When each representative presented his case to the others, he would have to explain why his national policy also would be good from a global point of view. If everybody did that, it would become much easier to evaluate who was right and who was wrong, and then bring beneficial pressure on all the countries involved.

Last but not least, governments would have to commit themselves to paying the highest possible respect to whatever would emerge from the deliberations of this triumvirate. This would be another difficult issue because of different constitutional arrangements in each country. Under the parliamentary democracy of Japan, the government represents the ruling party in Parliament. As a result, what the government decides has a better chance of being approved by Parliament. In other words, the government's commitment in international forums carries greater weight. Under a presidential system like that of the United States, the independent power of Congress is much greater and a commitment by the executive branch led by the president faces a risk of rejection in the legislature. Since the triumvirate's talks would be government talks, the different constitutional structures would create a fundamental problem. For example, in my own experience, either at the G-7 meetings or bilateral meetings between Japanese and U.S. officials, it became quite tiresome to hear American representatives tell us that although the government favored measures to reduce the budget deficit, controlling the deficit was really up to Congress, and the government could not control Congress. You feel quite hopeless when your counterpart tells you that he does not know whether his commitment will remain valid. However, one has to live in the real world. What we would need to secure is a firm public commitment from governments that they will make their genuine best efforts to implement the decisions of the meetings.

Certainly my proposal does involve a considerable amount of idealism. But none of it is very revolutionary, because I accept the basic structure and functioning of the system as it exists, and I hope to make it somewhat more smooth and efficient by grounding it in popular consensus. It may not be easy to find a thoroughly dispassionate set of representatives, but if we try to move in that direction and learn how to conduct our discussions by trying to balance national interests and global compatibility, we will make progress.

For a final moment, however, I would like to dream of something that would work perfectly in an ideal world. I would envision a situation in which the three countries agree to remove all restrictions on the use of their currencies, pledge they will have no exchange controls and no capital controls—and then agree to make all three currencies common legal tender in each others' countries. They would not have to surrender their monetary autonomy, nor intervene to support their currencies, nor commit to any fixed rate at all. They could, of course, agree to take concerted action in the exchange market or on their macroeconomic policies whenever they found it useful. But basically they would leave all that to the market, which would soon decide the respective rankings, roles, and values of the three currencies. Under such an arrangement, I believe that the exchange rates among the three major currencies would tend to be more stable because the market would react to each fundamental economic change more quickly and smoothly. For the moment, I concede this is sheer fantasy and I am not proposing it seriously. But it is comforting to hope that one day our sense of cooperation and international goodwill might make possible a system that would help draw us all closer together, not only as economic actors, but most of all as human beings.

12. Beyond Bretton Woods: A New Blueprint

Jeffrey Sachs

Benjamin Franklin, when asked what form of government had emerged from the American Constitutional Convention of 1787, replied: "A republic, if you can keep it." A delegate to the 50th-anniversary conference of the IMF and the World Bank, which was due to open on September 30th in Madrid, might describe today's world economy in similar terms: an integrated, free-market system—if you can keep it.

In 1994 the world is closer than ever before to the global, co-operative, free-market arrangements championed 50 years ago by the visionaries who met at Bretton Woods, New Hampshire. Pushed together by technology and the collapse of statist ideologies, the world's economies are now integrated not merely through trade in goods, but also through trade in services, finance and multinational production. The central task of the international economic institutions is to consolidate this achievement.

The stakes are high. China's emergence as a market economy is already pulling more than a billion people out of extreme poverty. India's 900m people stand to be next, as a result of the economic opening-up to the world that began there in 1991. Most of the 450m long-suffering citizens of Latin America are at last enjoying economic growth and low inflation as their countries rejoin the world system after decades of statist and autarkic development. And if much of the post-communist world remains mired in confusion, a few dynamic reformers—Poland, the Czech Republic, Slovenia, Estonia—are already showing a turnaround in growth and are seeking further integration into the world economy.

The IMF, the World Bank and the new World Trade Organisation (WTO), successor to the GATT, should play a decisive role in extending this process of global integration, by discharging four main tasks:

Helping the Ex-Communist Reformers.   Many countries, Russia and Ukraine most prominent among them, have abandoned statism but have not yet arrived at a viable market system. These countries need help. The IMF should continue to play the leading role, but if it is to succeed its policies will have to change.

Helping the Extremely Poor.   Dozens of countries, mainly in sub-Saharan Africa, are in such desperate straits that disease, civil unrest and collapsing infrastructure are overwhelming the capacities of economic policy-makers. These countries need more active and effective international support, best led by the World Bank.

Promoting Good Citizenship in International Trade.   The governments of America and Europe are engaged in a brazen, mercantilist battle for markets in China and the Middle East, twisting arms and bending foreign policy to grab commercial contracts. Protectionists continue to make mischief, seizing on all and any pretexts, ranging from vacuous anti-dumping cases to new challenges based on labour standards, as grounds to demand barriers to imports from low-wage countries. At the same time, many developing countries demand full access to developed-country markets while keeping their own markets closed. The main job of the new WTO should be to resist these tendencies with equal firmness, and to promote an even-handed commitment to open trade for all.

Extending the Framework of International Law.   International-trade rules are, in fact, just one instance of this broader task. The world system relies increasingly on international rules to govern commercial relations. For instance, currency convertibility is governed by Article VIII of the IMF Articles of Agreement; trade practices and intellectual property rights by the GATT and WTO; banking supervision by the Bank for International Settlements. Even the placing of communication satellites in orbit is managed by the International Telecommunication Union of the United Nations. But big holes remain in the legal fabric, and may yet threaten the global economic system.

THE RISKY ROAD TO CAPITALISM

In the beginning, the IMF's chief task was to monitor the global exchange-rate system. Lending to governments in financial distress was a subsidiary job. But the Fund lost its primary role in 1971 when the fixed-rate system collapsed. The bail-out side of its business assumed greater importance, the more so after the onset of the developing-country debt crisis in 1982. Since 1989 the IMF has been assigned the leading role in helping post-communist reformers.

To understand the IMF's role, and its shortcomings, it is important to see the IMF's bail-out function in the context of global integration. The IMF's clients are not, by and large, governments that have merely hit a bad financial patch and so need a temporary loan. (If this were the case, the financial markets could provide.) Its clients are governments that must contend with a total collapse of public confidence in the state, usually as a result of decades of bad economic policies. The IMF is right to lecture them about the need for fundamental change, but wrong to make this a substitute for quick financial help. The IMF has been obsessed with the problem of moral hazard—the danger that its loans will finance a resumption of bad management. As a result, it has been insensitive to the damage caused by prolonged insolvency of the state.

Bankrupt governments are usually willing to undertake drastic reforms. This is especially true under a new leader, such as Boris Yeltsin in Russia or Leonid Kuchma in Ukraine. The problem, typically, does not lie with the will to change, but with the difficulty of managing change when a government is enfeebled by an inherited financial crisis. Bankrupt governments are insecure. They cannot distribute largesse to buy off the opposition or keep their own partisans happy. Since their tenure is shaky, they lack credibility; in consequence they also lack the means to enforce the law, collect taxes and preserve the stability of the currency. In short, they are prone to fail.

Rarely does that failure mean a simple reversion to old practices; often it means a more dangerous state of affairs, including criminality, political extremism, civil unrest, hyperinflation, capital flight, and, in the worst cases, civil war. Yugoslavia's ethnic tinderbox was ignited by the insolvency of the Yugoslav federal government in the second half of the 1980s.

The IMF should see its main function as that of helping weak governments establish the credibility needed to carry through reform programmes. The basic fiscal problem is often as much one of public confidence in future policies as it is the size of a budget deficit *per se*. Brazil, Kirgizstan and Russia all had huge inflation in 1993 despite budget deficits comparable to those of many low-inflation OECD economies (see Table 12–1). The difference was that the high-inflation countries suffered from a flight from the currency and an unwillingness among public and foreign investors to hold government debt.

Rather than concentrating nearly all its efforts on budget-cutting, as it does now, the IMF should aim to combine fiscal restraint with ample foreign loans, exchange-rate stabilisation, increasing central-bank independence, and debt relief, all designed to restore confidence in the currency and in the government's ability to honour its (re-structured) debts. The package should mobilise sufficient support in the short term to ensure that the government can continue to provide essential services. Once stability is achieved, the reforming government can go on to more fundamental institutional reform in areas such as taxation.

A key step in restoring confidence lies in stabilising the exchange rate quickly—as has been demonstrated in many countries over the past ten years, among them Bolivia and Israel in 1985, Mexico in 1987, Poland in 1990, Argentina in 1991 and Estonia in 1992. An injection of foreign exchange is often required to set up a stabilisation fund; yet the IMF has preferred to play only a small role at the start of such reforms, albeit helping several countries to stay the course later on. Success in most cases has had to be homegrown, often with emergency support from America. The IMF continues to neglect currency stabilisation: it has held back money needed for stabilisation funds in Russia and Ukraine, and withheld support for Brazil's monetary reform in the summer.

The IMF should also help governments to mobilise international financing of budget deficits early in the reform process, and so minimise the risk that a fragile government might be toppled by hostile reaction to swingeing spending cuts and tax increases. Remarkably, the IMF has mobilised almost no fresh financing for the Russian budget since the fall of communism in 1991: almost all budgetary shortfalls have

TABLE 12–1   Spot the Difference

1993	DEFICIT, % OF GDP	M2, % OF GDP	INFLATION RATE, %
Developing economies			
Brazil*	0	11	2,490
Kirgizstan	8	4	1,366
Russia	10	12	940
OECD economies			
Greece	13	53	12
Portugal	8	89	6
Italy	9	60	5

*Brazil's deficit is net of inflation correction on public debt
Source: IMF; OECD; national statistics

been met by inflationary central-bank financing. Ukraine, too, has urgent need of budgetary support. The IMF can still redeem itself in both countries, but time is short. It would be tragic if reformers there were defeated not by lack of will on their own part, but by elementary mistakes at the IMF.

Here, as elsewhere, if the IMF succeeds, it can write itself out of the bail-out script within a few years. Now, once a government is creditworthy, it looks to private capital markets rather than to the IMF for its cues. Thus it was a credit-rating agency, Moody's, rather than the IMF, that provoked the tightening of credit in Turkey earlier this year. It was a team of money managers, not IMF officials, that helped to steer Mexican monetary policy after the assassination of the leading presidential candidate earlier this year. In recent months India's government was far more anxious about a bond-rating mission from Standard & Poor's than about the next visit of the IMF.

THE FORGOTTEN POOR

If its reforms are given a chance, Russia will prove not merely viable economically, but highly promising. The same cannot be said of Rwanda, or Sierra Leone, or dozens of other countries in Africa where misrule, disease and civil strife have left hundreds of millions untouched by the forces of global economic integration. Latin America attracted $190 a head in foreign capital inflows last year, Africa just $8 a head. Human capital is bleeding away as Africa's best and brightest leave to do menial jobs in the cities of America and Europe.

Africa is the most formidable challenge facing the World Bank in the next decade, one that will be best met by phasing out traditional project-financing operations and redirecting more of the Bank's resources towards Africa's urgent needs. The Bank's other main task is one at which it has lately improved: promoting and disseminating basic research on economic development.

The traditional project-financing role of the World Bank is rapidly becoming passé, as the Bank's own "World Development Report" indicates this year.* It rightly points out that world capital markets are mobilising project finance of a kind that was unthinkable a few years ago. The markets are channelling tens of billions of dollars into roads, ports, telecoms and power generators—and thereby supplanting the long-standing role of the Bank itself. Many countries are turning away the Bank's project loans because private ones are cheaper. The Bank will be left with projects that fail the market test. Increasingly, such projects will have to be viewed as a kind of aid, and, as such, restricted to the poorest countries.

Even if the Bank shifts its focus to Africa, the way ahead will be fraught with risk. Large-scale aid (beyond emergency relief) should be provided only to those countries ready to improve their governance through political and economic liber-

*"World Development Report 1994: Infrastructure for Development". World Bank/Oxford University Press

alisation. For such countries, however, the aid should be ample and timely. The Bank's greatest failure in the past has been to support the cockeyed schemes of African despots.

The Israeli-Palestinian peace process offers a useful precedent. In support of it, the Bank has mobilised $1.2 billion over three years for the 2m citizens of the occupied territories—$200 per person per year. The Bank notes that the purpose of this "emergency assistance programme" is "to provide tangible benefits to the Palestinian population quickly, equitably, and efficiently," as a foundation for sustainable development and peace. The programme spells out specific sources and uses of funds, down to the details of public administration and infrastructure. A similar inducement for a Nigeria or a Burundi opening-up to democracy would be equally valuable.

NEW RULES OF THE GAME

Even if the IMF meets its challenges in Russia and Ukraine, and the World Bank its own in Africa, the world economy will continue to be endangered by the extent to which international law trails behind international economic practice. The principal long-term goal of the IMF, the World Bank and the WTO should be to establish effective rules to facilitate international trade, finance and multinational production.

The Uruguay round was a remarkable step towards filling the gaps in international economic law. The resulting agreement is much more than a commitment to increased market access. It amounts to a bold and creative international code to govern trade in services, intellectual property rights, and some aspects of foreign investment and competition policy. Crucially, it sets up a plausible mechanism for resolving disputes, and hence for enforcing its provisions, among members.

Of course, this is only a start. The Clinton administration has so far failed to push ratification of the Uruguay round through Congress. This has given protectionists on the left and isolationists on the right time to mobilise opposition. For the moment, China and Russia are not even parties to the agreement. And detailed arrangements governing trade in services and foreign direct investment remain to be negotiated.

Surprisingly, international law governing financial flows has evolved less quickly than the rules governing trade. There have been no multilateral negotiations on financial flows comparable to those of the Uruguay round, even though the expansion of international flows of capital is at least as significant—and at least as much in need of new legal underpinning—as the growth of trade. The possibility of attracting large cross-border flows of investment is perhaps the single greatest spur to good economic policies among the developing countries today. Deepening such flows should be at the top of the international agenda.

The IMF's Articles of Agreement are all but silent as to capital flows. Under Article VIII, IMF members commit themselves (at least as a goal) to currency convertibility on the current account; they make no comparable commitment on capital flows. This neglect was understandable in 1944, when capital markets were moribund and were being viewed with great suspicion for their role in the 1930s. It is wholly inadequate today. The IMF should aim to create, through a new super-Article VIII, clear international responsibilities regarding capital movements, and so forestall another abrupt reversal in flows to developing countries of the kind that helped to trigger the debt crisis.

Agreed international rules for capital flows are needed not only for developing countries, many of which regulate capital movements heavily, but also for developed countries, including those that have supposedly unrestricted capital mobility. In almost all developed countries, regulatory agencies and finance ministries fix "prudential" limits to the international exposure of institutional investors and set trading rules (c.g., for global depository rights) that have a profound effect on the size and stability of international investment flows.

Even as we look to this new agenda, the IMF must act still to deal with one enduring legacy of the past. The developing-country debt crisis continues to impose heavy costs, most recently in Russia, because of inadequate legal tools for efficient work-outs of debt. The IMF should take as its new model the bankruptcy court as it functions under chapter 11 of America's bankruptcy code. In cases of sovereign debt, the main function of the IMF should be to provide a forum to which all of a country's creditors are brought for a comprehensive, across the board settlement. Current procedures are plagued by multiple negotiations, with the Paris Club, the London Club, suppliers and so on negotiating separately. This leads to strategic bargaining and to attempts to free-ride. Usually, comprehensive accords prove impossible in such circumstances.

IF YOU CAN KEEP IT

The IMF and World Bank have earned a moment of satisfaction at their annual meetings. They have played an important part in bringing the global economy to this moment of great promise. Never before has the world had the opportunity to adopt an international system built on law, in which the weak and strong are treated equally, and where all have a chance to benefit from an open, market-based, global economy.

It is ironic that the opinion leaders of many rich countries—in both America and Europe—are stumbling just as this new system is emerging. The vast majority of Americans take little heed of the new global system. The few who have heard of the World Trade Organisation view it with grumpy scepticism rather than seeing it for what it is—a fulfilment of American ideals pursued through 50 years of arduous effort.

The international bureaucrats assembled in Madrid have a special responsibility, therefore, to keep the global economy on the right path over the coming years. A moment of satisfaction, yes—and then it is back to the hard work of keeping the global system on course.

13. Bretton Woods Revisited: A Gift from the Cold War

The Economist

Global conflict inspired the architects of the Bretton Woods system to what now looks like remarkable audacity. America and Britain, with their wartime allies in attendance, set out to do nothing less than design the post-war economic order from scratch. Their goals were clear: to make reconstruction easier and to foster, through trade, economic integration of the kind that the world had not enjoyed since the 19th century. In setting those aims, the negotiators believed they had learnt the lessons of the 1920s and 1930s. During those years, breakdowns in trade and in the international monetary system, together with intolerable economic pressure on a defeated Germany, built the foundations of the second world war out of the wreckage of the first.

If reconstruction and integration were the aims at Bretton Woods, then the arrangements designed in 1944 were evidently a great success. In the two decades after 1945 the ruined economies of Europe and Japan grew faster than ever before (or since), achieving living standards broadly comparable with those in the United States. And reconstruction went hand in hand with integration. Over this period trade expanded (in real terms) even faster than output. It is no exaggeration to describe the first two post-war decades as a golden age of trade and growth, a time without parallel in the economic history of the world.

But to what extent do the Bretton Woods architects deserve the credit? On the face of it, events after 1970 only strengthen their claim. The cornerstone of their system was a regime of fixed exchange rates. It was this, many argue, that fostered the expansion of output and international trade after the 1940s. And the proof of this view is what happened when the agreement to peg currencies fell apart in the early 1970s.

In the late 1960s, partly because of the costs of the war in Vietnam, America began to suffer from rising inflation and heavy external deficits. Richard Nixon had to choose between devaluing the dollar (which would gravely undermine the Bretton Woods system) and inducing an economic slowdown (which would gravely disappoint America's voters). He chose to devalue. America suspended the dollar's link to gold. Before long, despite attempts to repair the system, the world's big economies shifted to the regime of freely floating exchange rates that continues to this day.

See what happened. The inflation of the 1970s, the disinflation of the 1980s; the slowing of growth worldwide, which shows no sign of reversing; outbreaks of protectionism, which interrupted the progress of liberalisation and recently brought the Uruguay round of trade talks to the brink of failure. Only when the system of fixed exchange rates had gone, you might argue, did it become clear how much it had mattered.

You might also argue that the other arrangements agreed to at Bretton Woods—which, unlike the exchange-rate system, survive in one form or another—continue to prove their worth. The International Monetary Fund (IMF) was created to supervise the system of fixed exchange rates, supplying short-term credit to countries suffering balance-of-payments difficulties and making sure that any realignment of the system's parities would be orderly and public-spirited. After 1973 the "surveillance" role no longer mattered and the credit-supplying role took on a quite different character. But the Fund soon found a new and equally important job in helping countries in financial distress—first in Latin America during the debt crisis of the 1980s and then in Eastern Europe and the former Soviet Union after the collapse of communism in 1989.

So the IMF has been nothing if not adaptable. The same goes for its Bretton Woods sister, the World Bank. Like the IMF, the Bank changed when circumstances said it must. With Western Europe rebuilt, it turned its attention, its advice and the money it tapped from the world's capital market to the third world—belatedly living up to its polite name, the International Bank for Reconstruction and Development.

Readiness to improvise has likewise been the hallmark of the General Agreement on Tariffs and Trade (GATT), the third pillar of the post-war economic order. Its designers foresaw an International Trade Organisation (ITO), with wide powers to promote liberal trade. In the end, America would not go along with that. In 1947, as a supposedly temporary measure, the GATT took the ITO's place—as neither a treaty nor an institution, but a bit of both. It succeeded splendidly nonetheless. In a series of ever more complicated negotiations, reinventing itself each time, the GATT supplied the forum in which the world economy moved by agreement from barter (the prevailing form of trade at the end of the war) to today's substantially open system.

Altogether, it seems, the Bretton Woods architects have much to be proud of: surely theirs was an impressive, and impressively long-lasting, legacy. In some ways, so it was. Undeniably, in the new jobs they have designed for themselves, both the IMF and the World Bank continue to do much economic good. Yet, despite all those achievements, the idea that the system designed at Bretton Woods has shaped the world decisively for the better these past 50 years is wrong.

BETWIXT CUP AND LIP

It is wrong, first of all, on a technicality: in few respects did the "Bretton Woods system" ever actually work as its inventors had proposed—not even before 1970. Doesn't this merely prove the adaptability of the institutions that Bretton Woods put in place? No, because those who praise the foresight of the Bretton Woods architects are also wrong in a deeper way.

Throughout, the arrangements that proved to matter were guided not by their blueprint—nor by any plan designed by economic technocrats to maximise the collective good—but mainly by the economic and strategic self-interest of the world's most powerful nation. It is here, in the question of where America's interests now lie, not in the question of what could be or should be, that the lessons for the future of the world economy must be sought.

Despite the economic might of the United States, the Bretton Woods plan for post-war economic institutions reflected British as well as American preoccupations—a mark of the intellectual domination of Maynard Keynes, who led the British team. America favoured fixed exchange rates and open trade (meaning fewer quantitative restrictions and less discrimination among trading partners). Britain, keen to retain its autonomy in economic policy, wanted movable exchange rates, trade controls, and preferential tariff arrangements (notably within the Commonwealth).

Bretton Woods left the trade questions unresolved. On currencies, it compromised. It proposed an exchange-rate regime that pegged currencies to gold or to the dollar (which was itself pegged to gold). Adjustments would be allowed, but only in exceptional circumstances and under the IMF's supervision. Controls on international flows of capital were allowed (granting governments some discretion in setting interest rates), but currencies were to be made convertible for current-account transactions—a measure calculated to expand the opportunities for international trade.

Keynes argued for a bigger and much better-financed institution at the centre—one that would make it easier for countries running external deficits to get credit (and thus avoid the need for tighter monetary and fiscal policies), and which would at the same time penalise countries with external surpluses (encouraging them to stimulate demand and thereby increase their imports). Such arrangements, Keynes believed, would reduce the tendency for the international monetary system to encourage deflationary policies. He did not get his way, but it did not matter very much. The early design quickly proved to be beside the point—and the economic order that subsequently emerged looked a lot like the one America had wanted all along.

The reason was the Marshall Plan. Despite the fact that the IMF and the World Bank had been designed to provide finance—short-term credit in the case of the Fund, long-term loans for reconstruction in the case of the Bank—they played only a small part in supporting Europe's recovery. The great bulk of the external resources used for that purpose were supplied by the Marshall Plan. The Fund actually barred countries receiving Marshall aid from using IMF resources. The Bank did lend to Europe, more than to any other region in its early years: between 1947 (when it made its first loan) and 1953 it committed loans of $753m. During the same period, however, the Marshall Plan supplied Europe with roughly 20 times as much.*

Marshall aid came with strings attached—much stricter "conditionality", in fact, than either the IMF or the World Bank has ever applied. Each recipient had to sign an agreement with America, promising to balance its budget, free prices (hith-

---

*"Managing the International Economy under the Bretton Woods System." By Barry Eichengreen and Peter Kenen. Forthcoming from the Institute for International Economics, Washington, DC.

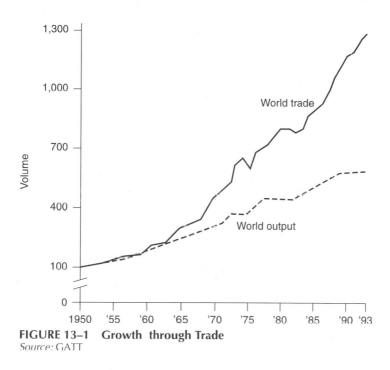

FIGURE 13–1 Growth through Trade
Source: GATT

erto controlled), halt inflation, stabilise its exchange rate and devise a plan for re-moving most trade controls.

From the beginning America also encouraged West European integration, in-sisting that recipients draw up a scheme to allocate American aid in collaboration with each other. Another new body was created for the purpose: the Organisation for Eu-ropean Economic Co-operation (OEEC), which later became the OECD. To pro-mote European integration, America even let countries receiving Marshall aid remove their controls on imports from the United States more slowly than they removed con-trols on imports from each other. Europe's drive to integrate politically and econom-ically, which later acquired a momentum all of its own, began at America's initiative.

What of the commitment, embodied in the IMF's articles of agreement, to make currencies convertible? Europe did not, in fact, hurry to restore current-account convertibility. Instead it set up yet another new body, a regional payments union, which stayed in operation until 1958. Finance to cover intra-European balance-of-payments deficits was provided not, as you might have imagined, by the IMF but by this new European Payments Union (EPU), helped by the Bank for International Set-tlements and the OEEC. The EPU was itself established using Marshall Plan lines of credit. Because of that, the new arrangements specified the dollar as both the unit of account and the means of settlement. This, in turn, led Europe's governments to maintain fixed dollar parities, instead of choosing (as Keynes had wanted, and as the Bretton Woods agreement, in principle, allowed) to make fairly frequent changes.

AMERICA ENGAGED

Thanks to the Marshall Plan, therefore, and not to the World Bank or the IMF, Western Europe's governments received the external support they needed to finance post-war reconstruction. By the same means, they were encouraged to move their economies from their wartime footing (of administered prices and a planned allocation of resources) to a liberal market system; to trade more freely with one another; and to fix their exchange rates quite rigidly.

Japan's equivalent of the Marshall Plan was the Dodge Plan. It worked in a similar way—among other things, establishing the dollar as the fixed anchor of the international monetary order. That is why Ronald McKinnon, a Stanford professor and an authority on international monetary history, has described the regime that was in place between 1950 and 1970 not as the "Bretton Woods system" but as the "Marshall-Dodge standard." This standard denied governments—with the exception of America's—the economic autonomy that the Bretton Woods architects believed they had built in. And, in Mr. McKinnon's view, that is the very reason why the arrangements which most economists still call the Bretton Woods system were such a success.

Although Mr. McKinnon is right that the "Bretton Woods system" was not designed at Bretton Woods, he may be wrong to argue that the post-war system of fixed exchange rates was chiefly responsible for that period's extraordinary economic success. Controversy rages over this question.

It is difficult to believe that the recovery of international trade in the 1950s and 1960s was not fundamental to the growth in output achieved during those years—but it is impossible to be sure how quickly trade would have expanded under a different monetary regime. Also, in the devastation caused by the war, Europe and Japan (and hence American exporters) had unparalleled opportunities for a burst of "catch-up" growth. The economic, as opposed to institutional, history of the post-war recovery is not straightforward.

But suppose that post-war institutions did have a lot to do with post-war economic success. Then it seems the credit for what was achieved during those years properly belongs to a fortunate convergence of American generosity, American self-interest and the collective good. Generosity, because the sheer scale of America's support for Europe and Japan after 1945 was remarkable; but self-interest too, because the institutions that actually emerged were shaped to reflect America's convictions and priorities.

In what way? First, America had indeed learnt the lessons of the 1920s and 1930s. Chief among these was that it could not spare itself pain by standing aside from the world. Between the wars, it had tried to do that—refusing to join the League of Nations, for instance, and in general accepting little or no responsibility for the development of the international economy. Despite this deliberate isolation, America's economy was devastated by the global economic depression of the 1930s, a catastrophe in which international economic linkages played a decisive role. Worse, the country was then dragged into the global war that the depression helped to cause. The broad lesson was well understood not only by America's leaders but by popular opinion: for its own sake, America had to lead the world to prosperity.

Second, after 1945 America was hugely self-confident. Its mighty industries had won the war. This victory belonged not just to shipbuilders or makers of aircraft and weapons, but to the whole infrastructure of military supply, which had spread to touch almost every part of the economy. Moreover, unlike the industries of Europe and Japan, America's were still intact. They wanted new markets to sell to. At least to begin with, these would be in Europe. At first, Marshall Plan money would be used directly to buy American exports. In the longer term it would serve the same purpose indirectly. Economic recovery in Europe—provided the region's markets were opened—posed no threat to American industry. Quite the opposite: it was exactly what American business wanted.

Third, by 1947 it was beginning to be clear that the defeat of Germany and Japan had left America to face a new and powerful adversary: Russia and its empire. In March of that year Harry Truman appealed to Congress for funds to support anti-communist forces in Greece, and proclaimed a broad new policy—the Truman doc-

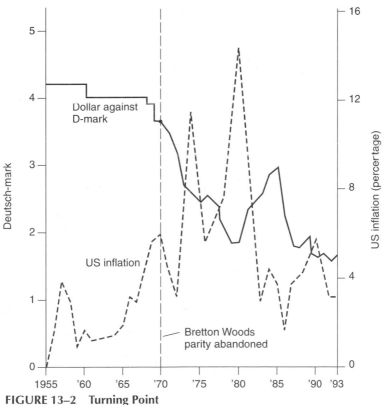

FIGURE 13–2   Turning Point
Sources: IMF; U.S. Department of Commerce

trine—that emphasised the need to keep communism in check worldwide. America was ever more sure that its political ideas would spread across the globe if only people were free to take them up. Foreign policy, including international economic policy, would strive to make this possible.

Equally, America was powerful, but not so powerful that it did not need allies. In this way too, recovery in Western Europe served American interests—especially if it could be secured in such a way that it not merely strengthened old friends, but also made strong friends of former enemies.

The Marshall Plan, undeniably an act of enormous generosity, can also be seen therefore as an act of extraordinary vision—a far-reaching programme of investment in markets, ideas and allies. The "Bretton Woods system," as it evolved in its early years, was made to serve the same broad goals. Departures from the spirit of the agreements of 1944 (for instance, the creation of the EPU using Marshall Plan resources, an innovation that badly undercut the IMF) are understandable when seen in this light.

As time passed, the system had to contend not merely with changes in the international economy but also with changes in American priorities. Certainly, there were plenty of the former. The proximate cause of the collapse of the fixed exchange-rate system in the early 1970s was economic: the regime could not deal with inflationary policies in the country whose currency anchored the system. And, before long, rebuilding a fixed-rate system came to look much more difficult for another economic reason. The expansion of international flows of capital (a trend driven mainly by improvements in technology) made defending a fixed set of parities much harder, and even (as Europe's exchange-rate mechanism demonstrated in 1993) impossible.

But the events of the early 1970s also reflect strategic considerations. By then Europe was reconstructed, highly integrated and (by and large) secure as an ally. America's management of the international economic order no longer needed to be guided by its old aims. Its narrow economic interest in devaluing the dollar could safely be pursued, even at some expense to its diminishing broader interest in the strength and openness of the world economy. Moreover, as the 1970s passed, and the oil-price rises brought recession and slowing growth to the United States, economically powerful friends in Europe and Japan began to look less like allies and more like competitors.

TOO POWERFUL TO LEAD?

In the past few years such calculations have again been overthrown by the collapse of communism. The implications for the international economic order—though likely to be profound—are still uncertain. Much depends on whether the transition to capitalism in the former Soviet empire succeeds. Also, in many parts of the third world, it is too soon to say that capitalism (lately embraced by governments of every political stripe) is secure. The transition from various kinds of anti-capitalism to market economics is painful; success cannot be taken for granted. And where it succeeds, the response of the industrial countries, including America, to the emergence of fierce new rivals is also in doubt.

On one question, however, history sheds some light. It is often argued that to-day's lack of international economic leadership reflects America's diminishing power. After 1945, the argument goes, the United States was strong enough to lead; as its power declined, so did its capacity to set the rules for the international system. The opposite view is more plausible. After 1947 America confronted a challenger that threatened its very existence. For as long as that was true, the United States would pay a price to organise and strengthen its allies. The economic elements of that policy—the "Bretton Woods system"—served everybody's interests. Its legacy is the prosperity enjoyed by today's industrial countries.

Now, America faces no such challenge. Not coincidentally, it increasingly sees economic strength beyond its borders as, at best, a mixed blessing. Whether the international economic order established by America after 1945 can survive its founder's indifference, or worse, remains to be seen.

14. The Evolution of the International Economic Order

W. Arthur Lewis

FINANCIAL DEPENDENCE

Europe has been a center of international finance for several centuries, as the Italians, the Dutch, and the British followed in each other's footsteps. Britain assumed the mantle of chief purveyor immediately after the Napoleonic war, but after a disastrous flurry with lending to Latin America in the 1820s, concentrated for the next three decades on Europe and North America, and did not lend significant sums to what is now the Third World until after the creation of the Indian Empire in 1857. Thereafter Britain was joined by France and Germany, and at the end of the century by the United States, which had previously been one of the largest borrowers. The development of the Third World did not begin until the last third of the nineteenth century when this flow of finance began to finance the railways, ports, and other infrastructure without which commerce could not move.

From *The Evolution of the International Economic Order* by W. Arthur Lewis. (Princeton, NJ: Princeton University Press, 1978).

Although foreign capital was important to the Third World, the Third World in the nineteenth century was not all that important to foreign capitalists. In 1913 only about one-third of outstanding investment was in the Third World (excluding Argentina). The bulk of the investment was in Europe, North America, and the other temperate countries of recent settlement. Foreign investment and imperialism do not coincide.

It is particularly important to note that foreign investment was not based on the rich countries lending to the poor countries. Per capita income was higher in the United States or Australia or Argentina, which were borrowers, than it was in the United Kingdom, France, or Germany, which were lenders. If income per head were the chief determinant of self-sufficiency in finance, we could not answer the question posed by opponents of foreign aid: namely, if Britain and France were saving enough to be lending in the middle of the nineteenth century, when they were not much richer than Ceylon or Brazil is today, why cannot the developing countries now save for themselves all the capital they need?

In the nineteenth century the distinction between the European lenders and the rich borrowers turned on differences in rates of urbanization. Those whose urban populations were growing by less than 3 percent per annum (France 1.0, England 1.8, and Germany 2.5) loaned, and those whose urban populations were growing by more than 3 percent per annum (Australia 3.5, United States 3.7, Canada 3.9, Argentina 5.3) borrowed.

Urbanization is a decisive factor because it is so expensive. The difference between the costs of urban development and rural development does not turn on the difference of capital required for factories and that required for farms. Each of these is a small part of total investment, and the difference per head is not always in favor of industry. The difference turns on infrastructure. Urban housing is much more expensive than rural housing. The proportion of urban children for whom schooling is provided is always much higher, at the stage where less than 60 percent of children are in school. The town has to mobilize its own hospital service, piped water supplies, bus transportation. In all these respects the towns require more per head in terms of quantity than rural areas, but even if quantities per head were the same, urban facilities would cost more in money terms than rural facilities. Rural people do more for themselves with their own labor in such matters as building houses, on working communally on village roads or irrigation facilities. When they hire construction workers they pay less, both because of a generally lower price level and because they are not faced with powerful construction unions. Rural people also do not hire architects.

The cause of these high rates of urbanization has been population growth—in Europe in the nineteenth century and in the developing countries in the second half of the twentieth century. Rural people have to move when population starts to grow, because this menaces the family farm. The family farm can be passed on intact if about two and one-half children per family survive to age of reproduction, of the eight or so born into the average rural family. As the number of survivors increases, the farm is threatened with dismemberment unless some sons move out. If there is plenty of land, as in West Africa, they can move out to make new farms or to seek employment on other new or expanding farms. If there is little new, cultivable land, they look to the towns. They will not go to the towns unless employment is known to be expanding there. If there is no work in the towns, or on other farms, the sons stay on the family's farm, which is then cut up into smaller and smaller pieces in the way with which we are so familiar in Southern Asia and the Middle East.

Therefore, in countries where all the land that can be cultivated without great expense is already occupied, the natural increase in the rural population seeks employment in the towns, once economic development has begun. The quantitative significance of this migration depends on two factors, the rate of natural increase of the population and the already existing ratio of urban to total population. At the end of the nineteenth century, Germany's population was growing at about 1.2 percent per annum. The urban population was 48 percent of the whole. To absorb the whole increase, the urban population had to grow at a rate of 1.2 divided by 48, i.e., by 2.5 percent per annum, which is exactly what it was doing. By this time emigration from Germany had virtually ceased. In Latin America, the population increases at about 3 percent per annum, and the urban population is already about 50 percent, so to absorb the whole natural increase the towns would have to grow at 6 percent per annum. This also is just about what the Latin American towns are averaging; the rural population remains constant while all the natural increase is accumulating in the towns. Asia and Africa cannot reach this condition because, though their population growth rates are about the same as the Latin American or even lower, say 2½ percent, their current urbanization level is lower still, say about 20 percent, so if the towns were to take all the natural increase they would have to grow at 12½ percent a year, which is virtually impossible.

The evidence suggests that in a complex industrial system whose interdependent parts must grow in some sort of balance if profitability is to be retained, employment in manufacturing and mining cannot grow faster than about 4 percent per annum. Japan has the fastest growth rate, and its industrial employment grew in the 1960s only at 3.8 percent a year. The figure for the United States in its heyday before the First World War was 3.5 percent a year. The U.S.S.R. reached 4.6 percent per annum in the 1930s but was then producing mainly armaments and factories to make armaments, which is a relatively simple system; in the 1960s, industrial employment in the U.S.S.R. grew only at 2.5 percent a year. It looks as if a complex industrial system cannot expand employment at more than 4 percent a year.

The problem is not so acute in Africa, where there is still plenty of land, as it is in South Asia, where there is not. Given its population growth rates, South Asia needs both more cultivable land and also more employment in agriculture per acre. These are its two highest priorities. This is not just a matter of providing work, over and above what non-agricultural activity can reasonably be expected to provide. It is also a matter of providing food for an exploding population. But even with all that can be done to make more employment in agriculture, rapid urbanization remains inevitable.

Urbanization would not be inevitable if industry could be spread around the countryside instead of concentrating in towns. This has been a deliberate objective of Mao's China. There are, however, two limits to what is possible. One is that people will migrate to the towns if they are allowed to do so; hence a system of permits to reside in the town, ruthlessly enforced, is an integral part of such a policy. And, second, industry is itself gregarious; most industrialists prefer to establish themselves in existing industrial centers, which already have not only the requisite physical infrastructure but also the network of institutions that binds industrial establishments together. One can work hard at establishing rural industries, but except in police states, success is bound to be limited.

The financial dependence of the developing countries on the developed is not due to their poverty, since even the richest countries have been borrowers. Neither does it derive from their unwillingness to save. Net domestic saving of the developing countries averaged about 10 percent a year in the 1960s, which is not very different from the ratios of Britain or France in the 1860s, when they were already lenders and not borrowers.

The developing countries' dependence for finance derives ultimately from their high rates of population growth, and intermediately from their high rates of growth of urbanization—around 5 percent per annum and more—to which this population growth gives rise. Population growth has already started to diminish (urbanization seems to be the basic constraint on population growth), but the dependency on borrowing will probably continue until the rate of natural increase drops to about one percent per year. Thus, it is likely to be with us at least until the end of this century.

It should be noted that dependence on international borrowing and dependence on foreign entrepreneurship are not the same thing. Britain was still borrowing from the Dutch in the eighteenth century, though not using Dutch entrepreneurship. The importance of direct private investment in the international flow is always greatly exaggerated, both by those who oppose it and by those who believe that it should be the principal channel for foreign transfers. The current scope for direct foreign investment is rather small. Plantations, public utilities, and mines were the usual sectors for private foreign investment up to 1929. The investment in plantation companies, which was associated with the movement of Indian and Chinese labor across the world, ended after the First World War as that movement ceased, and the investment of foreign capital in agriculture is now almost zero. Investment in public utilities is also at an end. Part of the reason for this is that it has become the conventional wisdom that public utilities should be in the public sector, so the private utilities are being bought out one after another. In addition, inflation kills public utilities because their costs rise faster than their prices, which are usually subject to elaborate public control. No knowledgeable person would put private money into Third World public utilities today. In the 1950s and 1960s the unprecedented growth of world industrial production created a large demand for minerals, including oil, and this sector became a magnet for foreign private investment. However, its very profitability has killed it. One after another, the governments are buying out the mineral enterprises, usually at substantially less than their market value, so this sector will no longer attract much private foreign investment. The other profitable sector was the financial sector, including banking and insurance. This sector took money out of the developing countries, rather than putting money in, so the developing countries have been clamping down here as well.

As these traditional sectors for private foreign investment fade out, the new sector is manufacturing industry. It is at present a reluctant contributor; it is the only sector in which Third World governments are actively encouraging foreign investment, and they are finding fewer takers than they would like. Here the emphasis is not on finance but on technology and management. The share of manufacturing in gross investment is rather small, and, if it were only a question of money, most developing countries could finance their manufacturing sectors without foreign involvement. The foreigner contributes two things, a market connection and managerial expertise. He may also contribute technology, but in the standard light-industry factory the technology is well known, and one can purchase a new cement factory or a new textile factory virtually off the rack. Advanced technology is relevant only in a few highly sophisticated industries such as computers, motor cars, or petrochemicals, and these are of immediate interest only to large, already industrially sophisticated countries such as Brazil, Mexico, or India. Current discussion of international investment as if it were mainly a problem of handling multinational corporations is quite out of perspective.

The developing countries will depend on foreign borrowing long after they have ceased to depend on foreign enterprise.* One should note that the Communist countries are now among the biggest debtors, alleged to be owing the Western world some $32 billion. It is the fast pace of urbanization that makes a country short of capital rather than a dependence on managerial expertise.

INTERNATIONAL FLUCTUATIONS

So much for the causes of financial dependence. I wish now to consider two disadvantages of this dependence that were already evident before the First World War. The first of these disadvantages is the vulnerability of debtors to international recession; the second is the speed with which the debt charges mount.

Exporters of primary products are vulnerable to international recession, whether they borrow or not, because the prices of their exports swing very widely over the course of the trade cycle. Various authors have sought to assess whether the degree of fluctuation was greater for agricultural or for industrial countries, using different definitions, and have reached different conclusions. The answer is not very important, for even if the fluctuations were equal, the agricultural countries could bear them less because their foreign exchange reserves are relatively smaller.

---

* I have said nothing about the need of oil-importing LDCs to borrow money to finance their balance of payments deficits because this is a separate problem, so large and urgent in itself that an immediate solution has to be found, in the shape of medium-term loans from oil-producing countries to LDCs, through one channel or another. In this paper I confine myself to the relationships that developed over the century up to 1973 since these are likely to continue for some time.

To the hazards inherent in the fluctuation of prices were added those of a simultaneous fluctuation in the flow of investment funds. This arose out of the miserly way Britain handled its adherence to the gold standard over the forty years before the First World War. The Bank of England kept very little gold—some say because gold yielded no interest, while others are more charitable. Whatever the reason, the consequence was that the Bank was forced to react to slight losses of gold, changing the Bank Rate an incredible number of times per year. Specifically, whenever Britain began to recover from cyclical recession there would come a point where the Bank began to lose gold, partly because the terms of trade would move adversely, and partly because international borrowers would temporarily withdraw gold to pay for purchases in other countries or at home. A financial crisis could occur, therefore, even before the trade cycle had reached its peak. The Bank Rate would go up sharply, and open market operations or their equivalent would be launched. At this point, overseas lending would be suspended because the stock exchange would react to the financial crisis, because the houses promoting such loans would think the moment inauspicious, and because those who held funds for foreign countries would keep them in London to earn the higher interest rates. So the borrowing countries were bereft of borrowing at the same time that prices moved against them.

Some of these stoppages were of long duration. The recessions of 1873, 1892, and 1929 turned into great depressions, with the final upturn into revival delayed for three or four years. Each of these recessions was marked by sharp declines in international investment. Borrowers could not meet their commitments, and a string of defaults (or as we would now call them "requests for rescheduling of debt") was inevitable. We tend to be shocked by such requests, but they are an old and intrinsic part of international investment. There was widespread defaulting in the 1820s, the 1840s, the 1870s, the 1890s, the 1930s, and the 1950s, and we are now waiting for the defaults of the end of the 1970s. The European capital market took such defaults in its stride. It knew that the borrowers would have to come back for more money, and could then be made to recognize outstanding obligations before becoming eligible for new borrowing. But the United States lost its temper when caught in the defaults of the 1930s, and with its "blue sky" laws, restricting the holding of foreign government bonds by financial intermediaries, effectively closed its long-term capital market to foreign governments, with unfortunate consequences for our day, which we shall discuss in a moment.

These great depressions with their long inroads into the flow of international investment were tied to what is now called the Kuznets cycle in the United States, which made the United States prosperous and depressed in alternate decades—prosperous in the 1880s, the 1900s, the 1920s, and the 1960s, and depressed in the 1870s, the 1890s, the 1930s, the 1950s, and the 1970s. Economists have forgotten the propensity of the U.S. economy to have these wide swings, with recession continuing for three or four years before a final upswing; and under the baleful influence of the National Bureau of Economic Research's three- to four-year reference cycles have come to believe that recessions usually last only 18 months. But this is quite unhistorical.

This shortness of memory has been aided by the fact that, not since the Second

World War have we had a really great depression of the old-fashioned kind. The United States went into recession in 1970, had a half recovery to 1973, and collapsed again. The graph of industrial production looks very much like that of the downturn of 1892, followed by the little recovery to 1895, renewed decline, and the long uphill climb, which took another seven years to get back on trend, in 1902. As on previous occasions a deep slump in building lies at the core of this Kuznets cycle. But the 1970 fall was not as great as that of 1893 because of our new built-in supports; and the rest of the industrial countries did not join in the downturn until 1974. So what we are in now is only a pale reflection of the long and deep depressions that we used to get every twenty years or so.

Another kind of fluctuation affecting international investment was the long swing in prices that we now call the Kondratiev swing, after the great Russian economist who first identified it. The sharp fall in the price level that lasted from 1873 to 1895 bore heavily on debtors. Somewhat to our surprise, the flow of international investment was not interrupted by the adverse movement of the terms of trade that was built into it from 1880 onward, but the rise in the real burden of debt certainly played a role in the heavy defaults of the 1870s and the first half of the 1890s. This long downswing of agricultural prices repeated itself between the wars, and again in the 1950s and 1960s. Agricultural prices rose sharply at the time of the Korean war, and then dropped continually until the end of the 1960s, when they turned upward again. However, the downward movement of prices was relatively small after 1955; nothing like the downswings of 1873 to 1895, or of 1920 to 1938. Now we seem to have started another long upswing of prices associated again with relative agricultural shortage, and if it persists it will help to erode the real burden of the debts contracted in the 1950s and 1960s.

It is not possible to guarantee LDCs against the consequences of long and deep recessions of the Kuznets variety, though the maintenance of multilateral and bilateral government lending through such recessions is certainly an improvement on the past. Neither can we guarantee against long downswings of the general price level of the Kondratiev variety, even though the world now seems determinedly set on continual price inflation. But we should be able to navigate the short three- to four-year cycle which has occurred in the United States since about 1890 and which also has its own name, the Kitchin cycle, after the economist who identified it or, as some would say, who invented it and sold it to the National Bureau of Economic Research.

These cyclical fluctuations in trade and investment have played havoc with the agricultural countries because their effect was multiplied as it passed through to the domestic economy. As the flow of foreign funds dried up, domestic income fell by more than the original decline in foreign exchange. This could be mitigated by devaluation. During the long decline in prices from 1873 to 1895, those countries which remained on the silver standard, such as India, escaped internal deflation; India's prices actually rose throughout this period. Some other countries, such as Argentina, Chile, and Brazil, let their currencies float up and down. It paid the agricultural classes to let the peso fall as prices fell in gold. This kept up their incomes in pesos and, by preventing the urban community from enjoying the lower gold prices of industrial imports, also moved the terms of trade in favor of the agricultural classes. Those agricultural countries that clung to the gold standard, such as Australia and many European colonies, paid the penalty of sharp internal swings. The case of the United States is particularly interesting. The United States had been borrowing overseas through the 1880s, and was caught in a foreign exchange jam in the first half of the 1890s both because of the decline of British lending and because of the very low prices of its agricultural exports. Whether to remain on the gold standard became an acute political issue that was not settled until the second half of the 1890s by a combination of the election of 1896, the rise in prices of agricultural exports, and an explosion of exports of manufactures in the second half of the 1890s. Milton Friedman has concluded:

> It should perhaps be noted explicitly that we do not intend to suggest that the alternative involving abandonment of the gold standard was economically undesirable. On the contrary, our own view is that it might well have been highly preferable to the generally depressed conditions of the 1890s. We rule it out only because, as it turned out, it was politically unacceptable.*

I think Professor Friedman must have changed his mind because, when lecturing in Israel in 1972 on the monetary problems of less developed countries, he advised that each such country should tie its currency to the currency of the country with which it did the most business, and just stay there.** He drew specific attention to the United States, which, he said, had thus "unified" the dollar with sterling at the end of the nineteenth century. In his 1972 view, this was an even better policy for a developing country than free floating.

There is in fact no easy path; this is a problem where every time you think about it you are liable to come to a different conclusion. Free floating is an obvious nuisance for countries with no organized forward markets. This is an important difference in the international economic order between the rich and the poor. But if an LDC maintains fixed rates of exchange all through the cycle, it has to pay the cost of higher unemployment levels as external prices fall; also, even in the absence of cyclical phenomena, it must keep a tight rein on internal prices, lest it be priced out of its export markets. If on the other hand it is known to be ready to devalue whenever it runs into balance of payments problems, no one will be willing to hold its currency. The onset of every minor difficulty would lead to a rush to sell and an exhaustion of its foreign reserves. Besides, devaluation is a dangerous medicine for an economy whose imports are large relative to national income. This was not so in the nineteenth century, when food was a small part of Third World imports, and when trade unions had not yet acquired the power to keep real wages constant or rising in all situations. Nowadays such an economy is likely to find itself on a treadmill, where devaluation raises domestic money incomes and prices, so setting off further devaluation *ad infinitum*. Firm control

---

* Milton J. Friedman and Anna J. Schwartz, *A Monetary History of the United States 1875–1960*. Princeton, N.J., 1963: Princeton University Press, p. 111.

** Milton J. Friedman, *Money and Economic Development*. New York, 1973: Praeger Publishers, pp. 44–48.

over the money supply and over the level of money incomes is a pre-condition for successful floating, especially if food and other consumer goods are a large proportion of
imports. Countries uncertain of their ability to pursue such policies will be reluctant
to use the tool of devaluation, especially if the trouble in the foreign balance is thought
to be temporary and cyclical.

What the situation requires is something the gold standard never had, namely
a lender of last resort. France and Germany could ride the cycle up to 1913 because
they kept huge hoards of gold. LDCs could not afford to do this. They could have afforded to hold larger foreign exchange reserves; but a debtor who holds large foreign
exchange reserves is a man who is borrowing at 6 percent to keep money in the bank
at 3 percent. Poor countries wish to avoid this. Britain avoided the same fate. Not only
did she hold very little gold, borrowing from France and Germany in times of strin
gency as in 1890 and 1907, but instead of holding exchange reserves in other countries' banks, she relied on having other countries hold their reserves in sterling in her
banks and on such reserves moving in and out at her convenience, as signaled by
changes in Bank Rate. This system worked for Britain until 1931, when it broke down.
It could never have worked for the less developed countries, since an LDC that raises
its bank rate is signaling a crisis that is more likely to drive money out than to bring
money in. We have to recognize that the instruments available to developed countries
for controlling the flow of foreign exchange over the trade cycle are simply not available to the developing countries. This is another of the clefts in the international economic order.

By 1939 it was clear that the foundation of any new international monetary system must be a lender of last resort, and this was built into the International Monetary Fund. Such a system is not easy to operate, and the IMF has had to learn its business painfully as it went along. It sounds straightforward to have an agency that passes
out money as industrial output in the developed countries declines and gets it back as
industrial output revives. This part of the problem gave little trouble before 1973,
since the cyclical movement was rather mild. IMF capacity to deal with it was also
strengthened by setting up compensatory financing, to help developing countries
whose exports have fallen off temporarily, and the EEC compensatory fund, which
serves the same purpose for its African, Caribbean and Pacific (ACP) associated nations, will also help. So also will the proposed commodity buffer stocks scheme, if it
gets off the ground.

But a lender of last resort is faced with many demands arising out of situations
that are not so obviously self-correcting, and for which long-term finance is more appropriate than short-term lending. One country runs out of foreign exchange because
it has experienced an unusual drought for three years running; how will it be able to
pay back temporary lending? Another country is in trouble because some new synthetic has cut its export prices in half. Another country has used suppliers' credits excessively to finance long-term investment, and now cannot meet its debt charges. Yet
another has been financing capital formation by inflation, and cannot face the unemployment that deflation will bring. The IMF faces two kinds of difficulties in dealing with such requests. One is where the deficit is due to the government's own poli-

cies, which the government refuses to change; this has led to the biggest quarrels. The other is where the appropriate remedy is not short- but long-term finance. To be a lender of last resort is not an enviable position, since one is inevitably faced with demands to which unrestricted short-term lending is not the appropriate answer. The availability of adequate long-term finance is a necessary condition for simplifying the role of short-term institutions.

15. The Changing Nature of World Power

Joseph S. Nye, Jr.

Power in international politics is like the weather. Everyone talks about it, but few understand it. Just as farmers and meteorologists try to forecast storms, so do leaders and analysts try to understand the dynamics of major changes in the distribution of power among nations. Power transitions affect the fortunes of individual nations and are often associated with the cataclysmic storms of world war. But before we can examine theories of hegemonic transition—that is, some of the leading efforts to predict big changes in the international political weather—we first need to recognize some basic distinctions among the terms *power, balance of power,* and *hegemony.*

POWER

Power, like love, is easier to experience than to define or measure. Power is the ability to achieve one's purposes or goals. The dictionary tells us that it is the ability to do things and to control others. Robert Dahl, a leading political scientist, defines power as the ability to get others to do what they otherwise would not do.[1] But when we measure power in terms of the changed behavior of others, we have to know their preferences. Otherwise, we may be as mistaken about our power as was the fox who thought he was hurting Brer Rabbit when he threw him into the briar patch. Know-

Joseph Samuel Nye, Jr. is director of the Center for Science and International Affairs at the Kennedy School of Government and director of the Center for International Affairs of the Faculty of Arts and Sciences, as well as Ford Foundation Professor of International Security and associate dean for International Affairs at Harvard University. He is the author of numerous books and articles on international affairs and foreign policy. This article draws from his recently published book *Bound to Lead: The Changing Nature of American Power* (BasicBooks, 1990).

From "The Changing Nature of World Power," by Joseph S. Nye Jr. *Political Science Quarterly,* Vol 105, No 2, Summer 1990, pp. 177–192. Reprinted by permission of *Political Science Quarterly.*

ing in advance how other people or nations would behave in the absence of our efforts is often difficult.

The behavioral definition of power may be useful to analysts and historians who devote considerable time to reconstructing the past, but to practical politicians and leaders it often seems too ephemeral. Because the ability to control others is often associated with the possession of certain resources, political leaders commonly define power as the possession of resources. These resources include population, territory, natural resources, economic size, military forces, and political stability, among others.[2] The virtue of this definition is that it makes power appear more concrete, measurable, and predictable than does the behavioral definition. Power in this sense means holding the high cards in the international poker game. A basic rule of poker is that if your opponent is showing cards that can beat anything you hold, fold your hand. If you know you will lose a war, don't start it.

Some wars, however, have been started by the eventual losers, which suggests that political leaders sometimes take risks or make mistakes. Often the opponent's cards are not all showing in the game of international politics. As in poker, playing skills, such as bluff and deception, can make a big difference. Even when there is no deception, mistakes can be made about which power resources are most relevant in particular situations (for example, France and Britain had more tanks than Hitler in 1940, but Hitler had greater maneuverability and a better military strategy). On the other hand, in long wars when there is time to mobilize, depth of territory and the size of an economy become more important, as the Soviet Union and the United States demonstrated in World War II.

Power conversion is a basic problem that arises when we think of power in terms of resources. Some countries are better than others at converting their resources into effective influence, just as some skilled card players win despite being dealt weak hands. Power conversion is the capacity to convert potential power, as measured by resources, to realized power, as measured by the changed behavior of others. Thus, one has to know about a country's skill at power conversion as well as its possession of power resources to predict outcomes correctly.

Another problem is determining which resources provide the best basis for power in any particular context. In earlier periods, power resources were easier to judge. According to historian A.J.P. Taylor, traditionally "the test of a Great Power is . . . the test of strength for war."[3] For example, in the agrarian economies of eighteenth-century Europe, population was a critical power resource because it provided a base for taxes and recruitment of infantry. In population, France dominated Western Europe. Thus, at the end of the Napoleonic Wars, Prussia presented its fellow victors at the Congress of Vienna with a precise plan for its own reconstruction in order to maintain the balance of power. Its plan listed the territories and populations it had lost since 1805, and the territories and populations it would need to regain equivalent numbers.[4] In the prenationalist period, it did not much matter that many of the people in those provinces did not speak German or felt themselves to be German. However, within half a century, nationalist sentiments mattered very much. Germany's seizure of Alsace-Lorraine from France in 1870, for example, made hope of any future alliance with France impossible.

Another change that occurred during the nineteenth century was the growing importance of industry and rail systems that made rapid mobilization possible. In the 1860s, Bismarck's Germany pioneered the use of railways to transport armies for quick victories. Although Russia had always had greater population resources than the rest of Europe, they were difficult to mobilize. The growth of the rail system in Western Russia at the beginning of the twentieth century was one of the reasons the Germans feared rising Russian power in 1914. Further, the spread of rail systems on the Continent helped deprive Britain of the luxury of concentrating on naval power. There was no longer time, should it prove necessary, to insert an army to prevent another great power from dominating the Continent.

The application of industrial technology to warfare has long had a powerful impact. Advanced science and technology have been particularly critical power resources since the beginning of the nuclear age in 1945. But the power derived from nuclear weapons has proven to be so awesome and destructive that its actual application is muscle-bound. Nuclear war is simply too costly. More generally, there are many situations where any use of force may be inappropriate or too costly. In 1853, for example, Admiral Matthew C. Perry could threaten to bombard Japan if it did not open its ports for supplies and trade, but it is hard to imagine that the United States could effectively threaten force to open Japanese markets today.

The Changing Sources of Power

Some observers have argued that the sources of power are, in general, moving away from the emphasis on military force and conquest that marked earlier eras. In assessing international power today, factors such as technology, education, and economic growth are becoming more important, whereas geography, population, and raw materials are becoming less important. Kenneth Waltz argues that a 5-percent rate of economic growth in the United States for three years would add more to American strength than does our alliance with Britain.[5] Richard Rosecrance argues that since 1945, the world has been poised between a territorial system composed of states that view power in terms of land mass, and a trading system "based in states which recognize that self-sufficiency is an illusion." In the past, says Rosecrance, "it was cheaper to seize another state's territory by force than to develop the sophisticated economic and trading apparatus needed to derive benefit from commercial exchange with it."[6]

If so, perhaps we are in a "Japanese period" in world politics. Japan has certainly done far better with its strategy as a trading state after 1945 than it did with its military strategy to create a Greater East Asian Co-Prosperity sphere in the 1930s. But Japan's security vis-à-vis its large military neighbors—China and the Soviet Union—depends heavily on U.S. protection. In short, even if we can define power clearly, it still has become more difficult to be clear about the relationship of particular resources to it. Thus, we cannot leap too quickly to the conclusion that all trends favor economic power or countries like Japan.

Like other forms of power, economic power cannot be measured simply in terms of tangible resources. Intangible aspects also matter. For example, outcomes generally depend on bargaining, and bargaining depends on relative costs in particular situations and skill in converting potential power into effects. Relative costs are determined not only by the total amount of measurable economic resources of a country but also by the degree of its interdependence in a relationship. If, for example, the United States and Japan depend on each other but one is less dependent than the other, that asymmetry is a source of power. The United States may be less vulnerable than Japan if the relationship breaks down, and it may use that threat as a source of power.[7] Thus, an assessment of Japanese and American power must look not only at shares of resources but also at the relative vulnerabilities of both countries.

Another consideration is that most large countries today find military force more costly to apply than in previous centuries. This has resulted from the dangers of nuclear escalation, the difficulty of ruling nationalistically awakened populations in otherwise weak states, the danger of rupturing profitable relations on other issues, and the public opposition in Western democracies to prolonged and expensive military conflicts. Even so, the increased cost of military force does not mean that it will be ruled out. To the contrary, in an anarchic system of states where there is no higher government to settle conflicts and where the ultimate recourse is self-help, this could never happen. In some cases, the stakes may justify a costly use of force. And, as recent episodes in Grenada and Libya have shown, not all uses of force by great powers involve high costs.[8]

Even if the direct use of force were banned among a group of countries, military force would still play an important political role. For example, the American military role in deterring threats to allies, or of assuring access to a crucial resource such as oil in the Persian Gulf, means that the provision of protective force can be used in bargaining situations. Sometimes the linkage may be direct; more often it is a factor not mentioned openly but present in the back of statesmen's minds.

In addition, there is the consideration that is sometimes called "the second face of power."[9] Getting other states to change might be called the directive or commanding method of exercising power. Command power can rest on inducements ("carrots") or threats ("sticks"). But there is also an indirect way to exercise power. A country may achieve the outcomes it prefers in world politics because other countries want to follow it or have agreed to a system that produces such effects. In this sense, it is just as important to set the agenda and structure the situations in world politics as it is to get others to change in particular situations. This aspect of power—that is, getting others to want what you want—might be called indirect or co-optive power behavior. It is in contrast to the active command power behavior of getting others to do what you want.[10] Co-optive power can rest on the attraction of one's ideas or on the ability to set the political agenda in a way that shapes the preferences that others express. Parents of teenagers know that if they have structured their children's beliefs and preferences, their power will be greater and will last longer than if they had relied only on active control. Similarly, political leaders and philosophers have long understood the power that comes from setting the agenda and determining the framework of a debate. The ability to establish preferences tends to be associated with intangible power resources such as culture, ideology, and institutions. This dimension can be thought of as soft power, in contrast to the hard command power usually associated with tangible resources like military and economic strength.[11]

Robert Cox argues that the nineteenth-century *Pax Britannica* and the twentieth-century *Pax Americana* were effective because they created liberal international economic orders, in which certain types of economic relations were privileged over others and liberal international rules and institutions were broadly accepted. Following the insights of the Italian thinker Antonio Gramsci, Cox argues that the most critical feature for a dominant country is the ability to obtain a broad measure of consent on general principles—principles that ensure the supremacy of the leading state and dominant social classes—and at the same time to offer some prospect of satisfaction to the less powerful. Cox identifies Britain from 1845 to 1875 and the United States from 1945 to 1967 as such countries.[12] Although we may not agree with his terminology or dates, Cox has touched a major point: soft co-optive power is just as important as hard command power. If a state can make its power legitimate in the eyes of others, it will encounter less resistance to its wishes. If its culture and ideology are attractive, others will more willingly follow. If it can establish international norms that are consistent with its society, it will be less likely to have to change. If it can help support institutions that encourage other states to channel or limit their activities in ways the dominant state prefers, it may not need as many costly exercises of coercive or hard power in bargaining situations. In short, the universalism of a country's culture and its ability to establish a set of favorable rules and institutions that govern areas of international activity are critical sources of power.[13] These soft sources of power are becoming more important in world politics today.

Such considerations question the conclusion that the world is about to enter a Japanese era in world politics. The nature of power is changing and some of the changes will favor Japan, but some of them may favor the United States even more. In command power, Japan's economic strength is increasing, but it remains vulnerable in terms of raw materials and relatively weak in terms of military force. And in co-optive power, Japan's culture is highly insular and it has yet to develop a major voice in international institutions. The United States, on the other hand, has a universalistic popular culture and a major role in international institutions. Although such factors may change in the future, they raise an important question about the present situation: What resources are the most important sources of power today? A look at the five-century-old modern state system shows that different power resources played critical roles in different periods. (See Table 15–1.) The sources of power are never static and they continue to change in today's world.

In an age of information-based economies and transnational interdependence, power is becoming less transferable, less tangible, and less coercive. However, the transformation of power is incomplete. The twenty-first century will certainly see a greater role for informational and institutional power, but military force will remain an important factor. Economic scale, both in markets and in natural resources, will also remain important. As the service sector grows within modern economies, the distinction between services and manufacturing will continue to blur. Information will

TABLE 15–1   Leading States and Major Power Resources, 1500s–1900s

PERIOD	LEADING STATE	MAJOR RESOURCES
Sixteenth century	Spain	Gold bullion, colonial trade, mercenary armies, dynastic ties
Seventeenth century	Netherlands	Trade, capital markets, navy
Eighteenth century	France	Population, rural industry, public administration, army
Nineteenth century	Britain	Industry, political cohesion, finance and credit, navy, liberal norms, island location (easy to defend)
Twentieth century	United States	Economic scale, scientific and technical leadership, universalistic culture, military forces and alliances, liberal international regimes, hub of transnational communication

become more plentiful, and the critical resource will be the organizational capacity for rapid and flexible response. Political cohesion will remain important, as will a universalistic popular culture. On some of these dimensions of power, the United States is well endowed; on others, questions arise. But even larger questions arise for the other major contenders—Europe, Japan, the Soviet Union, and China. But first we need to look at the patterns in the distribution of power—balances and hegemonies, how they have changed over history, and what that implies for the position of the United States.

BALANCE OF POWER

International relations is far from a precise science. Conditions in various periods always differ in significant details, and human behavior reflects personal choices. Moreover, theorists often suffer from writing in the midst of events, rather than viewing them from a distance. Thus, powerful theories—those that are both simple and accurate—are rare. Yet political leaders (and those who seek to explain behavior) must generalize in order to chart a path through the apparent chaos of changing events. One of the longest-standing and most frequently used concepts is balance of power, which eighteenth-century philosopher David Hume called "a constant rule of prudent politics."[14] For centuries, balance of power has been the starting point for realistic discussions of international politics.

To an extent, balance of power is a useful predictor of how states will behave; that is, states will align in a manner that will prevent any one state from developing a preponderance of power. This is based on two assumptions: that states exist in an anarchic system with no higher government and that political leaders will act first to reduce risks to the independence of their states. The policy of balancing power helps to explain why in modern times a large state cannot grow forever into a world empire. States seek to increase their powers through internal growth and external alliances. Balance of power predicts that if one state appears to grow too strong, others will ally against it so as to avoid threats to their own independence. This behavior, then, will preserve the structure of the system of states.

However, not all balance-of-power predictions are so obvious. For example, this theory implies that professions of ideological faith will be poor predictors of behavior. But despite Britain's criticism of the notorious Stalin-Hitler pact of 1939, it was quick to make an alliance with Stalin's Soviet Union in 1941. As Winston Churchill explained at the time, "If I learned that Hitler had invaded Hell, I would manage to say something good about the Devil in the House of Commons."[15] Further, balance of power does not mean that political leaders must maximize the power of their own states in the short run. Bandwagoning—that is, joining the stronger rather than the weaker side—might produce more immediate spoils. As Mussolini discovered in his ill-fated pact with Hitler, the danger in bandwagoning is that independence may be threatened by the stronger ally in the long term. Thus, to say that states will act to balance power is a strong generalization in international relations, but it is far from being a perfect predictor.

Proximity and perceptions of threat also affect the way in which balancing of power is played out.[16] A small state like Finland, for instance, cannot afford to try to balance Soviet power. Instead, it seeks to preserve its independence through neutrality. Balance of power and the proposition that "the enemy of my enemy is my friend" help to explain the larger contours of current world politics, but only when proximity and perceptions are considered. The United States was by far the strongest power after 1945. A mechanical application of power balance might seem to predict an alliance against the United States. In fact, Europe and Japan allied with the United States because the Soviet Union, while weaker in overall power, posed a proximate threat to its neighbors. Geography and psychology are both important factors in geopolitics.

The term *balance of power* is sometimes used not as a prediction of policy but as a description of how power is distributed. In the latter case, it is more accurate to refer to the distribution of power. In other instances, though, the term is used to refer to an evenly balanced distribution of power, like a pair of hanging scales. The problem with this usage is that the ambiguities of measuring power make it difficult to determine when an equal balance exists. In fact, the major concerns in world politics tend to arise from inequalities of power, and particularly from major changes in the unequal distribution of power.

HEGEMONY IN MODERN HISTORY

No matter how power is measured, an equal distribution of power among major states is relatively rare. More often the processes of uneven growth, which realists consider a basic law of international politics, mean that some states will be rising and others declining. These transitions in the distribution of power stimulate statesmen to form alliances, to build armies, and to take risks that balance or check rising powers. But the balancing of power does not always prevent the emergence of a dominant state. Theories of hegemony and power transition try to explain why some states that become preponderant later lose that preponderance.

As far back as ancient Greece, observers attempting to explain the causes of major world wars have cited the uncertainties associated with the transition of power. Shifts in the international distribution of power create the conditions likely to lead to the most important wars.[17] However, while power transitions provide useful warning about periods of heightened risk, there is no iron law of hegemonic war. If there were, Britain and the United States would have gone to war at the beginning of this century, when the Americans surpassed the British in economic and naval power in the Western Hemisphere. Instead, when the United States backed Venezuela in its boundary dispute with British Guyana in 1895, British leaders appeased the rising American power instead of going to war with it.[18]

When power is distributed unevenly, political leaders and theorists use terms such as *empire* and *hegemony*. Although there have been many empires in history, those in the modern world have not encompassed all major countries. Even the British Empire at the beginning of this century encompassed only a quarter of the world's population and Britain was just one of a half-dozen major powers in the global balance of power. The term *hegemony* is applied to a variety of situations in which one state appears to have considerably more power than others. For example, for years China accused the Soviet Union of seeking hegemony in Asia. When Soviet leader Mikhail Gorbachev and Chinese leader Deng Xiaoping met in 1989, they pledged that "neither side will seek hegemony in any form anywhere in the world."[19]

Although the word comes from the ancient Greek and refers to the dominance of one state over others in the system, it is used in diverse and confused ways. Part of the problem is that unequal distribution of power is a matter of degree, and there is no general agreement on how much inequality and what types of power constitute hegemony. All too often, hegemony is used to refer to different behaviors and degrees of control, which obscures rather than clarifies that analysis. For example, Charles Doran cites aggressive military power, while Robert Keohane looks at preponderance in economic resources. Robert Gilpin sometimes uses the terms *imperial* and *hegemonic* interchangeably to refer to a situation in which "a single powerful state controls or dominates the lesser states in the system."[20] British hegemony in the nineteenth century is commonly cited even though Britain ranked third behind the United States and Russia in GNP and third behind Russia and France in military expenditures at the peak of its relative power around 1870. Britain was first in the more limited domains of manufacturing, trade, finance, and naval power.[21] Yet theorists often contend that "full hegemony requires productive, commercial, and financial as well as political and military power."[22]

Joshua Goldstein usefully defines hegemony as "being able to dictate, or at least dominate, the rules and arrangements by which international relations, political and economic, are conducted. . . . Economic hegemony implies the ability to center the world economy around itself. Political hegemony means being able to dominate the world militarily."[23] However, there are still two important questions to be answered with regard to how the term *hegemony* is used. First, what is the scope of the hegemon's control? In the modern world, a situation in which one country can dictate political and economic arrangements has been extremely rare. Most examples have been regional, such as Soviet power in Eastern Europe, American influence in the Caribbean, and India's control over its small neighbors—Sikkim, Bhutan, and Nepal.[24] In addition, one can find instances in which one country was able to set the rules and arrangements governing specific issues in world politics, such as the American role in money or trade in the early postwar years. But there has been no global, system-wide hegemon during the past two centuries. Contrary to the myths about *Pax Britannica* and *Pax Americana*, British and American hegemonies have been regional and issue-specific rather than general.

Second, we must ask what types of power resources are necessary to produce a hegemonic degree of control. Is military power necessary? Or is it enough to have preponderance in economic resources? How do the two types of power relate to each other? Obviously, the answers to such questions can tell us a great deal about the future world, in which Japan may be an economic giant and a military dwarf while the Soviet Union may fall into the opposite situation. A careful look at the interplay of military and economic power raises doubt about the degree of American hegemony in the postwar period.[25]

Theories of Hegemonic Transition and Stability

General hegemony is the concern of theories and analogies about the instability and dangers supposedly caused by hegemonic transitions. Classical concerns about hegemony among leaders and philosophers focus on military power and "conflicts precipitated by the military effort of one dominant actor to expand well beyond the arbitrary security confines set by tradition, historical accident, or coercive pressures."[26] In this approach, hegemonic preponderance arises out of military expansion, such as the efforts of Louis XIV, Napoleon, or Hitler to dominant world politics. The important point is that, except for brief periods, none of the attempted military hegemonies in modern times has succeeded. (See Table 15–2.) No modern state has been able to develop sufficient military power to transform the balance of power into a long-lived hegemony in which one state could dominate the world militarily.

More recently, many political scientists have focused on economic power as a source of hegemonic control. Some define hegemonic economic power in terms of resources—that is, preponderance in control over raw materials, sources of capital, markets, and production of goods. Others use the behavioral definition in which a hegemon is a state able to set the rules and arrangements for the global economy. Robert Gilpin, a leading theorist of hegemonic transition, sees Britain and America, having created and enforced the rules of a liberal economic order, as the successive hegemons since the Industrial Revolution.[27] Some political economists argue that world economic stability requires a single stabilizer and that periods of such stability

TABLE 15–2   Modern Efforts at Military Hegemony

STATE ATTEMPTING HEGEMONY	ENSUING HEGEMONIC WAR	NEW ORDER AFTER WAR
Hapsburg Spain	Thirty Years' War, 1618–1648	Peace of Westphalia, 1648
Louis XIV's France	Wars of Louis XIV	Treaty of Utrecht, 1713
Napoleon's France	1792–1815	Congress of Vienna, 1815
Germany (and Japan)	1914–1945	United Nations, 1945

Source: Charles F. Doran, *The Politics of Assimilation: Hegemony and Its Aftermath* (Baltimore: Johns Hopkins University Press, 1971), 19–20.

have coincided with periods of hegemony. In this view, *Pax Britannica* and *Pax Americana* were the periods when Britain and the United States were strong enough to create and enforce the rules for a liberal international economic order in the nineteenth and twentieth centuries. For example, it is often argued that economic stability "historically has occurred when there has been a sole hegemonic power; Britain from 1815 to World War I and the United States from 1945 to around 1970. . . . With a sole hegemonic power, the rules of the game can be established and enforced. Lesser countries have little choice but to go along. Without a hegemonic power, conflict is the order of the day."[28] Such theories of hegemonic stability and decline are often used to predict that the United States will follow the experience of Great Britain, and that instability will ensue. Goldstein, for example, argues that "we are moving toward the 'weak hegemony' end of the spectrum and . . . this seems to increase the danger of hegemonic war."[29]

I argue, however, that the theory of hegemonic stability and transition will not tell us as much about the future of the United States. Theorists of hegemonic stability generally fail to spell out the causal connections between military and economic power and hegemony. As already noted, nineteenth-century Britain was not militarily dominant nor was it the world's largest economy, and yet Britain is portrayed by Gilpin and others as hegemonic. Did Britain's military weakness at that time allow the United States and Russia, the two larger economies, to remain mostly outside the liberal system of free trade? Or, to take a twentieth-century puzzle, did a liberal international economy depend on postwar American military strength or only its economic power? Are both conditions necessary today, or have modern nations learned to cooperate through international institutions?

One radical school of political economists, the neo-Marxists, has attempted to answer similar questions about the relationship between economic and military hegemony, but their theories are unconvincing. For example, Immanuel Wallerstein defines hegemony as a situation in which power is so unbalanced that

one power can largely impose its rules and its wishes (at the very least by effective veto power) in the economic, political, military, diplomatic, and even cultural arenas. The material base of such power lies in the ability of enterprises domiciled in that power to operate more efficiently in all three major economic arenas—agro-industrial production, commerce, and finance.[30]

According to Wallerstein, hegemony is rare and "refers to that short interval in which there is simultaneously advantage in all three economic domains." At such times, the other major powers become "*de facto* client states." Wallerstein claims there have been only three modern instances of hegemony—in the Netherlands, 1620–1650; in Britain, 1815–1873; and in the United States, 1945–1967. (See Table 15–3.) He argues that "in each case, the hegemony was secured by a thirty-year-long world war," after which a new order followed—the Peace of Westphalia after 1648; the Concert of Europe after 1815; and the United Nations–Bretton Woods system after 1945.[31] According to this theory, the United States will follow the Dutch and the British path to decline.

The neo-Marxist view of hegemony is unconvincing and a poor predictor of future events because it superficially links military and economic hegemony and has many loose ends. For example, contrary to Wallerstein's theory, the Thirty Years' War *coincided* with Dutch hegemony, and Dutch decline began with the Peace of Westphalia. The Dutch were not militarily strong enough to stand up to the British on the sea and could barely defend themselves against the French on land, "despite their trade-derived wealth."[32] Further, although Wallerstein argues that British hegemony began after the Napoleonic Wars, he is not clear about how the new order in the balance of power—that is, the nineteenth-century Concert of Europe—related to Britain's supposed ability to impose a global free-trade system. For example, Louis XIV's France, which many historians view as the dominant military power in the second half of the seventeenth century, is excluded from Wallerstein's schema altogether. Thus, the neo-Marxist historical analogies seem forced into a Procrustean ideological bed, while other cases are left out of bed altogether.

Others have attempted to organize past periods of hegemony into century-long cycles. In 1919, British geopolitician Sir Halford Mackinder argued that unequal growth among nations tends to produce a hegemonic world war about every hundred years.[33] More recently, political scientist George Modelski proposed a hundred-year cyclical view of changes in world leadership. (See Table 15–4.) In this view, a long cycle begins with a major global war. A single state then emerges as the new world power

TABLE 15–3   A Neo-Marxist View of Hegemony

HEGEMONY	WORLD WAR SECURING HEGEMONY	PERIOD OF DOMINANCE	DECLINE
Dutch	Thirty Years' War, 1618–1648	1620–1650	1650–1672
British	Napoleonic Wars, 1792–1815	1815–1873	1873–1896
American	World Wars I and II, 1914–1945	1945–1967	1967–

Source: Immanuel Wallerstein, *The Politics of the World Economy* (New York: Cambridge University Press, 1984), 41–42.

TABLE 15–4 Long Cycles of World Leadership

CYCLE	GLOBAL WAR	PREPONDERANCE	DECLINE
1495–1580	1494–1516	Portugal, 1516–1540	1540–1580
1580–1688	1580–1609	Netherlands, 1609–1640	1640–1688
1688–1792	1688–1713	Britain, 1714–1740	1740–1792
1792–1914	1792–1815	Britain, 1815–1850	1850–1914
1914–	1914–1945	United States, 1945–1973	1973–

Source: George Modelski, *Long Cycles in World Politics* (Seattle: University of Washington Press, 1987), 40, 42, 44, 102, 131, 147.

and legitimizes its preponderance with postwar peace treaties. (Preponderance is defined as having at least half the resources available for global order-keeping.) The new leader supplies security and order for the international system. In time, though, the leader loses legitimacy, and deconcentration of power leads to another global war. The new leader that emerges from that war may not be the state that challenged the old leader but one of the more innovative allies in the winning coalition (as, not Germany, but the United States replaced Britain). According to Modelski's theory, the United States began its decline in 1973.[34] If his assumptions are correct, it may be Japan and not the Soviet Union that will most effectively challenge the United States in the future.

Modelski and his followers suggest that the processes of decline are associated with long waves in the global economy. They associate a period of rising prices and resource scarcities with loss of power, and concentration of power with falling prices, resource abundance, and economic innovation.[35] However, in linking economic and political cycles, these theorists become enmeshed in the controversy surrounding long cycle theory. Many economists are skeptical about the empirical evidence for alleged long economic waves and about dating historical waves by those who use the concept.[36]

Further, we cannot rely on the long-cycle theory to predict accurately the American future. Modelski's treatment of political history is at best puzzling. For example, he ranks sixteenth-century Portugal as a hegemon rather than Spain, even though Spain controlled a richer overseas empire and swallowed up Portugal a century later. Likewise, Britain is ranked as a hegemon from 1714 to 1740, even though eighteenth-century France was the larger power. Modelski's categories are odd in part because he uses naval power as the sine qua non of global power, which results in a truncated view of military and diplomatic history. Although naval power was more important for countries that relied on overseas possessions, the balance in Europe depended on the armies on the continent. Britain could not afford to ignore its armies on land and rely solely on its naval power. To preserve the balance of power, Britain had to be heavily involved in land wars on the European continent at the beginning of the eighteenth, nineteenth, and twentieth centuries. More specifically, Modelski underrates the Spanish navy in the sixteenth century as well as the French navy, which outnumbered Britain's, in the late seventeenth century.[37] Some major wars, such as the Thirty Years' War and the Anglo-French wars of the eighteenth century, are excluded altogether from Modelski's organization of history.

Vague definitions and arbitrary schematizations alert us to the inadequacies of such grand theories of hegemony and decline. Most theorists of hegemonic transition tend to shape history to their own theories by focusing on particular power resources and ignoring others. Examples include the poorly explained relationship between military and political power and the unclear link between decline and major war. Since there have been wars among the great powers during 60 percent of the years from 1500 to the present, there are plenty of candidates to associate with any given scheme.[38] Even if we consider only the nine general wars that have involved nearly all the great powers and produced high levels of casualties, some of them, such as the Seven Years' War (1755–1763), are not considered hegemonic in any of the schemes. As sociologist Pitirim Sorokin concludes, "no regular periodicity is noticeable."[39] At best, the various schematizations of hegemony and war are only suggestive. They do not provide a reliable basis for predicting the future of American power or for evaluating the risk of world war as we enter the twenty-first century. Loose historical analogies about decline and falsely deterministic political theories are not merely academic: they may lead to inappropriate policies. The real problems of a post-cold-war world will not be new challenges for hegemony, but the new challenges of transnational interdependence.

NOTES

1. Robert A. Dahl, *Who Governs? Democracy and Power in an American City* (New Haven, Conn.: Yale University Press, 1961). See also James March, "The Power of Power" in David Easton, ed., *Varieties of Political Theory* (New York: Prentice Hall, 1966), 39–70; Herbert Simon, *Models of Man* (New York: John Wiley, 1957); and David Baldwin, "Power Analysis and World Politics," *World Politics* 31 (January 1979): 161–94.

2. See Ray S. Cline, *World Power Assessment* (Boulder, Colo.: Westview Press, 1977); Hans J. Morgenthau, *Politics among Nations* (New York: Alfred Knopf, 1955), chap. 9; and Klaus Knorr, *The Power of Nations* (New York: BasicBooks, 1975), chaps. 3, 4.

3. A.J.P. Taylor, *The Struggle for Mastery in Europe, 1848–1918* (Oxford, Eng.: Oxford University Press, 1954), xxix.

4. Edward V. Gulick, *Europe's Classical Balance of Power* (New York: W. W. Norton, 1955), 248–51.

5. Kenneth N. Waltz, *Theory of International Politics* (Reading, Mass.: Addison-Wesley, 1979), 172.

6. Richard N. Rosecrance, *The Rise of the Trading State* (New York: BasicBooks, 1986), 16, 160.

7. Robert O. Keohane and Joseph S. Nye, Jr., *Power and Interdependence* (Boston: Little, Brown, 1977), chap. 1. See also R. Harrison Wagner, "Economic Interdependence, Bargaining Power and Political Influence," *International Organization* 41 (Summer 1988): 461–84.

8. Keohane and Nye, *Power and Interdependence*, 27–29; Robert O. Keohane and Joseph S. Nye, Jr., "Power and Interdependence Revisited," *International Organization* 41 (Autumn 1987): 725–53.

9. Peter Bachrach and Morton S. Baratz, "Decisions and Nondecisions: An Analytical Framework," *American Political Science Review* 57 (September 1963): 632–42. See also Richard Mansbach and John Vasquez, *In Search of Theory: A New Paradigm for Global Politics* (Englewood Cliffs, N.J.: Prentice Hall, 1981).

10. Susan Strange uses the term *structural power*, which she defines as "power to shape and determine the structures of the global political economy" in *States and Markets* (New York: Basil Blackwell, 1988), 24. My term, *co-optive power*, is similar in its focus on preferences but is somewhat broader, encompassing all elements of international politics. The term *structural power*, in contrast, tends to be associated with the neo-realist theories of Kenneth Waltz.

11. The distinction between hard and soft power resources is one of degree, both in the nature of the behavior and in the tangibility of the resources. Both types are aspects of the ability to achieve one's purposes by controlling the behavior of others. Command power—the ability to change what others *do*—can rest on coercion or inducement. Co-optive power—the ability to shape what others *want*—can rest on the attractiveness of one's culture and ideology or the ability to manipulate the agenda of political choices in a manner that makes actors fail to express some preferences because they seem to be too unrealistic. The forms of behavior between command and co-optive power range along this continuum:

Command power	coercion	inducement	agenda-setting	attraction	Co-optive power

   Further, soft power resources tend to be associated with co-optive power behavior, whereas hard power resources are usually associated with command behavior. But the relationship is imperfect. For example, countries may be attracted to others with command power by myths of invincibility, and command power may sometimes be used to establish institutions that later become regarded as legitimate. But the general association is strong enough to allow the useful shorthand reference to hard and soft power resources.

12. Robert W. Cox, *Production, Power, and World Order* (New York: Columbia University Press, 1987), chaps. 6, 7.

13. See Stephen D. Krasner, *International Regimes* (Ithaca, N.Y.: Cornell University Press, 1983).

14. David Hume, "Of the Balance of Power" in Charles W. Hendel, ed., *David Hume's Political Essays* (1742; reprint, Indianapolis, Ind.: Bobbs-Merrill, 1953), 142–44.

15. Quoted in Waltz, *International Politics*, 166.

16. Stephen M. Walt, "Alliance Formation and the Balance of Power," *International Security* 9 (Spring 1985): 3–43. See also by Walt, *The Origins of Alliances* (Ithaca, N.Y.: Cornell University Press, 1987), 23–26, 263–66.

17. A.F.K. Organski and Jack Kugler, *The War Ledger* (Chicago: University of Chicago Press, 1980), chap. 1.

18. Stephen R. Rock, *Why Peace Breaks Out: Great Power Rapprochement in Historical Perspective* (Chapel Hill: University of North Carolina Press, 1989).

19. "New Era Declared as China Visit Ends," *International Herald Tribune*, 19 May 1989.

20. Charles F. Doran, *The Politics of Assimilation: Hegemony and Its Aftermath* (Baltimore: Johns Hopkins University Press, 1971), 70; Robert O. Keohane, *After Hegemony* (Princeton, N.J.: Princeton University Press, 1984), 32; Robert Gilpin, *War and Change in World Politics* (New York: Cambridge University Press, 1981), 29.

21. Bruce M. Russett, "The Mysterious Case of Vanishing Hegemony; or, Is Mark Twain Really Dead?" *International Organization* 39 (Spring 1985): 212.

22. Robert C. North and Julie Strickland, "Power Transition and Hegemonic Succession"

(Paper delivered at the meeting of the International Studies Association, Anaheim, Calif., March–April 1986), 5.

23. Joshua S. Goldstein, *Long Cycles: Prosperity and War in the Modern Age* (New Haven, Conn.: Yale University Press, 1988), 281.

24. James R. Kurth, "Economic Change and State Development" in Jan Triska, ed., *Dominant Powers and Subordinate States: The United States in Latin America and the Soviet Union in Eastern Europe* (Durham, N.C.: Duke University Press, 1986), 88.

25. The distinction between definitions in terms of resources or behavior and the importance of indicating scope are indicated in the following table. My usage stresses behavior and broad scope.

Approaches to Hegemony

	POWER RESOURCES	POWER BEHAVIOR	SCOPE
Political/military hegemony	Army/navy (Modelski)	Define the military hierarchy (Doran)	Global or regional
Economic hegemony	Raw materials, capital, markets, production (Keohane)	Set rules for economic bargains (Goldstein)	General or issue-specific

26. Doran, *Politics of Assimilation*, 15.

27. Keohane, *After Hegemony*, 32; Gilpin, *War and Change*, 144.

28. Michael Moffitt, "Shocks, Deadlocks and Scorched Earth: Reaganomics and the Decline of U.S. Hegemony," *World Policy Journal* 4 (Fall 1987): 576.

29. Goldstein, *Long Cycles*, 357.

30. Immanuel M. Wallerstein, *The Politics of the World-Economy: The States, the Movements, and the Civilizations: Essays* (New York: Cambridge University Press, 1984), 38, 41.

31. Ibid.

32. Goldstein, *Long Cycles*, 317.

33. Halford J. Mackinder, *Democratic Ideals and Reality: A Study in the Politics of Reconstruction* (New York: Henry Holt and Co., 1919), 1–2.

34. George Modelski, "The Long Cycle of Global Politics and the Nation-State," *Comparative Studies in Society and History* 20 (April 1978): 214–35; George Modelski, *Long Cycles in World Politics* (Seattle: University of Washington Press, 1987).

35. William R. Thompson, *On Global War: Historical Structural Approaches to World Politics* (Columbia: University of South Carolina Press, 1988), chaps. 3, 8.

36. Richard N. Rosecrance, "Long Cycle Theory and International Relations," *International Organization* 41 (Spring 1987): 291–95. An interesting but ultimately unconvincing discussion can be found in Goldstein, *Long Cycles*.

37. Paul Kennedy, *The Rise and Fall of the Great Powers: Economic Change and Military Conflict from 1500 to 2000* (New York: Random House, 1987), 99.

38. Jack S. Levy, "Declining Power and the Preventive Motivation for War," *World Politics 40* (October 1987): 82–107. See also Jack S. Levy, *War in the Modern Great Power System, 1495–1975* (Lexington: University of Kentucky Press, 1983), 97.

39. Pitirim Aleksandrovich Sorokin, *Social and Cultural Dynamics: A Study of Change in Major Systems of Art, Truth, Ethics, Law and Social Relationships* (1957; reprint, Boston: Porter Sargent, 1970), 561.

16. Realeconomik: The Convergence of National Security and Economic Interdependence

Martin and Susan J. Tolchin

We have no eternal allies and we have no perpetual enemies. Our interests are eternal and perpetual, and these interests it is our duty to perform. —Viscount Palmerston, foreign secretary of England, in 1848

We'll always have dependencies. We've got to change this to interdependency. It's okay if I buy D-RAMs from someone, as long as that person needs me for microprocessors. —Mike Kelly, director of manufacturing, DARPA

THE NEW GLOBALISM

A diagram of the General Dynamics F-16 fighter aircraft looks like a miniature United Nations, with several dozen components from all over the globe. Fuel pylons come from Denmark, Indonesia, Israel, and the U.S.; wing panels from the Netherlands and the U.S.; flaperon seats from Belgium and the U.S.; aft fuselages from Greece, Turkey, Belgium, and the U.S.; jet engines from the U.S., Turkey, and Belgium; and ventrals from South Korea, Israel, and the U.S.[1]

One of the genuine heroes of the Gulf War, the F-16 is a truly international product and an international effort. It is also an archetype of many similar global-defense products, showing how U.S. policy has intentionally, by design and congressional mandate, internationalized its defense industrial base. High-minded goals included the desire to arm our allies, strengthen them against their enemies, share our own technology, and learn new technologies and manufacturing methods. Initially, the U.S. armed its allies with its own products, but gradually other nations wanted to arm themselves and reap the profits offered by a healthy defense industry. When the U.S. wanted to continue to sell its own products, the price often included coproduction.

Budget constraints have forced the U.S. to consider cost above other factors driving procurement: if you can buy it cheaper, go ahead, even if it means sacrificing "Made in America" companies and products. Lower-cost labor, targeted trade and investment practices, and higher productivity have led to the purchasing of foreign components that are all too often cheaper and better than U.S. products, particularly those from companies that have become increasingly inefficient thanks to steady, non-competitive business from the Defense Department.

During the 1980s, DoD came under heavy criticism for sloppy and corrupt purchasing practices. Indeed, the term "defense mentality" has become synonymous with laziness, cost overruns, and a general lack of competitiveness—and sometimes downright fraud—referring to suppliers who have long since ceased to worry about the discipline of the marketplace or about especially vigorous oversight. The $600 toilet seat became a symbol for defense procurement, making it far more difficult for the Pentagon to win support for legitimate expenditures.

To a lesser extent, the U.S. has been forced to internationalize by countries whose trade positions strengthen their negotiating hand. These countries often insist that the U.S. company or government "offset" its profits with purchases from the same countries. At times, offsets can exceed profits—especially if the purchaser has no use for the products in question—but companies argue that in the long run winning market share will offset these losses, which they say can also be reduced by creative accounting practices and tax policies.

The mélange of policies that led to increased internalization is widely regarded as a positive development, in which the rest of the world could profit from freer trade by putting into practice the theory of comparative advantage. If Japan made better, cheaper semiconductors, aircraft-wing composites, and visual displays, all the better. Each country would develop its own market niche, and in the long run everyone would benefit, because market forces make more efficient manufacturing decisions than government bureaucrats, industry leaders, or politicians. The new world order also encompassed foreign policy: the more interdependent nations became, the less likelihood there would be of war; trading relationships would cement security relationships.

During this period of globalization, another development occurred that went virtually unnoticed: the wall collapsed between the defense industrial base and the industrial base. "There are few industries that are exclusively defense industries" any more, said Donald Atwood, deputy secretary of defense, observing a trend that has been largely ignored by his fellow policymakers. "DoD has a legitimate interest in the defense industrial base, but at the same time globalization has made us irretrievably dependent on foreign sourcing."

The ultimate irony was that the U.S. became "irretrievably dependent" during a period that represented the greatest military budget increase in history of a nation in peacetime—a wartime build-up without a war. U.S. defense procurement rose by 100 percent, to a level as high as it was during the Vietnam War. But without a critical-industries policy to influence decisionmakers, cost factors invariably predominated in many procurement decisions, thus accelerating the move toward internationalization and its byproduct, increased foreign dependence.

The response to foreign dependence served up a bland stew in which the flavors canceled themselves out; policies that were intended to *promote* U.S. industry led instead to further internationalization—and foreign dependence. For example: Congress passed a number of "Buy America" laws, along with a provision in the Defense

Production Act directing the president to limit the production of weapons systems to domestic manufacturers, within five years. The same Congress then turned around to give the secretary of defense the authority to waive many "Buy America" restrictions, and funded dozens of programs to stimulate R & D and codevelopment of new weapons with NATO allies.

Such inconsistencies inevitably led to problems in U.S.-Japan relations. The Japanese were understandably upset by the controversy provoked by the FSX agreement: why did the United States, they asked, accept with equanimity coproduction with its Western European allies, and then challenge a similar agreement with the Japanese? (Actually, the FSX went further than NATO agreements, in that the Japanese were asking the U.S. to codevelop a plane that the U.S. had no interest in acquiring for itself.)

National emergencies also breed inconsistency, when winning takes precedence over reducing foreign dependence. During the Gulf War, for example, the Defense Department debated waiving prohibitions against purchasing non-U.S. antifriction bearings for fear that U.S. manufacturers could not produce sufficient quantities for the ground war. U.S. manufacturers had already lodged complaints against the Navy for buying Swedish bearings and not abiding by those prohibitions, originally granted as a response to the U.S. bearing industry's arguments of unfair foreign competition.[2] The bearing industry had already taken a beating in 1983, when Treasury officials allowed the sale of New Hampshire Ball Bearing to the Japanese-owned Minebea Co., on the grounds that the sale would not compromise national security. The bearings industry can take cold comfort from the fact that they are not alone; the U.S. government has never stopped a sale to foreign investors on the grounds that losing a technology would constitute a threat to national security.

Globalization has also revealed inadequacies in U.S. technological development, especially in comparison with our major trading partners. It is painfully clear, for example, that Japan and the European Community have proved much more skilled at commercializing and producing technologies with civilian as well as military applications than the U.S. In other countries, particularly Japan, without public debates on whether government intervention is necessary or "industrial policy" is desirable, encouraging strategic technologies is a way of life. In World War II, for example, Yamaha, a manufacturer of musical instruments, shifted from producing pianos to aircraft parts, then went back to pianos after the surrender.

It is not a way of life for the United States, which remains content to keep civilian and military technologies separate despite all evidence linking them. Of the twenty "critical technologies" identified by the Department of Defense in 1990, fifteen are dual-use, including microelectronic circuits, software, robotics, photonics, superconductivity, and biotechnology. Japan not only leads in many of these technologies, but exports them to the United States for both civilian and military uses.[3]

U.S. policy fosters dual-use technology for military-security reasons, such as microelectronics and computers. But only in rare exceptions has the government provided public money to foster the development of commercial technologies or their applications. This is the key difference between the U.S. and Japan. In computers, for example, DoD funded university research in parallel processing through DARPA, even paying for the early products of start-up companies seeking to commercialize these new innovations. But for strictly commercial (as opposed to military-specific) computers, such companies were then on their own in the marketplace. In Japan, the process *begins* with the global commercial market as the prime objective.

Devastated by war, Japan and many of our NATO allies lacked the wherewithal to assume the role of either defending the world or funneling a lion's share of their resources into solely defense-related products; indeed, the Germans and Japanese were barred by law from developing a strong military capability. But they could rest secure in the knowledge that the United States would shoulder most of the responsibility for defending them against their common enemy, the Soviet Union, in exchange for keeping their own military presence to a minimum. The U.S. promoted and accepted this arrangement, since it suited the nation's postwar and Cold War foreign policy needs; no one wanted to see a re-emergence of the German or Japanese military traditions, even if it meant continued heavy expenditures on our part. At the same time, the long-term economic consequences of this world view tended to focus U.S. attentions and the nation's massive procurement budget on a somewhat narrower military view of defense, ignoring the defense industrial base and the issue of technologies related to—but not exclusive of—weapons or related products.

From the postwar years up to the 1990s, the emphasis was on superior military products, distinct from commercial products, leaving other nations free to focus on the marketplace. U.S. leaders focused on the very real threat of the Cold War and burgeoning Soviet military power, but were not responding at the same time to another vital national-security threat: the decreasing competitiveness of U.S. industries, particularly those involved in critical technologies. The United States' attitudes and policies in this area reflected great optimism on the part of its leaders and a feeling of economic superiority to the rest of the world—superiority unwarranted by the nation's rising budget deficits and foreign debt. In essence, while the world's economic express sped in one direction, the U.S. traveled the opposite way, often dissipating its vast economic and political resources. Thus, in the 1980s, while the U.S. negotiated the FSX agreement, the European Community supported the development and production of its own product, the Airbus, developed by an EC consortium, Airbus Industrie. Though it was widely criticized at the time by free-traders—mostly Americans—as a twenty-year financial drain, the Europeans are now enjoying the fruits of its commercial success—a quarter of the world's market for commercial jets—while the U.S. and Japan are stalled in an unproductive and conflict-ridden venture with virtually no commercial or military spin-off for the U.S. Similarly, MITI supported Nikon's efforts to build semiconductor optical steppers in spite of many generations of failure, while the U.S. government watched Perkin-Elmer flounder.

Many observers argued that the U.S. had lost its self-sufficiency in weapons production even before the Vietnam War, as corporations closely identified with the defense industrial base expanded into the international arena. Today, the contours of the defense industrial base are driven more often by the needs and policies of large multinational corporations, whose decisions often supersede those of nation-states—even countries as large and powerful as the United States.

The contours of the defense industrial base are also influenced by political conflicts within the defense industry, where a form of "class warfare" rages between U.S. prime contractors and the tens of thousands of smaller subcontractors that depend on the primes for their health and welfare. Large electronics and aerospace companies, for example, look for global partners as well as overseas subcontractors. This strategy opens foreign markets for their products, allows them to buy cheaper components, and helps them hold down prices and avoid fighting with DoD and Congress over cost overruns. Smaller companies argue that awarding defense business to foreign firms threatens their own existence. They warn that Asian and European firms seldom share their business, and that if they go out of business the defense mobilization base will further erode.[4] Excessive reliance on foreign subcontractors is a short-term strategy, they maintain, since foreign subcontractors raise their prices as soon as they corner the market. The conundrum continues. the primes then complain, as they have recently, that thousands of their U.S. suppliers have gone out of business, forcing them to depend on foreign suppliers.

Globalization is a fact of life, destined to continue and grow. This is reinforced by a new theory rationalizing the relationship between ownership and internationalization that has taken hold in the wake of an influential article in the *Harvard Business Review* by Robert Reich, a Harvard professor known in the past for his strong advocacy of industrial policy and government intervention in the marketplace. Departing from his former views, Reich now argues that ownership no longer matters in the global economy; what is important is how a corporation's behavior matches U.S. national needs: where its workers are hired and employed, and where its research, development, and engineering are located. U.S. corporations that export jobs and technology are far less valuable to the nation than foreign firms that bring jobs and technology to our shores. "Fifty-five percent of IBM's world employees are now foreign," argued Reich, "and the percentage is growing. . . . All told, more than 20 percent of the output of U.S. firms is now produced by foreign workers on foreign soil." At the same time that American firms increasingly locate their R & D and their engineering and complex fabrication facilities abroad, foreign firms have stepped up their investments here, hiring tens of thousands of American workers and locating labs and factories in the U.S. According to recent figures, foreign firms have invested the same amount of money in R & D in the United States as have U.S. firms. Many of these firms—particularly the Europeans—prefer to locate R & D close to the markets; moreover, they are eager to hire Americans and bring technology to the United States to prove they are good corporate citizens. Reich admits that Japanese firms are less likely than Europeans to hire Americans for high-ranking jobs, and are more likely to keep high-value components and R & D at home, but some, like Sony, are becoming more global in their approach.[5]

In this new world order, American interests no longer seem definable in narrow national terms. Reich argues that "the profitability of 'U.S.' corporations is beside the point" in an era of cross-border investing; and the "standard of living of Americans . . . depends far more on what it is that they *do* than it does on the assets they own." That American citizens control a corporation is no guarantee that the corporation will provide U.S. citizens with high-value jobs, or otherwise act in U.S. interests. Nor should it. Not even the most patriotic executives, says Reich, are "authorized by shareholders to forgo profitable opportunities abroad for the sake of improving the skills and competitiveness of the American workforce."[6]

Part of the problem in analyzing whether ownership matters is defining what constitutes a U.S. corporation. Decisions turning on corporate nationality have become increasingly important in direct proportion to the surge in foreign investment. In some cases, nationality seems confusing, as with the Ohio-based Honda Accord, which represented the leading auto import in Japan in 1988. How should government deal with Yamazaki Mazak, a Japanese machine-tool company with a $110-million screwdriver operation in Florence, Kentucky, when the company asked the Commerce Department to tighten up on Japanese machine-tool imports?[7] Sony, Thomson, Phillips, and other foreign multinationals are busily engaged in trying to get U.S.-government funding on the grounds that at least their affiliates are U.S. companies, creating jobs in the U.S.

In these cases, definition is everything, including criteria based on "incorporation papers, ownership shares, location of facilities and employment, citizenship of management and employees, reinvestment or repatriation of profits."[8] Others consider tax revenues the determining factor. The distinction can translate into millions of dollars, involving the potential denial of "national treatment" to a foreign corporation. A company that is clearly a "foreign company," for example, in certain cases can be denied government grants, access to technology, and tariff relief. Within the current confusing state of affairs, each case demands a unique response, depending on the criteria relevant to that situation. Buy America provisions in government procurement, for example, are based not on foreign ownership, but on content: products must have at least 50 percent U.S. content. The Defense Department's Foreign Owned, Controlled or Influenced (FOCI) criteria seek to ensure that a corporation's productive capability will be at the government's disposal during national emergencies, and that no unauthorized transfers of technology that could impede national security will occur. Domestic U.S. airlines must abide by a regulation—weakened by the Bush administration—that air carriers be at least 75-percent owned and controlled by U.S. citizens, who must also make up two-thirds of their board of directors and management.

Internationally accepted exemptions to broad definitions of corporate nationality include "national security and economic benefits." These, too, are somewhat murky concepts that can be channeled to anyone's advantage, depending on the skills and clout of a company's advocate. A leading advocate of a relaxed interpretation of Exon-Florio is Elliot Richardson, who heads the Association of International Investors in America. Mindful, perhaps, of all those companies incorporated in the Netherlands Antilles and other tax havens, Richardson argues that "one is operating under the wrong premise even to use the term 'foreign corporation,' because that assumes that the foreign corporation belongs to a country where it is incorporated, whereas it really belongs to a country where most of the shareholders are located. Some multinationals are integrated so well the host country doesn't think of them as 'foreign'; and, indeed, the multinational often doesn't respond to its host country." A more sophisticated approach, advises Richardson, would view multinationals as "centers around which decisions are made, where no country can claim first loyalty from the company, and where a company's first loyalty is to the shareholder. Northern Telecom—a Canadian multinational—resents being called a foreign corporation. The majority of its employees are here. The point is that the entity is accountable, country by country, to its subsidiary in that country."[9]

From the public's point of view, the confusion over definitions renders public policy inert. This means that, even though there are national security and economic benefits issues, they raise more questions than U.S. leaders are willing to answer.[10] United States leaders are also unwilling to tackle the task of what constitutes a U.S. corporation from a political point of view; for example, should U.S. subsidiaries of foreign corporations be considered U.S. corporations and be allowed to intervene in the political process even if they are clearly controlled by foreign parents?[11]

"The legal definition of a company is not the real definition," argued an official from DARPA, "because it does not tell you where the real decisions are made." "The real question is, 'Who is the banker?'" added Judy Larsen, a computer expert with Dataquest. "The real issue," says Ken Blalick of the Carnegie Corporation, "is one of corporate governance. Who are the shareholders? The institutional investors, the pension funds? We need a definition of the broader stakeholders—such as labor, local government—and until the major trading partners agree on a common definition, discussion is irrelevant."

From a corporate point of view, the new internationalism helps develop markets, adds flexibility to the manufacturing process, and lowers costs. Otis Elevator Co., for example, a division of United Technologies, was able to "save $10 million in design costs" and "cut its development cycle from four years to two" through "global deployment." Its newest, state-of-the-art elevator, the Elevonic 411, was developed by six research centers in five countries. Systems integration was done at the company's home base in Farmington, Connecticut; the motor drives that make the elevators ride smoothly were designed in Japan; the door systems in France; the electronics in Germany; the small-geared components in Spain.[12]

Ideally, the new globalism should protect national security if it works as it's supposed to, rendering ownership irrelevant and discounting public policies aimed at protecting security-related technologies. A foreign-owned firm, for example, that trains Americans and does its weapons manufacturing in the United States does more for U.S. security than an American-owned firm producing weapons and risking nationalization in another nation. For that matter, many argue that there are plenty of laws to take care of emergencies: the U.S. can always nationalize a foreign firm or—as it did with Iraqi firms—confiscate its assets when it presents a security threat.

CAVEAT GLOBALIST: INTERDEPENDENCE AND NATIONAL SOVEREIGNTY

The new globalism presents a picture of peace and prosperity, where nations take one another's interests to heart and competition takes a back seat to cooperation. Globalism presumes a world in which there is universal acceptance of these values, where nationalism has broken down and given way to a new world order—in short, a world that does not yet exist. The remarkable international coalition forged by President Bush in the Gulf War represented a triumph for globalism in international relations, but sparse evidence exists to show that national interests have become extinct in commercial relationships. Nationalism has in some cases been superseded by regionalism, but the emerging regional coalitions are often, if anything, even more powerful protectionists than their nationalistic predecessors. Watch the rising protectionism in the European Community, or in the less formalized alliances between Japan and the nations of Southeast Asia—or even between Japan and the EC—to see the effects of regional strength on trade and investment issues.

In much the same way that Europe figured out that nation-states would be stronger than the 300-odd duchies of the Holy Roman Empire, regional entities today present a more formidable challenge than do nations. In 1990–91, for example, the GATT almost collapsed over the EC's protection of its farmers—Belgian farmers allied with French farmers proved far more potent than Belgian farmers alone—while the U.S. struggled without much success to introduce investment issues onto the agenda. Though certainly an improvement over prewar trade chaos, the GATT round of trade talks hardly represents the comprehensive world order its founders and supporters intended it to be: today, almost half a century after its inception, the GATT finds itself confronting similar problems in managing the world trading system to those the United Nations treats in global government: it is better than nothing, an excellent framework of goals and objectives, occasionally surprising, and constantly improving, but not nearly enough on which to base the erasure of national borders from the trading map.

Political nationalism also seems alive and well, despite rumors of its early demise. Indeed, some of the most exciting—as well as chilling—developments appear to be occurring around the globe in the name of nationalism. Countries in Eastern Europe long subjugated by the Soviet Union have broken away to return to nation-statehood. Within the Soviet Union, the Baltics and other regions declared their national independence within days of the aborted coup in August 1991, with the Ukraine and other republics following suit before the end of the year. Some of the recent European nationalisms look as frightening as they did in their prewar configurations—Serbs versus Croats, the ugly anti-Semitism that has recurred along with the revival of Eastern European statehood, and the antiforeign violence plaguing a reunited Germany.

There are few signs that citizens are willing to subject their newly acquired national independence to the demands of an idealized global economy. Indeed, the very concept of a global economy is "hidden behind a set of euphemisms . . . 'coordination,' 'harmonization,' or 'negotiation,'" according to economist John M. Culbertson. "But the bottom line is . . . that the nation is not able to apply its own, independent policies in pursuit of its own ideas of what will work, and its own goals and values. Given the enormous range of ideologies and customs among today's nations . . . it seems that actually to bring the homogenization of mankind implied by the 'global economy' would require a miracle."[13]

If we accept the Panglossian premise that joining the global economy means increased reliance on the commercial and political good will of our allies, then Americans should also be aware of some troubling problems that intrude themselves on this scenario, including:

(1) The Reliability of Allies

The new globalism posits that it doesn't matter who owns our assets, because our allies will supply us with products, components, or whatever we need in peace and war; in other words, if we can buy it, we don't have to make it.

Or do we? Our history is replete with the risks of dependence on overseas suppliers, even when they are our most "reliable" allies and trading partners. Two Japanese suppliers, reflecting their nation's concerns with U.S. involvement in the Vietnam War, refused to supply parts for the war effort. Nor has the United States always proved such a reliable ally even to its best friends. Witness a recent case in which the U.S. refused to allow the sale of a Cray supercomputer to an Israeli university, despite a longtime relationship with Israel, the nation's only democratic ally in the Middle East. No reason was given, even though Cray supercomputers are sold worldwide and are commonly used in European and American universities. Brian Silver, the professor from the Technion Institute in Haifa who tried vainly to purchase the computer for his university, visited Washington and walked the corridors of the Pentagon as well as the State and Commerce Departments in a Kafkaesque effort to find out why his request was denied. No one gave him a straight answer, but the "subliminal message" he received was that the Pentagon feared the Israelis would tap into this technology to create more accurate missiles or, worse, a doomsday weapon. Silver's answer to them: How much more accurate would those missiles be than the ones "we used ten years ago to destroy an Iraqi nuclear reactor?" Besides, he added, Technion intended to use the Cray for "unclassified academic research. . . ."[14]

Identifying "reliable allies" is highly problematic. Specifically, how do we define our "allies," and how do we know if they will remain U.S. allies two or four or ten years from now? Also, even if our allies are reliable in terms of safeguarding our technologies, what about the companies based within their borders? Toshiba? Imhausen? Kongsberg?

There are also different categories of allies, chosen according to the nation's geopolitical needs at given moments in time. Few wish to be reminded today of how hard the U.S. cultivated Iraq as an ally in the 1980s, when Iraq fought Iran, and Iran was considered the nation's archenemy. During that period, U.S. policymakers turned a blind eye to some particularly heinous Iraqi violations of human rights, despite the best efforts of William Safire, the prescient *New York Times* columnist, who pounded away at Saddam Hussein's genocide against the Kurds, as he did against the German government's laissez-faire attitude toward companies that built chemical plants— "Auschwitz in the sand"—for Libyan dictator Muammar Qaddafi and the Iraqis.

No doubt the German government, in allowing these sales, also considered Iraq an ally. According to information uncovered in February 1991 by Congress, German companies were heavily involved in supplying Saddam with a host of products for his arsenal: over ninety German companies engaged in high-tech sales to Iraq, Libya, Syria, and Iran, with Iraq the biggest winner.[15]

American executives were not exactly choirboys during this period either, nor could federal oversight be characterized as vigorous. In the five years before the Gulf War, the U.S. approved sales of $1.5 billion in advanced technology and products to Iraq, including a sale of $695,000 in advanced data-transmission devices just one day before Iraq invaded Kuwait.[16]

U.S. support of Saddam involved more than the standard diplomatic back-patting: we armed, traded with, and transferred technology to him without looking too closely at his qualities as a long-term ally; Iraq's war with Iran was enough. "When the war's over," warned Senate Majority Leader George Mitchell, Democrat of Maine, "there is one lesson we must never forget: the dictator we help today may turn his weapons on us tomorrow. For ten years, U.S. policy favored Iraq. We can't repeat that kind of mistake. . . ."[17]

There are degrees of "allies" and, of course, at no time did U.S. leaders consider Iraq in the same category as Japan, the NATO countries, or even the nations of Latin America. Yet some troubling issues arise when allies we regard as genuinely "reliable" turn out to be fierce economic competitors. Even if we are chastened by our experience with Iraq and become more discriminating in the future about choosing our trading partners, we know that even the best of friendships with bona-fide allies can turn sour with a sudden shift in world conditions. In this scenario, our continued reliance on the "kindness of strangers" proves most naïve.

Trade tensions between the U.S. and Japan in the late 1980s produced a bitter reaction from the Japanese, many of whom were frustrated by what they considered U.S. domination of their affairs. Underestimating the lingering psychological effects of the Japanese defeat in World War II, U.S. diplomats were late in realizing some of the inherent problems in the U.S.-Japan alliance and found themselves unprepared for some of its ruder manifestations.

One such jolt came with the appearance in Japan, in 1989, of *The Japan That Can Say No*, a book co-authored by two icons of the Japanese establishment, Shintaro Ishihara, a best-selling novelist and member of the Diet, and Akio Morita, the articulate chairman of Sony and the most famous Japanese executive in America. Before Ishihara's part of the book was published two years later in a considerably watered-down American edition—Morita was too embarrassed by the bad publicity to allow his section to appear in English—an unauthorized photocopied translation of the entire original whipped through Washington, D.C. It riveted the attention of everyone lucky enough to get a copy, mostly members of Congress, academics, journalists, and key members of the executive branch. The CIA, DARPA, and electronics industry lobbyists are variously credited for translating and distributing the bootlegged version. What gripped readers was the book's unvarnished view of what Japan could do to the United States through its rapidly growing commercial leverage. Japan could "bring the United States to its knees within six months," wrote Ishihara, simply by withholding semiconductors. Even the sanitized version published in 1991 by Simon &

Schuster spent many weeks on *The New York Times'* best-seller list, fascinating American readers with its new and more realistic portrayal of Japan as first and foremost a mercantile state, and its argument that Japan should toughen its trade stance on the grounds that the entire U.S. nuclear arsenal depended on Japanese chips.[18] Although many pointed out that Ishihara represented a rightwing fringe element in Japanese politics, his views still scared Americans, particularly since his following seemed to be growing in size and influence, notably among the young. Unwittingly, Ishihara provided Americans with a healthy dose of skepticism, leading many to question the long-term reliability of an ally that harbored such deep-seated hostility.

Japan's behavior as a member of the Desert Storm coalition reinforced these concerns. Despite the efforts of Prime Minister Kaifu, Japan, which is highly dependent on Middle Eastern oil, only reluctantly supported the war, and only after considerable public debate, then refused to send even hospital ships into the war zone; a call for medical volunteers produced virtually no results. Fear of the resurgence of militarism in Japan offset that nation's desire to play a more substantial role in the community of nations; the result was a public posture of ambivalence. These cross-currents in Japan's internal politics played out against that nation's deeper and more long-standing mercantilism: the view that there was no need to go to war over oil, since it can always be bought on the open market. Most controversial was the effort it took to get Japan to fork over even a small part of its financial commitment to the effort. To put this in context, the initial Japanese commitment—not the actual check—of $4 billion was considerably less than the $6.6 billion Matsushita paid to acquire United Artists. Confronted with rising U.S. resentment over the issue, extensive arm-twisting on the part of the White House, and, finally, the desire to join the victory celebrations, Japan finally paid its full $13-billion share of the cost of the war. . . .[19]

The reliable-ally theory also raises the question: why are our allies trying to reduce their dependence on us at the same time that our dependence on them is rapidly increasing? "Japan's dependence on American defense technology is higher than Europe's dependence," stated a recent Defense Science Board study. "Yet as its no–foreign parts H-2 rocket and earlier go-it-alone FSX designs show, Japan is taking steps to reduce its dependence on American systems and subsystems."[20] The same trend appears to be growing in the European Community. For decades the Europeans "depended on U.S. defense technology in a way that is unacceptable and unthinkable to most Americans," concluded an OTA study. ". . . military dependence enhanced European security . . . and became a means of acquiring technology that could be used to rebuild their industrial bases. . . . Using U.S. technology as a base, they learned to build systems at home, systems that usually cost more and were somewhat less capable than systems available through U.S. foreign military sales programs." In the last analysis, the Europeans accepted a high degree of dependence to become more independent, for, "over time, the Europeans have been able to decrease their dependence on the United States substantially."[21]

"The good guys and the bad guys change over time," concluded the astute Tom Murrin, former deputy secretary of commerce in the Bush administration. "The worst-case scenario concerns military matters. We become dependent for sources of critically needed equipment on foreign sources. It may be in the self-interest of those foreign sources not to be dependable. Alexander Hamilton warned us about that two hundred years ago."

(2) Military Preparedness

Interdependence benefits the national defense in a variety of ways. It can bring down costs and allow DoD to keep an eye on technological developments from abroad. A problem arises, however, when the U.S. can only buy a product overseas: the risk grows greater as the choice of suppliers narrows. One major risk involves military preparedness in emergencies. DoD has to be able to respond quickly to threats to the national security: wars, skirmishes, and information revealing rapid technological advances in the hands of our enemies. Faced with the sale by Toshiba and its Norwegian partners of milling machines to the Soviet Union, DoD was suddenly confronted with the problem of how to deal with suddenly quieter Soviet submarines: how to detect them, and what to do about matching this new threat with appropriate technology of our own. "Techno-military competition is an interactive process of measure and countermeasure," concluded a high-level Pentagon task force. "DoD has to . . . be able to pulse its supplier base and get responses quickly. This base must be tightly linked, and completely accessible. . . . Its action-reaction loop must be tight."[22]

Foreign dependence puts the system at risk by loosening the links between producers and users, and assigning less importance to military needs. This relates to the reliable-ally theory: "Foreign firms are less sensitive to military needs, less responsive to any defense emergencies we may face, and harder to monitor in general." Defense officials also claim that foreign firms can be slow to respond to their timetables, such as "on-time" deliveries that may be critical in wartime. Since these firms often function beyond the reach of U.S. laws, DoD may find it cannot, for example, use the Defense Production Act to get deliveries on time from foreign companies, regardless of pressing needs. Desert Storm turned this fear into reality when DoD officials found themselves forced to rely on the intervention of cooperative foreign embassies who, in turn, were able to "influence" occasionally recalcitrant suppliers in their countries to give the war top priority.

Relying on foreign firms for chips occasionally puts DoD in another security bind: foreign suppliers cannot work on these products without access to sensitive information, which, according to Pentagon officials, is more likely to leak from foreign producers than from domestic companies. One more problem of great concern, the subject of private discussions among U.S. intelligence officials, is the possibility of the insertion of a "mole" (or electronic saboteur) on a chip; this might not be discovered for years, but could do great damage depending on where the chip was located—in a jet engine, a smart missile, or merely information storage. Communications and control systems are also highly dependent on semiconductor technology. In cryptography, for example, collecting intelligence as well as protecting existing communications depends on the availability of the most advanced generation of supercomputers and semiconductor devices. For these among other reasons, the National Security Agency decided to build its own semiconductor plant near its site at Fort Meade, Maryland. Building a semiconductor FAB from scratch today costs more than $500 million, about sixteen times the cost of a decade ago. . . .

Increased awareness of this problem has not solved it; on the contrary, the gap appears to be widening in defense as well as civilian-related technologies. Automakers report one-to-two-year delays in getting state-of-the-art machine tools from Germany. Producers of sophisticated computers and phone equipment have experienced late deliveries of high-speed chips from semiconductor divisions of their Japanese competitors. The gap is widening between the home and foreign introduction of Japanese chips and packaging technologies; chip manufacturers report delays in getting steppers and other related equipment.[23] Japanese companies at home reportedly show preference for Japanese affiliates in the United States; U.S. companies cite NEC's ability to obtain the latest Japanese-made equipment from Nikon Precision, Inc., for its plant in Rosedale, California, while they have been unable to obtain such equipment.

Even if the United States does not officially care where plants are located, other countries recognize the importance of keeping critical technologies within their borders. Xerox, for example, had to locate a factory in Japan in order to get etching equipment for print leads, according to officials at the Defense Department. DoD officials also complained that, when Nikon and Canon sold steppers to American companies, the ones they sold within the United States didn't have the same tables or level of accuracy as the ones they kept in Japan. Without the right tools, companies find it hard to go up the learning curve: one of several reasons the U.S. has remained ahead in software, according to some experts, is that U.S. companies managed to keep their tools at home.

The GAO has found that Japanese companies were withholding critical parts from U.S. manufacturers to give themselves an advantage over their American competitors. These charges have been heatedly denied by the Japanese, but the GAO collected dozens of examples, among them complaints from U.S. makers of flat-panel displays, critical to lap-top computers, and from manufacturers of medical devices and some military equipment, who charged that they couldn't get the latest Japanese parts for advanced versions of their products.[24] Japanese suppliers tell these manufacturers that the parts "are in short supply," according to James Hurd, CEO of Planar Systems Inc. of Portland, Oregon.[25] In the fast-moving world of computer technology, even a delay of a few months can be decisive in the race to be competitive, while declining competitiveness affects military preparedness.

(3) Holding On to Our Technological Edge

Michael Maibach, the government affairs manager for Intel, is one of the most eloquent spokesmen for high tech in the nation's capital. In 1992, he entered the Republican primary to run for the Silicon Valley seat of Representative Tom Campbell, who was campaigning for the Senate. Maibach quickly won the support of a large group of electronics-industry leaders, many of whom shared his views on U.S. competitiveness issues. The year before, holding in his hands a five-and-a-half pound laptop computer, he discussed the reasons for recent U.S. technology losses:

"This Compaq computer is the fastest-selling lap-top PC in the country. It uses an Intel 286 chip and a sixteen-bit microprocessor. Everything else is made in Japan. The overall box is made by Citizen Watch. Compaq didn't have the technologies, because they are not in the consumer-electronics business. They don't make ten million watches a year, like Citizen Watch. By making watches, Citizen Watch knows about miniaturization, flat-panel displays, and power management in a small area. The bottom line is: as consumer electronics and computer electronics merge, the U.S. is at a distinct disadvantage, because it no longer has a consumer-electronics business."

Maibach linked the loss of the television industry in the United States to the loss of the lap-top computer. "When you lose the television industry," he explained, "as we did as a result of dumping (from twenty-eight U.S. companies in 1967 to five in 1977 to one, Zenith, in 1987), you lose computers because you lose the technology for making screens."

It's the old story: U.S. companies pioneered the lap-top computer, and Japan perfected and commercialized it. American companies fell asleep for nearly a decade, from 1982, when the first ten-pound lap-top was introduced, to 1991, when they found Toshiba in control of half the world market for lap-tops. Meanwhile, Japanese electronics companies dominated the technologies critical to the manufacture of laptops: liquid-crystal-display screens, floppy-disk drives, and memory chips. The reason? The Japanese concentrated on such consumer-electronics products as calculators, camcorders, and watches, enabling them to perfect the miniaturization techniques necessary for producing notebook-sized computers. By 1991, U.S. companies were scrambling to enter joint ventures with Japanese companies. Whatever comes of these ventures, the Japanese now "control the key lap technologies . . . and seem destined to dominate in the laptop era"—all because they understood technology linkage.[26]

The missing links in the technology chain evoke a familiar epigram from *Poor Richard's Almanack*, published in 1785: "For Want of a Nail, the Shoe was lost; for want of a Shoe, the Horse was lost; for want of a Horse, the Rider was lost; being overtaken by the enemy all for want of Care about a Horse, a Shoe, a Nail." As we approach the twenty-first century, the lines become more blurred between fighting wars and trade wars, between economic and military strength, and between commercial and military products. . . .

For all their public promises about technology accompanying investments abroad, foreign firms often keep their leading-edge technologies at home until they have solidified their competitive edge. Hitachi, Ltd., for example, makes four-megabit computer memories in its Japanese factories, according to Paul Blustein, of the Tokyo bureau of the Washington *Post*, but will not start manufacturing those chips overseas in its U.S. and German plants until it is well along in its sixteen-megabit series.[27] From Hitachi's perspective, there is nothing inherently wrong with this strategy; it is simply good business practice.

The United States has seen its advantage eroded in a number of key areas, often the victim of foreign acquisitions, coordinated strategies by its economic competitors, and current difficulties in raising the capital to commercialize its inventions. U.S. technological slippage was epitomized by the case of Kubota, Japan's largest manufacturer of agricultural machinery. Kubota, which had never produced anything more complicated than a tractor, surprised the U.S. electronics industry when it announced its first advanced minicomputer was ready for export. How did Kubota move up the technological ladder so swiftly from tractors to supercomputers? By investing in several computer companies in Silicon Valley and later in Massachusetts, and then moving the blueprints to Japan. Some of those companies, like MIPS Computer Systems—where Kubota had initiated its high-tech U.S. investment with a 20-percent stake in MIPS' innovative semiconductor technology known as reduced instruction set computing (or RISC)—had enjoyed support from DARPA. This led inevitably to questions from critics about whether this was an efficient use of taxpayer dollars. Kubota's strategy, perfectly legal, traces the path of technology transfer through investment: the design, chips, and software were all American; the product, and later the profits, Japanese.[28] Just what this exported technology contributed to the further blunting of America's competitive edge is anyone's guess. Many U.S. companies found themselves forced to follow the same path: unable to find home-grown investors with a longer view than the quarterly payoff, they looked to the deep pockets and clearer vision of their offshore competitors.

Why does it matter, as long as we can buy technologies cheaper from abroad? The most troubling consequence of this argument, common among budget-minded policymakers, is that it lulls the nation into a false sense of national security, and takes away the urgency to invest in new technologies. "There's a big difference between being dependent on a foreign company for a component and dependent on a foreign company for an industry—particularly an industry strategically important for our future economic and military security," warned Dr. Richard Van Atta, of the Institute for Defense Analyses.

(4) Connecting Technology and Manufacturing

Part of the problem lies in the dichotomy between manufacturing and innovation in the U.S. You can't have one without the other. Talk of a "defense industrial base" conjures up visions of smokestacks belching pollutants into the air, grimy steel mills, and federal money being poured down a rathole. No one associates the futuristic landscape of a semiconductor FAB or a Los Alamos superconductivity lab with the tedium of an assembly line, a marketing plan, or the nitty-gritty of making products. In the case of semiconductors, for example, much of the critical technology resides in the manufacturing process; then, like the shoe and the horse and the nail, a synergy soon follows: manufacturing technology provides the "underpinning of the ability of the semiconductor industry to compete in the world market . . . [then] provides the revenues for firms to support research and development."[29]

In other words, technology develops best with a profitable commercial base: the higher the profits, the more money can be spent on R & D, which in turn can lead to even more lucrative products. Conversely, without a commercial base, technologies risk low productivity, low demand, and loss of world market share and eventually domestic market share. Scholars John Zysman and Stephen S. Cohen argued and documented this point eloquently in *Manufacturing Matters;* so did another influential work, *Made in America,* by a team of scholars from M.I.T.[30] Although many in the U.S. recognized this connection years ago, the Japanese acted on it, expending a growing percentage of their semiconductor profits on research and development at the same time they made sure that sales would increase to support that research. The results for the U.S. are now history: the U.S. semiconductor industry steadily lost market share, military dependence increased, and commercial dependencies increased as well.

For anyone who missed the lesson of technology and manufacturing, the point was driven home in December 1991, with the announcement that U.S. firms had leapfrogged their Japanese competitors in HDTV by showing that digital television was feasible, as against analog waves. Once again, Americans were on the cutting edge, but would not be there to reap the profits since the nation had lost its television industry over a decade before. Without a manufacturing base to support innovation, the best the inventors could hope for was royalty and license payments from those companies that still produced television sets.

(5) Retaining Engineering Know-how

The Kubota case debunked the view of those who scoff at the foreign challenge, arguing that in wartime the U.S. can always nationalize its foreign assets.

"If the Iraqis want to build a tank plant, it would be okay because we can always nationalize it; that's the argument," said Norman Augustine. "My caveat is that whatever is foreign-owned ought to have a self-sustaining capacity. If the manufacturing is here and the engineering in Japan, every two and a half years—the life cycle of semiconductors—you fall a generation behind. We need to have a plan. It could be denying or preventing foreign ownership. Or it could mean back-up plans for military hardware. This means accessing domestic sources and the capability for manufacturing military hardware. Foreign ownership is okay for trucks and tanks. Where technology is changing fast, you need something different."

Many security specialists agree that the power to nationalize provides little protection if the engineering know-how remains abroad. Chuck Kimzey, director of the now-defunct Defense Manufacturing Board, raised the example of the Italian-owned Baretta plant:

"Baretta, which manufactures nine-millimeter handguns, was required to build the plant here [in La Plata, Maryland]. The general intuitive feel is that, if you've got the production capability here, then we can appropriate. The question is, even if we appropriated the physical plant, where would we get the know-how to run it? It is the engineering know-how that is the real issue. Where does the engineering expertise reside? How do you make changes—to double or triple or quadruple production, to integrate American or other machine tools into a manufacturing system that we didn't design? The issue is not simply where the production facility is; it's where the engineering is."

(6) The Importance of an American Component: Dependence vs. Interdependence

A nation does not have to make 100 percent of a product; it can make as little as 10 percent of a product, as long as it retains the technology and the capacity to make that product in times of crisis. Sometimes these products are not profitable but are critical to the existence of other industries. Producers claim, for example, that there is no money in D-RAMs, but defense experts argue that the nation's economic and military security depend on them. To be truly interdependent, the nation must invest in whatever technologies it needs to keep its competitive edge.

But working out the details of such interdependence stumps the experts. How much market share does an industry need to remain in business? What kinds of volume, market share, and profit margins are necessary for an industry to keep its technological lead and at the same time attract capital?

"We'll always have dependencies," said Mike Kelly. "We've got to change this to interdependency." To accomplish that, the U.S. must make sure it retains the leverage to assure the flow of needed military equipment and supplies. This means the nation should attempt to diversify its dependencies so that others are as dependent on the U.S. for components as the U.S. is becoming on its trading partners. "If workstations are the industry of the future," Kelly continued, "then we need D-RAMs. It's okay if I buy D-RAMs from someone, as long as that person needs me for microprocessors."

That kind of interdependence hasn't occurred; in fact, quite the reverse. Once the world's leader in high technology, the U.S. today imports 97 percent of the silicon wafers needed for microelectronic circuits, used in advanced military hardware. Also imported: 97 percent of ceramic substrates, 95 percent of bonding wire, 80 percent of scanning electronic microscopes. One company, Kyocera, dominates the manufacture of ceramic substrates, which are used for certain defense and space applications, and that company is based in Japan.

In the case of D-RAMs, the U.S. has deepened its dependence on Japanese producers without any effort to offset that dependence with other products. Once dominated by U.S. producers, by 1986 the leading Japanese electronics manufacturers controlled 80 percent of the world D-RAM market and had surpassed all U.S. producers except IBM in technology. Many scholars and journalists have analyzed the reasons for this loss—predatory and aggressive pricing on the part of the Japanese manufacturers, U.S. slippage, inconsistent government policies, the financial and distributory advantages of Japanese cartelization and vertical integration[31]—but the most salient point is that it happened, and without any effective action on the part of the U.S. There were plenty of negotiations and policies, but, lacking as they were in both timeliness and consistency, they were doomed to cancel one another out.

Without comprehensive policies and effective government leadership, industry fell back on its own resources and decided to take matters into its own hands. Under the leadership of Sanford Kane of IBM, seven semiconductor producers organized a consortium, U.S. Memories, which sought to offset the industry's growing dependence by encouraging long-term investment by U.S. computer companies in U.S. D-RAM manufacturers. Immediately following the organization of U.S. Memories, D-RAM prices suddenly dropped—coincidentally?—and a D-RAM glut appeared on the world market; the flooded market produced a sharp drop in the enthusiasm of cost-conscious but shortsighted U.S. companies for investing in their future independence. Computer makers in the consortium, like Hewlett-Packard and Apple, found cheap D-RAMs from the Far East too hard to resist, and U.S. Memories too hard to support; also, it was alleged that representatives from Japanese companies were privately hinting to their U.S. customers that chips would become harder to get if competition from U.S. Memories became a reality. Not surprisingly, U.S. Memories folded in early 1990. The obituary notices were followed within days by an announcement from Japan's six largest D-RAM producers (who are also Japan's largest computer-makers) that they were cutting production and raising prices. Another coincidence? At the postmortem of the seven original companies, only IBM and DEC (Digital Equipment Corp.) were willing to lend their support and invest in U.S. Memories to preserve an American presence in a vital industry even if it meant paying more in the short run to help build up U.S. capability.

"It's true that there's no money in D-RAMs, but you're stuck," remarked Mike Kelly, for the U.S. must retain an independent capability in that vital technology if it wishes to remain a successful player in the twenty-first century. "The loss of super-conductivity [by itself] is not bad," added Kelly; "it's the loss of the technology that gets you to superconductivity. You have to strike a balance."

Not in the eyes of the government, however. Serious discussion about rising dependence takes place all the time within agencies like Defense and Commerce, but the follow-up is nil. At the White House in the 1980s there was virtually no sense of which sectors of the U.S. economy were critical to national security—such as energy resources, banking assets, and land—for fear that national security would be used as an excuse for protectionism—a not totally unfounded concern. . . .

"THEY ARE NOT US": ANOTHER LOOK AT COMPARATIVE ADVANTAGE

The surge of foreign investment in the U.S. has occurred in some measure because of the nation's recent inability to invest in itself. This represents a marked departure from past practice, which abounds with success stories of government investment in new and critical technologies. In the 1930s, airmail put the airline business aloft; in the 1950s, 75 percent of all computers were purchased by the government; in the 1960s, 70 percent of all chips went into military equipment. Industry after industry can point to initial boosts from government that put them on the map. And, conversely, took them off the map—the case with the airlines, the computer, and the chip industries. Because it is the nation's largest purchaser, government's investment policies can put an industry in orbit or destroy it through inattention, lax trade policies, and noncompetitive buying practices. Misdirected or not, government power is considerable when it comes to industrial health.

The 1980s era of laissez-faire ignored past successes and viewed government in a new light, heavily influenced by the doctrine of "comparative advantage." Simply put, this theory spoke to visions of an international economy, in which nations did what they did best, according to their natural advantages. If the Middle East was rich in oil reserves and Japan was not, Saudi Arabia could focus on producing oil while Japan made VCRs and other products more in keeping with its own advantages—a hardworking, productive, and well-educated labor force.

Influenced by this perspective, U.S. policymakers were content to abdicate a certain degree of self-sufficiency in order to promote the new world order, a vision they had promoted from the heady days of the postwar period to the present. If other countries were beating us in auto production, steel, computer chips, and machine tools, so be it; this just meant that we would have to search harder for products more suited to our own natural advantages. A dose of self-flagellation accompanied this view, much of it deserved. "Corpocracy" became the watchword of the late 1980s: U.S. corporations were caricatures of bloated bureaucracies, overpaid and shortsighted executives, and fickle stockholders who deserted companies in a flash at the slightest hint that dividends might be cut for R & D. Surely, these firms neither needed nor merited government help in the form of handouts or protection against foreign competition.

The doctrine of comparative advantage worked well in simpler times, when countries with forests cornered the lumber industry; those with oceans, fishing; and so on. Holding to this view obscures how this theory works today, as other governments adopt the former U.S. model and determine their own comparative advantages. Japan is a prime example: this nation—with almost no natural resources, vulnerable geographically to a host of predators, and highly dependent on other countries for energy—has, through a mix of public and private strategies, established itself as the premier manufacturer of automobiles as well as many other high-value technologies. Similarly, the Europeans concentrated on machine tools, commercial aircraft, and other technologies that had little to do with either their natural or comparative advantages, but a lot to do with their future industrial strength.

In other words, governments, not the invisible hand, made the difference in the fast-paced international marketplace in the capitalist world; nations that ignored that global fact of life did so at their own peril. Ahead of their time in recognizing that development in the early 1980s, Laura Tyson and John Zysman argued that "comparative advantage is not static but dynamic, and government policies that influence the comparative advantage of particular firms in particular sectors can alter the pattern [of] advantage over time." In the case of the U.S., the reverse occurs: "policies work to reduce our economic well-being over time," thanks to "market distortions induced by the policies of a foreign government" and ignored by our own. Using the semiconductor and automobile industries, the authors traced Japan's winning strategy in gaining a "long-term competitive advantage" over U.S. and European competitors long before it ever became a political issue. In fact, by the time it became a political issue, it was too late to reverse the trend. "In the presence of such distortions . . .

[which] may impose unacceptable adjustment costs on the U.S. economy . . . the presumption that markets automatically work well is called into question. . . ."[32]

Tyson argued several years later for a U.S. strategic investment policy on the grounds that "They [foreign corporations] are not us." Particularly when it comes to legitimate national-security concerns, government should resort to more stringent remedies to block takeovers and prevent the concentration of suppliers. In a critique aimed at debunking Robert Reich's "Who Is Us?" thesis, Tyson argues that ownership of U.S. assets *should* matter, on the grounds that "We are us"—that, despite "decades of substantial foreign direct investment by U.S. multinationals, the competitiveness of the U.S. economy remains tightly linked to the competitiveness of U.S. companies." U.S. companies still locate most of their operations within the United States; U.S. parents account for "78 percent of total assets, 70 percent of total sales, and 74 percent of the total employment of U.S. multinationals."

In other words, despite the tales of U.S. *maquiladoras* shipping jobs across the Mexican border, hemorrhaging globalism, and the "Company A and Company B" thesis, the data show something quite different when they track real companies, not hypothetical examples. In fact, like foreign multinationals, U.S. firms locate their higher-paying, higher-end jobs at home, as well as the bulk of their R-&-D budgets. "The average share of R & D activity undertaken by global companies outside their home countries is quite small. For Japanese companies it is negligible. . . . The leadership of American companies remains overwhelmingly American." Despite globalization, then, a "disproportionate share of U.S. multinationals, especially their high-wage, high-productivity, research-intensive activity, remains in the United States."[33]

When foreign firms have behaved "most like us," or acted in U.S. interests by substituting the more traditional "screwdriver" operations for plants that bring jobs and technology, Tyson argues, this has occurred only because U.S. policy has "encouraged them to do so," often through methods too subtle to document. Trade frictions, for example, brought many firms to the U.S.—firms that otherwise would have preferred to stay home and export their products—to ensure their future access to the nation's rich markets. The Europeans have always been more strategic on this issue. When Nissan located in France, for example, the host country demanded and got 80 percent local content. Even the British, the most laissez-faire-minded of the Europeans, "encourage" a variety of locational, content, and technology factors when foreign investors locate in their country. Recently, the Europeans have become more specific in their demands, deciding to forgo ownership in exchange for technology in the production of integrated circuits: They will "define origin . . . by the country where the 'process of diffusion' takes place." This new policy "encouraged" Japanese and American producers to establish semiconductor-fabrication plants in Europe.[34]

WHO IS IN CHARGE?

The criteria for the new globalism that regard companies in terms of the jobs, technology, and engineering they bring to the U.S., rather than nationality, make sense up to a point. That point fades, however, with the realization that no one is there to monitor whether foreign companies are living up to those expectations (or U.S. companies either, for that matter).

"Who is us?" is irrelevant without knowing "Who is in charge?" In the U.S., that question often remains unanswered, given the nation's fragmented, often *ad hoc*, approach to managing trade and investment problems. With the rapid turnover of trade officials, whose tenure in office averages less than two years, there is virtually no one with a sufficient grasp of history to preserve past gains or to prevent future losses. No wonder the U.S., unprotected by consistent leadership, so often finds itself ignored with impunity in the world trading system.

If government were powerful enough to intervene on questions as detailed as whether jobs, technology, or know-how were sited domestically, then perhaps ownership would not be important enough to make a difference, and more global criteria could be applied. At this point, at least in the United States, government agencies do not gather sufficient information to make policy on this issue, nor do they have the political will to ask questions or require answers. Moreover, the public sector all too often finds itself no match for the giant multinational corporations, whose budgets and power exceed those of most nations. The result, then, is that, with no one in charge, the nation has abdicated its industrial and technological future to the forces of the marketplace—a marketplace where other industrialized nations, well schooled in the lessons of comparative advantage, are very much in charge of their own destinies.

The U.S. must update its view of globalism to include the concept of a greater degree of independence within an interdependent world. The nation needs a new theory that progresses from *comparative* to *competitive* advantage, and that theory must cover "not only trade, but foreign investment," wrote Michael Porter, one of the country's leading thinkers in this field. "What a new theory must explain is why a nation provides a favorable *home base* for companies that compete internationally. The home base is the nation in which the essential competitive advantages of the enterprise are created and sustained. It is where a company's strategy is set, where the core product and process technology is created and maintained, and where the most productive jobs and most advanced skills are located. The presence of the home base in a nation has the greatest positive influence on other linked domestic industries and leads to other benefits in the nation's economy." What is clear is that other nations provide a "home base" more conducive to competitiveness than the U.S.[35]

From their home base, nations compete furiously for competitive advantage in high-profit, strategic technologies. The clashes that result from "technoglobalism" are worse than trade friction, because they involve rivalries among multinationals as well as rivalries among nations and regions whose market systems greatly influence their ability to compete. Japan, for example, does not want to give up the set of domestic laws, policies, and regulations that led to its worldwide successes in lap-top computers, D-RAMs, and HDTV. The EC and the U.S. chafe at their inability to penetrate that system or compete with different sets of rules. Even though Canada and the U.S. have joined together in a free-trade zone, the disequilibrium between their differing health-insurance systems and agricultural subsidies still gives them problems.[36]

TRUST BUT SOLIDIFY: FACING GLOBAL REALITIES

. . . The U.S. needs a new vision, a "realeconomik" that addresses its need to regain economic ground; otherwise, its role as a world leader will surely diminish over time. Until Iraq, most Americans were unaware that for the last decade their leaders had sacrificed energy self-sufficiency in order to purchase cheaper foreign oil. Talk of energy exploration and conservation soon followed the realization that interdependence didn't necessarily work in the mercurial environment of the Middle East.

It is true, of course, that no nation is an island, entirely self-sufficient and able to determine its own national strategies without regard to its neighbors, its allies, and the community of nations. However, some nations are less dependent and more secure than others, the degree largely determined by the health of their industrial base and technological advancement. It is the nature of interdependence that makes the difference, particularly when one side is more dependent on the other. The United States and Latin America, for example, are highly interdependent, yet the United States has far more power within that relationship. When Latin America wants to exert its influence, it often does so through negative means—angry demonstrations, defaulting on debts—often the only recourse of the powerless. Similarly, the colonies and Great Britain were highly interdependent; yet, as soon as they could, the colonies broke away from the shackles of the mother country. The moral is that in an interdependent world, there are better and worse sides on which to place the destiny of a nation.

NOTES

1. See U.S. Congress, Office of Technology Assessment, *Arming Our Allies: Cooperation and Competition in Defense Technology*, May 1990, pp. 42–43.
2. David Silverberg, "DoD May Use Foreign Bearings in Event of Desert Shield Conflict," *Defense News*, November 7, 1991, p. 25.
3. See U.S. Department of Defense, *Critical Technologies Plan*, prepared for the Committees on Armed Services, U.S. Congress, March 15, 1990, p. ES-1.
4. U.S. Congress, Office of Technology Assessment, *Arming Our Allies: Cooperation and Competition in Defense Technology*, May 1990, p. 12.
5. Robert Reich, "Who Is Us?," *Harvard Business Review*, January–February 1990, pp. 53–64; Robert Reich, "Does Corporate Nationality Matter?," *Issues in Science and Technology*, Winter 1990–91, pp. 40–44.
6. Reich, "Corporate Nationality," p. 42.
7. Zachary Schiller and Roger Schreffler, "Look Who's Taking Japan to Task," *Business Week*, June 4, 1990, p. 64.
8. John Kline, "Trade Competitiveness and Corporate Nationality," *Columbia Journal of World Business*, vol. 24, no. 3 (Fall 1989), p. 26.
9. From remarks made at the March 1990 meeting of the United Nations Association, a private group that addresses international issues.
10. It is even less surprising that within this context both national security and economic benefits are often sacrificed to looser interpretations of nationality and political sovereignty. See Kline, "Trade Competitiveness," p. 27.

11. Security-based exemptions rest on the concept of corporate noninterference in the internal affairs of states, which in turn rests on the government's ability to resist outside political influence that might be channeled through a foreign-based corporation. In the United States, foreign political influence has risen dramatically in proportion to the upsurge in foreign investment—so much so that foreign multinationals now control more than a hundred PACs in the U.S. through their U.S. subsidiaries. The justification? That their U.S. subsidiaries should be considered U.S. corporations, even if they are controlled by a foreign parent. See U.S. Senate, Hearing before the Committee on Finance, *Foreign Influence on the U.S. Political Process*, testimony of Susan J. Tolchin, September 19, 1991, p. 52; Martin and Susan Tolchin, *Buying into America: How Foreign Money Is Changing the Face of Our Nation* (New York: Times Books/Random House, 1988), chs. 1, 2, 8, 18.

12. William J. Holstein et al., "The Stateless Corporation," *Business Week*, May 14, 1990, p. 104.

13. John Culbertson, "The New Foreign Ownership in the U.S.: Its Causes and Implications," *Southern Business & Economic Journal*, January 1990, p. 90.

14. Brian Silver, "Computers, and a Sealed Room in Israel," *New York Times*, February 17, 1991, sec. 3, p. 13.

15. Iraq did business with a majority of the companies (Libya came in second), including Imwako GMBH, a company that sold Iraq "magnets for its uranium enrichment plant" and made "technical improvements on SCUD-B missiles." Other sales that warranted congressional attention include: The Messerschmidt-Boelkow-Blohm (MBB) sales list ("fuel air explosive technology, . . . SAAD-16 chemical and missile weapons development plant, combat helicopters, . . . antitank rockets, and electronics and testing for Condor 2 missiles"); Pilot Plant's "chemical warfare plant"; Loi Industrial Furnace Facilities' "furnaces for cannon installation"; Walter Thosti Boswai (WTB)'s "Construction of four nerve case plants"; Water Engineering Trading GMBH (WET)'s "Chemical substances for manufacture of nerve gases"; Imhausen-Chemie's "chemical warfare plant"; and Hofberger Bau's "buildings for chemical weapons facilities." See U.S. Congress, Subcommittee on Commerce, Consumer Protection and Competitiveness, Committee on Energy and Commerce, *Iraq's Efforts to Acquire U.S. Technology and the Need for Legislation to Give the President Additional Authority to Seize Iraqi Interests in U.S. Firms*, February 21, 1991.

16. Sales also included: advanced computers, and "graphics terminals that could be used to design rockets and analyze their flights, machine tools, computer mapping systems and imaging devices for reading satellite pictures." A great deal of this technology was later destroyed by allied bombing aimed at Iraq's chemical and nuclear-weapons plants. Commerce Department officials claimed they tried to tighten their policies after Saddam Hussein "threatened to use poison gas on Israel . . . but were rebuffed in interagency meetings by top officials of the State Department." (Stuart Auerbach, "$1.5 Billion in U.S. Sales to Iraq, Washington *Post*, March 11, 1991, pp. A1, A16.)

17. According to a study published by the Simon Wiesenthal Center in 1991, the White House instructed the Pentagon to yield to the Commerce Department and permit export licenses to Iraq for dual-use technologies that could be employed for war or peace. Citing Commerce documents, the study showed that, between 1986 and 1990, four hundred export licenses for Iraq were approved and only seventy-seven turned down. The approved technologies ranged from computer systems to imaging technology to high-temperature furnaces that could be used in a nuclear program. Stephen Bryen, formerly deputy undersecretary of defense for trade-security policy, confirmed a 1986 National Security Directive that urged the Pentagon to be "more forthcoming on Iraq," listing specific cases where the Pentagon's Defense Technology Security Agency had "obstructed the export of technology to Iraq." Commerce official Dennis Kloske was, in essence, fired several months following the publication of the directive, after testifying before Congress that the White House and the State Department had ignored his warn-

ings to limit American technology to Iraq months before the invasion of Kuwait. The White House denied that Kloske—undersecretary for export administration—was being fired, but Kloske's remarks, distinctly out of character for official Washington, almost invited his dismissal. "I decided to employ the only option available to a bureaucrat," he told Congress. "I tried to tie up all sales in red tape." (Clyde H. Farnsworth, "Official Reported to Face Ouster After His Dissent on Iraq Exports," *New York Times,* January 10, 1991, pp. A1, D2.)

18. Shintaro Ishihara, *A Japan That Can Say No,* New York: Simon & Schuster, 1991.
19. Paul Blustein, "In Japan, the Politics of Hesitation," Washington *Post,* February 17, 1991, p. C2.
20. U.S. Department of Defense, Defense Science Board, *Critical Industries: A New Strategy for the Nation's Defense Industrial Base,* May 1990, p. 7.
21. U.S. Congress, Office of Technology Assessment, *Arming Our Allies,* p. 36.
22. U.S. Department of Defense, Defense Science Board, *Keeping Access to the Leading Edge: A Consolidated Executive Summary by the Industrial Base Committee to the Defense Science Board,* June 6, 1990, p. 5.
23. U.S. Department of Defense, Defense Science Board, *Keeping Access,* p. 8.
24. U.S. General Accounting Office, International Trade, *U.S. Business Access to Certain Foreign State-of-the-Art Technology,* September 1991.
25. G. Pascal Zachary, "U.S. Probes Allegations of Withholding of Parts," *Asian Wall Street Journal,* January 21, 1991, p. 1.
26. Deidre A. Depke et al., "Laptops Take Off," *Business Week,* March 18, 1991, pp. 118–24.
27. Paul Blustein, "Japan Inc. Stretches Its Global Foothold," Washington *Post,* March 24, 1991, p. H7.
28. David E. Sanger, "U.S. Parts, Japanese Computer," *New York Times,* September 7, 1988, p. D1.
29. U.S. Department of Defense, Defense Science Board, *Defense Semiconductor Dependency,* February 1987.
30. John Zysman and Stephen S. Cohen, *Manufacturing Matters: The Myth of a Post-Industrial Economy* (New York: Basic Books, 1987); Michael L. Dertouzos et al., *Made in America: Regaining the Productive Edge* (Cambridge, Mass.: M.I.T. Press), 1989.
31. Charles Ferguson, "Computers and the Coming of the U.S. Keiretsu," *Harvard Business Review,* July–August, 1990, p. 66.
32. The formula: insulating their own domestic markets, retaining a secure home base (which leaves plenty of room for mistakes), and pouring lots of resources into research, development, management, and engineering. The Americans did the reverse: instead of reinforcing their strengths and enhancing their ready-made comparative advantages, U.S. companies went for cheap labor, tolerated laissez-faire neglect on the part of their leaders, and ignored modern management techniques that their Japanese competitors adopted with alacrity. (Laura D'Andrea Tyson and John Zysman, *American Industry in International Competition* [Ithaca, N.Y.: Cornell University Press, 1983], p. 34.)
33. Laura D'Andrea Tyson, "They Are Not Us: Why American Ownership Still Matters," *American Prospect,* no. 4 (Winter 1991), pp. 37–48. Tyson uses some data from the work of Raymond Mataloni, Jr., "U.S. Multinational Companies: Operations in 1988," *Survey of Current Business,* 70 (June 1990), pp. 31–44; and John Dunning, "Multinational Enterprises and the Globalization of Innovatory Capacity," paper presented at University of Reading, September 1990.
34. Tyson, "They Are Not Us."
35. Michael E. Porter, "Competitive Advantage," *Harvard Business Review,* March–April 1990, p. 85. See also Michael E. Porter, *The Competitive Advantage of Nations,* (New York: Free Press, 1990).
36. Sylvia Ostrey, a professor at the University of Toronto and former Canadian trade offi-

cial, calls this "system friction," or friction among the consumer-oriented, short-term pluralist market economy of the U.S., which favors minimal government involvement; the European social market economy, with its extensive government involvement in business as well as the promotion of social welfare; and the Japanese managerial market economy, unique for its long-term, producer orientation, government involvement in business, and ability to weather external shocks. Recognizing that there can never be any true reconciliation of policies among those systems, she calls for greater multilateral cooperation, especially in the area of investment and technology, where "asymmetry of access to investment and technology"—or absence of reciprocity—is becoming a growing political problem. (Sylvia Ostrey, "Technology and the Global Economy: International Responses," unpublished monograph, International Policy Conference, OECD, Montreal, 1991. See also Sylvia Ostrey:, *Governments and Corporations in a Shrinking World* (New York: Council on Foreign Relations, 1990).

17. Who Are the Copy Cats Now?

The Economist

Japan is not just an exporter of cars and video-recorders; it is becoming an exporter of ideas as well. As the charts show, it is no longer merely a borrower of other people's technology. The first chart maps trends in the way Japan's businesses buy foreign technology—through licenses, patent fees, royalties and the like. Payments made by Japan have risen over the past two decades (from $2.7 billion in 1970 to $3 billion in 1985 in constant prices). But in the 1980s Japanese firms have also begun to earn handsome sums in the same way. In relative terms, receipts rose far more, from $373m to $898m in 1970–85. (Japan also now spends less of its research and development budget on foreign ideas.)

The second chart displays some trends in the American patent system. In 1975 65% of new patents in America were for the inventions of Americans; 9% were for the work of Japanese inventors; 8½% Germans; and 7½% British and French inventors combined. In the following decade America's share fell by ten percentage points, to less than 55%. West Germany's share rose a bit, Britain's dropped a bit, and the French stayed much the same. Japan's slice more than doubled to almost 19%. Japanese inventors now own more new patents in America than those from Britain, Germany and France.

Where does the Japanese technology go? The table, produced by matching patent classes with standard industrial classifications, offers some clues. By 1985 Japanese inventions accounted for 20% of new ceramics patents, 23% in primary

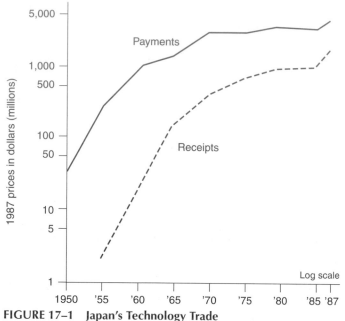

FIGURE 17–1   Japan's Technology Trade
Source: U.S. Department of Commerce; US Patent and Trademark Office;
Bank of Japan

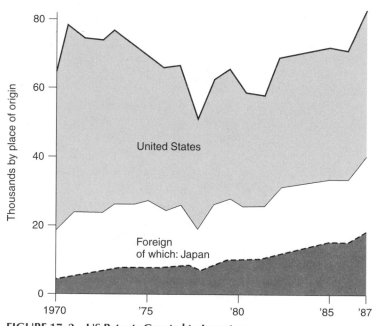

FIGURE 17–2   US Patents Granted to Inventors
Source: U.S. Department of Commerce; US Patent and Trademark Office; Bank
of Japan

TABLE 17–1 Japanese-Invented US Patents		
	SHARE OF TOTAL PATENTS GRANTED %	
SIC CATEGORY	1975	1985
Food	8	11
Textiles	10	17
Chemicals & allied products	10	15
Petroleum	3	6
Rubber	10	18
Ceramics*	8	20
Primary metals	13	23
Fabricated metals	5	12
General machinery	7	15
Office-computing & accounting machines[†]	13	33
Electrical machinery	10	21
Communications equipment & electronic components	13	26
Motor vehicles	7	23
Aircraft & parts	10	30
Professional & scientific instruments	12	23
All fields	9	19

*Stone, clay, and glass products.
[†]Includes computers
Source: National Science Foundation

metals, 26% in communications equipment, 30% in aircraft and their parts, and 33% in office-computing and accounting machines.

Admittedly, patents—and the earnings from them and their kin—are crude measures of how technologically advanced a country is. Take the payments, for example: as Japanese firms have invested abroad in the 1980s, they have used royalties and patent fees to repatriate profits from their plants overseas. That accounts for at least some of the move towards balance.

Patent figures, too, should be treated with caution. Some of the industry-sector figures (aircraft parts, for instance) are suspect, because it is hard to link industrial and patent classifications. Nevertheless, Japanese patents are cited more often than average in later patents—which is reckoned a good indicator of how useful an invention turns out to be.

Whatever the problems of measurement, the direction of change is clear. It is also clear that the change is fast. Buying technology was necessary to help Japan develop in the 1950s and 1960s. As the country's technological prowess grew, those imports became less important. In several areas—textiles, chemicals, iron and steel, motor vehicles—Japan already enjoys a surplus in royalty and fee payments. In short, it is becoming an exporter of technological ideas.

THE MODEL T REVISITED

Do not lose perspective. America still has more scientists and engineers, spends more on research, and publishes more scientific papers than Britain, France, West Germany and Japan put together. Yet the flow of technology is changing direction—from Japan, instead of to it. There are two main reasons why.

• *Riches.* After the second world war America dominated the world's human and capital resources. In the 1950s its command of technological resources began to reflect that fact. Since then the rest of the world has been catching up, first in Europe and later in Asia. Japan's growth has been the most startling. Japanese national income per head in 1968 was a mere 30% of America's; by 1988, it had grown to 120%.

• *Priorities.* Japan has poured money and men into R&D. The number of scientists and engineers per 10,000 people has risen steadily since the early 1960s. In America it peaked in 1969. By 1986 Japan had a higher proportion of its population engaged in R&D than America did. Since the early 1970s Japan has also spent more of its national income on non-military R&D than America.

There is another thing. The distinction between two parts of manufacturing—design and production—is breaking down. For the second time in the twentieth century (the first was the arrival of mass-produced cars in the 1920s), the process of production calls for just as much technological expertise as does the design of a product. For instance, a dozen or so firms around the world have designed prototype four-megabit dynamic random-access memory chips, which will be the next generation of computer memories: the few that manage to perfect the production process will own a secret worth billions of dollars. Production technology is what Japanese companies are especially good at. Luckily for them, it counts for far more in the 1980s than it has done for half a century.

OVERCOMING THE ISLAND SPIRIT

Quick though it has been to acquire technological prowess, Japan is slower to send its new knowledge abroad. One simple reason for this is the complexity of the Japanese language. Relatively few westerners have mastered it—leaving much of Japanese science a distant secret (see box). More than ten times as many Japanese scientists leave home to study than arrive in Japan from abroad. It does not help that Japan's big national universities, with reputations for research, are part of the civil service and do not admit foreigners as faculty members.

Much of Japan's liveliest work is done in corporate laboratories, where staff are hired immediately after graduation and linger until they retire. There is little of the mobility that marks many science careers in the West. Who—outside an inner circle of specialists—could name Japan's equivalent of the West's best pure-research centres, such as AT&T Bell Laboratories in New Jersey, or CERN, the particle-research centre near Geneva? Something similar is true of more down-to-earth commercial technologies. Although Japanese firms send staff abroad to pick up expertise in the research departments of foreign companies—around 100 are at Boeing in America, for example—few foreigners ever penetrate Japanese laboratories.

Japanese companies are undoubtedly reluctant to let their technological secrets fly the coop. Just as reluctantly, though, they are starting to change. Paradoxically, it is the fear of protectionism that has overcome their reluctance. In Asia, Japanese firms have been forced to swap technology for access to markets. The subsidiaries of Japanese companies and joint-venture partners from Bangkok to Taipei are using Japanese technology to make everything from steel to semiconductors, from cars to computers.

TRANSLATE THINE ENEMY

Washington, DC

After the humiliation of Russia's *Sputnik* launch in 1957, the American government gave its own space programme a big kick. It also began to translate Russian scientific journals. Many Washingtonians think something similar should be done to counter the "threat" from Japan. Americans know little about research in Japanese laboratories. That is only partly because of secretiveness. It is also because Americans fail to make use of available information.

There are probably fewer than 1,000 American scientists who speak Japanese. And years of technological superiority have made American managers think of fact-finding trips abroad as little more than paid holidays. More seriously, although the benefits of finding out about some piece of Japanese technology would often outweigh its cost to industry as a whole, sometimes no single firm will find it profitable to do the legwork. Hence the calls for government help.

A paper by Dr. Christopher Hill of the Congressional Research Service, written 18 months ago, offered some rough calculations of what various options might cost.

- Take airmail subscriptions to every Japanese technical journal: $1m a year (there are about 10,000 of them). Translate them all into English: $80m a year. (But it would take 1,000 full-time translators. America does not have that many.)

- Send two engineers in each of 20 specialities to visit five locations abroad; get them to publish reports of what they saw: $2m. Send 100 researchers to Japanese universities or laboratories: $5m a year.

- Give tax credits for such things as translation and Japanese consultants: $50m a year. Set up ten automatic-translation research programmes: $10m.

The National Science Foundation has begun to send a few scientists to Japan. In other respects, progress have been mixed. Some information-brokers are doing well selling raw or processed news about Japanese technology. Others have gone bust. One of the three that closed down in 1988 was the American Electronics Association's newsletter on Japanese electronics. When the AEA wrote to 17,000 of its members advertising the newsletter, it got just 21 orders.

In America and Western Europe the picture is more subtle. To avoid import quotas and high tariffs, Japan's companies have invested far from home. Intended or not, the result is a significant transfer of technology. Take the car business. When Ford set up an American-based joint venture with Mazda, it subcontracted some transmission manufacturing work to the Japanese company. Even though Mazda employees worked from the same blueprints, they churned out better parts. Both firms worked to the same engineering tolerances, but the accuracy of Mazda's machining was higher than specified.

A similar tale comes from Britain. Nissan's plant in Washington, near Newcastle, is shaking up the local car industry, not with new-fangled equipment brought over from Japan, but because Nissan has mastered the management of its manufacturing process.

Or consider the steel industry, where Japanese continuous-casting techniques are giving America's sluggish producers new ideas. (In continuous casting, metal is processed more as it would be on a production line, instead of being made in single ingots that have to be rolled.) National Steel is half-owned by a Japanese company; Kawasaki Steel has bought Armco; several other American steel companies have joint ventures with firms from Japan. As a result, Japan earns more than six times as much in technology fees and royalties in the iron and steel industry than it pays out.

So much for brawny businesses. In the brainy ones, Japanese firms are forced to be open with their technology for a different reason: the high costs of market entry. It can cost several hundred million dollars to set up an advanced chip-manufacturing plant, and not even the biggest Japanese electronics firm dares go it alone. Hitachi is selling Texas Instruments the secrets of how to stack semiconductors on a single silicon chip, not out of altruism, but because it needs Texas Instruments' expertise in other areas, such as software.

REMEMBER MAUDSLEY'S LATHE

Such developments are all very well, a Japanophobe might say, but who did the basic research for these technologies in the first place?

True, America, and probably Western Europe too, are striding comfortably ahead of Japan across the fields of basic (ie, pure) research. But it is not so long ago that Europeans levelled against America the complaints that Americans now aim at Japan. At the Great Exhibition of 1851 British industrialists strolling around the Crystal Palace in London were horrified at the quality of the latest American guns. Unfair, they said. The dastardly colonials were using a British idea (a new lathe designed by a Mr Maudsley) to mill weapons with greater precision than the British. Then they had the cheek to sell Britons the fruits of their own basic research. Later, Britain made similar complaints about radar, penicillin, polyesters, computerised-tomography medical scanners—and much more.

In Japan, as in America in its time, basic research is proving a more delicate flower to cultivate than the hardier plants of industrial R&D. Japan produces less than

9% of the world's scientific literature compared with America's 35%. And the share of Japanese R&D spending devoted to basic research actually declined in the first half of the 1980s, from 15% to 13%.

Here, too, there are signs of change. The structure of university research in Japan remains largely unreformed: the curriculums still encourage people to learn by rote, not to think for themselves; professors are still promoted according to seniority rather than brains. But private companies are beginning to set up more imaginative research laboratories, where employees are encouraged to think beyond the next Walkman model. One such is Canon's laboratory at Atsugi, opened in 1985, which employs 300 people to do largely ruminative work on artificial intelligence, fibre-optic technology, new materials and electronics. It is structured more on (relatively) free-thinking American lines than as a rigid Japanese hierarchy.

Private firms alone cannot transform Japanese research. That will take a new approach to government intervention too, as some Japanese civil servants recognise. No longer can the Ministry of International Trade and Industry (MITI) and the seminationalised telephone company, NTT, marshal temporary consortia to zoom in on hand-picked research programmes. The telephone company is now—at least nominally—a private firm and MITI is not the dragon it was. The industries over which it once held sway (largely by controlling the allocation of capital in the 1950s) were the heavy ones, like steel and shipbuilding, that are now in relative decline. The new industries—semiconductors and biotechnology—have no tradition of obeisance to MITI.

Hauling in technology from abroad and spreading it on domestic industry like imported butter was the old challenge for Japanese policy-makers. The new one is to raise the quality of basic research in permanent organisations (not short-term groupings like MITI's *ad hoc* consortia). And bureaucrats are not the best people to decide where to direct such research.

Nevertheless, progress has been made. The telecommunications ministry has a Key Technologies Programme that has seeded a few permanent research centres. So has the ambitious "fifth-generation" computer project (which was announced as a great leap forward in artificial intelligence and so far is little more than an arthritic hop). Where short-term government projects continue, they are for the first time being opened to foreign companies. IBM is collaborating with ten Japanese firms on an education-ministry project to develop a distributed parallel processor. Four foreign universities have joined the Hayashi subatomic-particle project run by the Science and Technology Agency.

THE ENEMY WITHIN?

Oddly, American policy-makers are looking towards Japan's 1960s-style consortia just when Japan is turning away from them. One example is Sematech, a collection of American firms, partly financed by the federal government, which is supposed to bring America's computer-memory makers back into the market from which Japanese firms drove them in the mid-1980s (largely by investing more and charging less).

Yet Sematech excludes foreign companies from its co-operative research. Given that even its participants think they sometimes need access to foreign technology (witness Texas Instruments' deal with Hitachi), that must be misguided.

In another respect, though, Sematech is spot-on: it is piping government money to civilian rather than explicitly military science. The relationship between technological supremacy and military spending is changing. In the 1960s it was a safe bet that billions of dollars poured into space programmes or new missiles would eventually help American firms in their commercial pursuits. But technology no longer just spins off from military research into the market; often it spins on, in the other direction. High-definition television, designed for film buffs and sharp-eyed *sumo* fans in Japan, will be useful to the next generation of weapons—in, for example, fighter aircraft whose missiles are launched by people using video displays much like those found in arcade games.

Such developments ought to provoke new thoughts about America's spending on military research. Suppose—just suppose—that the billions devoted to defence-related R&D (currently about 30% of all American R&D) do little for American technology off the battlefield. That would be more worrying for America than any threat from the other side of the Pacific.

Part III

State-Market
Tensions Today

Part III applies many of the approaches, themes, and concepts dealt with in the first two parts of the reader to different nations and groups of nations. State-market relations are organized differently among the nations of the European Union (EU), the North American Free Trade Area (NAFTA), Japan and the United States, and the nations currently involved in the transition from communism to capitalism or some other sort of national political economy. Members of the EU and NAFTA are also involved in integrating their economies and political systems to some extent.

The growth and success of the EU is due in part to the willful policies of its leaders in using the benefits of freer and more efficient markets to help member nations overcome the forces of history, culture, and nationalism that have historically divided them. In the 1990s, the EU has achieved great success, expanding to 15 member states in 1995 with a long list of other nations knocking on the door, applications in hand. It would be easy for EU leaders to be smug and complacent now. This would be a mistake, *The Economist* argues in "Survey: The European Union." The EU faces real challenges in both its economic and political spheres. Europe must find ways to improve both its system of markets and its system of democracy if it is to realize in the long run more economic gains. All of today's problems will be compounded as the EU grows eastward in the future, encompassing the formerly communist states of eastern and central Europe.

Contrary to the optimistic outlook of *The Economist,* Godfrey Hodgson is not so sanguine about the future of the EU. In "Grand Illusion," Hodgson outlines many of the issues that stand to divide EU officials and undermine the European consciousness of people. Hodgson argues that economics cannot overcome the political divisiveness. Although the common objective of standing strong against communism went a long way in holding EU members together until the late 1980s, the expense associated with unifying Germany, growing numbers of immigrants throughout the EU, and failure to deal with war in the former Yugoslavia threaten to pull it apart. Hodgson does not rule out the possibility of economic success for the EU "if" the right decisions are made, but he worries that failure of officials to generate significant economic growth throughout the EU heightens the possibility that integration will give way to disintegration.

Another attack on economic liberal ideas is made by Collingsworth, Goold, and Harvey in their short piece "Time for a Global New Deal." Whereas liberals usually praise integrative efforts in the EU, NAFTA, and GATT, Collingsworth et al. view these and other developments through largely structuralist lenses. They are critical of the extent to which the international production structure is now dominated by multinational corporations, whose efforts to generate wealth have resulted in exploiting cheap labor in developing nations. Collingsworth et al. reject arguments about free trade and want the United States to lead a global effort to support new social legislation that protects the rights of workers the world over. International competition should not be allowed to drive workers' wages below minimum standards of living. Drawing on the analogy of the U.S. New Deal legislation of the 1930s and also some of the ideas of Keynes, Collingsworth et al. contend that such legislation will not only improve wages and working conditions but also increase the purchasing power of the poor. New global standards for workers everywhere, but in LDCs especially, promise to generate more economic growth throughout the world.

The role of Japan in the international political economy is a hotly debated topic. Many have speculated that Japan will become the next global economic hegemon and even a military hegemon to complement its financial power and influence. Takashi Inoguchi explores four possible international and complementary roles Japan might adopt in the next 25 to 50 years. He outlines some of the attitudes and opinions of the Japanese people. His argument is that Japan is not likely to, nor does it desire to, become a hegemon of the stature of Great Britain or the United States (i.e., Pax Nipponica). Japan's domestic social, political, and economic problems are likely to constrain it in the near future.

The transition from classical socialism (or communism as it is often called) to capitalism or market socialism is more than a change in systems of IPE; it is also a change in the fundamental conditions of life for the millions of people who are affected. In his *Foreign Affairs* article titled "Russia's Work Ethic," Kyril Tidmarsh considers the effects of 70 years of communist rule and central control on the work ethic and psychology of Russian workers. Have Russians forgotten how to work? Can they adapt, in a reasonable period of time, to the conditions of Western-style markets? Will they be able to take responsibility for their own actions? The answers to these questions are critical, Tidmarsh argues, for both Russian capitalism and—perhaps more important—for Russian democracy.

China has the longest experience in liberal market reforms among the Communist nations, and has achieved, some would argue, the best results. In recent years, however, China has moved toward much more radical market reform. China's reform program has been acceptable and feasible, according to Fan Gang of the Chinese Academy of Sciences. In his essay "Dual-Track Transitions in China" from the European journal *Economic Policy,* Fan argues that China's pattern of economic reforms that mix elements of socialism with economic liberal-market policies and strategies has recently been tailored to China's specific needs. Shock therapy would have been unacceptable in earlier years, but a continued policy of gradual transformation of the economy is unacceptable now. The reader is challenged to consider whether China's success provides insights that can be transferred to other states and markets in transition.

18. The European Union

The Economist

FAMILY FRICTIONS

It is easy to caricature the European Union: a dozen countries squabbling over subsidies, 18,000 Brussels bureaucrats quarrelling over perks and 567 Strasbourg parliamentarians moaning about their relative lack of power and fame. Meanwhile, even as economies switch from recession to recovery, a tenth of the EU'S workers remain without jobs. No wonder that in June's elections for the European Parliament, the turn-out (despite compulsory voting in three EU countries) was barely 56%. An opinion poll this summer suggested that only one in two Europeans thought their countries had benefited from EU membership. A cynic might well ask: if this union did not exist, would anyone bother to invent it?

Actually, yes. There are perfectly sound reasons for Europe's nations to join together. As a Belgian prime minister, Théo Lefèvre, once pointed out in a cutting reference to fading imperial powers: "In Western Europe there are now only small countries—those that know it and those that don't know it yet." Some 31 years later that argument for collective strength applies just as much to the countries of Central and Eastern Europe, freed from communism and now queuing up to join the EU.

Why, then, the caricature? One reason is cultural: the free-trading British and some others mistrust the expensive interventionism of the agricultural and regional policies of the European Union (as the European Community declared itself to be when members signed the Maastricht treaty in 1992). A union in which some contribute much more than others, and receive much less in return, seems wrong to them. A second reason is popular bewilderment. If politicians stumble over the arithmetic of "qualified-majority voting" and the "blocking minority", and if Eurocrats have trouble working out the minutiae of the common agricultural policy, what chance has the man on the Paris metro? It is easier to lampoon than to understand.

But the biggest reason is that Europe's leaders promised what they could not deliver. The "single market," with the economy-boosting free flow of capital, goods, people and services, opened on January 1st last year, only to coincide with the worst recession since the 1930s. The "common foreign and security policy," launched by the Maastricht treaty, was mocked by Bosnian blood shed on the EU's doorstep. And the Maastricht journey towards "economic and monetary union" (EMU, in the EU's acronymic jargon for the achievement of a single European currency) was abruptly sidetracked—not least by high German interest rates, which made Europe's economic troubles worse. Add the painful process by which the German parliament, the last to act among the 12 national parliaments, ratified the Maastricht treaty in October last year, and even the most gung-ho Euro-enthusiasts feel somewhat abashed.

Perhaps that is why the quarrels over Europe's post-Maastricht future are becoming so ugly, two years ahead of a special intergovernmental conference on the subject. There is talk of a two-tier European Union, of "concentric circles" of commitment, of multi-tracks and multi-speeds, of some countries "being more equal than others". Is this grand endeavour doomed to disintegrate under the strains of its own diverging ambitions?

Such questions would be less troubling if Europe felt more confident. After the dismal recession of the early 1990s, most EU economies are rebounding. France and Germany, for example, are having to double the cautious growth predictions for 1994 that they made in January. Yet still the gloom lingers. The main reason for this is that recovery is shortening dole queues by barely a smidgen (see Figure 18–1); and half of the queues consist of people jobless for more than a year.

When that dismal record is compared with the job-creating records of America and Japan, even the most arrogant Eurocrat or government minister must worry about the future. Last December the European Commission (the EU's executive) issued a special report on growth, competitiveness and employment. This quickly provoked responses from virtually every government and industrial lobby. But there is no miracle cure for Europe's joblessness short of thinning the welfare cushion that makes unemployment preferable to many sorts of work. The unemployed might then price

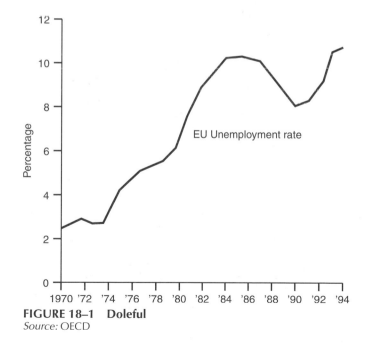

FIGURE 18–1   Doleful
Source: OECD

TABLE 18–1   Cushy Numbers

INDICATORS OF QUALITY OF LIFE, LATEST	EU	UNITED STATES	JAPAN
GDP per head, $	17,978	24,601	33,908
Total education expenditure, as % of GDP	5.3	7.0	5.0
Working hours per year	1,771	1,945	2,017
Unemployment benefits, as % of government spending	3.3	1.5	0.7
Life expectancy, years	76.3	75.6	78.6
TVs, per 100 people	44	81	62
Homicides, by males, per 100,000 males	1.6	12.4	0.9

Sources: UN; IMD: World Economic Forum

themselves into some kind of job. And even this hard-headed logic can work only up to a point. Already Europe's big cities are scarred by ghettoes of the unemployed, un-educated and disaffected—an "underclass-in-waiting," the politicians fear, if Europe deflates the welfare cushion too far and too fast.

Just as there is no miracle cure, perhaps there is no painless one either. Euro-peans take for granted a quality of life that many others might envy (see Table 18–1). GDP per head is generally higher in America and Japan, but few Europeans believe that America's extra purchasing power makes up for its horrendous murder rate, or that Japan's is adequate compensation for what Sir Roy Denman, a now-retired Eu-rocrat, once described as "living in rabbit hutches." What sensible Parisian or Roman office worker would envy his job-insecure counterpart in crime-ridden Washington, DC, or the exhausted *sarariman* making his daily two-hour commute to central Tokyo?

The question is how to sustain Europe's quality of life. Unfortunately for the German car worker, with his six weeks' holiday a year, or the disabled Belgian who receives benefits equal to 97% of the average industrial wage, many trends in pro-ductivity, unemployment, debt and demography are working against their interests.

A JOB-DESTROYING MACHINE

Margaret Thatcher will never find a place in a pantheon of the EU's champions. That will be reserved for "true Europeans", such as Messrs Monnet, Adenauer, De Gasperi, Delors, Kohl and Mitterrand. The Iron Lady may have impressed with her intelli-gence (Jacques Delors, president of the European Commission, admits his admira-tion for Britain's prime minister of the 1980s), but she dismayed with her handbag-waving pursuit of narrowly defined national interests. If she is happy to be rid of Brussels (the derisive shorthand for the EU's affairs and institutions), the feeling is re-ciprocated.

Even so, future historians may yet place Lady Thatcher on an EU honour roll. After all, it was she who insisted on counting every ecu that went into and out of the community's budget, so highlighting which countries were net contributors and which net beneficiaries. Moreover, it was her Micawberish determination to balance Britain's own books and lessen the role of the state that spawned privatisation programmes across the whole of the union and beyond. Even the *dirigiste* French now sometimes praise market forces and the reduction of government spending as though they mean it. Much of the Thatcherite message has become Europe's conventional wisdom.

But in the end Europe would have got the message even without Mrs Thatcher. The countries of Europe are, quite simply, living beyond their means. Social benefits, from family allowances and unemployment assistance to sickness pay and old-age pensions, are paid for by taxation and corporate earnings. If tax rates are too high, corporate earnings could fall and workers be laid off, meaning that tax revenues would flag or even fall—so tax rates would have to rise even higher. Individuals can try to escape from this vicious circle through the black economy: let no taxman benefit from bargains struck between willing householders and willing window-cleaners. Employers can seek refuge by laying off workers or moving their businesses to a friendlier country.

The escape route of governments, however, is to borrow, and this produces a second vicious circle of tax revenues being used to service the public debt instead of to build roads, hospitals and schools. When the Maastricht treaty set out the route towards a single currency, one of the signposts was that a country's gross public debt should not exceed 60% of its GDP. Belgium's level last year was almost 150%; Greece's almost 110%; Italy's almost 120%. Those numbers are signs not so much of recent recession but of prolonged irresponsibility. The governments of all three countries are having to make annual interest payments on their debt equivalent to at least a tenth of their GDP (see Figure 18–2).

To escape through borrowing is a mere illusion, and the longer it is indulged the more damaging it becomes. Any Cassandra can see that over time a country's interest rates will have to rise, its infrastructure will deteriorate and its quality of life will gradually decline. Is that to be Europe's fate?

The real escape would be to find ways of helping Europe's jobless back to work. As the social costs of unemployment fell, tax revenues would rise and tax rates could fall, and happy employers would make bigger profits and so bigger investments. That virtuous circle, however, is hard to create.

To Thwart Cassandra

One reason is that governments have to live with the mistakes of their predecessors. In Italy those predecessors—a succession of venal, Christian Democrat-dominated coalitions—handed out state pension-rights like confetti. Italy's pensioners (almost a quarter of them claiming disability pensions) now soak up two-fifths of government spending. If the government of Silvio Berlusconi is to fulfil its promise to cut both debt and tax, it must reduce spending on pensions and on other aspects of a generous welfare state. Yet Mr Berlusconi was told in June by the Constitutional Court

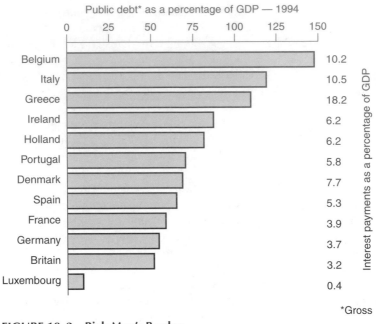

FIGURE 18–2   **Rich Man's Burden**
Sources: OECD; European Commission

that he could not renege on $19 billion-worth of unpaid state pensions. And because Italy has the world's lowest fertility rate, the number of pensioners will grow faster than the number of workers whose efforts support them.

Italy's problems are bad but not unique. Statutory charges on labour—that is, the sum of taxes and obligatory social-security contributions—now account for around two-fifths of the EU'S GDP. In 1970, they took just over a third. By comparison, the proportion in America has remained stable at just below 30%, and in Japan it has risen from just under 20% to just over 30%. One reason for the proportional increase in Europe is that economic growth has slowed. But—welcome to another vicious circle—a cause of that slowdown has in turn been the burden on employment and wealth creation of the statutory charges. Businessmen are deterred from investing and hiring by the extra cost.

Changes in the demographic profile will make the burden still heavier. At the moment every 100 European workers are supporting almost 40 retired people; in ten years' time, unless unemployment falls dramatically, this grey pressure on the workforce will rise, to almost 50 pensioners per 100 workers. No wonder EU governments are trying to stabilise or cut back on statutory charges as a proportion of GDP, for example by raising retirement ages (as in Italy) or by changing the rules (as in Britain) for inflation-linked pensions or by encouraging greater reliance on private pensions.

Enter Delors

All of which is expressed in admirable detail in that special report on growth, competitiveness and employment—commonly known as "the Delors white paper"—which was laid before last December's Brussels summit of Europe's heads of government, and portentously subtitled "the challenges and ways forward into the 21st century."

The stark conclusion of the white paper and other reports is that Europe's taxes, social obligations and rising real wages—plus the high interest rates that resulted from the cost of German unification—have combined to stretch public finances, reduce corporate profits, constrain investment and inhibit the creation of jobs. Comparisons with America and Japan reveal a Europe that is singularly bad at creating employment even when its economies are booming. Over the past three decades, as America was adding to its store of jobs at a rate of 1.8% a year, the countries of the EU were managing an annual average growth of just 0.24%. In the past two decades America has created 30m private-sector jobs, Europe just over 10m (see Figure 18–3).

Even in the second half of the 1980s, a boom period when Europe had recovered from the oil shocks of the 1970s and was investing for the impending "single market", the number of jobs rose by only 1.3% a year. That meant that even though Europe created 9m new jobs (mostly in the public sector), its unemployment rate fell

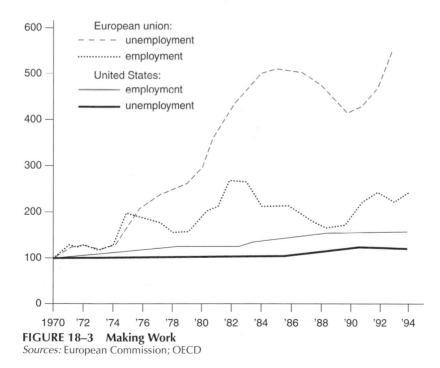

FIGURE 18–3 Making Work
Sources: European Commission; OECD

from its 1985 peak of 10.8% to a still dismal 8.3% in 1990. Today the EU is back on that nasty peak with around 18m people, more than a tenth of the workforce, looking (at least in theory) for jobs. By contrast, America's jobless rate is about 6% and Japan's 3%.

You might conclude that Europe has a lot to learn from both America and Japan. Yet it is understandably reluctant to imitate what it sees. Japan has a culture of life-time employment (now eroding) and a willingness to accept wafer-thin profit margins and tiny share dividends. For its part, America's capitalism is too raw for most European stomachs. Whereas article 2 of the Maastricht treaty specifically calls for "a high level of employment and of social protection," the American model combines a high level of employment with a low level of social protection. The result is that an American in the bottom tenth of the workforce earns less than two-fifths of median pay; his European counterpart earns more than two-thirds.

Britain's Conservative government may find inspiration in the American way—on the grounds that a low-paid job is better than no job at all—but the EU's other governments tend to shudder. Continental Europeans cherish the concept of "solidarity", the notion, held by Socialists and Christian Democrats alike, that people have a moral duty to help each other. To them, the American way smacks of an unnecessary drive to "align our costs on those of our competitors in the developing countries: socially unacceptable and politically untenable," in the words of the white paper.

What, then, is the remedy? The white paper's prescription mixes a dose of Adam Smith, a touch of Colbert and a hint of central planning. Let there be deregulated labour markets, lower taxes on labour and less profligate social spending—but also government-encouraged research into areas of high technology and a government-commanded infrastructure policy to create "trans-European networks" (TENS) of motorways, railways, energy pipelines and telecommunications links. Let there also, in order simultaneously to make up for the lost taxes on labour and to protect the environment, be new taxes on energy use.

Mix and Match

Whether such a cocktail can be swallowed in one go is perhaps irrelevant. The point is that it contains at least one ingredient for every taste. The British will savour the stress on deregulation, the French the emphasis on high-speed railways, businessmen the stress on telecommunicating "superhighways," and so on. Politically, Mr Delors's white paper is superbly adroit, not least in the way that it preserves a strong role—in co-ordinating the TENS, for example—for the European Commission.

That may sound somewhat snide. But the sneers will increase if the financial arithmetic goes astray. The white paper talks of financing needs that amount to 400 billion ecus ($492 billion) over the next 15 years, including by the end of this century 200 billion ecus for transport projects and 30 billion ecus for energy networks. Mr Delors argues that such amounts can be raised easily, since much of the money is already there in the spending plans of member countries, and the private sector will happily provide the lion's share of what is not. But the figures are large enough to alarm the EU's finance ministers—who have vetoed Mr Delors's plan for the commission to issue "Union bonds" (a clever ploy to increase the Commission's power) to help pay for the TENS. As for the private sector, the example of building a tunnel between England and France is one that will persuade most companies to proceed with caution.

It is possible to cavil at many bits of the white paper. Europe's industrialists, for example, reckoning that their energy bills are already on average 33% higher than in America, are particularly upset by the proposed energy taxes. But if the union is to fulfil the potential of its single market, it needs to make a bigger collective investment in infrastructure. The finance ministers may worry, but Mr Delors is adept at outflanking them. In June, at their summit in Corfu, the union's heads of government turned visionary and approved an early start for the first 11 transport projects, and an urgent examination of nine "priority" energy schemes. The challenge now is for Europe's industrialists and businessmen to seize the opportunity.

A QUESTION OF CULTURE

Carving gracefully through the dazzling sky of south-west France, an Airbus A340 is put through its paces. On the tarmac, other aircraft, slim A320s and bulky A310s, listen in their fresh airline liveries, newly rolled out from the hangers that contain yet more airframes in various states of completion. The spirit of corporate pride at Airbus's Toulouse headquarters is almost tangible: Airbus aircraft are glamorous symbols of effective European co-operation in high technology.

The feeling is much the same thousands of miles away on America's Pacific coast: a new Boeing 777 climbs on its test flight high above Seattle; the 747s—the original jumbo-jets—roll profitably off the Everett assembly line; and the workforce applauds yet more examples of America's high-tech superiority. And the passengers for these aircraft? Whether they fly in a Boeing or an Airbus, few will notice any difference.

If they are European taxpayers, perhaps they should. Airbus is constituted under French law as a *Groupement d'Intérêt Economique,* which means that its accounts are available only to its four shareholders: France's state-owned Aérospatiale and Germany's Deutsche Aerospace Airbus (each with a 37.9% holding); privatised British Aerospace (20%); and Spain's state-owned CASA (4.2%). Whereas Boeing's profitability is a matter of public record ($1.2 billion net profit last year on revenues of $25.4 billion), Airbus's is invisible, hidden in the books of its shareholders. How, then, does one judge the success of Europe's best-known high-technology consortium?

By the amount of its subsidies, say Boeing folk, whose guesstimates start at $26 billion. By the excellence of the products and their share of the market, counters the team in Toulouse, adding that Boeing has enjoyed subsidies of its own from defence-contracting and federal research projects.

Both sides have a point. Since its first airliner entered service 20 years ago, Airbus has gained 30% of the market, compared with Boeing's 60%; in the next decade

Airbus hopes to win a 50% share. Given that Boeing is America's single biggest exporter and that 80% of Airbus sales are beyond the national boundaries of its shareholders, the argument is a constant irritant in transatlantic relations—the Americans and Europeans are, indeed, still quarrelling over a subsidies agreement concluded two years ago.

Over time, the subsidies issue may fade. Airbus is making profits on its A320 and may well do so on other models, too. Moreover, aerospace is a murky and incestuous world: probably half of any Airbus by value will go to contractors and engine makers in America, and they can lobby Washington as much as Boeing can. The real issue is whether Airbus's progress has been worth the taxpayers' investment. Lady Thatcher always had her doubts—but in the end her government, like its predecessor, stumped up the necessary "launch aid." By contrast, the Germans had rather fewer misgivings, and the French and Spanish none at all.

Some will say the difference is yet another example of Anglo-Saxon perversity, forgetting that Lady Thatcher's predecessors, both Labour and Conservative, were often very willing to pour the state's money into industrial ventures. In fact, the difference was doctrinal: Thatcherism decreed that governments had no business picking industrial winners—not least because, the Airbus example notwithstanding, they usually picked losers.

That Thatcherite dogma was surely right. The sectors in which Europe leads or matches the rest of the world—pharmaceuticals, retailing, fashion, recorded music—are precisely those in which governments have interfered least. Where they have interfered most, they have usually failed. Look at Europe's history of loss-making state-owned airlines and steel companies, or at Groupe Bull, France's struggling, state-controlled computer maker. Some inefficient state companies, such as Belgium's telephone utility, have made profits—but only by being monopolies. And some state companies, such as France Télécom, have given good service—but at prices which would have been too high in a free market.

Perhaps the dogma is a mite simplistic: some transport economists argue that the heavily subsidised French rail system is a much better deal for French taxpayers than the lightly subsidised British system is for British ones. Meanwhile, Airbus apologists will argue that it is a special case: aerospace is a business with lots of high-tech spin-offs, plenty of "value-added," and significant for defence.

Maybe. But it is worth remembering that aerospace sales are smaller than those of, say, cigarettes. In order to prosper, Europe needs to compete across the board, and grow new firms and industries. Ron Woodard, president of Boeing's Commercial Airplane Group, notes that the net worth of Bill Gates's Microsoft, a software company that did not even exist 20 years ago, is bigger than Boeing's, and yet "you could put all their assets in one of our parking lots."

It is a good point. Europe's real problem is that it has no Microsofts, even though European brains are presumably as good as American ones, and its schools are arguably better. Why is Palo Alto in California crammed with the "start-up" companies that may provide tomorrow's Microsoft or Intel, while France's Sophia Antipolis science park, nestling in pine-clad hills just above the Côte d'Azur, is still struggling after 25 years to produce a home-grown Apple alongside such foreign residents as AT&T and Digital Equipment Corporation?

The answer is not an absence of raw material. Europe is full of small and medium-sized enterprises, ie, those with fewer than 500 employees. The European Commission reckons they provide 70% of EU jobs, including 29% provided by firms with fewer than ten employees. In the computer business there are almost 6,000 small companies. Yet somehow it is hard to see them sprouting rapidly to become the size of Microsoft, Apple or Compaq.

As for Europe's bigger computer companies, such as Italy's Olivetti and Germany's Siemens Nixdorf, they are having a hard time adjusting to a slowing market. As one EU official publication delicately puts it: "The key weakness in Europe seems to lie in its inability to integrate research, development and innovation in an overall strategy which both exploits and orients them." That sentence could have been written for Philips of Holland: a brilliant innovator of electronic gadgets which others, notably the Japanese, have then gone on to exploit more successfully.

The Wrong Mood

The explanation for this mismatch of talent and commercial success lies in a mix of history, geography and culture. For all its size, America has a common language and a well-defined view of the way the world should work. The "American dream" inspires New Yorkers in the same way as Los Angelenos. If you fail with one American start-up, then you move on to another. By contrast, the EU is a patchwork of individual nations, with different cultural values from one another—if your European start-up fails, don't bother to try again—and mutually incomprehensible languages (nine official ones at the moment, with more to come).

One result is that while a Californian whizz-kid, of whom there are many, will face few obstacles in selling to Floridians, his Danish equivalent, a rare species, will have real problems in selling to Italians. And despite a wave of privatisations, the age of national champions in Europe is not quite over: France seems obsessed with keeping Groupe Bull alive; Italy protects private-sector Fiat by limiting Japanese car imports; almost every government, except the holier-than-thou British (who privatised British Airways a decade ago), protects and subsidises its flag-carrying airline.

If the European Union lived up to its political rhetoric, none of this would be happening. State aids would be disappearing; national borders would no longer equal market borders; and Europe's inherent creativity would be inspiring entrepreneurs by the thousand. Unfortunately, rhetoric and reality have yet to coincide.

A SINGULAR MARKET

Free movement for Europe's workers, goods, services and money—if there is one thing that squabbling Europeans can always agree on it is the importance of the "single market." And rightly so. A union that has internal frontiers is both a contradiction in terms and, since more trade creates more wealth, an economic opportunity forgone.

Hence a lingering mood of celebration. From January 1st last year, Europe's internal barriers (but for a few "temporary" exceptions) have disappeared: Spanish lorry drivers who once needed 70 forms to cross a frontier can now truck oranges to Holland unhindered by customs officers and border police; German banks can open branches in Italy; Greek students can attend Danish universities as of right. From January 1st this year these same freedoms of the EU's single market have been extended to Austria, Finland, Iceland, Norway and Sweden to form the European Economic Area (add EEA to the list of acronyms). The result is a market more populous than America's, more valuable than China's.

Fine, except that it has all taken so long; that the freedoms are not fully exploited; and that so many in the union still try to limit the market's potential.

The four freedoms of the single market are part of the 1957 Treaty of Rome, establishing what was then called the European Economic Community, with its "common market". Unhappily there remained an uncommon number of differing technical standards, incompatible taxes and laws, close relationships between governments and their national companies: even without tariffs and quotas, protectionism still flourished at the ultimate expense of consumers.

The desire to end that protectionism is enshrined in the Single European Act, agreed in 1985 "with the aim of progressively establishing the internal market" over a period expiring at the end of 1992. The momentum owed much to the determination and vision of Jacques Delors, newly arrived as commission president; but also to the nitpicking efficiency of Lord Cockfield, a British commissioner who listed and relentlessly pursued 300 actions (later consolidated into 282 pieces of legislation) that had to be accomplished by member governments to establish a single market.

Has it all paid off? Up to a point, certainly. Intra-EU trade as a proportion of all EU countries' trade has risen from just over half in 1985 to around three-fifths today: take in the whole of the EEA and the proportion rises to more than two-thirds. German students now escape overcrowded lecture halls at home by attending universities in Britain; north European pensioners retire in the sunny south. Only Britain, Ireland and—at least for the moment—Denmark still insist on frontier checks on EU visitors. Cross-frontier mergers and acquisitions (a simple way of exploiting the single market) rose from 2,190 in 1987 to 4,553 in 1992.

Yet the single market has fallen disappointingly short of its original expectations. In 1988 one lot of experts convened by the European Commission was predicting that the single market in its first five or six years would lower the EU's prices by 6%, create 2m new jobs, increase output by 4.5% and "put Europe on an upward trajectory of economic growth into the next century." There is still time for this body, the Cecchini committee, to be proved right; but in the single market's first year the EU's GDP shrank by 0.3% and its unemployment rose to 10.5% of the workforce. Meanwhile, some of the best business users of Europe's single market have been non-Europeans— Japan's car makers and electronics companies, for example, or a whole swathe of Americans, selling everything from IBM computers to McDonalds hamburgers.

The disappointment should not really be a surprise. For Europe's smaller companies the barriers of different languages and legal systems remain daunting. So, too, does the amount of paperwork. Customs formalities may have disappeared for lorry drivers. But until 1997, when value-added tax on goods is supposed to be charged in their country of origin rather than, as now, in the country of final sale, the paperwork of VAT charges and VAT refunds remains a nightmare. And in the absence of a single currency there are still exchange-rate risks in venturing from home. Whatever the potential of an unfamiliar pan-European market, many a small company is bound to prefer to opt for the comfort of a familiar national one.

That choice is unavailable to non-Europeans, some of whom had started seeing Europe as a single market long before Mr. Delors arrived in Brussels. Ford of Europe, for example, was created by joining Ford's British and German subsidiaries as long ago as 1967 (when de Gaulle was still resolutely blocking Britain's membership of the European Community). But enthusiasm on a large scale came in the late 1980s when foreign firms could suddenly foresee a Europe free of national protectionism. Japan's direct investments in Europe amounted between 1970 and 1984 to $8.8 billion; from 1985 to 1993, they totalled $74.6 billion (see Figure 18–4).

About two-fifths of those Japanese investments went to Britain: a Nissan factory in the north of England, a Toyota one in Derbyshire, a Sony plant in Wales. Why Britain? In a survey this year by the Japan Institute for Overseas Investment, by far the main reason given by the investors themselves was the English language, better understood by Japanese managers than any other European language and familiar also from Japanese plants in America. Yet some Europeans cite another reason—

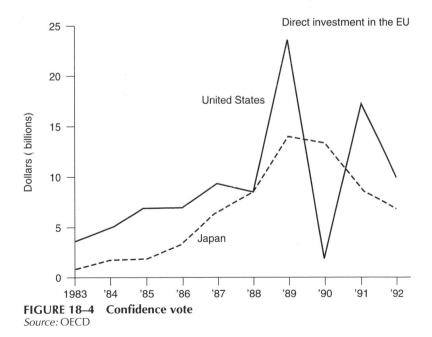

FIGURE 18–4   Confidence vote
Source: OECD

Britain's willingness, with financial incentives for foreign investors, to be the "Trojan horse" by means of which Europe's rivals will invade its fortress.

Unfair Competition

This accusation, with its implicit nationalism, illustrates the greatest problem for the single market: the readiness of member governments to conspire against their own creation.

At one level, this conspiracy consists of agreed delays in the single market: no free trade in insurance until July this year; none in investment services until January 1996; no compulsion to liberalise basic telephone services until 1998 (and up to five years later in poorer countries, so as to protect utilities such as Greece's from being crushed by the likes of Britain's BT or America's AT&T).

At another level, there are convenient parliamentary delays. Of the 282 measures needed to create the single market, some 222 have to be "transposed" into legislation in the member countries. The commission may boast that 87% of the necessary national laws have been passed, but only half of the 222 measures have been passed by all 12 member states. While the Danes and British have been the most active legislators, the Greeks, French, Spanish and Irish have been rather slower. The delays could, of course, be innocent. But cynics note that the worst ones are in public procurement, where by the end of 1993 only 59% of required national laws had been passed; company law (60%); intellectual and industrial property, such as designs, inventions and databases (61%); and insurance (73%).

Delays of this sort cost taxpayers dear: in public procurement, for example, which was worth some 595 billion ecus in 1990, the last year for which figures are available, the Cecchini report calculated that open competition could be saving member countries some 21 billion ecus a year. And yet the non-national share of contracts is stuck at 5% in public services and even less in public works. Worse still, few unsuccessful bidders complain, for fear that they would be ignored in future bids.

But the greatest insult to a free and single market remains the use of state aid. Provided it does not distort competition, this is allowed by the Treaty of Rome but it is perennially open to abuse—witness the loss-making survival of national airlines and state-owned makers of steel, ships and cars. What makes the abuse all the easier is that the treaty in effect condones the existence of state monopolies: telecommunications, postal services, energy and transport are all "reserved sectors."

Even in cases where monopolies have been legislated away, the market can be manipulated. From the beginning of last year Europe's airlines have been free to fly where, when and at what prices they want, save only for "cabotage" (the right to fly domestic routes in a foreign country)—and even that restriction will be gone by April 1997. Theoretically, therefore, Europe's skies are now as free and competitive as America's. And yet governments protect their national carriers both by restricting foreign airlines' access to their airports and by pressing the European Commission to approve yet more state aid for airlines that in a free market would go out of business. It is a form of blackmail: if the subsidies are not approved, then thousands will be made redundant, governments will be under pressure and life will be made very uncomfortable for independent-minded commissioners.

With suitable promises to restructure the airline so that it will supposedly never need another subsidy, the blackmail usually works. In July the commission approved $7.1 billion in state aid to Air France, TAP of Portugal and Olympic of Greece. Herman De Croo, head of a committee that had advised the commission to be stricter with subsidies and link them explicitly to privatisation, reckons that commission approval since August 1991 has added up to $10.35 billion in airline subsidies—"roughly $10m a day". Against this background, advocates of a single, free-trading European market may be tempted to despair.

They should not, for three reasons. The first is that state sectors, and therefore state subsidies, are getting smaller and will get smaller still—if only because privatisation and budgetary discipline can hardly be avoided by governments attempting to meet the Maastricht treaty's criteria for economic and monetary union. The second is that rules for the single market are decided not by unanimity among Europe's governments, but by qualified majority voting—so the illiberal will find it harder to defy the liberal, assuming the liberal are in a majority. The third is that market forces, once unleashed, are hard to resist. Assume success for commission plans to liberalise telecommunications and postal services and introduce competition into energy markets, and Europe as a giant zone of truly free trade will finally have arrived. The European Union's challenge, however, is to make itself into something rather bigger than that. . . .

1996 AND ALL THAT

Variable geometry, multi-track, multi-speed, two-tier, hard core, concentric circles, à la carte, deepening, widening . . . More than ever, Europe's politicians are mixing their metaphors.

The confusion stems from the part of the Maastricht treaty that calls for a conference of member states in 1996 "to examine those provisions of this Treaty for which revision is provided, in accordance with the objectives set out in Articles A and B." Those objectives are economic and monetary union, "ultimately including a single currency;" a common foreign and security policy, "which might in time lead to a common defence;" and "close co-operation on justice and home affairs."

These are big ambitions. The job of the 1996 intergovernmental conference is to correct any mistakes the Maastricht drafters may have made in the "process of creating an ever closer union among the peoples of Europe." Since there are some profound disagreements over what this union should mean, the 1996 debate could be extremely lively.

Why then has it started prematurely? The best explanation is that Germany, which now holds the six-month rotating presidency of the union, has a vision of an expanding, federalist Europe for which it feels that national electorates, and fellow governments, need to be prepared. After all, one lesson of the Maastricht process—

shown by the wafer-thin referendum majority in France in 1992 and the need for Denmark to hold a second referendum in 1993—is that Europe's leaders can easily misread the public mood. Even those who do not share Germany's vision will concede that some kind of EU reform is inevitable.

Age Limits

As presently constituted, the EU can barely cope with the present, let alone the future. Bear in mind that this is a club of unequals. Member states range from unified Germany, with 80m people, to tiny Luxembourg with a mere 395,000. They range in wealth from Denmark, with a GDP per head of over 21,000 ecus, to Greece, with about 7,500 ecus. Now look at three main institutions.

The commission is a body of permanent civil servants and government appointees which administers EU business and proposes and drafts legislation. The Council of Ministers, attended by appropriate government ministers from the member countries, is the EU's legislature, the only one in the democratic world which normally deliberates in secret. The European Parliament, which holds its committee meetings in Brussels but its plenary sessions in Strasbourg, is the one EU body directly elected by the union's citizens and yet has few of the powers of any national parliament and counts for less than either the council or the commission.

This structure was designed for a club of six, and it has just about coped with the doubling to 12. But how can it deal, the rule-book unchanged, with a club that in the next two decades could expand to a membership of a score or more?

The bigger the club, the tougher it will be to maintain an acceptable balance between large countries and small. Of the six founding members, France, West Germany and Italy had big populations; Holland, Belgium and Luxembourg small ones. Today the big members have been joined by Britain, with Spain close behind, and the small countries have been bolstered by Ireland, Denmark, Greece and Portugal. Harmony of sorts is maintained by a system of checks and balances: big countries have more votes in the Council of Ministers so that they cannot be out-voted by a gaggle of small ones. In turn, small countries are protected by a system of weighted voting. Of the council's 76 votes, 54 are currently needed to form a "qualified," or decisive, majority—and only 23 are therefore needed to form a blocking minority.

So far, so good. The present arithmetic means that the big five, with 48 votes between them and representing four-fifths of the union's population, can muster a qualified majority only if they gain the support of at least two small states. Similarly, to get their way the small states need the backing of three big states. Conversely, two big countries can form a blocking minority if they can get the support of any small country other than Luxembourg. Roughly speaking, a qualified majority normally represents 70% of the EU'S people, a blocking minority 30%.

The problem is the future. From January 1st the EU is supposed to grow, by four more countries, to 16 members. Extend the arithmetic and the qualified majority will go up to 64 votes out of 90 (see Table 18–2); and the blocking minority to

TABLE 18–2   Little and Large

1994	POPULATION EST. M	VOTES IN COUNCIL
Germany	81.6	10
Britain	58.2	10
Italy	58.1	10
France	58.0	10
Spain	39.2	8
Holland	15.4	5
Greece	10.5	5
Belgium	10.1	5
Portugal	9.4	5
Sweden	8.8	4
Austria	8.0	4
Denmark	5.2	3
Finland	5.1	3
Norway	4.3	3
Ireland	3.6	3
Luxembourg	0.4	2

Sources: European Commission; OECD

27. By John Major's pocket calculator that means that Britain, Germany and Holland, a liberal economic group, would be unable to form a blocking minority against illiberal nonsense even though they would represent over 40% of the union's population. By contrast, eight small countries could gang together and get 27 votes even though they represent only 12% of the European Union's people.

Viewing this as an unacceptable shift in the union's balance, Britain threatened until last March to hold up the accession treaties with the applicant countries. Then a compromise was reached: if two big countries wanting to block a decision could not gather the 27 votes needed, fellow members would try for a "reasonable" period to reach a compromise acceptable to them.

The British have a point—it is already bizarre that Germany should have only one council vote for every 8m people while Luxembourg has one for every 198,000—and the point will grow more obvious if tiddlers such as Malta and Cyprus join the union. But, in practice, council meetings tend to be bazaar-like bargaining sessions in which calculators are seldom needed. Of some 233 single-market decisions taken in the five years to last December only 91 actually went to a vote. The implicit message of Britain's obduracy was that it is more important to be able to block legislation than to pass it.

Is such an attitude sustainable in an expanding union? True followers of Monnet would say that no minority should be allowed to paralyse the European process. The concept of majority voting was in the original Treaty of Rome and was put into effect for all legislation affecting the single market. The aim must surely be to increase the scope for majority voting, not to go backwards towards more of the unanimity still needed for such areas as taxation and foreign policy—and for the revision of the treaties and the acceptance of new members.

On the other hand, no club can be happy if some members are constantly over-ruled, especially if it is a club of conflicting interests and rival cultures. And that it surely is. Some members, such as Germany, Holland, Denmark and Britain, instinctively believe in free trade and open markets; others, such as France and Spain, mistrust market forces that they cannot influence. Some, notably Germany and Britain, put into the communal budget far more than they get out, while others, especially Greece, Ireland, Spain and Portugal, do the reverse. There are plenty of what John Major once called "fault lines" to threaten the union's solidity. . . .

19. Grand Illusion: The Failure of European Consciousness

Godfrey Hodgson

"A spectre stalks Europe," wrote Karl Marx in 1848, "the spectre of communism." It is tempting to say that the specter that stalks Europe today is the fall of communism. Certainly, many of Europe's current discontents are direct or indirect consequences of the sudden collapse of the threat that dominated European political realities for almost fifty years.

If the western European economy is entering a more sluggish phase, as it seems to be doing, it is largely because of the downturn in the German economy. If the German economy is stumbling, for the first time to any significant extent since the early 1950s, it is because the cost of reunification with the formerly communist east is far higher than anyone anticipated; it is higher than the powerful western economy—which everyone had expected to be the engine of growth not only for western Europe but for the whole of eastern Europe as well—can bear without higher interest rates, declining growth, hard choices, and consequent social tension.

Godfrey Hodgson is former foreign editor of the *Independent* of London and author of *An American Melodrama*.

From "Grand Illusion: The Failure of European Consciousness." *World Policy Journal*, Vol X, No 2, Summer 1993. Reprinted by permission.

If there is social tension over immigration, specifically, it is true that it is not limited to the countries exposed to flows of migrants from the former communist countries. There are growing pressures from both asylum seekers and economic migrants, legal and illegal, from sub-Saharan Africa, the Maghreb, Turkey, the Middle East, and parts of Asia. But by far the largest and most immediate problems are represented by the hundreds of thousands of migrants who have already reached Germany and (to a significantly lesser extent) other western European countries, and by the hundreds of thousands more who are pressing on the relatively more prosperous of the former communist countries—Poland, the Czech Republic, Slovakia, and especially Hungary—but whose goal is the better-paid jobs and more generous social services of Germany, Austria, Switzerland, Italy, and points west.

If there is cynicism, political paralysis, fear for the future—and all these specters stalk Europe—it is above all because of the impotence of Europe's political leaders in the face of the horrors of civil war in the former Yugoslavia, and their awareness that what has been happening in Bosnia today could happen on an even larger scale elsewhere to the east tomorrow.

Above all, if there is an atrophy of the will to build European institutions, and the way the good ship Maastricht is wallowing and bucketing in rough seas is only the most conspicuous evidence of that failure of will, the most obvious explanation also points to the collapse of communism as the principal reason. For forty-five years, the conventional wisdom has it, Western Europe simply had to stick together, first to build the economic and political strength that would keep communism out, and second to be able to talk to the United States on a more equal footing than even the strongest of Europe's individual states could hope to do. Now that the external threat is removed, the argument goes, centripetal forces that were restrained by the greater need for unity over two generations have reasserted themselves, and the result is the destruction of the will to build Europe, even the rise of a new perception that building Europe is no longer necessary or relevant.

I believe that the collapse of communism, while unquestionably one of the immediate explanations of what is happening in Europe, is the proximate, not the profound, cause of Europe's present purposelessness and perplexity. No part of central, eastern, or southeastern Europe has been "normal" since 1941.

Essentially, there has been no normality since 1914. Before communism, there was the nightmare of nazism. And the Nazis not only massacred Jews and Gypsies. They also sent to the concentration camps Communists, socialists, trade unionists, intellectuals, liberals, Christians: anyone, in a word, who might have provided leadership in any sphere against the Nazi regime. So the whole of Europe east of a line from Lübeck to Trieste had been deprived of freedom at least since 1941. But even in the 1920s, there were few countries where there was anything even distantly resembling democratic government: only in Czechoslovakia was there a reasonably effective working democracy. So the whole of central and eastern Europe is like a valley that has been drowned by a dam. Cultures, nations, religions, ideals, and values were all submerged for at least two, and in many cases three, generations.

CONFRONTING THE PAST

Since 1989, with astonishing speed, the dam has broken. The water has drained away. And—surprise, surprise!—what is there to be seen is what was there before . . . only covered with layers of slime. So, depressingly, there is anti-Semitism in Poland. *The Protocols of the Elders of Zion* sells briskly in cheap editions in bookstalls around the War- saw railway station. A Roman Catholic bishop, a man with an exceptional education, fluent in several languages, openly blames the Jews for Poland's political problems. "But, Monsignor, there are only a few thousand Jews left in Poland." It didn't deflect him. So, in the former Yugoslavia, the Serbs call the Croats *Ustacha*, the name of the pro-German guerrillas of the early 1940s, as if fifty years had been for nothing; and the Croats have forgotten none of the atrocities of the Second World War or of the Balkan wars. Indeed, the Serbs have not forgiven those of the kinsfolk who, perse- cuted as followers of the Bogomil heresy, converted to Islam when the Turks con- quered them after the battle of Kosovo in 1389. The Slovaks have not forgotten their differences with the Czechs, or with the Hungarians. The Hungarians have not for- gotten their lost Magyar kinsfolk in Romania or in the Vojvodina. And so the litany of irredentist claims, long memories, and obscure hatreds goes on.

There are, of course, serious dangers for Europe in these unforgotten quarrels. What if the Hungarians take advantage of their neighbors' troubles to try to create a Greater Hungary, as the Serbs are trying, so far unresisted by the European powers or by the United Nations, to build a Greater Serbia? And there are even more fright- ening hypotheses than that, if you want to scare yourself. What if the Germans were to claim Silesia and the other lands Stalin stripped from them and added to Poland in the west to compensate Poland for the lands he had stolen in the east? What if the Islamic powers were to take the part of their Muslim brothers in Bosnia or, for that matter, in Azerbaijan? Such nightmares, I believe, I hope, are not likely to come true. But the point is that after what has happened in Yugoslavia, after the speed with which not just the communist empire, but the tsarist empire it replaced has fallen apart, cen- tral and eastern European countries can no longer avoid confronting their distant, as well as their more recent, pasts.

The same, however, is also true of western Europe, and more particularly of Germany. There has been a good deal of emphasis, not least in the United States, on those events since reunification that recall the catastrophe of 1933–45: intolerance and hostility toward immigrants, vicious, and even lethal, attacks on Turks and other foreigners, stray but persistent incidents of anti-Semitism. Since 1989, Germany has absorbed hundreds of thousands of immigrants, including *Volksdeutsch*, or ethnic Ger- mans from the Volga and other parts of the former Soviet Union, as well as from Tran- sylvania (some of whose families left the present territory of Germany anywhere from two to five centuries ago), as well as asylum seekers from as far away as Sri Lanka and immigrants from Turkey, Russia, and the Middle East. It is clear that the Germans' considerable tolerance and generosity toward foreigners is beginning to wear thin. Unlike in such "new countries" as the United States, Australia, Canada, or Argentina, there is no general feeling anywhere in Europe that immigration is in and of itself a good thing. Still less is there the feeling that is so strong in the United States that it is the purpose of the nation to forge people of different nationalities into a new people. Several European countries, most notably France, have in fact welcomed very large numbers of immigrants over the past century. A recent advertisement in *Le Monde*, calling for the defense of the French language against corruption by foreign (especially Anglo-American) influences was signed by notables, some of whose parents or grand-parents, to judge from their surnames, must have spoken one of more than twenty different European or North African languages. Immigration policy is a problem for all Europeans, and, rightly or wrongly, the majority of policymakers in every European country believe that there is a limit, and not necessarily a very high limit, to the number of immigrants it would be "safe" to admit.

This does not mean, however, that Europe is about to see a wave of anti-immigrant feeling wash through its political process, still less that we are about to witness pogroms against Turkish immigrants in Germany, Bangladeshis in Britain, or Maghrebians in France. Nonetheless, all-too-frequent acts of violence have taken place against these groups. In 1979, Margaret Thatcher was able, with cynical ease, to prick the bubble of the anti-immigrant National Front by making a few speeches about how she sympathized with those who did not want their country to be "swamped" by people of "a different culture." Almost unnoticed amid the journalistic breast-beating about the National Front in France, the traditional parties of the Right have quietly performed the same trick. Because they have made understanding noises about the racial fears of ordinary people, the air is going out of Jean-Marie Le Pen, or at least out of his pretensions to be considered a national political figure of the front rank.

Immigration, I would contend, is a major issue in western Europe only because of two more fundamental problems. The first is the comparative lack of economic dynamism. The fact is that it has been almost twenty years since rapid economic growth in Germany, Italy, France, and the Low Countries was replaced by relative stagnation. Not since the twin oil shocks of the 1970s has there been anything comparable to the growth rates of 10 percent per year or more that Germany, France, and Italy achieved in the 1950s and 1960s. Moreover, there is reason to suppose that in each case those very high growth rates were the result of probably unrepeatable circumstances.

TWO DECADES OF STAGNATION

In France and Italy, millions of workers moved from marginal agricultural jobs into urban, industrial, or service employment at relatively high wages. In West Germany, where the urban proportion of the populations was already higher than in France, and much higher than in central and southern Italy, the economy benefited from massive migration from the east and from the stimulus of reconstruction after the spectacular deconstruction of 1944–45. Postwar Britain, whose internal migration from country to town had been essentially completed long before 1914, witnessed the collapse of the traditional three-cornered system of imports and exports between its domestic manufacturing industry, the Empire's primary producers, and the United States, thereby missing out on the spectacular growth experienced elsewhere.

It is hard to see where a new wave of hypergrowth is likely to come from for any of the European countries in the immediate future. Still, it is not necessary to be unduly pessimistic on the economic front. If appropriate political courses are laid down and followed with determination—although this is quite a big "if"—there is no reason why Britain and France should not continue to be very successful exporters (even if too high a proportion of their manufacturing exports are in the vulnerable defense and luxury sectors). Cyclical factors promise reasonable growth in Britain and, perhaps after an interval, in France, where in any case the recession has been less severe than in Britain, or even than in the United States. Germany ought—again, subject to political considerations—to begin to reap the return on the spectacularly large investments that it has made both in the former East Germany and elsewhere in eastern Europe. And there is still plenty of ground to be made up by industrialization, urbanization, modernization, and income growth in Spain, Portugal, Ireland, and Greece, not to mention in the four countries that European politicians hope will be able to join an expanded European Community by the year 2000: Poland, Hungary, Slovakia, and the Czech Republic. Even Slovenia and Croatia have reasonable hopes of growing prosperity, within the German/Austrian economic zone, and the Baltic states can expect to form part of the Nordic bloc, which enjoys very high levels of income.

Economic prosperity in western Europe, while by no means automatic, is likely to be available to governments that show themselves able to make the right decisions. And a prosperous western Europe, especially if it has a prosperous Germany as its "Middle West," will pull along with it first the stronger countries of the second rank, then the others—if the political framework is strong enough to carry the burdens put on it, and if the political will is present.

SPLINTERED LOYALTIES

The question of political will is at the core of the European problem. When I compare western Europe with the United States, I must conclude that America's decisive advantage is in the political sphere. Not that the quality of U.S. politicians is spectacularly superior, even though the Clinton administration does seem to be responding to new realities with greater realism than any major government in Europe. Nor do I believe that American institutions, as such, are demonstrably superior to those of the more advanced European democracies. For every advantage inherent in the separation of powers, for example, there are disadvantages; nor can it be said that successive presidents in Washington have been conspicuously more effective in responding to economic difficulties than the chanceries and central banks of Europe.

The clear and enviable advantage of the United States rests in the realm of national self-consciousness, identity, loyalty, and unity. It is here, and not in the problems of transition brought on by the collapse of communism, that the true crisis in Europe lies. The great task for European politics in 1993 is the same task Europe failed to perform in 1913. The European political system at the beginning of the twentieth century was simply inadequate to deal with the changes inherent in the process of modernization that had taken place over the previous fifty or sixty years. Europe was ruled by five jagged-edged imperial nation-states (including France as an imperial republic). Between them there lay an ancient and murderous rubble of disputed provinces and resurgent nationalisms, each obsessed with lateral rivalries, as well as by their self-righteous hostility to the imperial power: thus Hungarians repressed Croats while trying to emancipate themselves from Germans, and Poles cast covetous eyes on Ukraine, even as they gallantly vindicated the principles of liberty against Russia, and so on ad infinitum.

The five, maneuvering, sometimes with vertiginous diplomatic cunning, sometimes with crass clumsiness, between other dead and rising stars, resurgent Italy and dynamic Scandinavia, comatose Spain and moribund Turkey, thought only of their own interests and glory. None had developed a mass democracy satisfactorily combined with republican institutions or constitutional monarchy, though Britain and France were closest to having viable institutions. In France, however, the deep division between the revolutionary tradition of 1789, 1830, 1848, and 1871 and those elements in the national life that still refused to accept the Republic scored fault lines that were to shiver in 1871 and shatter in 1940. In Britain, unnoticed under the elegant generosity of Edwardian upper class rule, intellectual and institutional paralysis had set in; the British did not comprehend how much their country's wealth and power depended not only on domination of India and Africa, but also on unrealistic assumptions about the loyalty of Ireland, South Africa and, in the remoter future, of the "white dominions," and even of Scotland.

These historical flaws, however, were nothing compared with the catastrophic political failures of the three empires of central and eastern Europe. Russia was an unreconstructed autocracy. Austria had abandoned parliamentary democracy for the personal rule over a brawling multinational empire of a tragically inadequate octogenarian. And Germany combined industrial and intellectual dynamism and modernity to an extreme degree with dynastic folly, sclerotic political institutions, and a neurotic inability to confront and exorcise strange demons of insecurity and rage from the past.

Until a few years ago, it was possible to argue that the Europe of 1913 had been swept away by the tragic history of two world wars, by the collapse of the Versailles system and the triumph of nazism, and by the success of new European institutions. It is not easy to make any such assumption today.

THE DISSIPATION OF WILL

The most striking aspect of the European scene today is the feebleness of any European consciousness. As it happens, I have recently traveled extensively in France, Germany, and Italy, all of which I know well already, and I live in Britain. I have also visited Russia and five other countries in eastern Europe, some more than once. Nowhere did I find, as Tocqueville found in the ancien régime, "the same institutions." Even less did I find a common European spirit.

This is most glaring in the four main countries of western Europe. The media in all four scarcely even report European affairs as such. In Britain, to the extent that newspapers and television have a serious political agenda at all, they focus on the monarchy and its discontents, on the "Eurosceptic" wing of the Conservative party, weak in numbers but powerful in its showing in the press, and on the economic and political tribulations of the Major government. In France, the media have been concerned with the decline and fall of the Socialist government to the exclusion of almost all else. In Italy, there has been an orgy of (justified) national soul searching over corruption, the Mafia, and the need for fundamental reform of the Italian political system. And in Germany, the press has dealt mainly with reunification and its various consequences and implications. British newspapers print little about German politics, and that little is largely unfriendly. French newspapers print little about Italy, and that is mostly amused. German newspapers are contemptuous of Britain, Italian television is alarmist about Germany, and French newspapers are full of *schadenfreude* about everyone.

The Bosnian crisis has thrown this lack of a common political identity and consciousness into relief. The first response of the Powers, to use, appropriately in this context, the term current in the year 1900, was to pursue ancient and largely irrelevant national interests. The British foreign secretary explained to any who would listen that it was self-evidently absurd to intervene militarily in a country as far away as Croatia, although Zagreb is only seven hundred and fifty miles from London, but he had enthusiastically advocated intervention in the Falklands (eight thousand miles) and the Persian Gulf (three thousand miles). The French, mindful of the Little Entente of the 1920s, flirted with an alliance with Serbia; while the Germans, instinctively, it seemed, responding to the legacy of 1914—or was it 1941?—or perhaps to the number of German families who vacation on the Dalmatian coast or the number of Croat *gastarbeiter*, sided with Zagreb. To be sure, these atavistic reactions did not last long, but they were succeeded by inaction, induced by near paralysis.

Bosnia is only the most signal and, to date, the most tragic example of this absence of a European consciousness and a unified European political will. The same hesitations, masking different perceptions of national interest and, at bottom, unreconstructed national envies and rivalries, underlie the inability to act decisively in support of democracy in Russia. Even more catastrophically, they account for the dissipation of will in relation to the development of Europe's own institutions.

Britain is the most conspicuous example. While perhaps no more than two dozen Conservative members of Parliament will oppose the Maastricht Treaty to the bitter end, the British government has reacted as though the most significant aspect of the treaty was the part John Major managed to talk Britain out of. No one knows how a referendum on Maastricht would go. But it is a fair bet that the chief reason why Major is so set against one is because he is not sure that he could win it. A substantial section of British political and public opinion cherishes the quite unrealistic idea that some sort of link with the United States is an alternative to wholehearted commitment to Europe.

If Britain is the most unmistakably lukewarm member of the European Community, nowhere is white heat to be felt. The French make it all too plain that they think European institutions are an excellent thing, so long as they continue to come up with rulings that favor French interests. Italy is the most European-minded among the big countries; but the Italians are preoccupied with their own problems, and they are not above using the European machinery for more or less outrageous financial scams, public or private. As for the Germans, they have clearly put the reunification of their country above the strengthening or the expansion of the European Community, and their reluctance to see the almighty mark replaced by a European currency suggests that at bottom they are no more singing "Europa über alles" than the British are singing "Rule, Europa!" or the French are abandoning the bloodthirsty chauvinism of the "Marseillaise" for the idealistic internationalism of Schiller's "Ode to Joy," music by Ludwig van Beethoven.

The lack of commitment to the idea of community, not monetary union, immigration policy, or even the Serbian challenge to the peace of Europe, is the problem Europeans most urgently need to address. Heroic efforts toward creating a European community were made, under American sponsorship, by the European founding fathers. They did not, however, carry the European peoples along with them. Especially in Britain, but everywhere else as well, the European institutions and the European project have remained remote, inaccessible, a little elitist, more than a little suspect. The collapse of communism has made them seem a little less necessary. The prospect of dramatic change, brought on by conflicts, the movements of populations, and general uncertainty, has made the tackling of the twin political tasks of deepening and widening the community seem less urgent, when in fact it ought to have made them more necessary than ever. Opportunities are slipping away; great, perhaps irreversible, changes are taking place without the sanction and blessing of Europe. Almost unnoticed, Europe is failing again, as it failed before 1914, to make itself collectively responsible, through rational and democratic processes and institutions, for its own peace and prosperity. In the process, it is making conflict—political and economic with the United States, political, and conceivably military, with its neighbors—ultimately more probable.

20. Time for a Global New Deal

Terry Collingsworth
J. William Goold
Pharis J. Harvey

The clash between capitalism and communism is over, and the winners have set about making the world a safe and efficient place for business. The reality is plain enough. Nike is making its famously expensive athletic shoes in Indonesia, where its women workers labor long hours for a meager $38 a month. Wal-Mart, K-Mart and Sears, the great American retail icons, are having their shirts made in Bangladesh by culturally passive Islamic women toiling 60 hours a week and making less than $30 a month. The companies sell the shirts in the United States at U.S. prices. The labor cost per shirt is roughly four cents. They assert the need to lower costs in order to remain competitive, but their main competitors are all there in Bangladesh as well, enjoying the same windfall of cheap labor.

At the same time, the major industrialized economies are experiencing an alarming, lingering recession. Trade unions in the United States and Europe protest massive job cuts and the lowering of living standards. Japanese workers face the end of the one certainty that motivated their untiring devotion to sacrifice for the national interest—the lifetime employment system. It is no longer in Sony's or NEC's interest to employ expensive Japanese workers when Thai and Malaysian workers will do the same job for much less. The lengthy debate over the North American Free Trade Agreement (NAFTA) exposed similar stories of U.S. companies shifting production to Mexico, making use of highly productive workers kept cheap by the labor policies of a government more interested in keeping investors happy than in ensuring a decent wage for its citizens.

These examples illustrate how a global economy has allowed multinational companies to escape developed countries' hard-won labor standards. Today these companies choose between workers in developing countries that compete against each other to depress wages to attract foreign investment. The free trade philosophy for creating a prosperous global economy is in practice denying workers their share of the fruits of wealth creation. First World components are assembled by Third World

Terry Collingsworth is General Counsel, International Labor Rights Education and Research Fund, and Program Director for the Asian-American Free Labor Institute in Bangladesh and Nepal. J. William Goold is Vice President, International Labor Rights Education and Research Fund, and Legislative Director and Press Secretary for Representative George E. Brown, Jr. Pharis J. Harvey is Executive Director, International Labor Rights Education and Research Fund.

workers who often have no choice but to work under any conditions offered them. Multinational companies have turned back the clock, transferring production to countries with labor conditions that resemble those in the early period of America's own industrialization.

"TRICKLE DOWN" TRADE

The U.S. lacks a responsible or comprehensive global trade policy and has effectively delegated the policymaking to multinational companies, which have fiercely resisted any efforts to regulate worker rights globally. They successfully blunted attempts to include meaningful labor standards in NAFTA and prevented the inclusion of any "social clause" in the General Agreement on Tariffs and Trade (GATT) and the European Community Charter. Their resistance is easy to understand. What is more difficult to comprehend is the lack of real political debate over the long-run implications of America's current trade policies, which seem to assume that the global trading system will somehow on its own create expanding markets and advance larger U.S. interests. The defining principle of U.S. trade policy today echoes that famous General Motors maxim: what's good for U.S.–based multinationals is good for America.

The debate in the United States over "free trade" has ignored the need for trade to be fair to workers' interests. For all of candidate Bill Clinton's criticism of President Bush's plans for a NAFTA without worker protection, he ultimately championed a treaty with largely symbolic side agreements on labor and the environment. "Protectionists" epitaphs are hurled at any American union that decries how its members are losing jobs as U.S. companies search for cheap labor around the globe. No one is fooled that the unions are doing much more than protecting their interests, and their position is derided for that reason. At the same time, however, the free-trade position of the multinationals is passed off as representing not merely their own interests but America's as well. Their many trade lawyers and economists are earning substantial fees peddling a global version of free-trade, "trickle down" economics.

A more accurate description of the position of the multinational corporations is that regulation is good only if it protects their interests and bad if it eats into their profits. If they truly believe in lifting global regulation to leave trade free, they have been moving in exactly the opposite direction. The Dunkel draft of GATT is encyclopedic and the final version of NAFTA exceeded 2,000 pages. There was never any pretense that these agreements were intended to remove regulations. They were efforts to remove tariffs and to agree on a comprehensive set of regulations governing global trade that are designed primarily to protect property rights. In these negotiations, the business community fought for and won a complex series of regulations that protected their property interests and set the rules for the global economy. That there was not a word about the fundamental rights of workers in the thousands of pages of rules reflects the priorities of those doing the negotiating, rather than any principled opposition to trade regulation.

The usual response to such criticism is that global trade law is not an appropriate forum for social legislation. For example, the current debate over the pending Harkin-Brown bill, which would ban from U.S. markets any product made with child labor, has brought fourth assurances from the free-traders that, while they naturally abhor the use of child labor, it violates the purity of trade law to link it with social legislation. Trade is trade, business is business, and social legislation must stand on its own. Never mind that it is precisely the indigent conditions of developing countries in a global economy that allows many multinational companies to escape U.S. labor laws and to reduce the costs of an integral part of production.

The position of the multinationals fundamentally ignores the recent history of linking social legislation to the trading system—to great social and economic benefit. There are numerous examples, but the most compelling comparison is with the New Deal legislation. As President Roosevelt declared in a message to Congress on the 1937 Fair Labor Standards Act, the first nationally applicable law setting minimum labor standards and outlawing child labor: "Goods produced under conditions which do not meet a rudimentary standard of decency should be regarded as contraband and ought not to be allowed to pollute the channels of interstate commerce."

Roosevelt was making the moral argument, which back then seemed sufficient, but the practical key to his vision comes in the final clause. The only recourse available to combat the growing problem of states engaging in cutthroat competition, leaving their citizens and workers without adequate living standards, was to use the power of Congress to regulate interstate commerce. The premise was that when one state was willing to undercut other states, not only did this affect other states' ability to maintain higher standards, but it also resulted in a downward bidding spiral that depressed purchasing power. National legislation was required to set a floor below which no state could descend in competing for jobs and investment. The federal labor laws enacted under the New Deal not only improved wages and working conditions but also increased purchasing power and contributed to the postwar economic boom. Workers became consumers and fueled the engine of unparalleled economic growth, saving the large manufacturing firms from ruination largely of their own creation.

NEW WORLD CONSUMERS

Setting aside the morality of multinational companies using impoverished workers who are unable within their political systems to fight for better conditions, it also makes no economic sense to continue to treat labor standards as irrelevant to trade policy. When they reduce their expensive U.S., European or Japanese work forces, the multinationals displace workers who until recent years were dynamic consumers with steadily rising purchasing power. Their replacement workers in Bangladesh, Indonesia and Mexico are often earning subsistence wages. While this new class of worker would also like to buy televisions and VCRs, their primary needs are food and shelter. The effect is to diminish one consumer class without building up an equivalent class. In Keynesian terms, supply is exceeding demand, which inevitably leads to surplus, recession and more. The global economy suffers not from a shortage of productive capacity but from a lack of broad-based consumer purchasing power, especially in developing countries.

Compounding this problem is the fact that the global economy has helped dissipate individual governments' efforts to use fiscal and monetary tools to achieve economic growth. National measures to increase aggregate demand often merely increase consumption, while the investment, production and employment benefits occur in other countries. These international "leakages" substantially weaken domestic economic policies. Stimulus in one country, if other economies remain stagnant, simply increases imports and immigration into the expanding economy.

In the future, achieving real economic growth in the United States will require policies to attain coordinated growth in the global economy. The key to promoting global growth is to create expanding broad-based consumer demand in developing countries. For this to happen, however, new international trade and investment policies must make it possible for agricultural and industrial workers to receive a rising share of the benefits of increased productivity and economic expansion.

It is thus in the interest of all countries to cooperate to reduce the obstacles to real growth in developing countries. Part of this strategy must be global agreement on binding trade and investment rules to protect fundamental worker rights and minimum international labor standards. This idea is not a new or radical policy departure. GATT's 1947 preamble contains an important message that subsequent generations of free traders have forgotten: "Relations among countries in the field of trade and economic endeavor should be conducted with a view to raising standards of living and ensuring full employment." What has been lacking in recent decades is the collective political will to make the protection of basic worker rights an essential part of the regulatory system that encourages global economic growth. The time has come to recognize internationally what the Great Depression forced America to realize nationally: actively advancing worker living standards is critical to boosting their overall purchasing power and to achieving sustainable real growth. This is true for developed and developing countries alike.

TOWARD GLOBAL STANDARDS

Today policies are needed to begin a global New Deal. Progress toward globally applicable worker rights and labor standards should be the cornerstone of a forward-looking trade policy that does more than maximize short-run profits. It should provide the basis for first creating and then sustaining a global consumer class, encourage true efficiencies in production and stop the destructive downward bidding spiral of the labor conditions and wages of workers throughout the world. If uniformly enforced, no single company or country could gain a competitive advantage and be rewarded in the global market for engaging in exploitive labor practices, removing the argument that such practices are necessary for companies to remain competitive.

Using existing models from other forms of globally applicable legislation, beginning in the mid-1980s Congress passed a series of laws that directly linked unilateral trade benefits with respect for worker rights. Five laws were ultimately enacted requiring compliance with "internationally recognized worker rights." The most effective has been the Generalized System of Preferences Act (GSP), which grants developing countries duty-free status on many exports to the United States conditioned on compliance with a five-factor worker rights standard. Using standards developed by the International Labour Organisation (ILO), based on conventions agreed to by most of the world's countries, the GSP standard was designed to have universal application. Most of the rights are absolute, meaning that they are not dependent upon a country's relative economic condition. Thus, to be eligible, all countries must respect the rights to associate and bargain collectively, the two most important worker rights that allow independent trade unions to form and to negotiate for whatever share of the economic pie is available. In addition, countries cannot use forced or compulsory labor or child labor and must provide reasonable conditions for worker health and safety. A final requirement is that there must be a national mechanism for establishing a generally applicable minimum wage law, which necessarily should take into account a country's level of economic development. There are several possible formulas for evaluating whether the minimum wage level is adequate, including tying wage increases to productivity gains.

The GSP law has created a forum for challenging systemic violations of worker rights as a means for any country to seek competitive advantage in international trade. It allows interested parties to petition the U.S. Trade Representative to deny countries that violate worker rights duty-free access to the U.S. market. But the law contains unacceptably vague language that has allowed successive presidents to undermine its enforcement. The GSP law must be reauthorized by September 1994. An important step toward a more enlightened global trade policy would be for the Clinton administration to strengthen the worker rights provisions of the GSP law and to extend this linkage to other U.S. trade laws and the GATT.

There is much more that the United States could do if it takes the lead in adding respect for workers to the agenda of global trade policy. The opportunity to use NAFTA to create a regional model for enforceable labor standards was largely missed. Ultimately, however, a global solution is required. While the ILO is currently the only international body responsible for globally monitoring worker rights, it has no enforcement power. Further, its tripartite charter between employers, governments and worker groups substantially reduces its ability directly to confront governments and employers.

In order properly to link worker rights with global trade, organizations dedicated to protecting worker rights need to have a voice in GATT, where global trading rules are made and enforced. GATT needs a substantive social clause that, much like the GSP standard, would either be directly enforceable or allow individual countries to take retaliatory action against noncomplying countries. Previous efforts to include such a clause have not made it to a working-group phase for discussion. The issue of a social clause has simply not been viewed as a priority by GATT's business-minded negotiators, including those from the United States.

Trade is not an end in itself. It is time to give life to the GATT preamble and harness trade for the purpose that free-traders claim—to strengthen the world economy by enhancing the purchasing power of workers and allowing them to have access to the goods they make. There is no need to wait for trade's benefits to "trickle down" to workers living in poverty if minimum standards can help ensure them reasonable living conditions. The United States should use its influence in the world market to make acceptance of a GATT social clause a top priority, for the good of its own workers, for workers in other countries, and as the basis for sustainable and fairly distributed global economic growth.

21. Four Japanese Scenarios for the Future

Takashi Inoguchi

Japan is in an era of transition. Behind a facade of confidence in their country's future, many Japanese feel adrift in the world of the late twentieth century.[1] The Japanese energy that is currently directed overseas is no longer based, as it was in the 1960s, on a nationally orchestrated strategy. Governments are no longer sure how to guide society, or with what goals. And Japanese society itself displays its loss of faith in the belief-system so dominant in the 1960s. Today the almost blind belief of that period in the loyalty to big business firms has lost its appeal. It is not an exaggeration to say that in the 1980s Japan had been improvising its responses to the unfamiliar challenges from within and without on an hoc basis, tenaciously adhering to time-honoured ways of doing things.

Bereft of a sense of direction, and uncertain about the future, Japan has been haunted by a vague angst about its future which has led it sometimes to hedge, and at least to limit, its commitment to the demands, requests and suggestions coming from overseas that Japan, now a global economic power, should take on more global responsibility.[2] As one observer aptly put it,

> Japan, in fact, does not seem to be pursuing any reasoned search for a secure place in an uncertain world, much less a plan to dominate it, but rather an energetic, opportunistic drift reminiscent of the early 1930s, with freebooting individuals and companies out giving their country a bad name while native people back home believe, like the king of Spain, that hoarding gold will make them rich. Japan has had far too many eggs—defense, trade and technology—in one US basket, considering how uncertain the US seems to be about what to do next.[3]

From "Four Japanese Scenarios for the Future," by Takashi Inoguchi. This article first appeared in *International Affairs* (London), Vol 65, No 1, Winter 1988–89. Reprinted by permission.

One of the salient themes which emerged in the directionless Japanese society of the 1980s is an emphasis on traditional values: values such as perseverance, frugality, diligence, effort, family, community, sacrifice, humility, the spirit of harmony and deference for the elderly. This fact is instructive. The problem is that these traditional values cannot be the basis for Japanese principles in guiding Japanese global policy. Former Prime Minister Noboru Takeshita's favourite saying, "When you do something, sweat by yourself and give credit to others," may be the epitome of humility, generosity and altruism, but it cannot be the sole organising principle of Japanese diplomacy. The same can be said about economic efficiency and profitability. They cannot dominate other considerations when the dollar's volatility could shake down the world economy or when the United States makes it imperative for its allies to implement tighter measures on technological transfer to communist countries.

Apart from these traditional values and economic criteria, which are too vague to allow one to fathom how the Japanese would like to see the world evolve, what are Japan's conceptions of its global position and its global roles? In other words, how is the country shaping its scenarios of the future worlds in which Japan will occupy a not unimportant position? This chapter addresses these and related questions, especially in relation to burden sharing and power sharing with the United States in the management of the world economy and international relations.

I will present below four Japanese scenarios of the world system in 25–50 years' time, making a clear distinction between the economic and the political and security arrangements envisaged in each scenario. In each scenario, Japan's role and the degree of burden sharing/power sharing with the United States will also be indicated. Next, the feasibility of the four scenarios will be discussed in terms of three major conditions, assessing the relative feasibility and desirability of each scenario. The United States and Japan will be the primary focus, though other major actors, no less important to Japan than the United States, will be touched upon as much as possible. Lastly, I will reflect on my findings in the light of the dominant aspirations and apprehensions of the Japanese.

But before these four scenarios are introduced, more straightforward, if somewhat prosaic opinion poll results will be presented. To know what opinion polls reveal is important since the scenarios of the future that follow are inevitably those conjured up largely by educated elites and do not necessarily represent the prevailing moods and sentiments of ordinary Japanese people.

JAPAN'S EXTERNAL ROLE: OPINION POLL RESULTS

A 1987 opinion poll provides useful data on how the Japanese people see Japan's external role. The Public Relations Department of the Prime Minister's Office commissions annual polls on Japanese diplomacy. The poll conducted in October 1987[4] contains one question relevant to our interest. "What kind of roles do you think Japan should play in the community of nations? Choose up to two from the list below." The list had five items:

1. Japan should make contributions in the area of international political affairs such as the improvement of East–West relations and the mediation of regional conflicts.
2. Japan should consolidate its defence capability as a member of the Western camp.
3. Japan should contribute to the healthy development of the world economy.
4. Japan should co-operate in the economic development of developing countries.
5. Japan should make contributions in scientific, technological and cultural exchanges.

Not surprisingly, the respondents overwhelmingly preferred roles outside the security and political realms. Item 3 registered 50.4 per cent; item 4, 34 per cent and item 5, 31 per cent, the three together adding up to 115.4 per cent out of a total of 162 per cent. By contrast, item 1 recorded 24.2 per cent, while item 2 registered only 7.8 per cent. It is very clear from these figures that the Japanese are disinclined to accept a major political or security role in the world.

Another poll (1986) conducted by an academic team permits us to compare the priorities attached by respondents to the domestic and international roles the government should play.[5] It allowed for multiple choices from among a list of priorities:

1. Preventing crime and securing people's safety (law and order).
2. Promoting technological innovation and raising productivity and production efficiency of the economy as a whole (economic power).
3. Increasing defence capability and consolidating national security.
4. Building roads, schools and hospitals and making life comfortable (standard of living).
5. Enhancing patriotism and strengthening the solidarity of the nation (national solidarity).
6. Promoting adjustment with foreign countries in economic fields and improving the world economy as a whole (global economic welfare).
7. Increasing taxes for those who can afford it and taking care of the poor and needy (social welfare).
8. Managing the economy to prevent inflation and unemployment (domestic economic management).

Instead of asking, "To which task do you want to see the government attach its first priority?," the poll stated: "There are many kinds of government policies nowadays. What do you think about the emphasis which government puts on each of them? Choose one of the following answers: (1) much more emphasis, (2) a little more emphasis, (3) keep as it is, (4) a little less emphasis, (5) no emphasis, (6) don't know and (7) no answer.

To make comparison simple, we will look only at responses for the first answer—much more emphasis. The following order of priorities emerges:

1. Domestic economic management (55.7 per cent).
2. Law and order (55.7 per cent).
3. Social welfare (45.2 per cent).
4. Standard of living (44.5 per cent).
5. Economic power (29.7 per cent).
6. Global economic welfare (27.8 per cent).
7. National solidarity (18.8 per cent).
8. National security (11.3 per cent).

In order to make comparison across different polls possible, I must make an admittedly crude assumption. If global economic welfare is said to correspond roughly to Japan's contribution in the economic field, and national security is said to correspond roughly to Japan's contribution in the security field, then two things are immediately clear: first, the overwhelming primacy of domestic priorities and, secondly, the overwhelming weight given to economic contributions compared to security contributions in Japan's desired role in the world. All this is not surprising. However, it is very important to keep in mind that, given the preoccupation with internal affairs and the avoidance of a commitment to security matters, public acceptance of the kind of world role for Japan that is envisaged by the Japanese government and expected by foreign countries can come only slowly.

It is true that overall public acceptance of Japan's greater role in the world, whether of an economic nature or otherwise, has been steadily increasing for the last few years, especially during the tenure of the Nakasone Cabinet (1982–7). But this has been largely a grudging acceptance, coming only after the government had made a series of carefully calculated incremental moves without arousing too much opposition.[6] We can recall the recent breakthrough in 1987 when the defence budget exceeded the limit of 1 per cent of GNP,[7] and also various measures enabling enhanced security co-operation with the United States, including the Japanese decision to allow participation in the US Strategic Defense Initiative (SDI) programme. But what is seen by the Japanese government as the barrier of public acceptance is still very much in evidence when it comes to Japan's security role in the world.

One recent event reinforces the impression gained from these polls. When the United States and many other NATO countries were sending naval boats to the Persian Gulf in 1987 under the US flag, the suggestion to send the Maritime Safety Agency's boats, put forward by the Prime Minister and the Foreign Ministry, was defeated in Cabinet discussions because of opposition from the Ministry of Transport (which has the Maritime Safety Agency under its jurisdiction). The Cabinet Secretary played a crucial role in siding with the Minister of Transport and with public opinion.[8] It is only against such a background that we can accurately assess Japan's conceptions of global roles, to which I now turn.

THE FOUR SCENARIOS

The following four scenarios of the world in the next 25–50 years are seen by the Japanese as "visions of the future."[9] Although in some respects they overlap, they represent differing views on the future of global development, the distribution of economic and military power, and institutions for peace and development. It should also be mentioned that these scenarios have not been sketched out by the Japanese alone; both Japanese and non-Japanese have articulated their preferences, given a future in which Japan will play an enhanced role.

Pax Americana, Phase II

This image of the future was first articulated by the Americans. It is the image of an America retaining its leading position in the world and making full use of its advantage in having created the institutions of post-Second World War order and security. This scenario depicts an America experienced in forging the "balanced" or globalist view of the Western Alliance and deftly prodding and cajoling its allies into enlightened joint action. The outline of this scenario was first made during the latter half of the 1970s, when the post-Vietnam trauma was still strong and when Soviet global influence was somewhat exaggeratedly felt in the United States. In the parlance of American political scientists, the key word was "regimes"—rules and practices in international interest adjustment—whereby the United States would retain its enlightened hegemony and control the direction of world development. Such phrases as "after hegemony" and "cooperation under anarchy"—both used as book titles—epitomise the primary thrust of policy and academic interest in articulating this model of the future.[10]

This image has been intermittently put forward in different forms. Confident in the retention of America's cultural hegemony in the Gramscian sense, Bruce Russett, a Yale political scientist, criticised the declaration of America's decline and imminent demise by likening it to the premature report of the death of Mark Twain. More directly and bluntly, Susan Strange of the London School of Economics has asserted that US hegemony has not yet gone; the lament on "after hegemony" is the favourite habit of American self-indulgence, she says. More recently, Paul Kennedy of Yale has described the revival of American composure and confidence, combined with the sombre recognition of the inevitability of national decline in the longer term.[11]

In Japan, this image of America's future has been a consistent favourite. Naohiro Amaya, a former vice-minister in MITI was fond of talking about "*Go-Bei*" ("later United States"), as if the United States prior to Vietnam was called "*Zen-Bei*" ("earlier United States"). This is an analogy with the later Han dynasty of China, which was restored after 17 years of disappearance and survived for another two centuries. Similarly, Yasusuke Murakami, a well-known economist, has argued that the hegemonic cycle that has been observed for the last few centuries has ceased to repeat itself largely because the world economy has been transformed from something based on individual national economies to a much more integrated structure. His scenario delineates an America which is an enlightened and experienced *primus inter pares* in an increasingly multipolar world.[12]

This image has been a favourite one, not least because it encourages the basic retention of Japan's traditional concentration on an economic role with no drastic increase in its security role, which is largely delegated to the United States. Although Japan's profile in the world has changed a great deal in the 1980s, the Japanese preference for limiting the country's commitment to military matters, many of which are generally deemed to have dubious utility, has not been altered.

Japan's roles in Pax Americana Phase II are not significantly different from its present ones. Essentially, these are primarily of an economic nature, with the bulk of global security shouldered by the United States. Even if Japan–US security cooperation is accelerated, this basic division of labour is unlikely to change. Even if Japan were to enhance its out-of-area security co-operation by sending warships to the Persian Gulf to shoulder the cost of oil imports, it would be bolstering the US-dominated world rather than becoming a main security-provider in the region. Even if Japan were to increase its security-related assistance to some Third World countries like Pakistan, Turkey, Papua New Guinea and Honduras, the security leadership of the United States would remain strong. Needless to say, there are those who argue that Japan will start in due course to exert influence by accumulating credit in the United States and other countries. But in this scenario Japanese self-assertiveness will be restrained by various domestic and international factors.

Japan's regional roles in this scenario will be heavily economic. More concretely, Japan will become the vital core of the Pacific growth crescent, encompassing three areas: (1) northern Mexico, the Pacific United States and Canada; (2) Japan and (3) the Pacific—the Asian NICs, coastal China, the Association of Southeast Asian Nations (ASEAN) countries and Oceania.[13] The incorporation of the second and the third economic groups into the extended US economic zone will be a vital factor in a US revival. In short, Japan's role in this scenario will be to link the US economy with the Asian Pacific economies in a more balanced manner than today. In this scenario, the current US efforts to liberalise the Pacific Asian markets, revalue local currency–dollar exchange rates and promote burden sharing in development aid, finance and international security will be given further momentum. At the same time, Pacific Asian nationalistic anti-Americanism will be considerably restrained. Perhaps it is important to note that Pax Americana Phase II will need a no less vigorous Western Europe. An enlarged and enhanced European Community (EC) will remain a pillar of this scenario. But if it degenerates into regional protectionism of the sort that can be glimpsed in the tougher EC anti-dumping policy on printing machines, through arrogance derived from an expected enlarged size and power, then it will elicit a negative reaction from the United States and Japan.

"Bigemony"

This second scenario for the future has been propagated by economists and businessmen, fascinated by the rapid development and integration of what Robert Gilpin, a Princeton political scientist, calls the *"nichibei* [Japan–US] economy." That is to say, the economies of Japan and the United States have become one integrated economy of a sort. C. Fred Bergsten, an economist who worked as a senior bureaucrat in the Carter administration and is now Director of the Institute for International Economics, coined the world "bigemony," which denotes the primordial importance of the United States and Japan in managing the world economy. Zbigniew Brzezinski, National Security Advisor to President Carter, coined the expression "Amerippon" to describe the close integration of the American and Japanese manufacturing, financial and commercial sectors, and indeed the two economies as a whole. This image of the future has been enhanced by the steady rise in the yen's value compared to the US dollar, and the concomitant rise in Japanese GNP, now registering 20 per cent of world GNP.[14]

In Japan this image has been put forward most forcefully by former Prime Minister Yasuhiro Nakasone. In one of his meetings with President Reagan, he suggested that the two countries should forge a single community of the same destiny, although what he envisaged focused on security rather than on economic aspects of the bilateral relationship.[15] It must be noted that Japanese images of the future have tended to focus on Japan–US relations, to the dismay of Europeans and Asians, let alone other Third World countries. This tendency itself shows the strength of this second scenario.

Japan's roles in the "bigemony" scenario may appear to some to be very similar to those envisaged in Pax Americana Phase II. However, economic power becomes military power almost inevitably, and Japan does not constitute the historic exception to this rule.[16] But the form in which Japan's economic power will be translated into military power needs close attention. Under "bigemony" the technical, economic and strategic co-operation/integration between the United States and Japan will become formidable, and of the largest scale in history. It is therefore not difficult to foresee, for instance, advanced fighter aircraft being developed jointly and manufactured primarily for Japanese use, with Japanese finance, though with American know-how, and also sold to third countries under the label, "Made in the United States." The large-scale strategic integration between these two countries as developed in the Pacific in the 1980s will come to be seen as a good testimony of the bigemonic roles Japan can play in security areas.

Japan's regional role in "bigemony" is an acceleration of the features presented in Pax Americana Phase II. A gigantic Pacific economic community will be forged, with Japan's role reminiscent of the role played by the corridor stretching from northern Italy through northeastern France, the Rhineland and the Low Countries to southern Britain in modern European economic development. Under this scenario, the potentially heated contest between the United States and Japan over the structural framework of Pacific Asia's economic relationship with the United States will be largely dissipated. Currently, Pacific Asia faces increasingly clear alternatives as to its economic framework: either a US-led free-trade regime established through a bilateral agreement with the United States, or a regional community with de facto Japanese initiatives, which would try to retain a free-trade zone even if North America and Western Europe fell into the temptation of protectionism and regionalism of a malign kind.[17] Furthermore, the strategic integration of many countries in the region may make it hard to accommodate the Soviet Union within an invigorated bigemonic structure, thus relegating it to a far less important status than it currently occupies, unless some other countervailing moves are continuously taken. In this scenario Western Europe, though large in size and high in income level, will be increasingly localised within Europe and its immediate vicinity. This picture reminds one of Immanuel Wallerstein's scenario of the future predicting the formation of two de facto blocs, one comprising the United States, Japan and China, and the other both Western and Eastern Europe.[18]

Pax Consortis

Japan's third scenario portrays a world of many consortia in which the major actors proceed by busily forging coalitions to make policy adjustments and agreements among themselves—a world in which no single actor can dominate the rest. This scenario resembles Pax Americana Phase II in its crude skeleton with its "regimes" and "cooperation under anarchy." However, the major difference is that the thrust of the third scenario rests on the pluralistic nature of policy adjustment among the major actors, whereas that of the first conveys the desirability or necessity (or even the hoped-for inevitability) of "administrative guidance" or "moral leadership" by the state that is *primus inter pares*—the United States. This third image is favoured by many Japanese, not least because Japan is averse to shouldering large security burdens. It is also favoured because Japan is not completely happy about America ordering everyone around, especially when it only grudgingly admits its relative decline.

Kuniko Inoguchi, a Sophia University political scientist, articulates this scenario most eloquently and forcefully in the context of the American debate on post-hegemonic stability of the international system.[19] The image has also been put forward by former Vice-Minister Shinji Fukukawa of MITI, which favours minimising the role of military power. Recently, MITI and the Ministry of Foreign Affairs, conscious of the increasing intrusion by other ministries into foreign affairs, have been trying to use national security and the Western Alliance as a stick to discipline other ministries which might otherwise move in an "irresponsible" direction (as in the Toshiba case, when it came to light in 1987 that the Toshiba company had sold equipment to the Soviet Union which the United States claimed was in breach of the CO-COM agreement on technology transfer). The image of Pax Consortis accords on the whole with the pacifist sentiments of most Japanese.

Japan's role in the Pax Consortis scenario is two-fold. First, with the superpowers' strategic nuclear arsenals increasingly neutralised either by the de facto US–Soviet detente process or by technological breakthroughs, Japan's primary role is that of quiet economic diplomacy in forging coalitions and shaping policy adjustments among peers, no one of which is predominant. Secondly, Japan's role is that of helping to create a world free from military solutions. That would include, if possible, the diffusion of anti-nuclear defensive systems to all countries and the extension of massive economic aid tied to ceasefire or peace agreements between belligerent parties. Japan's primary regional role in this scenario would be that of co-ordinator or promoter of the interests of the Asian Pacific countries which have not been fully represented either in the UN system or in the economic institutions of the industrialised countries, such as the OECD. Japan's secondary regional role is that of moderator, especially in security areas.[20] This might include acting as an intermediary and attempting to achieve reconciliation between North and South Korea, or the provision of neutral peacekeeping forces in Cambodia and/or Afghanistan in order to facilitate reconstruction through massive aid flows from such multilateral institutions as the Asian Development Bank (ADB). Western Europe will loom larger in this scenario than in the other three. In line with its role is such forums as the Western seven-power summits, Western Europe will continue to play an even larger role, having been traditionally quite adept in those situations where multiple actors adjust conflicting interests. The increasing economic ties between Western Europe and Pacific Asia will also encourage thinking along the lines of this scenario.[21]

Pax Nipponica

A fourth image of the future, "Pax Nipponica," was first put forward by Ezra Vogel, a Harvard sociologist, who in 1979 published a book entitled *Japan as Number One*. It is a world in which Japanese economic power reigns supreme. This scenario has been propagated by those Americans who are concerned about the visible contrast between the United States' relative loss of technological and manufacturing competitiveness and Japan's concomitant gain. Ronald Morse of the US Library of Congress, for example, published an article entitled "Japan's Drive to Pre-eminence."[22] This view has also been gaining power in Japan, reflecting both the noticeable rise in the value of the Japanese yen compared to the US dollar and other currencies and Japan's leading position as a creditor country. The steady rise of Japanese nationalism, in tandem with what the Japanese call the internationalisation of Japan, is contributing to the strength of this scenario, because the intrusion of external economic and social forces into Japanese society stimulated nationalistic reactions against internationalisation.

Japan's role in this scenario is best compared to that of Britain during the nineteenth century, when it played the role of balancer among the continental powers, its global commercial interests presumably helping it to fulfil this role. As for Pax Consortis in its fullest version, a prerequisite for the advent of Pax Nipponica is either the removal of the superpowers' strategic nuclear arsenals or the development of an anti-nuclear defence system. Without the neutralisation of nuclear weapons, Japan's leading role in the security area would be minimised, and Pax Nipponica in its fullest form would not be realised. In this scenario, Japan's regional role will coincide with its global role, as its pre-eminent position will enable it to play the leading role in the Asian Pacific region as well.

These scenarios offer substantially different visions of Japan's future. I will now consider what conditions must prevail if they are to be realised.

REQUIREMENTS FOR THE FOUR SCENARIOS

To what extent are these scenarios feasible? Under what conditions will the scenarios come into being? In attempting to answer these questions, I will first identify three factors which seem to distinguish these scenarios from each other, and secondly, speculate on the feasibility of each scenario in the next 50 years.

There appear to be three major factors which are crucial in distinguishing these scenarios from each other—(1) the effective neutralisation of strategic nuclear arsenals, (2) scientific and technological dynamism and (3) the debt of history.

Neutralising the Nuclear Arsenals

It is the arsenals of strategic nuclear forces that have allowed the United States and the Soviet Union to retain their superpower status and global influence. Whether these weapons will become obsolete—in other words, whether they cease to be a crucial factor determining global development—remains to be seen. Whether the United States or the Soviet Union or any other country will be able to arm itself with a defensive weapons system which makes it immune to nuclear attack is another question which needs to be answered, and the American SDI and its Soviet counterpart are directly related to this factor. The Conventional Defense Initiative, in which the United States has recently proposed that Japan be jointly involved, may be included as a miniature version of a less ambitious yet more solid kind of effort. Ronald Reagan's fascination with the SDI and Japan's quiet effort to build the CDI may simply reflect what might be called a "Maginot line" complex surfacing again years after its failure.[23]

If such a revolutionary weapons system is realised, strategic nuclear arsenals will be neutralised. Unless this happens, the fourth scenario, Pax Nipponica, will have difficulty in emerging because while superpower status is based on ownership of strategic nuclear weapons, both the United States and the Soviet Union will remain superpowers despite all their economic difficulties. In a similar vein, the third scenario, Pax Consortis, will not materialise into a system comprising both economic and security regimes without a similar neutralisation of strategic forces. With the disarmament process between the United States and the Soviet Union slowly making progress, strategic nuclear forces may not make much difference in determining global developments. There are those who, arguing in favour of Pax Consortis, maintain that nuclear weapons and even military power in general have already ceased to be a major factor in international politics and that economic interdependence has deepened sufficiently to make war an obsolete instrument for resolving conflicts of interests, at least among OECD countries and in direct East–West relations. Even granting that military power has become less important, I would argue that what is sometimes called the "Europeanisation of superpowers," in Christoph Bertram's phrase, will progress so slowly as to make it hard to envisage the fully fledged scenarios of Pax Consortis or Pax Nipponica inside the twentieth century. Needless to say, those who argue for Pax Consortis talk about it in a somewhat nebulous future most of the time.

Scientific and Technological Dynamism

The second factor concerns the innovative and inventive capacity of nations—how vigorous they are in making scientific and technological progress and in translating it to economic development. Needless to say, forecasting technological development is not easy. However, even a cursory examination of the social propensity to innovate seems to tell us that the Americans have been the most innovative nation, with the Japanese following on steadily behind. Such conditions as open competition, abundant opportunities, a strong spirit of individualism and freedom and high social mobility, which are observed in the United States, compare very favourably to conditions in Japan.

There is another argument, however, which completely opposes this, that is to say, that Japanese technological innovation has been making steady progress. The following evidence is adduced for the argument:

1. The number of licences obtained by Japanese companies and individuals in the United States has come very close to that of the United States itself. In 1987, the top three companies were all Japanese firms—Canon, Hitachi and Toshiba (in that order).[24]
2. More articles by Japan-based authors have appeared in *Chemical Abstracts* than by authors from any other country for several years.
3. The United States in the first 30 years of this century produced as few as five Nobel Prize winners, which is about on a level with Japan's seven winners for the 40-year period since 1945.[25]

Yet as far as general innovativeness is concerned, the United States seems likely to enjoy its dominant position at least until the end of the twentieth century. If this argument is sufficiently strong, then the first scenario gains force.

The Legacy of History

The third factor is related to the memory of the peoples of the nations occupied in the Second World War of their treatment, primarily at the hands of the Germans and the Japanese. As the former Secretary-General of the Chinese Communist

Party, Hu Yaobang, once said to Toyoko Yamazaki, a Japanese novelist, the memory of people who have suffered from war disappears only 80 years after the event. His evidence for this is the Boxer intervention in China in 1900, which has virtually been forgotten, whereas he argues that the memory of the second Sino–Japanese war of 1937–45 will not disappear from the memory of the Chinese for another 40 years. With the question of their wartime atrocities still a politically controversial issue, as shown by international reaction to Japanese official visits to the Yasukuni Shrine in Tokyo (which contained the remains of Japanese war criminals) and President Reagan's 1985 conciliatory visit to the Bitburg cemetery (which contained the graves of Waffe-SS men), Japan or West Germany cannot play a leading role without facing many barriers.[26] Pax Nipponica is inherently difficult because of this factor.

THE FOUR SCENARIOS RECONSIDERED

Let me now examine the four scenarios in the light of the three factors discussed above.

Pax Americana, Phase II

Whether Pax Americana Phase II is realised or not will critically depend on factor 2—scientific and technological dynamism. The argument for this scenario tends to be based on the free spirit, open competition and dynamic character of American society, which it is thought will help the United States to reinvigorate its innovative and inventive capacity.

In my view, this scenario has a fairly high feasibility if the present predicament is managed well. For that purpose two policies are essential: first, close Japan–US macroeconomic policy co-operation and, secondly, the full-scale interlinking of the US economy with the Asian Pacific economies under US leadership. Whether the United States can achieve this without igniting Asian nationalism against it remains to be seen.

"Bigemony"

The feasibility of "bigemony" depends critically on factor 3—the debt of history. In other words, it is still an open question whether Japanese pacifist feeling can be overcome and whether the East Asian neighbours can be at ease with Japanese leadership in regional and global security matters, even a leadership based on co-operation with the Americans. To be feasible, therefore, this scenario requires very close friendship between the United States and Japan as a precondition for overcoming the debt-of-history problem. The argument against this scenario is that the steady progress of Japan–US economic integration and defence co-operation has been accompanied by recurrent and at times almost explosive friction between the two countries, which augurs ill for the future.

In my view, the "bigemony" scenario can progress only slowly and steadily, in a moderate manner, as technological progress and economic dynamism push Japan and the United States closer together.

Pax Consortis

The feasibility of Pax Consortis depends critically on factor 1—nuclear neutralisation. This is conceivable in the distant future, but certainly not in the foreseeable future. For the two superpowers to relinquish superpower status and revert to less important roles will take time, even assuming that their decline has already begun. One may recall Edward Gibbon's remark that it took another 300 years for the Roman empire to disappear after its inevitable decline and demise were declared by Tacitus. It is utterly beyond speculation whether and how an unknown perfect anti-nuclear defensive weapon system might be developed and deployed. The weaker form of Pax Consortis, one could argue, is more feasible. One may cite the inability of the superpowers to have much influence on the course of events in Nicaragua and Afghanistan, for example; the increasing importance of monetary and economic policy co-ordination and consultation among the major powers; increasing international collaboration in research and development; and the very frequent formation of consortia in manufacturing and financial activities. Needless to say, conventional forces will become more important when nuclear weapons are neutralised. Thus arms control—a kind of consortium—in conventional forces will become an important focus under Pax Consortis.

Pax Nipponica

The feasibility of Pax Nipponica depends critically on factors 1 and 2—neutralisation of nuclear weapons and scientific and technological dynamism. If both factors are realised together, the historical factor may become less important. But the difficulty of neutralising nuclear weapons has already been mentioned. It must also be emphasised that the obstacles to Japan taking security leadership will not be easy to surmount. First, it will not be easy to persuade the overwhelmingly pacifist Japanese public. Second, it is not easy to see Japan shouldering the burden of the level of overseas armed forces the United States currently possesses for a prolonged period of time. It could easily lead Japan to suffer the kind of inefficiency that the Soviet Union has been so painfully experiencing. Thus estimates of Japan's likely scientific and technological dynamism will also affect the likelihood of Pax Nipponica.

In my view, Japan's innovative and inventive capacity for the next 10–20 years should not be underestimated. But beyond that period, the expected fall in demographic dynamism and associated social malaises that are bound to arise, such as the overburdening of the small productive working population for extensive social welfare expenditure and for Japan's increased contributions for international public goods, seem to augur ill for this scenario.

To sum up, it seems to me that scenarios one and two—Pax Americana, Phase

II and bigemony—are more likely than scenarios three and four in the intermediate term of 25 years, while in the longer term of 50 years a mixture of Pax Americana, Phase II and Pax Consortis seems more feasible. Of the two scenarios feasible in the medium term, Pax Americana, Phase II is the more desirable because it entails fewer risks to the United States as well as to the rest of the world. The effort necessary to sustain the US hegemonic position in its fullest form, whether alone or jointly with Japan or other allies, may cause more stresses than benefits. In the longer term, a soft landing on a Pax Consortis seems desirable.

CONCLUSION

These four scenarios are, admittedly, incomplete. Yet their delineation is useful in order to know better what kind of futures the Japanese have in mind in their assiduous yet uncertain search for their place in the world. Some readers may be struck by the fact that these scenarios reflect peculiarly Japanese aspirations and apprehensions. The weight of the past not only lingers on, but fundamentally constrains the Japanese conception of the world. Any drastic restructuring of Japan's foreign relations away from the ties with the United States seems virtually impossible to the majority of Japanese. It is instructive to learn that in Japan only 7.2 per cent of the population are neutralists, who want to abrogate the country's security treaty with the United States, while in West Germany as many as 44 per cent are neutralists.[27]

The same thing can be said of the three major factors. First, the debt of history to the Pacific Asian neighbours has been deeply felt as a major constraining factor in our scenarios. It is as if an anti-Japanese alliance in Pacific Asia were always ready to be forged, despite that near half-century since the war, just because Japan once crossed a certain threshold of misconduct. Secondly, the neutralisation of nuclear weapons has been the dream of most Japanese since 1945, when two nuclear bombs were dropped on two Japanese cities. Thirdly, the innovative and inventive capacity of nations is one of those things many Japanese have long felt lacking within themselves. Perhaps reflecting that, they waver between unnaturally timid and exceedingly bold estimates of their own scientific and technological capacity.

Some may argue that my overall scenario—a soft-landing scenario proceeding from Pax Americana, Phase II to the Pax Consortis—is more than mildly optimistic. This may be true. It is arguable that this optimism is somewhat unfounded when the United States, the architect of the post-war order, is beset by severe problems. The point is that a large majority of responsible Japanese leaders have found it virtually impossible to think beyond a world where the United States is of primary importance to Japan and where the Japan–US friendship is a major pillar of global stability. My delineation of four scenarios, including the Pax Nipponica and bigemony, should not be understood as a disclosure of non-existent plans for Japan to become a world supremo, or co-supremo. Rather, it should be interpreted as a manifestation of the kind of independent impulse long suppressed, yet only recently allowed to appear on a very small scale in tandem with Japan's rise as a global economic power. The Japanese are perplexed as they continue to rise in influence. Under what combination of the four scenarios Japan will stand up on the world stage remains a matter for our common interest.

NOTES AND REFERENCES

Some of the material in this article is drawn from an earlier paper by the author, entitled "Japan's global roles in a multipolar world" and presented to the Council on Foreign Relations, New York, in 1988. Professor Inoguchi gratefully acknowledges the constructive comments on that article by Shafiqul Islam and Brian Woodall, as well as the contributions of members of the Council's study group on Japan's role in development finance.

1. T. Inoguchi, *Tadanori to Ikkoku Hanei Shugi o Koete* (Beyond free-ride and prosperity-in-one-country-ism) (Tokyo: Toyo Keizai Shimposha, 1987); T. Inoguchi, "Tenkanki Nihon no Kadai" (Japan's Tasks at a Time of Transition), *Nihon Keizai Shimbun* (1, 8, 15, 22 and 29 November 1989).

2. T. Inoguchi, "The Ideas and Structures of Foreign Policy: Looking ahead with Caution," in T. Inoguchi and D. I. Okimoto (eds), *The Political Economy of Japan, Vol. 2: The Changing International Context* (Stanford, CA: Stanford University Press, 1988) pp. 23–63, 490–500; T. Inoguchi, "Japan's Images and Options: Not a Challenger but a Supporter," *Journal of Japanese Studies*, 12(1) (Winter 1986) pp. 95–119; T. Inoguchi, "Japan's Foreign Policy Background," in H. J. Ellison (ed.), *Japan and the Pacific Quadrille* (Boulder, CO: Westview, 1987) pp. 81–105.

3. M. Sayle, "The Powers that Might Be: Japan is no sure bet as the next global top dog," *Far Eastern Economic Review* (4 August 1988) pp. 38–43.

4. Department of Public Relations, Office of the Prime Minister, *Gaiko ni Kansuru Yoron Chosa* (Opinion Poll on Diplomacy) (Tokyo: Office of the Prime Minister, April 1988).

5. Joji Watanuki *et al.*, *Nihonjin no Senkyo Kodo* (Japanese Electoral Behaviour) (Tokyo: University of Tokyo Press, 1986).

6. T. Inoguchi, "Trade, Technology and Security: Implications for East Asia and the West," *Adelphi Papers*, 218 (Spring 1987) pp. 39–55; T. Inoguchi, "The Legacy of a Weathercock Prime Minister," *Japan Quarterly*, 34(4) (October–December 1987) pp. 363–70.

7. When the 1987 fiscal budget draft was revealed early in 1987, it surpassed the 1 per cent limit. But because in 1987 GNP increased much more vigorously, defence expenditure became less than 1 per cent of GNP at the end of the 1987 fiscal year. On the opinion polls, see Nisihira Sigeki, *Yoron ni Miru Dosedai Shi* (Contemporary History through Opinion Polls) (Tokyo: Brain Shuppan, 1987) p. 295.

8. *Asahi Shimbun* (30 October 1987); see also K. Chuma, "Nihon no Yukue o Kangaeru" (Thinking about Japan's Future Direction), *Sekai* (December 1987) pp. 85–98.

9. T. Inoguchi, "Tenkanki Nihon no Kadai," *Nihon Keizai Shimbun* (15 November 1987).

10. Stephen Krasner (ed.), *International Regimes* (Ithaca, NY: Cornell University Press, 1983); Robert O. Keohane, *After Hegemony: Cooperation and Discord in the World Political Economy* (Princeton, NJ: Princeton University Press, 1984); Kenneth A. Oye (ed.), *Cooperation Under Anarchy* (Princeton NJ: Princeton University Press, 1985).

11. B. Russett, "The Mysterious Case of Vanishing Hegemony: or, Is Mark Twain Really Dead?," *International Organization*, 39(2) (Spring 1985) pp. 207–31; S. Strange, "The Persistent Myth of Lost Hegemony," *International Organization*, 41(4) (Autumn 1987) pp. 551–74; P. Kennedy, *The Rise and Fall of the Great Powers* (New York: Random House, 1987).

12. N. Amaya, *Nihon wa Doko e Ikunoka* (Whither Japan?) (Tokyo: PHP Institute, 1987); Y. Murakami, "After Hegemony," *Chuo Koron* (November 1985).

13. C. I. Bradford and W. H. Branson (eds), *Structural Change in Pacific Asia* (Chicago, IL: University of Chicago Press, 1987); P. Drysdale, *International Economic Pluralism: Economic Policy in East Asia and the Pacific* (Sydney: George Allen & Unwin, 1988).

14. R. Gilpin, *War and Change in World Politics* (Cambridge: Cambridge University Press, 1981); R. Gilpin, *The Political Economy of International Relations* (Princeton, NJ: Princeton University Press, 1987).

15. T. Inoguchi, "The Legacy of a Weathercock Prime Minister."

16. Kennedy, *The Rise and Fall of the Great Powers.*

17. T. Inoguchi, "Shaping and Sharing the Pacific Dynamism," paper presented at a symposium on "Japan's Growing External Assets: A medium for growth?," Centre for Asian Pacific Studies, Lingnan College, Hong Kong (22–4 June 1988).

18. I. Wallerstein, 'Friends as Foes', *Foreign Policy* (Fall 1980) pp. 119–31.

19. K. Inoguchi, *Posuto Haken Sisutemu to Nihon no Sentaku* (An Emerging Post-hegemonic System: Choices for Japan) (Tokyo: Chikuma Shobo, 1987).

20. T. Inoguchi, *Tadanori to Ikkoku Hanei Shugi o Koete.*

21. T. Inoguchi, "Shaping and Sharing the Pacific Dynamism."

22. E. Vogel, *Japan as Number One* (Cambridge, MA: Harvard University Press, 1979); E. Vogel, "Pax Nipponica?," *Foreign Affairs*, 64(4) (Spring 1986) pp. 752–67; R. A. Morse, "Japan's Drive to Pre-eminence," *Foreign Policy*, 69 (Winter 1987–88) pp. 3–21.

23. On the CDI pushed by the US Congress see D. C. Morrison, "Earth Wars," *National Journal* (1 August 1987) pp. 1972–5; R. L. Kerber and D. N. Frederiksen, "The Conventional Defense Initiative/Balanced Technology Initiative," *Defense Issues*, 2(36) pp. 1–5. I am grateful to Jefferson Seabright for enabling me to read these and other related materials.

24. *Nihon Keizai Shimbun* (26 March 1988).

25. *Ashai Shimbun* (evening edition, 24 March 1988).

26. P. Katzenstein, "Supporter States in the International System: Japan and West Germany," paper prepared for the conference on "Globalized Business Activities and the International Economy," Research Institute of International Trade and Industry, Tokyo (23–4 June 1988).

27. On the West German figure, see "Disarmament is a Long Word and Takes a Long Time to Say," *The Economist* (30 July 1988); on the Japanese figure see Sayle, "The Powers that Might Be."

22. Russia's Work Ethic

Kyril Tidmarsh

HAVE THEY FORGOTTEN HOW TO WORK?

Optimists look to the market and democratic pluralism as the motors for driving Russia, the great outsider, back into the fold of "normal" economic and political development. Seeking aid and investment from the West, President Boris Yeltsin and his economists point to Russia's vast natural resources as collateral for loans and capital. Little is said, however, of another critical factor: the Russian labor force. While the technology can be imported, the essential human element cannot.

In city and country alike workers exhibit a long-suffering passivity and what the labor newspaper *Trud* called "a psychology of permanent dependence." With little pride in their inadequately remunerated work, and for years aware that they were anything but masters of their own proletarian country, the resignation of Russia's workers leaves them ill-prepared for the rough-and-tumble free market. Russian Prime Minister Viktor Chernomyrdin said at this year's World Economic Forum in Davos, Switzerland, "Without discipline and hard work we will achieve nothing. We cannot live as they live in the West and work as we work in Russia." For three generations a negative selection process systematically weeded out workers of the greatest drive, know-how and resilience, giving rise to a pervasive, cowed apathy and scheming work ethic, with the liveliest initiatives directed at seeking maximum personal gain with a minimum expenditure of effort.

Soviet communism has left a demoralized and dissatisfied Russian work force. What use will the world's poorest white workers make of new economic opportunities? Will they take advantage of novel freedoms and credits to hoist their country again to the respectable growth rates and vigor that it knew at the beginning of the century? Or will the Russian worker remain unproductive and unenterprising even in a democratic environment?

COLLECTIVIST ROOTS

Even before the 1917 Bolshevik takeover Russia's rural and urban working classes were conditioned by a traditional collectivist mentality. Individual effort and achievement tended to be regarded with suspicion. The peasant mentality was molded by the "mir," or commune, whose ponderous collective decision-making and parcelling out of land and jobs tended to induce mediocrity. That communal tradition—of "being like everyone else"—would later be revived by Stalin.

Migrating peasants within tsarist Russia transported those same group habits to the urban setting. There workers would form "artels," or cooperatives, sharing accommodations and tools to meet deadlines often set as part of some crash program. The artel did not inspire development of a settled class of craftsmen. Rather it was an ad hoc arrangement to survive along familiar lines in an unfamiliar setting.

Bought and sold like chattels until just two generations before the revolution, suffocated by the local-level commune and subjugated by Moscow's imperial autocracy, the Russian *moujik* was treated as a commodity, plagued, in the words of a nineteenth-century Russian historian, by "a curse of laziness."

It was only near the end of the nineteenth century, barely fifty years after the abolition of serfdom, that Russian agriculture began to change. By the eve of World War I half of peasant households held their own land under hereditary private tenure, and a Western form of individual ownership had slowly insinuated itself within the traditional system of communal tilling and joint village responsibility. Across central

Russia and into the endless expanses of underpopulated Siberia, a new class of farmer had begun to coalesce, displaying a level of productivity that made Russia the world's largest grain supplier. A network of railways connected a number of major urban centers containing a new class of industrial worker.

But World War I and the Bolshevik seizure put an abrupt end to any progress made by Russia along a Western path of development. Almost immediately the Bolshevik regime launched a systematic attack on the independent peasant farmer. The policy was principally motivated by apprehension—to preempt the relatively new class of independent and prosperous peasants from resisting accelerated industrialization at the expense of the farm sector.

Apart from the short respite provided by Lenin's so-called New Economic Policy from 1924–28, the entire Soviet period represented a return to collectivist roots and a consistent attack on the principle of intensive small-scale farming. In place of individual tilling collectivized peasants were reduced to executing orders from above. Surplus labor was syphoned off to cities, as well as to forced labor camps. For many years rural emigration provided what was considered an inexhaustible supply of cheap labor for factories. From 1951–79 an average of 1.7 million persons per year were uprooted from the countryside.

The collectivization process, begun ruthlessly in 1928, had the effect of eliminating the most competent part of the farm community. Stripped of what was considered by the Communist Party to be a potentially obstreperous class, the countryside was left with the weaker brethren. The peasant was again tied to a feudal master in the form of the *kolkhoz*, whose "elected" chairman was in fact a party nominee. Systematically decimated and mismanaged, the countryside and its captive inhabitants underwent unprecedented degradation. The well-rounded and competent owner-farmer was replaced by a narrowly specialized *kolkhoz* worker tied to a particular sector of farm work.

The impact of the Soviet regime on the industrial working class, in whose name the Bolsheviks created the "dictatorship of the proletariat," was no less destructive. In the years following the revolution what remained of Russia's skilled and unionized European-style working class was swamped by a massive influx of peasantry, toting a traditional communalist and conformist mentality. By 1928 the total number of workers in industry had increased fivefold, and sufficient housing and social services could not be provided for the new arrivals. Flimsy temporary housing became permanent, a situation that persists to the present day.

This radical process of urbanization and collectivization contributed to the destruction of traditional working-class attitudes. Entire nations were moved from one end of the Soviet Union to the other, frequently finding themselves in a hostile ethnic setting with racial tensions simmering barely below the surface, a situation hardly conducive to productive teamwork.

The Soviet working class was also atomized by the party's systematic efforts to destroy all horizontal links among professional and other groups. The concept of a nongovernmental organization independent of the Communist Party—let alone an independent trade union—simply ceased to exist until recent times. Social cohesion was further undermined by the fact that social benefits were increasingly provided by enterprises for their own employees, rather than by government for society as a whole. The Communist Party, the armed services and the great ministerial institutions tended to look after their own to the exclusion of outsiders. Like those institutions, individuals were also in competition for limited facilities and resources. Workers came to look out for number one, shirking any nobler goal or national motivation. All this, of course, ran exactly contrary to espoused party ideology.

BRAVE NEW INCENTIVES

From the start Lenin emphasized compulsory work and quantity output rather than quality, telling an American visitor, "I will force a sufficient number of people to work fast enough to produce what Russia needs." For decades to come the Soviet population would be conditioned to depersonalized work—a rupture of professional traditions—and to distrust government policies. Not only were individual efforts virtually unrewarded but any display of initiative could be dangerous. Forced labor camps nurtured a universal revulsion for work among prisoners and guards alike. This "Gulag complex" eventually spilled over to grip the entire country.

As the "workers' paradise" evolved into the dictatorship of Stalin and his heirs a shameful social contract took shape: the worker suffered a low standard of living but in return gained the right to have sloppy work accepted. According to *Sovetskaya Rossiya*, for instance, four out of every hundred kilograms of butter produced was substandard; one in every three television sets had to be returned to its Leningrad factory. Constant invocation to greater effort, bogus "socialist competition" campaigns and policies aimed at leveling incomes gave rise to a culture of slack and sloppy workmanship. Despite party propaganda touting the superiority of everything Soviet, the shoddiness of Soviet goods became legendary, even within the country itself. The August 1991 putsch against Mikhail Gorbachev failed, according to a quip, because it was "made in the U.S.S.R."

Probably no factor was more destructive of working-class professionalism than the leveling of wages and the narrowing of differentials, regardless of skill and output. The number of pay grades was cut after the Second World War, and in Nikita Khrushchev's time the difference between the highest and lowest paid fell to 1.5 times from 3.5 previously. One effect was the appearance of labor shortages in the most demanding sectors. If qualifications and output were not appropriately reflected in the pay packet, why aspire to jobs demanding greater skill or application?

In 1988, for example, there were only 60 operators for every 100 available lathes. Many of the millions of job slots that remained vacant tended to be filled by unproductive personnel—generally linked to management—such as propagandists, chauffeurs and secretaries. This category of freeloaders, who came to be known as "snowdrops," nonetheless took up a vital share of limited welfare, housing and social services.

Particularly undesirable "dirty" jobs eventually had to be remunerated with inappropriately high pay, giving rise to what sociologist Natalia Rimashevskaya called the "inversion" phenomenon in Soviet wage policy. Low-skilled workers thus became higher paid while the high-skilled saw their pay decline. "Wages," she wrote, "gradually lost their role of being a material incentive."

A fast-growing class of workers, commonly known as "bich" (taken from the Russian for "formerly educated person") abandon their underpaid, dead-end niches for highly paid manual labor, often in less developed parts of the country. By 1991 they numbered some six million persons.

Unable to improve their situation through regular jobs, others turned to moonlighting in repair, maintenance and services, forming a large shadow economy. In the countryside the best efforts of collective and state farms, and much pilfered inputs and equipment, were directed toward private gain. It is a widely quoted fact that private peasant plots, constituting barely three percent of land, made up for the inefficiency of the farm sector proper. These plots, for example, in the 1980s produced more than half the country's potatoes.

Such trends led to a markedly differentiated society. A 1989 survey found that 86.5 percent of families were "poor," 11 percent fell into the middle income category and 3.3 percent were described as "rich." Awareness of the gulf separating the gray working-class majority and dismally underpaid professionals from the small elite of worker-technicians and privileged nomenklatura generated resentment.

Industrial wage-fixing also contained a built-in productivity disincentive. Every operation had a quantitative labor "norm" that workers had to fulfill for basic pay. Productivity above the norm was sometimes rewarded. It was well known, however, that dramatic or continuous norm-beating would lead to an upward revision of the work goal. For decades, therefore, the system encouraged workers to produce below potential.

An abundance of cheap and, for many years, forced labor led to a preference for all kinds of labor-intensive methods—hence the spectacle of automated production lines terminating with teams of old women manually removing the end product. In a jobs-for-all society it was advantageous and indeed necessary to use this vast pool of workers rather than to invest in machinery. The effect, however, was to strengthen the feeling on both sides of industry that the worker was a common and expendable commodity.

Tolerance, even to the present day, of various forms of compulsory labor underscored the low value placed on the worker. Although the Gulags have been closed, there were recently almost a million people in corrective labor institutions, with *Izvestia* noting that the "entire corrective labor system is used to turn a profit." Even today the language of these prison workers is little different from that developed by Gulag laborers, a vocabulary filled with an untranslatable stable of verbs describing various forms of work-shirking (*mantulit, kantovatsia, temnit*).

Much use is also made of military conscript manpower, particularly in civil construction projects. It 1990 some 20 ministries contracted the armed forces to provide 540,000 workers, estimated to cost one-twentieth of civilian labor. Barely paid or trained, the stroibat laborer's lack of motivation is proverbial and, by the time he is demobilized, on-the-job training in malingering has taken its toll.

In the cities there is also the larger category known as "limitchiks." With urban residence permits (*propiska*) severely restricted, those falling over the limit are granted conditional authorization to work. They have no residence rights, other than in the lodging provided by their employer. Since such permits are not transferable, limitchiks are tied to that enterprise. For the first ten years they are denied the right even to sign on to waiting lists for individual housing—or to start a family. These workers rightly consider themselves exploited and for that reason display little motivation. Such unjust degradation of workers has contributed to the demoralization of wide swaths of the labor force.

A labor policy depending on low-wage, low-productivity employment also tends to require low skills and low education. It is, however, one of the inexplicable paradoxes of the Soviet system that the educational and vocational training systems churned out large numbers of skilled workers. This absurd mismatch made those skills virtually superfluous, as large numbers were employed in occupations well below their professional and trade capabilities. The phenomenon is particularly striking in the medical and health fields, where training costs are especially high. It was estimated in 1990 that more than half of unskilled jobs were filled by workers with more than the obligatory primary schooling.

Ensuring job dissatisfaction led to various forms of escapism. Many workers simply fled their jobs, seeking better outlets for their abilities. Workers tended to move restlessly from job to job, producing high labor fluidity, which reached frightening proportions in the Brezhnev years. Even under Gorbachev, in 1988, for example, 20 per cent of the working population changed jobs. Others drifted into the criminal underworld. Some simply became vagrants.

BELIEF IN QUICK-FIXES

The long-suffering passivity caused by such labor practices may explain the remarkable restraint of labor protest in Russia. The few strikes since Stalin's death tended to take the form of spontaneous explosions against extreme injustice rather than organized movements aimed to improve labor conditions. The 1989 Kuzbass miners strike followed six months of patient waiting while demands were examined at no fewer than seven official levels. In Krasnoyarsk the same year the miners' committee actually dispatched a telegram to the minister of mines stating that even the most severe disputes should not be resolved by strikes. Orderliness was one of the most significant features of the massive industrial action that finally did take place. The strikes were silenced by government promises but so far, despite worsening conditions, there has been no work stoppages on the same scale.

A general deterioration of public health, years of privation and environmental pollution may also contribute to worker lethargy. Upon retirement at age 55 an average miner's life expectancy in 1990 was barely five more years. The recent anti-alcohol campaign claimed that there were over 50 million alcoholics in the Soviet Union; every fifth woman of childbearing age undergoes an abortion annually.

Disillusionment and distrust of government policies is strengthened by revelations that many grandiose Soviet claims had been little but deception. Propaganda about miraculous worker achievements promoted a vision of eventual communist utopia. In 1935 one worker was supposed to have turned out 102 tons of coal in a single six-hour shift—seven times the norm—thus demonstrating the party could inspire almost superhuman feats. Glasnost has since revealed such claims as total fraud.

This mythology contributed to a deeply ingrained belief in quick-fix solutions. Such misplaced faith is now reinforced daily in the media by tales of the apparently effortless production of material goods under capitalism. The working class is heartened to expect affluence at once. Encouraged by Western politicians and bankers, people now harbor the illusion that within a few hundred days or some other tangible time span, given help from Washington or Brussels, they can acquire what the democracies took centuries to achieve.

THE SPECTER OF PRIVATIZATION

Relaxing economic controls has not yet produced a commercial gold rush but an extremely slow start-up of those small- and medium-sized enterprises that had been expected to boom. Liberalization has led to much buying and selling of state property but no significant growth in the artisan activity that could create self-employment for workers with initiative.

The same can be seen in agriculture. In suburban areas weekend farming has increased, concentrating mainly on marketable vegetables and meats such as poultry and pork. Proper agricultural workers, however, remain wary. Few farmers are able to remember the days before collectives. But many well recall the confiscatory currency reform, compulsory state loans and arbitrary adjustments to the size of private plots. Perhaps most painful was Khrushchev's sudden ban on private cattle. It was a traumatic experience when the family cow, usually the most cherished possession in millions of households, had to be handed over to the *kolkhoz*.

This background explains why the recent schemes for land leasing have been met with profound distrust. Even today, legislators' reluctance to adopt guaranteed, nonreversible decollectivization reinforces prevailing suspicions and unwillingness to invest more effort in the land. Rural workers are too accustomed to orders from above, fixed holidays and miserable social benefits in order to risk going it alone, except on micro-plots.

The reluctance of farm workers to acquire land for themselves has given rise among reformers not only to exasperation but also, ironically, to calls for forcible privatization. Thus if the former owner-farmer no longer exists and if the collective farm worker is afraid to take responsibility, then the solution should be simply to privatize by the well-tried method of compulsion. This is the same instant-solution mentality that gave rise to the past's painful and catastrophic social engineering. That it can still be enunciated today points to the profound impact of the Soviet experience and of ideological cramming.

The latest Russian revolution was by no means a clean break. The Soviet regime was not destroyed; it just ground to a halt. The key people of the ancien régime simply changed hats, leaving in place the familiar framework of labor-management relations. It is not easy for these people to grasp that the market mechanism does not function by the planners' fiat and that new methods of consultation and remuneration are needed to motivate an inert labor force.

Even though central Moscow and St. Petersburg have come to resemble vast bazaars, it is difficult to think of a country less culturally prepared for individual enterprise. According to academician Leonid Abalkin, one of Gorbachev's early economic advisers, the seeds of private enterprise in Russia are being sown in hopelessly infertile human soil. In his view the country has spent too long "moving backwards," struggling against excellence in all domains. What was missing, he argued, was "the culture, the attitude to work and human relations—which take generations to nurture."

Individuals in the West believe they can improve their situation through greater effort and skill. The Russian reflex, on the other hand, is to pull back the successful to achieve some kind of equality in poverty. A survey of workers' attitudes in 120 industrial establishments found that over half the respondents believed that material improvement would not come due to any change in their own motivation but rather as the result of some administrative action taken by the state.

LEARNING TO WORK

In many respects perestroika can be compared to Western Europe's Reformation. The medieval church and the Communist Party both gave ethical meaning to immobile societies. Both saw capitalism as destructive of a natural order where everyone knew his place. Both failed.

The difference is that the church had to make way for an ethic of thrift and personal advancement that reflected the realities of an expanding commercial society. The Reformation took place in a society in which individualism was already the prevailing philosophy. In contemporary Russia, on the other hand, the old regime collapsed of its own accord, unable to compete with the outside world. It did not, unfortunately, succumb to pressure from upwardly mobile workers or an ambitious middle class.

Consolidation of a "civil society"—rule of law, privatization, an effective banking and credit system, progressive taxation—will be able to revive a productive work ethic and harness Russian talent. It can confidently be expected that political stability, significant Western investment and a well-managed transfer of technology will quickly do wonders for Russia's rusting smokestack industries, dangerous nuclear power stations and polluted environment.

But institutional change alone will not suffice to extricate millions of Russian workers from the mind-set created by many years of subordination to communalist and command systems. That will take time. Painfully, Russian society will have to accommodate a commercial and consumption culture for which it is ill prepared. Real paychecks and social justice will certainly transform the scene, but they will not speedily improve a work ethic based on the principle that "they pretend to pay us, we pretend to work." Revival of a healthy, skilled and motivated work force will require prolonged exposure to an enterprise culture in which pay and position are tied directly to effort and the quality of work.

23. Dual-Track Transition in China

Fan Gang

In 1993, China registered the highest GNP growth rate (13.4%) in the world and a recognizable acceleration of market-oriented reform. In the previous year, a kind of market economy ("socialist market economy") was officially adopted by the ruling Communist Party as the goal of system reform. As some formerly socialist countries are still suffering from economic recession and political turmoil, China has suddenly become a "model" for successful economic restructuring, e.g., Chen *et al.* (1992), and Gelb *et al.* (1993).

The goals of this paper are twofold. First, it explains the fundamental causes and characteristics of China's gradual market-oriented reform strategy. Second, the paper identifies the problems that the gradual reform strategy has left for further reforms.

The problem of policy choice is studied by focusing on two related questions. The first question is why "shock therapy" could not be accepted by the Chinese in the late 1970s or even now, and why "gradualism" was not acceptable or is no longer acceptable in some other nations in the late 1980s. The second question is why China has been successful so far in conducting its "gradual reform" in the 1980s, while others failed during the same period. The first question is about the "acceptability" of different reform approaches, and it is the subject of Section 1. The second question is about the "feasibility" of different reform approaches, and is discussed in Section 2.

The gradual reform strategy has delayed the resolution of several fundamental

I have benefited from discussion with and comments from Leszek Balcerowicz, Georges de Menil, Jeffrey Sachs, Sheng Wong, Juro Teranishi, Wang Limin, Wing Thye Woo, Zhang Shuguang and Zuo Dapei. I am grateful to the Maison des Sciences de l'Homme, the Ford Foundation and the Chinese Academy of Social Sciences for supporting my research.

From "Dual-Track Transition in China," by Fan Gang. *Economic Policy: A European Forum*, Georges de Menil and Wing Thye Woo, eds., December 1994, pp. 99–122. Reprinted by permission.

issues. The postponement of reforms in these areas has created forces that are destabilizing the economy. Section 3 discusses the problems of the "dual-track" system, and Section 4 traces the post-1978 output cycles to the decentralization policies of the reform programme.

1. ACCEPTABILITY: THE POLITICAL ECONOMY OF REFORM

1.1. The Pre-Reform Economic Situation

China's overall economic reform has never been "radical" as compared with Eastern European countries and the Former Soviet Union (EEFSU). Political reform has yet to take place after fifteen years of economic reform, mass privatization is not on the agenda; price reform has been gradual; exchange rates were not unified until very recently; and so on. The general objective model is the ambiguous "Socialist Market Economy."

Gradualism was adopted at the end of 1978 not because there were no proposals for more radical reform programmes but because a majority of society and the leadership were not in favor of them. The fact was that the Chinese economic situation in the late 1970s was "too good" for a radical reform package to be adopted. Following the end of the decade-long Cultural Revolution in 1976, China registered 7.8% national income growth in 1977 and 12.3% in 1978 before the reform started in 1979. At that time, most ordinary people had not yet totally lost their trust in the old system because, first, they had not suffered zero or negative income growth like the Eastern Europeans and Russians did (see Figure 23–1 for comparison of growth trends in different countries), and, second, they felt that the Chinese technocrats had had no chance to carry out their "optimal" economic plans due to the frequent political upheavals since the late 1950s. It was hence popularly believed that the most important problem for the economy was the failure of the "political-struggle-first" doctrine; and not defects in the basic institutional structure of the system. Such "methodological mistakes" could easily be overcome by concentrating on economic construction.

The noticeable recovery of economic performance immediately after the end of the Cultural Revolution seemed to many people evidence of the virtues of the old system. It was hence natural for a majority of people not to choose an abrupt change of their life when their real income was not only growing but was also expected to continue to grow under the current regime. Compared with the seventy-year old Soviet system which finally ran into deep crises in the late 1980s, forty years of socialist history was too short to exhaust the energy of China's economic machine.

In contrast, a radical reform programme was actually demanded by the EEFSU societies in late 1980s after their political change. In 1989 when the revolution took place, the gradual approach was unacceptable to the majority. The Russian referendum in April 1993, 3 years later, still supported the radical approach. Similarly, the

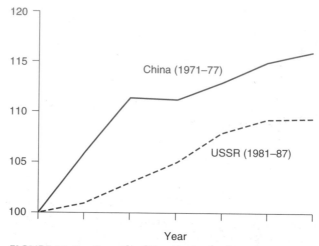

FIGURE 23–1   Growth of Per Capita Real Income
Sources: China Statistics Yearbook, 1993, China Statistics Press,
1993; *Statistical Yearbook of the Soviet Union,* 1985 and 1988,
USSR Statistics Press.

Notes: For China, the index refers to per capita consumption;
1971 = 100. For the USSR, 1981 = 100.

economists who designed the "shock therapy" package could not have sold it to the
EEFSU societies if there were other alternatives under the prevailing circumstances
(the lack of real authority of central government, for instance). Furthermore, gradual
reform had been tried before the 1989 social crises. The previous gradual reforms
were undertaken not because people were myopic or "conservative" but because the
old system at that time had not yet entered its terminal crisis. China's old system (the
state sector) has not yet reached its end even after fifteen years of reform. What has
happened in China so far is mostly the growth of a new system paralleling the old one.

The hypothesis advanced here is that the radicalness or gradualness of the reform process is a function of, among other things, the extent to which the economy
has stagnated and declined on the eve of the reform. Specifically, the lower the growth
potential of the old system, the stronger are the incentives and the willingness to pursue radical reform.

1.2. The Ceaselessly Changing Objective Models

China's gradual reform also has been characterized by gradual changing of its
reform objectives. Unlike the majority of Poles and Russians who were clear about
their desire to "return to Europe" and to adopt a private market economy, the Chinese had neither a clear idea nor consensus about where to go. What the Chinese

knew was merely that the conventional centrally-planned system was not working well and that some changes were necessary in order to promote economic growth.

Consequently, China has proceeded through a lengthy path of readjusting reform objectives, from "a planned economy with some market adjustment," to "a combination of plan and market," and now to "a socialist market economy." The changes in objectives reflect, first, the increasing knowledge in China about the merits of different resource allocation mechanisms, and, second, and more fundamentally, the changes in the social balance between various interests groups and the changes of economic structure resulting from the process of reform and development itself. As the non-state sector grows rapidly and the state sector continues its decline, people become more convinced about the superior efficiency of the market system and hence offer less resistance to more profound changes.

1.3. The Role of Government

The discussion above suggests that "gradualism" is less an "adopted approach," or "chosen strategy," but more of an *ex post* description of an unintended evolutionary process. Very few people really knew in 1978 how to implement gradual reform. Participants might have known what the first "piece" should be, but might not know what the next piece should be. Indeed the term "piece-meal approach" is a more accurate description than "gradualism."

For example, the rural "household contract responsibility system," which later turned out to be the most important step in starting the whole reform process, was banned by the government in 1979 and only "adopted" later after it had become widely practiced by the peasants. Again, when the rural economy was liberalized, few policy-makers would have predicted that there would be a dynamic rural industry sector. In fact, most policy-makers and some leading pro-reform economists were against the development of township and village enterprises (TVEs) for a long time. More recently, the retrenchment programme of 1989–91 included serious measures to crack down on TVEs and private businesses in order to increase the dominance of the state sector. These measures were abandoned later only because the state authority could not afford the sharp fall in tax revenue caused by the crack-down.

Another example is that even to date, the leadership and many reformists are still convinced that expanding state-owned enterprises' (SOEs') autonomy without changing ownership is the way to perfect the system of socialist ownership and to solve the current problems in the SOEs. They put their major effort into reforming the state sector and left the non-state sector to grow "spontaneously" by itself. It is hence ironical that the development of the non-state sector has been counted by the Chinese policy-makers as one of their major achievements.

1.4. Decentralization and Bottom-up Innovation

Do Chinese policy-makers have something to offer for improving reform methodology? Perhaps.

One notable feature is the pragmatic and flexible attitude of the Chinese government. As it did not see the need to clarify everything in concepts before taking actions, it did not spend much time on argument ("No argument [on principles]" has even become an official approach in dealing with controversies) and simply allowed different norms to exist ("groping for stone to cross river"). When something new but controversial appeared, the "no-encouragement-but-no-ban" policy was applied. This may not be the best way to deal with the transformation, but under certain circumstance, it may create the conditions for a better approach to emerge.

While the decentralization of decision-making powers to local governments and enterprises under the unchanged public ownership framework have created a number of new problems (to be discussed in Section 4), it has turned out to be a dynamic mechanism for various new forms of economic arrangements to emerge. Experiments of different reform programs at various levels were encouraged; "special economic zones" were set up; various "special treatments" to different regions were extended; and local initiatives were respected.[1]

Now, more and more Chinese people understand that the market cannot be planned or created in planned ways. What needs to be planned may be only the first of several steps toward removing restrictions to institutional innovations by ordinary people and putting reform vehicles on track.

2. FEASIBILITY: THE DIFFERENT STRUCTURAL CONDITIONS

2.1. The Pre-Existence of a Repressed Non-State Sector

The different fates of gradualism in different countries at various times were actually pre-determined by their initial economic structures (Fan, 1993; and Sachs and Woo, 1994). Gradualism is more possible in an under-developed (under-industrialized) economy with a huge surplus rural labour force like China than in an "over-industrialized" and "over-state-sector-dominated" country like Poland. Until the end of the 1970s, Chinese peasants' incomes were declining (absolutely and relatively) compared to those of the urban population (see Figure 23–2). The pre-existence of a repressed sector—peasant agriculture as in China—in which people earned a stagnant subsistence income and had a strong demand for change and new opportunities, provided a labour force that was ready to pursue new economic activities. It was the development of a new non-state sector emerging from a previously repressed non-state sector that made the first stage of reform a Pareto improvement.

---

1. This means that the "M-form hierarchy" (Qian and Xu, 1993) is mainly the result of the decentralization reform rather than the pre-condition for a special approach to reform to be taken. As Zhang (1993) pointed out: "It was (former) Premier Zhao Ziyang's strategy to use local governments to fight against more conservative central ministerial bureaucrats. To some degree this strategy was shared by Deng Xiaoping . . . As pointed out by Shi (1993), decentralization of reform governance was a feature of the central leaders' style of governing the reform.

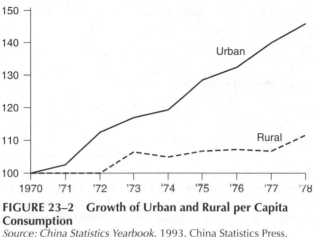

FIGURE 23–2　Growth of Urban and Rural per Capita Consumption
Source: China Statistics Yearbook, 1993, China Statistics Press, 1993.

The different approaches to reform may also be defined in terms of ways of dealing with the old system. If it were feasible to develop a new non-state sector first, the original state sector could (and, maybe, should) be kept alive for a while in order to avoid immediate resistance from the people who still benefit from it. If, however, the new sector cannot be established without moving resources from the old sector, then political reform must come first before any real economic reform (cutting subsidies to the SOEs, for instance) can be undertaken.

One important question is: can the new sector develop fast enough to outpace the increasing need to keep the declining old sector alive? As long as the state sector is dominant but suffering losses, it will use every possible means (explicit or implicit) to extract subsidies from the other sectors. Furthermore, it will win in policy-making if "majority rule" is followed.[2] Thus, if the new sector cannot grow fast enough and become strong quickly enough to retain some of its surplus (after paying for the subsidies) to add to its capital accumulation, it will always be repressed and not attractive enough to draw out more state employees.

From this perspective, China had two special conditions that permitted incrementalist reform. First, China started reform when the state sector was not so worn down that it needed heavy subsidies like the former Soviet firms in the late 1980s. In 1978, subsidies to loss-making SOEs accounted for only 3.21% of GDP, an amount that was easily covered by moderate growth. Second, rural reform and liberalization

---

2. Sachs and Woo (1994) argue that the pro-reform government should cut subsidies to push more state employees to leave the state sector for the more attractive non-state sector. The problem is whether the cuts would be accepted. The recent change in Russian government policies to the state sector show how strong the state sector is. It seems that whether the state would cut the subsidies to state firms does not depend on its willingness to do so, but on the deterioration of the state's capacity to mobilize resources from the other sectors, i.e., tax the non-state enterprises.

of private economic activities in the presence of a huge rural labour surplus could generate growth rapid enough to outpace the speed at which the subsidies to SOEs were increasing.

2.2. The Government's Authority

Another condition favorable for gradualism is the political continuity of the government. The Chinese government never lost the administrative ability to control the reform path and to keep changes moving gradually. Furthermore, it did not totally denounce the old system and announce a commitment to something totally different. In contrast, a government, that was established through political revolution and owed its legitimacy to the promise of a radically new system, would not be able to make changes gradually and still maintain its authority. The lesson appears to be that under "post-revolutionary" conditions, gradualism is not only unacceptable but also infeasible.

2.3. The Path of Least Resistance

The fact that Chinese reform started in agriculture has led many observers to conclude that the optimal reform strategy would have a "leading sector approach," e.g. Chen *et al.* (1992). I offer two comments about this recommendation.

(1) When the economy as a whole has not run into an overall systemic crisis that requires an overall radical reform programme, remedial measures will be demanded and carried out on a sector-by-sector basis. From the political perspective of implementing sequential reforms, the most important feature of the leading sector is that it is the sector with the least resistance to reform and therefore the easiest sector in which to carry out reforms. An early success is important in persuading the other sectors also to adopt the reforms. This is why gradual reforms in China have been taken in an "easy-to-hard sequence," see Zhang (1993). So if gradualism is the only acceptable and feasible strategy, one should find out which sector is of "the least resistance" and start reform there.

This reasoning suggests that Goldman's (1991) conclusion that the agricultural sector should always be the first to be reformed makes as little sense in political terms as it does in economic terms. There is no basis to believe that the agricultural sector in an industrialised country like the Czech Republic would automatically be the sector most eager to undertake reform. Woo (1994) stresses the above political consideration to explain the sequencing of reforms, and he advances the hypothesis that the largest sector is generally the most "reform-demanding" sector because its crisis by definition is the gravest one faced by the economy.

(2) For an economy which is not significantly differentiated in terms of ownership, development level, income disparity, labour mobility, or relationship with the state, the "leading sector approach" would not work. The resistance to reform in this case may be evenly distributed and no sector can play a "leading role." In this case,

to choose a particular sector to start the reform may create more rather than less conflict.

3. THE DUAL-TRACK TRANSITION

3.1. Honoring Previous "Implicit Contracts"

The "dual-track system" in China was first used in price reform, and it has been extended to cover almost all economic transactions.[3] The most important dual-track system has been the reform of the ownership structure which has created a dual-track economy: the development of a new system that parallels the unreformed old system. China's rapid economic growth can be attributed mainly to the dynamic development of the "new track non state sector" which consists of private and semiprivate enterprises, community-owned rural industrial enterprises, foreign joint-ventures and individual businesses (see Table 23–1).

The virtue of the dual-track system is that it honors the "implicit contract" previously set according to socialist principles. The implicit contract guarantees the worker that, regardless of her work effort, she would receive at least the minimum wage and various benefits which include health insurance, free housing, retirement pension and jobs for her children. Even though this implicit contract system may reduce the efficiency of the market economy, it has to be recognised that it has already become part of people's vested interests. To keep the "old track" is to respect the vested interests under the old system. The gain from the maintenance of the distorted incentives is that the resistance to reform is reduced. This explains why governments have tended to pursue a dual-track approach to reform if at all possible. It is only when this approach fails and the old government collapses, that the new government—free of the obligation to respect previous contracts—can pursue radical reforms and enter into new contractual obligations.

3.2. Convergence of the Two Tracks?

The real question is not whether the government should follow a dual-track system, but whether the two tracks should converge into one as rapidly as possible. The success of dual-track transition depends mainly on the success of the new track. If the growth rate of the new sector is higher than that of the old sector, then the old system will, in the long run, shrink to zero as a proportion of the economy. In other words, if the old system stops expanding and everything else grows, a dual-track transition will end in the space of one generation, without explicit reform actions having been taken against the old system.

---

3. The most notable exception is credit markets where interest rates are still tightly controlled by the central government (although black market rates are widely in effect).

TABLE 23–1   The Development of Non-State Sectors (All Percentages)

	1980	1981	1982	1983	1984	1985	1986	1987	1988	1989	1990	1991	1992
Output value of non-state industry as % of total OVI	24.0	25.3	25.6	26.6	30.1	35.2	37.7	40.3	43.2	43.9	45.4	47.1	51.9
Non-state employment as % of total employment	81.1	80.9	80.9	81.1	82.1	82.0	81.8	81.7	81.6	81.7	81.8	81.7	81.7
State budgetary revenue from non-state sectors as % of total state revenue	18.0	21.2	21.3	22.3	23.0	29.6	25.4	28.6	31.6	33.2	33.6	36.1	n.a.
Retail sales of non-state sector as % of total sales	48.6	50.1	51.3	53.0	54.5	59.6	60.6	61.4	60.5	60.9	60.4	59.8	58.7

Source: China Statistical Yearbook, State Statistical Bureau of People's Republic of China (English edition), 1991, 1992.

Price reform has followed this idealised dual-track transition for a number of markets. In 1992, most Chinese provinces removed all controls on food prices. This was the "final punch" of a process of step-by-step price reforms over the past ten years. When convergence of the two tracks finally took place, the food products sold at officially fixed prices accounted for less than 15% of total consumption and the free market prices were about twice the official prices. Naturally, under these conditions, the "final punch" did not cause "shocks."

A similar thing happened in the foreign exchange market. The unification of the official exchange rate and the "swap market exchange rate" occurred at the end of 1993 when the differential between the two rates was about 50%. But at that time, only 20% of foreign exchange transactions were still subject to the official exchange rate. In this case, it is noteworthy that the "rationed" component of foreign exchange sales did not decrease in absolute size over time, it only shrank relative to the size of the "new track."

In practice, an expansion of the old system (in absolute size) has occurred quite frequently. This is because the state has used the revenue from the more productive new sectors both to compensate those who suffer losses because of the transformation and to expand the old inefficient sector. The latter type of subsidy is usually justified on the grounds of strengthening the competitiveness of the SOEs through techno-logical upgrading. The result is that the old track has not shrunk proportionately as rapidly as it should have.

From a supply-side perspective, the non-state sector has become the major con-tributor to China's GDP—52% of industrial output in 1992, and an estimated 57% in 1993. In 1992, about 80% of the increment of GDP was from the non-state sec-tor. On the expenditure side, however, the state sector has remained dominant. In 1992, 79% of total bank credits went to the state sector.[4] In 1993, over 70% of total social investment in fixed assets was for projects in the state sector. This was a higher share than in the previous year. The number of state employees as a proportion of the total labour force has not changed in the past 15 years; in some years, it even increased. The number of state enterprises has also increased (see Table 23–2).

Corruption is another reason for the survival and expansion of the "old track." For example, in the process of price reform, the old track was frequently expanded not only because of pressures from SOEs seeking more resources at low official prices, but also because of rent-seeking by government officials. The higher the share of pro-duction that is designated as "planned sales," the higher will be the free market price, and, hence, the greater the amount of resources that can be diverted to the corrupt officials. The result was that for a long time, planned sales were not fixed as they were supposed to be, but increased instead. Sometimes what shrank was the "market track"

---

4. It should be noted that, as bank loans are given to state enterprises at low interest rates (about 10%), and the non-state sector is willing to pay higher rates (about 20%), the state enterprises re-lend some of these credits to non-state firms in the black market and earn interest differentials (that may be higher than their profits). No data is available on the volume of credits which have been "transferred" in this way. But a reasonable estimate is no more than 30% of credits to the state sector.

TABLE 23–2   The State Sector in the Chinese Economy to Date

	1978	1980	1985	1988	1989	1990	1991	1992	1993
State sector investment as % of total investment	n.a.	66.6[a]	66.1	61.4	61.3	65.6	65.9	67.1	70.3
State fixed investment as % of NI[b]	20.9	20.2	23.9	23.5	19.2	20.3	21.9	25.2	n.a.
State employees as % of labour force	18.5	18.9	18.0	18.4	18.2	18.2	18.3	18.3	n.a.
Credit to state sector as % of total credits[c]	n.a.	n.a.	80.9	79.3	80.1	80.3	80.0	79.0	n.a.

Source: China Statistical Yearbook, 1993.
Notes: a 1983; b NI = National Income = GNP — Depreciation; c Including credits from the state banking system and "rural credit unions."

instead of the "planned track." This is one of the reasons why the dual-track price system has lasted for so long.

The lesson is clear: the most important challenge in a gradual transition may not be how to speed up the growth of the new track, but how to assure that the old track does not grow as well. The old track cannot be simply ignored as many advocates of gradual transition have suggested, because it will not wither away voluntarily. It may, on the contrary, not only prosper as a parasite of the new track because of its considerable political clout, but may also metastasize and crowd out the new track.

3.3. "Transitional Corruption" and "Spontaneous Privatization"

Corruption is no doubt a source of economic distortion, income disparities and social unrest. But it appears that wide-spread corruption may be unavoidable for a declining public ownership economy during the transformation. "Capitalistization" (Zhang, 1993) of some government officials, openly or underground, may be the way to make everyone better off, because it shifts officials from previous positions under the old system to new ones with a minimum of residence.

Wang and Li (1993) have estimated that, in 1992, official corruption, wage-drift ("wage eats profits and capital"), and stealing has siphoned off at least 100 billion yuan worth of state assets, or about 5% of total state assets. A survey in Shanxi province shows that up to 40% of state assets has been dissipated in the past 10 years. Meanwhile, household savings in the form of both bank deposits and financial assets have increased rapidly. For an economy in which mass privatization with a fairer redistribution of property rights could not be accepted, such gradual "spontaneous privatization" seems to be an unavoidable part of the process of moving towards the market. The unpleasant possibility during the historical stage of "initial capital accumulation" is that the big money may be the most "dirty" money.

It is imperative that legal protection of private property rights be quickly established in order to reduce the "decapitalization" and "capital flight" that are occurring. In recent years, personal purchases of luxury consumer goods have been running disproportionately high for the level of overall economic development, and Hong Kong banking sources have estimated that about US$10 billion of capital fled abroad annually. Capital flight amounted to one-third of the gross capital inflow in 1993. This suggests that private property rights have not been sufficiently protected and private investment in the domestic market has not been properly encouraged.[5]

The present level and form of "transitional corruption" have not given rise to many problems, because many corrupt officials used their power and privileges to obtain money from the state for their own businesses and then left their positions in the government. One cannot be sanguine, however, that the nature of corruption will not evolve into types that would stop economic growth. One such danger lies in the conversion of planning power into "licensing power." The disturbing signs are that the approval process has become longer in recent years for many kinds of business and projects, and that the number of profit-oriented companies run by government departments has increased greatly. There is a positive sign, however, in that the demand for further changes is also increasing.

3.4. Remaining Hardcore Problems and "Sequential Features"

The gradual approach in its essence is an "easy-to-hard" reform sequence. It starts with the easy problems and leaves the hard problems until later. In contrast, the radical approach tackles the hard problems at the beginning. As the question of which approach is better can be answered only after all problems have been solved in both approaches, one should therefore be very careful when making comparisons in the middle of the reform process.

In terms of economic optimality, a "hit-the-core-problems-first" radical programme is more justifiable because it maximizes efficiency gains and minimizes implementation costs of the reform. On the other hand, an "easy-to-hard" gradual programme is more justifiable on the grounds of minimizing the political costs of reform.[6] Clearly, the reform costs are different in different economic and political situations. So an "optimum sequence" cannot be defined without specifying the circumstances under which the reforms are being implemented.

The three most hardcore problems remaining in the Chinese economy today are: (1) Factor price reform, including interest rates and prices for oil, coal and some other basic raw materials; (2) Ownership reform of the state sector, including the state-owned banks (SOBs); and (3) Government reform, including reform of the fiscal system.

---

5. Of course, if an individual's assets were proved after due process to be illegally obtained ("dirty"), they should be seized and the individual punished. If "dirtiness" cannot be established, then the individual's assets should be protected as long as they stay reinvested in the national economy.

6. "Political costs" of system reform refer to the economic resources wasted because of political conflicts. It may take the form of a reduction in output, and I have argued in Fan (1993) that this reduction is necessary to economic restructuring.

4. DECENTRALIZATION AND MACROECONOMIC STABILIZATION

4.1. Decentralization and Liberalization

For a centrally planned economy, market-oriented reform must involve the decentralization of decision-making powers. The broader definition of decentralization may include removing restrictions to private activities, or more generally, all kinds of non-state[7] economic activities, and decentralizing decision-making powers to individuals and private business people. The narrower definition of decentralization, however, may only refer to granting decision-making powers to the lower-level state agencies from the central authority, i.e., to local governments, to state-owned enterprises (SOEs) and to state-owned banks (SOBs, plus other state financial institutions if any). In short, it is decentralization within the state sector without change of ownership structure. Under this narrower definition of decentralization, actions of removing restrictions to private economic activities should be referred as "economic liberalization."

Decentralization within the state sector and economic liberalization of private activities may be correlated with each other. When the local governments have autonomy to pursue their own interests, they may find that it is in their interests to promote and protect local private or non-state business, as long as the latter would provide more "local revenues." This is one of the major reasons why the non-state sectors have been developing so rapidly. On the other hand, decentralization within the state sector may encourage so-called "spontaneous privatization" as it may result in the spread of corruption and "flowing-out" of state assets to private hands or the "capital depletion" of state enterprises. But decentralization within the state sector itself is not the same thing as liberalization of private activities.

4.2. Decentralization Within the State Sector

The reform of the state sector so far has mainly remained a process of decentralization without change of ownership.[8] It has involved almost all decision-making on production, pricing, investment, trade, expenditure, income distribution, taxation, and credit allocation. The following institutional innovations have played important roles in the process:

---

7. This term is quite often used by Chinese economists to refer to a broader range of economic organizations, from private businesses, cooperative firms, semi-private or shareholding companies, and collective or community-owned businesses such as Township and Village Enterprises (TVEs). These economic organizations are mostly new since the economic reform, and differ from state enterprises as they do not follow some regulations applicable to the state sector. Most forms of non-state enterprise are transitional—they are still evolving with the changes in the entire institutional environment.

8. Some fundamental steps towards reforming state ownership have taken place recently. The experimental "share-holding" state corporation that was started in 1988 allowed only 10% of shares to be sold to individuals. In 1993, comprehensive restructuring of state ownership was adopted by the Central Committee of the Chinese Communist Party (October, 1993) and the first Corporation Law was passed by the National People's Congress (December, 1993). Various experiments in corporatization will be made in 1994.

(a) The "Budgetary Contracting System" (BCS, since 1980, see Zhong, 1990).[9] This was the major device for re-shaping fiscal relations between central and local government. Under the BCS, the central government shares revenues (taxes and profit remittances) with local governments in the following way: (1) The central and local governments collect revenues on separate tax bases according to the administrative subordinate relationship (different levels of government tax different payers); (2) Each provincial government signs a contract with the central government fixing the amount of revenue remittances for a specified period of time. For provinces that run budget deficits, the contract will be on the subsidies to be transferred by the centre to local government.

(b) The "Contract Responsibility System" (CRS, since 1985) for state enterprises. Under this system, SOEs pay a fixed amount of taxes and profits to the state and retain the rest for themselves. In principle, as long as SOEs can deliver the tax-cum-profit remittances specified in the contracts, the government will not interfere with their operations.

(c) Direct borrowing. Since 1985, state grants for operating funds and fixed asset investments have been replaced by bank loans. Local governments and SOEs are allowed to borrow directly from banks. The proportion of SOEs' funds that is raised externally has been increasing dramatically over the years (see Fan and Woo, 1993). Since 1991, local governments and SOEs are also allowed to borrow directly from workers, households and other institutions. Similarly, the local branches of the central bank (People's Bank) and the state specialized banks are also allowed some discretion in formulating their lending policies.[10] The fact is that direct credit control (through "credit quotas" or "credit ceilings") imposed by the central authority has been in force most of the time.

The decentralization reforms have created a "decentralized state sector." "Autonomous" local governments, SOEs and local SOBs have increasingly important roles in determining resource allocation, while the central authority has become less influential in resource allocation within the unchanged ownership framework. It should be noted, however, that the giving up of power by the centre has not always been voluntary. The impetus for decentralization at later stages has been pressure from local governments and SOEs. The step-by-step reform in the past 14 years has often reflected erosion of the resistance of the central authority to these pressures for decentralization.

9. New changes are being attempted in taxation and revenue sharing. The new attempts include redistribution of tax revenues by categories (instead of by taxpayers) between central and local government in order to increase the share of central revenue, rebuilding the revenue transfer mechanism, and redefining the division of expenditure responsibilities between central and local government.

10. The local branches of state banks (the central bank and the state commercial banks) are to a great extent "truly local." The officials of local banks are part of a larger hierarchy, usually appointed by higher supervisors within the bank system. In reality, they are directly under the supervision of local authorities and benefit from local prosperity. They have generally always done their best to meet the loan requests of local officials and local SOEs, albeit somewhat constrained by central regulations—see Bowles (1989).

Many people still believe that a market system could be created by changing managerial incentive systems and that a market economy could be compatible with state ownership. Many economists (Chinese and foreign) have praised the decentralization and measured the progress of reform by the amount of decision-making powers that have been given up by the central government. The decentralization reform may have improved the technical efficiency of the state sector.[11] But if we look at the allocative efficiency and intertemporal stability, it must be understood that the decentralized state sector is the major institutional cause of macroeconomic instability and of the divergent development of regional economies. In addition to the ordinary factors of structural changes in the "take-off" stage of economic development, China's increasing inflation and fluctuations are to a great extent caused by the redistribution of fiscal power, increasing budget deficits, growing subsidy credits ("policy loans") to state enterprises, and the phenomenon of "locally initiated monetary expansion."

4.3. The Redistribution of Fiscal Power and Central Budget Deficits

The fiscal situation can be summarized by two facts: total government budgetary revenue declined from 31% of GNP in 1978 to 16.6% of GNP in 1992; and central budgetary expenditure fell from over 60% of total budgetary expenditure in the 1970s to 39.7% in 1992.[12] The relative fall in budget revenue is due to two major reasons: the fall in revenue remitted by SOEs and the rise of the "revenue-hiding-in-local-economies" phenomenon.

Despite the (possible) improvement in productivity, the profitability of SOEs has been deteriorating since the decentralization reform. Wage payments, bonuses, fringe benefits, and "publicly-financed consumption" (which are often disguised as costs) have increased dramatically and disproportionately. The overcompensation of workers has caused profits remitted to the government to decrease as a proportion of total value-added (see Fan and Woo, 1993). Budget subsidies to loss-making SOEs have also increased (see Table 23–3). Besides, under the enterprise "Contract Responsibility System" (CRS), the amount of remitted taxes and profits are pre-set. So when production grows, remittance will fall as a proportion of total revenue. Meanwhile, under the CRS, SOEs are still not responsible for their losses in practice even

---

11. There are four major factors which determine the productivity of state enterprises: (1) management (operational incentive structure and decision-making process for "agents"); (2) outside environment (planning or market); (3) technological inputs; and (4) the ownership form ("principal-agent" incentives and responsibility). Decentralization may improve the first three. That is why it is not surprising to observe improvement in SOEs' total factor productivity or technical efficiency (see Jefferson *et al.*, 1992), but the extent of the improvement remains controversial (see Woo *et al.* 1994). These improvements, however, do not disprove the importance of the ownership factor, which may become the key "bottle-neck" for further improvement.

12. Budgetary revenues includes domestic government borrowing but excludes foreign debts (source: *Chinese Statistics Yearbook*, 1993).

TABLE 23–3 The Financial Performance of Major State Enterprises[a]

	1978	1980	1985	1988	1989	1990	1991	1992
Profit rates	15.5	16.0	13.2	10.4	7.2	3.2	2.9	2.7
Profits + taxes as % of total asset value	24.2	24.8	23.5	20.6	17.2	12.4	11.8	9.7
Profits + taxes as % of output value	24.9	24.1	21.8	17.8	14.9	12.0	11.6	11.4
Revenues from state sector as % of total revenue	n.a.	82.0	70.4	68.4	66.8	66.4	63.9	n.a.
Total losses (billion yuan)	4.2	3.4	3.2	8.1	18.0	34.9	36.7	36.9
Total losses as % of total profits	8.2	5.8	4.3	9.1	24.2	39.8	91.3	69.0
Total losses as % of total profits + taxes	5.3	3.7	2.4	4.6	10.1	23.2	22.1	19.0
Losses as % of budget revenue	3.8	3.2	1.7	3.1	6.1	10.5	10.2	8.9
Subsidies for losses (billion yuan)	n.a.	n.a.	32.5	44.6	59.9	57.9	51.0	44.4
Loss-subsidies as % of budgetary revenues	n.a.	n.a.	14.3	17.0	20.3	17.4	14.1	10.7

Source: China Statistical Yearbook, 1990–1993.

Note: a Large- and medium-sized state enterprises with independent accounting.

though they are supposed to be in theory. For those enterprises that make unexpectedly large profits, their revenue remittances do not increase beyond the contracted amounts. Consequently, government revenue is destined to fall because of this institutionalized asymmetry.

The central government revenue is mainly dependent on taxes and profit remittances from the large and medium-sized SOEs. But since the financial performance of these enterprises has been below average, there has been a fall in central government revenue relative to total revenue.

Another cause for the relative decline in total budget revenue and central budget revenue is the change in central-local fiscal relations. Under the "Contracting Budgetary System" (CBS), the amount of revenue transfer between local and central government is also pre-set by contracts that were determined by a one-to-one bargaining process between the central and provincial governments. (The provincial governments would then negotiate tax contracts with the lower down local governments). As the negotiated amounts are heavily influenced by the tax payments of the previous periods, central revenue growth has not kept up with the growth of the local economies. Moreover, to retain more revenues in the local economies, local governments have increasingly concealed their revenue bases. Local governments would allow local enterprises to under-report their taxable revenues and, in return, the enterprises would make contributions to local development projects when the local governments indicate their needs for funds. Such types of concealed-revenue arrangements have played increasingly important roles in the recent development of local economies. According to some surveys, such concealed funds amount to 40–70% of the explicit revenue of local governments (Sen and Zhu, 1993).[13] If this kind of "out-of-budget" local government revenues were added to the total government revenue, government revenue would not have fallen so much.

As the result of the decline in budget revenue, budget deficits and government borrowing from the banks have been rising (see Table 23–4). Furthermore, central government support for the development of poor regions has tapered off.

4.4. Subsidy Credits

An increasingly significant cause of inflation is the increase in policy loans to loss-making SOEs. The SOEs have gained more and more autonomy, but their budget constraint has remained soft. With the government's ability to subsidize the loss-making enterprises declining, bank loans have become a more important means of keeping these enterprises afloat. It is estimated that one-third of SOEs have explicit losses, and that another one-third of SOEs have "hidden losses" which refer to the accumulation of unpaid inter-enterprise debt. It is well known that the reported explicit losses understate the true losses substantially. According to a 1992 survey of 300 large and medium-sized SOEs carried out by the State Economic and Trade Commission,

---

13. That is, when the local government collects 100 yuan as a "budgetary revenue," it receives another 40 to 70 yuan as "out-of-budget revenue." They get 140 to 170 yuan in total.

TABLE 23–4 Budget Deficits

	1978	1980	1983	1985	1988	1989	1990	1991	1992
Budget revenues[a] as % of GNP	31.2	23.3		21.5	17.7	17.5	17.7	17.0	16.6
Growth index of total deficit			100	99.1	284.3	305.3	419.0	540.3	737.4
Total deficit as % of budget revenue[a]				3.7	13.3	12.7	15.5	18.4	21.8
Growth index of budgetary borrowing from banks			100	137.8	288.9	343.0	401.4	535.1	621.9

Source: China Statistical Yearbook, 1990, 1993.

Note: a Revenues include domestic government borrowing, but exclude foreign borrowing.

the average ratio of total debt to total assets was 180%. Other surveys suggest that the ratio was almost up to 200%.

As the policy loans are something of a "must," the central authority have encountered a dilemma in macroeconomic stabilization. It wants to curtail monetary expansion to cool down the over-heated economy, but it is not able to reduce credits to loss-making enterprises which are using these credits to maintain the wage levels of their employees. So, in practice, a tight credit policy hurts only profitable enterprises.

4.5. Locally Initiated Monetary Expansion

The most important cause of inflation and economic fluctuations in the past decade has been monetary expansion initiated by pressures exerted at the local level. Decentralization reform has produced strong "local public-ownership economies." Each region is led by a coalition of local governments, SOEs, and SOBs, and the regions compete with each other for bank credits to finance local growth. It is not market competition that they engage in, but competition under soft budget constraints.

Under the centrally planned system, regions would constantly demand for more investment projects. Now, under the decentralized system, they can make most decisions on investment by themselves.[14] Great pressures are put on the local banks for investment loans and in most cases local banks collude with the local governments and local enterprises. Diversion of credit and innovative financing have become common practices since the early 1980s. Innovative financing has taken forms that include requests for more credits from the central monetary authority, issuance of de facto "IOUs" to depositors, and misappropriation of funds from central projects to local projects, leaving the central projects to be financed by additional credits (see Zhong and Hong, 1990, and Oi, 1992). Since 1991, local governments and SOEs have also had the right to issue bonds to the public.

It is extremely difficult to test the hypothesis that the increase in money supply since 1978 has, to an increasing extent, been initiated by the local governments and SOEs. What we do know is that the actual money supply has always been greater than the money supply target set at the beginning of the period, and that banks usually extended more credits than allowed by their credit quotas without obtaining clearance first.

Table 23–5 shows that the enlargement of the difference between the planned money supply and actual money supply is correlated with the path of decentralization. First, the "actual-plan ratio" in column 3 and 6 were unusually high in the years of high inflation. Second, the years with high actual-plan ratios were years in which greater autonomy were granted to local economies and SOEs. Third, the years where

---

14. Local autonomy on investment projects has expanded over time. For example, in 1984, the limit on investment projects that a provincial authority could approve was raised from RMB10 million to RMB30 million. In 1992, this limit was raised to RMB50 million. Furthermore, nearly all "nonproductive investment projects" (apartment buildings, for instance) are under the jurisdiction of local governments. The result was that 82.7% of total investment in fixed assets in the state sector in 1992 was labeled "local projects" (Tang, 1992), and there was a 45.4% increase in total investment spending by the state sector in 1992.

TABLE 23–5   Planned and Actual Money Supply (in Billion Yuan)

	INCREMENT OF CREDIT			INCREMENT OF CASH		
	A PLANNED	*B ACTUAL*	*B/A*	*C PLANNED*	*D ACTUAL*	*D/C*
1983	354	378	1.07	60	90.7	1.51
1984	423	988	2.34	80	262.3	3.28
1985	715	1,486	2.09	150	195.7	1.30
1986	950	1,685	1.77	200	230.5	1.15
1987	1,225	1,442	1.17	230	236.1	1.03
1988	n.a.	1,518	n.a.	200	679.5	3.40
1989	n.a.	1,851	n.a.	400	210	0.53
1990	1,700	2,757	1.60	400	300	0.75
1991	2,100	2,878	1.37	500	533	1.07
1992	2,800	3,804	1.38	600	1,158	1.93

Sources: Zhong (1990) and Xie (1993).

the extra-plan ratios were low were years when local autonomy was curbed by the central government as part of a "retrenchment" programme. Of course, the data in Table 23–5 are only suggestive rather than definitive of the locally-initiated-monetary-expansion hypothesis. Other factors that could have contributed to the increase of the actual money supply were not controlled for.

5. CONCLUDING REMARKS

My conclusion is that the economic transformation experiences to date do not show that either approach to reform, radicalism or gradualism, is unconditionally better than the other. Rather, by comparing the initial economic and social situations and special economic structures, the only conclusion is that each approach may be a "constrained optimum" that reflects what is politically acceptable and economically feasible in each case. This does not mean that whatever happened was always right. It just shows that each approach has its own logic. Any comparison between Chinese reform and EEFSU reform is necessarily a difficult task. There have been only three years of radical reform in EEFSU. China, on the other hand, has been implementing reforms for over 15 years. Initial successes of Chinese reform should not be misjudged as superiority.

By saying that both approaches to reform are "constrained optimum," I am not saying that there is no need for improvements in reform strategies and implementation policies in both cases. Given that China is likely to stay on gradualism, there could be better gradualism. The policy recommendations presented here, for example, would render the reform process more efficient.

As pointed out above, there are several hardcore challenges facing China: ownership reform, macroeconomic stabilization, regional and rural-urban income disparity and political reform. Fortunately, positive signs are emerging.

Corporatization is becoming a widely accepted idea and ownership reform of the state sector is not only on the policy agenda but is also no longer a subject of political criticism. More and more state enterprises are being sold to, or merged with, non-state companies. Property rights in rural industries are being redefined and redistributed among members of local communities. Most important of all, knowledge about the market economy is rapidly growing. In short, China's market-oriented reform has become irreversible.

One thing is certain: any improvement of the situation in EEFSU (such as what has happened in Poland) will accelerate Chinese reform by giving China lessons on how to deal with difficulties, and putting more pressure on the Chinese government to catch up faster with the West.

REFERENCES

Bowles, Paul (1989). "Contradictions in China's Financial Reforms: the Relationship Between Banks and Enterprises," *Cambridge Journal of Economics.*

Chen, Kang, Gary Jefferson and Inderjit Singh (1992). "Lessons from China's Economic Reform," *Journal of Comparative Economics.*

Fan Gang (1993). "Two Kinds of Reform Costs and Two Approaches to Reform" (in Chinese), *Economic Research Journal.*

Fan Gang and Wing Thye Woo (1993). "Decentralized Socialism and Macroeconomic Stability: Lessons from China," Working Paper No. 112, World Institute for Development Economics Research, The United Nations University, July.

Gelb, Alan, Gary Jefferson & Inderjit Singh (1993). "The Chinese and East European Routes to Reform," manuscript, NBER Eighth annual Macroeconomics Conference.

Goldman, Marshall (1991). *What Went Wrong With Perestroika?* Norton.

Jefferson, Gary, Thomas Rawski and Yuxin Zheng (1992). "Growth, Efficiency and Convergence in China's State and Collective Industry," *Economic Development and Cultural Change.*

Oi, Jean C. (1992). "The Shifting Balance of Power in Central-local Relations: Local Government Response to Fiscal Austerity in Rural China," mimeo, Harvard University.

Qian, Yingyi, and Xu Chenggang (1993). "Why China's Economic Reforms Differ: The M-form Hierarchy and Entry/Expansion of the Non-state Sector," *The Economics of Transition.*

Sachs, Jeffrey and Wing Thye Woo (1994). "Structural Factors in the Economic Reforms of China, Eastern Europe, and the former Soviet Union," *Economic Policy.*

Sen, Tanzhen and Zhu Gang (1993). "A Study of Out-of-system Government Revenue of Township and Village," *Jingji Yanjui (Economic Research Journal).*

Shi, Z. Jeffrey (1993). "Reform for Decentralization and Decentralization for Reform: a Political Economy of China's reform," mimeo, University of Maryland.

Tang, Zongkun (1992). "Decline of Profits and Reproduction Capability of State Enterprises' (in Chinese), *Jingji Yanju (Journal of Economic Research).*

Wang, Chenghua and Xintao Li (1993). "The Losses of State Assets" (in Chinese), *Financial and Economic Studies.*

Woo, Wing Thye (1994). "The Art of Reforming Centrally-Planned Economies: Comparing China, Poland and Russia," *Journal of Comparative Economics.*

Woo, Wing Thye, Wen Hai, Yibiao Jin and Fan Gang (1994). "How Successful Has Chinese Enterprise Reforms Been? Pitfalls in Opposite Biases and Focus," *Journal of Comparative Economics.*

Zhang, Weiying (1993). "Decision Rights, Residual Claim and Performance: A Theory of How Chinese Economy Works," Nuffield College, Oxford, mimeo.

Zhong, Pengrong (1990). *A Study of China's Inflation* (in Chinese), Jianxi People's Press.

Zhong, Pengrong and Tonghu Hong (1990). *Macroeconomics* (in Chinese), Beijing: Economic Sciences Press.

Xie, Ping (1993). "Monetary Policy During the Transition towards the Market Economy," Working Paper, The People's Bank of China.

Part IV

IPE North and South

Part IV examines a variety of issues and problems surrounding different nations and groups of nations organized into what have typically been referred to as the Northern industrialized and Southern LDCs. One key issue of conformation between the rich North and poorer South is the "development dilemma." Examined here are some of the forces that have helped some of the newly industrialized countries (NICs) achieve some level of development while other LDCs still struggle to overcome tremendous odds in their effort to grow and raise their standard of living. The success of Taiwan, Singapore, South Korea, and Hong Kong is often cited as a model for other nations to copy if they want to develop. Other readings focus on development strategies for African nations and the large and important role that multinational corporations (MNCs) or transnational corporations (TNCs) play in the development process.

In "How Africa Can Prosper," Robert S. Browne examines some of the problems African nations have experienced in their effort to economically develop. By the 1980s traditional economic development strategies designed to encourage growth through trade were judged to be ineffective. The motivation for African integration is not so much to enhance efficiency of an economic liberal sort, but rather constitutes an effort to overcome dependency on export-led development and to achieve self-reliance. The World Bank and other international finance institutions frown on these strategies, preferring that LDCs adopt structural adjustment policies of the neoclassical economic liberal variety. Browne argues that most African nations would benefit from efforts to promote regional integration and increase intraregional trade. He examines several efforts to do so. As in the case of the EU and integration efforts in Asia, politics and even war still separates nations and works against the success of African unity.

If African nations are having a difficult time developing, the NICs have become success stories and models to many other nations. "Asia's Emerging Economies" by *The Economist* surveys the Asian NICs and tries to outline the tangible and intangible elements of a successful development strategy. To some extent influenced by the Japanese model of export-led growth (see the paper by Karl J. Fields in Part II), these nations have undergone record growth over a relatively short period of time. *The Economist* suggests that economic liberal policies that limited welfare payments and stressed productivity and international competitiveness were big lessons. However, a mercantilist outlook on the role of the state in guiding the economy, easy access to the American economy and technology, and a "relatively equal distribution of incomes and relatively low taxes" also helped motivate workers. Other "intangibles" were recognized to be "the coherence of a society, (and) its commitment to common ideals, goals and values." What many officials and business leaders fear is that the Asian Tigers will not be able to sustain the growth they have achieved. Labor is cheaper in nations nearby, new investment from Japan and other nations is not guaranteed, and political conditions inside and outside the region remain unpredictable, especially developments in China. Perhaps there are two lessons here for all LDCs. In the case of many of the NICs, one lesson is that success in the past does not guarantee continued success in the future. Second, academics and other experts may have a good understanding of the many factors and conditions that contribute to underdevelopment or that get in the way of an LDC's development. As of yet, however, there is no fool-proof strategy nations can adopt that will guarantee that they will successfully overcome their development problems.

In his classic essay, "Multinationals and Developing Countries: Myths and Realities," Peter F. Drucker sheds more light on the development process. Drucker explores and debunks four accepted propositions about MNCs, the basis of which are found in structuralist descriptions of MNCs. Drucker challenges many of the structuralist arguments against MNCs, in particular that LDCs are important to MNCs and that MNCs exploit LDCs. Drucker also challenges other commonly held assumptions about LDCs, for instance, that they lack capital. What LDCs lack is the ability to make the most of their resources. In contrast to Collingsworth et al. in Part III, Drucker faults MNCs for neglect and indifference to LDCs rather than exploitation of them. He believes MNCs to be one of the few trump cards of the LDCs. He goes on to argue that those LDCs with limited capacity to trade or acquire foreign aid are compelled to depend on investment to support their development efforts. MNCs may as yet be the best chance LDCs have to become integrated into the larger world economy.

Like Drucker, William Greider has recently become a prolific writer. In "The Global Marketplace: A Closet Dictator," Greider would agree with Drucker that MNCs have "obvious benefits as a modernizing influence on the world." Yet whereas Drucker views integration into the world economy as a good (economically liberal) thing, Greider believes that the "new version of internationalism" promulgated by MNCs "will continue to undermine America's widely shared prosperity" and subvert "the nation's ability to set its own political standards." He documents the many cases of MNC exploitation and abuse in Mexico, and the efforts by the United States to accommodate MNCs. Yet, as MNCs freely move around the world, jobs and taxes are lost at home, weakening local labor and environmental laws and ultimately the nation's sovereignty. The closet dictator—the marketplace—promises to unravel democracies. In language that sounds quite Marxist in tone, Greider would have people in the United States and different nations cooperate with one another to form new democratic alliances in an effort "to impose new political standards on multina tional enterprises and on their own governments."

Energy and oil are issues that concern almost all nations. Because of their critical role in the industrialization and development process, these two related issues have been of utmost importance but also of some dispute between nations of the North and South. In his article "Oil and Power After the Gulf War" Robert J. Lieber outlines the role that the Organization of Petroleum Exporting Countries (OPEC) played in setting oil prices in the early and late 1970s. Since then it appears that the scarcity of oil and other resources is not the issue of crisis proportions that many forecasted it would be. Yet, Lieber argues that there is good reason to believe the contrary. He suggests that had a few events associated with the recent Persian Gulf war turned out differently, oil prices might be back up where they were in the 1970s. The price and availability of oil is conditioned just as much by economic conditions as it is politics. Arab countries such as Iran, Iraq, and Saudi Arabia, who have been at war with one another during the past fifteen years and continue to remain political adversaries, are key players in the international economy given their control over major oil fields. This situation, coupled with the fact that the United States and other industrialized nations remain quite dependent on oil imports, makes for a potentially volatile situation.

24. How Africa Can Prosper

Robert S. Browne

Africa has looked on with dismay as the world has raced down the contradictory tracks of GATT-led free trade, on the one hand, and the European Union and NAFTA, on the other. As it has become more evident that Europe and the United States are distancing themselves from a full commitment to free trade in favor of the erection of regional trading blocs, Africa has become increasingly concerned about where it will fit within this new trading paradigm.

Consisting of some 47 national entities, most of which are economic midgets, Africa[1] is acutely aware that the already weak bargaining power of its component states is further eroded when they must confront, not a single nation, but an integrated regional trading entity. One notable consequence of this concern has been the rejuvenation within Africa of the movement for regional economic integration.

Regional integration has been a live issue in Africa since the early years of independence. Such stalwarts as Ghana's Kwame Nkrumah, leader of black Africa's first successful national independence struggle, recognized early on the vulnerability of an Africa brought into independence as a number of small and economically nonviable national units rather than as a limited number of larger, integrated units. His warnings went unheeded, however, as ever larger numbers of mini-states sought independence, complete with national flags, presidents, and parliaments, thereby creating vested interests in these new, often artificial national entities. Leaving aside the serious problems of irredentism and fractured tribal groupings that these colonially determined frontiers aroused, the economic irrationalism that they imposed on the continent is proving to be devastating. It is this economic irrationalism that is being exacerbated by the enhanced trading disparities produced by the new passion for regional trading blocs.

Although foreign assistance has been one major source of funds for such economic development as Africa has experienced since independence, foreign trade has actually been Africa's principal source of revenue. This commerce has taken place almost exclusively with non-African countries; only about 4 percent of Africa's recorded trade has been intra-African. With the exception of South Africa, the economies of Africa depend primarily on the export of primary commodities, either agricultural products or natural resources, and the import of manufactured goods. Because their economies are small, the African countries are price-takers rather than price-makers—that is, they exercise little influence over the prices of either their ex-

Robert S. Browne is an international economic development consultant and former U.S. executive director of the African Development Fund.
From "How Africa Can Prosper," by Robert S. Browne. *World Policy Journal,* Vol XI, No 3, Fall 1994, pp. 29–39. Reprinted by permission.

ports or their imports. Given the volatility of commodity prices and the chronic tendency toward decline in the terms of trade, Africa's prospects for achieving a greater degree of economic independence are dim unless its trading power can be enhanced.

Despite their articulated concern over Africa's poor growth record, the developed countries have persisted in maintaining policies that perpetuate rather than alleviate Africa's dependency relationship, suggesting at best some ambivalence as to what global role the developed countries truly envision for Africa. For example, developed countries continue to impose the insidious practice of "tariff escalation," by which the tariff rate rises with the degree of processing to which an imported commodity has been subjected, thus effectively precluding Africa from developing an industrial sector around its substantial mining and agricultural interests. The recently completed Uruguay Round of GATT negotiations largely ignored Africa's needs and approved many provisions likely to prove detrimental to Africa's interests.[2] Faced with such an uncompromising climate, it is not surprising that Africa is seeking to shore up its own regional strengths in the hope that the playing field of international trade can be prevented from tilting even further to its disadvantage.

A SPLINTERED CONTINENT

Although intra-African trade appears to have been widespread in precolonial Africa, the arrival of imperialism shifted the focus of Africa's trading activities toward Europe. The transport networks built by the colonial powers were designed to evacuate products to the port and thence to Europe, not to link the colonies with one another. Thirty years after independence, there are still few roads or railways connecting the major African cities. The air travel network has developed on a similar pattern: most African countries have frequent, direct air connections to at least one European capital, but the swiftest air connections between many African countries, including not-so-distant neighbors, is often by way of Europe. There are even places where telephone communications still must be routed via Europe, despite the relative proximity of the caller and the called. Such clumsy linkages are not only expensive and time consuming; they constitute a palpable barrier to the development of any meaningful business relationships among neighboring countries. Fortunately, new communications technology offers a means for eventually sidestepping these longstanding communications blockages, although the emergence of a telecommunications superhighway in Africa lies far in the future.

The obstacles to intra-African trading go well beyond transportation and communication barriers. One of the most frequently cited problems is that the economies of most African countries—especially those that are neighbors—simply do not complement one another. Most African countries produce primary commodities, either agricultural or mineral, which they export overseas. Few use these products in any significant quantity, and rarely can they be used in the unprocessed form in which they are generally exported. Africa does produce some consumer goods—such as cigarettes, clothing and textiles, beverages, household utensils, and furniture—and a few countries produce more sophisticated items such as electrical appliances, batteries, tires, and pharmaceuticals. In one or two countries, steel and a smattering of industrial items are manufactured. There is a modest intra-African trade in these items.

Given the nonviable economic size of most African national markets, regional markets are essential for the development of an industrial sector. Currently, domestic production (other than of primary commodities) is generally domestically consumed, either because the scale of production is insufficient to permit exports or because there is little external demand for the products. These products are generally not competitive in overseas markets, and neighboring countries often either make identical items or else feel that they can purchase better quality items from overseas, and at cheaper prices. This is sometimes true because the domestically produced items are primitive or flawed—but more often is the case because a foreign (generally European) manufacturer is willing to "tailor" prices to local conditions, or to offer more favorable credit terms to an African importer than neighboring African exporters can afford.

The lack of a mutually acceptable transaction currency constitutes another impediment to intra-African trade. The remnants of the colonial mentality, plus the nonconvertability of most African currencies, result in the demand that intra-African trade be carried out in hard currency. The spectacle of two African countries trading with one another but insisting on payment only in dollars, francs, or pounds is an egregious contradiction to the continent's widely articulated commitment to pan-Africanism. Nonetheless, it is common practice.

Tariff and nontariff barriers, together with a lack of harmony in customs nomenclature and procedures, differing trading philosophies and marketing arrangements, varying exchange-control arrangements, and large disparities in size and level of economic development among neighboring states are significant impediments to regional cooperation and integration. Labor and capital immobility and bureaucratic requirements of unimaginable obscurity and unpredictability also serve to discourage African regional economic cooperation.

THE WILL AND THE WAY

Although the foregoing obstacles to integration are formidable, they are not insurmountable. Most can be overcome if African governments have the will to do so. The politics are not easy, however, because the benefits of integration generally accrue in the long term, whereas the costs are immediate. Intellectually, there is a strong push within Africa for regional economic cooperation and integration. Its rationale lies in the belief that Africa should reduce its excessive dependence on export-led development and work toward a strategy of collective self-reliance. Even at the level of heads of state, the Organization of African Unity has issued a steady stream of calls for greater economic integration. Among the more notable were the Lagos Plan of Action, which emerged in 1980 from a special economic summit meeting of African heads of state and called on Africa to create a common market by the year 2000. This plan was updated at the 1991 OAU summit meeting, which fathered a treaty outlining an African Economic Community it envisaged to be operating by 2025. The treaty has been ratified by two-thirds of its signatory governments and is now in force.

Many steps led to the emergence of this treaty, and much effort will be required to transform it into a genuine operating entity. Since independence, most African countries have been content to follow their pre-independence patterns of economic development, which essentially consisted of using their land either to grow or mine products for sale abroad and then using the proceeds to import the goods they needed. This so-called export-led development strategy worked fairly well throughout the early years of independence, but by the mid-1970s Africa's economic growth had begun to stagnate, and by the 1980s, had turned negative in many countries.

Although the reasons for this economic decline were varied, one of the more visible was that Africa's terms of trade were steadily deteriorating. The prices that Africa was receiving for its exports were declining as the prices of its imports were rising, and there was virtually nothing that Africa, as an exporter of primary commodities, could do about it. Setting the prices of either its exports or its imports lay outside its control, and its pleas for the enactment of global measures to stabilize the prices, if not the quantities, of its exports fell on deaf ears.

Alarmed by the continent's growing impoverishment, Africa's economic development intellectuals began to call for a reduction in the excessive dependence on exports and the initiation of a program of collective self-reliance. By self-reliance they meant that Africa should begin to directly produce the things it needed, rather than producing goods for export and then purchasing its needs with the proceeds of the sales. Recognizing that most African countries are too small to offer markets that could attract major investment, they called on African governments to focus on the creation of regional markets, adding "collective" to the self-reliance concept and gradually winning the endorsement of every African head of state and government at a special summit meeting in 1980.

Africa's enthusiasm for collective self-reliance and for the regional integration concept was not widely shared within the donor community. The World Bank, particularly, was highly skeptical of the wisdom of placing serious reliance on regional integration and was adamantly opposed to Africa departing in any way from the export-led development strategy that had become the prevalent development theology within World Bank circles. A full explanation for the bank's coolness toward African regional integration has, to my knowledge, never been articulated. But its overt hostility to any breaching of the export-led development strategy presumably derives from its blind adherence to classical Ricardian "comparative advantage" theory and to its belief that import-led substitution strategies had invariably resulted in overly protected and highly inefficient industrial ventures by their borrowing members (principally in Latin America).

Within African circles, some credence is given to a "conspiracy" explanation, which argues that the World Bank and its bosses, the developed countries, find it in their interests to keep the African countries as mainly exporters of raw materials and importers of manufactured items rather than to assist them in becoming tenacious industrial competitors, as the newly industrialized countries of East Asia have become.

The fact that the economic competition from low-wage developing countries is an increasingly controversial issue in the domestic policies of the major industrialized nations undoubtedly lends credibility to this perspective.

A part of the World Bank's resistance to this new strategic thinking coming out of Africa can also be attributed to the strains that arose when the bank insisted on structural adjustment programs as the solution to Africa's economic disarray and as a condition for obtaining loans. Space does not permit a discussion of this controversy here; suffice it to say that neither the World Bank nor the African countries seem to have understood that a strategy of collective self-reliance need not be seen as a natural enemy of properly framed structural adjustment programs. Indeed, if properly conceived, they should reinforce one another.

A spirited intellectual debate swirled around these issues during most of the 1980s. The World Bank's insistence on export-led development rested heavily on its prediction of an imminent halt in the long-term decline of primary commodity prices, and when this prediction proved to be grossly incorrect, the bank seems to have (ever so slightly) softened its resistance to the self-reliance concept.

Whereas in its first landmark report on sub-Saharan development in 1982 the World Bank devoted only a few, relatively innocuous sentences to regional integration, by 1989, in its second major report on sub-Saharan Africa, it included an entire chapter on the topic, even though the bank's strong preference for the export-led development strategy remained virtually undiminished. More recent statements by the bank suggest that it may be coming to accept a more African perspective on what really needs to be done to stimulate genuine growth and development in Africa (although the availability of the requisite funds is in serious doubt).

THEORIES OF UNITY

In Africa, the drive for regional integration is perceived as a survival mechanism, although its overall objectives are not dissimilar to NAFTA's. The hope is that regional economic integration will stimulate intra-African trade and provide, within Africa, a market potential of sufficient breadth to attract investment capital to the region. African countries give intra-African trade priority because these countries believe they can ultimately establish a more stable market for the sale of African-made products than the overseas export market provides. In any case, because Africa lags so far behind the rest of the world in technological skills, it cannot aspire to be a competitive producer in the short term. A protected internal market offers the only opportunity for Africa to move up the technology learning curve.

In the years since independence, Africa has spawned a plethora of regional organizations, of which half a dozen or so are striving to weld countries together into strong (sub)regional entities. Most of them seek to increase intra-African trade via the collective reduction of myriad trade barriers, although one entity, the Southern Africa Development Coordination Conference (SADCC), placed its initial emphasis on encouraging functional, single-country projects of a multinational nature, such as the construction of national roads and railways designed to facilitate commerce among neighboring states.

Regional economic integration did not begin with Africa, of course, and there is a substantial history of such undertakings in Latin America and elsewhere. Development theory holds that regional integration follows five steps—the creation of:

- a preferential trade area (liberalization of trade barriers among members);
- a free trade zone (abolition of trade barriers among members);
- a customs union (a common tariff policy among members);
- a common market (free movement of factors of production and of commodities within the region); and
- an economic community (harmonization of national monetary and economic policies among member countries).

Full economic integration arrives only after all these stages have been successfully completed and is characterized by the unification of economic and social policies of the members under a supranational authority. A common currency and a central bank are implicit therein. In Africa, the merging of the several (sub)regional economic communities to be developed across the continent over the next 30 years will create the proposed African Economic Community.

The foregoing sequence is not invariable, and it only approximates the African experience. Perhaps the biggest departure from it was the early creation of a common currency, the CFA franc (Communauté Fianancière Africaine), for 13 of France's former African colonies. Since 1948, France has underwritten the CFA franc under a formal agreement, which obliges the African participants to take 65 percent of their foreign exchange holdings in the French Treasury and to accept limits on the management of their international monetary affairs. The blessing of having a freely convertible common currency affords these countries an unusually high degree of solidarity within their region. France's motivation for structuring and maintaining the CFA monetary zone, which for 45 years unfailingly underwrote this African currency at the fixed rate of 50 CFA francs to 1 French franc, was clearly the desire to maintain some of the trappings of empire, as well as to retain its hold over the colonial market. A by-product, however, has been to knit together these former colonies in a closer relationship than is enjoyed by most of the rest of Africa. Probably not coincidentally, trade among this CFA-using group of countries has been running at about 9 percent of total trade—more than double the rate in the rest of Africa—which is probably a reflection of the relative monetary stability provided by the convertibility of the CFA and French francs.

During its early years, the CFA arrangements undoubtedly worked to the benefit of France because the African members generally ran surpluses in their trade balances. During the 1980s, however, the collapse of commodity prices reversed this situation and the CFA became a drain on the French Treasury, sparking speculation that France might abandon it. More urgently, the CFA gradually became seriously overvalued, leading to disastrous distortions and serious economic hardship in CFA-using countries. Calls by the International Monetary Fund and World Bank for a devaluation of the CFA long fell on deaf ears, but in early 1994 the CFA/French franc exchange rate was finally reduced from 50 to 1, which had prevailed since 1948, to a new rate of 100 to 1.

Currency unification is only one of many goals for which countries normally strive in seeking to achieve regional integration. In the building of the European Union, for example, currency unification was left to the end and still remains an unrealized goal. Normally, once the creation of a regionally integrated entity has been agreed to, the reduction of tariff and nontariff barriers within the region is designated as the area for priority attention. This has certainly been the pattern in the two largest regional economic integration efforts that have been made in sub-Saharan Africa, the Economic Community of West African States (ECOWAS) and the Preferential Trade Area of Eastern and Southern Africa (PTA).

THE WEST AFRICAN DILEMMA

ECOWAS, the largest of the African regional integration organizations (in terms of population), consists of 16 nations in West Africa. It boasts a total population of 179 million, of which one country, Nigeria, accounts for 100 million, or 56 percent of the total. Nine francophone states join with five anglophone and two lusophone states to constitute this entity, which was created in 1975. ECOWAS is committed to the following program:

- to liberalize trade, eventually eliminating tariffs between member nations and leading to some pooling of resources;
- to create a West African Common Market similar to the European Union;
- to form a united front against lender nations when renegotiating foreign debt financing;
- to legalize free movement of citizens between one ECOWAS state and another;
- to create a common currency for the region; and
- to improve telecommunications and road systems to link member states.

ECOWAS has thus far placed its major emphasis on trade liberalization and on the free movement of citizens within the region. It has had little success with the former. At its inception, ECOWAS designated a number of targets for tariff reduction and tariff harmonization. They were to be achieved in stages, with the goal of having a full customs union in place within 15 years, that is, by 1993. Unfortunately, by 1993, targets scheduled to be met in the early 1980s had not yet been reached, and there was little expectation that they would be met anytime soon. Clearly, the ECOWAS member states are either unwilling or unable to carry through on the commitments that they had adopted, a phenomenon that has been repeated elsewhere in Africa.

Both unwillingness and inability probably play a role in these disappointing results. Most African countries depend heavily on customs duties as a major, sometimes *the* major, source of government revenues. Compared with alternative revenue-raising vehicles, the tariff is an easier tax to enact and to administer, and states are reluctant to give it up.

A hopeful step toward the encouragement of trade within West Africa was the creation of the West African Clearinghouse. The role of the clearinghouse is to enable ECOWAS members to trade with one another with minimal use of hard currency. Via the clearinghouse, traders can carry out their transactions using local currencies, needing to settle only their *net* balances in hard currencies at periodic intervals. Although an excellent idea, it has not worked out well in practice, in part because some countries are persistently tardy in settling their balances, which impacts negatively on others. Of course, CFA-using countries need this facility only when they trade with non-CFA ECOWAS members.

ECOWAS has also made a strong effort to facilitate the mobility of labor within the region, also with mixed results. An ECOWAS-created travel document permits citizens of member countries to move about within the region much more easily than before, both as tourists and as migrants. This signal achievement, however, has been marred by several mass expulsions of nationals of other member countries under the stress of local pressures. Free movement of peoples is clearly not yet the order of the day.

ECOWAS has also attempted to attract new investment capital by promising investors access to a 16-nation, tariff-free market. The potential economies of scale are real, but luring investors depends on fulfilling promises, as well as on a host of additional factors, including the overall climate for investment in the region. Unfortunately, the failure to deal effectively with this latter problem, plus the meager progress achieved in the creation of even a preferential trading area, has meant that investment in West Africa remains low.

Another set of obstacles frustrating ECOWAS's pursuit of regional integration has been differences in size, wealth, and stage of development of its members. This is a classic problem faced by all regional integration efforts. Where there are great disparities in any of these factors, the costs and benefits that emerge will be unequally distributed, with poorer countries usually getting the least benefit but often bearing the most cost. To keep the regional arrangement alive, measures have been introduced to minimize such inequities, either through bureaucratic or financial incentives, or via direct cash transfers to the losers from a compensation fund to which the winners ideally contribute.

The ECOWAS Fund for Cooperative Compensation and Development has been created specifically to make compensatory funding available. But member states have made only desultory contributions to the fund: other than the construction of a splendid headquarters building and the establishment of a special telecommunications modernization fund, its achievements have not been significant. This is especially disappointing to the smaller and poorer countries, who looked to the fund to balance the disparity between themselves and their giant Nigerian neighbor. France has also created a similar fund to ease inequities within the regional economic associations that it has created among its former colonies.

In brief, except for the CFA monetary zone, West Africa can point to only very modest progress down the path of economic integration, with the convertible CFA franc perhaps the most successful program. The CFA zone has been a mixed blessing, however. Some vocal ECOWAS members complain bitterly that the presence of the tightly linked CFA-using group of countries within the all-encompassing regional community of West Africa has proved to be an obstacle to an effective economic integration program for the overall West African region.

Indeed, under French leadership, the francophone states have grouped themselves into several special-purpose economic associations whose objectives parallel the ECOWAS program and inhibit the effectiveness of the larger grouping. These associations have been accused of driving a wedge into West African solidarity and of being little more than nefarious tools for maintaining French influence within independent Africa.

ASPIRATIONS AND REALITY

East Africa has no regional economic organization devoted solely to it. The largest and perhaps the most effective of Africa's regional economic integration organizations carries the clumsy title of the Preferential Trade Area for Eastern and Southern Africa, or PTA. The geographic reach of this 18-nation entity sweeps from the Horn of Africa down the entire eastern coast and then across the south to the Atlantic coastal countries of Namibia and Angola. Although apartheid South Africa was excluded from membership, the PTA does include the two national enclaves geographically surrounded by South Africa—Lesotho and Swaziland—as well as the Indian Ocean island nations of Mauritius and Comoros.

Despite the fact that the overwhelming number of PTA members are English speaking, it is culturally and linguistically a diverse organization, encompassing Africa's two major lusophone countries, Mozambique and Angola, the former Belgian colonies of Rwanda and Burundi, the former Italian colony of Somalia, and former French-ruled Djibouti.

The PTA has fared better than ECOWAS, although it, too, set ambitions tariff-reduction targets only to have them repeatedly postponed because of noncompliance by member states. On the other hand, it has created a clearinghouse that has succeeded in attracting 50 percent of intra-PTA trade. Although it is not free of problems, as of mid-1993 the PTA clearinghouse had never experienced a default, not even from Somalia.

Other successful innovations within the PTA include the creation of a traveler's check that is usable within the 18-country region, thereby eliminating the need for intra-region travelers to carry several currencies with them or to change their money at each frontier. Equally helpful has been the adoption of the Road Customs Transit Declaration document (RCTD), which enables transport vehicles to travel among PTA-member countries without being subjected to frequent inspections and redocumentation of their cargoes. This practice had traditionally been a major deterrent to interstate, and even to intrastate, shipping. A PTA report claims that on the Mombasa-Kampala-Kigali-Bujumbura corridor the introduction of the RCTD permitted trucks to achieve turn-around times of two per month instead of one per month. The 1986 creation of the PTA Development Bank is also seen as a positive action to facilitate the mobilization of capital for regional investment in multinational projects. It has, however, been slow in getting launched and as yet has little to show in the way of results.

Because it is not yet even a preferential trade area, but aspires to become much more than just that, the PTA recently voted to rename and restructure itself into the Community of Eastern and Southern Africa, or COMESA. Its mandate remains essentially unchanged and differs little from that of ECOWAS.

The need to provide a more ambitious name for the PTA arose from the growing tension between it and the Southern Africa Development Community (SADC), the other major economic integration effort in the southern Africa region.

The SADC consists of the nine southern-most PTA member states plus Botswana. The SADC (until recently officially known as the southern Africa Development Coordinating Conference, or SADCC) has long had a competitive relationship with the PTA. It was created in 1980 to strengthen the states contiguous to or closely affected by South Africa and to enable them to resist the destabilizing aggression, both economic and military, that emanated from South Africa as the anti-apartheid struggle intensified.

At its inception, the SADCC has no pretensions of becoming a common market or an economic union, instead limiting itself to developing functional projects. Over the period 1982–92, the SADCC obtained funding for an impressive number of projects, mainly in the transport sector. The best known of these was the reconstruction of the Beira Corridor—roadway, railway, and port—which created a usable transport network across Mozambique and provided several of the landlocked SADCC member countries with an alternative to South African railways for the evacuation of their exports.

With the crumbling of the apartheid regime, the original mission of the SADCC dissolved. This led the SADCC membership, in 1992, to reformulate itself into a new organization, the southern African Development Community. Its objective is similar to that of the PTA/COMESA: the achievement of development and growth for the region through regional integration and self-reliance. Among the specific tasks that is set for itself was the elimination of "obstacles to the free movement of capital and labor, goods and services, and of the peoples of the Region generally, among Member States."[3]

Earlier in 1992, the PTA heads of state had voted to merge the SADCC into the PTA, in view of the high degree of overlap in the membership and objectives of the two organizations. But eight months later, meeting as the heads of state of the SADCC, the same PTA member countries completely reversed their position and created instead the SADC, in a turnabout stunning even for Africa. The overlap of membership, the duplication of purpose, and the strains of competition between these organizations argue strongly for a harmonization or merging of their efforts. Whether human and political sensitivities will allow this to take place without external pressure remains to be seen.

A POWERFUL NEW PLAYER

A major contemporary concern in both groupings is the prospect of a post-apartheid South Africa seeking membership in one or both of the organizations. The South African economy is larger than the economies of all ten SADC countries combined, and an SADC staffer once publicly mused that he did not know whether it would be a question of South Africa joining the SADC or of the SADC joining South Africa. Clearly, the emergence of post-apartheid South Africa will have profound effects throughout the region. An often-expressed fear among SADC members is that foreign investors seeking to locate in southern Africa are likely to be attracted to the highly sophisticated South African economy in preference to the neighboring countries. Within both South Africa and the United States, one hears frequent reference to South Africa's "destiny" to become the engine of growth for all of southern Africa, and even for the whole continent. Such comments are cause for considerable alarm within the other countries of the region, all of whom have made serious sacrifices on behalf of the South African liberation struggle but who now fear the possible effect that this powerful new player may have on the region.

Regrettably, the rhetoric of African unity is often contradicted by the reality of African existence, which has been characterized by an astonishing amount of warfare in the post-independence years, mostly of an internecine nature. Many of these wars have been instigated and fueled by the big powers as part of their Cold War strategies (as in Zaire, Angola, Mozambique, Ethiopia, and Somalia), but there has also been a dismaying number of internally generated wars (as in Sudan, Liberia, and Rwanda).

Despite these persistent struggles, Africa's leaders make great pronouncements in support of regional economic integration. Unfortunately, their actions fall considerably short of their rhetoric. Their failure to comply with their own tariff-reduction commitments, their cavalier attitude regarding the removal of bureaucratic impediments to trade and foreign investment, even when from African sources, and their reneging on agreed-upon immigration policies for citizens of member states all belie their verbal commitments.

This contradiction is further emphasized by the widespread failure of many member states to pay their dues and meet their other financial obligations to their respective regional associations. While these delinquencies may be understandable in light of the austere budgetary situation in which most of Africa finds itself, the other failures are less excusable and may indicate that, at least at the highest levels of government, regional economic integration is not viewed as a priority issue.

On the other hand, summit meetings of ECOWAS, the PTA, the SADC, and some of the smaller regional groupings not discussed here generally attract a surprisingly good turnout of heads of state. Nevertheless, it must be admitted that the real push for African regional economic integration comes from the intellectual community, which probably sees more clearly than the politicians that without a regional integration strategy, Africa can never hope to pull itself up from the global economic cellar.

THE AMERICAN EFFORT

Although the United States has not been particularly supportive of Africa's efforts at regional integration, Congress, largely at the initiative of members of the Congressional Black Caucus, annually earmarked $50 million for the SADCC from 1989 to 1993. This was a fairly modest sum compared to contributions of some other Western donor countries, but, coming from the world's major economic power it was a very important symbol of support. Unfortunately, it was dropped from the 1994 aid bill as part of an agreement between Congress and the Clinton administration that there would be no designation of funds (except for Israel and Egypt) in forthcoming assistance legislation. Considering the confusion of roles that has developed between the SADC and the PTA, cessation of these funds comes at an opportune moment. Perhaps now the two organizations will see the need either to merge or at least to allocate the work between them in a rational manner so that donors will better know how to proceed.

Over the years, there has been some minor funding provided by the United States for some of the other African regional integration programs but never any major commitment to these organizations. Happily, in the restructured foreign assistance program that is gradually emerging in Washington, explicit mention is expected to be made of the need for increased attention to regional economic integration efforts, so the outlook is promising.

Exactly what is the U.S. interest in this whole topic, if any? Does the United States have an interest in seeing that the African economies are placed on a sound growth path, and is regional economic integration the best means for putting Africa on this path?

With regard to the former, there is plenty of evidence that the answer is yes. To be sure, the debate over NAFTA brought to the surface the concerns that Americans have about the increasing difficulty that developed countries face in competing with the lower wage costs of the Third World. At times it seems that the nation is having second thoughts about the wisdom of having built up the Japanese, Korean, and Taiwanese economies in view of the way these countries are now sucking up American jobs. Are the African conspiracy theorists right in suspecting that the West fears the emergence of additional rivals for the jobs of its labor force and therefore prefers to see Africa remain principally an exporter of primary commodities and an importer of manufactured goods and services?

This case can probably be made, in fact probably is being made at this very moment in some corridor of power. But it is a short-sighted judgment from a number of points of view. Morally, it is indefensible to condemn millions of people to a near hopeless existence when the means exist to assist them. Economically, an expanding and developing Africa, even one inwardly focused, would offer a tremendous market for all sorts of U.S. goods and services that Africa will be unable to produce at home for many years. Environmentally, Africa's rich endowment of natural resources, which are of use to all the world, is fast eroding away due to the poverty of its people, a result that harms everyone. And politically, the vast and growing disparity between the wealth of the developed countries and the poverty of the poor ones is a time bomb waiting to explode. It is in everyone's interest that it be defused, but, regrettably, after three "Decades of Development," the gap continues to widen.

An African woman, appearing recently on a cable television program, made the trenchant observation: "The rich must learn to share their wealth; otherwise the poor will be obliged to share their poverty." This was not meant as a threat, but it eloquently dramatizes why it is strongly in the U.S. interest to assist Africa to move toward a sustained and sustainable growth path.

Having accepted that it is in the U.S. interest to accelerate the economic development of Africa, the question becomes whether regional economic development is the best means for achieving this. By now it is fairly clear that Africa's mini-states are generally too small to become viable, self-supporting entities, and the same is only slightly less apparent for the others, except for the half dozen largest ones. Although a political consolidation is really called for, so radical a solution is not likely in the foreseeable future. A strategy of regional economic integration, however, can create attractive target areas for investment capital and offers a slender chance for weaning Africa from its heavy dependence on others. Obviously, regional economic integration is not the whole answer to Africa's problems. Dramatic changes in other African policies and practices are needed as well.

The disappointing progress achieved thus far in African regional economic integration does not inspire confidence in the prospects for this strategy, but there is virtually no alternative—certainly not within a democratic framework. Directly, and through its influence in the World Bank, the United States can give a serious push to the regional integration effort by affording it maximum support and visibility. Although this largely means money, it also means America using its influence in subtler ways. By creating incentives for African countries to seek foreign assistance on a regional basis rather than solely on a national basis, the United States can help to replace the competition for aid monies with a spirit of cooperation among neighboring countries.

When the African states ratified the treaty establishing the African Economic Community, they may have displayed excessive optimism in setting 2025 as their target date, given the many decades that Europe has already spent pursuing a similar, and as yet unachieved goal. The date may indeed be unrealistic, but the goal is absolutely correct, and regional economic integration provides the road map to get there.

NOTES

1. References to Africa apply solely to sub-Saharan Africa.
2. For example, provisions of the Agreements on Trade-Related Investment Measures (TRIMs) and Trade-Related Intellectual Property (TRIPs) and the refusal to phase out the Multi-Fibre Agreement. TRIMs oblige governments to lift laws regulating foreign investment, passed to ensure that investment contributes to development (via requirements to hire local personnel, domestic-content regulations, and similar obligations). TRIPs allow transnational corporations to patent new seeds and other life forms being introduced as replacements for existing Third World seed stocks. Developing-country farmers will not only be beholden to foreign suppliers for seeds but also will be obliged to pay a monopoly price for such items. The Multi-Fibre Agreement is a longstanding arrangement permitting developed countries to place severe limits on the volume of textile imports. Developing countries had hoped that this agreement would be terminated at the Uruguay Round of the GATT talks; instead, it was extended for another decade.
3. Treaty of the Southern African Development Association, Article 5, Section 2(d). Issued at Windhoek, Namibia, August 17, 1992.

25. Asia's Emerging Economies

The Economist

BURNING BRIGHT

Four decades ago, Asia seemed condemned to poverty. Half of Japan's workforce was in the fields; the other half in factories that were only 15% as productive as America's. "Made in Japan" meant gimcrack. Shanghai, previously one of Asia's most dynamic cities, had fallen to Mao's Communists; its refugees streamed on to a hopeless little island called Taiwan. Korea was poorer than Sudan and on the brink of a devastating civil war. Hong Kong and Singapore were busy little ports, but not a lot more. A pundit, asked to choose the Asian cities of the future, would probably have chosen Manila, Rangoon, and Saigon.

Today, two of that trio are basket cases and Manila is rapidly heading that way. While they have languished, Japan has emerged as the world's industrial superpower. The four economic "tigers" of East Asia—South Korea, Taiwan, Singapore and Hong Kong—have forged the fastest industrial revolutions the world has ever seen. Behind them are another four countries which are getting close to the point of industrial take-off—Thailand, Malaysia, Indonesia and, most interestingly, China.

China and south Korea, the two largest economies in the group, grew on average three times faster than the OECD economies during the 1980s. All eight economies have proved that they can sustain growth rates of over 7% a year. At that speed an economy doubles in size each decade.

Assuming that Asia's super-competitive economies keep growing two-to-three times faster than the older industrial economies, by 2000 the average Taiwanese will be richer than most New Zealanders and catching up fast with most Australians. Hong Kongers will be richer than their erstwhile colonisers, the British, and Singaporeans better off than Italians. South Koreans, the poorest of the tigers' people with GDP per head of just over $6,000 a year, will be as wealthy as the Irish. By the middle of the 21st century there will have been a shift in economic power away from Europe and North America to the western side of the Pacific Rim.

The benefits of growth have been remarkably evenly distributed, so that "the material conditions of life, even for the unskilled, have been transformed in a single generation," writes Robert Wade, the author of one of the best books on the tigers.* Throughout the arc of countries that sweeps down from South Korea to Indonesia, there is profound optimism that life will continue to get better and a readiness to work hard to ensure that it does.

"The key question is, if countries have access to more or less the same technology and the same resources, and they all operate essentially free-market systems, competing on a level playing-field, what makes some more successful than others?" So asks Lee Kuan Yew, the prime minister of Singapore for 31 years until he stepped down last year.

The answer, Mr. Lee believes, lies in what he calls "the intangibles." By this he means "the coherence of a society, its commitment to common ideals, goals and values." The vital intangibles are a "belief in hard work, thrift, filial piety, national pride." These qualities are now often labelled Confucianism. This cultural explanation of East Asia's rise makes some observers uneasy. Not long ago Confucian societies' obsession with the veneration of elders was touted as a reason why they were condemned to remain inflexible and poor. Besides, Confucianism as it is now defined is not unique to East Asia; it is almost identical to the Calvinist work ethic described by Max Weber in 1904.

Chi-Chu Chen, of Taiwan's International Commercial Bank of China, has an altogether simpler explanation: "What is the difference between Taiwan and unsuccessful poor countries? My conclusion is we are economic animals, probably the greediest people on earth. The most important thing is to give the man in the street an incentive to work. Here self-interest has been given a free rein."

Learning the Lessons

The success of the tigers makes it easy to gloss over the differences in the way the government of each has encouraged its people to better their condition. Hong Kong is the only one that can claim to be laissez-faire (although, even there, two-fifths

---

*Governing the Market: Economic Theory and the Role of Government in East Asian Industrialisation. Princeton University Press

of housing is subsidised by the government). Singapore, the other city state, has one of the most *dirigiste* governments on earth, now devoting itself to creating an "attractive package" for global companies looking for a base in the region. South Korea's equally interventionist government has concentrated on keeping foreign companies out, while feeding credit to rear a handful of wholly-Korean, world-scale companies. By contrast with Korea, Taiwan's industrial structure, with a workforce of 8.3m employed in over 150,000 factories, could have been incubated on a different planet.

There are, however, some fundamental lessons that have been learnt in common.

• The priority of state action should be economic development, defined not by the government's ability to hand out welfare payments to the less privileged, but rather by growth in output, productivity and, above all, international competitiveness. Resource-poor countries with small domestic markets can grow only if they sell abroad. The tigers have been so successful at penetrating overseas markets that today their combined merchandise exports are twice those of all the countries in Central and Latin America, even though the latter have six times the population and are on the doorstep of the world's largest single market.

• Rapid growth is impossible without a commitment to markets and private property. In Taiwan the government leaves companies to do whatever they want, within the bounds it has set. In sluggish India, on the other hand, the government has tried to control everything and ended up serving only the vested interests of Indian big business.

• Markets do not have to be completely free. Apart from Hong Kong, the state has guided markets with instruments formulated by an elite bureaucracy—"an economic general staff," as Mr Wade calls it. There are numerous institutions for consultations between the bureaucrats and business—what else are golf courses for? A researcher at the Korea Development Institute, the government's economic think-tank, says that no one is sure how many laws there are in South Korea regulating intervention in individual industries—it might be over 1,000. Some of these efforts to guide the market have paid off, others have flopped. But Korea's government, and those of the other tigers, have been careful to get prices right so that producers can always tell if their goods are internationally competitive.

• A relatively equal distribution of incomes and relatively low taxes motivate workers. The pay differential between a production-line worker for Samsung, Korea's largest company, and its president is nine-fold. At any American company of a comparable size, the differential would be closer to 100. The feeling that everyone is in the same boat has been one of the factors that has allowed the tigers' governments to get away with being authoritarian for so long. It has given governments the power to push through unpopular measures in times of economic crisis, which in East Asia means whenever growth slips below 5% a year.

• The last lesson is probably the most important: investing in education pays in spades. The tigers' single biggest source of comparative advantage is their well-educated workers.

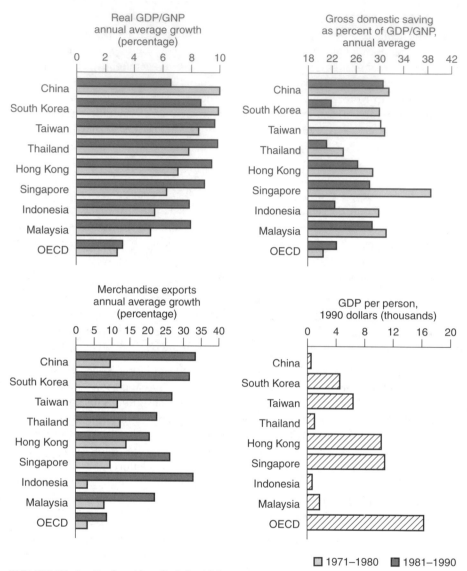

FIGURE 25–1   Racing Ahead of the Rich
Sources: Asian Development Bank; OECD; EIU

These lessons have been studied by the tigers' neighbours, who are now applying some of them. Almost everything about China's political future is uncertain. However, the momentum built up by the economic reforms introduced by Deng Xiaoping in 1979, which began the long process of opening up China's economy to the world, now looks irreversible, especially in the southern coastal provinces. China will have the fastest-growing economy in Asia during the first half of this decade.

The collapse in raw-material prices in the mid-1980s pushed the commodity exporters of South-East Asia—Thailand, Malaysia and Indonesia—into a recession, prompting all three to introduce fundamental reforms. They lifted old restrictions on foreign investment and deregulated their economies. The results have been impressive. Thailand was the world's fastest-growing economy in the second half of the 1980s. Indonesia's manufactured goods now earn more abroad than its exports of oil and gas. Earlier this year the Malaysian government unveiled its masterplan to make Malaysia a "fully developed country" by 2020. Economic growth of 7½% a year—the plan's basic premise—seems entirely possible.

But not easy. Asia's emerging economies are at a crossroads. They have done the simple bit. Move Thais or Indonesians out of a paddy field into a textile mill and you get a sharp increase in productivity, without much increase in skills. Can the second generation of emerging economies build on their present modest industrial base before their rising costs force foreign investors to look elsewhere?

A still more intriguing challenge faces the first generation of emerging economies. They have perfected the art of taking apart other people's products and working out how to make them almost as well and a whole lot cheaper. Now that they are becoming high-cost economies, the tigers must work out how to develop and market their own products, an altogether more difficult proposition. Easy access to the American market, which has helped to cover up some of their earlier mistakes, may no longer be available.

This survey is not about the doctrinal disputes between economic liberals and believers, like Mr Wade, in the "governed market." Instead, it will dwell on the engine-room—the companies that have driven growth and will succeed or go bust in the restructuring that lies ahead.

Emerging Asia is spawning a new generation of companies that, within 10–15 years, will be almost as well-known as Toyota, Sony and Mitsubishi are today. Japan has taught them that comparative advantage over competitors is not inherited, it is created. Taiwan and Korea can draw on some of the most technically-skilled labour available anywhere in the world. China has hundreds of millions of people who, given the chance, are the same as Hong Kongers—dynamic and industrious. The Chinese diaspora in Hong Kong, Taiwan and farther afield has the skills and capital to develop China.

These rapidly expanding companies have a raw entrepreneurialism that requires observers to ask not what will make them grow, but what can stop them? As a sign on an office wall in Taipei demands, "Why aren't you a millionaire yet?"

RISK AND REWARD

Tony Chao, from Taiwan, runs a clothing factory in an industrial estate near Sri Lanka's main airport. He has found an unusual niche. His workers sew hideous clothes—stone-washed denim mini-skirts covered in sequins are a popular line. They are shipped to Vladivostok and loaded onto the trans-Siberian railway. A couple of crates get pushed off at each stop into the arms of consumers desperate to buy any-thing.

Economic miracles are created by thousands of Tony Chaos, always on the look-out for a new market or product. Some 150 years ago, hard-faced men from Manchester were scouring the world for opportunities in just the same way. In Asia today's hard-faced men follow one of two different styles of doing business: the Japan-ese or the Chinese.

The emerging economies of Asia are Japan's backyard. Japanese companies and their products are everywhere. Millions of Asians go to work in a Japanese car, sit in an office cooled by Japanese air conditioners, try to sell their products to a Japan-ese company. After work, yuppies in Kuala Lumpur had for *karaoke* bars, the Japan-ese fad sweeping Asia even faster than McDonald's.

The 1990s version of a kinder and gentler Greater Asian Sphere of Co-Pros-perity makes some Japanese nervous. "We are very afraid of the political problems created by the over-dominance of Japanese business in some Asian markets," says a senior official in the planning department of Japan's Ministry of Foreign Affairs. "Japanese companies are in general indifferent to calls for more local involvement. In particular, they are slow to promote non-Japanese." How long will it be before mem-ories of how Japan behaved in the second world war create an anti-Japanese backlash in the countries now emerging in Japan's wake?

The answer is a very long time indeed. The economic animals of East and South-East Asia are realists and know that for the foreseeable future they will need Japan more than it needs them. Their pragmatism has ensured that the old wounds have not festered. The clearest indication so far of this was Emperor Akihito's tour of Thailand, Malaysia and Indonesia in September, the first time a Japanese emperor had visited South-West Asia and the first time one had apologised, obliquely, for "the horrors of that unfortunate war." A Malaysian cabinet minister suggested that the em-peror's visit was less controversial than one by George Bush would have been.

Korea has the most difficult relationship with Japan, its former coloniser. Ko-reans delight in explaining to visitors how Japanese culture is a bastardised version of the Korean original. Their businessmen bridle at suggestions they do business in a Japanese way. It is clear, however, that the *chaebol* which dominate the Korean econ-omy are self-conscious imitations of the *zaibatsu* which built Japan. The Korean con-glomerates show the naked aggression that wealth has now blunted in Japan. Their only concern about over-dominance is that they may not achieve it.

When Hyundai decided to build ships in 1973, it began by constructing the world's largest shipyard. Its competitors laughed, and then went bust. Since then Hyundai has become the first big entrant into the world market for cars since the Japanese in the 1960s. POSCO is now lauded by the World Bank as "arguably the world's most efficient producer of steel," which is ironic given that the Bank refused to back the company in the early 1970s because Korea was deemed to have no comparative advantage in steel. In the early 1980s four *chaebol* led a charge into semiconductors (see Table 25–2). A few billion dollars later, in 1988, Samsung introduced its own four megabyte DRAM (dy-namic random access memory) chip only six months behind Toshiba.

1990 sales in dollars (billions)

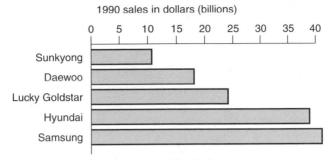

FIGURE 25–2   Top 5 Korean Chaebol
Source: WI Carr

Samsung's corporate motto is, "We do business for the sake of nation-building." The government has returned the favour by underwriting the company's riskiest ventures. Under the leadership of Lee Kun-hee, the third son of Samsung's founder, Samsung aims to become one of the ten biggest companies in the world by the turn of the century.

The Chinese are different. "A company for carrying on an undertaking of Great Advantage, but no-one to know what it is," is how the South Sea Company described itself in 1711. The description could well be applied to many Chinese conglomerates today. The tycoon is the only person who knows how the cash flows around the myriad companies he has single-handedly created. Minority shareholders are at his mercy.

This is not the least of the typical Chinese company's faults. According to the canons of western management theory, it gets most things wrong. Its strategy is usually centred on quick trading profits, rather than the long term. Personal relationships are exploited to win monopolies. One can exercise iron control over the activities of sprawling conglomerates between whose parts there is no attempt at synergy. The Salim Group, for example, was founded in Indonesia by Liem Sioe Liong and prospered thanks to presidential favours—Mr Liem supplied General Sukarno while he was in the jungle fighting the Dutch. Today Mr Liem presides over 300 subsidiaries, which account for about 5% of Indonesia's GDP.

Any company that has got that big must be getting something right. Hong Kong, with a population of 5.9m, had 13 (American-dollar) billionaires at last count. The Sophonpanich family in Thailand and the Kuoks in Malaysia rival the Liems in wealth. Indonesia's Chinese minority, only 5% of the total population, controls an estimated 75% of corporate assets. For the past 30 years Malaysian politics has been dominated by efforts to redistribute wealth from the Chinese minority to the Malay majority. Half of Thailand's GDP is produced by Bangkok, a Chinese city in Thai disguise.

The life blood of a Chinese company is *guanxi*—connections. Penetrating layers of *guanxi* is like peeling an onion: first come connections between people with ancestors from the same province in China; then people from the same clan or village; finally, the family. It does not matter much whether a Chinese businessman is in Hong

Kong or New York, he will always operate through *guanxi*. But these networks do not enforce conformity. Chinese tend to be far less concerned with consensus than the Japanese. As long as they honour their word and look after their own, they can do whatever they want.

This environment offers Chinese companies some fundamental advantages. The networks of *guanxi* are now global; so are the companies they spawn. The patriarch sits in Hong Kong, looking after the finances; number-one son runs the factories in China or Thailand; number-two son went to a top university in America and now works as a genteel form of industrial spy in California.

The network functions like a living organism, excelling at producing products quickly and cheaply. This is why Hong Kong has supplanted Italy as the world's top producer of fashion goods. It is how tiny Taiwanese companies run rings around giants in the personal-computer market.

The paradox is that the strength of centralised control, usually under one man, is also the Chinese company's weakness. The founding dynast cannot live much longer. In some cases there is no obvious successor; in others the empire is too big to be handed over to one man. Most tycoons are choosing the same solution—bringing in the suits with MBAs to run their companies after they are gone.

Li Ka-shing, Hong Kong's richest man, has gone furthest down this route. His family holding company, Cheung Kong, is run in the traditional way. But its biggest asset is its controlling stake in Hutchison Whampoa, one of Hong Kong's oldest trading houses, which is run (like the other *hongs*) by westerners.

In Indonesia the Soeryadjaya family is bringing in professional managers to run its Astra empire. It is trying to make more of the components for the Toyotas, Hondas and BMWs it assembles for the Indonesian market. Astra has even started to sponsor a special programme at INSEAD, the business school outside Paris. In Singapore, Kwek Hong Png, the 79-year-old chieftain of the Hong Leong group, has brought in the local head of IBM as his group's managing director.

Doubtless some Chinese-owned companies will evolve into conventional (in a western sense) companies. Others will go bust. The point is that within the Chinese diaspora, there will always be a new generation of tycoons on the make.

And what of European and American companies? "In some Asian markets, western companies were dominant historically. Many of them have given up this position without much of a fight, rather like the fall of Singapore in 1941," says Kevin Jones, a principal in McKinsey's office in Tokyo. It is all too easy for western companies to find reasons not to take Asia seriously: protectionism excludes them from some markets; they need to conserve their resources to fight off the Japanese at home; the market may be growing fast, but it is small now; and so on. The problem is that by the time a market is attractive, it will often be too late.

Western companies have been successful in areas where their Asian rivals are weakest, especially services and brand names. Citicorp has taken a 20-year view on the development of its retail-banking network. It is poaching the richest customers from local rivals. Toyota uses Inchcape, a British trading house, as its distributor in several markets. Procter & Gamble has learnt from its disasters in Japan in the late

1970s and is now expanding in emerging Asia. Unilever, its main rival, is the biggest consumer-products company in Indonesia, the world's fifth most populous country.

The list could go on. It cannot change the fact that western companies are bit-part players. Asia's miracle economies are being driven by Asian companies.

TRIUMPHANT ABROAD

Japanese and Chinese business indulged in an orgy of investment in the second half of the 1980s. Now that capital has become more expensive and the emerging economies are temporarily sated with investment, it is possible to discern the outlines of what has, and has not, happened.

Imagine it is late 1986 and you are managing a consumer electronics factory in Japan. Your business is in trouble. The deal struck at the Plaza Hotel the year before has doubled the value of the yen—the currency your manufacturing costs are based in—against the dollar, the currency of your biggest export market. Your workers are expensive and it is hard to find anyone to do jobs that involve the three Ks—*kitamai, kiken* or *kitsui* (dirty, dangerous or tough). The currencies of your most aggressive competitors, the Taiwanese and Koreans, have risen only slightly against the dollar and they are snatching market share away from you. What do you do?

One answer was to move as much of your manufacturing as possible offshore to lower-cost countries, preferably with currencies loosely pegged to the dollar. Between fiscal years 1988 and 1990, Japanese companies made 2,494 investments worth $11 billion in Indonesia, Malaysia, Singapore and Thailand. The latter has been the darling of Japanese companies: by 1990 they were opening factories in Thailand at the rate of one every 2½ days. Thomas Zengage, a management consultant in Tokyo, calls the process "Operation Sushi Storm."

South Korean and Taiwanese firms have turned from interested observers to imitators. As their own costs have risen, they have had three choices: move production offshore; make something else with more value added; or go bankrupt. Many companies have chosen the first route because it offers a quicker return than spending on research and development. During 1990 cumulative foreign investment by Korean companies doubled to $2.3 billion (still a low figure for an economy with exports worth roughly $72 billion this year). Taiwan's foreign investments are harder to track, because so much has been funnelled through the overseas Chinese network to avoid Taiwan's tax and other regulations. But in at least one country—Malaysia—Taiwan has replaced Japan as the largest single investor. Taiwanese companies invested M$6.3 billion ($2.3 billion) there during 1990.

The lucky recipients find it hard to avoid complacency. This could hurt them. Cheap labour is the only attraction most poor countries can offer potential investors. It can be used to establish an industrial base of textile plants and simple assembly lines. Many developing countries then fail to leap to a virtuous cycle of industrialisation, in which an ever higher proportion of value is added by domestic producers capable of producing export-quality goods.

However cheap their workers are, there is always somewhere where people will work for less. Vietnam's cost advantage explains why Asia's smart money expects the nation to grow so rapidly from its low base—Vietnamese GDP per head is officially $200—once the Communist Party loses its grip on power. Rapid increases in wages and land prices in Thailand and Malaysia could force manufacturers in the most labour-intensive industries to start another Operation Sushi Storm—the shift into Vietnam, China and Bangladesh.

Second, whereas South-East Asia had few competitors as an attractive site to build a factory in the mid-1980s, the collapse of communism in Europe, the European single market and the mooted North American free-trade area have created some interesting new possibilities. . . .

The third point is that T-shirts from Taiwan cost only 50% more than those from Thailand, though Taiwan's factory wages are four times higher. As you move up-market, this productivity gap between the well-educated workers of the tigers and the less skilled workers of South-East Asia gets wider.

Setting a Standard

The managers of Japanese factories in South-East Asia do not like talking about productivity gaps. When asked how their workers are performing, they smile politely and say that it is just like home. As they talk, the hit squads from head office are probably scratching their heads over how to get quality and productivity up to the required levels. One big Japanese electronics firm, Sharp, has sent teams to 150 of its suppliers in Thailand in an effort to raise their standards.

Japanese companies are wondering when it makes sense to move factories offshore. It is always worth making consumer products close to the intended market, because this allows you to cater to each market's foibles and helps to undercut protectionist pressure. But when it comes to mega-industries, it may not be sensible to move factories to developing Asia. A senior executive at Mitsubishi Motors explains: "Basically we are not transferring manufacturing to Asian countries—their only advantage is cheap labour. In our industry you need economies of scale and a large network of reliable suppliers. Most components are still cheaper when they are made in Japan. In some markets we can't even source plastic bags locally—we have to import them from Japan." His ideal factory floor does not swarm with cheap labour. It is deserted, the work done by robots, with zero defects.

In other words, moving production offshore is a way to delay the sunset over some low-technology industries. But it dodges the challenge of making a high-cost economy competitive through the development of domestic technology and services.

For the second generation of emerging economies—Thailand, Malaysia and Indonesia—the implications are worrying. Japanese investment, the fuel for their rapid growth over the past four years, is slowing. Many Japanese companies have now built the factories they will need to meet the expected growth in domestic demand in these three markets over the next five years or so. That frees them to concentrate on the American and European markets. (To put things in perspective, Japanese companies had invested $40.3 billion in manufacturing plants in North America by the end of 1990, double their investment in all of Asia.)

This slowdown in foreign investment comes at a difficult time. Thailand, Malaysia and Indonesia are expected to have current-account deficits ranging from $4 billion to over $8 billion (in Thailand's case) this year. Their recent success means they will have no difficulty in financing these deficits. But what about their underlying trade deficits with Japan? Indonesia is the only country in South-East Asia that has a trade surplus with Japan, thanks to its reserves of oil and gas. Thailand has the biggest deficit—in 1990 it was $5 billion. Conventional wisdom argues that this deficit has been caused by imports of capital equipment and will start to close as soon as the new plant is working. What this argument ignores is that much of the equipment is to meet domestic demand, and it will need a constant stream of Japanese spare parts. To pay for them, Thai, Malaysian and Indonesian producers will either have to penetrate the Japanese market—succeeding where so many others have failed—or they will have to outrun the tigers in the rest of the world.

The halcyon days are over in South-East Asia, at least for the time-being. For the front runners of the late 1980s, a lot of hard pounding lies ahead. One more challenge they will have to face is competition from the rising star of the 1990s—southern China.

GEOGRAPHY AND GEOMETRY

If it were not part of China, Guangdong province would be a decent-sized country with a population of 63m. As an economic unit, it has two advantages over the rest of China, and is about to acquire a third. First, its people, the Cantonese, have traded with the outside world for centuries. In Hong Kong and the other outposts of the Chinese world, they are world-class businessmen. Secondly, Beijing's control over its southern provinces has always been haphazard. The main benefit to Guangdong is an ironic one—it was starved of investment during the 1960s and 1970s, which means that today it has far fewer of the grotesquely inefficient state-owned enterprises that are bleeding the rest of China white. Thirdly, in 1997 the remaining artificial barriers will fall between Guangdong and one of the world's best natural harbours, which comes equipped with highly sophisticated trading and financial services: Hong Kong.

Guangdong's emergence began in 1979, when Deng Xiaoping launched reforms which returned control of the land to the peasants. In the next six years, rural incomes more than doubled in the whole of China. More importantly for Guangdong, Mr Deng made China as open to world trade as any other large developing economy. He created 14 open coastal cities, relaxing restrictions on foreign investment. In addition (and using Singaporean advice), he established five "special economic zones" (SEZs) with added incentives for investors. Three of the SEZs are in Guangdong.

The result has been over a decade of astonishing progress. During the 1980s Guangdong's output grew at an average rate of 13% a year in real terms, meaning the economy doubled in size every six years. Shenzhen, just across the border from Hong Kong, has grown from 100,000 people to over 2m; its output grew by 47% a year during the 1980s.

Official Chinese statistics are among the worst in the world. The "gross value of industrial and agricultural output"—China's version of GDP—does not include services. Guangdong's output-minus-services in 1990 were valued at $44.2 billion. Anyone who has seen Shenzhen yuppies spend more on one dinner than Mr Deng earns in two months will realise that Guangdong's service industries are far more developed than the rest of China's, where the world Bank guesses they account for 20% of GDP. One guess is that Guangdong's GDP is $78 billion—or $1,230 a head.

The fuel for Guangdong's boom has been investment by foreign companies. By June this year they had started over 15,000 ventures in the province, at a cost of over $20 billion. Four-fifths of this money came from Hong Kong companies, enticed by the fact that building a new factory in Guangdong costs one-fifth what it would in Hong Kong. It is also cheaper than it would be in the two obvious alternative sites in South-East Asia (see Figure 25–3). While manufacturing employment in Hong Kong has fallen from 900,000 jobs in the early 1980s to 720,000 now, Hong Kong companies have created over 2m new jobs in Guangdong.

Gordon Wu, an infectiously optimistic Hong Kong businessman, argues that the transformation of Guangdong has only just begun: "Not many people outside Hong Kong realise yet what Guangdong can manufacture and export. Nor do they raelise that Guangdong has the best of both worlds—access to the world market through Hong Kong as well as to the internal market. Give China another 25 years and the whole country can be at Guangdong's level today. By then, Guangdong will be where Taiwan is today, or probably even better."

Hopewell Holdings, Mr Wu's company, is trying to turn this vision into reality. It is in the process of building a six-lane highway through Guangdong. Mr Wu predicts that phase one—the 123 kilometres from Hong Kong to Guangzhou (Canton)—will be open by June 1993, one year ahead of schedule. It will cut the travelling time between the two cities from an infuriating six hours to 90 minutes. Once it is complete, Hopewell will go on to build a ringroad around Guangzhou and another highway from there to Macau. Guangdong will end up with 305 km of decent road; to-

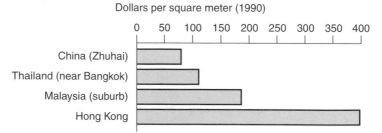

Dollars per square meter (1990)

FIGURE 25–3   Average Cost of Standard Factory Construction
Source: McKinsey & Co

day it has none. Mr Wu then hopes to build another 500 km of highway from Guangzhou to Hengyang, a town on the Yangtze river in Hunan province. If he can get the finance to build this road, it would be the first modern artery into the interior of China.

Good roads will give Hong Kong's tycoons access to more of Guangdong. This will help to contain labour costs by enabling factories to move away from the Pearl River delta into the province's hinterland. That is an added bonus, but in Guangdong, as in South-East Asia, cheap labour alone is not enough. What gives Guangdong its edge is the quality of its labour. "Friends with factories all over Asia say that Thailand and Malaysia just cannot compare with China. If you need quality and quick delivery, then you have to go to the Pearl River delta," says Kayser Sung, the publisher of *Textile Asia*.

The industrial prosperity is radiating outwards. Neighbouring Fujian has its own centre of growth in Xiamen (Amoy), which has attracted $3.5 billion in foreign investment, one-third of it from Taiwan, almost visible across the Taiwan Strait. Imagine that the Chinese empire run from Beijing were to disintegrate—Guangdong, Fujian, Taiwan and Hong Kong could form the Republic of Southern China. This new country would have a population of 120m and a combined GDP of roughly $310 billion, which would put it on a par with Brazil.

Though this may seem unlikely, or at least not imminent, it is next to impossible to predict what will happen in China. Optimists, like Mr Wu, argue that Beijing needs its tax revenues from Guangdong too much to do anything silly. Besides, Guangdong shows the way ahead for the rest of China. The pessimists, many of whom lost everything after the fall of Shanghai, counter that it is impossible to overestimate the communists' ability to kill the goose—and they point to the latest moves in Beijing that show the hardliners strengthening their position. There will be no clear answers until Mr Deng dies and the leanings of his eventual successor become apparent. . . .

THE PROBLEMS OF SUCCESS

So far this has been a survey of almost unrelenting optimism. Now for three doubts. None is insurmountable. But, if they are not dealt with, the tigers will lose the spring in their prowl and the second generation of emerging economies may forfeit its chances of reaching the next stage.

The first is a problem of success: growth has overwhelmed the infrastructure. Few governments have the effrontery to ask for taxes to rebuild a country's transport system just in case its economy doubles in size over the next decade. The exception is Singapore, whose government has never flinched from acting long before the need is apparent. Thus, Singapore is one of the few cities in emerging Asia with traffic that moves; its eerily efficient Changi airport sometimes seems almost deserted.

Contrast that with Hong Kong, where Kai Tak airport is so overburdened that airlines have to send their aircraft to Manila overnight to find parking space. Or with South Korea, where 600 new cars roll on to Seoul's streets every day. Kim Jong Gie, the director of planning at the Korea Development Institute, estimates that the government will have to spend at least $10 billion a year on infrastructure between now and 1996 just to stop things getting worse. Mr Kim would rather not think about the possible cost of rebuilding the North.

All these sums are dwarfed by Taiwan's. Its government says—with an ambition that strains belief—that it will spend NT$8 trillion ($302 billion) over the next six years on upgraded ports, new airports, superhighways and high-speed trains. The doubts concern not so much money, as will.

In the tigers, as well as in Indonesia and Malaysia, the will is there and things are moving. The Chinese government does not have the money to do much and would not use it to help the southern provinces if it did. But it does not seem to mind letting people like Mr Wu do the job for it. The same cannot be said of Thailand. Mr Wu would like to build a mass-transit system in Bangkok, where traffic now moves at an average speed of less than 8 km an hour. His proposal has joined a dusty pile of other plans for mass-transit systems, some of them now 12 years old. It is impossible to quantify how much foreign investment Thailand has already forgone because of its over-burdened infrastructure, but future growth will clearly be hostage to improvements in the country's physical condition.

The second problem is also a by-product of success, but it is harder to solve. Asia's industrial revolutions have been the fastest ever; they have also been the dirtiest.

Laundering the Profits

There were two environmental lessons that Asia's emerging economies could have learnt from Japan's experience. The first is that you can go hell-for-leather for growth and worry about cleaning up the pollution once you are rich. The second lesson is the gospel as now preached by the Keidanren, Japan's powerful industrial lobby: it can be 100 times cheaper to prevent the muck from coming out of the pipe than cleaning it up once it has.

Sadly, most of emerging Asia has chosen to learn the first lesson. (Once again, Singapore is the exception. It went green years ago.) Taiwan's limit on emissions of sulphur dioxide by factories is 750 parts per million, five times the limit applied in Los Angeles.

Until recently, South Korea and Hong Kong were not much better. As a result, vocal environmental lobbies have sprung up in all three countries. One effect of their pressure has been an effort by industry to shift its dirtier processes to countries that do not ask too many questions. The Thailand Development Research Institute recently looked at investment applications by foreign firms whose activities would produce significant amounts of hazardous waste. Between 1987 and 1989 such applications rose from 25% of the total to 55%. The institute calculates that the country now produces 2m tons of hazardous waste a year, and forecasts that this will triple by the turn of the century.

Thailand's problems will be dwarfed by the environmental consequences of

China's rapid growth. China relies on low-quality coal for three-quarters of its power. It is already the world's fourth largest producer of greenhouse gases (after America, the Soviet Union and Brazil). Pity the ozone layer once all 1.2 billion Chinese can afford CFC-using fridges and air-conditioners.

History suggests that during industrial revolutions people will tolerate horrendous living conditions as long as they feel their lot is improving. What the governments of Asia's emerging economies should not forget is that it is the poor who suffer most from pollution. If they start to suspect, for whatever reason, that they are not benefiting from growth, the social stability on which economic growth depends could disappear.

The third doubt is financial. Asia's emerging economies have savings rates significantly higher than the average for members of the OECD. The question is how efficiently these savings are channelled. The paradox is that the region's most dynamic economies have the most primitive financial systems.

This applies particularly to South Korea and Taiwan. Credit has been the fuel of South Korea's growth. The biggest *chaebol* are massively indebted: Samsung's electronics subsidiary, for example, took on debt equal to seven times its equity in order to finance its push into semiconductors. The industrial planners' main lever of control has been their ability to direct cheap credit to the borrowers they favour. Current-account surpluses in South Korea between 1986 and 1989 gave the government a chance to overhaul the country's financial system; but the technocrats would not give up their source of influence, and the current account has since slipped back into deficit. One result of this failure to reform is that big and small companies are forced to rely on the "informal" market for much of their short-term finance. A financial executive of one of the larger *chaebol* was unable to start an interview until he had rounded up some overnight cash, for which he had to pay 23%.

Taiwan's companies are less willing to borrow—in part because of a Chinese dislike of debt, in part because the island's banks will not normally lend to small and medium-sized companies. The competition for cash in the informal market is harsh: "It's just like the Serengeti—only the fit survive," says one banker. Until early 1990 the stockmarket was one way for small, fit companies to finance expansion—helped by spectacular speculative excess. On at least one day in early 1990, turnover in the Taipei market was greater than that on the Tokyo and New York stock exchanges combined. Then the bubble burst. Taipei's punters are an "ignorant, credulous and unsophisticated bunch," says one sniffy investor in Hong Kong.

Taiwan's version of the stockmarket as casino has caught on elsewhere. In the first half of this year it was quite normal for half the turnover on Bangkok's exchange to be trading in the shares of stockbrokers, who make their profits from trading in shares. In Jakarta there are twice as many registered stockbrokers as there are listed companies.

The governments involved must perform the delicate balancing act of continuing to liberalise their financial systems, while at the same time introducing effective regulation. Until they do this, Hong Kong and Singapore will retain their traditional roles as bolt-holes for much of the region's spare cash.

THREATS ABROAD, OPPORTUNITIES AT HOME

What would happen to Asia's emerging economies if the United States took shelter behind protectionist walls? For all their bluster, American politicians cannot forget that America needs Japan's capital and that their voters like Japanese gadgets. Emerging Asia is a much easier target than mature Japan. In the last presidential campaign, it was a Hyundai car from South Korea that drew Richard Gephardt's greatest ire.

East Asia was the great beneficiary of Reagonomics; its trade surpluses mirror America's trade deficit. America is the largest single market for the exports of each of Asia's emerging economies. Hong Kong's reliance on the American market has actually increased. Greater protectionism in America would be a disaster for emerging Asia.

Or would it? Measures designed to restrict Asia's most competitive exporters have often had the opposite effect. Voluntary restraint agreements (in reality anything but voluntary) placed on the export of Japanese cars to America handed windfall profits to Japanese producers, because demand then comfortably exceeded supply. The notorious Multi-fibre agreement, which for the past 31 years has rigged world trade in textiles and clothing has become a source of competitive advantage for the Hong Kong producers it was meant to hit. Its quota system gives them a degree of protection against lower-cost producers.

But if congress lost its senses and reintroduced Smoot-Hawley protectionism, even Asia's wiliest exporters would have a hard time turning this to their advantage. The remote threat that this could happen has had one positive effect: it has forced Asia's emerging companies to realise that there is a whole world they have barely touched.

In the late 1980s the acid test for most companies from the four tigers was whether they could sell in the American market. They read about Europe's plans for 1992, but tended to see Europe as a tricky place, best ignored. Now, however, Taiwanese and South Korean sales teams are combing Europe, including Eastern Europe, for opportunities. South Korea's government has offered the Soviet Union $3 billion in tied aid, in the hope that Korean firms can seize market share before the Japanese go wading in. Nor is Europe the only area of interest. Daewoo Telecom has signed a contract to provide 20,000 fax machines and several hundred telephone exchanges to Iran.

The Wealth Next Door

The biggest new market, however, is not exotic at all; it is right next door. Emerging Asia is the world's fastest-growing consumer market.

Two factors are driving the market's growth. The first is the rise in earnings. The second is demography. In Asia's emerging economies life expectancy is rising while infant mortality is dropping. As the number of young adults as a proportion of the whole population increases, so does the number of households. South Korea had 8.1m households in 1980; it will have 14.7m by 2005. Most of these new households will be in the cities. In Thailand, Indonesia and Malaysia, the population of the large cities is growing at 3½–4% a year, while the rural population remains unchanged.

Because there will be more urban households and smaller families, with both parents working, the structure of consumer demand will be transformed. There will be a housebuilding boom, followed by a sharp rise in demand for consumer durables, particularly for labour-saving things like washing machines and microwaves. An urban middle class will want more ways to pass its leisure time, so expect to see the world's biggest Disneyland somewhere in southern China by the early 21st century. It will also want better education for its children, and better health care for the growing number of old people.

This opportunity also presents companies with a problem. They need to establish a foothold before each market is established, but that means tackling markets that are mostly too small to be profitable.

There are, however, three factors that are making it much easier to tackle emerging Asia's markets. First, Asian consumers are among the most brand-conscious in the world. This creates a rare opening for western companies with strong brands. Mercedes, BMWs and Volvos are the only non-Japanese cars commonly seen in Asian traffic jams, and they are getting more common. Johnny Walker chose Thailand as the first country in the world to launch its Blue Label whisky, which is distinguishable only by the colour of its label and a price ten times higher than Black Label. McDonald's already has 59 restaurants in Hong Kong.

Second, Asia's rich consumers are becoming more accessible. Most urban households own a television. Satellite technology is weakening governments' grip on broadcasting, which as a result is becoming more commercial. Earlier this year a joint venture between Hutchvision, controlled by Li Ka-shing, China's CITIC and Cable & Wireless, a British telecommunications company, launched AsiaSat 1. The satellite's footprint covers 2.7 billion people from Tehran to Taipei. Star TV will be beamed free into any home with a dish.

At the same time, retailing is getting much more sophisticated. Japanese chains like Isetan, Sogo and Seibu are leading the way. Yaohan has gone the furthest. In Japan it is a medium-sized chain of supermarkets. Kazuo Wada, Yoahan's idiosyncratic founder, decided that land prices in Japan made the cost of expanding there prohibitive. So he moved his head office and family to Hong Kong three months after the Tiananmen Square massacre ("Rents were cheap then," he explains). He opened his first Chinese store in Shenzhen two months ago, and is now negotiating to build the biggest store in Asia in Pudong, a massive new development in Shanghai.

Mr Wada has few illusions about China. Its government is a nightmare to deal with, he says, and only the Special Economic Zones are ready for slick retail operations; "the rest of the country will not be ready until the next century." In the meantime Mr Wada is concentrating on establishing reliable suppliers in China and opening more stores in the expanding suburbs of South-East Asia.

The third factor that is making Asia's consumer markets more accessible is probably the most important. The barriers which have until now hobbled intra-Asian trade are being dismantled. This makes it possible for producers to start thinking about tackling several markets from one base, rather than going through the laborious process of establishing a factory in each market.

At the moment Hong Kong and Singapore are the only emerging Asian economies which are practising free trade, although the others are now moving in the right direction. By the end of 1990 Taiwan had cut its average tariff to 5.8%. It aims to reduce it to 3.5% by 1993. South Korea's target for 1993 is 7.9%. Last year Indonesia cut tariffs on 2,500 imports and removed 370 non-tariff barriers. Anand Panyarachun, Thailand's prime minister, has come up with an interesting proposal to turn the Association of South-East Asian Nations (ASEAN) into a free-trade area.

The demolition of the still-high trade barriers within Asia would give added impetus to the already rapid growth of intra-Asian trade. And, if past trends are a guide, Japan will eventually replace America as the world's biggest market. These two factors mean that Asia's emerging economies will be away, on a self-sustaining cycle of growth. Not much can stop them then; except, perhaps, politics.

A QUESTION OF GOVERNMENT

This survey has deliberately left politics to the end, in part because that is where most Asians would put it; in part because the political lessons to be drawn from the emerging economic powers of Asia are the most sobering.

Over the past quarter of a century of dazzling growth, there has not been a transfer of power to another political group in any of the economies. China remains a communist dictatorship. Singapore, Indonesia and Malaysia have each been ruled by the same authoritarian party since achieving independence. South Korea and Taiwan have begun to liberalise, but for the time being are still run by the old guard. Hong Kong is a colony. Thailand appears to be an exception, but is not really. While its generals and civilian politicians take it in turns to govern and to serve as a disloyal opposition, a small group of technocrats rules the country. This group's first loyalty is to the king, who gives stability to the nation.

Is the lesson, then, that it is only possible to double the size of an economy each decade with an authoritarian government at the helm? Not necessarily. What has made emerging Asia's governments exceptional is that they have been economically enlightened.

Many Asian businessmen would define enlightenment in one word: stability. Asia's strong governments have rarely flinched from taking tough measures to maintain macroeconomic stability. Just as important, they have ensured that economic policies are predictable. At the same time they have kept their economies in shape through controlled exposure to international competition. . . .

This protection was often paid for by discriminatory taxes on farming, thus impoverishing farmers. Asian governments realised, in the words of Lee Kuan Yew, that they "must create an agricultural surplus to get their industrial sector going." Rich and industrious rice-farmers have been the foundation of Asia's industrialisation.

In Japan, South Korea, Taiwan and China, investments to make farming more productive were accompanied by radical land reform. The link with income equality is self-evident. The Philippines' failure to introduce serious land reform is the main reason why it is the sick man of South-East Asia and not an emerging economy.

The Challenge of Change

The example of the Philippines shows how hard it is to implement land reform, except in the aftermath of war or revolution. There are easier ways to encourage the even spread of wealth; none matters more than education. A study carried out in Malaysia found that one extra year of schooling increased a man's wages by an average of 16% and a farmer's output by 5%. Indonesia has just made a painful transition from being an oil-dominated economy to one led by industry. During the transition, its government cut capital investment, but it maintained its current spending on education and other basic social services. The most impressive consequence was the poor's share of GDP actually increased during a difficult period of adjustment.

For the second generation of emerging economies, making sure the poor benefit from growth is vital. They are larger countries than the first generation, and less racially homogeneous. In Indonesia and Malaysia, there is an endemic risk of a backlash against Chinese businessmen when things do not go quite so well. In Thailand average household incomes in Bangkok are ten times higher than they are in the north-east, where one-third of the population lives. The widening gulf between the prosperity of China's coastal provinces and the poverty of its interior will inevitably cause political tension. That is why, despite the potential of the Hong Kong–Guangdong economy, many of the colony's brightest will continue to leave—along with an estimated $3 billion of Hong Kong money put each year into Vancouver's banks and property.

The other three tigers—Singapore, South Korea and Taiwan—are facing a different set of political problems. To get to the next stage, their businesses need a well-educated, flexible workforce—people who will be more politically demanding. But will the old guard be willing to loosen its grip?

In Singapore, Lee Kuan Yew stood down towards the end of 1990 after 31 years as prime minister, handing power to his annointed successor, Goh Chok Tong. Mr Lee remains in the cabinet as senior minister without portfolio; is son, Lee Hsien Loong, serves as deputy prime minister. Mr Goh called an election at the end of August in an effort to win his own mandate, but ended up losing an unprecedented four seats to the opposition (out of a total of 81 seats). Some observers therefore assume that the Lees, *père et fils*, will take back the reins of power. Even so, Singapore's road to political liberalisation is likely to remain one-way.

The same is true in Taiwan and South Korea. In the mid-1980s Taiwan's President Chiang Chingkuo began to prepare for the end of martial law and for a freer electoral system. Its parliament has since become famous for its televised fisticuffs. Yet these are positive signs of the vigour of Taiwanese society and of its increasing openness. No one has taken the trouble to learn the rules of polite political exchange yet, but they will.

South Korea is facing three rounds of national elections next year. Although there could be an upset, President Roh Tae Woo is expected to win all three. What matters is that the result will have been decided not in an army barracks but by the Korean people. The fact of most Koreans' daily lives is that their civil liberties are now respected, not infringed.

Over the past quarter of a century, the governments of emerging Asia have based their claim to popular support on their ability to sponsor, or at least to preside over, a rapid increase in prosperity. This is unlikely to change as they move from authoritarianism towards democracy. Asian businessmen exude self-confidence. Those who worry about their leaders' ability to keep up with change can always seek solace in the words of an observer of the first industrial revolution, Adam Smith: "Though the profusion of government must undoubtedly have retarded the national progress of England towards wealth and improvement, it has not been able to stop it."

26. Multinationals and Developing Countries: Myths and Realities

Peter F. Drucker

Four assumptions are commonly made in the discussion of multinationals and the developing countries—by friends and enemies alike of the multinational company. These assumptions largely inform the policies both of the developing countries and of the multinational companies. Yet, all four assumptions are false, which explains in large measure both the acrimony of the debate and the sterility of so many development policies.

These four false but generally accepted assumptions are: (1) the developing countries are important to the multinational companies and a major source of sales, revenues, profits and growth for them, if not the mainstay of "corporate capitalism;" (2) foreign capital, whether supplied by governments or by businesses, can supply the resources, and especially the capital resources required for economic development; (3) the ability of the multinational company to integrate and allocate productive resources on a global basis and across national boundaries, and thus to substitute transnational for national economic considerations, subordinates the best national interests of the developing country to "global exploitation;" (4) the traditional nineteenth-century form of corporate organization, that is, the "parent company" with wholly owned "branches" abroad, is the form of organization for the twentieth century multinational company.[1]

II

What are the realities? In the first instance, extractive industries have to go wherever the petroleum, copper ore or bauxite is found, whether in a developing or in a developed country. But for the typical twentieth-century multinational, that is a manufacturing, distributing or financial company, developing countries are important neither as markets nor as producers of profits. Indeed it can be said bluntly that the major manufacturing, distributive and financial companies of the developed world would barely notice it, were the sales in and the profits from the developing countries suddenly to disappear.

Confidential inside data in my possession on about 45 manufacturers, distributors and financial institutions among the world's leading multinationals, both North American and European,[2] show that the developed two-thirds of Brazil—from Bello Horizonte southward—is an important market for some of these companies, though even Brazil ranks among the first 12 sales territories, or among major revenue producers, for only two of them. But central and southern Brazil, while still "poor," are clearly no longer "underdeveloped." And otherwise not even India or Mexico—the two "developing" countries with the largest markets—ranks for any of the multinational companies in my sample ahead even of a single major sales district in the home country, be it the Hamburg-North Germany district, the English Midlands or Kansas City.

On the worldwide monthly or quarterly sales and profit chart, which most large companies use as their most common top-management tool, practically no developing country even appears in my sample of 45 major multinationals except as part of a "region," e.g., "Latin America," or under "Others."

The profitability of the businesses of these companies in the developing countries is uniformly lower by about two percentage points than that of the businesses in the developed countries, except for the pharmaceutical industry where the rate of return, whether on sales or on invested capital, is roughly the same for both. As a rule, it takes longer—by between 18 months to three years—to make a new operation break even in a developing country. And the growth rate—again excepting the pharmaceutical industry—is distinctly slower. Indeed, in these representative 45 businesses,

---

1. The author acknowledges his indebtedness for advice and helpful criticism to Dr. Tore Browaldh, Chairman of Svenska Handelsbanken and recently a member of the U.S. Group of Eminent Persons studying multinationals, and to Dr. Ernst Keller, President of Adela Investment Co., S.A., Lima, Peru.

2. I have no data on Japanese-based multinationals; but in developing countries the Japanese are still mainly engaged in extractive and raw-material-producing business.

75 to 85 percent of all growth, whether in sales or in profits, in the last 25 years, occurred in the developed countries. In constant dollars the business of these 45 companies in the developed world doubled—or more than doubled—in the last 10 to 15 years. But their business in the developing countries grew by no more than one-third during that period if the figures are adjusted for inflation.

Published data, while still scarce and inadequate, show the same facts. Only for the extractive industries have the developing countries—and then only a few of them—been of any significance whether as a source of profits, as loci of growth, or as areas of investment.

The reason is, of course, that—contrary to the old, and again fashionable, theory of "capitalist imperialism"—sales, growth and profits are where the market and the purchasing power are.

To the developing country, however, the multinational is both highly important and highly visible.

A plant employing 750 people and selling eight million dollars worth of goods is in most developing countries a major employer—both of rank and file and of management—and a big business. For the multinational parent company, employing altogether 97,000 people and selling close to two billion dollars worth of goods a year, that plant is, however, at best marginal. Top management in Rotterdam, Munich, London or Chicago can spend practically no time on it.

Neglect and difference rather than "exploitation" is the justified grievance of the developing countries in respect to the multinationals. Indeed, top management people in major multinationals who are personally interested in the developing countries find themselves constantly being criticized for neglecting the important areas and for devoting too much of their time and attention to "outside interests." Given the realities of the business, its markets, growth opportunities and profit opportunities, this is a valid criticism.

The discrepancy between the relative insignificance of the affiliate in a developing country and its importance and visibility for the host country poses, however, a major problem for the multinationals as well. Within the developing country the man in charge of a business with 750 employees and eight million dollars in sales has to be an important man. While his business is minute compared to the company's business in Germany, Great Britain or the United States, it is every whit as difficult—indeed it is likely to be a good deal more difficult, risky and demanding. And he has to treat as an equal with the government leaders, the bankers and the business leaders of his country—people whom the district sales manager in Hamburg, Rotterdam or Kansas City never even sees. Yet his sales and profits are less than those of the Hamburg, Rotterdam or Kansas City sales district. And his growth potential is, in most cases, even lower.

This clash between two realities—the personal qualifications and competence, the position, prestige and power needed by the affiliate's top management people to do their job in the developing country, and the reality of a "sales district" in absolute, quantitative terms—the traditional corporate structure of the multinationals cannot resolve.

III

The second major assumption underlying the discussion of multinationals and developing countries is the belief that resources from abroad, and especially capital from abroad, can "develop" a country.

But in the first place no country is "underdeveloped" because it lacks resources. "Underdevelopment" is inability to obtain full performance from resources; indeed we should really be talking of countries of higher and lower productivity rather than of "developed" or "underdeveloped" countries. In particular, very few countries—Tibet and New Guinea may be exceptions—lack *capital*. Developing countries have, almost by definition, more capital than they productively employ. What "developing" countries lack is the full ability to mobilize their resources, whether human resources, capital or the physical resources. What they need are "triggers," stimuli from abroad and from the more highly developed countries, that will energize the resources of the country and will have a "multiplier impact."

The two success stories of development in the last hundred years—Japan and Canada—show this clearly. In the beginning, Japan imported practically no capital except small sums for early infrastructure investments, such as the first few miles of railroad. She organized, however, quite early, what is probably to this day the most efficient system for gathering and putting to use every drop of capital in the country. And she imported—lavishly and without restrains—technology with a very high multiplier impact and has continued to do so to this day.

Canada, in the mid-1930s, was far less "developed" a country than most American republics are today. Then the liberal governments of the 1930s decided to build an effective system for collecting domestic capital and to put it into infrastructure investments with a very high "multiplier" effect—roads, health care, ports, education and effective national and provincial administrations. Foreign capital was deliberately channeled into manufacturing and mining. Domestic capital and entrepreneurs were actually discouraged in the extractive and manufacturing sectors. But they were strongly encouraged in all tertiary activities such as distribution, banking, insurance and in local supply and finishing work in manufacturing. As a result a comparatively small supply of foreign capital—between a tenth and a twentieth of Canada's total capital formation—led to very rapid development within less than two decades.

There is a second fallacy in the conventional assumption, namely that there is unlimited absorptive capacity for money and especially for money from abroad. But in most developing countries there are actually very few big investment opportunities. There may be big hydroelectric potential; but unless there are customers with purchasing power, or industrial users nearby, there is no economic basis for a power plant. Furthermore, there is no money without strings. To service foreign capital, even at a minimal interest rate, requires foreign exchange. At that, loans or equity investments as a rule constitute a smaller (and, above all, a clearly delimited) burden than grants and other political subsidies from abroad. The latter always create heavy obligations, both in terms of foreign and domestic policy, no matter where they come from.

A developing country will therefore get the most out of resources available abroad, especially capital, if it channels capital where it has the greatest "multiplier impact." Moreover, it should channel it where one dollar of imported capital will generate the largest number of domestic dollars in investment, both in the original investment itself and in impact-investment (e.g., the gas stations, motels and auto repair shops which an automobile plant calls into being), and where one job created by the original investment generates the most jobs directly and indirectly (again an automobile industry is a good example). Above all, the investment should be channeled where it will produce the largest number of local managers and entrepreneurs and generate the most managerial and entrepreneurial competence. For making resources fully effective depends on the supply and competence of the managerial and entrepreneurial resource.

According to all figures, government money has a much lower multiplier impact than private money. This is, of course, most apparent in the Communist-bloc countries; low, very low, productivity of capital is the major weakness of the Communist economies, whether that of Russia or of her European satellites. But it is true also of public (e.g., World Bank) money elsewhere: it generates little, if any, additional investment either from within or from without the recipient country. And "prestige" investments, such as a steel mill, tend to have a fairly low multiplier impact—both in jobs and in managerial vigor—as against, for instance, a department store which brings into existence any number of small local manufacturers and suppliers and creates a major managerial and entrepreneurial cluster around it.

For the multinational in manufacturing, distribution, or finance locating in a developing country, rapid economic development of the host country offers the best chance for growth and profitability. The multinational thus has a clear self-interest in the "multiplier" impact of its investment, products and technology. It would be well advised to look on the capital it provides as "pump priming" rather than as "fuel." The more dollars (or pesos or cruzeiros) of local capital each of its own dollars of investment generates, the greater will be the development impact of its investment, and its chance for success. For the developing country the same holds true: to maximize the development impact of each imported dollar.

The Canadian strategy was carried on too long; by the early 1950s, Canada had attained full development and should have shifted to a policy of moving its own domestic capital into "superstructure" investments. But though the Canadian strategy is certainly not applicable to many developing countries today—and though, like any strategy, it became obsolete by its very success—nevertheless it was highly successful, very cheap and resulted in rapid economic growth while at the same time ensuring a high degree of social development and social justice.

What every developing country needs is a strategy which looks upon the available foreign resources, especially of capital, as the "trigger" to set off maximum deployment of a country's own resources and to have the maximum "multiplier effect." Such a strategy sees in the multinational a means to energize domestic potential—and especially to create domestic entrepreneurial and managerial competence—rather than a substitute for domestic resources, domestic efforts and, even, domestic capital. To make the multinationals effective agents of development in the developing countries therefore requires, above all, a policy of encouraging the domestic private sector, the domestic entrepreneur and the domestic manager. If they are being discouraged the resources brought in from abroad will, inevitably, be wasted.

For by themselves multinationals cannot produce development; they can only turn the crank but not push the car. It is as futile and self-defeating to use capital from abroad as a means to frighten and cow the local business community—as the bright young men of the early days of the Alliance for Progress apparently wanted to do—as it is to mobilize the local business community against the "wicked imperialist multinational."

IV

The multinational, it is said, tends to allocate production according to global economics. This is perfectly correct, though so far very few companies actually have a global strategy. But far from being a threat to the developing country, this is potentially the developing country's one trump card in the world economy. Far from depriving the governments of the developing countries of decision-making power, the global strategy of the multinationals may be the only way these governments can obtain some effective control and bargaining leverage.

Short of attack by a foreign country the most serious threat to the economic sovereignty of developing countries, and especially of small ones, i.e., of most of them, is the shortage of foreign exchange. It is an absolute bar to freedom of decision. Realizing this, many developing countries, especially in the 1950s and early 1960s, chose a deliberate policy of "import substitution."

By now we have all learned that in the not-so-very-long run this creates equal or worse import-dependence and foreign-exchange problems. Now a variant of "import substitution" has become fashionable: a "domestic-content" policy which requires the foreign company to produce an increasing part of the final product in the country itself. This, predictably, will eventually have the same consequences as the now discredited "import substitution," namely, greater dependence on raw materials, equipment and supplies from abroad. And in all but the very few countries with already substantial markets (Brazil is perhaps the only one—but then Brazil is not, after all, "developing" any longer in respect to the central and southern two-thirds of the country) such a policy must, inevitably, make for a permanently high-cost industry unable to compete and to grow. The policy creates jobs in the very short run, to be sure; but it does so at the expense of the poor and of the country's potential to generate jobs in the future and to grow.

What developing countries need are *both*—foreign-exchange earnings and productive facilities large enough to provide economies of scale and with them substantial employment. This they can obtain only if they can integrate their emerging productive facilities—whether in manufactured goods or in such agricultural products as fruits and wine—with the largest and the fastest-growing economy around, i.e., the world market.

But exporting requires market knowledge, marketing facilities and marketing finance. It also requires political muscle to overcome strongly entrenched protectionist forces, and especially labor unions and farm blocs in the developed countries. Exporting is done most successfully, most easily and most cheaply if one has an assured "captive" market, at least for part of the production to be sold in the world market. This applies particularly to most of the developing countries, whose home market is too small to be an adequate base for an export-oriented industry.

The multinational's capacity to allocate production across national boundary lines and according to the logic of the world market should thus be a major ally of the developing countries. The more rationally and the more "globally" production is being allocated, the more they stand to gain. A multinational company, by definition, can equalize the cost of capital across national lines (to some considerable extent, at least). It can equalize to a large extent the managerial resource, that is, it can move executives, can train them, etc. The only resource it cannot freely move is labor. And that is precisely the resource in which the developing countries have the advantage.

This advantage is likely to increase. Unless there is a world-wide prolonged depression, labor in the developed countries is going to be increasingly scarce and expensive, if only because of low birthrates, while a large-scale movement of people from pre-industrial areas into developed countries, such as the mass-movement of American Blacks to the Northern cities or the mass-movement of "guest workers" to Western Europe, is politically or socially no longer possible.

But unless the multinationals are being used to integrate the productive resources of the developing countries into the productive network of the world economy—and especially into the production and marketing systems of the multinationals themselves—it is most unlikely that major export markets for the production of the developing countries will actually emerge very quickly.

Thus, the most advantageous strategy for the developing countries would seem to be to replace—or, at least to supplement—the policy of "domestic content" by a policy that uses the multinationals' integrating ability to develop large productive facilities with access to markets in the developed world. A good idea might be to encourage investment by multinationals with definite plans—and eventually firm commitments—to produce for export, especially within their own multinational system. As Taiwan and Singapore have demonstrated, it can make much more sense to become the most efficient large supplier worldwide of one model or one component than to be a high-cost small producer of the entire product or line. This would create more jobs and provide the final product at lower prices to the country's own consumers. And it should result in large foreign-exchange earnings.

I would suggest a second integration requirement. That developing countries want to limit the number of foreigners a company brings in is understandable. But the multinational can be expected to do that anyhow as much as possible—moving people around is expensive and presents all sorts of problems and troubles. Far more important would be a requirement by the developing country that the multinational integrate the managerial and professional people it employs in the country within its worldwide management development plans. Most especially it should assign an adequate number of the younger, abler people from its affiliate in the developing country for from three to five years of managerial and professional work in one of the developed countries. So far, to my knowledge, this is being done systematically only by some of the major American banks, by Alcan, and by Nestle. Yet it is people and their competence who propel development; and the most important competence needed is not technical, i.e., what one can learn in a course, but management of people, marketing and finance, and first-hand knowledge of developed countries.

In sum, from the point of view of the developing countries the best cross-national use of resources which the multinational is—or should be—capable of may well be the most positive element in the present world economy. A policy of self-sufficiency is not possible even for the best-endowed country today. Development, even of modest proportions, cannot be based on uneconomically small, permanently high-cost facilities, either in manufacturing or in farming. Nor is it likely to occur, let alone rapidly, under the restraint of a continental balance-of-payments crisis. The integration of the productive capacities and advantages of developing countries into the world economy is the only way out. And the multinational's capacity for productive integration across national boundaries would seem the most promising tool for this.

V

That 100-percent ownership on the part of the "parent company" is *the* one and only corporate structure for the multinational, while widely believed, has never been true. In so important a country as Japan it has always been the rather rare exception, with most non-Japanese companies operating through joint ventures. Sears, Roebuck is in partnership throughout Canada with a leading local retail chain, Simpson's. The Chase Manhattan Bank operates in many countries as a minority partner in and with local banks. Adela, the multinational venture-capital firm in Latin America, and by far the most successful of all development institutions in the world today, has confined itself from its start, ten years ago, to minority participation in its ventures, and so on.

But it is true that, historically, 100-percent ownership has been considered the preferred form, and anything else is likely to make unity of action, vision and strategy rather difficult. Indeed, restriction of the foreign investor to less than 100-percent control or to a minority participation, e.g., in the Andean Pact agreements or in Mexico's legislation regarding foreign investments, is clearly intended as restraint on the foreigner, if not as punitive action.

But increasingly the pendulum is likely to swing the other way. (Indeed, it may not be too far-fetched to anticipate that, a few years hence, "anti-foreign" sentiment may take the form of demanding 100-percent foreign-capital investment in the national company in the developing country, and moving toward outlawing partnerships or joint ventures with local capital as a drain on a country's slender capital resources.)

The multinational will find it increasingly to its advantage to structure ownership in a variety of ways, and especially in ways that make it possible for it to gain access to both local capital and local talent.

Capital markets are rapidly becoming "polycentric." The multinationals will have to learn so to structure their businesses as to be able to tap any capital market— whether in the United States, Western Europe, Japan, Brazil, Beirut or wherever. This the monolithic "parent company" with wholly-owned branches is not easily capable of. When companies, for example the West Europeans, raise money abroad, they often prefer financial instruments such as convertible debentures, which their own home capital markets, or the United States, do not particularly like and cannot easily handle. There is also more and more evidence that the capital-raising capacity of a huge multinational, especially for medium-term working capital, can be substantially increased by making major segments of the system capable of financing themselves largely in their own capital markets and with their own investing public and financial institutions.

But capital is also likely to be in short supply for years to come, barring a major global depression. And this might well mean that the multinationals will only be willing and able to invest in small, less profitable and more slowly growing markets, i.e., in developing countries if these countries supply a major share of the needed capital rather than have the foreign investor put up all of it.

That this is already happening, the example of Japan shows. Lifting restrictions on foreign investment was expected to bring a massive rush of take-over bids and 100 percent foreign-owned ventures. Instead it is now increasingly the Western investor, American as well as European, who presses for joint ventures in Japan and expects the Japanese partner to supply the capital while he supplies technology and product knowledge.

Perhaps more important will be the need to structure for other than 100-percent ownership to obtain the needed managerial talent in the developing country. If the affiliate in the developing country is not a "branch" but a separate company with substantial outside capital investment, the role and position of its executives become manageable. They are then what they have to be, namely, truly "top management," even though in employment and sales their company may still be insignificant within the giant concern.

And if the multinational truly attempts to integrate production across national boundaries, a "top management" of considerable stature becomes even more necessary. For then, the managers of the affiliate in a developing country have to balance both a national business and a global strategy. They have to be "top management" in their own country and handle on the local level highly complex economic, financial, political and labor relations as well as play as full members on a worldwide "system management" team.[3] To do this as a "subordinate" is almost impossible. One has to be an "equal," with one's own truly autonomous command.

---

3. For a full discussion of this organization design, see my recent book *Management: Tasks; Responsibilities; Practices,* New York: Harper & Row, 1974, especially Chapter 47.

VI

Domestically, we long ago learned that "control" has been divorced from "ownership" and, indeed, is rapidly becoming quite independent of "ownership." There is no reason why the same development should not be taking place internationally—and for the same two reasons: (1) "ownership" does not have enough capital to finance the scope of modern large businesses; and (2) management, i.e., "control," has to have professional competence, authority and standing of its own. Domestically the divorce of "control" from "ownership" has not undermined "control." On the contrary, it has made managerial control and direction more powerful, more purposeful, more cohesive.

There is no inherent reason why moving away from "100-percent ownership" in developing countries should make impossible maintenance of common cohesion and central control. On the contrary, both because it extends the capital base of the multinational in a period of worldwide capital shortage and because it creates local partners, whether businessmen or government agencies, the divorce between control and direction may well strengthen cohesion, and may indeed even be a prerequisite to a true global strategy.[4]

At the same time such partnership may heighten the development impact of multinational investment by mobilizing domestic capital for productive investment and by speeding up the development of local entrepreneurs and managers.

Admittedly, mixed ownership has serious problems; but they do not seem insurmountable, as the Japanese joint-venture proves. It also has advantages; and in a period of worldwide shortage of capital it is the multinational that would seem to be the main beneficiary. Indeed one could well argue that developing countries, if they want to attract foreign investment in such a period, may have to *offer* co-investment capital, and that provisions for the participation of local investment in ownership will come to be seen (and predictably to be criticized) as favoring the foreign investor rather than as limiting him.

VII

The multinational, while the most important and most visible innovation of the postwar period in the economic field, is primarily a symptom of a much greater change. It is a response to the emergence of a genuine world economy. This world economy is not an agglomeration of national economies as was the "international economy" of nineteenth-century international trade theory. It is fundamentally autonomous, has its own dynamics, its own demand patterns, its own institutions—and in the Special

---

4. On very different grounds, Professor Jack N. Behrman, former Assistant Secretary of Commerce in the Kennedy Administration and a man with encyclopedic knowledge of how the multinational economy works, reached similar conclusions. See his *Decision Criteria for Foreign Direct Investment in Latin America*, New York: Council of the Americas, 1974.

Drawing Rights (SDR) even its own money and credit system in embryonic form. For the first time in 400 years—since the end of the sixteenth century when the word "sovereignty" was first coined—the territorial political unit and the economic unit are no longer congruent.

This, understandably, appears as a threat to national governments. The threat is aggravated by the fact that no one so far has a workable theory of the world economy. As a result there is today no proven, effective, predictable economic policy: witness the impotence of governments in the face of worldwide inflation.

The multinationals are but a symptom. Suppressing them, predictably, can only aggravate the disease. But to fight the symptoms in lieu of a cure has always been tempting. It is therefore entirely possible that the multinationals will be severely damaged and perhaps even destroyed within the next decade. If so, this will be done by the governments of the developed countries, and especially by the governments of the multinationals' *home* countries, the United States, Britain, Germany, France, Japan, Sweden, Holland and Switzerland—the countries where 95 percent of the world's multinationals are domiciled and which together account for at least three-quarters of the multinationals' business and profits. The developing nations can contribute emotionalism and rhetoric to the decisions, but very little else. They are simply not important enough to the multinationals (or to the world economy) to have a major impact.

But at the same time the emergence of a genuine world economy is the one real hope for most of the developing countries, especially for the great majority which by themselves are too small to be viable as "national economies" under present technologies, present research requirements, present capital requirements and present transportation and communications facilities. The next ten years are the years in which they will both most need the multinationals and have the greatest opportunity of benefiting from them. For these will be the years when the developing countries will have to find jobs and incomes for the largest number of new entrants into the labor force in their history while, at the same time, the developed countries will experience a sharp contraction of the number of new entrants into their labor force—a contraction that is already quite far advanced in Japan and in parts of Western Europe and will reach the United States by the late 1970s. And the jobs that the developing countries will need so desperately for the next ten years will to a very large extent require the presence of the multinationals—their investment, their technology, their managerial competence, and above all their marketing and export capabilities.

The best hope for developing countries, both to attain political and cultural nationhood and to obtain the employment opportunities and export earnings they need, is through the integrative power of the world economy. And their tool, if only they are willing to use it, is, above all, the multinational company—precisely because it represents a global economy and cuts across national boundaries.

The multinational, if it survives, will surely look different tomorrow, will have a different structure, and will be "transnational" rather than "multinational." But even the multinational of today is—or at least should be—a most effective means to constructive nationhood for the developing world.

27. The Global Marketplace: A Closet Dictator

William Greider

With the end of the Cold War burdens, Americans were understandably inclined to turn inward and attend to the many neglected priorities at home. But American democracy is now imprisoned by new circumstances—the dynamics of the global economy—and this has produced a daunting paradox: Restoring the domestic political order will require a new version of internationalism.

The rise of transnational enterprises and production systems, the easy mobility of capital investment and jobs from one country to another, has obvious benefits as a modernizing influence on the world. It searches out lower costs and cheaper prices. But its exploitative effects on both rich and poor nations remain unchecked.

As a political system, the global economy is running downhill—a system that searches the world for the lowest common denominator in terms of national standards for wages, taxes and corporate obligations to health, the environment and stable communities. Left unchallenged, the global system will continue to undermine America's widely shared prosperity, but it also subverts the nation's ability to set its own political standards, the laws that uphold the shared values of society.

The economic consequences of globalized production have already been experienced by the millions of U.S. industrial workers who, during the last two decades, were displaced when their high-wage jobs were transferred to cheaper labor in foreign countries. This transformation, more than anything else, is what has led to the declining real wages in the United States and the weakening manufacturing base. The deleterious impact on American wages is likely to continue for at least another generation.

But the economic effects are inseparable from the political consequences. The global competition for cost advantage effectively weakens the sovereignty of every nation by promoting a fierce contest among countries for lower public standards. If one nation's environmental laws are too strict or its taxes seem too burdensome, the factory will be closed and the jobs moved elsewhere—to some other nation whose standards are lax, whose government is more compliant.

For ordinary Americans, traditionally independent and insular, the challenge requires them to think anew their place in the world. The only plausible way that citizens can defend themselves and their nation against the forces of globalization is to link their own interests cooperatively with the interests of other peoples in other nations—that is, with the foreigners who are competitors for the jobs and production

From "The Global Marketplace: A Closet Dictator," in *The Case Against Free Trade: GATT, NAFTA, and the Globalization of Corporate Power.* (San Francisco: Earth Island Press, 1933), pp. 195–217. Copyright © Simon & Schuster, New York.

but who are also victimized by the system. Americans will have to create new democratic alliances across national borders with the less prosperous people caught in the
same dilemma. Together, they have to impose new political standards on multinational enterprises and on their own governments.

The challenge, in other words, involves taking the meaning of democracy to a
higher plane—a plateau of political consciousness the world has never before reached.
This awesome task does not begin by examining Americans' own complaints about
the global system. It begins by grasping what happens to the people at the other end—
the foreigners who inherit the American jobs.

On the outskirts of Ciudad Juarez, across the river from El Paso, Texas, the sere
hillsides are a vast spectacle of human congestion. A canopy of crude huts and cab-
ins, made from industrial scraps, is spread across the landscape, jammed together like
a junkyard for abandoned shipping crates. The houses are not much more than large
boxes, with walls of cardboard and floors made from factory pallets or Styrofoam
packing cases. The tar-paper roofs are held in place by loose bricks; an old blanket or
sheet of blue plastic is wrapped around the outhouse in the yard. Very few homes have
running water and many lack electricity. Streets are unpaved and gullied. There are
no sewer systems. For mile after mile, these dwellings are visible across the countryside—dusty, treeless subdivisions of industrial poverty.

The *colonias* of Ciudad Juarez are like a demented caricature of suburban life
in America, because the people who live in Lucio Blanco or Zarogoza or the other
squatter villages actually work for some of America's premier companies—General
Electric, Ford, GM, GTE Sylvania, RCA, Westinghouse, Honeywell and many others. They are paid as little as fifty-five cents an hour. No one can live on such wages,
not even in Mexico. With the noblesse oblige of the feudal padrone, some U.S. companies dole out occasional *despensa* for their struggling employees—rations of flour,
beans, rice, oil, sugar, salt—in lieu of a living wage.

In addition to the cheap labor, the U.S. companies who have moved production
facilities to the Mexican border's *maquiladora* zone enjoy the privilege of paying no
property taxes on their factories. As a result, Ciudad Juarez has been overwhelmed
by a burgeoning population and is unable to keep up with the need for new roads, water and sewer lines and housing. The migrants who came from the Mexican interior
in search of "American" jobs become resourceful squatters, scavenging materials to
build shelters on the fast-developing hillsides. In time, some of these disappointed
workers decide to slip across the border in the hope of becoming real Americans.

"A family cannot depend on the *maquila* wage," explained Professor Gueramina
Valdes-Villalva of the Colegio de la Frontera Nortre in Juarez, an experienced critic
who aided workers at the Center for Working Women. "If you evaluate what these
wages translate into in purchasing power, you see a steady deterioration in what those
wages provide. They can't buy housing because there is a housing shortage. When
they go into the squatter situation, they can't invest in public services. We have a shortage of water, sewers, electricity, streets. The city is pressed heavily by the two sectors
who do not pay taxes—the *maquiladora* companies and the minimum-wage workers.

"The saddest thing about it is, not only does the city become unbearably unlivable, but then the city becomes unproductive too. As the city deteriorates, it becomes more expensive for companies to locate here. For the first time last year, we had negative growth in Juarez. Some of the employers are leaving. We can see the companies looking at their other options. Eastern Europe has become very attractive to them."[1]

If Americans wish to visualize the abstraction called the global economy, the need only drive across the U.S. border into Mexico and see the human consequences for themselves, from Matamoros and Juarez to Nogales and Tijuana. A vast industrial belt of thirteen hundred plants has grown up along the border during the last twenty years, encouraged by special duty-free provisions but fueled primarily by low wages and the neglect of corporate social obligations.

By moving jobs to Mexico, companies not only escape higher industrial wages, but also U.S. laws and taxes, the legal standards for business conduct on health and safety and social commitments that were established through many years of political reform in America. Mexico has such laws but it dare not enforce them too energetically, for fear of driving the companies elsewhere.

The *maquiladora* factories, notwithstanding their handsome stucco facades and landscaped parking lots, are the modern equivalent of the "sweatshops" that once scandalized American cities. The employers are driven by the same economic incentives and the Mexican workers in Ciudad Juarez are just as defenseless. The Juarez slums reminded me of the squalid "coal camps" I saw years before in the mountains of Eastern Kentucky. Those still-lingering "pockets of poverty" were first created in the late nineteenth century by the coal and steel industries and they employed the very same industrial practices—low wages, neglect of public investment, dangerous working conditions, degradation of the surrounding environment, the use of child labor.

The well-being of Americans is intertwined with this new exploitation, not simply for moral reasons or because most of the Mexican plants are owned by American companies, but because this is the other end of the transmission belt eroding the structure of work and incomes in the United States. Jobs that paid ten dollars or eleven dollars an hour in Ohio or Illinois will cost companies less than a tenth of that in Ciudad Juarez. The assembly work turns out TV sets, seatbelt harnesses, electrical switches and transformers, computer keyboards, disposable surgical garments, luggage locks, battery packs and a long list of other products.

Juarez, of course, is but a snapshot of the much larger reality around the world. Corporate apologists often point out that if the American jobs did not migrate to Mexico, they would go somewhere else—Singapore or Brazil, Thailand or now perhaps Eastern Europe—where the consequences would be less easily observed by Americans. This is true. The easy mobility of capital is the core element in the modern global economy. It is made possible by invention, brilliant planning and the new technologies that connect corporate managers with far-flung factories and markets and allow them to relocate production almost anywhere in the world.

To confront the effects of the global system, Americans must educate themselves about the world—to understand not only their own losses but also what is happening to others. Ciudad Juarez (or any other border city) is an excellent place to start, mainly because it starkly refutes so many of the common assumptions surrounding globalization. Aside from profit, the justifying and widely accepted rationale for global dispersion of production is the benefit to the poor, struggling masses. Their economies, it is said, will move up to a higher stage of development and incomes will rise accordingly. The auto workers in Ohio will lose, certainly, but the new auto workers in Juarez will become middle-class consumers who can afford to buy other products made in America. Thus, in time, everyone is supposed to benefit.

On the streets of Juarez, the workers tell a different story: Their incomes are not rising, not in terms of purchasing power. They have been falling drastically for years. These workers cannot buy American cars or computers. They can barely buy the basic necessities of life.

Fernando Rosales had just quit his job at Chrysler, where he assembled safety harnesses, because it paid the peso equivalent of only $4.20 a day. While he builds a squatter house in Lucio Blanco, Rosales searches for work as an auto mechanic, away from the *maquila* plants.

"I came here six years ago, thinking I would better myself, but I won't be able to do that," Rosales said. "It's been very difficult. The only benefits I had were transportation—they sent a bus for us—and one meal a day. Maybe for the government, it's okay. But for the people it really is shameful that American companies pay such low wages."

"The wages are very low, that's just the way it is," said Daniel Fortino Maltos, twenty-one years old and married with a baby. He works for General Electric at a plant making capacitors, as does his wife. "Young people generally leave after a few months or a year because the salary is so low, they can't make it," he explained.

Outside Productos Electricos Internacionales, another GE plant, a group of teenage workers on their lunch break described the same conditions. "The turnover is roughly every three months," said Fernando Rubio. "They just bring new ones in. There is such a big demand for workers, people can leave and go elsewhere." General Electric operated eight plants in Juarez, more than any other company.

Many of the workers blame the Mexican government for their condition, not the American employers. An older woman, Laura Chavez, who just quit her job at Delmex, a General Motors plant, expected to find another easily because of the extraordinarily high turnover in the *maquila* factories. "Look, it's not enough," she said. "If you're going to be living off that salary, it's not enough. I don't blame the companies. I blame the Mexican government because the wages are whatever the government requires."

In Mexico, the federal government does periodically raise the legal minimum-wage level but, for the last decade, the increases have lagged further and further behind the rising cost of living—thus providing cheaper and cheaper labor for the American employers.

Indeed, the *maquiladora* industry boasts of this attraction in the glossy publication it distributes to prospective companies. In 1981, the industry association reported, the labor cost for a *maquila* worker was $1.12 an hour. By the end of 1989, the real cost had fallen to 56 cents an hour.[2]

What these workers have surmised is correct: Their own government is exploiting them too. Mired in debt to American banks since the early 1980s, Mexico has been desperate to raise more foreign-currency income to keep up with its foreign-debt payments. Aside from oil, the *maquiladora* industry provides the country with its largest influx of U.S. dollars, and the Mexican government has attracted more U.S. enterprise by steadily depressing the wages of the workers. If it had not, Mexico might have lost the jobs to its principal low-wage competitors (Singapore or Taiwan or South Korea) and lost the precious foreign-currency income it needed to pay its bankers.

Wages for workers are, thus, falling on both ends of this global transmission belt. The people who lost their premium manufacturing jobs in the United States are compelled to settle for lower incomes. But so are the Mexican peasants who inherited the jobs. On both sides of the border, workers are caught in a vicious competition with one another that richly benefits the employers.

The wage depression in Mexico is an extreme case, but not at all unique in the world. In many of the other countries attracting global production, similar exchanges occur that victimize workers and their communities and often benefit the country's established oligopoly of wealth and political power. The CEO of an American clothing company was asked if his company's imported goods from China might, in fact, have been manufactured with slave labor. "Everybody is a slave laborer," he replied. "The wage is so cheap."[3]

Instead of an experienced workforce, the *maquiladora* zone has created a bewildering stream of young people tumbling randomly from one job to another.

"We have begun to see more fourteen-year-olds in the plants—children fourteen to sixteen years old," Valdes-Villalva said. "The *maquila* workers are very young on the whole, we're talking sixteen to twenty-one years old. Usually, the companies are careful to see that the youngest girls and boys get permission slips from their parents.

"Workers do not age in this industry—they leave. Because of the intensive work it entails, there's constant burnout. If they've been there three or four years, workers lose efficiency. They begin to have problems with eyesight. They begin to have allergies and kidney problems. They are less productive."

The workers themselves matter-of-factly describe the reality of children who have left school for these jobs. "Quite a lot say they are sixteen but I know they are probably thirteen or fourteen or fifteen years old," said Sylvia Facoln at the GE plant. "I know of people who are less than fourteen years old and I myself brought one of them to work here. It's very common in all the *maquilas*."

The scandal of major American corporations employing adolescent children to do the industrial work that once belonged to American adults has been documented in many settings, yet it provokes no political response in either Washington or Mexico City. The *Arizona Republic* of Phoenix ran a prize-winning series on the *maquiladora* across from Nogales, Arizona, where, among other things, the reporter found thirteen-year-old Miriam Borquez working the night shift for General Electric (the same company that cares deeply about educating disadvantaged minorities at home).

The girl quit school to take the job, she explained, because her family needed the money. They were living in a nine-by-sixteen tin hut. The *Arizona Republic*'s conservative editorial page lamented: "Has greed so consumed some businessmen that human lives in Mexico are less valuable than the next saxophone shipped to the U.S. from Sonora?"[4]

Maquiladora officials always protest their innocence in this matter. Mexican labor laws permit them to hire fourteen-year-olds if their parents grant permission. These laws are faithfully observed, the officials explain, but companies cannot always verify the true age of young job applicants and children sometimes forge permission slips from parents or use someone else's documents. This is sometimes true, according to Ignacio Escandon, an El Paso businessman familiar with the Juarez labor market, but the excuse hardly relieves the corporations of their moral burden. "The companies don't ask many questions," Escandon said. "The demand for labor is constant."

There is a general lack of political scrutiny. Beyond anecdotes, no one knows the real dimensions of the exploitation. The use of child labor is one of the many aspects of the Mexican *maquiladora* that has never been authoritatively investigated, since neither government has much interest in exposing the truth.

Environmental damage from the *maquiladora* plants, likewise, has never been squarely examined by federal authorities though gross violations have been cited in numerous reports and accusations from private citizens and some state agencies. The National Toxics Campaign described the U.S.-Mexican border as already so polluted with dangerous chemicals that it may become "a two-thousand-mile Love Canal."

For years, Professor Valdes-Villalva and her associates have tried to track down what the companies do with the toxic chemicals that are brought into the Mexican plants. Mexican law requires that imported hazardous materials must be shipped back to the United States, but the researchers could only find customs documents covering less than 5 percent of the volume. They suspect—but can't prove—that the bulk is trucked to illegal dumps in the interior, future Superfund sites waiting to be discovered by Mexican authorities.

The health consequences that frightened American citizens when they first encountered the casual disposal of toxic wastes in their own communities now worry Mexican citizens too. Like the Americans before them, the concerned Mexicans are confronted by official denial and a lack of reliable information to confirm or refute their fears.

"What most concerns me is the health within the plants," Valdes-Villalva said. "This is where we are lacking. We have no money for research, but we hear these complaints from workers. We find high levels of lead in blood samples. We have situations in which we find a tremendous amount of manic-depressives, which does not follow the usual amount in the population. So what I'm beginning to think is that this is a central nervous system disorder, physical not psychological. It could be solvents. It's heavily concentrated in the electronics industry. There's also a tremendous number of Down's syndrome children. Other disorders you find in high incidence are cleft palates and other deformities."

Like the American citizens who have formed thousands of grassroots political organizations to combat industrial pollution, Mexican citizens who summon the courage to protest are utterly on their own—aligned against both industry and government, without the resources to challenge the official explanations or the political influence to force the government to act. But, of course, the Mexican citizens are in a much weaker position to undertake such political struggles. Their communities are impoverished. Their national economy depends crucially on these factories. Their own democratic institutions are weak and underdeveloped or corrupted.

The situation seems overwhelming, but not entirely hopeless. Along the border and elsewhere, some people of both nationalities are beginning to grasp the fact that citizens of neither nation can hope to change their own conditions without the support of the other. Mexicans cannot hope to stand up to General Motors or GE from the *colonias* of Ciudad Juarez. Nor can Americans expect to defend their own jobs or their own social standards without addressing the hopes and prospects and afflictions of their impoverished neighbors.

Genuine reform will require a new and unprecedented form of crossborder politics in which citizens develop continuing dialogues across national boundaries and learn to speak for their common values. Only by acting together can they hope to end the exploitation, not just in Mexico but elsewhere across the global production system. This kind of sophisticated internationalism has not been characteristic among Americans, to put it mildly.

That is the daunting nature of the global political dilemma. People like Valdes-Villalva have already seen it clearly and so do some Americans. A Coalition for Justice in the *Maquiladoras* was formed in 1991 by more than sixty American environmental, religious, community and labor organizations, including the AFL-CIO, in order to speak out against the injustices and confront the multinational corporations with demands for civilized conduct. Leaders from the Mexican *maquiladora* communities are being brought to the United States to spread the word to Americans on the true nature of the global economic system.[5]

"Moral behavior knows no borders," Sister Susan Mika, president of the coalition, declared. "What would be wrong in the United States is wrong in Mexico too."

Valdes-Villalva described the new democratic imperative:

"In order for workers to protect themselves, they have to see that they are tied to workers worldwide," she said. "It is the transnational economy that is undermining labor. A new union has to emerge that crosses national borders and makes a closer relationship among workers—a new kind of union that cooperates worldwide. Companies can make agreements among themselves about markets and production. The only competition in the global economy is between the workers."

Wolfgang Sachs, the German social critic, offered a mordant metaphor to describe the antidemocratic qualities of the global economy. The global marketplace, he said, has become the world's new "closet dictator."

"The fear of falling behind in international competition has become the predominant organizing principle of politics, North and South, East and West," Sachs wrote. "Both enterprises and entire states see themselves trapped in a situation of relentless competition, where each participant is dependent on the decisions of all other players. What falls by the wayside in this hurly-burly is the possibility for self-determination."[6]

For Americans, this is a new experience, profoundly at odds with national history and democratic legacy. We are now, suddenly, a nation whose citizens can no longer decide their own destiny. The implications offend the optimism and self-reliance of the American character, eclipsing our typical disregard for the rest of the world. Citizens of most foreign nations—smaller, less powerful and more dependent on others—have had considerable practical experience with the limitations and frustrations of global interdependency. Americans have not. They are just beginning to discover what global economics means for their own politics.

ACORN, the grassroots citizens' organization, discovered, for instance, that the prospect for financing low-income housing—a major priority for its members—had been seriously damaged by a new banking regulation that assigns an extremely high risk rating to bank lending for multifamily housing projects. "This will be a disaster for poor people unless Congress intervenes immediately," Jane Uebelhoer of ACORN testified. "This is outright government red-lining and it will be the end of low-income home ownership in Detroit, in Chicago, in New York and elsewhere."[7]

But the new credit regulation did not flow out of any legislation enacted by Congress and the president. It was a small detail in an international agreement forged among the central bankers from a dozen industrial countries, including the United States. The central bankers met periodically in Basel, Switzerland, for several years as the Committee on Banking Regulations and Supervisory Practices, trying to reconcile the different banking laws of competing nations and creating a "level playing field" that would standardize the capital requirements for banks.

America's representative (and the leading promoter of the agreement) was the Federal Reserve, the nonelected central bank that enjoys formal insulation from political accountability. While America's most important multinational banks were consulted beforehand, no consumer representatives were included in the Federal Reserve's deliberations nor were any of the groups that speak for low-income home buyers.[8]

"When we talk to the federal regulators," Chris Lewis, an ACORN lobbyist, complained, "they say to us: 'Oh, that's an international treaty, we can't possibly do anything about that.' So now we have housing policy determined by central bankers with no accountability whatsoever."

American politics, in other words, is moving offshore. The nature of the global economy pushes every important political debate in that direction—further and further away from the citizens. As companies become multinational, able to coordinate production from many places and unify markets across national boundaries, they are taking the governing issues with them. From arcane regulatory provisions to large questions of national priorities, the corporations, not governments, become the connecting strand in offshore politics, since they are the only organizations active in every place and coping with all the world's many differences.

Arguments that were once decided, up or down, in the public forums of democratic debate are now floating off into the murk of international diplomacy and deal making. They are to be decided in settings where neither American citizens nor their elected representatives can be heard, where no institutional rules exist to guarantee democratic access and accountability.

Environmental activists discovered, for instance, that U.S. proposals for the current round of international trade negotiations would effectively vitiate domestic laws on food safety by assigning the question of standards to an obscure UN-sponsored commission in Rome. If the nation (or a state government) enacts laws on pesticides or food additives that exceed the health standards set by the Codex Alimentarius Commission in Rome, then other nations can declare that the environmental standards are artificial "trade barriers" designed to block foreign products and, therefore, subject to penalties or retaliation.

The goal proclaimed by trade negotiators is to "harmonize" environmental laws across the boundaries of individual nations to encourage freer trade. But that objective, inevitably, means lowering U.S. standards. Indeed, that is the objective for major components of American agribusiness, including the multinational chemical manufacturers who are enthusiastic supporters of what is blandly called "harmonization."

The Codex is an obscure agency utterly unknown to ordinary citizens, but the multinational companies that help devise its standards are well aware of its significance. At a recent session of the commission, the American delegation included executives from three major chemical companies—Du Pont, Monsanto and Hercules—serving alongside U.S. government officials. Among other things, the Codex standard permits DDT residues on fruit and vegetables that are thirty-three to fifty times higher than U.S. laws allows.[9]

As environmentalists and some allied farm groups have argued, the current round of GATT negotiations is actually aimed at fostering a new generation of deregulation for business—without the inconvenience of domestic political debate.

"The U.S. proposals (for GATT) represent a radical attempt to preempt the authority of its own citizens and the citizenry of other countries to regulate commerce in the pursuit of environmental and social ends," David Morris of the Institute for Local Self-Reliance in St. Paul, Minnesota, declared. "It is an attempt to impose a laissez-faire philosophy on a worldwide basis, to allow the global corporations unfettered ability to transfer capital, goods, services and raw materials across national boundaries."

Other citizen groups and interests, from sugar growers to insurance companies to state governments, have also discovered that global politics is encroaching on their domains. Japan protests that state-set limits on U.S. timber harvesting constitute a GATT violation. European trade officials complain that the state of Maine's new law on throwaway bottles is an artificial trade barrier that the federal government should preempt in accordance with the international trade agreement.

The centrifugal diversity of the American federalist system, in which states can legislate and experiment independent of the national government, is thus headed for collision with the leveling, homogenizing force of the global marketplace. One or the other will have to yield power and prerogatives.[10]

American democracy is ill equipped to cope with offshore politics, both in its institutional arrangements and in its customary responses to foreign affairs. Treaty making and diplomacy belong traditionally to the presidency, even though the U.S. Senate must ratify the results, and there is a time-honored tendency to defer to the chief executive in negotiating foreign relations so that the nation may speak with one voice.

The overall political effect of globalization is to further enhance the power of the presidency—just as the Cold War did—at the expense of representative forums, public debate and accountability. Once an issue has become part of high-level diplomatic exchanges, all of the details naturally become murkier, since negotiators do not wish to talk too freely about their negotiating strategies. The discussions often literally move offshore and behind closed doors—more irregular deal making that will have the force of law.

When international deals are being struck, it matters enormously who is doing the bargaining and who is in the room offering expert advice. The so-called G7, for instance, meets regularly to "coordinate" economic policies among the major industrial nations (including fiscal policy, a realm the Constitution assigns to Congress). Yet there is no visible procedure—much less legislated agenda—by which the Treasury secretary or the Federal Reserve chairman is empowered to make international economic policy for the nation. Those two officers, by their nature, represent a very narrow spectrum of American interests—mainly banks and the financial system—and they cannot be expected to reflect the full, rich diversity of American perspectives on economic issues. Bankers are well represented, but who speaks for the home builders or the auto industry or machine tools or the farmers?

Substantial institutional reforms are needed, obviously, to prevent global politics from gradually eclipsing the substance of democratic debate and action. At the very least, that would mean democratizing reforms to ventilate the U.S. negotiating routines in a systematic way so that everyone can follow the action. It might also require refusal to participate in any international forum or agency that lacks democratic access to the information and decision making. If the chemical companies can lobby the Codex in Rome for weaker health standards, then surely any other American citizen should be able to sit at the table too. When central bankers meet in Basel to decide U.S. housing policy, then housing advocates should also be in the room.

The first, overriding imperative, however, is to defend the nation's power to govern its own affairs. If democracy is to retain any meaning, Americans will need to draw a hard line in defense of their own national sovereignty. This is not just about protecting American jobs, but also about protecting the very core of self-government—laws that are fashioned in open debate by representatives who are directly accountable to the people. Among other things, this challenge requires Congress to confront the presidency and restrain it—to refuse to grant the chief executive the power to bargain away American laws in the name of free trade or competitiveness or any other slogan.

Offshore politics threatens the ability of free people to decide the terms of their own social relations; it allows the closet dictator to decide things according to the narrow interest of "efficiency." The "harmonizing" process begins with the regulatory laws that business interests consider meddlesome and too expensive, but the attack will lead eventually to the nation's largest social guarantees, welfare or Social Security or health, since those programs also add to the cost of production and thus interfere with the free-flowing commerce among boundaryless companies.

Who will decide what is equitable and just for American society? A closed meeting of finance ministers in Geneva? An obscure group of experts in Rome coached by corporate lobbyists? Such questions have already penetrated the fabric of self-government. Americans, in addition to their other-democratic burdens, need to get educated on the answers.

The concept of the "boundaryless company" has now become commonplace among executives of major multinational corporations. They are American companies sort of but not really, only now and then when it suits them. IBM, the flagship of American industrial enterprise, is composed of 40 percent foreign employees. Whirlpool is mostly not Americans. GE puts its logo on microwaves made by Samsung in South Korea.[11] Chrysler buys cars from Mitsubishi and sells them as its own. America's most important banks operate legally authorized "foreign facilities" right in Manhattan for the benefit of depositors who wish to keep their money "offshore."

The question of what is foreign and what is American has become wildly scrambled by global commerce. The multinational enterprises, unlike Americans generally, are already securing alliances in this fierce world of global competition—networks of joint ventures, coproduction and shared ownership with their ostensible rivals in the world, including state-owned enterprises in foreign nations. Every U.S. auto company has become partners one way or another with its competitors, the Japanese car companies. Producers of electronic equipment, computers, even aircraft have melded their American citizenship in similar arrangements.

Multinational executives work to enhance the company, not the country. The president of NCR Corporation told *The New York Times:* "I was asked the other day about United States competitiveness and I replied that I don't think about it at all." A vice-president of Colgate-Palmolive observed: "The United States does not have an automatic call on our resources. There is no mindset that puts this country first." And the head of GE Taiwan, where so many U.S. industrial jobs have migrated, explained "The U.S. trade deficit is not the most important thing in my life . . . running an effective business is."[12]

John Reed, CEO of Citibank, America's largest troubled bank, has said he is actively scouting options for moving the corporation headquarters to a foreign country in order to escape U.S. banking laws. "The United States is the wrong country for an international bank to be based," Reed declared. Meanwhile, his bank's deposits are protected by the U.S. taxpayers and his lobbyists in Washington actively promote a multi-billion-dollar government bailout to save large commercial banks like Citibank from insolvency.[13]

These men are merely expressing the prevailing values of the "stateless corporation," as *Business Week* called it. This creature operates most successfully when it discards sentimental attachments like patriotism and analyzes global opportunities with a cold, clear eye. Some of these same corporations, it is true, wave the flag vigorously when bidding for defense contracts or beseeching the U.S. government for tax subsidies, but their exuberant Americanism dissipates rapidly when the subject is wages or the burden of supporting public institutions.

Their weak national loyalty has profound implications for the nation's politics because these men, on the whole, are also influential voices in shaping the outlines (and often the close details) of national economic policy—not just for trade policy, but for taxation and government spending priorities. Politicians in both parties (especially the Republican party) defer to their worldly experience. Most economists and political commentators have embraced their argument that America's future prosperity will be best served by a laissez-faire regime in which governments get out of the way and let the marketplace develop its global structure.

But here is the blunt question: Can these people really be trusted to speak for the rest of us? How can they faithfully define America's best interest when their own business strategies are designed to escape the bounds of national loyalty? The impressive fact about ordinary Americans is that, despite years of education and propaganda, they still cling stubbornly to their skepticism about the global economy. With the usual condescension, elite commentators dismiss the popular expressions of concern as uninformed and nativist, the misplaced fears of people ill equipped to grasp the larger dimensions of economics.

Ordinary citizens generally form their economic opinions and perceptions, not from distant abstractions or even from the endless tides of propaganda, but from their own commonsense values and their own firsthand experiences. Common sense tells people that it cannot be good for America's long-term prosperity to lose millions of high-wage manufacturing jobs. Even if this hasn't affected their own employment, it means that middle-class families are losing the wherewithal to be viable consumers, and sooner or later, that has to hurt the overall economy.

The majority of Americans are not wrong on their unsophisticated skepticism. The new reality of global competition generates a vicious economic trap for worldwide prosperity: a permanent condition of overcapacity in production that ensures destructive economic consequences. Simply put, the world's existing structure of manufacturing facilities, constantly being expanded on cheap labor and new technologies, can now turn out far more goods than the world's consumers can afford to buy. That is, more cars, computers, aircraft, appliances, steel and so forth are made than the marketplace can possibly absorb.

The auto industry is an uncomplicated example: Auto factories worldwide have the capacity to produce 45 million cars annually for a market that, in the best years, will buy no more than 35 million cars. "We have too many cars chasing too few drivers," a Chrysler executive remarked. The economic consequences are obvious: Somebody has to close his auto factory and stop producing. This marketplace imbalance in supply and demand is the larger reality that underlies the fierce competition for advantage among companies and among nations—the awesome force driving everyone toward the lowest common denominator.

Whose factory must be closed to bring the worldwide supply into balance with the worldwide demand? Whose workers will be laid off? The older, less modern factories are closed first, of course, but also the plants that pay the highest wages and the ones where government provide less generous tax subsidies to the employer. American workers in steel and autos and other industries have had a lot of experience watching this process at work—seeing factories they knew were viable and productive suddenly declared obsolete. But so will workers in the less abundant nations. This process closed Ohio factories and someday it will close Mexico's. So long as global productive capacity exceeds global demand by such extravagant margins, somebody somewhere in the world has to keep closing factories, old and new.

The companies have no choice. They must keep moving their production, keep seeking the lowest possible costs and most favorable political conditions, in order to defend their market shares. Eventually, as economist Jeff Faux has written, South Korea will be losing jobs to cheap labor in Thailand and even China may someday lose factories to Bangladesh. The popular notion among struggling nations that they can someday become the next South Korea—as the reward for a generation or so of the degradation of their workers—is fatally at odds with the logic of permanent overcapacity. The Mexican *maquiladora* cities thought they were going to become the next South Korea, but instead they may be the next Detroit.[14]

In fundamental economic terms, the globalization process produces three interlocking economic consequences that together are deleterious to everyone's wellbeing. First, it destroys capital on a large scale by rendering productive investments useless to the marketplace. That is the meaning of closing viable factories that can no longer meet the price competition: The invested capital is lost, the idle factories are written off as tax losses. Modernizing production with new technologies always produces this destruction, of course, but the global dispersion of production lives on it—like a game of checkers in which advantage goes to the player who made the last jump.

Second, the overcapacity permanently depresses wage levels worldwide, since no workers anywhere can organize and bargain very successfully against the threat of a closed factory, whether they are well-paid Americans or impoverished peasants working somewhere in the Third World.

Finally, these two effects—the instability of capital investment and the depression of wages—combine to guarantee that global demand can never catch up with global supply. New consumers for the world's output, to be sure, emerge with new development, but other existing consumers are lost, as their jobs are lost or their wages decline in real terms. So long as the process is allowed to run its course, the flight will continue downhill—too many factories making too many goods for a marketplace where too many families lack the wherewithal to buy them.

It does not require great political imagination to see that the world system is heading toward a further dispersion of governing power so the closet dictator of the marketplace can command things more efficiently, from everywhere and nowhere. The historic paradox is breathtaking: At the very moment when western democracies and capitalism have triumphed over the communist alternative, their own systems of self-government are being gradually unraveled by the market system.

To cope with this complicated new world, every government naturally seeks to centralize its command of policy and thus become more hierarchical, less democratic. Societies like Japan have a natural advantage because they already practice a feudal form of state-administered capitalism, dominated by a one-party monopoly in politics, managed through government-assisted cartels and insulated from popular resistance. Some elites in the United States, though they do not say so directly, would like to emulate the efficiency of the Japanese political structure—equipping the chief executive with even more authority and putting citizens at even greater distance from government.

For many years, a wishful presumption has existed that, in time, the hegemony of global corporations would lead the way to the construction of a new international political order—world institutions that have the representative capacity to govern equitably across national borders. That prospect is not at hand in our time.

On the contrary, what is emerging for now is a power system that more nearly resembles a kind of global feudalism—a system in which the private economic enterprises function like rival dukes and barons, warring for territories across the world and oblivious to local interests, since none of the local centers are strong enough to govern them. Like feudal lords, the stateless corporations will make alliances with one another or launch raids against one another's stake. They will play weakening national governments off against each other and select obscure offshore meeting places to decide the terms of law governing their competition. National armies, including especially America's, will exist mainly to keep the contest free of interference.

In that event, the vast throngs of citizens are reduced to a political position resembling that of the serfs or small landholders who followed church or nobility in the feudal system. They will be utterly dependent on the fortunes of the corporate regimes, the dukes and barons flying their national flag. But citizens will have nothing much to say about the governing of these global institutions, for those questions will have moved beyond their own government. If national laws are rendered impotent, then so are a nation's citizens.

A different vision of the future requires great political imagination—a new democratic sensibility in which people in many places manage simultaneously to overcome their sense of helplessness. A single nation is not helpless before these forces, despite what conventional wisdom teaches, and the United States especially is not helpless. Citizens have enormous potential leverage over the global economy if they decide to use it through their own national governing system. A corporation's behavior abroad is not separable from its home country because it enjoys so many special benefits at home.

In the United States, a multinational corporation that wishes to be treated as an American citizen for the purposes of the law and government benefits can be made to play by America's rules, just as Japan's are, or else surrender all the tax subsidies, government contracts and other considerations, including national defense, that American taxpayers provide.

Why should Americans, for instance, provide research and development tax subsidies for corporations that intend to export their new production and to violate common standards of decency by exploiting the weak? Why should American military forces be deployed to protect companies that do not reciprocate the national loyalty?

These are among the many contradictions created by the global system that only nationalism can reconcile. American law cannot police the world and need not try, but it can police what is American. To take the starkest example, no U.S. company should be treated as a lawful entity, entitled to all the usual privileges, if its production is found to exploit child labor in other countries. The same approach applies across the range of corporate behavior, from environmental degradation to ignoring tax laws.

The American political system also has enormous leverage over the behavior of foreign-owned multinational enterprises—access to the largest, richest marketplace in the world. Because of that asset, the United States could lead the way to new international standards of conduct by first asserting its own values unilaterally. If trade depends upon price advantages derived mainly from poverty wages for children or defenseless workers prohibited from organizing their own unions or factories that cause great environmental destruction, this trade cannot truly be called free.

The purpose of asserting America's political power through its own marketplace would be to create the incentive for a new international system of global standards, one which all the trading nations would negotiate and accept. For a start, the United States ought to reject any new trade agreements that do not include a meaningful social contract rules that establish baseline standards for health, labor law, working conditions, the environment, wages. The U.S. government might also prohibit the familiar tax-dodging practices of companies that exploit communities as the price for new jobs. Indeed, companies ought to post community bonds when they relocate—guaranteeing that they will not run away from their obligations to develop roads and schools and the other public investments.[15]

Fundamentally, it is not just the exploited workers in the United States who need a higher minimum-wage law. The world economy needs a global minimum-wage law—one that establishes a rising floor under the most impoverished workers in industrial employment. A global minimum-wage law would recognize, of course, the wide gaps that exist between rich and poor, but it could establish flexible ratios aimed at gradually reducing the differences and prohibiting raw exploitation like that in the *maquiladora* zone in Mexico. No one imagines that world incomes will be equalized, not in our time certainly. But, as nations move toward equilibrium, they ought to be governed by a global economic system that pushes the bottom up rather than pulling the top down.

The democratic imperative is nothing less than that: to refashion the global economy so that it runs uphill for everyone, so that it enhances democracy rather than crippling it, so that the economic returns are distributed widely among all classes instead of narrowly at the top.

NOTES

1. Professor Gueramina Valdes-Villalva, whom I interviewed in July 1990, worked for many years to aid the exploited *maquiladora* workers and to challenge the practices of the companies. She died in a plane crash in Texas on February 13, 1991. My guides and translators in Ciudad Juarez were two Americans, Sister Maribeth Larkin, an organizer with EPISO, the IAF organization in El Paso, and Ignacio Escandon, a businessman who is active in EPISO.

2. The statistics on falling labor costs are from *Twin Plant News: The Magazine of the Maquiladora Industry,* May 1990.

3. The "slave labor" remark was quoted by Lane Kirkland, president of the AFL-CIO, speech to the American International Club of Geneva, June 24, 1991.

4. The *Arizona Republic* and reporters Jerry Kammer and Sandy Tolan of Desert West News Service won the Robert F. Kennedy journalism award for their series on the Nogales industries, published in April 1989. *The Wall Street Journal* published a harrowing account of a twelve-year-old working in a Mexican shoe factory and described child labor as general throughout the country—exploiting five to ten million underage workers. See Matt Moffett, "Working Children: Underage Laborers Fill Mexican Factories," *Wall Street Journal,* April 8, 1991.

5. Formation of the Coalition for Justice in the *Maquiladoras* was reported in the newsletter of the Federation for Industrial Retention and Renewal, Spring 1991. Coalition members include FIRR, the National Toxics Campaign, the Interfaith Center for Corporate Responsibility, the AFL-CIO and a variety of others.

    Some major labor unions such as the food and commercial workers' are beginning to develop their own strategies for cross-border politics with similar unions in Europe, Asia and Latin America, having discovered that they are up against the same companies and similar labor practices, regardless of their own nation.

6. Wolfgang Sachs, of the Essen Institute for Advanced Studies, wrote in *New Perspectives Quarterly,* Spring 1990.

7. Jane Uebelhoer of ACORN testified before the Senate Banking Committee, April 4, 1990.

8. The international agreement signed by the Federal Reserve and other central banks created a system of risk-based capital ratios for banking—capital requirements geared to the level of risk in each bank's portfolio. Housing suffered because the Federal Reserve assigned a 100 percent risk ratio for multifamily projects—a rating identical to the most speculative business loans—which would raise the cost of such lending for banks. The central bank, in effect, had promulgated a credit-allocation policy that would discourage investment in low-income housing—when the nation faced an obvious shortage. Federal regulators claimed that they were bound by international agreement, but the fact is that other nations' central banks were prepared to assign a more favorable risk rating to housing than was the Federal Reserve.

9. Details on Codex standards and the influence of American chemical companies are from Eric Christensen, "Food Fight: How GATT Undermines Food Safety Regulations," *Multinational Monitor,* November 1990. The GATT negotiations reached an impasse in early 1991 on other economic issues but presumably will resume.

10. Examples of GATT objections to U.S. state laws were recounted by Bruce Stokes, "State Rules and World Business," *National Journal,* October 27, 1990.

11. Details on IBM, Whirlpool and GE microwaves are from Robert B. Reich, *The Work of Nations: Preparing Ourselves for 21st Century Capitalism,* Alfred A. Knopf, 1991.

12. The three corporate executives from NCR, Colgate-Palmolive and GE were quoted by David Morris, "Trading Our Future."

13. John Reed's efforts to relocate Citicorp in a foreign country were described as his "pet

project" by *The Wall Street Journal,* August 9, 1991. Lloyd Cutler, whose Washington law firm represents Citibank, has proposed a vast recapitalization of commercial banks by the Federal Reserve.

14. The contours of the global process were described by the Economic Policy Institute's director, Jeff Faux, "Labor in the New Global Economy," *Dissent,* Summer 1990.

15. Lane Kirkland, president of the AFL-CIO, spoke for this idea in terms of labor rights: "A trade policy that encourages or tolerates the spectacle of corporations roaming the world in search of the cheapest and most repressed labor is more perversely protectionist than any tariff or quota, and serves in the last analysis to restrict and undermine markets and lower standards the world over. In the interest of basic fairness and the continued elevation of the human condition, the denial of workers' rights should be clearly defined internationally as the unfair trading practice it is, through the incorporation of a social clause in the General Agreement on Tariffs and Trade." Speech to American International Club of Geneva, June 24, 1991.

28. Oil and Power After the Gulf War

Robert J. Lieber

What are the implications of the Gulf War for the world oil market and for global energy security? On initial examination, there would seem to be little cause for concern, and no fewer than three separate factors contribute to such a conclusion. First, the devastating defeat suffered by Iraq suggests that both past and future military threats can be minimized. Second, the success with which producing and consuming countries managed to cope with the purely oil-related components of the Gulf crisis suggests that both the supply and the price of petroleum are manageable. Third, regardless of policy choices made by these countries, elasticities of both supply and demand appear to insure that world energy markets can and will cope with potential disruptions.

However, an assessment of oil and power in the aftermath of the Gulf War provides evidence for concluding that the risks were in fact very substantial and that avoidance of serious upheaval was by no means inevitable. This interpretation rests not only on analysis of the Gulf crisis itself, but also on the lessons of the two oil shocks

From "Oil and Power After the Gulf War," by Robert J. Lieber. *International Security,* Vol 17, No 1, Summer 1992, pp. 155–176. Copyright © 1992 the President and Fellows of Harvard College and of the Massachusetts Institute of Technology. Reprinted by permission.

Robert J. Lieber is professor and Chairman of the Department of Government at Georgetown University. His most recent books are *No Common Power: Understanding International Relations* (HarperCollins, 2d ed., 1991), and *Eagle in a New World: American Grand Strategy in the Post–Cold War Era,* co-edited with Kenneth Oye and Donald Rothchild (HarperCollins, 1992).

of the 1970s, as well as on experience from the following decade. In this light, each of the three arguments above proves less reassuring.

In the military realm, the extraordinary victory of the American-led coalition in an air war lasting just over five weeks and a ground war of 100 hours has given rise to a virtual consensus on both the invincibility of the coalition and the inevitability of its triumph. However, cases both old (the debacle of Australian and other British Empire forces at Gallipoli against the Ottoman Turks in 1915[1]) and more contemporary (the failure of Desert One, the American effort to rescue the Iranian-held hostages in April 1980[2]), and even the ambiguous consequences of Israel's 1982 war in Lebanon,[3] suggest that the triumph of the forces of modern or Western powers over those of less technically-advanced Middle Eastern regimes cannot simply be taken for granted.

Moreover, timing proves to have been crucial. Had Saddam Hussein's forces promptly followed their August 2, 1990, invasion and occupation of Kuwait by a drive into Saudi Arabia, the Saudis and Americans would have lacked the military means to stop the hundreds of thousands of troops and the thousands of armored vehicles under the command of the Iraqi dictator. At best, this might have triggered a longer, less successful, and far more costly war. At worst, Saddam might have controlled the Saudi Gulf Coast ports and major Saudi oilfields, leaving the United States with two unwelcome options: to mount a military campaign without the benefit of the Saudi ports and facilities and to risk the kind of destruction later seen in Kuwait on a still vaster scale against the oilfields of Saudi Arabia, or to acquiesce in Iraq's control of almost half the world's proved oil reserves, as well as the likelihood of Saddam's domination of the remainder of the Gulf oil producers.

The cutoff of Kuwaiti and Iraqi oil from world oil markets was managed, but with a costly volatility in world oil prices. Saudi Arabia increased its own oil production by more than 3 million barrels per day (mbd), approximately the amount previously supplied by Iraq, and other countries more than made up the shortfall caused by the loss of Kuwait's production. On the demand side, the countries of the International Energy Agency (IEA), led by the United States, eventually took measures to signal both their ability and their will to reduce demand and subsequently to release oil from their strategic stocks. Nonetheless, the United States and the IEA countries were slow to announce their intent to draw down stocks, and these delays appear to have been costly.

While markets did work, the temporary run-up of prices proved costly in terms of inflation and in tipping a weakening American economy into a serious recession.[4] Moreover, one lesson of the 1973–74 and 1979–80 oil shocks is that markets often over-shoot, and that inelasticities of both supply and demand for energy can make the adjustment process long and very costly. Indeed, even with the supply and demand effects largely under control, initial uncertainties and market psychology caused oil prices to triple. These surged from a pre-crisis level of $13 per barrel in May 1990, to a peak of over $40 per barrel in the early autumn, before falling back to the $20 per barrel range.

In sum, the experience of the Gulf crisis—as well as the evidence of the past two decades—leaves little reason for complacency, and the case thus deserves careful examination. The remainder of this article attempts to do so, first, by assessing oil as a problem in international politics and political economy, in terms of the need for integrating both economic and political dimensions of analysis. It then considers the status of oil from Iraq and the Persian Gulf along with problems posed by the fact that two-thirds of proved world petroleum reserves are located in the Gulf region. Next, the article turns to specific consideration of Iraqi and Saudi oil, and the way in which the global oil system reacted to the crisis. Finally, a number of policy implications are examined.

OIL AS A PROBLEM IN POLITICAL ECONOMY

A reliable understanding of the role of oil in international politics and international political economy has proven elusive. A principle reason for this is that too many observers approach the subject through perspectives that are narrowly economic or, conversely, mostly political. These interpretations, in their most pristine forms, can be considered as "ideal types."

From the vantage point of the exclusively economic perspective, it is simply assumed that the market mechanism will provide an eventual equilibrium for supply and demand.[5] Thus if shortages of oil develop, prices will rise until the available supply matches demand. Higher prices will have the effect of causing additional supplies of oil and other forms of energy to be developed and brought to market. At the same time, higher prices will result in reduced demand as buyers seek to economize by conserving or by switching to other forms of energy.

From the economic perspective, policies aimed at protecting energy security or incorporating externalities are seen as largely irrelevant, and the risks of energy crises are seen as minimal.[6] Moreover, the economic perspective points to both the unintended consequences and to the failure of deliberate governmental policies. For example during the 1970s, price regulation and allocation policies for oil and natural gas did not prevent, and may even have fostered, spot shortages, gas lines, congressional stalemate, and political recrimination, and they were ultimately discarded. Also unsuccessful and later abandoned was the expensive synthetic fuels program initiated by the Carter administration.

However, the economic perspective itself remains seriously deficient when used in isolation. For one thing, it tends either to minimize the importance of the Organization of Petroleum Exporting countries (OPEC) in shaping the world oil system, or else to suggest that long-term market factors make it largely impossible for OPEC to have a lasting impact. Moreover, this approach tends to overlook the implications of geography, particularly the fact that no less than 67 percent of proved world oil reserves are located in the Persian Gulf area, one of the most politically unstable regions on earth. In addition, market imperfections and barriers to market entry, in terms both of cost and time, are disregarded. Yet, regardless of market signals, it costs many billions of dollars and takes many years to find and develop a new oil field or develop particular energy sources. Finally, an exclusively economic perspective does not successfully meet an historical reality test. That is, given the costly and disruptive cases of the 1973–74 and 1979–80 oil shocks, it fails to provide a convincing explanation for why such disruptions may not be repeated.

Conversely, analyses of oil which are essentially—or even exclusively—political also provide only a one-dimensional perspective. These approaches tend to minimize the role of market phenomena. They thus have overstated the threat of oil embargoes, exaggerated the relationship between world oil supply and the Arab-Israeli conflict, and inflated the fundamental power of individual oil-producing countries. After each of the 1970s oil shocks, the political approach tended to assume that oil prices would continue to rise indefinitely.

To be sure, many of the prevailing economic (or political) interpretations are more complex than these ideal types convey. For example, one of the more sophisticated market-oriented interpretations, which sees economic forces tending to push oil prices lower over the long term and tends to downplay the risk of future oil shocks, nonetheless incorporates policy recommendations for the United States that go well beyond merely letting the market take its own course.[7] Thus, Eliyahu Kanovsky urges that the United States take steps to limit its vulnerability to Middle East supply disruptions through actions such as incentives for Third World states to pursue oil exploration and development, as well as the introduction of American fiscal and regulatory policies to encourage domestic energy efficiency and conservation.

In reality, oil can be understood most effectively through integrating insights from both economics and politics. Without this synthesis, there exists the kind of problem identified by Robert Gilpin, in which political scientists tend to overlook the role of markets, while economists often neglect the importance of power and the political context of events.[8]

Oil issues in the Middle East take on a broad significance because they encompass both political and economic dimensions and because they often have consequences that spread far beyond regional confines. Under certain very specific circumstances, events occurring in the Gulf can reverberate halfway around the world, and do so almost instantaneously. The most dramatic (though least common) pattern is that of an oil shock, defined as a profound disruption of the existing supply and price system. However, two major phenomena must be present simultaneously for such an event to take place. One is the existence of a tight or precarious balance between supply and demand, in which available world oil supplies only just manage to satisfy world oil demand and there is little or no additional unused production capacity. The second component is some major event (war or revolution being the most pertinent) that triggers a disturbance in existing supply patterns. When these two circumstances intersect, and only then, the result is an oil shock.

The political economy of world oil thus involves an integrated world system. All countries that import or export petroleum are linked to it. Developments occurring anywhere in the system that have a bearing on the demand or supply for oil, whether political or economic in nature, affect the overall balance of that system. Hence, when a serious disequilibrium occurs, the effects are felt globally. For example, even if the United States imported little or no Middle East oil, the fact that it imports any oil—

and that its oil imports provide nearly 50 percent of its total petroleum supplies—means that it is almost instantly affected.

IRAQ AND PERSIAN GULF OIL

Prior to the outbreak of the Gulf crisis and war, Iraq was producing 3.4 million barrels of crude oil per day.[9] This represented a 20 percent increase over average output for 1989 and meant that Iraq had regained its level of peak production set in 1979, the last full year prior to the Iran-Iraq war. Even at the July 1990 figure, however, Iraq's oil output accounted for just 5.7 percent of world production.[10]

By another measure, however, Iraq's importance to the world oil system is significantly greater. In terms of proved oil reserves, Iraq is second only to Saudi Arabia. (See Table 28–1.) Set against a world total of just under one thousand billion barrels, the Saudis, with 260 billion barrels, hold approximately 26 percent of the world total. Iraq has 100 billion barrels, equivalent to 10 percent, and is followed closely by the United Arab Emirates (98 billion barrels), Kuwait (97 billion barrels), and Iran (93 billion barrels). By contrast, the next largest group of producers, Venezuela, the Soviet Union, and Mexico, fall in the 51–59 billion barrel range. For its part, the United States has just 26 billion barrels, or the equivalent of only 2.6 percent of world proved reserves.

The significance of Iraq's position, particularly in the crisis, thus becomes more evident. As of August 2, 1990, not only did the regime of Saddam Hussein control both its own reserves and those of Kuwait—and thus some 20 percent of the world figure—but it directly menaced Saudi Arabia. Iraq thus was in position to dominate—either directly or indirectly—56 percent of all proved reserves, when oil of the rich but militarily inconsequential United Arab Emirates is counted.

To grasp the implications of this, it is essential to understand the importance of Gulf oil—and of OPEC more broadly—along with the reasons why this importance seems to wax and wane at various intervals. In brief, the volatility is due to a phenomenon which one analyst has called "the OPEC multiplier."[11] Oil-importing countries, due to a combination of political and economic reasons, have tended to rely on OPEC oil as a last resort. They prefer, where possible, to utilize domestic oil and energy resources. If they must resort to imports, they next seek supplies from non-OPEC countries. But when these other avenues are no longer available or are fully utilized, they must turn to OPEC suppliers. As a consequence, changes in the demand for OPEC oil can be disproportionate to overall changes in world oil demand.

When world demand falls, the reductions thus affect OPEC to a greater extent than other suppliers. In the case of the United States, where total oil demand fell by more than 3.6 mbd—or almost 20 percent—between 1978 and 1983, domestic oil production continued at levels near full capacity, and imports of non-OPEC oil actually increased. At the same time, U.S. imports of OPEC oil fell sharply, dropping from 5.7 to 1.8 mbd (a reduction of 68 percent).[12]

However, the OPEC multiplier works in the opposite direction as well. During

TABLE 28–1 **Proved Oil Reserves**

COUNTRY	BILLION BARRELS	PERCENT OF WORLD
Saudi Arabia	260.3	26.3
Iraq	100.0	10.1
United Arab Emirates	98.1	9.9
Kuwait	96.5	9.7
Iran	92.9	9.4
Venezuela	59.1	6.0
USSR	57.0	5.8
Mexico	51.3	5.2
United States	26.3	2.7
China	24.0	2.4
Libya	22.8	2.3
Nigeria	17.9	1.8
Algeria	9.2	0.9
Norway	7.6	0.8
Indonesia	6.6	0.7
India	6.1	0.6
Canada	5.6	0.6
Egypt	4.5	0.5
Oman	4.3	0.4
Yemen	4.0	0.4
United Kingdom	4.0	0.4
Others	32.9	3.1
WORLD TOTALS:	991.0	100.0

Notes: Based on data from *Oil and Gas Journal*, December 30, 1991, for reserves recoverable with present technology and prices. Data for Saudi Arabia and Kuwait include half of the Neutral Zone. UAE includes Abu Dhabi, Dubai, Ras al-Khaimah, and Sharjah. Figure for USSR is "explored reserves," including proved, probable and some possible. Author's calculations for "others" and percentages. Due to rounding, sum of percentages exceeds 100.0.

the last half of the 1980s, a combination of economic growth, cheaper oil prices, and gradual decreases in American oil output caused an upsurge in world oil demand. At the time, most of the non-OPEC suppliers were producing at or near capacity, and so demand for OPEC oil rose rapidly. U.S. imports of OPEC oil increased by 2.5 mbd, to a level of 4.3 mbd. Global demand for OPEC oil surged from a low point of 16.6 mbd in 1985 to 24.3 mbd by the spring of 1990. At the time, OPEC still possessed several mbd of unused capacity, but much of this was concentrated within Saudi Arabia and other nearby areas in the Gulf.

IRAQI AND SAUDI OIL IN THE GULF CRISIS

In the weeks following the Iraqi invasion of Kuwait, the United Nations embargo against Iraq's oil exports had the effect of removing approximately 4.0 to 4.3 mbd from world supplies of crude oil.[13] World crude oil markets, reacting initially to the threat of war in the Gulf and then to the loss of oil from Iraq and Kuwait, saw a dramatic run-up in prices. As a result of growing tensions in the region, prices which had been as low as $13 per barrel for Saudi light crude oil in June 1990 had already climbed to $20 by mid-July. By August 2, the day of the invasion, oil reached $24 per barrel. Not surprisingly, prices moved steeply higher in the following weeks, peaking at $40.42 on October 11.[14]

Set against world oil production of some 60 million barrels per day, Iraqi and Kuwaiti oil exports before the crisis amounted to approximately 7 percent of the global total. A shortfall of this magnitude, had it not been offset by production increases elsewhere, would have been in the same range as the one that triggered the 1973–74 oil crisis, and would have been larger than the 4 percent shortfall experienced during the second oil crisis in early 1979.[15]

Moreover, even though a supply shortage did not materialize, the economic impacts of sharply higher oil prices threatened to be significant. Thus, had oil remained at an average price of $30 per barrel for all of 1991, instead of receding to $20 by late January, the industrial democracies of the Organization for Economic Cooperation and Development (OECD) would have seen 2 percent additional inflation, 0.5 percent reduction in gross national product (GNP) growth, and an adverse $90 billion shift in the balance of trade.[16] By themselves, these effects would have been less damaging than the results of the 1970s oil shocks (the numbers for inflation and balance of trade, for example, were only one-third those of the earlier period[17]), but they could nonetheless have been significant factors in tilting the world economy into recession. Moreover, even the relatively brief price "spike" that did occur exacerbated economic problems in Eastern Europe and parts of the Third World, and damaged certain industries (e.g., aviation, automobiles) in the more prosperous Western countries.

In reality, despite the loss of Iraqi and Kuwaiti crude oil, and fears that terrorism or war could further reduce supplies of oil from the Gulf, sufficient oil production increases became available to offset the potential shortfall. Almost 80 percent of this production came from Persian Gulf states and from other member countries of OPEC, with smaller amounts from producers elsewhere around the world. However, Saudi Arabia proved to be the greatest source of increased production.

Between December 1989 and December 1990, Saudi production of crude oil rose by nearly 2.9 mbd, to a level of almost 8.6 million barrels per day. (See Table 28–2.) In other words, although a great deal of additional activity took place elsewhere, including not only production increases, efforts to curtail or defer demand, and a January 17, 1991, pledge by the twenty-one states of the International Energy Agency to make available 2 mbd from their reserves,[18] more than two-thirds of the

TABLE 28-2   Production of Crude Oil

PRODUCERS	DECEMBER 1989	DECEMBER 1990	CHANGE	
Iraq	3.000 mbd	0.425 mbd	−2.575 mbd	
Kuwait	2.090	0.075	−2.015	
Total loss:				−4.590
Estimated Global Loss (net of domestic consumption):				−4.0 to 4.3
Saudi Arabia	5.696	8.570	+2.874	
Iran	2.900	3.300	+0.400	
Libya	1.201	1.500	+0.299	
Algeria	1.110	1.210	+0.100	
Qatar	0.395	0.370	−0.025	
UAE	2.406	2.400	−0.006	
Net Additions from Persian Gulf:				+3.642
Venezuela	1.977	2.340	+0.363	
Mexico	2.476	2.660	+0.184	
Indonesia	1.434	1.550	+0.116	
Nigeria	1.854	1.950	+0.096	
Total of Other Major Net Additions:				+0.759
Other Totals				
Arab OPEC	15.897	14.550	−1.347	
Persian Gulf	16.529	15.182	−1.347	
Total OPEC	24.605	24.280	−0.325	
World	61.320	60.449	−0.871	

Note: Numbers are given in millions of barrels per day (mbd).

Source: Author's calculations from data in *Monthly Energy Review* (Washington, D.C.: U.S. Department of Energy, Energy Information Administration, March 1991), pp. 118–119.

reduction in oil from the Gulf was made up by Saudi Arabia alone, with less than 20 percent coming from outside the Middle East.[19]

Elsewhere, net additions to world supplies came from Iran (0.4 mbd), Venezuela (0.36), Libya (0.3), Indonesia (0.1), Algeria (0.1), Nigeria (0.1), with lesser amounts from a variety of other producers around the world. One important factor worked in the opposite direction, however; due to a continuing decline in Soviet production, between December 1989 and December 1990, the reduction there came to more than 1 mbd. In total, world oil production in December 1990 was 60.4 mbd. Despite the Gulf crisis, this was just 0.9 mbd below the figure of a year earlier. With a reduction in world demand of some 1 mbd in response to the sharply higher price of crude oil, as well as the subsequent decision by the United States and other IEA countries to make available additional oil from stocks,[20] world oil supplies remained adequate.

In sum, no real oil crisis developed. The shortfalls from Iraq and Kuwait were effectively offset. By mid-January of 1991, oil prices fell below $20 per barrel, thus returning close to their pre-invasion levels and then fluctuating in a narrow range around that figure during the Gulf War and its aftermath.

Given this result, as well as the post-crisis commitment of the Saudis to maintaining high levels of oil production, the gradually increasing flow of Kuwaiti oil, and the prospect that some amounts of Iraqi oil will eventually be exported again, there might appear to be grounds for complacency: a potentially destabilizing loss of supply from two major producing countries was absorbed with no major crisis, while the accompanying surge in oil prices subsided within five months.

However, a closer look suggests reasons why the ability to experience a potential crisis without severe disruption cannot be taken for granted. The single most important factor here remains the role of Saudi Arabia. Had the Saudis been unable or unwilling to respond as they did, the history of the Gulf crisis would have been far different. First, an Iraqi invasion of Saudi Arabia during the earliest days of the crisis would have been beyond the ability of the Saudis themselves—or of the American forces in their initial deployments—to repel. Saudi oil fields are concentrated in the vicinity of Ras Tanura, less than 200 miles from the Kuwaiti border, and these could have been seized by a determined Iraqi assault. In such circumstances, even had the Saudis retained any kind of nominal independence, it is unlikely they could have been in a position to do anything except acquiesce in whatever demands Saddam would have placed upon them and their resources.

Initially, on August 4, the U.S. Central Intelligence Agency (CIA) reported that Saddam's forces already numbered more than 100,000 men, and that the only obstacle between the Iraqis and the Saudi oil fields was a Saudi National Guard battalion of less than 1000 men.[21] At that moment, the U.S. ability to mount a military operation was extremely problematic. In the event, the American deployments succeeded because they had the full cooperation of the Saudi government, access to Saudi ports, and the use of a vast infrastructure of modern airbases. Without these requisites, an American military effort aimed at driving the Iraqi invaders out of both Saudi Arabia and Kuwait would have been exceptionally difficult and costly, if the Bush administration had even opted to attempt it. The widespread diplomatic, political, and military support that the American-led coalition enjoyed would also have been far more difficult to assemble under circumstances in which Saddam's triumph looked self-evident and the costs of reversing it unsustainable.[22]

The subsequent Iraqi destruction and torching of Kuwait's oil wells in the midst of the allied military triumph also suggest that even a successful American assault on the Iraqi forces in Saudi Arabia would have resulted in unprecedented destruction of oil facilities. The threatened reduction, or actual disappearance, of 8.5 million barrels in oil supply (as measured against Saudi Arabia's December 1990 oil production) would have triggered a disastrous crisis in world oil supplies. Its consequences in shortfalls of petroleum for the world economy, staggering price increases, alliance disarray, and political blackmail can only be imagined.

As a consequence, by mid-August 1990, Saddam Hussein would have been in a position to exercise control over the oil resources of Kuwait and Saudi Arabia, along with those of Iraq. With 46 percent of the world's proved reserves of crude oil subject to his direct dictate, and with his Gulf neighbors painfully aware of his ability to use any means at his disposal, the Iraqi president would have gained access to a vast source of present and future wealth. Moreover, based on the record of the past two decades, there is every reason to believe that these resources would have permitted him to purchase the most modern forms of technology and arms, including missiles and nuclear weapons technology.

The sobering conclusion of this scenario is that oil-importing countries and Iraq's Middle Eastern and even European neighbors have been fortunate in what did *not* happen after August 2, 1990. Despite the shattering military defeat of Iraq and the destruction of much of its most dangerous weaponry, the avoidance of disaster was by no means inevitable.

IRAQ AND WORLD OIL: PAST AND FUTURE PATTERNS

Saddam Hussein's seizure of Kuwait had multiple causes, not least the Iraqi leader's characteristic over-reaching with its disastrous consequences. Nonetheless, important economic considerations are quite evident as well. During the decade of the 1980s, Iraq spent approximately $100 billion on its military. By mid-1990 the country had accumulated an international debt of approximately $90 billion,[23] on which interest payments amounted to some $8–10 billion per year. With world oil prices at $20 per barrel, exports of 3 mbd would generate less than $20 billion per year in revenues. Moreover, by June 1990, with both Iran's and Iraq's oil exports having increased following the end of their bloody war in 1988, oil prices had slipped to as low as $13 per barrel. At that figure, Iraq would earn approximately $14 billion per year, barely enough to cover debt service and imports of necessities. Given the costs of reconstruction following the Iran-Iraq war, the demands of the Iraqi economy and popular expectations, and Saddam's continuing and grandiose military spending predilections, the Iraqi leader sought means of increasing his country's revenues. Thus the resources and income afforded by the seizure of Kuwait, as well as the prospect of exerting leverage over Saudi Arabia and hence influence over world oil prices, offered a tempting target for the Iraqi leader.

In the aftermath of the Gulf War and continuing United Nations sanctions on oil exports, Iraq's economy has had an acute need for oil revenues. This reality provides some opportunity for external actors to influence that country's conduct. Sooner or later, however, Iraq will resume oil exports. When it does, the amounts involved can grow rather quickly. Indeed, just two months after the war ended, a CIA estimate concluded that within three months after restrictions were lifted, Iraq could be producing 1 mbd. And, with the investment of an additional $1.5 billion to repair pumping facilities, output could have reached 2.7 mbd by the end of 1992.[24]

Given Iraq's indebtedness, estimated costs of $30 billion to repair destruction caused by the latest war, and UN-mandated reparations of as much as $50 billion to pay for the destruction and looting in Kuwait,[25] Iraq will continue to have a pressing long-term need for export revenues. This provides motivation for Saddam, or his eventual successors, to seek ways of encouraging higher world oil prices. Moreover, it also suggests an underlying danger. It is that, barring major changes in existing circumstances, Iraq will have its own reasons for seeking to intimidate its neighbors.

Apart from efforts to shape oil production and pricing policies, the aims of such pressure could also include obtaining financial assistance (in less polite terms, blackmail), influencing other countries' defense and foreign policies, and causing changes in the internal regime structure of adjacent states.

As long as the United States remains committed to regional security, whether in terms of troop presence or via longer-term security arrangements with an unambiguous American commitment, this potential intimidation from Iraq will not have much effect. The role played by the United States was unique in opposing the Iraqi takeover of Kuwait, in orchestrating UN condemnation and sanctions, and finally in leading an international coalition in a brief, devastating war against Iraq. However, if the United States proves unable to sustain a long-term commitment, or if regional states are unwilling or unable to collaborate in the maintenance of it, then Iraq will eventually find ways to reassert strength within the region. Under such circumstances, the regime of Saddam Hussein (or a successor regime with comparable interests and values) will continue to threaten both longer-term regional stability and the prevailing Persian Gulf oil regime. Although even in the absence of this threat there would remain internal and external sources of instability, for example Islamic fundamentalism and the uncertain nature of Iran's role, nonetheless Saddam and Iraq represent a demonstrably significant danger to their neighbors.

The oil dimension of this incorporates two distinct elements. One is that Iraq—having previously attacked four of its neighbors (Iran, Kuwait, Saudi Arabia, and Israel) and having bitter quarrels (Syria) or uneasy relations with others (Turkey)—could again find itself in a conflict or war. If so, the danger to oil facilities, whether intentional or not, is present. Alternatively, if Iraq succeeds in regaining regional power and influence, this may lead to an attempt to manipulate oil production for the purpose of increasing world prices. To be sure, the economic and market dimensions of the political economy of oil make it uncertain whether Iraq could ever succeed in these efforts. The experience of the OPEC countries in the 1980s suggests that this is a difficult task. On the other hand, if Iraq ultimately did manage to exert control over its neighbors, or succeed in intimidating them, the results could be quite different.

The interplay among politics and economics also means that if Iraq finds ways to regain a measure of economic strength and to loosen the sanctions upon itself, oil revenues can again be translated into offensive military power which once more could jeopardize the security of the region. Unless a UN embargo on weapons exports can be sustained and rigorously enforced, at least some arms manufacturing countries will seek markets for their exports of tanks, aircraft, missiles, chemical weapons, and nuclear weapons technology. The pressing financial predicament of the emergent East European economies, the problems of Latin American manufacturers such as Brazil and Argentina, and the behavior of China make this a long-term problem. Indeed, post–Gulf War accounts of a Czech decision to supply T-72 tanks to Syria, of China's shipment of M-9 missiles to Syria and construction of a nuclear "research" reactor in Algeria, and of an Argentine Condor II surface-to-surface missile program financed by Iraq[26] provide evidence that any sustained effort to control the export of advanced offensive weapons to the region will face great difficulties. Moreover, even with an embargo, the capability of Iraq's existing defense industrial base, coupled with the leakage of technology from outside sources, particularly from the former Soviet Union, presents an additional problem.

SUMMING UP

The principal developments in world oil over the past two decades have come largely as surprises, and many of these have run directly counter to conventional wisdom among policymakers, analysts, and scholars. Such cases include the tightening world oil market after 1970, the oil shocks of 1973–74 and 1979–80, the oil gluts (and accompanying price reductions) of 1976–78 and especially of the mid-1980s, and Iraq's August 1990 invasion of Kuwait.

The long-term pattern of oil supply and price, along with the broader stability of the Middle East, depends on a complex interplay of elements that are economic, political, and military. Such factors as the fate of the Ba'athist regime of Saddam Hussein, the availability of oil revenues to finance a rearming of Iraq, the durability of the U.S. commitment to regional security, the role of Saudi Arabia and the stability of its regime, the pattern of long-term oil and energy demand outside the region, declining Russian oil production, the inability of the United States to implement an energy policy to reverse its rising dependence on imported oil, and the risk of renewed warfare within the region can all interact. In other words, economic and energy variables partially determine political and military outcomes and vice versa.

In sum, the fact that the first great crisis of the post–Cold War era did not produce a severe oil shock should not be grounds for complacency. A reconsideration of the three optimistic but widely shared notions cited at the start of this article suggests grounds for caution.

First, despite the crushing defeat of Iraq and the destruction of much of its military infrastructure, Saddam Hussein has survived the initial aftermath and managed a bloody suppression of uprisings by Shi'ites in Southern Iraq and Kurds in the North. Although he has been subjected to a continuing oil and weapons embargo, the durability of these restraints is problematic over the long term. Absent a change of regime, Saddam and his Ba'athist leadership could eventually pose a renewed regional threat. Moreover, the crisis that began in August 1990 could have had a far more dangerous outcome if Saddam had sent his forces into Saudi Arabia immediately or the U.S. administration had been less effective in gaining United Nations support, assembling an unprecedented international coalition, and ultimately gaining congressional approval for its actions.

Second, the ability of oil producers and consumers to weather the crisis owed a great deal to the willingness and ability of Saudi Arabia to increase production. However, had Saudi oil facilities been disrupted by the crisis, or had its leaders decided not to boost production (or had they been prevented from doing so), the economic and political consequences of the crisis would have been far more serious.

Third, while the market mechanism functioned successfully, both in the recent crisis and in moderating the policies of OPEC countries during the past decade, the market does have its limits. For example, markets tend to overshoot. Thus, in the aftermath of Iraq's seizure of Kuwait, and despite the factors that allowed producing and consuming countries to avoid serious disruption, panic buying resulted in a price spike to more than $40 per barrel. Moreover, markets by themselves cannot change geography, in this case the concentration of two-thirds of the world's proved oil reserves in the Gulf area. These supplies remain potentially vulnerable to military or political events that have nothing to do with markets, but which can have an enormous impact on oil supply and price.

Indeed, even though markets can and do have benign effects in regulating supply and demand for oil and energy, market imperfections have consequences as well. These include the role of OPEC in influencing (though by no means determining) world oil supply and price, and time delays before markets regain equilibrium. While it is true that the price spikes of 1973–74 and 1979–80 ultimately proved reversible, the damage done to Western and developing country economies during these two shocks was quite serious. By one estimate the Group of Seven industrial counties lost $1.2 trillion in economic growth as a result of the two oil shocks.[27] In addition, the developing countries' grave problems of indebtedness, which have plagued their economies and societies during the 1980s and early 1990s, are in part a legacy of these "temporary" oil price disturbances.

While the picture that emerges of Iraq and the world oil system in the aftermath of the Gulf crisis and war can provide reassurance, at the same time it gives reason for caution. An awareness of the interrelated political and economic dimensions of the problem, and a willingness to draw lessons from the 1990–91 crisis, as well as those of 1973–74 and 1978–79, is essential if future threats to energy security are to be avoided as well.

POLICY IMPLICATIONS

Comprehension of a problem does not automatically dictate the response. Moreover, the urgency of the problem will vary due to factors which may be only modestly influenced by policy choices. In the present case, these include future levels of oil and energy production outside the Persian Gulf, the global supply and demand balance for oil, and the degree of instability and conflict which actually take place within the Gulf area. Nonetheless, the broad outlines of an appropriate U.S. policy can be suggested.

Iraq's invasion of Kuwait and the subsequent crisis and war suggest continuing need for the United States to maintain some mix of forces capable of intervening effectively in the Gulf. Obtaining international collaboration also appears important, to achieve legitimacy, effectiveness, and funding. In the specific case of Iraq, the ability of the United States to organize and lead a coalition with the support of the UN Security Council was not only important internationally, it was also a prerequisite for obtaining congressional authorization for the use of force. The alternative to American leadership in the crisis would have been international inaction.

In retrospect, the postwar survival of Saddam Hussein, and the resistance of his regime to compliance with UN Security Council resolutions requiring identification and destruction of facilities for production of nuclear and chemical weapons and missiles, provide reason to conclude that the war was brought to a close too early. Key units of the Republican Guard which sustains the Ba'athist regime should have been destroyed. Moreover, allowing Saddam's forces to use attack helicopters against uprisings by Shi'ites in the south and Kurds in the north was also short-sighted. As long as Saddam Hussein's regime endures, the stability of the Gulf area will remain particularly vulnerable.

The role of Saudi Arabia is central. Indeed, the Saudis' importance to the world oil system is even greater than previously suggested. While the most commonly reported numbers, including those officially used by the Saudis themselves, credit the kingdom with 260 billion barrels of proved reserves, the actual figure is much more likely to be in the range of 320–330 billion barrels.[28] This represents approximately one-third of the global total.

After a long period of internal evolution and debate following the oil shocks of the 1970s, the Saudi political system has managed to demonstrate a much greater durability than might have been expected. Although the long-term stability of the Saudi system and its political evolution remain imponderables, the Saudi leadership has made a series of choices which commit it to energy, economic, and security policies aligning its own future with that of the United States and the other industrial democracies. It has also displayed a certain degree of pragmatism toward other regional issues and the Arab-Israel conflict. But the war and the unprecedented deployment of American forces in the kingdom do not mean that the Saudis have chosen to embrace a substantial and on-going U.S. force deployment. From their standpoint, the fact that the United States was willing to lead a world-wide coalition and to deploy a half-million troops even without having a formal treaty or large permanent bases in Kuwait or Saudi Arabia leads them to conclude that they can retain this commitment with only modest additional steps involving force deployments or signed agreements. For both Saudi Arabia and the United States, dealing with the long-term development of this security relationship will be a complex task.

More broadly, American and international efforts to reduce the proliferation of missiles and of chemical, biological, and nuclear weapons in the Gulf region may contribute to stability, or at least reduce the scope of destruction in the event of future wars there.

The United States must cooperate with International Energy Agency countries for dealing with a future crisis. However, the United States should seek agreement on earlier use of strategic stocks in the event of a potential crisis. Both the United States and the IEA were slow to commit themselves to announcing stock draw-downs in the 1990–91 crisis. By acting earlier, they could have alleviated the kind of market panic that drove prices to over $40 per barrel. Their announcement of willingness to use the strategic reserve in August or September 1990 could have blunted the price spike significantly, and thus reduced its negative economic effects.[29]

The criterion for judging domestic policies is not the unattainable goal of energy independence. Instead, it is the reduction of oil consumption and imports and thus the lessening of U.S. vulnerability in the event that some kind of serious disruption arises in the future. The United States should adopt a more coherent and sustained program to encourage energy efficiency and conservation, including the use of tax policies to encourage more efficient use of gasoline.[30] It should strive for a robust, diverse energy mix with incentives for domestic production of oil and natural gas, encouragement of clean-burning coal technologies, maintaining a viable nuclear power option, pursuing more ambitious policies for research and development of new technologies (including solar energy), and increasing the Strategic Petroleum Reserve to its originally intended target of one billion barrels.

Finally, there remains the question of whether the need for policy can correspond with the capacity for policymaking, or whether this intersection represents a very "small set." The years since the first oil crisis in October 1973 do not provide a great deal of encouragement. While there do exist elements of effective policy response (e.g., creation of the International Energy Agency, passage of the Corporate Average Fuel Economy (CAFE) standards for automobile fuel efficiency, and establishment of the Strategic Petroleum Reserve), these tend to be exceptions. Thus the Carter administration found itself in a long policy stalemate in 1977–78 over a series of energy issues, particularly natural gas, until the oil crisis brought on by the fall of the shah in early 1979. During the 1980s, the Reagan administration largely deemphasized energy policy and dismantled much of what had existed.[31] The Bush administration began by seeking development of a National Energy Strategy (NES) with the aim of reducing dependence on imported oil, but the Department of Energy recommendations were watered down by the White House before their release in early 1991. The remaining proposals became stalled in Congress until the issue of drilling for oil in the Alaskan National Wildlife Refuge (ANWR) was finally removed.

This experience suggests a sobering conclusion. It is that while the United States generally has an impressive capacity for responding to crisis, its policy process is far less effective in providing coherent policy responses in noncrisis situations. This is especially true for issues such as energy security which are themselves complex, involve huge resource allocation choices, tend to engage the attention of tenacious advocates and institutions on opposite sides, and rarely attract strong executive branch leadership. It thus may be the case that while the broad elements of an effective policy are more or less evident, their implementation may await the time of some future crisis in energy security.

NOTES

1. A brief account of the Gallipoli expedition and debacle can be found in David Fromkin, *A Peace to End All Peace: The Fall of the Ottoman Empire and the Creation of the Modern Middle East* (New York: Avon, 1990), pp. 150–187. For a comprehensive treatment, see Alan Moorehead, *Gallipoli* (New York: Harper and Brothers, 1956).
2. See, for example, Gary Sick, *All Fall Down: America's Tragic Encounter with Iran* (New York: Random House, 1985), pp. 296–302.

3. In particular, see Avner Yaniv's assessment of what he terms a "Pyrrhic victory," as well as the unforeseen domestic and international political reverberations, in Yaniv, *Dilemmas of Security: Politics, Strategy and the Israel Experience in Lebanon* (New York: Oxford University Press, 1987), pp. 117ff and 216–284.

4. The annual "Economic Report of the President" subsequently concluded that the rapid rise in oil prices and uncertainties accompanying the crisis with Iraq were among the factors that tipped the U.S. economy, then only barely growing, into recession in the third quarter of 1990. See John M. Barry, "Administration's Annual Economic Report Presents Lower Expectations," *Washington Post*, February 6, 1992, p. A14.

5. For example, the initial National Energy Policy Plan of the Reagan administration held that market forces could increase petroleum investment and production, and it also held that this approach should be applied in times of crisis: "In the event of an emergency, preparedness plans call for relying primarily on market forces to allocate energy supplies." Summary of National Energy Policy Plan, U.S. Department of Energy, *Energy Insider*, Washington, D.C., August 3, 1981, p. 3.

6. For example, the Reagan administration initially made clear that it would not use governmental action or resources to reduce oil imports or oil consumption. And, despite the previous decade of experience with international energy instability, it held the view that, "Achieving a low level of oil imports at any cost is not a major criterion for the nation's energy security and economic health. Even at its current high price, imported oil is substantially less expensive than available alternatives." Quoted in *Energy Insider*, August 3, 1981, p. 3. Moreover, as late as 1985, the administration advocated a "moratorium" on filling the Strategic Petroleum Reserve during the 1986 fiscal year. *New York Times*, February 5, 1986.

7. See Eliyahu Kanovsky, *OPEC Ascendant? Another Case of Crying Wolf*, Policy Papers No. 20 (Washington, D.C.: Washington Institute for Near East Policy, 1990), pp. x and 53–56. An earlier paper by the same author argued that competition for market share and revenue needs of oil exporters, along with advances in oil exploration and production, energy efficiency, and the conclusion of the Iran-Iraq war, would hold down the price of oil for the foreseeable future. Kanovsky, *Another Oil Shock in the 1990s? A Dissenting View*. Policy Papers No. 6 (Washington, D.C.: Washington Institute for Near East Policy, 1987.) See also the discussion of Kanovsky's approach by Hobart Rowen, *Washington Post*, May 12, 1991, p. H16.

8. Robert Gilpin, *U.S. Power and the Multinational Corporation: The Political Economy of Direct Foreign Investment* (New York: Basic Books, 1975), pp. 4–5.

9. *Monthly Energy Review* (Washington, D.C.: U.S. Department of Energy, Energy Information Administration, March 1991), Table 10.1a, p. 118.

10. Percentage calculations throughout this paper are those of the author. World crude oil production in 1990 amounted to 60.072 mbd; *Monthly Energy Review*, March 1991, Table 10.1b, p. 119.

11. For elaboration of the concept, see Bijan Mossavar-Rahmani, "The OPEC Multiplier," *Foreign Policy*, No. 52 (Fall 1982), pp. 136–148.

12. In 1978, "petroleum products supplied" (i.e., total demand for petroleum) in the United States amounted to 18.847 mbd. By 1983 the figure had declined to 15.231. *Monthly Energy Review*, March 1991, p. 17.

13. As of December 1989, Iraq had been producing 3.0 mbd and Kuwait 2.1. By December 1990, these figures had fallen to 0.425 for Iraq and a mere 0.075 for Kuwait. Counting domestic uses of various kinds, the combined reduction of nearly 4.6 mbd was greater than the two countries' net exports, together estimated in the range of 4.0 to 4.3 mbd.

14. With the exception of the June figure, all prices are for light sweet crude oil quoted on the New York Mercantile Exchange; see *New York Times*, October 12, 1990, and March 1, 1991.

15. See Robert J. Lieber, *The Oil Decade: Conflict and Cooperation in the West* (Lanham, Md.: University Press of America, 1986), especially pp. 13–43.

16. Data from "The World Economy: Third Time Lucky," *The Economist* (London), August 11, 1990, p. 23.

17. The increased wealth transfer at $30 per barrel from the OECD countries would have been on the order of 0.6 percent of GNP, whereas in each of the 1970s oil shocks, the figure was 2.0 percent. In addition, compared with a hypothetical OECD inflation increase of 2 percent for 1991, the actual net increase for the Group of Seven leading industrial countries ("G7") in the 1974 shock was 6.1 percent (i.e., rising from 7.9 percent in 1973 to 14.0 percent in 1974). In the second oil shock, the inflation rate of the G7 increased by almost 6 percentage points. See "The World Economy: Third Time Lucky."

18. With the aim of reducing market volatility related to the Gulf War, the IEA countries agreed to make available approximately two million barrels per day from their governmental reserves and to take conservation measures to reduce demand by an additional 500,000 barrels per day. However, in implementing the plan at the end of January, 1991, Agency officials noted that oil would only be sold if oil companies indicated a need to buy it. See Steven Greenhouse, "International Energy Agency Affirms Plan to Tap Stocks," *New York Times*, January 29, 1991. This represented the first time since the IEA's creation in 1974 that its emergency draw-down system was put into effect. Shortly after the end of the war, on March 6, the IEA ended emergency sales of oil. For details, see Steven Greenhouse, "International Energy Agency Ends Emergency Oil Sales," *New York Times*, March 7, 1991.

19. Note that figures for oil supply from the Gulf and OPEC, as well as world figures, often vary depending on the particular source quoted, differing time periods, and other factors. For reasons of consistency, except when otherwise noted, data used in this paper comes from the *Monthly Energy Review* of the Energy Information Administration, US Department of Energy.

20. OECD stocks would have been sufficient to provide 2 mbd for an additional 4.5 years. Data on stocks from International Energy Agency, reported in *The Economist*, August 11, 1990, p. 21.

21. Bob Woodward, *The Commanders* (New York: Simon and Schuster, 1991), p. 248. Moreover, during the first two weeks of American force deployments, the situation remained precarious, and both U.S. Chief of Staff General Colin Powell and Secretary of Defense Dick Cheney are reported to have believed that Saddam Hussein's forces would have had the upper hand. Ibid., pp. 278, 282–285.

22. A counterargument is that a more powerful and threatening Iraq might make it easier to muster support from other regional powers such as Iran and Syria, which might be expected to balance rather than bandwagon in their behavior. Moreover, Stephen Walt's work provides evidence of alliance formation in the Middle East in which state behavior is driven by reaction to threat. See Walt, *The Origins of Alliances* (Ithaca: Cornell University Press, 1987). However, practical—indeed brutal—regional realities work to minimize balancing. Saddam would have achieved a *fait accompli*. Moreover, against his demonstrated willingness to use violence with extreme ruthlessness against his internal and external adversaries, as well as his ability to wield both bribery and blackmail, the ability of his neighbors to effectively align themselves with the United States would have been highly problematic. In particular, having been militarily defeated after an eight-year war in which their cities were exposed to demoralizing Scud attacks, the Iranians' willingness and ability to play an active role in an anti-Saddam coalition, let alone balance by aligning themselves with America (the "Great Satan"), would have been improbable.

23. Laurie Mylroie cites this figure, noting that it represented a $10 billion increase over the previous two years, i.e., from the time of the cease-fire with Iran. See Mylroie, *The Fu-

ture of Iraq, Policy papers No. 24 (Washington, D.C.: Washington Institute for Near East Policy, 1991), p. 29.

24. These calculations assumed that mutual agreement on lifting the sanctions would have been achieved, and that Western countries would have agreed to sell oil equipment to the Iraqis. However, Iraq rejected the UN terms for resuming initial limited oil exports and as of April 1992 no agreement had yet been reached. The CIA report is described in Patrick E. Tyler, "Hussein's Ouster is U.S. Goal, But at What Cost to the Iraqis?" *New York Times*, April 28, 1991.

25. *New York Times*, May 15, 1991, p. A16.

26. The Condor II project was a secret program organized by the Argentine air force, over which government officials had little control. After his election as president, Carlos Menem initially found himself in a bureaucratic battle with the air force over the program, which had become a sensitive issue in relations with the United States in the aftermath of the war with Iraq because Argentina had aided Iraq's missile development program. See Nathaniel C. Nash, "Argentine's President Battles His Own Air Force on Missile," *New York Times*, May 13, 1991, p. 1. Subsequently the program was halted.

27. Daniel Yergin, "Crisis and Adjustment: An Overview," in Yergin and Martin Hillenbrand, eds., *Global Insecurity: A Strategy for Energy and Economic Renewal* (Boston: Houghton Mifflin, 1982), p. 5.

28. From interviews by the author with officials in Saudi Arabia, October 8–14, 1991. The official figure of 260 billion barrels does not include 30 billion barrels of light sweet crude oil in the more recently discovered al-Hawta field.

29. The case for early release of the SPR has been made, for example, by the Chairman of the Energy and Power Subcommittee of the House Committee on Energy and Commerce, Congressman Philip Sharp. See Sharp, "How Bush Made the Recession Worse," *Washington Post*, December 19, 1991, p. C7. Also see Sharp's exchange of letters with Deputy Energy Secretary Henson Moore, *Washington Post*, January 23 and February 10, 1992.

30. The OECD has noted that energy prices and energy taxes are far lower in the United States than in Western Europe and Japan; gasoline sells in the United States for one-third its price in Italy and France. The OECD annual report on the American economy concludes that higher U.S. energy taxes would be consistent with enhanced energy security and with environmental goals. See Steven Greenhouse, "OECD Forecasts Slow U.S. Recovery From Recession," *New York Times*, November 26, 1991.

31. For an evaluation of Reagan administration energy policy, see Robert J. Lieber, "International Energy Policy and the Reagan Administration: Avoiding the Next Oil Shock?" in Kenneth A. Oye, Robert J. Lieber and Donald Rothchild, eds., *Eagle Resurgent? The Reagan Era in American Foreign Policy* (Boston: Little, Brown, 1987), pp. 167–189.

Part V

Global Problems Today

Part V examines several IPE problems that all nations and other international actors face or encounter at one time or another. These issues are oil and energy, food and hunger, and the environment; They also involve one or more international structures. The authors use a variety of IPE approaches to explain the causes and some of the possible solutions to these problems.

Garrett Hardin's "The Tragedy of the Commons" is a must read for every student of IPE. Hardin, a biologist, uses an analogy—cattle herders overpopulating their communal grazing area, the "commons," with cattle to the point of ruining the commons and themselves—to argue that the earth's resources are finite. The problem of growing population cannot be solved by some new technology; thus we (and presumably our governments) must make hard choices if we are to keep from destroying ourselves. Hardin advocates limiting the freedom of people to have more children in order to limit pollution and prevent our ultimate demise. This article is important because of the issues it raises and its connection to other IPE problems. At the level of the individual, Hardin establishes that as individuals we all act as "free riders" to the extent that we continue to consume resources as though there was an unlimited supply of them. His work is popular with those neo-Malthusians who view population as not only one of the chief causes of hunger in the world, but also a cause of the damage done to the environment, especially in Third World nations. At a macroeconomic level, Hardin also establishes a central dilemma that everyone concerned about hunger and the environment must face—the limited resources of the earth—and what to do about it.

Martin Diskin's work "Lack of Access to Land and Food in El Salvador" rejects the overpopulation–lack of food thesis that was so popular in the 1950s and 1960s. Diskin also rejects the "trickle-down" approach to development so often touted by Western development experts to overcome hunger problems. Diskin's analysis is primarily structuralist in tone. The state often acts in the interest of the private sector and the wealthy elite. U.S. support of El Salvador's development efforts in the 1980s was conditioned in part by efforts to combat communist and other popular movements in the nation. For Diskin, what should matter is individual food security before industrial development. Achieving food security entails the state's involvement in guaranteeing peasants access to land and redistributing food and the nation's wealth to the masses of the people. The state is a positive instrument that should be used to accomplish these objectives. However, as in many other Central and Latin American countries (as well as in other LDCs), a state that promotes reform is more than likely to continue to encounter political and economic resistance from the wealthy elite—who would go so far as to terrorize and even kill their own people in order to maintain control over the land.

The exact relationship of hunger and environmental problems to population continues to be a hotly debated topic. Donella H. Meadows outlines the major variations of Malthus' assertion that the population of the earth will overtax the ability of mankind to feed itself. In her article "Seeing the Population Issue Whole," she explores four major positions about this issue and argues that they are all part right and yet part wrong. The "Blues" are market-oriented development types who believe that new technologies and efficiencies associated with the production process will win the day. "Reds," like Martin Diskin (we are asserting here), would solve problems of political and economic inequality first in order to overcome hunger and population problems. "Greens" worry about the tendency to over-consume resources pursuant to industrialization and development. Finally, the views of "Whites" overlap with many of the views of the other groups but want to empower people to solve their own problems. Meadows argues that instead of each group arguing about which position is correct, we should all be taking stock of our values and goals related to our political, economic, and social systems and work together to develop new ideas as to how to reconcile conflicting interests involved with solving these problems.

Michael G. Renner's work ties together at least two different IPE issues, namely security and the environment. Renner's thesis is simple: although the popular image of the Persian Gulf war was that of a victory for the United States and its allies, the damage done to the local ecology was of monumental proportion. After cataloguing some of the damage done to the land, air, and bodies of water in the region, Renner raises questions about the "conduct of war and the protection of the natural environment," suggesting that these objectives were, and will continue to be in the future, incompatible. After reading Renner, one cannot help but wonder about the political, social, and economic costs of the "Gulf War syndrome" that has affected the health of many soldiers (along with some of their family members) who fought that war.

This section concludes with two essays about the United States and the IPE. With increasing global interdependence, the day is long past when any nation—even the United States—can consider its own problems and policies in isolation from those of the shrinking globe. Global problems condition domestic policies and define the realm of effective political action. These final essays make clear the degree to which national interests are linked to global concerns at this point in history.

Joseph S. Nye, Jr., raises the issue of "the vision thing" or what the Bush administration referred to as "the new world order" after the Persian Gulf war. Although it is not clear to the United States what that order is, Nye deals with many of its component parts. First is the distribution of power or, as realists refer to it, the "balance of power." The end of the Cold War promises to see liberal capitalism compete with indigenous political movements of all sorts and many other variations of ethnic national and religious movements. Second, nationalism is likely to compete with increasing transnationalism—movement across borders encouraged not only by developments in the international economy such as increased MNC activity, but also by the development of new global communication systems, the proliferation of nuclear weapons, the international drug trade, the spread of diseases, and growing environmental problems.

Nye expects the United States to be torn between its own interests and its assumed role and responsibility in solving many of these problems. Picking up where he left off in his earlier work on "The Changing Nature of World Power," Nye argues that the United States should pursue two goals at the same time: a distribution of military power that secures itself and its allies, and a new world order in which liberal political values of self-determination and individual and human rights are recognized and institutionalized. Whereas the United States no longer wants to be the "world's policeman," Nye asserts that it cannot retreat from influencing developments in the IPE through multilateral institutions because the new world order "can hurt, influence or disturb the majority of people living in the United States."

David P. Calleo is Dean Acheson Professor of European Studies at the Paul H. Nitze School of Advanced International Studies of the Johns Hopkins University. In his provocative essay, "Can the United States Afford the New World Order?", he explores the critical relationship between the domestic problems of the United States and its international role and responsibilities. Calleo asks whether the United States has the domestic strength necessary to continue as global hegemon. He finds that the United States economy has changed in recent years, and is weakened by slow growth and high debt. But the world has also changed; Japan and Europe are now much stronger and more able to bear the burdens of global leadership. In essence, Calleo rejects the "hegemonic stability" thesis that one state—in this case the United States—must accept the burden of political and economic leadership. He favors "devolution," whereby the United States would help craft a cooperative global framework that is consistent with its domestic needs and viable within the increasingly interdependent world of foreign relations.

29. The Tragedy of the Commons

Garrett Hardin

At the end of a thoughtful article on the future of nuclear war, Wiesner and York[1] concluded that: "Both sides in the arms race are . . . confronted by the dilemma of steadily increasing military power and steadily decreasing national security. *It is our considered professional judgment that this dilemma has no technical solution.* If the great powers continue to look for solutions in the area of science and technology only, the result will be to worsen the situation."

I would like to focus your attention not on the subject of the article (national security in a nuclear world) but on the kind of conclusion they reached, namely that there is no technical solution to the problem. An implicit and almost universal assumption of discussions published in professional and semipopular scientific journals is that the problem under discussion has a technical solution. A technical solution may be defined as one that requires a change only in the techniques of the natural sciences, demanding little or nothing in the way of change in human values or ideas of morality.

In our day (though not in earlier times) technical solutions are always welcome. Because of previous failures in prophecy, it takes courage to assert that a desired technical solution is not possible. Wiesner and York exhibited this courage; publishing in a science journal, they insisted that the solution to the problem was not to be found in the natural sciences. They cautiously qualified their statement with the phrase, "It is our considered professional judgment. . . ." Whether they were right or not is not the concern of the present article. Rather, the concern here is with the important concept of a class of human problems which can be called "no technical solution problems," and, more specifically, with the identification and discussion of one of these.

It is easy to show that the class is not a null class. Recall the game of tick-tack-toe. Consider the problem, "How can I win the game of tick-tack-toe?" It is well known that I cannot, if I assume (in keeping with the conventions of game theory) that my opponent understands the game perfectly. Put another way, there is no "technical solution" to the problem. I can win only by giving a radical meaning to the word "win." I can hit my opponent over the head; or I can drug him; or I can falsify the records. Every way in which I "win" involves, in some sense, an abandonment of the game, as we intuitively understand it. (I can also, of course, openly abandon the game—refuse to play it. This is what most adults do.)

The author is professor of biology, University of California, Santa Barbara. This article is based on a presidential address presented before the meeting of the Pacific Division of the American Association for the Advancement of Science at Utah State University, Logan, 25 June 1968.

The class of "No technical solution problems" has members. My thesis is that the "population problem," as conventionally conceived, is a member of this class. How it is conventionally conceived needs some comment. It is fair to say that most people who anguish over the population problem are trying to find a way to avoid the evils of overpopulation without relinquishing any of the privileges they now enjoy. They think that farming the seas or developing new strains of wheat will solve the problem—technologically. I try to show here that the solution they seek cannot be found. The population problem cannot be solved in a technical way, any more than can the problem of winning the game of tick-tack-toe.

WHAT SHALL WE MAXIMIZE?

Population, as Malthus said, naturally tends to grow "geometrically," or, as we would now say, exponentially. In a finite world this means that the per capita share of the world's goods must steadily decrease. Is ours a finite world?

A fair defense can be put forward for the view that the world is infinite; or that we do not know that it is not. But, in terms of the practical problems that we must face in the next few generations with the foreseeable technology, it is clear that we will greatly increase human misery if we do not, during the immediate future, assume that the world available to the terrestrial human population is finite. "Space" is no escape.[2]

A finite world can support only a finite population; therefore, population growth must eventually equal zero. (The case of perpetual wide fluctuations above and below zero is a trivial variant that need not be discussed.) When this condition is met, what will be the situation of mankind? Specifically, can Bentham's goal of "the greatest good for the greatest number" be realized?

No—for two reasons, each sufficient by itself. The first is a theoretical one. It is not mathematically possible to maximize for two (or more) variables at the same time. This was clearly stated by von Neumann and Morgenstern,[3] but the principle is implicit in the theory of partial differential equations, dating back at least to D'Alembert (1717–1783).

The second reason springs directly from biological facts. To live, any organism must have a source of energy (for example, food). This energy is utilized for two purposes: mere maintenance and work. For man, maintenance of life requires about 1600 kilocalories a day ("maintenance calories"). Anything that he does over and above merely staying alive will be defined as work, and is supported by "work calories" which he takes in. Work calories are used not only for what we call work in common speech; they are also required for all forms of enjoyment, from swimming and automobile racing to playing music and writing poetry. If our goal is to maximize population it is obvious what we must do: We must make the work calories per person approach as close to zero as possible. No gourmet meals, no vacations, no sports, no music, no literature, no art. . . . I think that everyone will grant, without argument or proof, that maximizing population does not maximize goods. Bentham's goal is impossible.

In reaching this conclusion I have made the usual assumption that it is the acquisition of energy that is the problem. The appearance of atomic energy has led some to question this assumption. However, given an infinite source of energy, population growth still produces an inescapable problem. The problem of the acquisition of energy is replaced by the problem of its dissipation, as J. H. Fremlin has so wittily shown.[4] The arithmetic signs in the analysis are, as it were, reversed; but Bentham's goal is still unobtainable.

The optimum population is, then, less than the maximum. The difficulty of defining the optimum is enormous; so far as I know, no one has seriously tackled this problem. Reaching an acceptable and stable solution will surely require more than one generation of hard analytical work—and much persuasion.

We want the maximum good per person; but what is good? To one person it is wilderness, to another it is ski lodges for thousands. To one it is estuaries to nourish ducks for hunters to shoot; to another it is factory land. Comparing one good with another is, we usually say, impossible because goods are incommensurable. Incommensurables cannot be compared.

Theoretically this may be true; but in real life incommensurables *are* commensurable. Only a criterion of judgment and a system of weighting are needed. In nature the criterion is survival. Is it better for a species to be small and hideable, or large and powerful? Natural selection commensurates the incommensurables. The compromise achieved depends on a natural weighting of the values of the variables.

Man must imitate this process. There is no doubt that in fact he already does, but unconsciously. It is when the hidden decisions are made explicit that the arguments begin. The problem for the years ahead is to work out an acceptable theory of weighting. Synergistic effects, nonlinear variation, and difficulties in discounting the future make the intellectual problem difficult, but not (in principle) insoluble.

Has any cultural group solved this practical problem at the present time, even on an intuitive level? One simple fact proves that none has: there is no prosperous population in the world today that has, and has had for some time, a growth rate of zero. Any people that has intuitively identified its optimum point will soon reach it, after which its growth rate becomes and remains zero.

Of course, a positive growth rate might be taken as evidence that a population is below its optimum. However, by any reasonable standards, the most rapidly growing populations on earth today are (in general) the most miserable. This association (which need not be invariable) casts doubt on the optimistic assumption that the positive growth rate of a population is evidence that it has yet to reach its optimum.

We can make little progress in working toward optimum population size until we explicitly exorcize the spirit of Adam Smith in the field of practical demography. In economic affairs, *The Wealth of Nations* (1776) popularized the "invisible hand," the idea that an individual who "intends only his own gain," is, as it were, "led by an invisible hand to promote . . . the public interest."[5] Adam Smith did not assert that this was invariably true, and perhaps neither did any of his followers. But he contributed to a dominant tendency of thought that has ever since interfered with positive action based on rational analysis, namely, the tendency to assume that decisions reached individually will, in fact, be the best decisions for an entire society. If this assumption is correct it justifies the continuance of our present policy of laissez-faire in reproduction. If it is correct we can assume that men will control their individual fecundity so as to produce the optimum population. If the assumption is not correct, we need to reexamine our individual freedoms to see which ones are defensible.

TRAGEDY OF FREEDOM IN A COMMONS

The rebuttal to the invisible hand in population control is to be found in a scenario first sketched in a little-known pamphlet[6] in 1833 by a mathematical amateur named William Forster Lloyd (1794–1852). We may well call it "the tragedy of the commons," using the word "tragedy" as the philosopher Whitehead used it[7]: "The essence of dramatic tragedy is not unhappiness. It resides in the solemnity of the remorseless working of things." He then goes on to say, "This inevitableness of destiny can only be illustrated in terms of human life by incidents which in fact involve unhappiness. For it is only by them that the futility of escape can be made evident in the drama."

The tragedy of the commons develops in this way. Picture a pasture open to all. It is to be expected that each herdsman will try to keep as many cattle as possible on the commons. Such an arrangement may work reasonably satisfactorily for centuries because tribal wars, poaching, and disease keep the numbers of both man and beast well below the carrying capacity of the land. Finally, however, comes the day of reckoning, that is, the day when the long-desired goal of social stability becomes a reality. At this point, the inherent logic of the commons remorselessly generates tragedy.

As a rational being, each herdsman seeks to maximize his gain. Explicitly or implicitly, more or less consciously, he asks, "What is the utility *to me* of adding one more animal to my herd?" This utility has one negative and one positive component.

1. The positive component is a function of the increment of one animal. Since the herdsman receives all the proceeds from the sale of the additional animal, the positive utility is nearly +1.
2. The negative component is a function of the additional overgrazing created by one more animal. Since, however, the effects of overgrazing are shared by all the herdsmen, the negative utility for any particular decision-making herdsman is only a fraction of −1.

Adding together the component partial utilities, the rational herdsman concludes that the only sensible course for him to pursue is to add another animal to his herd. And another; and another. . . . But this is the conclusion reached by each and every rational herdsman sharing a commons. Therein is the tragedy. Each man is locked into a system that compels him to increase his herd without limit—in a world that is limited. Ruin is the destination toward which all men rush, each pursuing his own best interest in a society that believes in the freedom of the commons. Freedom in a commons brings ruin to all.

Some would say that this is a platitude. Would that it were! In a sense, it was learned thousands of years ago, but natural selection favors the forces of psychological denial.[8] The individual benefits as an individual from his ability to deny the truth even though society as a whole, of which he is a part, suffers. Education can counteract the natural tendency to do the wrong thing, but the inexorable succession of generations requires that the basis for this knowledge be constantly refreshed.

A simple incident that occurred a few years ago in Leominster, Massachusetts, shows how perishable the knowledge is. During the Christmas shopping season the parking meters downtown were covered with plastic bags that bore tags reading: "Do not open until after Christmas. Free parking courtesy of the mayor and city council." In other words, facing the prospect of an increased demand for already scarce space, the city fathers reinstituted the system of the commons. (Cynically, we suspect that they gained more votes than they lost by this retrogressive act.)

In an approximate way, the logic of the commons has been understood for a long time, perhaps since the discovery of agriculture or the invention of private property in real estate. But it is understood mostly only in special cases which are not sufficiently generalized. Even at this late date, cattlemen leasing national land on the western ranges demonstrate no more than an ambivalent understanding, in constantly pressuring federal authorities to increase the head count to the point where overgrazing produces erosion and weed-dominance. Likewise, the oceans of the world continue to suffer from the survival of the philosophy of the commons. Maritime nations still respond automatically to the shibboleth of the "freedom of the seas." Professing to believe in the "inexhaustible resources of the oceans," they bring species after species of fish and whales closer to extinction.[9]

The National parks present another instance of the working out of the tragedy of the commons. At present, they are open to all, without limit. The parks themselves are limited in extent—there is only one Yosemite Valley—whereas population seems to grow without limit. The values that visitors seek in the parks are steadily eroded. Plainly, we must soon cease to treat the parks as commons or they will be of no value to anyone.

What shall we do? We have several options. We might sell them off as private property. We might keep them as public property, but allocate the right to enter them. The allocation might be on the basis of wealth, by the use of an auction system. It might be on the basis of merit, as defined by some agreed-upon standards. It might be by lottery. Or it might be on a first-come, first-served basis, administered to long queues. These, I think, are all the reasonable possibilities. They are all objectionable. But we must choose—or acquiesce in the destruction of the commons that we call our National Parks.

POLLUTION

In a reverse way, the tragedy of the commons reappears in problems of pollution. Here it is not a question of taking something out of the commons, but of putting something in—sewage, or chemical, radioactive, and heat wastes into water; noxious and dangerous fumes into the air; and distracting and unpleasant advertising signs into the line of sight. The calculations of utility are much the same as before. The rational man finds that his share of the cost of the wastes he discharges into the commons is less than the cost of purifying his wastes before releasing them. Since this is true for everyone, we are locked into a system of "fouling our own nest," so long as we behave only as independent, rational, free-enterprisers.

The tragedy of the commons as a food basket is averted by private property, or something formally like it. But the air and waters surrounding us cannot readily be fenced, and so the tragedy of the commons as a cesspool must be prevented by different means, by coercive laws or taxing devices that make it cheaper for the polluter to treat his pollutants than to discharge them untreated. We have not progressed as far with the solution of this problem as we have with the first. Indeed, our particular concept of private property, which deters us from exhausting the positive resources of the earth, favors pollution. The owner of a factory on the bank of a stream—whose property extends to the middle of the stream—often has difficulty seeing why it is not his natural right to muddy the waters flowing past his door. The law, always behind the times, requires elaborate stitching and fitting to adapt it to this newly perceived aspect of the commons.

The pollution problem is a consequence of population. It did not much matter how a lonely American frontiersman disposed of his waste. "Flowing water purifies itself every 10 miles," my grandfather used to say, and the myth was near enough to the truth when he was a boy, for there were not too many people. But as population became denser, the natural chemical and biological recycling processes became overloaded, calling for a redefinition of property rights.

HOW TO LEGISLATE TEMPERANCE?

Analysis of the pollution problem as a function of population density uncovers a not generally recognized principle of morality, namely: *the morality of an act is a function of the state of the system at the time it is performed.*[10] Using the commons as a cesspool does not harm the general public under frontier conditions, because there is no public; the same behavior in a metropolis is unbearable. A hundred and fifty years ago a plainsman could kill an American bison, cut out only the tongue for his dinner, and discard the rest of the animal. He was not in any important sense being wasteful. Today, with only a few thousand bison left, we would be appalled at such behavior.

In passing, it is worth noting that the morality of an act cannot be determined from a photograph. One does not know whether a man killing an elephant or setting fire to the grassland is harming others until one knows the total system in which his act appears. "One picture is worth a thousand words," said an ancient Chinese; but it may take 10,000 words to validate it. It is as tempting to ecologists as it is to reformers in general to try to persuade others by way of the photographic shortcut. But the essence of an argument cannot be photographed: it must be presented rationally—in words.

That morality is system-sensitive escaped the attention of most codifiers of ethics in the past. "Thou shalt not . . ." is the form of traditional ethical directives which make no allowance for particular circumstances. The laws of our society follow the pattern of ancient ethics, and therefore are poorly suited to governing a complex, crowded, changeable world. Our epicyclic solution is to augment statutory law with administrative law. Since it is practically impossible to spell out all the conditions under which it is safe to burn trash in the back yard or to run an automobile without smog-control, by law we delegate the details to bureaus. The result is administrative law, which is rightly feared for an ancient reason—*Quis custodiet ipsos custodes?*—"Who shall watch the watchers themselves?" John Adams said that we must have "a government of laws and not men." Bureau administrators, trying to evaluate the morality of acts in the total system, are singularly liable to corruption, producing a government by men, not laws.

Prohibition is easy to legislate (though not necessarily to enforce); but how do we legislate temperance? Experience indicates that it can be accomplished best through the mediation of administrative law. We limit possibilities unnecessarily if we suppose that the sentiment of *Quis custodiet* denies us the use of administrative law. We should rather retain the phrase as a perpetual reminder of fearful dangers we cannot avoid. The great challenge facing us now is to invent the corrective feedbacks that are needed to keep custodians honest. We must find ways to legitimate the needed authority of both the custodians and the corrective feedbacks.

FREEDOM TO BREED IS INTOLERABLE

The tragedy of the commons is involved in population problems in another way. In a world governed solely by the principle of "dog eat dog"—if indeed there ever was such a world—how many children a family had would not be a matter of public concern. Parents who bred too exuberantly would leave fewer descendants, not more, because they would be unable to care adequately for their children. David Lack and others found that such a negative feedback demonstrably controls the fecundity of birds.[11] But men are not birds, and have not acted like them for millenniums, at least.

If each human family were dependent only on its own resources; *if* the children of improvident parents starved to death; *if,* thus, overbreeding brought its own "punishment" to the germ line—*then* there would be no public interest in controlling the breeding of families. But our society is deeply committed to the welfare state,[12] and hence is confronted with another aspect of the tragedy of the commons.

In a welfare state, how shall we deal with the family, the religion, the race, or the class (or indeed any distinguishable and cohesive group) that adopts overbreeding as a policy to secure its own aggrandizement?[13] To couple the concept of freedom to breed with the belief that everyone born has an equal right to the commons is to lock the world into a tragic course of action.

Unfortunately this is just the course of action that is being pursued by the United Nations. In late 1967, some 30 nations agreed to the following[14]:

> The Universal Declaration of Human Rights describes the family as the natural and fundamental unit of society. It follows that any choice and decision with regard to the size of the family must irrevocably rest with the family itself, and cannot be made by anyone else.

It is painful to have to deny categorically the validity of this right; denying it, one feels as uncomfortable as a resident of Salem, Massachusetts, who denied the reality of witches in the 17th century. At the present time, in liberal quarters, something like a taboo acts to inhibit criticism of the United Nations. There is a feeling that the United Nations is "our last and best hope," that we shouldn't find fault with it; we shouldn't play into the hands of the archconservatives. However, let us not forget what Robert Louis Stevenson said: "The truth that is suppressed by friends is the readiest weapon of the enemy." If we love the truth we must openly deny the validity of the Universal Declaration of Human Rights, even though it is promoted by the United Nations. We should also join with Kingsley Davis[15] in attempting to get Planned Parenthood-World Population to see the error of its ways in embracing the same tragic ideal.

CONSCIENCE IS SELF-ELIMINATING

It is a mistake to think that we can control the breeding of mankind in the long run by an appeal to conscience. Charles Galton Darwin made this point when he spoke on the centennial of the publication of his grandfather's great book. The argument is straightforward and Darwinian.

People vary. Confronted with appeals to limit breeding, some people will undoubtedly respond to the plea more than others. Those who have more children will produce a larger fraction of the next generation than those with more susceptible consciences. The difference will be accentuated, generation by generation.

In C. G. Darwin's words: "It may well be that it would take hundreds of generations for the progenitive instinct to develop in this way, but if it should do so, nature would have taken her revenge, and the variety *Homo contracipiens* would become extinct and would be replaced by the variety *Homo progenitivus*".[16]

The argument assumes that conscience or the desire for children (no matter which) is hereditary—but hereditary only in the most general formal sense. The result will be the same whether the attitude is transmitted through germ cells, or exosomatically, to use A. J. Lotka's term. (If one denies the latter possibility as well as the former, then what's the point of education?) The argument has here been stated in the context of the population problem, but it applies equally well to any instance in which society appeals to an individual exploiting a commons to restrain himself for the general good—by means of his conscience. To make such an appeal is to set up a selective system that works toward the elimination of conscience from the race.

PATHOGENIC EFFECTS OF CONSCIENCE

The long-term disadvantage of an appeal to conscience should be enough to condemn it; but has serious short-term disadvantages as well. If we ask a man who is exploiting a commons to desist "in the name of conscience," what are we saying to him? What does he hear?—not only at the moment but also in the wee small hours of the night when, half asleep, he remembers not merely the words we used but also the nonverbal communication cues we gave him unawares? Sooner or later, consciously or subconsciously, he senses that he has received two communications, and that they are contradictory. (i) (intended communication) "If you don't do as we ask, we will openly condemn you for not acting like a responsible citizen"; (ii) the unintended communication) "If you *do* behave as we ask, we will secretly condemn you for a simpleton who can be shamed into standing aside while the rest of us exploit the commons."

Everyman then is caught in what Bateson has called a "double bind." Bateson and his co-workers have made a plausible case for viewing the double bind as an important causative factor in the genesis of schizophrenia.[17] The double bind may not always be so damaging, but it always endangers the mental health of anyone to whom it is applied. "A bad conscience," said Nietzsche, "is a kind of illness."

To conjure up a conscience in others is tempting to anyone who wishes to extend his control beyond the legal limits. Leaders at the highest level succumb to this temptation. Has any President during the past generation failed to call on labor unions to moderate voluntarily their demands for higher wages, or to steel companies to honor voluntary guidelines on prices? I can recall none. The rhetoric used on such occasions is designed to produce feelings of guilt in noncooperators.

For centuries it was assumed without proof that guilt was a valuable, perhaps even an indispensable, ingredient of the civilized life. Now, in this post-Freudian world, we doubt it.

Paul Goodman speaks from the modern point of view when he says: "No good has ever come from feeling guilty, neither intelligence, policy, nor compassion The guilty do not pay attention to the object but only to themselves, and not even to their own interests, which might make sense, but to their anxieties."[18]

One does not have to be a professional psychiatrist to see the consequences of anxiety. We in the Western world are just emerging from a dreadful two centuries-long Dark Ages of Eros that was sustained partly by prohibition laws, but perhaps more effectively by the anxiety-generating mechanisms of education. Alex Comfort has told the story well in *The Anxiety Makers;*[19] it is not a pretty one.

Since proof is difficult, we may even concede that the results of anxiety may sometimes, from certain points of view, be desirable. The larger question we should ask is whether, as a matter of policy, we should ever encourage the use of a technique the tendency (if not the intention) of which is psychologically pathogenic. We hear much talk these days of responsible parenthood; the coupled words are incorporated into the titles of some organizations devoted to birth control. Some people have proposed massive propaganda campaigns to instill responsibility into the nation's (or the world's) breeders. But what is the meaning of the word responsibility in this context? Is it not merely a synonym for the word conscience? When we use the word responsibility in the absence of substantial sanctions are we not trying to browbeat a free man in a commons into acting against his own interest? Responsibility is a verbal counterfeit for a substantial *quid pro quo.* It is an attempt to get something for nothing.

If the word responsibility is to be used at all, I suggest that it be in the sense Charles Frankel uses it.[20] "Responsibility," says this philosopher, "is the product of definite social arrangements." Notice that Frankel calls for social arrangements—not propaganda.

MUTUAL COERCION, MUTUALLY AGREED UPON

The social arrangements that produce responsibility are arrangements that create coercion, of some sort. Consider bank-robbing. The man who takes money from a bank acts as if the bank were a commons. How do we prevent such action? Certainly not by trying to control his behavior solely by a verbal appeal to his sense of responsibility. Rather than rely on propaganda we follow Frankel's lead and insist that a bank is not a commons: we seek the definite social arrangements that will keep it from becoming a commons. That we thereby infringe on the freedom of would-be robbers we neither deny nor regret.

The morality of bank-robbing is particularly easy to understand because we accept complete prohibition of this activity. We are willing to say "Thou shalt not rob banks," without providing for exceptions. But temperance also can be created by coercion. Taxing is a good coercive device. To keep downtown shoppers temperate in their use of parking space we introduce parking meters for short periods, and traffic fines for longer ones. We need not actually forbid a citizen to park as long as he wants to; we need merely make it increasingly expensive for him to do so. Not prohibition, but carefully biased options are what we offer him. A Madison Avenue man might call this persuasion; I prefer the greater candor of the word coercion.

Coercion is a dirty word to most liberals now, but it need not forever be so. As with the four-letter words, its dirtiness can be cleansed away by exposure to the light, by saying it over and over without apology or embarrassment. To many, the word coercion implies arbitrary decisions of distant and irresponsible bureaucrats; but this is not a necessary part of its meaning. The only kind of coercion I recommend is mutual coercion, mutually agreed upon by the majority of the people affected.

To say that we mutually agree to coercion is not to say that we are required to enjoy it, or even to pretend we enjoy it. Who enjoys taxes? We all grumble about them. But we accept compulsory taxes because we recognize that voluntary taxes would favor the conscienceless. We institute and (grumblingly) support taxes and other coercive devices to escape the horror of the commons.

An alternative to the commons need not be perfectly just to be preferable. With real estate and other material goods, the alternative we have chosen is the institution of private property coupled with legal inheritance. Is this system perfectly just? As a genetically trained biologist I deny that it is. It seems to me that, if there are to be differences in individual inheritance, legal possession should be perfectly correlated with biological inheritance—that those who are biologically more fit to be the custodians of property and power should legally inherit more. But genetic recombination continually makes a mockery of the doctrine of "like father, like son" implicit in our laws of legal inheritance. An idiot can inherit millions, and a trust fund can keep his estate intact. We must admit that our legal system of private property plus inheritance is unjust—but we put up with it because we are not convinced, at the moment, that anyone has invented a better system. The alternative of the commons is too horrifying to contemplate. Injustice is preferable to total ruin.

It is one of the peculiarities of the warfare between reform and the status quo that it is thoughtlessly governed by a double standard. Whenever a reform measure is proposed it is often defeated when its opponents triumphantly discover a flaw in it. As Kingsley Davis has pointed out,[21] worshippers of the status quo sometimes imply that no reform is possible without unanimous agreement, an implication contrary to historical fact. As nearly as I can make out, automatic rejection of proposed reforms is based on one of two unconscious assumptions: (i) that the status quo is perfect; or (ii) that the choice we face is between reform and no action; if the proposed reform is imperfect, we presumably should take no action at all, while we wait for a perfect proposal.

But we can never do nothing. That which we have done for thousands of years is also action. It also produces evils. Once we are aware that the status quo is action, we can then compare its discoverable advantages and disadvantages with the predicted advantages and disadvantages of the proposed reform, discounting as best we can for our lack of experience. On the basis of such a comparison, we can make a rational decision which will not involve the unworkable assumption that only perfect systems are tolerable.

RECOGNITION OF NECESSITY

Perhaps the simplest summary of this analysis of man's population problems is this: the commons, if justifiable at all, is justifiable only under conditions of low-population density. As the human population has increased, the commons has had to be abandoned in one aspect after another.

First we abandoned the commons in food gathering, enclosing farm land and restricting pastures and hunting and fishing areas. These restrictions are still not complete throughout the world.

Somewhat later we saw that the commons as a place for waste disposal would also have to be abandoned. Restrictions on the disposal of domestic sewage are widely accepted in the Western world; we are still struggling to close the commons to pollution by automobiles, factories, insecticide sprayers, fertilizing operations, and atomic energy installations.

In a still more embryonic state is our recognition of the evils of the commons in matters of pleasure. There is almost no restriction on the propagation of sound waves in the public medium. The shopping public is assaulted with mindless music, without its consent. Our government is paying out billions of dollars to create supersonic transport which will disturb 50,000 people for every one person who is whisked from coast to coast 3 hours faster. Advertisers muddy the airwaves of radio and television and pollute the view of travelers. We are a long way from outlawing the commons in matters of pleasure. Is this because our Puritan inheritance makes us view pleasure as something of a sin, and pain (that is, the pollution of advertising) as the sign of virtue?

Every new enclosure of the commons involves the infringement of somebody's personal liberty. Infringements made in the distant past are accepted because no contemporary complains of a loss. It is the newly proposed infringements that we vigorously oppose; cries of "rights" and "freedom" fill the air. But what does "freedom" mean? When men mutually agreed to pass laws against robbing, mankind became more free, not less so. Individuals locked into the logic of the commons are free only to bring on universal ruin; once they see the necessity of mutual coercion, they become free to pursue other goals. I believe it was Hegel who said, "Freedom is the recognition of necessity."

The most important aspect of necessity that we must now recognize, is the necessity of abandoning the commons in breeding. No technical solution can rescue us from the misery of overpopulation. Freedom to breed will bring ruin to all. At the moment, to avoid hard decisions many of us are tempted to propagandize for conscience and responsible parenthood. The temptation must be resisted, because an appeal to independently acting consciences selects for the disappearance of all conscience in the long run, and an increase in anxiety in the short.

The only way we can preserve and nurture other and more precious freedoms is by relinquishing the freedom to breed, and that very soon. "Freedom is the recognition of necessity"—and it is the role of education to reveal to all the necessity of abandoning the freedom to breed. Only so, can we put an end to this aspect of the tragedy of the commons.

NOTES

1. J. B. Wiesner and H. F. York, *Sci. Amer.* 211 (No. 4), 27 (1964).
2. G. Hardin, *J. Hered.* 50, 68 (1959); S. von Hoernor, *Science* 137, 18 (1962).
3. J. von Neumann and O. Morgenstern, *Theory of Games and Economic Behavior* (Princeton Univ. Press, Princeton, N.J., 1947), p. 11.
4. J. H. Fremlin, *New Sci.*, No. 415 (1964), p. 285.
5. A. Smith, *The Wealth of Nations* (Modern Library, New York, 1937), p. 423.
6. W. F. Lloyd, *Two Lectures on the Checks to Population* (Oxford Univ. Press, Oxford, England, 1833), reprinted (in part) in *Population, Evolution, and Birth Control*, G. Hardin, Ed. (Freeman, San Francisco, 1964), p. 37.
7. A. N. Whitehead, *Science and the Modern World* (Mentor, New York, 1948), p. 17.
8. G. Hardin, Ed. *Population, Evolution, and Birth Control* (Freeman, San Francisco, 1964), p. 56.

9. S. McVay, *Sci. Amer.* 216 (No. 8), 13 (1966).
10. J. Fletcher, *Situation Ethics* (Westminster, Philadelphia, 1966).
11. D. Lack, *The Natural Regulation of Animal Numbers* (Clarendon Press, Oxford, 1954).
12. H. Girvetz, *From Wealth to Welfare* (Stanford Univ. Press, Stanford, Calif., 1950).
13. G. Hardin, *Perspec. Biol. Med.* 6, 366 (1963).
14. U. Thant, *Int. Planned Parenthood News,* No. 168 (February 1968), p. 3.
15. K. Davis, *Science* 158, 730 (1967).
16. S. Tax, Ed., *Evolution after Darwin* (Univ. of Chicago Press, Chicago, 1960), vol. 2, p. 469.
17. G. Bateson, D. D. Jackson, J. Haley, J. Weakland, *Behav. Sci.* 1, 251 (1956).
18. P. Goodman, *New York Rev. Books* 10(8), 22 (23 May 1968).
19. A. Comfort, *The Anxiety Makers* (Nelson, London, 1967).
20. C. Frankel, *The Case for Modern Man* (Harper, New York, 1955), p. 203.
21. J. D. Roslansky, *Genetics and the Future of Man* (Appleton-Century-Crofts, New York, 1966), p. 177.

30. Lack of Access to Land and Food in El Salvador

Martin Diskin

Few circumstances reveal national priorities or values of governance more clearly than the distribution among a national population of the most basic form of national wealth, food. If food security means the promise that all citizens of a country will be guaranteed a basic diet, then virtually no country in the world lacks the means to accomplish this. Measured by food produced per capita, and by the financial means to make up production shortfalls, almost all countries in the world still qualify.[1] Yet, in 1991 endemic malnutrition and systematic deficiencies in nutritional intake still plague much of the world. Although these deficiencies are most obvious in the Third World, developed countries such as the United States contain pockets of undernutrition and hunger as well.[2]

There is no single route to food security. But we may generally distinguish two paths by which governments claim to achieve this universally accepted goal. First is the idea that food security can only be achieved as a by-product of a successful economic system. That is, high national output and profits will lead to more absolute wealth that will in turn achieve better distribution of this wealth, and the population will have greater access to food. This can occur either through an employment effect (higher wages, fringe benefits) or through government spending made possible by

Reprinted from "Lack of Access to Land and Food in El Salvador," by Martin Diskin in Scott Whiteford and Anne E. Ferguson, *Harvest of Want: Hunger and Food Security in Central America and Mexico,* (Boulder, CO: Westview Press, 1991).

higher tax revenues from the productive system. This is the "trickle-down," or the "rising-tide-floats-all-boats," idea.

The other general approach states that the government's primary obligation to its population is to feed it, whatever the costs and whatever the measures that need be taken. This is sometimes characterized as a "basic-needs" approach (Weeks & Dore 1982) or as a human right (Catholic Institute for International Relations 1987, 2–3). The basic-needs approach usually envisions serious state intervention to marshal and direct the necessary resources, to control the distribution system, to enact the necessary legislation, and to carry out the required research (Barraclough 1982). Such a policy is independent of the gross domestic product, balance of payments, or other measures of the economic health of the government. It has been called "the logic of the majority" in the Nicaraguan case.

The trickle-down school focuses on strengthening the climate for capital accumulation. It is usually associated with capitalist systems, where market forces constitute the major means of ordering the economy. It tends to see the state as legitimate only if it facilitates the activities of the private sector and limits its own regulatory power. It regards its solution to food problems as ultimately more efficient because it focuses on production efficiency, although it may entail some possible short-term discomfort or even suffering of those most in need. A corollary of this vision is that those who cannot feed themselves are usually deficient in some respect, that is they don't have the necessary drive, intelligence, education, or "culture," to enter the market and provide for themselves.

Trickle-down approaches founder because the control for the downward evolution of benefits is often in the hands of those who profit. As individuals they do not feel responsible for reducing hunger and claim that the market is the final arbiter, the invisible hand that decides who benefits and who languishes in poverty. One difficulty with this view is that it typically ignores distribution factors. That is, if national aggregate outputs are high, that does not guarantee that food security exists. Further, it is unclear at what point the national wealth begins to trickle down or what the mechanisms are to ensure this outcome. These are matters for visible hands (for an analysis of how government policy helped achieve more equitable income distribution in Taiwan, see Kuo, Ranis, and Fei 1981).

In capitalist Third World countries, the state often acts in agreement with the private sector. As a result, policies that increase taxes, raise wages, guarantee welfare through health care, social security and other redistribution measures are absent. With a state that does not advocate for the poor, a private sector that does not acknowledge the need for improving welfare, and a military that shores up the status quo, the system may be called a "reactionary despotism" as Baloyra terms it for the Salvadoran case (1982), or, in Jeane Kirkpatrick's formulation, an autocracy where

> traditional autocrats leave in place existing allocations of wealth, power, status, and other resources, which in most traditional societies favor an affluent few and maintain masses in poverty. But they worship traditional gods and observe traditional taboos. They do not disturb the habitual patterns of family and personal relations. Because the miseries of

traditional life are familiar, they are bearable to ordinary people who, growing up in the society, learn to cope, as children born to untouchables in India acquire the skills and attitudes necessary for survival in the miserable roles they are destined to fill (Kirkpatrick 1982, 49–50).

Thus, security is achieved, not by providing enough, but rather through the "tradition" and "habit" of favoring an affluent few. And, of course, this is not food security. For redistributive measures to be carried out, something more than ordinary rationality, or common decency, must provide the stimulus. In El Salvador the "traditional autocracy" has developed its own momentum and maintained inequality even where the population's poverty is a source of economic and political instability.

The autocratic system is able to claim stability through the imposition of violently sanctioned order. This order contributes to efficiency through the suppression of the wage rate and curtailment of workers' rights (Cambranes 1985). In Central America, the highly profitable cotton industry yielded wealth for the planters at the cost of substandard wages for harvest workers and unacceptably high use of chemical inputs that increased yields and costs, injured workers, and poisoned the environment (Williams, 1986, chap. 3; Leonard 1987, 144–159). This vaunted efficiency is achieved through control over other aspects of the social and economic system (taxes, exchange rates, credit, suppression of dissent) that increase profit (White 1973, 121–127). It does not reflect real competitiveness or market pressure. Investment in research, plant breeding, cultivation practices, and technology are not the basis of this efficiency (Pino Cáceres 1988).

The logic of the majority regards the state as the agent of the masses, often in opposition to an elite, and as associated with socialist governments. Concerned with mass problems such as large-scale food deficits, the state often proposes collective solutions, such as communes, state farms, and agricultural cooperatives. It may invest national resources in research to stabilize food production and increase yields (such as drought-resistant seed strains, open-field pollination practices to allow farmers to experiment themselves) and to train the rural poor in agronomy and farm management. It may intervene in the price structure of food to subsidize urban populations with cheap food. The logic of the majority is a moral commitment, but at the same time it shores up political support for the government.

However, popular support for such governments may in turn disguise inefficiency. The inefficiencies observable in socialist food-security planning are often cited as evidence for the lack of feasibility of socialism itself (Colburn 1986 writing about Nicaragua; Powelson 1987, chap. 1). Inefficiency may co-exist with steady progress in providing more food to the poor. Moving toward food security sometimes creates difficulties because of the increased demand and consumption (Utting 1987).

Not all situations are so black and white. No government is openly supportive of widespread hunger and starvation. Nor does any country devote its resources exclusively to the eradication of hunger. In all cases, national policy is a blend of pragmatic considerations, political party or interest group competition, the economic condition of the country, and foreign policy. These dynamics determine who the most significant clientele of the state is (Barraclough 1970). The returns to this clientele help define political will, that is, the level of priority a government assigns to the food-security question.

In each case, the various priorities are ordered differently, and this ordering gives us a glimpse into the national political will. Although the trickle-downers may correctly speak about the efficiency of their system, success in accomplishing higher aggregate output is no guarantee of greater food security. Likewise, those who propose collective solutions may have to live with lower efficiency but may, through state intervention, make this output travel farther. However, insuring that the GDP is equitably distributed to the population is no guarantee that the system is self-sustaining. So, it may be that productive efficiency and effective distribution (or redistribution) are either independent of each other or are inversely related, that is, low efficiency is related to equitable food distribution and high efficiency to stratification and inequity.

An example of the latter would be Cuba, where, although yields of sugar and other crops have not been high under a collective productive regime, none doubt that basic needs, particularly food security, are provided to all. In fact, by way of dramatic contrast, the yields per surface area of sugar on the northeast coast of Brazil are higher than in Cuba, even though sugar is produced there on small holdings. But Northeast Brazil is an area of endemic hunger, even starvation (Gross and Underwood 1971). Cuba, in the words of the 1982 report of the Joint Economic Committee of the U.S. Congress, guarantees food security to its people through a "highly egalitarian redistribution of income that has eliminated almost all malnutrition, particularly among young children" (quoted in Benjamin, Collins, and Scott 1984, 90).

Recent research on the quality of life suggests that high GDP and equity of distribution are probably unrelated (UNDP 1990). Studies such as these suggest that political will alone is necessary to resolve problems of inequitable distribution of national wealth.

FOOD SECURITY AND SOCIAL CHANGE

I treat the case of El Salvador, where the distribution of food reflects the distribution of other national resources. That is, a large percentage of the population lives in a constant state of deprivation. That same sector earns the lowest incomes, has access to the least amount of land or is landless, and has virtually no opportunity to express itself in an organized fashion in defense of its interests. Since a military coup in October 1979, a series of reform measures have been designed to change this situation and to benefit the lowest socioeconomic sector. The Military Proclamation of October 15, 1979, found that the social inequities were "the result of the antiquated economic, social and political structures that have traditionally prevailed in the country, structures that do not offer the majority of the inhabitants the minimum conditions essential for their human self-fulfillment" (quoted in Americas Watch and American Civil Liberties Union 1982, 260). This proclamation was an abrupt rupture with an ancien régime and expressed goals that went far beyond the food question; in this paper I analyze the government's activities and successes in achieving that specific goal.

THE PRE-COUP FOOD SITUATION

During the 1970s, El Salvador was a country composed of two worlds. A small elite, numerically inconsequential, controlled most of the land, and the majority of the population (including almost all the rural population) lived at a level below what was necessary to survive. 40.9 percent of the rural population was landless in 1971, up from 11.8 percent in 1961 (Deere and Diskin 1984, 18), and 70.9 percent of all farms were below 2 hectares in size (compare Table 30–1). Agricultural production patterns also reflected the duality. 77.9 percent of maize, 78.3 percent of beans, and 82.3 percent of sorghum (grown for human consumption in El Salvador) were produced on farms 10 hectares or less (Deere and Diskin 1984, 21). In contrast, 74 percent of coffee and 89.3 percent of sugar was produced on farms over 20 hectares in size (Deere and Diskin 1984, 21). Basic grains constituted only 10.1 percent of the market value of all crops; coffee, cotton, and sugar accounted for 83.6 percent of the market value of all crops (Deere and Diskin 1984, 22).

The landless and land-poor (numbering more than 350,000 families) survived through a combination of cultivation and wage work that generally deepened their poverty each year. The vast bulk of the poor depended to a considerable degree upon wages to complete family income (see Table 30–2). The rural poor, those working less than 2 hectares of land, or the landless, earned only a portion of their income from farm work on their own land. Those working one hectare or less earned 60 percent of family income on their own land. The landless earned 72 percent of their income through wage labor on others' farms. In 1975, 75 percent of rural households fell below a threshold that would enable them to buy the minimal diet (Deere and Diskin 1984, 7, table 3). In February 1968, when the minimum wage was 2.25 colones/day for agricultural work, many campesinos preferred the old, lower wage of 1.50 colones/day because they customarily received three meals. The sad conclusion is that they could not feed themselves adequately on .75 colones/day. At .75/day virtually all the landless and land-poor population would have earned too little to meet basic food requirements (CDIA 1968, 78).

In general, 1975 incomes for the rural poor represent a real decline compared to 1961 (see Table 30–3). The income of landless families fell 16 percent in that period, and the income of families who worked one hectare or less dropped by 20 percent (Deere and Diskin 1987, 7). This drop in real income was also accompanied by shifts in land tenure. For farms of one hectare or less, ownership fell from 43 percent in 1950 to 28.5 percent in 1971 (see Table 30–4). Ownership of farms from 1–2 hectares fell from 52.7 percent in 1950 to 31.4 percent in 1971 (Deere and Diskin 1984, 19). Thus, with smaller farms, even smaller income shares were staying with those who worked the land.

Although farms one hectare and less in size accounted for 49 percent of all

TABLE 30–1 Changes in Land Distribution, El Salvador, 1950–1971

FARM SIZE (HECTARES)	1950				1961				1971			
	NO. FARMS	%	AREA (HECTARES)	%	NO. FARMS	%	AREA (HECTARES)	%	NO. FARMS	%	AREA (HECTARES)	%
-.99	70,416	40.4	35,203	2.3	107,054	47.2	61,366	3.9	132,464	49.0	70,287	4.8
-1.99	35,189	20.2	48,013	3.1	48,501	21.4	68,542	4.3	59,063	21.9	81,039	5.6
-4.99	34,868	20.0	106,973	7.0	37,743	16.6	117,470	7.4	43,414	16.0	131,985	9.1
-9.90	14,064	8.1	99,446	6.5	14,001	6.2	98,791	6.2	15,598	5.8	110,472	7.6
10–19.99	8,875	5.1	122,477	8.0	8,524	3.8	117,426	7.4	9,164	3.4	126,974	8.7
20–49.99	6,660	3.8	206,334	13.5	6,711	3.0	208,628	13.2	6,986	2.6	215,455	14.8
50–99.99	2,107	1.2	147,640	9.6	2,214	1.0	154,704	9.8	2,238	0.8	154,164	10.6
100–999.99	1,881	1.1	459,119	30.0	2,023	0.9	505,582	32.0	1,878	0.7	437,939	30.2
1000 or more	145	0.1	305,118	19.9	125	0.1	248,919	15.7	63	0.0	123,579	8.5
Total	174,204	100	1,530,323	99.9	226,896	100.2	1,581,428	99.9	270,868	100.3	1,451,894	99.9

Source: Dirección General de Estadísticas y Censos (DGEC): Censo Agropecuario 1950, 1961, and 1971 (El Salvador, 1950, 1961, and 1971).

TABLE 30–2 Composition of Annual Net Income by Source, El Salvador, 1975 (Percentages)

FARM SIZE (HECTARES)	FARM INCOME				NONFARM INCOME				
	CROPS	FRUITS	ANIMAL	SUB-TOTAL	WAGE WORK	TRADE	OTHER[a]	SUB-TOTAL	TOTAL
Landless	—	20	8	28	52	14	6	72	100
Less than 1	25	26	8	59	31	7	3	41	100
1.0–1.9	34	28	13	75	19	5	1	25	100
2.0–4.9	64	18	10	92	6	2	0	8	100
5.0–9.9	74	12	7	93	2	4	1	7	100
10.0–50.0	74	9	11	97	2	2	2	6	100

[a]Other includes artisan production income, remittances, and rental payments.

Source: United Nations Development Programme (UNDP). *Realidad campesina y desarrollo nacional*, Project ELS/73/003, vol. 7. San Salvador, 1976, p. 83.

TABLE 30–3 Average Rural Household Income, El Salvador, 1961–1975 (1975 colones)

FARM SIZE (HECTARES)	1961			1975		
	NO. OF HOUSEHOLDS	%	AVERAGE INCOME	NO. OF HOUSEHOLDS	%	AVERAGE INCOME
Landless	30,451	12	940	166,922	41	792
Less than 1	107,054	42	1,252	138,838	34	1,003
1–9.9	100,245	39	1,752	94,330	23	2,287
10–50	19,957	7	6,010	7,927	2	6,342
Total	257,707	100		407,387	100	

Source: UNDP. *Realidad campesina y desarrollo nacional*, Project ELS/73/003, vol. 7. San Salvador, 1976, p. 75.

TABLE 30–4   Changes in Land Tenure by Farm Size, El Salvador, 1950–1971

	OWNERSHIP	NONOWNERSHIP[a]	TOTAL
1950			
Farm size (hectares)			
1 and less	43.0	57.0	100.0
1–2	52.7	47.3	100.0
all farms	61.9	38.1	100.0
1971			
Farm size (hectares)			
1 and less	28.5	71.5	100.0
1–2	31.4	68.6	100.0
all farms	39.9	60.1	100.0

[a]Includes, primarily, *arrendamiento simple* and *colonia*.
Source: Dirección General de Estadísticas y Censos (DGFC), 1950 and 1971.

farms, they received only .8 percent of total agricultural credit. Farms in the 1–10 hectare category, accounting for 43.7 percent of all farms, received only 12.5 percent of credit (Deere and Diskin 1984, 23). Wages increased during the previous decade by 78.1 percent for coffee harvesters (the maximum) and fell 18.2 percent for permanent farm workers (the minimum); the general cost of living went up by 95.2 percent (Deere and Diskin 1984, 34, table 18).

The consequences of this poverty were reflected in the most sensitive indicator of welfare: the nutritional status of children. In a study conducted by INCAP (Instituto de Nutrición de Centro América y Panamá) in 1965–1967, 78 percent of Salvadoran children were undernourished, of whom 25 percent were "moderately" undernourished, and 3.2 percent "severely" affected. Survey data for 1976–1978 indicate improvements, although the situation was still far from acceptable. Sixty-four percent of children tested were malnourished, 12 percent moderately and .9 percent severely[3] (USAID 1985, 80 92).

A carefully controlled study in the mid-1970s that looked at malnutrition among children according to their precise economic niche indicated that permanent residents on coffee plantations suffered from the greatest degree of malnutrition. They differed from the land-poor and landless in the greater frequency of third degree malnutrition, 2.2 percent (Valverde et al., 1980).

These measures of malnutrition have their counterparts in the poor state of rural health, education, housing, and life expectancy. The slight improvements in nutritional status in 1976–1978 reported in the INCAP study probably reflected the greater number of urban workers who benefited from a certain amount of industrialization, but the rural situation remained critical. Perhaps the worst aspect of this was that, with no institutional change, the global situation was headed for explosion. Efforts to promote change, whether government-inspired or through participation from below, were consistently met with repression.

During the late 1970s, food-production levels were higher in El Salvador than in any other Central American country (Leonard 1987, 213, table A.23). El Salvador's economy was also growing at a vigorous rate (5.9 percent in 1960–1970) (de Janvry 1981, 36), but the rural income distribution worsened, with the Gini coefficient of income distribution changing from .52 in 1961 to .68 in the early 1970s (Deere and Diskin 1984, 7). High rates of economic growth and production levels, coupled with profound human misery, cast the trickle-down theory in real doubt. When presented with the previous details, members of the Salvadoran private sector argued that even higher levels of growth were needed before the trickle-down effect could begin. The president of the private-sector association ANEP (Asociación Nacional de la Empresa Privada) told me in 1984 that general benefits would flow when the private sector made a sustained annual growth of 35 percent. The following year he amended this to a mere 19 percent, citing Taiwan as the relevant precedent. The logic of this argument is hermetic, because the preconditions to achieve this end would give such total control over the society to the private sector that whether trickle-down would occur at that time or not would not matter.

During this period of growth in production, population was growing at a vigorous rate, 3.1 percent between 1950 and 1971, with a 3.5 percent rural rate and a 2.9 percent urban rate (Banco Mundial 1979, 11). Although the numbers may suggest that poverty is the inexorable outcome of high population growth, Durham's research clearly shows that land-use patterns contribute much more to rural impoverishment than population growth (Durham 1979). In the 1960s and 1970s, agricultural employment opportunity was higher than the growth rate of the rural labor force. "Between 1961 and 1971, the rural labor force increased by 2.2 percent, i.e., 0.4 percent less than the growth rate of agricultural employment" (Deere and Diskin 1984, 31). Per capita cereal production was decreasing in the period 1975–1981, as was general per capita food production in 1974–1982 (Leonard 1987, 214). At the same time, El Salvador had a positive balance of food trade in the 1981–1983 period of $330.3 million. This meant that the deficit in cereals, meat, dairy products, fruits, vegetables, and animal and vegetable oils of $103.9 million was counterbalanced by revenues of $434.2 million, of which coffee revenues accounted for $419.3 million (Leonard 1987, table A.26 215). In macroeconomic terms, this process may be called development, that is, the value of the shortfall in food production is more than compensated for by coffee revenues. But that positive balance was not used to benefit the rural poor.

AGRARIAN REFORM—A WAY TO FOOD SECURITY?

The military coup of 1979 specifically sought to redress the social injustice that the agro-export system ("the majority") had wrought. The junior officers who seized power felt that by eliminating the repression, corruption, and arbitrary anti-democratic behavior, they could increase yields, better distribute farmland, and therefore increase family incomes. The most important means to accomplish this was an agrarian reform.

The kind of agrarian reform envisioned was the product of considerable debate during the 1970s (see Table 30–5). It would have had rather severe acreage limitations on landholdings (about 50 hectares), would have offered technical and financial support to the new beneficiaries, and would have encouraged the formation of peasant-run cooperatives (Alvarenga 1977, 139–140). In late 1979 and early 1980, there was widespread support for establishing agricultural cooperatives as well as for titling small holdings. At least, the members of the civilian-military junta supported such measures. They were joined in this by the Ministry of Agriculture and Cattle (MAG), members of labor and church organizations, and academics. Had the reformist tone of the junior officers who accomplished the coup prevailed, that tone would likely have shaped the agrarian reform decree. In fact, the American Embassy believed, just days before the decree was issued, that the document would reflect such intentions.[4]

But between the formation of the junta on October 15, 1979, and the emission of Decree 153 (the Basic Law of Agrarian Reform, March 6, 1980) the political complexion of the government changed drastically (Dunkerley 1982; Armstrong and Schenk 1982; Montgomery 1982; Baloyra 1982). Behind-the-scenes negotiations were going on between the junta, the MAG, ISTA (Instituto Salvadoreño de Transformación Agraria), UCS (Unión Comunal Salvadoreña), the American Embassy, the Salvadoran military, and the rural oligarchy. The reformers seemed to be losing ground as the military old guard assumed more prominent positions in the government. The military stamp was seen in the intensification of repression against all forms of government opposition activity. The installation of then Col. García to the junta and the Ministry of Defense and the retention of Gen. Jaime Abdul Gutiérrez meant a decline in power for the original reformist officers such as Col. Majano. Demonstrators were shot down in the streets, while the junta was seeking a negotiated accommodation with them through the implementation of reforms.

Because of these events, the decree was different than expected. It placed the upper limit on land ownership at 100 hectares and ordered the confiscated lands to be made into peasant cooperatives. The next day an implementing decree made it clear that only properties over 500 hectares would be "intervened" immediately, confiscation of the remainder would be indefinitely postponed. At that time, an emergency suspension of civil liberties was also decreed, giving near total power to the military, something it had held in any event, without benefit of decrees.

On April 26 of the same year, decree 207 was passed by the junta. This stated that small-holding tenants, that is, renters, sharecroppers, and other nonowning cultivators, would become owners of the lands they worked, up to a limit of 17 acres. Although the authors of this decree intended that its effect would be immediate, it became the slowest and most problematical part of the land-reform program. Instantly dubbed the "most sweeping land reform in the history of Latin America" by its United States supporters (Prosterman and Temple 1980), it was supposed to lead to increased family-farm production of basic grains. That would, in turn, help fuel industrial development that would feed back into increased agricultural production through improved technology. This spiral of economic development and recovery would involve so many of the rural poor[5] that the pool of recruits for the FMLN

(Farabundo Martí National Liberation Front) guerrilla force would dry up and the country would "escape the threat of a civil war" (Prosterman and Temple 1980, 4). This was not to be.

Any effort at agrarian reform was fiercely opposed by the landowners and their military allies. The confiscation of lands over 500 hectares, Phase I, was done very soon after decree 153 was issued.[6] The military saw to it that landowners did not resist, but at the same time, it unleashed a wave of terror in the countryside. This double message meant that the new or potential beneficiaries of reform should not become too exuberant in seeking to use their new status to promote more changes. It was a message stating that reformism would be limited and that it would not threaten the power of the military or the rural elite that still maintained holdings (see Table 30–6). Not only was this form of "implementation" of the reform a hardship, but the economic burdens of the new cooperative members of these properties were overwhelming. Overcompensation of former landowners (an informal bribe) and the systematic decapitalization of properties left new cooperatives with an agrarian debt too large to pay.[7] Added to that were difficulties in obtaining credit and technical assistance: The new cooperatives were left to sink or swim, with the former landowners hoping for failure.

Decree 207 hardly sparked an instant transfer of land; it took almost a year before anything was done at all. When new financial and bureaucratic machinery was finally put in place, eligible peasants were faced with an impenetrable thicket of rules, procedures, and paperwork that had to be initiated by each campesino, all in an environment of increasing lethal violence.

Those who benefited from either measure, that is, Phase I and decree 207, moved from a status of technical landlessness to one of only technical landownership. This was so for different reasons. Phase I beneficiaries were severely circumscribed by regulations that prevented the full exercise of ownership and did not grant them the assistance needed to run the new properties. Many new cooperatives were run by the more highly skilled staff of the previous landowner, so for the field hands it meant only a change in bosses. There was no increase in wages because returns from harvests were controlled by the agrarian agency and the bank. There was almost never enough of a surplus to improve the status of the rural poor beneficiaries. If there was a surplus, the government agrarian reform agency (ISTA) placed that money in re-

TABLE 30–5   Estimated Benefits at Beginning of Agrarian Reform (1981)

	AREA		BENEFICIARIES	
	# OF HECTARES	*% OF TOTAL LAND IN FARMS*	*# OF FAMILIES*	*% OF RURAL POPULATION*
Phase I	223,000	15.4	50,000	11.9
Phase II	343,000	23.6	50,000	11.9
Phase III	175,000	12.1	150,000	35.7
Total	741,000	51.1	250,000	59.5

Source: Diskin 1988.

TABLE 30–6   Agrarian Reform Outcome vs. Original Estimated Goals

	AREA (HA.)	% OF GOAL	% OF FARMLAND	# FAMILIES BENEFITED	% OF GOAL	% OF RURAL FAMILIES
Phase I	218,566	98	15.1	31,259	68	7.5
Phase II			NEVER IMPLEMENTED			
Phase III	96,566	55	6.7	37,500	25	8
Total	315,132	42	21.8	68,759	28	15.5

Source: Diskin 1989.

stricted noninterest bearing accounts to keep against payments on the agrarian debt. The technical support needed to manage complex activities such as cotton production was very difficult to obtain, especially if the cooperative leadership was composed of former peasant field hands rather than the previous skilled managers associated with the previous landowners. A peasant I interviewed in May 1988 told me that the difference between his condition now and before the reform was only that he now had more days of work each year but not an increase in the wage rate or a dividend from profits on sales.

For 207 beneficiaries, there was a constant diet of violence and intimidation. Instead of upward of 150,000 beneficiary families as originally stated, as of June 16, 1988, only about 37,500 families actually received land (FINATA 1988) Although there is some indication that these beneficiaries have taken their ownership seriously, improved their lands, invested in improvements, and experienced a slight increase in family income (MAG-OSPA-PERA 1985, 105–110), their numbers are so few as to not have any impact on the rural sector in general.

IMPACT OF REFORM, THE WAR, AND U.S. AID ON FOOD SECURITY

The agrarian reform of 1980 was an effort to redistribute land among an impoverished rural mass. The institutional tension between landowners, the private sector, the military, labor unions, peasant organizations, and church groups, did not change significantly. The only real change was in the intensification of the conflict into a full-blown civil war.

The data available show that the condition of the rural poor has since deteriorated. The most recent report of the congressional Arms Control and Foreign Policy Caucus entitled "Bankrolling Failure" describes some of this situation. For FY 1988, U.S. Aid to El Salvador exceeded El Salvador's own contribution to its budget. The United States contributed $608 million compared to the $582 million national budget (Hatfield, Leach, and Miller 1987, 1–2). This enormous subsidy to El Salvador, if consistent with the publicly stated U.S. foreign policy goals, should be used primarily to implement reforms, improve welfare, and contribute to the Salvadoran military's effort to defeat the insurgency. President Reagan and his secretary of state often said that the military portion of the aid served as a "shield" behind which reforms could be carried out.[8] However, a close examination of the real destination of this aid convinced the caucus that "*Three dollars of U.S. aid were devoted to the war and its effects in 1987 for every one dollar used to address its root causes*" (Hatfield, Leach, and Miller 1987, 2, emphasis theirs). The U.S. government acknowledged that its highest priority was given to the war by calling this pattern of aid transitional to assistance for reform and development (USAID 1985, 63). Worse still, a significant portion of this aid was administered directly by the Salvadoran military, although this is in contravention of U.S. law that prevents the use of food aid for "military or paramilitary purposes" (Hatfield, Leach, and Miller 1987, 9). This skewed pattern of U.S. aid accompanied a sharp deterioration in living standards, a worsening economic system, and a "collapse of political will" (Hatfield, Leach, and Miller 1987, 20).

In 1991, after eight years of a stalemated war, the social changes that have occurred may best be described as a rebirth of the political power of the rural oligarchy and the private sector. The enormous growth in the military budget has greatly increased the political influence of the military. In opposition to this was the growth of peasant organizations (some within the agrarian reform and others outside its structure), a renewed militancy of the labor movement, and an increased military capability of the guerrilla forces.

U.S. support for rural development has focused more and more on private agricultural development. USAID has advocated a process of rural privatization during the past few years. For campesinos who will be relocated on presently abandoned agrarian reform properties, for new beneficiaries who will be placed on Phase I properties, and for new beneficiaries who will be placed on land to be bought by the government—all of these groups would be given titles for small, privately owned plots. Rather than consider that the lack of social change, that is, the failure to break the power of the rural oligarchy, has impeded healthy agrarian change, AID has come to think that the reasons for stagnation in production, the continuing low levels of rural welfare (New York Times, Oct. 16, 1988), and the continued oppression of rural organizations lie in the existence of cooperative forms of production. Little attention is given to the continuing institutionalized violence, the difficulties of obtaining credit for small producers, or the domination of rural affairs by the large growers' associations. About all that is agreed upon is that the conditions of campesinos in El Salvador remain abysmal.

It should be noted that of the two general strategies to achieve food security, U.S. spending strongly favors the trickle-down approach. It justified the military portion of the aid package as a necessary measure to create the conditions for development. "AID spends over 40 percent of the local currencies generated by U.S. aid on guarantees and lending programs for business, rather than on basic needs and long-term development projects" (Hatfield, Leach, and Miller 1987, 19).

Under the Reagan administration there was a spate of new, semigovernmental agencies such as the Bureau of Private Enterprise, the Trade Credit Insurance Corporation, and the Center for International Private Enterprise, which was created expressly to stimulate and aid the private sector throughout Central America and in other countries. These groups in conjunction with other U.S. government institutions such as the Overseas Private Investment Corporation (OPIC), the Export-Import Bank (EXIMBANK), the National Endowment for Democracy (NED), in turn spawned many local business groups and think tanks for the private sector (Barry and Preusch 1988, chap. 3). Through the use of portions of the U.S. assistance budget such as Economic Support Funds, PL480 (Title I) food assistance, roughly 75 percent of USAID spending in Central America was destined for "stabilization," that is, support for the financial structure of the recipient country (direct aid to the private sector). Very little USAID spending has addressed the social causes of the conflict (Barry and Preusch 1988, 21).

OUTCOME AND UPDATE

The economic devastation created by the war and the depopulation of certain areas caused by military actions left the country in disastrous financial condition. Now, in 1991, roughly half a million Salvadorans live outside their country because of the war and government repression. Many people living in displaced persons camps in El Salvador or in United Nations–supervised camps in Honduras have returned to their home villages. Under and unemployment rose to 50 percent (Hatfield, Leach, and Miller 1987, 19). Consumption declined 30 percent in the first four years of the war (Hatfield, Leach, and Miller 1987, 19). A 23 percent drop in purchasing power coupled with a 32 percent inflationary rise in 1986 pushed many of the rural poor into a desperate situation (Hatfield, Leach, and Miller 1987, 19). A 1985 study of the nutritional status of children of displaced families showed that among this stressed portion of the population, conditions were worse than ever previously recorded. Only 28.8 percent of these children were normal and 28.1 percent were in grades 2 and 3 (moderate and severe malnutrition) with 5.9 percent in grade 3 (USAID 1985, 83, table 8-1). The highest rate of grade 3 malnutrition (7 percent) was found among children living in the marginal urban sections of San Salvador (USAID 1985, 86–87, table 8-3). These figures contradict the usual idea that the urban environment offers the most economic opportunity and reflect the fact that displaced people in camps were probably eating better because of international assistance and the efforts of different institutions, including religious agencies, that care for these people. The disastrous outcome for urban displaced children reflects the extreme downturn of the national economy.

Agricultural production has diminished considerably. This downturn was caused in part by low market prices for the principal export crops and also reflects the private sector's efforts to withhold production in order to obtain concessions from the government. This has been especially true in the case of cotton production.

The disastrous condition of the rural poor would be worse yet were it not for the high level of subsidy that U.S. aid represents and the generosity of numerous PVOs (private voluntary organizations) that maintain a presence there (Arias 1989, 79, 93). Government data from 1985 show that about 3 million people fall below a level of absolute poverty, that is, below what is required for their physical reproduction, even if they spend 100 percent of their income on food (CENITEC 1989, 11).

This situation has worsened since then. The cost of food has risen about 400 percent since 1978, with most of the increase occurring during the past two years (Centro Universitario 1990); the increase in 1989 was about 33 percent (Instituto de Investigaciones 1990). By 1989 real wages had fallen to between 32 and 43 percent of 1978 levels (Instituto de Investigaciones 1990).

If the setbacks were merely momentary reverses in a well-conceived reformist plan, the continued application of more of the same should bear fruit for the population as conditions stabilize. However, should the war end tomorrow, the underlying problems of rural poverty, food insecurity, and inequity of land ownership would still be present. That is, the underlying institutional obstacles to fair distribution of national wealth would remain to be attacked. The continuation and ferocity of war is an indication of the resistance to change by the private sector and military.

The conditions described developed under the Christian Democratic administration of President Duarte, a lifelong reformer. Duarte failed to realize the thorough implementation of the agrarian reform because of corruption within his administration and his inability to challenge the continuing veto exercised by the traditional right-wing alliance of the military and the oligarchy. When the government passed into the hands of the ARENA (Alianza Republicana Nacionalista) party in 1988 (municipal and legislative elections) and 1989 (presidential elections), a very different developmental philosophy took over.

ARENA's view of private-sector-driven development (ECA 1989; Universidad Centroamericana 1988) dovetailed nicely with USAID free-market guidelines (Lievano and Norton 1988; Norton 1990). In the macroeconomic sphere it signaled the end of price supports to consumers, devaluation of the currency as a stimulus to agro-export production, and elimination of protective tariffs. In effect, wage controls and the suppression of union activity continued apace, ostensibly to prevent an inflationary spiral. It also meant privatization of government-owned assets, private marketing arrangements (including foreign trade of coffee), the return of banks to private hands, and the attempted breakup of agrarian reform cooperatives by issuing individual titles to each member of the cooperative.

What the future also holds is a probable reduction of the U.S. subsidy because congress is beginning to question the efficacy of continued aid. Hence, the resolution to these severe problems is yet to materialize. USAID seeks to return to a "free market" situation that might grant slightly more access to rural private property. But there is no reason to believe that now the invisible hand will successfully order Salvadoran society where it has failed in the past.

CONCLUSION

The two forms of political will (trickle-down and logic of the majority) seem to present clear tradeoffs and challenges. Trickle-down has a capacity to benefit the population, but the question remains regarding the location of the trigger point in national income formation. Must the Salvadoran economy await a steady 19 percent annual growth rate as the private sector advocates? That would place the economy in the realm of phantasy. All we know is that in El Salvador, high rates of growth in the GDP are possible with declines in the general level of welfare.

The logic-of-the-majority approach permits rapid changes in production patterns and distribution of food and therefore the elimination of hunger. But can this approach lead to significant enough levels of growth in the GDP to consolidate these immediately obtainable benefits? It can guarantee the protection of the population from the worst effects of hunger, but can it overcome inherent inefficiency and frequent bureaucratic torpor?

For both cases there is another significant aspect. Each system requires social order and support, or at least quiescence and lack of active opposition. El Salvador has pursued a policy, through war and peace, of emphasizing a leading sector, the private agrarian and industrial producers, as the engine of development. The welfare of the bulk of the population is left to a loaded market environment. For two decades, more and more people have experienced declining real incomes and standards of living. Order and legitimacy have been obtained through intimidation by military and paramilitary means from the 1880s to the present. But with changes in church leadership, the rise of rural organizations, new political parties, and an active guerrilla insurgency, the legitimacy of the Salvadoran state and government is itself in jeopardy. In no other way can the success of the FMLN be explained (Bacevich et al., 1988). U.S. policy, guided by a "low-density conflict" strategy has advocated reform to win "hearts and minds" but has not offered adequate financial and political support to accomplish the original goals of agrarian reform.

The 1980s have seen some efforts and much talk about reforms. These efforts have been carried out in order to moderate the disenchantment of the rural population, to create "small-scale capitalists" who would increase production by means of "an agricultural sector someday as conservative and efficient as South Korea, Taiwan, and Japan" (U.S. Embassy Cable, March 4, 1980b). But, as we have seen, this has not been the outcome of policy. What the "reactionary despots" (Baloyra 1982) seem unable to see is that the way to end the war is to end the historic injustice the oligarchs and much of the military are fighting to preserve. Preservation of this injustice is a formula for disaster, and this is what we are presently seeing.

El Salvador in the 1980s shows that the primary goal for the Salvadoran government and the United States is to win a counter-insurgency war rather than to benefit the vast bulk of the population and thereby erase the fundamental sources of the conflict. The near future will clarify whether this war can be won without the support of a population that has been repeatedly abused in the name of this policy. If the U.S.-supported project triumphs, then trickle-down will have the opportunity to demonstrate that it can improve the welfare of the majority. If not, the conflict will continue to needlessly claim innocent lives.

NOTES

1. In cases such as famines in the horn of Africa, adequate food supplies, although not derived from local production, could be given to those in need were it not for political and military factors.

2. Although the United States enjoys the highest per capita income in the world, there was a measurable and growing amount of hunger in 1991. The significance, indeed the existence of this phenomenon, was the subject of intense debate and polemics. The Reagan administration said at various times that its programs were adequate for the problem, there was more welfare fraud than genuine hunger, and some of the hungry preferred food handouts to work. Opponents of the administration accused it of callousness and indifference to human suffering.

3. (The categories "mild," "moderate," and "severe" are terms referring to weight-for-age data measured against the Iowa reference scale for acceptable child growth.) Children are called normal if they are within 90 percent of the Iowa range for their age, mildly malnourished if they are within 75–89.9 percent, moderately malnourished if they are within 60–74.9 percent, and severely malnourished if they are under 60 percent on the Iowa scale. This so-called Gomez classification is normally presented as grades 1 (mild), 2 (moderate), and 3 (severe) (USAID 1985, 81–82).

4. Three days before decree 153 was issued, Professor Roy Prosterman, described by Ambassador White as a "prominent land-reform expert," briefed the embassy staff about the law to be issued. Prosterman had enjoyed privileged access to all the participants in the agrarian reform negotiation. He spoke about a 35-hectare limit on the best lands. He called this sort of reform "good" and "not radical," referring to the much lower retention limits of the Taiwanese and Japanese reforms (U.S. Embassy Cable, March 3, 1980a).

5. In Alexander Haig's 1984 book, *Caveat,* he remembers it this way, "In March 1980, this junta headed by Duarte, announced a land reform program that expropriated all estates larger than 1,250 acres and promised to grant 90 percent of all other arable land to peasant cooperatives or sharecroppers" (Haig 1984, 126).

6. Phase I, the only well-implemented part of the reform, was carried out in the reformist euphoria of early 1980. The Christian Democrats entered into a pact with the military whereby they would enter the governing junta and grant it a certain legitimacy in return for the military's promise to implement the agrarian reform.

7. This was because decree 153 specified in article 30 that the agrarian debt, i.e., the amount given to ex-landlords, was to be repaid to ISTA (Instituto Salvadoreño de Transformacion Agraria) (MAG 1980, 35–36).

8. Before Secretary of State Schultz, Secretary of State Alexander Haig put it this way, "The Salvadoran armed forces needed equipment and training so they could guarantee the safety of their government while the process of land redistribution and social and economic reform was completed" (Haig 1984, 124).

REFERENCES AND BIBLIOGRAPHY

Alvarenga, Ivo P. (1977). *Temas de Derecho Agrario y Reforma Agraria.* San Jose: Editorial Universitaria Centro Americana (EDUCA).

Americas Watch Committee and the American Civil Liberties Union (1982). *Report on Human Rights in El Salvador, January 26, 1982.* New York: Vintage Books.

Arias, Salvador (1989). *Seguridad o Inseguridad Alimentaria: Un Reto Para la Región Centroamericana.* Perspectives Para el Año 2000. San Salvador: UCA Editores.

Armstrong, Robert, and Janet Shenk (1982). *El Salvador: The Face of Revolution.* Boston: South End Press.

Bacevich, A. J., J. D. Hallums, R. H. White, and Thomas F. Young (1988). *American Military Policy in Small Wars: The Case of El Salvador.* Working Group Study. Cambridge: The John F. Kennedy School of Government.

Baloyra, Enrique (1982). *El Salvador in Transition.* Chapel Hill and London: The University of North Carolina Press.

Banco Mundial (World Bank) (1979). *El Salvador: Cuestiones y Perspectivas Demográficas.* Washington, D.C.: Banco Mundial.

Barraclough, Solon (1970). "Agricultural Policy and Strategies of Land Reform." In *Masses in Latin America,* edited by Irving Louis Horowitz. New York: Oxford University Press, 95–171. (1982). *A Preliminary Analysis of the Nicaraguan Food System.* United Nations Institute for Social Development, Food Systems and Society Series. Geneva: United Nations.

Barry, Tom, and Deb Preusch (1988). *The Soft War: The Uses and Abuses of U.S. Economic Aid in Central America.* New York: Grove Press.

Benjamin, M., J. Collins, and M. Scott (1984). *No Free Lunch: Food and Revolution in Cuba Today.* San Francisco: Institute for Food and Development Policy.

Cambranes, J. D. (1985). *Coffee and Peasants in Guatemala.* CIRMA/Plumsock Mesoamerican Studies, South Woodstock, Vermont: CIRMA.

Catholic Institute for International Relations (1987). *Right to Survive: Human Rights in Nicaragua.* London: Catholic Institute for International Relations.

CENITEC (Centro de Investigaciones Tecnológicas y Científicas) (1989). "Las Dimensiones de la Pobreza Extrema en El Salvador." *Cuadernos de Investigación,* no. 1 (Feb.). San Salvador: CENITEC Dirección de Investigaciones Económicas y Sociales.

Centro Universitario de Documentación e Información (1990). "Consideraciones Macroeconomicas en Torno al Problema de la Extreme Pobreza." *Proceso* 445 (Sept. 26). San Salvador: Universidad Centroamericana "José Simeón Cañas."

CIDA (Comité Interamericano de Desarrollo Integral (1968). *El Salvador: Características Generales de la Utilización y Distribución de la Tierra.* Mexico City: CIDA.

Colburn, Forrest D. (1986). *Post-Revolutionary Nicaragua: State, Class, and the Dilemmas of Agrarian Policy.* Berkeley, Los Angeles, London: University of California Press.

Deere, C. D., and M. Diskin (1984). "Rural Poverty in El Salvador: Dimensions, Trends, and Causes." World Employment Program Research Working Paper 10–6/WP64. Geneva: International labor Organization.

de Janvry, Alain (1981). *The Agrarian Question and Reformism in Latin America.* Baltimore: Johns Hopkins University Press.

DGEC (Dirección General de Estadísticas y Censos) (1954). I Censo Agrario, 1950. San Salvador: DGEC. (1967). II Censo agrario, 1961. San Salvador: DGEC. (1975). III Censo agrario, 1971. San Salvador: DGEC.

Diskin, Martin (1989). "El Salvador: Reform Prevents Change." In *Searching for Agrarian Structure and Agrarian Reform in Latin America,* edited by William C. Thiesenhusen. Boston: Unwin Hyman.

Dunkerly, James (1982). *The Long War: Dictatorship and Revolution in El Salvador.* London: Junction Books.

Durham, William H. (1979). *Scarcity and Survival in Central America: Ecological Origins of the Soccer War.* Stanford: Stanford University Press.

ECA (Estudios Centroamericanos) (1989). "La Política de Reforma Agraria de ARENA." *Estudios Centroamericanos,* no. 492 (Oct.). San Salvador Universidad Centroamericano "José Simeón Cañas," pp. 843–846.

FINATA (Financiera Nacional de Tierras Agricolas) (1988). *Decreto No. 207: Situacion del Proceso de Ejecucion.* June 16, 1988, San Salvador: FINATA.

Gross, Daniel R., and Barbara A. Underwood (1971). "Technological Change and Caloric Costs: Sisal Agriculture in N. E. Brazil." *American Anthropologist* 73: 725–740.

Haig, Alexander M. (1984). *Caveat: Realism, Reagan, and Foreign Policy.* New York: MacMillan.

Hatfield, Mark O., J. Leach, and G. Miller (1985). *U.S. Aid to El Salvador: An Evaluation of the Past, a Proposal for the Future.* February, U.S. Congress, Washington, D.C.: Arms Control and Policy Caucus. (1987). *Bankrolling Failure: United States Policy in El Salvador and the Urgent Need for Reform.* A Report to the Arms Control and Foreign Policy Caucus, U.S. Congress. Washington, D.C.: Arms Control and Policy Caucus.

Instituto de Investigaciones Economicas (1990). "Necesidades Básicas y Deterioro de las Condiciones de Vida." *Coyuntura Económica* Year 5, no. 28 (Jan.-Feb.): 17–19. San Salvador: Universidad de El Salvador.

Kirkpatrick, Jeane J. (1982). *Dictatorships and Double Standards: Rationalism and Reason in Politics.* New York: The American Enterprise Institute and Simon and Schuster.

Kuo, Shirley, Gustav W. Y. Ranis, and John C. H. Fei. (1981). *Taiwan Success Story: Rapid Growth with Improved Distribution in the Republic of China, 1952–1979.* Boulder: Westview Press.

Leonard, Jeffrey H. (1987). *Natural Resources and Economic Development in Central America: A Regional Environment Profile.* New Brunswick and Oxford: Transaction Books.

Liévano, Mirna, and Roger Norton (1988). "Food Imports, Agricultural Policies and Agricultural Development in El Salvador, 1960–1987." Washington, D.C.: Robert Nathan Associates.

MAG (Ministerio de Agricultura Y Ganaderia) (1980). *Legislacion de la Junta Revolucionaria de Gobierno Aplicable al Proceso de Reforma Agraria.* Departamento de Informacion Agropecuaria. Santa Tecla, El Salvador: MAG.

MAG-OSPA-PERA (1985). *Segundo Perfil de Beneficiarios del Decreto* 207. Document PERA-1-04-86. San Salvador: MAG-OSPA-PERA.

Mision Interagencial del Sistema de Naciones Unidas (1986). "La Pobreza Rural en El Salvador: Elementos Basicos Para Una Politica Campesina." Informe de la Mision (Version Preliminar), January 1986. San Salvador: MISNU, 21–29.

Montgomery, Tommie Sue (1982). *Revolution in El Salvador: Origins and Evolution.* Boulder: Westview Press.

Norton, Roger (1990). *An Assessment of the Recent Agricultural Policy Reforms in El Salvador.* San Salvador: USAID.

PAHO (Pan American Health Organization) (1986). *Health Conditions in the Americas, 1981–1984.* Vol. 2, Scientific Publication no. 500. Pan American Health Organization. Pan American Sanitary Bureau. Regional Office of the World Health Organization, Washington, D.C.: PAHO.

Pino Cáceres, Jose Eduardo (1988). "Crisis Estructural de la Caficultura Salvadorena. Una Hipotesis Alarmante." *Presencia* Year 1, no. 1 (April–June), San Salvador.

Powelson, John P., and Richard Stock (1987). *The Peasant Betrayed: Agriculture and Land Reform in the Third World.* Boston: Oelgeschlager, Gunn, and Hain in association with the Lincoln Institute of Land Policy.

Prosterman, Roy L., and Jeffrey M. Riedinger (1987). *Land Reform and Democratic Development.* Baltimore and London: Johns Hopkins University Press.

Prosterman, Roy L., and Mary Temple (1980). "Land Reform in El Salvador." *Free Trade Union News* 35, no. 6 (June). Published by the Department of International Affairs, AFL-CIO.

UNDP (United Nations Development Program) (1976). "Realidad Campesina y Desarrollo Nacional." Project ELS/73/003, vols. 5 and 7. San Salvador: UNDP. (1990). *Human Development Report 1990.* New York: Oxford University Press.

Universidad Centroamericana (1988). "Parcelación o Colectivación: Dilema de la Reforma Agraria en El Salvador." In *Realidad Economico-Social.* San Salvador: Universidad Centroamericana "José Siméon Cañas," 363–368.

USAID (United States Agency for International Development) (1985). *Baseline Survey of the Displaced Population.* Contracting Corporation of America. AID Project no. 519-0178-C-00-5237-00. San Salvador: USAID. (1986). *Congressional Presentation.* Fiscal Year 1987, Annex III. Latin America and the Caribbean. Washington, D.C.: USAID.

U.S. Embassy (1980a). "Analysis of El Salvador's Land Reform Law." Cable sent to Dept. of

State, March 3. San Salvador: U.S. Embassy. (1980b). "Land Reform Decree Nears Final Version." Cable sent to Dept. of State, March 4. San Salvador: U.S. Embassy.

Utting, Peter (1987). "Domestic Supply and Food Shortages." In *The Political Economy of Revolutionary Nicaragua,* edited by Rose Spalding. Boston, London, Sydney: Allen and Unwin.

Valverde, V., et al. (1980). "Lifestyles and Nutritional Status of Children from Different Ecological Areas of El Salvador," in *Ecology of Food and Nutrition.* Vol. 9, 167–177.

Weeks, John F., and Elizabeth W. Dore (1982). "Basic Needs: Journey of a Concept." In *Human Rights and Basic Needs in the Americas,* edited by Margaret E. Crahan. Washington, D.C.: Georgetown University Press.

White, Alastair (1973). *El Salvador.* New York and Washington, D.C.: Praeger Publishers.

Williams, Robert G. (1986). *Export Agriculture and the Crisis in Central America.* Chapel Hill and London: University of North Carolina Press.

Wolfe, Marshall (1981). *Elusive Development.* United Nations Research Institute for Social Development and Economic Commission for Latin America. Budapest: Statistical Publishing House.

31. Seeing the Population Issue Whole

Donella H. Meadows

The debate has been going on for almost two hundred years, since the Reverend Thomas Robert Malthus, in reaction to a group of optimistic French writers, penned his famous dictum in his 1798 *Essay on the Principle of Population:* "Taking the population of the world at any number . . . the human species would increase in the ratio of—1,2,4,8,16,32,64,128,256,512,&c, and subsistence as—1,2,3,4,5,6,7,8,9,10,&c."

Since then, the label *Malthusian* has been attached to those who believe that the human population could push or is pushing against the earth's resources. Their opponents, the anti-Malthusians, hold that this fear is not only exaggerated but dangerous. At best, they believe, it expresses too little faith in the adaptive, creative potential of humankind. At worst, they say, it allows some people to declare other people too numerous, a threat to the planet—with horrendous social consequences.

The optimists sometimes are called *cornucopians* or Marxists, since Marx was one of the harshest critics of Malthus. Other labels for the two sides have been *anti-*

Donella H. Meadows is an adjunct professor in the Environmental Studies Program at Dartmouth College.

natalists or *ecofreaks* for the Malthusians and *pronatalists* or *technotwits* for the anti-Malthusians.

Whatever the labels, since Malthus wrote, the human population has grown by a factor of six, and total human energy use by a factor of one hundred or so. Human life expectancy has increased nearly everywhere. The forest cover of the earth has been cut by a third and the area of undisturbed wetlands by half. The composition of the atmosphere has been altered by human-generated pollution. Hundreds of millions of people have starved to death; thousands of species have gone extinct. Mines and oil wells have been depleted—and new ones have been discovered. The economy has gone on growing.

One reason the argument continues is that history offers such mixed evidence. If you are part of the richest 20 percent of the world's population, you can easily read the past as an uninterrupted human triumph over the limits of the earth. If you are among the desperately poor, you might well agree with Malthus. As he put it, *A Summary View of the Principle of Population* (1880), "The pressure arising from the difficulty of procuring subsistence is not to be considered as a remote one which will be felt only when the earth refuses to produce any more, but as one which actually exists at present over the greatest part of the globe."

Or, as ecologist Garrett Hardin put it, writing in the November 1972 issue of the *Bulletin of the Atomic Scientists,* "Malthus has been buried again. (This is the 174th year in which that redoubtable economist has been interred. We may take it as certain that anyone who has to be buried 174 times cannot be wholly dead.)"

If a debate persists with passion for nearly two centuries, it must be true not only that the evidence is complex enough to support both sides, but also that each side is actively sifting the evidence, accumulating only that which supports preconceived notions. If people are doing that, there must be more to the argument than a scientific disagreement. There must be emotional investment as well. The protagonists in the Malthusian debate are not so much searching for truth as they are acting on commitments to see the world their way, and refusing to see it otherwise.

That shouldn't be surprising, science historian Thomas Kuhn would say, because even supposedly scientific debates have their ideological content. All human beings develop ego involvement with their own beliefs. They do so especially when the beliefs are fundamental, when they touch on the nature of humanity, the purpose of existence, the question of how we relate to nature and to each other. For centuries, scientists could not look objectively at the idea that the earth was not at the center of the universe. Many still have trouble with the idea that the earth is finite.

At least that's how I see it, as a person who has been active in the Malthusian debate but who has become less interested in winning than in understanding the intransigent nature of the discussion. I assume the argument resists resolution partly because the issues it raises are so complex and partly because they are so emotional. What I wonder is, what could we see if we were willing to approach the question of human population growth and planetary limits purely scientifically? What if we could divest ourselves of hopes, fears, and ideologies long enough to entertain all arguments and judge them fairly?

What we would see, I think, is that all sides are partly right and mostly incomplete. Each is focusing on one piece of a very complex system. Each is seeing its piece correctly. But because no side is seeing the whole, no side is coming to wholly supportable conclusions.

In short, to resolve the Malthusian conundrum and to find a way of thinking and acting that can guide a growing population to a sufficient and supportable standard of living within the earth's limits, we need all points of view. We need to treat them all with respect. We need to integrate them.

There are more than two points of view. The argument is not simply pro- and anti-Malthus. To begin what I hope will be a more comprehensive discussion, I will describe four sides of the debate here, with the understanding that many people put elements of these four together in their own unique combinations, and that there are other points of view as well. To avoid traps of labeling, I will use colors to characterize each side—though even colors carry emotional loads, as you will see.

Because of space limitations, I will have to simplify what are in each case self-consistent, sophisticated human worldviews. I will try to do so fairly (though probably no one can do that) so that the wisdom as well as the weakness in all these views will be apparent.

THE BLUES

The Blue view of the Malthusian question focuses on the possibility of keeping capital growing faster than population, so everyone can be better off. Progress, as defined by this view, comes from the accumulation of productive capital, from the building of infrastructure (roads, dams, ports) to make that capital more effective, and from the education of humans to make them more skilled and inventive in producing output from capital.

An important part of the Blue model is the assumption that capital grows most efficiently in a market system, where it is privately owned, where those who make it grow are directly rewarded, and where government interferes minimally.

Blues see living demonstrations of the workability of their view all around them. The world's most vibrant, diverse, productive, and innovative economies are those where industry is strong and where people reap material incentives for hard work, cleverness, or willingness to sacrifice in the present to invest for the future. Singapore, South Korea, and Taiwan are examples of successful development under the Blue model—and the United States, Japan, or Europe represents a vision for all the world's people of where that model can lead.

The Blues focus on raising the total level of output, not on the distribution of that output. They assume that concentrations of wealth are necessary to spur investment and that wealth will "trickle down" to enrich everyone.

Some Blues worry about population growth as a drain on investment—if too much is needed for consumption, schools, health care, and the like, then not enough will be available to plow back into the economy. Others, at the anti-Malthusian extreme, don't see even very rapid population growth as a problem at all. They see every new mouth as equipped with two new hands. The problem, in their eyes, is not how to slow the multiplication of people but how to multiply capital fast enough to put tools and machines in those hands so the new arrivals can earn their own way and even produce a surplus.

Blues see the human economy with great clarity. They see the natural world, from which raw materials come and to which wastes and pollution flow, only dimly—as a set of opportunities, a cost of production, or a source of government regulation—not as a complex system in its own right and certainly not as a limited or vulnerable one.

Insofar as Blues admit that raw materials or the earth's ability to absorb pollution may be constrained, they assume that human technology and the market system can adjust. If a resource becomes scarce, if a pollution stream becomes unbearable, a cost will rise, prices will incorporate that new cost, and a technical change will bring about more efficiency or a substitute or an abatement process. There have been many examples of this kind of adjustment, from beneficiation technologies that yield metals from poorer ores to catalytic converters that have reduced the average pollution emission per car by as much as 85 percent.

Blues assume that human beings are basically competitive, individualistic, and motivated by material gain. They believe that there are real differences in merit and competence among people. Justice in this model means appropriate rewards for productivity. Injustice means rewarding those who are not productive with goods or services taken from those who are. One of the strongest assumptions in the Blue model is that promoting the good of individuals and companies will add up to the good of the entire system.

THE REDS

Reds are quiet these days, subdued by the collapse of the former Soviet Union. But their way of looking at the world has by no means disappeared; nor, would they say, has it been invalidated. What the Reds see more clearly than anyone else is the way societies systematically enrich those who already are rich, leaving the poor behind.

Reds do not assume that the enriched ones reap just rewards of superior productivity, while the left-behind ones fail because they are unwilling to work or invest. They point out many social processes, from interest payments to differential educations to the distribution of political power, that reward those who already have won and condemn many to lives of continuous losing.

Reds want to fix these inequities and oppressions. They envision a community of people working together to control resources and produce goods. It is a community that respects every person as a full member, sharing both work and output. Red assumptions about human nature are, of course, quite different from those of Blues. Reds believe that people care about the welfare of others and that no one can be truly happy while others are miserable. They believe that people respond to opportunities to serve the larger society, not just to material rewards. Justice to a Red means meeting the needs of all and never discriminating against the least fortunate.

In the Red view, labor—not capital and not natural resources—is the most critical factor of production. Therefore, people should be rewarded for their labor. Some Reds harbor a deep streak of resentment toward people who earn through rents or dividends or other payments related to ownership rather than work.

Most Reds do not trust the free market alone to add up to the common good. They see the need for social control of the economy to keep it functional and equitable. The Soviet Union, modern Reds would say, was not a real example of their philosophy at work—it was too large to manage centrally, and there was too much greed and corruption at the top. For examples of their model at its best, most Reds would point to cooperatives and worker-controlled industries all over the world, or to the mixed socialist-capitalist economies of Scandinavia.

Most Reds, like Blues, see development in terms of large-scale industry but with factories controlled by representatives of their workers. Historically, Reds have not been much concerned about population growth or the environment. They have assumed that people with tools, land, education, and political empowerment will regulate their own numbers. Like Blues, Reds see economic growth as good in itself and as a key to solving social problems. They have not until recently focused on natural resources. The possibility of a limited earth is not easy to accommodate within the Red philosophy.

THE GREENS

If Blues turn their attention to the growth of capital and technology and Reds are especially conscious of labor and patterns of distribution, Greens keep their eyes on resource depletion and pollution. They see not capital, not labor, but materials and energy as the most critical factors of production. They are worried about the size of the economic system relative to the size that nature can support. Whereas both Blues and Reds strive to make economies grow bigger, those who see the world through Green lenses fear that economies and population can grow too big to be sustainable.

Progress, according to Greens, should bring people to a state of sufficiency, not one of constant material growth. The key word is *enough*—enough food, clothing, shelter, education, and health care, and also enough clean water, green trees, and unspoiled natural beauty. The major threats to achieving this vision are production methods that waste resources and populations and economies that stress ecosystems.

The path to development, in this view, is to reduce excessive human demands for both production and reproduction. That means stabilizing or even diminishing populations, moderating material wealth, and choosing technologies that enhance, rather than destroy, the natural world. Greens are as technologically optimistic as Blues and Reds but only when it comes to technologies they like. They believe solar energy can work but not nuclear power. They think materials can be recycled almost indefinitely but not taken from the earth indefinitely. Greens are less likely than Blues or Reds to call upon a generalized technology to solve all problems. No technology, say the Greens, will allow continuous expansion of population and production on a limited planet.

From the Green point of view, both the market and social-equity measures may be necessary in an ideal world, but they will do no good if they are not contained within a mind-set of harmony with the environment. This mind-set would admit that human beings are both communal and individualistic, both greedy and altruistic, but it also would assume that humans have evolved in relationship with nature, that they require continued contact with nature to be truly happy, and that functioning ecosystems are needed to support a functioning economy. Both justice and pragmatism, from the Green point of view, must ensure the welfare of all species, not just *Homo sapiens.*

Green thinkers favor incentives for small families and disincentives for large ones. They favor either adjustments to the market, so that real environmental costs are contained within prices, or strong regulatory measures to prevent public and private actors from destroying resources. Most Greens are not as fond of coercion as Blues think they are, but, as with all these points of view, there is a range of opinion even within a single camp. Some Greens would be quite willing to use the police power of society to protect nature from greedy or senseless depredation. They would argue that crimes against nature are, directly or indirectly, crimes against humanity as well.

Blues tend to see Greens as Reds in disguise. Reds tend to see Greens as elitists who live at the ends of long, winding roads and who do not care about the struggle for economic justice. In fact, Greens do not fit on the Red-Blue spectrum at all.

THE WHITES

The White view combines some aspects of all the previously mentioned colors (which is why I have dubbed it white), but it rejects their centralist, we-will-tell-you-how-to-behave tone. Whites see any policy as worthwhile only if it comes out of the wisdom and efforts of the people. Their emphasis is not on revolutionary redistribution or population control or building factories or planting trees but on empowering people to take control of their own lives. They care less about what should be done and more about who decides.

This model sees progress as local self-reliance. An important concept to the Whites is appropriate technology—technology that uses tools that can be manufactured and maintained at the local level, that uses nearby resources and skills, and that yields products needed close at hand. The best agents for development in this view might be facilitators (something on the order of Peace Corps workers) who are familiar with modern technologies (vaccines, for instance, or how to hybridize plant varieties). A facilitator should know how to tap outside resources and knowledge, when necessary, but should come from, live with, and feel himself to be one of the people.

From the White point of view, all other ideologies originate from citified, intellectual people who confuse their compassion for the poor with their own personal agendas. Environment, class conflict, and the free market are abstractions that show their worth only when applied to specific questions like how to make a particular field grow more grain, or how to allocate the water from a new irrigation system, or how to design a biogas energy system or get a fair price for fish.

According to Whites, big loans for big industry are likely to trample real development; very small loans are what is needed. Market incentives are fine as long as they help little businesses compete instead of reinforcing the power of big businesses. Land reform, family planning, health care, education, reforestation, and prevention of soil erosion are all okay as long as they are planned and controlled by local people. They are not okay if they are promoted by central authorities.

Many White organizations are strongly environmental—such as the rubber tappers in Brazil—because people often have considerable knowledge of local resources and a direct stake in preserving them. But Whites see the environment as a *working* environment, one within which and from which people live, not one that is kept pristine for the admiration of tourists.

The White view of human nature is very positive. It assumes that even the most common people (and especially the most common people) can be entrepreneurial, communal, industrious, moderate in their material demands, and gentle to their environment—if they are free to be that way. Justice in this view means removing the obstacles that keep people from taking control of their own lives.

THE CLASH OF MODELS; THE CONSOLIDATION OF MODELS

I have simplified each of these views greatly, but not as much as they simplify each other. Each side has a tendency to define itself by its own more moderate beliefs and to see the other sides at their extremes.

I could go on to describe how the various parties call upon their own stables of biased experts, how they use the same words in different ways, how they seize upon different indices of good or bad performance, how they commit egregious logical errors. But I want to dwell here not on the ways these protagonists differentiate themselves from one another, but on how their arguments overlap—and are coming together.

Reds the world over are experimenting with the undeniable efficiencies of the market. Some Blues are recognizing that one does not have to pitch out the market completely to impose upon it standards of social justice and environmental stewardship. White development leaders I know are asking themselves how they can scale up, how they can use the skills of large-scale management without losing the ability to listen to the people. Greens are admitting that nature can be preserved without dashing the hopes of human beings, and they are learning the hard way that equating the human population with an out-of-control cancer is not an auspicious beginning for a political discussion. The earth itself is making clear to people from the Himalayas to the World Bank that their visions of development have to rest upon a foundation of a healthy, functioning planet.

The Greens are correct: Population growth that causes people to level forests and overgraze lands exacerbates poverty. The Reds are correct: The helplessness of poverty creates the motivation for parents to have many children, as their only hope of providing for themselves. The Blues are right: Economic development can bring down birthrates. The Whites are right: Development schemes work only when they are not imposed from on high. The Greens are right: Family planning alone is not enough to stabilize populations. The Reds are right: Populations stabilize when all people have a real economic stake in their society.

Capital can be the scarcest factor of production at some times and places, labor at other times and places, materials and energy and pollution-absorption capacity at still others. The limits the Greens point out really are there. So are the injustices the Reds want us to see. So are the market and technical responses the Blues have faith in. And so is the wisdom of the people that the Whites respect.

The earth almost certainly is more resilient than the Greens think it is, and less so than the Blues think it is. The collapse of industrial society because of populations and economies growing past the earth's carrying capacity is not inevitable. It also is not impossible.

What would we do about population, development, and environment if we allowed ourselves to see from all these viewpoints at once? My guess is that at first we would not so much change policy as alter the way we advocate, choose, and implement policy. We would be less doctrinaire and more open to learning. Instead of seeing the results we want to see from the social and technical experiments going on in the world, we would try to see what actually is happening. We would proceed more experimentally. We probably would learn that different continents, cultures, and communities require different blends of the policies advocated by the various points of view, but that in general all the policies being advocated are needed to one extent or another.

Most parts of the world need more productive capital. The places that already are overcapitalized need more efficient, resource-conserving, nonpolluting, elegant capital. Every nation on earth needs technologies that produce the same final result from less energy, material, and labor. True ingenuity and productivity should be rewarded quickly and unambiguously; at the same time, the inequities that stifle ingenuity and productivity should be removed.

Population growth should be slowed and finally stopped everywhere. The way to do that is through both fertility-control technologies and people-based, empowering economic development.

Mindless, wasteful consumption also should be slowed and stopped. How to do that is hard for us in the rich parts of the world to imagine, because it is the change that will affect us most. I believe it is also the change that will free us and delight us most. First, it will involve rethinking our economics enough to get our prices and indices of success (such as the GNP) to reflect real costs and human values. Second, it will require greater sophistication about the goal of growth, which will be seen as a means, not an end. Some kinds of growth are needed and welcome; others are excessive and destructive. We have to be able to differentiate. Finally, I think, we have to distinguish our material needs, which are undeniable, from our nonmaterial needs. The latter, which also are undeniable, involve everything from self-esteem to salvation and cannot be met by material accumulation. Getting that straight—seeing, for example, that a car is a means of transportation, not a means of self-importance—is key not only to "saving the earth" but to real happiness.

In the final analysis, if we were to admit the relevance of all points of view, we would see that we need to pay as close attention to the earth's energy and material flows as we do to our economy's money flows. We need to keep resource accounts, like bank accounts, and never commit the foolishness of spending down our capital while calling it income. If we did that, we would discover that our planet is enormously bountiful but not infinite. We would see how to achieve our human dreams without destroying either the resources or the natural magnificence that will allow future generations to achieve their dreams.

The scarcest resource is not oil, metals, clean air, capital, labor, or technology. It is our willingness to listen to each other and learn from each other and to seek the truth rather than seek to be right. Because we have not done that, another resource has become critically scarce: time. With the world population growing now by 95 million a year, 90 percent of whom are born in poor nations; with forests, soil, water, and ecosystems being degraded around the world; with people to educate and factories to build and new technologies to develop, there is no time to continue the Malthusian argument fruitlessly for another two hundred years.

32. Military Victory, Ecological Defeat

Michael G. Renner

Military historians are likely to remember the recent Gulf War as a modern-day *blitzkrieg,* a triumph of "smart bombs" and other high-tech wizardry. However, while the fighting was brought to a swift conclusion, the onslaught against the environment continues with undiminished ferocity. The Gulf War now ranks among the most ecologically destructive conflicts ever.

Kuwait is liberated, but the region has been transformed into a disaster zone. Hundreds of oil fires are severely polluting the atmosphere; oil deliberately spilled onto the ground and into the Persian Gulf is tainting aquifers and poisoning marine life; attacks on refineries, petrochemical plants, and chemical and nuclear facilities have likely released substantial quantities of toxic materials; damage to public utilities

Michael G. Renner is a senior researcher at the Worldwatch Institute. His work focuses on the links between military activities and the environment.

From "Military Victory, Ecological Defeat," by Michael G. Renner, *World Watch,* July/August 1991, pp. 27–33. WorldWatch Institute. Reprinted by permission.

and roads could trigger health epidemics and famine; the massive movement of troops and their heavy equipment has imperiled an already fragile desert ecology. Kuwaiti officials think the environmental damages may be more severe than the material losses of the war.

But the disparity in the response to the military and environmental aspects of the conflict could hardly be more pronounced. To force Iraq out of Kuwait, no expense or effort was spared. An alliance of more than two dozen countries was carefully crafted, the United Nations machinery for collective security was thrown into high gear, and hundreds of thousands of soldiers and huge amounts of equipment were ferried halfway around the globe.

By contrast, assessing and tackling the ecological consequences of the conflict has been a much lower priority. For example, the effort to contain and clean up the massive oil spill in the Gulf in February was hampered by lack of money and poor coordination among various Saudi government agencies. Attempts to monitor the impacts of oil fires and to put them out also seem woefully inadequate. An air-quality testing lab in Kuwait has not been repaired, and fire-fighting equipment has been slow in coming.

The Gulf War demonstrates the need for the international community to set up a mechanism to cope with the ecological damage arising from armed conflicts. In a broader sense, though, it shows that wars and environmental protection are incompatible. Although international environmental-protection agreements are necessary, the most important step that can be taken is to work for peaceful means of resolving conflicts.

TOWERING INFERNO

Kuwaiti officials estimate that as many as 6 million barrels of oil are going up in flames every day—almost four times the country's oil production per day prior to the Iraqi invasion, or 9 percent of the world's petroleum consumption. Some scientists, including Paul Mason of the British government's Meteorological Office, believe the volume of burning oil is smaller. Beyond dispute, however, is the fact that immense clouds of smoke block the sunlight and turn day into night. In April, daytime temperatures in affected areas were as much as 27 degrees Fahrenheit below normal.

Fire fighters have never confronted so many fires burning simultaneously and in such close proximity. By May, workers had put out only 60 of the 500 to 600 fires, primarily the smaller and more accessible ones. Experts estimate that it will take at least two years to extinguish all of the blazes. By that time, Kuwait may have lost as much as 10 percent of its 92 billion barrels of proven oil reserves—either through combustion or structural damage to its oil reservoirs.

The atmospheric pollution resulting from these fires is almost unprecedented, comparable only to large-scale forest fires and volcanic eruptions. Assuming a burn rate of 6 million barrels per day, as much as 2.5 million tons of soot may be produced in a month—more than four times the average monthly emissions in the entire United

States in 1989 (the last year for which data are available). In addition, more than 1 million tons of sulfur dioxide and approximately 100,000 tons of nitrogen oxides may be released each month.

The clouds of oil smoke also contain large amounts of toxic and potentially carcinogenic substances such as hydrogen sulfide, benzene, and other hydrocarbons. Overall, according to a U.S. Environmental Protection Agency (EPA) estimate in March, roughly 10 times as much air pollution was being emitted in Kuwait as by all U.S. industrial and power-generating plants combined.

The stew of contaminants makes breathing a hazardous undertaking. Rare is the news story about postwar Kuwait that does not mention the sore throat from which virtually everyone seems to suffer. Kuwaiti hospitals are filled with people fallen ill from exposure to the air pollution, and doctors advise those with chronic respiratory problems not to return to Kuwait. Although considerable uncertainty persists concerning the long-term toll on human health, many air pollutants are thought to cause or aggravate a wide range of conditions, including blood disorders, respiratory problems such as asthma and bronchitis, coronary ailments, cancer, and possibly genetic damage. Scientists now acknowledge that prolonged exposure to even low levels of smog—the product of reactions between nitrogen oxides and hydrocarbons in the presence of sunlight—may cause irreparable lung damage. Young children and the elderly are particularly at risk.

Because Kuwaiti oil has a high sulfur content, acid rain—of which sulfur dioxide is a principle component—is expected to afflict the Gulf region and adjacent areas. Acid deposition (which does not always require rain) is known to destroy forests and reduce crop yields. It can also activate several dangerous metals normally found in soil—including aluminum, cadmium, and mercury—making them more soluble and therefore more of a threat to water supplies and edible fish. "Black rain"—soot that is washed out of the skies or eventually falls back to the ground—is coating people, animals, buildings, and crops with an oily, black film.

The effects of air pollution depend not just on the quantity of contaminants released, but on atmospheric conditions that change with the seasons. Summer is a particularly bad time for pollution in the Gulf because of diminished air-cleansing winds and rains, and increased atmospheric inversions that trap pollutants under stagnant layers of air.

THE GEOGRAPHY OF POLLUTION

The densest smoke is found over Kuwait, eastern Iraq, and western and southern Iran. In Kuwait, scientists with the British Meteorological Office recorded 30,000 soot particles per cubic meter of air, 1,000 parts per billion of sulfur dioxide and 50 parts per billion of nitrogen oxides at an altitude of 6,000 feet—about 30, 20, and 10 times, respectively, the levels in a typical city plagued by air pollution.

As far as 1,000 miles away—in parts of Bulgaria, Romania, Turkey, and the Soviet Union that border on the Black Sea—smog levels caused by the oil fires are as serious as the smog found anywhere in Europe under normal conditions, according to Paul Mason. A much larger area—from the waters of the Nile to the snows of the Himalayas—is susceptible to acid rain and soot fallout, according to the Max Planck Institute for Meteorology in Hamburg, Germany.

The burning of such large amounts of oil over long periods could generate enough soot and smoke to diminish solar radiation, thereby lowering daytime temperatures and reducing the amount of rainfall. One ounce of soot can block about two-thirds of the light falling over an area of 280 to 340 square yards. In Kuwait, the amount of solar energy reaching the ground is at times reduced by more than 90 percent. Reduced photosynthesis combined with the deposition of soot and other toxic materials could imperil crops.

Whether such an effect would extend beyond the Gulf region depends on how high the soot climbs and how long it remains there. That, in turn, depends on a range of factors, including the combustion characteristics of the oil fires, the size of the soot particles, and general atmospheric conditions. Intense fires, such as those involving hydrocarbons, create convective currents that give smoke a strong updrift. The finer the particles, the higher they rise, the longer they stay aloft, and the more efficient they are at blocking sunlight, according to Paul Crutzen, director of atmospheric chemistry at the Max Planck Institute for Chemistry in Mainz, Germany. Many small particles appear to be present in the smoke clouds, according to scientists from the British Meteorological Office who gathered samples from a plane in April.

The soot would need to rise to about 35,000 feet for the jet stream to pick it up and carry it around the globe. During April, the smoke plume was reported to be hovering at altitudes of no more than 12,000 feet, with small quantities found as high as 20,000 feet. But the same hot summer weather that helps create temperature inversions near the ground could cause greater updrafting and thus make some of the smoke climb higher. By early May, the U.S. National Oceanic and Atmospheric Administration (NOAA) reported that soot levels at about 20 times above normal readings were recorded at the Mauna Loa Observatory in Hawaii. Presumably, the Kuwaiti oil fires, some 8,000 miles away, are the source of the soot. Despite the elevated soot levels, NOAA does not expect any "significant" environmental impact in North America.

At the same time that it is potentially causing a short-term cooling, the Kuwaiti oil conflagration is also contributing to the long-term phenomenon of global warming. It may add as much as 240 million tons of carbon to the atmosphere in the course of a year—about 4 percent of the current global annual carbon release. This is comparable to the amount produced by Japan, the world's second-largest economy and fourth-largest emitter of carbon dioxide from fossil fuels. Since carbon emissions need to be slashed by at least 20 percent by the year 2005 just to slow climate change, the Kuwaiti oil fires send us another step in the wrong direction.

Nothing in human experience could help model and predict the precise consequences of the Kuwaiti oil blaze. The Gulf region thus has become a huge air pollution laboratory. Unfortunately, the subjects of these dangerous pollution experiments are people, plants, and animals.

OIL ON THE WATER

The oil spilled into the Gulf waters is posing a severe test for marine ecosystems. Estimated at more than 3 million barrels by the Saudi Meteorology and Environmental Protection Administration, the Persian Gulf oil spill roughly equals the largest in history—the Ixtoc well blowout in the Gulf of Mexico in 1979—and is 10 times the size of the Exxon Valdez accident.

Following spills during the eight-year Iran-Iraq war, the Persian Gulf was already a highly stressed environment in poor condition to withstand additional ecological assaults. A relatively shallow sea, it is essentially a closed ecosystem with only a narrow outlet to the Arabian Sea through the Strait of Hormuz. Because Kuwaiti oil is of a "light" variety, up to 40 percent of it may have evaporated. The warm waters of the Gulf allow the remaining oil to decompose fairly rapidly, but significant amounts will foul shorelines or poison the sea bottom. The Saudi government was apparently ill-prepared for dealing with a disaster of such magnitude. By early April, only about half a million barrels of oil had been recovered, and it was clear the focus of the effort was to protect the country's desalination plants.

Considerable harm to Gulf fish and other wildlife—including porpoises, turtles, and seabirds—seems inevitable since many nesting and spawning grounds have been soaked in oil. At least 14,000 birds were killed along the Saudi shore. Some areas are so contaminated that they had to be declared off-limits to fishing, threatening the livelihoods of commercial and subsistence fishers. The Saudi shrimp industry, for example, has been wiped out and is considered unlikely to recover before the end of the decade. Extensive damage to coral reefs and sea grasses also has occurred, according to the EPA. If large quantities of plankton are killed, the entire ecosystem may be threatened.

DESERT WASTELAND

The presence of more than 1 million soldiers with their immense arsenals has placed severe strains on the already fragile desert ecology of Kuwait, Saudi Arabia, and Iraq. Normally inhabited only by Bedouins, the desert of the Arabian peninsula cannot bear such a massive burden. Desert vegetation is sparse, but it helps to stabilize and protect the soil. Tanks and other vehicles have disrupted and compacted the soil and destroyed plants whose root systems are often close to the surface. As a result, the ground in many areas has been rendered susceptible to accelerated erosion. Seeds that lie dormant for large parts of the year, but which spark to life during spring rains, were likely affected.

If a significant portion of the desert vegetation is destroyed, dry spells might be lengthened and the ecological balance could be tipped into long-term decline. It may take hundreds of years for the desert to recover from the massive pre-war maneuvers and the tank battles, according to John Cloudsley-Thompson, an expert on desert ecology at the University of London. The Libyan desert, for example, still bears heavy scars from World War II combat, as do portions of the Negev in Israel from fighting in 1967 and 1973, and parts of the Mojave in southern California from maneuvers in the early 1940s.

The military presence has additional consequences. The armed forces routinely handle massive amounts of highly toxic materials to maintain and operate their tanks, jet fighters, and other pieces of equipment. Experience on U.S. military bases suggests that these substances could severely contaminate underground water supplies (see "War on Nature," May/June 1991) if they're not properly handled. The inhospitable Saudi environment, with its blistering heat and gritty sand, forced the allied troops to use special lubricants of a more toxic nature, according to the U.S. Congressional Research Service, and generally larger amounts of hazardous materials than in more moderate climates. Exposure to even trace amounts of these chemicals through drinking, skin absorption, or inhalation can cause cancer, birth defects, and chromosome damage, and may seriously impair the function of the liver, kidneys, and central nervous system.

Another long-term peril stems from unexploded bombs and mines littering large parts of Iraq and Kuwait. The U.S. Air Force says it dropped 88,500 tons of explosives. The Pentagon generally assumes a 10-percent dud rate, meaning that almost 9,000 tons of explosive material must be cleared. Even an intensive recovery effort will likely fail to detect many of them, as experience from previous wars suggests. Gar Smith reports in *Earth Island Journal* that as much as 20 percent of the 1 million land mines laid by Iraq may remain undetected after cleanup efforts. Clearing the bombs is extremely difficult. Some of the "smart bombs" can only be disarmed with special tools and techniques that may be unavailable to Iraq. According to a report by the San Francisco-based Arms Control Research Center, some of these bombs are magnetically triggered. Any metal tool, such as a farmer's hoe or plow, could detonate them.

CHEMICAL WARFARE

The veil of military secrecy and post-war chaos in Iraq have precluded a full assessment of the effects of allied air attacks on Iraq's chemical, biological, and nuclear facilities and its refineries and petrochemical plants. Many of these facilities are located close to civilian population centers along the Tigris and Euphrates rivers. The incineration of materials produced and stored at these installations may well have generated a variety of deadly toxins, including cyanide, dioxin, and PCBs.

Reports in the German press, including such well-respected newspapers as *Frankfurter Rundschau* and *Handelsblatt*, suggest that toxic vapors escaped following air raids on chemical facilities, killing scores of Iraqi civilians. The nerve gases tabun and sarin, which Iraq has admitted possessing, evaporate rapidly and thus do not pose a persistent hazard. But another agent in the Iraqi arsenal, mustard gas, which is a mutagen and a carcinogen, is much longer-lived. A spokesman for the Patriotic Union of Kurdistan, an Iraqi opposition group, asserted in early February that allied attacks against chemical and ammunition plants led to widespread contamination of water resources.

VICTOR OR VANQUISHED?

Sadly, the environmental disaster in the Gulf was preventable. In the months leading up to the outbreak of armed conflict, the alternatives of resorting to military force or relying on economic sanctions were debated, but the latter option was given too little time to work. Sanctions may have been less swift and certain than force, but would likely have spared many lives and avoided the tragic environmental effects.

That Saddam Hussein would set the torch to Kuwait's oil wells was no secret; he repeatedly threatened to do so if attacked by the U.S.-led coalition. The U.S. and British governments even commissioned studies about the potential environmental impact of such an act, but proceeded with their military plans anyway. The responsibility for the environmental destruction lies with Saddam Hussein's regime, but the devastation was either underestimated by the allied governments or considered an acceptable price of victory.

With such results, it is difficult to distinguish between victor and vanquished. Indeed, the war's ecological impact extends far beyond the battlefield, blurring the distinction between the combatants and countries that were not party to the conflict and had no say over its course.

In light of the Gulf War's ecological devastation, the time has come for the world community to consider creating a stronger convention for the protection of the environment in war. The existing United Nations "Convention on the Prohibition of Military or Any Other Hostile Use of Environmental Modification Techniques" is tailored to proscribe use of the environment as a weapon. A 1977 amendment to the 1949 Geneva Protocols prohibits means of warfare that are intended or expected to damage the environment and, in consequence, jeopardize the health and lives of the civilian population.

Neither agreement, however, includes any enforcement mechanisms and both were ignored by the belligerents in the Gulf War. Establishing such mechanisms, including trade embargoes and other nonviolent sanctions against offenders, would be an important first step. Next, lowering the threshold at which the prohibitions apply and making more explicit what acts they cover would give them more practical meaning.

But even a strengthened international code is of limited value. The conduct of war and the protection of the natural environment are fundamentally incompatible objectives. War on the environment is, unfortunately, nothing new. From the Punic Wars in the third century B.C. on, armies have poisoned wells, salted soils, and destroyed crops to foil the enemy. However, over time, the environmental impact of warfare has grown as sophisticated technology has boosted the firepower, range, and speed of weapons. In addition, modern industries present many high-profile targets whose destruction can wreak environmental devastation on a vast scale.

It was after the dawn of the atomic age that nations gradually came to realize that nuclear arsenals, if used, would destroy what they were supposed to defend. Now, in the wake of the Gulf War and its immense environmental toll, conventional warfare, too, may come to be seen as a less-acceptable means of settling conflicts.

33. What New World Order?

Joseph S. Nye, Jr.

The 1991 Persian Gulf War was, according to President Bush, about "more than one small country; it is a big idea: a new world order," with "new ways of working with other nations . . . peaceful settlement of disputes, solidarity against aggression, reduced and controlled arsenals and just treatment of all peoples." Not long after the war, however, the flow of White House words about a new world order slowed to a trickle.

Like Woodrow Wilson's fourteen points or Franklin Roosevelt's four freedoms, George Bush's grand rhetoric expressed the larger goals important for public support when a liberal democratic state goes to war. But after the war, when reality intruded, grand schemes turned into a liability. People were led to compare the war's imperfect outcome with an impossible ideal. The proper standard for judgment should have been what the world would look like if Saddam Hussein had been left in possession of Kuwait. The victory lost its lustre because of an unfair comparison that the president inadvertently encouraged, and recession shifted the political agenda to the domestic economy. The White House thus decided to lower the rhetorical volume.

II

The administration faces a deeper problem than mere political tactics. The world has changed more rapidly in the past two years than at any time since 1945. It is difficult to keep one's conceptual footing within such fundamental shifts in politics. Familiar concepts fail to fit a new reality. It is worth recalling that it took Americans several years to adjust to the last great shift in the late 1940s. But the Bush administration, famous for eschewing "the vision thing," added to the confusion because it had never really thought through what it meant by the concept it launched. Neither the admin-

Joseph S. Nye, Jr., is Director of the Harvard Center for International Affairs and author of *Bound To Lead: The Changing Nature of American Power.*

From "What New World Order?" by Joseph S. Nye, Jr. Reprinted by permission of *Foreign Affairs*, Vol 71, No 2, Spring 1992. Copyright © 1992 by the Council on Foreign Relations, Inc.

istration nor its critics were clear about the fact that the term "world order" is used in two very different ways in discussions of world politics.

Realists, in the tradition of Richard Nixon and Henry Kissinger, see international politics occurring among sovereign states balancing each others' power. World order is the product of a stable distribution of power among the major states. Liberals, in the tradition of Woodrow Wilson and Jimmy Carter, look at relations among peoples as well as states. They see order arising from broad values like democracy and human rights, as well as from international law and institutions such as the United Nations.

The problem for the Bush administration was that it thought and acted like Nixon, but borrowed the rhetoric of Wilson and Carter. Both aspects of order are relevant to the current world situation, but the administration has not sorted out the relation between them.

From the realist perspective there is definitely a new world order, but it did not begin with the Gulf War. Since order has little to do with justice, but a lot to do with the distribution of power among states, realists date the new world order from the collapse of the Soviet empire in eastern Europe in the autumn of 1989. The rapid decline of the Soviet Union caused the end of the old bipolar order that had persisted for nearly half a century.

The old world order provided a stability of sorts. The Cold War exacerbated a number of Third World conflicts, but economic conflicts among the United States, Europe and Japan were dampened by common concerns about the Soviet military threat. Bitter ethnic divisions were kept under a tight lid by the Soviet presence in eastern Europe. A number of Third World conflicts were averted or shortened when the superpowers feared that their clients might drag them too close to the nuclear abyss. The various Arab-Israeli wars, for example, were brief. In fact some experts believe that a stronger Soviet Union would never have allowed its Iraqi client to invade Kuwait. If so Kuwait can be counted as the victim rather than the cause of the new world order.

Some analysts see the collapse of the Cold War as the victory of liberal capitalism and the end of the large ideological cleavages that drove the great international conflicts of this century. There is no single competitor to liberal capitalism as an overarching ideology. Rather than the end of history, the post-Cold War world is witnessing a return of history in the diversity of sources of international conflict. Liberal capitalism has many competitors, albeit fragmented ones. Examples include the indigenous neo-Maoism of Peru's Shining Path guerrilla movement, the many variants of Islamic fundamentalism and the rise of ethnic nationalism.

This does not mean that the new world politics will be "back to the future."[1] There is an enormous difference between the democratically tamed and institutionally harnessed nationalisms of western Europe and the revival in eastern Europe of untamed nationalisms whose ancient animosities were never resolved in the institutional structure of state communism and the Soviet empire.

---

1. See John Mearsheimer, "Back to the Future: Instability in Europe After the Cold War," *International Security,* Summer 1990.

Moreover national boundaries will be more permeable than in the past. Nationalism and transnationalism will be contending forces in the new world politics. Large transnational corporations distribute economic production according to global strategies. Transnational technological changes in communications and transportation are making the world smaller. Diplomacy occurs in real time; both George Bush and Saddam Hussein watched Cable News Network for the latest reports. Human rights violations and mass suffering in distant parts of the globe are brought home by television. Although Marshall McLuhan argued that modern communications would produce a "global village," his metaphor was misleading because a global political identity remains feeble. In fact nationalism is becoming stronger in most of the world, not weaker. Instead of one global village there are villages around the globe more aware of each other. That, in turn, increases the opportunities for conflict.

Not all transnational forces are benign any more than all nationalisms are malign. Transnational drug trade, terrorism, the spread of AIDS and global warming are cases in point. With time, technology spreads across borders, and the technologies of weapons of mass destruction are now more than a half century old. The collapse of the Soviet Union removes two of the factors that slowed the spread of nuclear weapons in the old world order: tight Soviet technological controls and influence over its client states. The United States cannot escape from these transnational problems, and few of them are susceptible to unilateral solutions. Like other countries in the new world order, the United States will be caught in the dialogue between the national and the transnational.

III

The United States will need power to influence others in regard to both transnational and traditional concerns. If the old world order has collapsed, what will be the new distribution of power? Over the past few years of dramatic change, different observers have claimed to discern five alternatives.

Return to bipolarity. Before the failure of the August coup and the final collapse of the Soviet Union, some argued that a newly repressive Soviet or Russian regime would create a harsh international climate and a return to the Cold War. But even if the coup had succeeded, it would not have restored bipolarity. The decline of the Soviet Union stemmed in large part from overcentralization. Stalin's system was unable to cope with the Third Industrial Revolution, in which flexible use of information is the key to successful economic growth. The return of the centralizers might have created a nasty international climate, but rather than restoring Soviet strength, recentralization would have continued the long-term decline of the Soviet economy. The same would be true for a centralizing Russian dictatorship.

Multipolarity. This is a popular cliché that drips easily from the pens of editorialists, but if used to imply an historical analogy with the nineteenth century it is highly misleading, for the old order rested on a balance of five roughly equal great powers while today's great powers are far from equally balanced. Russia will continue to suffer from economic weakness, and its reform is a question of decades, not years. China is a developing country and, despite favorable growth, will remain so well into the next century. Europe is the equal of the United States in population, economy and human resources. Even after the December 1991 summit at Maastricht, however, Europe lacks the political unity necessary to act as a single global power.

Japan is well endowed with economic and technological strength, but its portfolio of power resources is limited in the hard military area as well as in the cultural and ideological appeal that provides soft power. Japan would have to make major changes in its attitudes toward military power as well as in its ethnocentricity before it would be a challenger on the scale of the United States.

Three economic blocs. Those who devalue military power argue that Europe and Japan will be superpowers in a world of restrictive economic blocs. An Asian bloc will form around the yen, a western hemisphere bloc around the dollar and a European bloc (including remnants of the former Soviet Union) will cluster around the European Currency Unit (according to optimists) or the deutsche mark (in the view of pessimists). Others foresee a European versus a Pacific bloc.[2]

There are three problems with this vision. First, it runs counter to the thrust of global technological trends. While regional trade will certainly grow, many firms would not want to be limited to one-third of the global market and would resist restrictive regionalism. Second, restrictive regional blocs run against nationalistic concerns of some of the lesser states that need a global system to protect themselves against domination by their large neighbors. Japan's Asian neighbors do not want to be locked up in a yen bloc with Japan. There will continue to be a constituency for a broader international trade system.

Most important, however, this vision is too dismissive of security concerns. With large nuclear neighbors in turmoil, both Europe and Japan want to keep their American insurance policies against uncertainty. The second Russian revolution is still in its early years, and China faces a generational transition. It is difficult to imagine the United States continuing its security guarantees in the context of trade wars. The end of the Cold War was not marked by European and Japanese calls for withdrawal of American troops. European and Japanese security concerns are likely to set limits on how restrictive the economic blocs become.

Unipolar hegemony. According to Charles Krauthammer, the Gulf War marked the beginning of a Pax Americana in which the world will acquiesce in a benign American hegemony.[3] The premise is correct that the collapse of the Soviet Union left the world with only one superpower, but the hegemonic conclusion does not follow. For one thing the world economy is tripolar and has been since the 1970s. Europe, Japan and the United States account for two-thirds of the world's product. In economics, at least, the United States cannot exercise hegemony.

Hegemony is also unlikely because of the diffusion of power through transna-

2. Jacques Attali, *Lignes d'Horizon*, Paris: Foyard, 1990.

3. Charles Krauthammer, "The Unipolar Moment," in *Rethinking American Security: Beyond Cold War to New World Order*, Graham T. Allison and Gregory F. Treverton, eds., New York: Norton, 1992.

tional interdependence. To cite a few examples: private actors in global capital markets constrain the way interest rates can be used to manage the American economy; the transnational spread of technology increases the destructive capacities of otherwise poor and weak states; and a number of issues on the international agenda—drug trade, AIDS, migration, global warming—have deep societal roots in more than one country and flow across borders largely outside of governmental control. Since military means are not very effective in coping with such problems, no great power, the United States included, will be able to solve them alone.

Multilevel interdependence. No single hierarchy describes adequately a world politics with multiple structures. The distribution of power in world politics has become like a layer cake. The top military layer is largely unipolar, for there is no other military power comparable to the United States. The economic middle layer is tripolar and has been for two decades. The bottom layer of transnational interdependence shows a diffusion of power.

None of this complexity would matter if military power were as fungible as money and could determine the outcomes in all areas. In describing Europe before 1914, the British historian A.J.P. Taylor wrote that the test of a great power was the ability to prevail in war. But military prowess is a poor predictor of the outcomes in the economic and transnational layers of current world politics. The United States is better placed with a more diversified portfolio of power resources than any other country, but the new world order will not be an era of American hegemony. We must be wary of the prison of old concepts.

The world order after the Cold War is sui generis, and we overly constrain our understanding by trying to force it into the procrustean bed of traditional metaphors with their mechanical polarities. Power is becoming more multidimensional, structures more complex and states themselves more permeable. This added complexity means that world order must rest on more than the traditional military balance of power alone. The problems encountered by the Bush administration at the end of the Gulf War are illustrative. The traditional approach of balancing Iran and Iraq was clearly not enough, and U.N. resolutions 687 and 688 (which dealt with Iraq's weapons and refugees) went deep into areas of national sovereignty.

The realist view of world order, resting on a balance of military power, is necessary but not sufficient, because it does not take into account the long-term societal changes that have been slowly moving the world away from the Westphalian system. In 1648, after thirty years of tearing each other apart over religion, the European states agreed in the Treaty of Westphalia that the ruler, in effect, would determine the religion of a state regardless of popular preference. Order was based on the sovereignty of states, not the sovereignty of peoples.

The mechanical balance of states was slowly eroded over the ensuing centuries by the growth of nationalism and democratic participation, but the norms of state sovereignty persist. Now the rapid growth in transnational communications, migration and economic interdependence is accelerating the erosion of that classical conception and increasing the gap between norm and reality.

IV

This evolution makes more relevant the liberal conception of a world society of peoples as well as states, and of order resting on values and institutions as well as military power. Liberal views that were once regarded as hopelessly utopian, such as Immanuel Kant's plea for a peaceful league of democracies, seem less far-fetched now that political scientists report virtually no cases of democracies going to war with each other. Current debates over the effects of German reunification, for example, pit against each other realists who see western Europe going back to the troubled balance of power, and liberals who fault such analysis for neglecting the fact that unlike 1870, 1914 or 1939, the new Germany is democratic and deeply enmeshed with its western neighbors through the institutions of the European Community. Moreover the interactions between democratic politics and international institutions reinforce each other.

Of course the game is still open in post-Cold War Europe, and Europe is very different from other parts of the world such as the Middle East, where traditional views of the balance of military power are still the core of wisdom. But the experience of Europe (and the democratic market economies more generally) suggests that in at least parts of this hybrid world, conceptions of divisible and transferable sovereignty may play an increasing part in a new world order. The complex practices of the European Community are a case in point.

These liberal conceptions of order are not entirely new. The Cold War order had norms and institutions, but they played a limited role. During World War II Roosevelt, Stalin and Churchill agreed to a United Nations that assumed a multipolar distribution of power. The U.N. Security Council would enforce the doctrine of collective security and nonaggression against smaller states while the five great powers were protected by their vetos.

Even this abbreviated version of Woodrow Wilson's institutional approach to order was hobbled, however, by the rise of bipolarity. The superpowers vetoed each other's initiatives, and the organization was reduced to the more modest role of stationing peacekeepers to observe ceasefires rather than repelling aggressors. The one exception, the U.N. role in the Korean War, proved the rule; it was made possible only by a temporary Soviet boycott of the Security Council in June 1950. When the decline of Soviet power led to Moscow's new policy of cooperation with Washington in applying the U.N. doctrine of collective security against Baghdad, it was less the arrival of a new world order than the reappearance of an aspect of the liberal institutional order that was supposed to have come into effect in 1945.

But just as the Gulf War resurrected one aspect of the liberal approach to world order, it also exposed an important weakness in the liberal conception. The doctrine of collective security enshrined in the U.N. Charter is state-centric, applicable when borders are crossed but not when force is used against peoples within a state.

Liberals try to escape this problem by appealing to the principles of democracy and self-determination. Let peoples within states vote on whether they want to be protected behind borders of their own. But self-determination is not as simple as it sounds. Who decides what self will determine? Take Ireland, for example. If Irish people voted within the existing political boundaries, Ulster would have a Protestant majority, but if the Irish voted within the geographical boundaries of the island, Ulster would be encompassed within a Catholic majority. Whoever has the power to determine the boundaries of the vote has the power to determine the outcome.

A similar problem plagues Yugoslavia. It seemed clear that relatively homogeneous Slovenia should be allowed to vote on self-determination, but a similar vote in Croatia turns Serbs in some districts into a minority who then demand a vote on succession from an independent Croatia. It is not surprising that issues of secession are more often determined by bullets than ballots.

Nor are these rare examples. Less than ten percent of the 170 states in today's world are ethnically homogeneous. Only half have one ethnic group that accounts for as much as 75 percent of their population. Most of the republics of the former Soviet Union have significant minorities and many have disputed borders. Africa is a continent of a thousand ethnic and linguistic peoples squeezed within and across some forty-odd states. Once such states are called into question, it is difficult to see where the process ends. In such a world, federalism, local autonomy and international surveillance of minority rights hold some promise, but a policy of unqualified support for national self-determination would turn into a principle of enormous world disorder.

V

How then is it possible to preserve some order in traditional terms of the balance of power among sovereign states, while also moving toward international institutions that promote "justice among peoples?"

International institutions are gradually evolving in just such a post-Westphalian direction. Already in 1945, articles 55 and 56 of the U.N. Charter pledged states to collective responsibility for observance of human rights and fundamental freedoms. Even before the recent Security Council resolutions authorizing postwar interventions in Iraq, U.N. recommendations of sanctions against apartheid in South Africa set a precedent for not being strictly limited by the charter's statements about sovereignty. In Europe the 1975 Helsinki Accords codified human rights. Violations can be referred to the European Conference on Security and Cooperation or the Council of Europe. International law is gradually evolving. In 1965 the American Law Institute defined international law as "rules and principles . . . dealing with the conduct of states and international organizations." More recently the institute's lawyers added the revealing words, "as well as some of their relations with persons." Individual and minority rights are increasingly treated as more than just national concerns.

Of course in many, perhaps most, parts of the world such principles are flouted and violations go unpunished. To mount an armed multilateral intervention to right all such wrongs would be another source of enormous disorder. But we should not think of intervention solely in military terms. Intervention is a matter of degree, with actions ranging from statements and limited economic measures at the low end of the spectrum to full-fledged invasions at the high end. The U.N. Security Council and regional organizations may decide on limited nonmilitary interventions. Multilateral infringements of sovereignty will gradually increase without suddenly disrupting the distribution of power among states.

On a larger scale the Security Council can act under chapter seven of the U.N. Charter if it determines that internal violence or development of weapons of mass destruction are likely to spill over into a more general threat to the peace in a region. Such definitions are somewhat elastic—witness the imposition of sanctions against Rhodesia in the 1960s. The reasons for multilateral intervention will gradually expand over time. Although Iraq was a special case because of its blatant aggression, Security Council resolutions 687 and 688 may create a precedent for other situations where mistreatment of minorities threatens relations with neighbors or where a country is developing weapons of mass destruction in violation of its obligations under the Nonproliferation Treaty.

In other instances groups of states may act on a regional basis to deal with internal fighting, as Nigeria and others did by sending troops to Liberia under the framework of the Economic Community of West African States. In Yugoslavia the European Community employed the threat of economic sanctions as well as observer missions in an effort to limit the violence. In Haiti members of the Organization of American States imposed economic sanctions in response to the overthrow of a democratically elected government. None of the efforts was fully successful, but each involved intervention in what are usually considered domestic affairs.

It may also be possible to enhance U.N. capabilities for independent actions in cases where the permanent members do not have a direct interest. The gains for collective security from the Gulf War would be squandered, for example, if there were no international response to a Rwandan invasion of Uganda or a Libyan incursion into Chad. A U.N. rapid deployment force of 60,000 troops formed from earmarked brigades from a dozen countries could cope with a number of such contingencies as determined by the Security Council.

Such a fighting force, as contrasted to traditional peacekeeping forces, could be formed around a professional core of 5,000 U.N. soldiers. They would need frequent joint exercises to develop common command and operational procedures. The U.S. involvement could be limited to logistical and air support and, of course, the right to help control its activities through the Security Council and the military staff committee. Many details need to be worked out, but an idea that would have been silly or utopian during the Cold War suddenly becomes worth detailed practical examination in the aftermath of the Cold War and Gulf War.

Such imperfect principles and institutions will leave much room for domestic violence and injustice among peoples. Yugoslavia is an immediate example, and it will not be alone. But the moral horrors will be less than if policymakers were to try either to right all wrongs by force or, alternatively, to return to the unmodified Westphalian system. Among the staunchest defenders of the old system are the poorly integrated postcolonial states whose elites fear that new doctrines of multilateral intervention by the United Nations will infringe their sovereignty. The transition to a liberal vision of a new world order is occurring, but not smoothly. Liberals must realize that the evolution beyond Westphalia is a matter of decades and centuries, while realists must recognize that the traditional definitions of power and order in purely military terms miss the changes that are occurring in a world of transnational communications and instant information.

VI

What is the American national interest in promoting a new world order? As election-year rhetoric asks, why not put America first? The country faces a number of serious domestic problems. The net savings rate has dropped from about 7.5 percent of gross national product in the 1970s to about 4.5 percent today. The federal budget deficit eats up about half of net private savings. The educational system is not producing a high enough level of skills for continuing progress in an information-age economy. In terms of high school dropouts the United States is wasting a quarter of its human resources compared to five percent for Japan. There is a need for investment in public infrastructure. Clearly we need to do more at home.

But Americans should beware of a false debate between domestic and foreign needs. In a world of transnational interdependence the distinction between domestic and foreign policy becomes blurred. The real choice that Americans face is not between domestic and foreign policy, but between consumption and investment. President Bush has said that the United States has the will but not the wallet. The opposite is closer to the mark. The United States spends about 31 percent of gross national product on government at all levels, while most European countries spend closer to 40 percent. The United States is a rich country that acts poor. America's U.N. dues are a relative pittance, and many countries see our failure to pay them as proof of our hypocrisy about a new world order. Similarly Europeans cite our low levels of aid and question our seriousness and relevance to stability in postcommunist eastern Europe. The American economy could support a few more percentage points of gross national product to invest at home while helping to maintain international order.

But why spend anything on international order? The simple answer is that in a world of transnational interdependence, international disorder can hurt, influence or disturb the majority of people living in the United States. A nuclear weapon sold or stolen from a former Soviet republic could be brought into the United States in the hold of a freighter or the cargo bay of a commercial airliner. Chaos in a Middle Eastern country can sustain terrorists who threaten American travelers abroad. A Caribbean country's inability to control drugs or disease could mean larger flows of both across our borders. Release of ozone-depleting chemicals overseas can contribute to a rise in skin cancer in the United States. With more than ten percent of U.S. gross national product exported, American jobs depend upon international economic conditions. And even though not a direct threat to U.S. security, the human rights violations brought home to Americans by transnational communications are discomforting. If the rest of the world is mired in chaos, and governments are too weak to deal with their parts of a transnational problem, the U.S. government will not be able to solve such problems alone or influence them to reduce the damage done to Americans.

In addition, even after the Cold War the United States has geopolitical interests in international stability. The United States has a continuing interest that no hostile power control the continent of Europe or that European turmoil draw us in under adverse circumstances, as happened twice before in this century. While such events now have a much lower probability and thus can be met with a much reduced investment, a wise foreign policy still takes out insurance against low probability events. Given the uncertainties in the aftermath of the Soviet collapse, an American security presence, even at greatly reduced troop levels, has a reassuring effect as European integration proceeds. The United States has an interest in a stable and prosperous western Europe that gradually draws the eastern part of the continent toward pluralism and democracy. The primary role will rest with the Europeans, but if the United States were to divorce itself from the process, we might find the future geopolitical situation far less stable.

The United States also has geopolitical and economic interests in the Pacific. The United States is the only country with both economic and military power resources in the region, and its continued presence is desired by Asian powers who do not want Japan to remilitarize. Japan's current political consensus is opposed to such a military role, and Japanese leaders realize it would be destabilizing in the region. With a relatively small but symbolically important military presence the United States can help to provide reassurance in the region, while encouraging Japan to invest its economic power not in military force but in international institutions and to help share the lead in dealing with transnational issues.

In realist terms the United States will remain the world's largest power well into the next century. Economists have long noted that if the largest consumer of a collective good, such as order, does not take the lead in organizing its production, there is little likelihood that the good will be produced by others. That was the situation in the 1920s when the United States refused to join the League of Nations or cooperate in preserving the stability of the international economy. Isolationism in the 1920s came back to haunt and hurt Americans a decade later. There is even less room for neo-isolationism today.

Why not simply leave the task of world order to the United Nations? Because the United Nations is the sum of its member nations and the United States is by far the largest member. Large scale U.N. efforts like the repulse of Iraq will continue to require the participation of the world's largest power.

The United States correctly wants to avoid the role of world policeman. The way to steer a middle path between bearing too much and too little of the international burden is to renew the American commitment to multilateral institutions that fell into abeyance in the 1980s. The use of multilateral institutions, while sometimes constraining, also helps share the burden that the American people do not want to bear alone. Multilateralism also limits the resentments and balances the behavior of other nations that can lead them to resist American wishes and make it harder for Americans to achieve national interests.

While the Bush administration failed in its policies toward Iraq before and at the end of the Gulf War, its actions in organizing the multilateral coalition that expelled Iraq from Kuwait fit the national interest in a new world order. The administration combined both the hard power of military might and the soft power of using institutions to co-opt others to share the burden. Without the U.N. resolutions it might have been impossible for the Saudis to accept troops and for others to send troops. Nor is it likely that the United States could have persuaded others to foot nearly the entire bill for the war. Had there been no response to Iraq's aggression and violation of its obligations under the Nonproliferation Treaty, the post-Cold War order would be far more dangerous.

In short the new world order has begun. It is messy, evolving and not susceptible to simple formulation or manipulation. Russia and China face uncertain futures. Regional bullies will seek weapons of mass destruction. Protectionist pressure may increase. The United States will have to combine both traditional power and liberal institutional approaches if it is to pursue effectively its national interest. We want to promote liberal democracy and human rights where we can do so without causing chaos. The reason is obvious: liberal democratic governments are less likely to threaten us over time. We will need to maintain our alliances and a balance of power in the short run, while simultaneously working to promote democratic values, human rights and institutions for the long run. To do less is to have only a fraction of a foreign policy.

34. Can the United States Afford the New World Order?

David P. Calleo

The answer depends both on the nature of the new world order and on what is meant by "afford." The latter consideration should come first, since it helps clarify the real issue—the distinction between America's capabilities and priorities.

David P. Calleo is Dean Acheson Professor of European Studies at the Paul H. Nitze School of Advanced International Studies, the Johns Hopkins University.
From "Can the United States Afford the New World Order?" by David P. Calleo. The SAIS Review, Vol 12, No 2, pp. 23–33. Reprinted by permission.

WHAT CAN AMERICA AFFORD?

It may sound boastful to say that the United States is the only real superpower. Nevertheless, it seems true—certainly in a military sense. America's military budget is roughly three times that of Britain, France and Germany combined, and ten times that of Japan. The U.S. more than balanced the old Soviet Union in strategic nuclear power, has a fleet unchallenged on any ocean, a formidable and highly mobile land army and a huge air force. Technologically, these forces are unmatched.

If history is any guide, America's military spending could be still much larger. America's military outlays, in constant dollars, are close to their highest level since World War II. But they have fallen dramatically as a percentage of GNP from the levels of the 1950s and 1960s. The huge military buildup in the Reagan years, while it pushed the level of real annual defense outlays up by roughly 50% over 1980, only raised the ratio of military spending to GNP from 4.90% in 1980 to a high of 6.45% in 1986—still far below the 7.5% to 9.6% range of the 1960s, or the 10.2% to 14.4% range between 1952 and 1959. The United States may also be regarded as the only superpower in a political and diplomatic sense. As many analysts have been at pains to stress, America has a unique ability to rally other nations to common purposes. Through NATO, the U.S. has long exercised the leading role in organizing Europe's collective security. America's military relationship has been still more hegemonic with Japan. Years of competition have developed into a special relationship with the Soviets as well.

The Gulf War highlighted these American strengths. The U.S. provided the great bulk of both the military force and the diplomatic initiative. The coalition included not only substantial forces from Britain and France, but also from several Middle Eastern countries, together with strong diplomatic support from the Soviet Union, and substantial Japanese, German and Middle Eastern financial contributions. Indeed, America's allies more or less paid the operating costs of the American forces. If the Gulf War defines the new world order, the United States seems well able to afford it.

A LESS OPTIMISTIC VIEW: THE FISCAL CRISIS

Allied contributions, of course, defrayed only the war's direct operating costs. They did not cover the huge capital investments needed to create the American forces, nor the high costs of keeping the men and equipment for similar operations in the future. America's dazzling military performance, moreover, was the reward earned by the enormous military buildup of the Reagan years. But that buildup had already lost its forward momentum around 1987. The erosion thereafter has reflected not so much a lessening enthusiasm for military strength, as an acute federal budgetary crisis. Federal borrowing needs were 6.6% of the GNP in fiscal 1990 and 7.4% or $422 billion in fiscal 1991.

Deficits on this huge scale go back to the fiscal year 1982, when Reagan's mili-

tary buildup coincided with his tax cut. The predictable budgetary shortfall was supposed to be made up from rapid economic growth following the "supply-side" tax cuts
of 1981, and from large cuts expected in the government's civilian spending. In fact,
neither growth nor cuts in civilian spending filled the budgetary gap. Meanwhile, tight
monetary policy and the indexing of tax brackets blocked those regular tax increases
through inflation that had helped to mitigate earlier deficits.

Soaring federal deficits were a major issue in the 1984 presidential elections.
The Democratic candidate, Walter Mondale, called for major tax increases, while
President Reagan reiterated his support for heavy cuts in civilian spending. Mondale
was defeated but Reagan, reelected, failed to achieve civilian cuts on the necessary
scale. The same pattern was repeated in the 1988 elections—when George Bush defeated Michael Dukakis.

WHY U.S. DEFICITS ARE SO INTRACTABLE

The reasons why neither tax increases nor civilian spending cuts have proved to be viable reflect more than a simple failure of leadership. A quick look at what might be
called America's "fiscal profile," shown here in comparison with that of France and
Germany, suggests why.

American levels of both taxation and civilian spending are much lower than in
France or Germany. This reflects a different American division of labor between public and private sectors. Logically, the weight of taxation ought to be considered in relation to the extent of public goods provided. Government in the U.S. provides far
fewer civilian "public goods" than government in France. America's private sector has
a much larger role in providing pensions, health care, education, the arts, urban or
rural amenities, or infrastructure in general. Seen in the light of this fact, U.S. taxes
are very high in proportion to the civil goods delivered to the taxpayer. Indeed, when
direct government transfers to private households are deducted, American tax levels
are as high as European. When all civilian public goods are taken into account, American tax levels seem much higher in relation to what is returned. And since this different division between public and private sectors means that the American taxpayer

TABLE 34–1   Total Government Outlays and Receipts
Percentage of GDP

	1967		1977		1988	
	OUTLAYS	*RECEIPTS*	*OUTLAYS*	*RECEIPTS*	*OUTLAYS*	*RECEIPTS*
U.S.	30.5	27.1	31.6	29.9	36.3	31.5
Germany	38.6	36.7	47.8	44.7	46.6	43.7
France	39.0	38.2	44.6	41.1	50.3	47.1

Source: OECD, *Economic Outlook*, 48 (Paris: OECD, December 1990), p. 189–90.

has to provide much more for himself, he not unreasonably resists having to pay anything like European taxes. Considering the direct return to himself, his taxes are already comparatively high.

There is, as yet, no drive to push American civil spending to European levels. The American middle class has never experienced the same linkage between its own welfare and security and higher government spending. Whereas Europe's welfare state is by and large for the middle class, America's is for the poor. The greatest benefits for the well-to-do American taxpayer probably come from tax exemptions rather than direct benefits. Thus, there is nothing like the same constituency for higher spending—or taxes.

Two additional considerations also inhibit tax increases in the U.S. In some critical fields—particularly health care—the American division between public and private sectors seems notably less efficient than in France. Medical care costs the American economy proportionately much more than the French, with no correspondingly obvious superiority in quality. At the same time, the American system leaves roughly 17 percent of the population without formal insurance coverage (1987 figures). Such high medical costs are a further squeeze on private budgets in America. The significance of our bloated health sector is difficult to exaggerate. Virtually the entire increase in the American consumption in the 1980s can be accounted for by the rising cost of medical care.

Reluctance to pay higher taxes is also reinforced by the stagnation in household incomes. Figures show median household incomes in the United States virtually stationary from 1973 to 1987. Improvement was confined mostly to the upper brackets and attributable in many cases to more households with a second wage earner. This stagnation of household incomes seems closely tied to the shift from jobs in manufacturing to jobs in services. Average wages in American services have been a mere 44% of those in manufacturing (1987 figures)—a disparity explained presumably by the low level of productivity growth in the service sector. The recompense is that the U.S. has a relatively low level of unemployment. In any event, stagnant household incomes in the U.S. reinforce the reluctance to pay higher taxes.

While all these conditions reinforce resistance to higher taxes, they also help explain the reluctance to cut the comparatively low level of civilian spending still further. America's swelling "underclass" causes widespread anxiety and indignation, as does the deteriorating physical infrastructure and environment. Disaffection with the educational system is widespread, and the perception is growing that public spending in general is inadequate to sustain growth and competitiveness.

Taken together, these considerations explain America's political paralysis before its huge federal deficits. That paralysis could not have continued, however, except for the relative ease with which the deficits have been financed, despite a very low level of domestic saving. Thanks to its huge economy, and the dollar's international role, the U.S. has been able to summon a substantial part of the rest of the world's savings. The high level of borrowing has not produced the same acute discomfort that would be normal elsewhere. Thus, even if political leaders on all sides deplore the deficit, there is no compelling reason to adopt bold and painful policies to reverse it. It is eas-

TABLE 34–2 Government Spending and Household Taxes
Percentage of GDP, 1986

	NET HOUSEHOLD TAXES (1)	NET GOVERNMENT DISBURSEMENTS (2)	GOVERNMENT CONSUMPTION FOR WELFARE GOODS AND SERVICES (3)	HOUSEHOLD TAXES LESS WELFARE (1)–(3)	GOVERNMENT DISBURSEMENTS LESS WELFARE (2)–(3)
U.S.	14.7	20.0	9.0	5.7	11.0
Germany	20.4	26.6	16.3	4.1	10.3
France	16.4	24.8	13.9	2.5	10.9

(1) Direct taxes and social security contributions paid by households plus government receipts from indirect taxes *minus* current transfers by government.

(2) Total government disbursements *minus* current transfers.

(3) Government consumption expenditure for general public services, public order and safety, education, health, soial security and welfare, housing and community amenities, and recreational, cultural and religious affairs.

Source: United Nations, *National Accounts Statistics: Main Aggregates and Detailed Tables, 1987* (New York: United Nations, 1990). Detailed Tables for France, pp. 474–511; for West Germany, pp. 525–574; and for the United States, pp. 1586–1639. French government consumption figures are for 1985.

icr to hope that "growth" or beneficent catastrophe will rescue the nation from its debts.

Without radical policies, however, relief is unlikely. The huge deficits are structural rather than merely cyclical. In 1989, after six years without a recession and with unemployment at only slightly more than 5%, the federal deficit was still around $160 billion. Increasingly, growing interest costs themselves augment the deficit significantly. Interest charges, 8.89% of annual federal spending in fiscal 1980, were 14.77% in 1990. In recent years, moreover, the budget has been devastated by having to bail out one sector after another of the financial industry. Arguably, the country's financial disarray is not unrelated to the monetary manipulations practiced to keep financing the huge debt. Over the past decade, interest and exchange rates have gyrated as much as 50% or more within a year or two. In a market economy, these are not ideal conditions for financial stability, nor for serious long-term investment to restore rapid growth.

Long-term trends in the civilian economy do not point toward an improvement in the fiscal situation. Like Europe, America's population is aging, which implies higher social security and medical costs. Depreciating infrastructure and inadequate education and health care are seen as deeply detrimental to long-term growth and competitiveness. The finances of many local governments are precarious. Hopes for significant overall cuts on the civilian side of the federal budget thus seem patently unrealistic. Instead, powerful trends are pushing for higher civilian spending on the not implausible grounds that more is needed to keep the economy competitive. By comparison, the Soviet collapse makes the prospects for military cuts seem much more promising.

CUTS IN THE MILITARY BUDGET

Defense has been losing its budget share since fiscal 1987, although it has scarcely yet fallen in constant dollars. Administration plans earlier this year called for defense to consume 19.6% of the federal budget in 1995, down from 23.9% in 1990. These projections included highly sanguine assumptions about growth and interest rates. Congressional reactions and the President's most recent arms-control proposals suggest that cuts may be much deeper. Some analysts have argued that defense cuts already underway will undermine America's capacity to project its military power. Some have argued, for example, that a comparable American effort in the Gulf War would not be possible by the middle of this decade. So far, only procurement—among the four major functions—has been hard hit. Annual authorizations for expenditures declined 30.4% in real terms from 1985 to 1990, and administration estimates earlier this year projected an additional 23% drop by 1995. Other functions are now expected to be hit seriously as well. In administration estimates earlier this year, personnel was scheduled to lose 21% of its real budgetary authority by 1995; operations and maintenance 20.4%; and research 14.6%.

All such projections are uncertain, and their military consequences still more so. Whatever happens, the U.S. will remain an immense military power. Recent force projections envisage armed forces of some 1,795,000 men and women on active duty. No cuts, moreover, are yet projected for the thirteen aircraft carriers. With defense spending that will still dwarf everyone else's, the problem will be less the lack than the mal-deployment and waste of funds, particularly if the Pentagon loses effective control over its budget. Present circumstances make the huge military budget highly vulnerable. Unrealistic plans and commitments are likely to be swept aside. Military weakness will result from the ensuing chaos rather than any real lack of funds. It thus seems critically important that there be a realistic correspondence between dreams of a new world order and budgetary realities.

DEFINING THE NEW WORLD ORDER: HEGEMONY VERSUS DEVOLUTION

Operational definitions of the new world order are likely to be considerably less ambitious than the official rhetoric of recent years implies. For obvious reasons, the United States is not about to withdraw from the world. But it will certainly be forced to pay more attention to balancing its domestic and foreign priorities. America's allies should probably expect the old issue of "burden-sharing" to revive with new intensity.

Traditionally and logically, there are two broad formulas for burden-sharing. The first calls for the United States not only to maintain the strategic global balance but also to take the lead in organizing and sustaining a series of standing regional alliances. In this traditional model, allies provide forces, facilities and subventions. But the Americans take charge and themselves provide substantial forces. This has been the pattern for NATO and for the Japanese-American security relationship. These two alliances, by themselves, have traditionally accounted for a large proportion of American military spending. NATO alone, it has been claimed officially, has been responsible for roughly half of America's defense outlays.

In this "hegemonic" model of burden-sharing, the principal issue is the great imbalance between American and allied contributions. Since America's allies are advanced industrial societies, formidably competitive and as rich per capita as the U.S., Americans naturally demand larger contributions. Such demands are undercut, of course, by America's determination to continue playing the leading role in the regional alliances. Under such circumstances, hegemonic burden-sharing has had its political limits. Various administrations have looked for clever formulas to sustain hegemony "on the cheap." Hence, in the 1950s, President Eisenhower's enthusiasm for "massive retaliation," and tactical nuclear war-fighting. Such periods, when undiminished geopolitical ambitions were sustained with reduced military forces, were invariably followed by a rediscovery of the Soviet threat and a major rearmament. Thus, Eisenhower's "more bang for the buck" was succeeded by Kennedy's "missile gap" and "flexible response." Nixon and Ford's detente was followed by the "window of vulnerability" and the massive Reagan rearmament that actually began under

Carter. America's military budgets have thus had a cyclical character—which has, on balance, contributed to their inefficiency.

In theory, American administrations have always had a major alternative: to go beyond hegemonic burden-sharing to what might be called "burden-sharing by devolution." In this latter alternative, the United States would expect its major allies to take the lead in managing the defense of their own regions. The formula has been the basis of various visionary plans over the years—a European Defense Community, a European pillar in NATO, or a European SACEUR. The early Nixon Administration awaited a "pentagonal" world order and counted on regional "surrogates" like Iran. But as the reactions of Secretary of State Henry Kissinger indicated during the 1973 oil crisis and "Year of Europe," the U.S. has, in fact, been reluctant to relinquish its leadership. Kissinger, for example, objected to being confronted with decisions emerging from a European Community in which the United States did not participate.

European leaders like Michel Jobert were quick to note the anomalies in the American position. But neither side of the Atlantic was greatly dissatisfied with a status quo that left European military security primarily in American hands. Only the Americans were ready and able to provide Europe with a credible nuclear deterrent to the Soviet military threat. The alternatives were either questionable militarily (and politically), like an extended French deterrent for Germany, or explosive politically, like a German national deterrent.

The price for American protection, moreover, was minimal. American hegemony in NATO did not keep France from developing a nuclear deterrent or fighting major colonial wars, nor deter Germany from its *Ostpolitik*, nor France and Germany from their own special cooperation. Nor did it interfere with Europe's economic and political integration. True, as the Soviets reached strategic parity with the Americans, extended deterrence grew more problematic and therefore dangerous. Hence the intense missile and SDI debates of the 1970s and early 1980s. It is not unlikely that the combination of a deteriorating strategic balance, plus America's growing fiscal difficulties would, sooner or later, have forced a major shift toward an American devolution of military hegemony in Europe. Certainly the need for it was increasingly taken for granted by experts on both sides of the Atlantic.

Before any such transformation could mature the Soviet system itself collapsed. This has left Europe without its threat and the United States without its global rival. But, it has also left the United States with its deteriorating fiscal problem, together with its urgent need for massive foreign borrowing to finance it. Since the success of the new European order, and ultimately the world's as well, requires the economic, political and social transformation of the old Soviet sphere, and this will require immense capital resources, America's own voracious foreign borrowing works at cross purposes with its wider geopolitical interests. The rational way out presumably lies in some major improvement of the American fiscal situation. Cuts in military spending seem the most promising prospect.

This chain of reasoning coexists uneasily with the vision of the U.S. as the world's unique superpower and global hegemon. On the contrary, it points toward a new world order with a more plural division of labor and responsibility. It does not imply the end of a close transatlantic alliance, but it seems hard to reconcile with the continuous presence of large and expensive American forces in Europe, or with an indefinite American management of European defense.

If economic considerations had been foremost, America's role in Europe's security arrangements would probably have changed long ago. But with the Soviet army massively deployed in Central Europe, the hegemonic American protectorate seemed essential, whatever the costs and other difficulties. What are the military threats that might determine the transatlantic relationship in the post–Cold War era?

TOMORROW'S THREATS AND THEIR IMPLICATIONS

What was the Soviet Union no longer appears aggressive but continues to possess a nuclear arsenal that rivals America's. Its weakness and volatility is a threat in itself. Any prudent European security policy for the coming years must, therefore, sustain a reasonable deterrent. Some form of transatlantic alliance remains desirable, sealed by the continuing presence of some American forces and legitimized and coordinated by some kind of NATO structure.

NATO arrangements, however, will inevitably change. Forward defense, with large standing armies equipped with short-range nuclear weapons, is already being abandoned. American withdrawals have been underway and European forces are being reduced and transformed. The new threats arise in Europe's unstable periphery— in the Mediterranean and Middle East, and in Central and Eastern Europe.

The Gulf War and the Yugoslav crisis have crystallized the threats, but the relevant "lessons" remain unclear. Both the military and political conjuncture of the Gulf War was so unique that it seems an unsound model for the future. In both the Mediterranean and the East, the European interest lies not simply in deterring or repelling military attacks, but in promoting peaceful "modernization" to bring prosperity and stability over the long term. To do so, European governments will need to mobilize more effectively their commercial, investment and political resources. In both regions, Europeans have greater economic resources and interests than the Americans. During the Cold War, with its overriding Soviet military threat, military security was left primarily to U.S. initiative, while European governments played a much greater role in economic and political relations. In present circumstances, European states may grow more uncomfortable with their military dependence. They may come to feel that their economic and political approach needs to be backed up by a more serious collective military capacity of their own, if only to give themselves more leverage over American policy.

The disadvantages of Europe's lack of a coordinated military posture of its own may prove particularly distressing in the Yugoslav case, a European crisis where Americans are loath to take the lead. In the Cold War, Europe's military need was a static, all-or-nothing deterrence. In the future, its security problems will require a much broader and active political-economic approach, but one that will include the capacity for limited military interventions, coordinated with that broader approach. It will probably be harder to keep the military and civilian spheres of policy separated. In a situation where the European contribution and initiative is more important than the American, NATO seems an unlikely locus for Europeans to coordinate their grand policy, at least so long as NATO is organized around American hegemony. There are, of course, obvious limits to this shift. Americans will continue to have a vital interest in European security, even when they no longer take the lead in managing it. Europeans will continue to need the U.S. as an ultimate stabilizer of its own internal equilibrium. Each will need the other to sustain the global order that will be in the interest of both. In summary, the sort of security problems that seem most likely in Europe's future suggest a new transatlantic military relationship—one in which the Americans should remain as partners, but where the primary initiative in managing European problems shifts toward the major West European states.

American governments may resist, but will also be influenced by the logic of their fiscal situation. Like Europe, or the Soviet Union, the United States faces a vast agenda of economic, social, and political problems in adapting its own continental system to a fast-changing and increasingly competitive world. America's fiscal crisis is a warning signal that its domestic challenges cannot be ignored without damaging the springs of its national power. And because America's unproductive borrowing places heavy demands on the world's supply of free capital, it also threatens Europe's prospects and the world's prosperity and financial order in general.

Over time, the United States may thus be expected to make way for a more self-assertive Europe. While the fate of Europe and America are inextricably linked, no American government can expect to manage successfully Europe's problems as well as its own. Partnership will continue to be essential, but hegemony is going out of fashion. There is not, after all, any shortage of opportunities for American leadership elsewhere in the world.

In the end, making this more rational form of burden-sharing in our alliance operational will depend more on the Europeans than on the Americans. The real question is how soon a self-assertive European confederacy will appear to master the problems of the continent. Much obviously will depend on how the European Community progresses in its next stage. The character of the new confederacy will doubtless influence the quality of transatlantic relations. American officials sometimes fear a Community so mechanically widened and deepened that it becomes a sort of federalist automaton, too inflexible to negotiate with outsiders. A Europe more widened than deepened is superficially a more convenient prospect. But a Europe lacking the machinery for coordinating policies among its major states, and therefore excessively vulnerable to internal bickering and outside manipulation, would not be in the real interest of a United States that intends to address its own problems seriously.

Probably the best European structure, for American as well as European purposes, would be inclusive enough to stabilize the East, but with a Western core cohesive and compact enough to provide firm and coherent leadership from within Europe itself. With such a core, Europe could be an effective partner and also have the flexibility to negotiate transatlantic problems. Such a Europe, however, would be the critical element in any new world system. Its existence would go a long way, in itself, toward constituting a broader global order based on a more regional division of responsibility, and reflecting a more complex and plural distribution of resources and power. In effect, developing a satisfactory world order that America can afford over time now depends heavily on Europe's success in dealing with its own problems. Close family that we are, we are condemned to interdependence.